Ducati 600, 620, 750 & 900 2-valve V-Twins
Service and Repair Manual

by Penny Cox and Matthew Coombs

Models covered

600SS. 583cc. 1994 to 1997
620S. 618cc. 2003
M600. 583cc. 1994 to 2001
M620. 618cc. 2002 to 2005
750SS. 748cc. 1991 to 2002
M750. 748cc. 1991 to 2002
900SS. 904cc. 1991 to 2002
900SL. 904cc. 1992 to 1997
M900. 904cc. 1993 to 2002

All Dark, Sport and Special editions included

(3290-272-5AE3)

© Haynes Publishing 2005

ABCDE
FGHIJ
KLMNO

2

A book in the **Haynes Service and Repair Manual Series**

ISBN **978 0 85733 986 7**

Library of Congress Control Number – 2005928908

Printed in Malaysia

Haynes Publishing
Sparkford, Yeovil, Somerset BA22 7JJ, England

Haynes North America, Inc
859 Lawrence Drive, Newbury Park, California 91320, USA

Contents

LIVING WITH YOUR DUCATI

Introduction

Doctor T and The Desmos	Page	0•4
Acknowledgements	Page	0•7
About this Manual	Page	0•7
Model development	Page	0•8
Bike spec	Page	0•8
Safety first!	Page	0•10
Identification numbers	Page	0•11
Buying spare parts	Page	0•11

Daily (pre-ride) checks

Engine oil level	Page	0•12
Clutch fluid level	Page	0•13
Suspension, steering and final drive	Page	0•13
Brake fluid levels	Page	0•14
Legal and safety checks	Page	0•15
Tyres	Page	0•16

MAINTENANCE

Routine maintenance and servicing

Specifications	Page	1•2
Recommended lubricants and fluids	Page	1•3
Component locations	Page	1•4
Maintenance schedule	Page	1•5
Maintenance procedures	Page	1•6

Contents

REPAIRS AND OVERHAUL

Engine, transmission and associated systems
Engine, clutch and transmission   Page   **2•1**

Fuel system – carburettor models   Page   **3A•1**

Fuel system – fuel injection models   Page   **3B•1**

Ignition system   Page   **4•1**

Chassis components
Frame and suspension   Page   **5•1**

Brakes, wheels and tyres   Page   **6•1**

Fairing and bodywork   Page   **7•1**

Electrical system   Page   **8•1**

Wiring diagrams   Page   **8•25**

REFERENCE

Tools and Workshop Tips   Page   **REF•2**

Security   Page   **REF•20**

Lubricants and fluids   Page   **REF•23**

Conversion factors   Page   **REF•26**

MOT test checks   Page   **REF•27**

Storage   Page   **REF•32**

Fault finding   Page   **REF•35**

Fault finding equipment   Page   **REF•44**

Index   Page   **REF•48**

Doctor T & The
Desmos

by Julian Ryder

More than any other factory, with the possible exception of Norton, the history of Ducati is the history of its racing. From the early days with the lightweight singles in 125 cc Grand Prix racing to the bevel-drive V-twins winning the Imola 200, Mike Hailwood's legendary return to the Isle of Man, a hatful of World TT Formula 2 titles with the Pantah, Daytona Battle of the Twins success with Marco Lucchinelli, the triumphant entry to Superbike racing with the high-tech 888 and then the mighty 916, racing has shown the way. Every one of these victories is engraved on the minds – and hearts – of racing enthusiasts all over the world, there is a romance about Ducati that only an Italian factory could generate. This is underlined by the personal nature of these achievements.

The early success and the credit for laying down the ground rules for every Ducati design since the early '50s is universally acknowledged to belong to the late Fabio Taglioni, an engineer who was as well-known and revered as his designs. Although the man himself was not over-fond of the limelight, he was elevated to the status of demigod by the Ducati faithful. When Taglioni, the man who made desmodromic valve operation work on racing and production motorcycles, stepped down, Massimo Bordi took over and produced a motorcycle that more than matched the best that the giant Japanese corporations could produce. Yet the new 851 Superbike was still recognisably a Ducati. It was a V-twin and it had desmodromic valve operation but it also had fuel injection, water-cooling and four-valve heads. More surprisingly, it eschewed the fashion for aluminium beam frames and stuck with the tubular steel ladder frame that came in with the Pantah in 1980. The 851 and its descendants, the 888, the 916, and the 996 went on to World Superbike glory and in true Ducati tradition created unprecedented demand for its street bikes.

Despite the dominance of the Italian Ducati factory in Superbike racing in the UK, Europe, Australia and the USA, as well as at World Championship level, the company is relatively new. Ducati didn't start making motorcycles until 1950 with a then typically Italian range of small, lightweight bikes. The marque's first giant leap forward came with the arrival of one of the two men who would come to embody Ducati's inimitable Italian flair: Fabio Taglioni.

Fabio Taglioni

Taglioni joined Ducati as boss of the technical, planning and experimental department after four years at the small Mondial company where he had worked on their DOHC single-cylinder Grand Prix racers. His job was the complex one of kick-starting the racing programme which had to also fulfil the function of development testbed for the production models.

In under a year from Taglioni's arrival the 98 cc Grand Sport was launched into the highly-competitive 100 cc racing class. This engine was a unit-construction OHC motor with nothing in common with Ducati's earlier pushrod motors or the two-stroke competition. Looking at one of those early GSs you can easily spot the genes of what was to follow, for the overhead camshaft was driven by a bevel-gear-drive via a near vertical shaft enclosed in polished tube that ran up the right-hand side of the barrel. This was the layout that would be followed not just in the 125 cc, DOHC Grand Prix single that was Taglioni's next creation, but in every Ducati built up to 1980. But Taglioni's stroke of genius did not hit the tracks until 1956. The racing world was shaken by the instant success of the new Ducati, basically a standard GS racer with Desmodromic valve gear. In the 125 cc Swedish Grand Prix factory rider Degli Antoni lapped the entire field and set new race and lap records on his way to victory. It was the new bike's first race.

The principle of Desmodromic valve operation is simple: the valves are both opened and closed positively. Instead of being closed by a compressed valve spring extending they are closed by a rocker operated by a third camshaft sighted centrally between and geared to the inlet and exhaust camshafts. Desmodromic valve operation wasn't new, James Norton had roughed out plans for such a system before 1910 and the fabulous pre-War Mercedes W196 Grand Prix car had it. The advantages are self-evident,

The 250 Desmo single

The 900 Darmah

higher rev limits thanks to the prevention of valve 'float' at high revs. That first desmo 125 GP bike revved to 12,500 and was regularly taken to 15,000 rpm by factory testers. Here was a way of allowing four-strokes to rev on without self-destructing. If the principle is simple, the precision needed to make it work in practice most certainly isn't and desmodromics remained in the realms of race-track exotica until 1968 when a 250 and 350 single were launched after being unveiled at the Cologne Show the previous year.

The desmo singles, especially the last yellow, disc-braked versions of the early '70s, introduced a whole generation of enthusiasts to the joys of Ducati ownership. This was, however, not usually an unalloyed joy. Taglioni was above all an engine man and the factory personnel's somewhat, er, Mediterranean attitude to quality control showed through in the experience of ownership. The stories of peeling chrome and self-destructing electrics were by no means apocryphal. These singles were the first Ducatis to be exported in numbers and seemed to addict riders for life or put them off anything Italian for life in equal numbers.

Changes at the Factory

Unfortunately, while the Ducati company was a world leader in innovation, it was noticeably inept at making a profit. In 1971 it was taken into government 'controlled administration', equivalent to the USA's Chapter 11 bankruptcy, to give it temporary respite from its creditors. Not that this prevented the factory from pulling off one of the most astonishing victories in racing at the Imola 200 in 1972.

Taglioni had designed a V4 in the mid-1960s with the aim of cracking the American market, but the project never got beyond the prototype stage. Instead, it was announced in 1970 that Ducati would build a V-twin based on half the V4. That doesn't seem strange today, but back then the V-twin layout was regarded as an antiquated curiosity. The first V-twins (Taglioni preferred L-twin as the front cylinder was near horizontal) used conventional valve springs, the first Desmo V-twin appeared in 1972 for the prestigious Imola 200. Paul Smart was signed up at short notice to ride the bike alongside factory tester Bruno Spaggiari. They finished first and second, beating factory Triumphs, Nortons and Hondas plus the seemingly almighty combination of Giacomo Agostini and the factory MV Agusta as well as an impressive array of private and semi-works Kawasakis, etc. Just like with the 125 GP racer, this was the desmo twin's first race.

This was the race that founded what is now regarded as the classic family of Ducatis, the bevel-drive desmo V-twins. The first production bikes were a batch of 25 Imola replicas, known as the 750SS, just enough to homologate the model for the new F750 world

The 900 GTS

championship. As with later Ducatis, demand far outstripped supply and led to the development of a whole range of bikes. As we'd come to expect, the motor was a gem but the bits wrapped round it were not for the nervous. American magazine Cycle found a slew of faults on their test bike, the most famous of which, a fly trapped for ever in the glass-fibre moulding of the petrol tank, has passed into legend.

The bevel-drive V-twins would go on into the '80s in a variety of guises, the most desirable of which is probably the 900SS, a bigger version of the original Imola replicas. The less-sporty and slightly more civilised versions, like the Darmah, GTS and the S2 simply didn't embody what Ducati was about in the way the Super Sports models did. There was, though, one more bevel-drive 900, and this one wasn't just the result of one of racing's greatest moments but of some quick thinking in the marketing department as well. The event that led to the creation of the 900SS MHR (Mike Hailwood Replica) was the return of Mike Hailwood to the Isle of Man TT. The man regarded as the finest rider ever to grace a racing motorcycle retired from F1 car racing after a bad accident at the Nurburgring in 1974; he chose a Ducati for his comeback to the world stage after a couple of low-profile races in Australia. The 1978 F1 TT was Mike's first Island ride in 11 years and he was 38 years old, yet he won and won convincingly.

While the world of motorcycling went

collectively mad, Ducati took advantage of this unexpected success. Mike's bike had of course been a factory special, but the fully-faired version of the 900SS with its red, white and green paintwork went from being a 500-unit limited edition to the factory's best seller for several years. In fact the last ever bevel-drive V-twins were Mille MHRs. Incidentally, the Isle of Man victory gave Hailwood and Ducati a world title, for the F1 TT was effectively a one-race world championship. The V-twin had Ducati's first world title, something the old 125 never had the reliability to do, especially after the great Degli Antoni was killed.

Racing success or not, the road-going bevel-drive Dukes still had many of the problems of the old singles. The antidote to the frankly old-fashioned nature of the big twins was launched in 1980: the Pantah. The resemblance to the bevel-drive bikes was obvious, although the tunnel housing the shaft drive to the cams was gone, replaced by a polished plate over the toothed belts that would operate the desmodromic valve gear of every new Ducati from now on. The same rocker covers were used, making the engine look a lot more like the old lump than it actually was. The frame was new, too. The old double cradle was gone and in its place was a double ladder frame made of short, straight steel tubes. Like the belt-driven cams, this design set the pattern for every future Duke.

The new belt-driven V-twins couldn't

The M900 Monster

compete with the multi-cylinder opposition in F1 competition, but the 600 cc Pantah was a natural for F2 competition. The British importer entered veteran Tony Rutter on a Pantah-engined bike in the 1981 TT, which he duly won. He also won the world title that year and for the following three years. The last Ducati to be built and sold to the public while Ducati was still being run by the Italian government agency was the F1, a 750 cc belt-drive motor in a chassis that bore a very strong resemblance to the works F2 bikes – despite the seeming conflict in the designations.

Now the F2 championship and even the Battle of the Twins class that the F1 did so well in were all very well, but they were very small beer compared to the F1 title of '78 and the new Superbike class that was starting to take hold in the USA. It looked as if Ducati were set to fade away completely under the dead hand of Italian bureaucracy, or at best become one of those small, enthusiasts-only marques.

Cagiva Take-over

In 1985 Ducati was bought by the Castiglioni brothers, owners of the Cagiva Group which already owned the old Aermacchi/Harley-Davidson set-up, who were looking to expand their industrial empire to include a major motorcycle manufacturer with which to take on the Japanese. Ducati turned out to be the obvious choice, and they gained an instant North American dealer network by buying the Swedish Husqvarna concern as well.

There was no way the ageing Ducati line-up was going to be able to compete with the Japanese, so the new chief engineer, Massimo Bordi was given the funds to develop a new-generation desmo Ducati. The result was the 851, a completely new motorcycle that nevertheless was very much in the tradition of Taglioni's work, which first saw the light of day at the 1986 Bol d'Or. The motor was a 90° V-twin but to endow it with performance on a par with the four-cylinder Japanese opposition it featured fuel injection

and water-cooling plus four valves per cylinder operated, of course, desmodromically. The frame was a steel trellis very much along the lines of the Pantah's.

This is the bike that was developed into the first Superbike racer, the 888, which appeared for the first ever World Superbike Championship race at Donington Park in 1988. Marco Lucchinelli took the new bike to an overall win on its debut. The 888 and its descendants, the 916 and 996, have gone on to win all but three of the World Superbike Championships so far run. This success in what is an increasingly high-profile class, both at the world and domestic level, increased demand for Ducatis drastically, helped by the fact that the depressed value of the Italian Lire on international markets kept prices well below the Japanese competition.

A completely new line was unveiled in 1993, the Monster. Here was a bike as far removed from Ducati tradition as you could imagine, a boulevard cruiser using the old air-cooled motors and built for show, not go. Amazingly, it became a best seller. Further diversification came with the ST sports tourers, which met with critical acclaim but not such impressive sales figures.

Unfortunately, this was not necessarily a recipe for commercial success. The Castiglioni brothers, like many other Italian industrialists, were caught up in the incredibly tangled political situation. The rise in interest rates after the fall of the Socialist government saw them unable to service their loans and on the lookout for cash. Customers noted a difficulty in getting motorbikes, suppliers noted a difficulty in getting paid. That resulted in a new company, Ducati Motor SpA, which came into being in September 1996 as a

The 900SS Supersport

joint venture between the Castigionis and the Texas Pacific Group, an American investment fund. By 1998, Texas Pacific owned the whole company. The result was a massive increase in personnel, investment in new machinery, a redesign of the corporate logo, and a happier time for customers in general. And while Ducati continues to win races, there are sure to be plenty of them.

The 2-valve V-Twins

All the 600, 620, 750 and 900 cc V-twins in this manual were first designed and produced after the Castiglionis took over Ducati. They therefore have much better quality control and ancillary components than used to be the case. Despite this, the sports versions bear a very strong visual relationship to the old bevel- and belt-drive twins. This is deliberate, a tug on the heart strings. And indeed the basic bore and stroke dimensions show you where the designs came from: the 750 shares its bore and stroke with the F1 of 1985, but the 900's 92 x 68 mm bears no relation to the dimensions of the original 900SS. What you have is the Pantah motor updated with oil cooling to the heads and packaged in a very sporty chassis that's meant to remind you very strongly of the old 900, a trick it performs very well.

The 600, 750 and 900SS (Supersport) models are all in the traditional Ducati vein, sportsters with few concessions to comfort. The 900SL (Superlight) differs from the 900SS in its use of lightweight carbon fibre material for the mudguards, clutch and sprocket covers and a single seat. The 750 and 900SS were redesignated Supersport or Sport models in 1998 and had a total bodywork redesign with Marelli fuel injection replacing

The 600SS Supersport

the carbs fitted to earlier engines. These models were eventually superseded by the 1000SS which marked another generation of the two-valve twin. Never having made a great impact on the buoyant 600 market, the 600SS was discontinued at the end of 1997, but reborn as a 620 Sport for 2003 using the improved 618cc engine fitted to the previous year's M620 Monster.

The Monster is a totally different beast from the Supersport range. It uses the same motor but packages it in a way that has nothing to do with sports riding. It's an unfaired muscle bike in the style of Yamaha's V-Max. It wasn't designed for the Curva Grande at Monza but

for wheelieing past the cafes down on the sea front near Misano. Historically, Ducati have not been good at non-sportsters but the Monster has a proven sales record, and marked a style which other manufacturers have been quick to follow. The original M750 and M900 models evolved to using fuel injected engines towards the end of their model run, but were eventually superseded by the twin-spark M800 and M1000 models, and also by the 4-valve 916/996cc S4 and S4R. The smallest Monster remains in the current range having received fuel injection and an extra 35cc capacity when the M620 came along in 2002.

Acknowledgements

Our thanks are due to Bridge Motorcycles of Exeter and Riders of Bristol who provided the machines featured in this manual, and to Mel Rawlings AIRTE of MHR Engineering who carried out some of the mechanical work. Thanks are also due to Guy Crossley who provided the M900 model.

We are especially grateful for the help of Ducati UK for providing technical advice and literature. NGK Spark Plugs (UK) Ltd supplied the colour spark plug condition photographs and the Avon Rubber Company provided information on tyre fitting. The Ducati introduction, 'Doctor T & The Desmos' was written by Julian Ryder.

About this Manual

The aim of this manual is to help you get the best value from your motorcycle. It can do so in several ways. It can help you decide what work must be done, even if you choose to have it done by a dealer; it provides information and procedures for routine maintenance and servicing; and it offers diagnostic and repair procedures to follow when trouble occurs.

We hope you use the manual to tackle the work yourself. For many simpler jobs, doing it yourself may be quicker than arranging an appointment to get the motorcycle into a dealer and making the trips to leave it and pick it up. More importantly, a lot of money can be saved by avoiding the expense the shop must pass on to you to cover its labour and overhead costs. An added benefit is the sense of satisfaction and accomplishment that you feel after doing the job yourself.

References to the left or right side of the motorcycle assume you are sitting on the seat, facing forward.

We take great pride in the accuracy of information given in this manual, but motorcycle manufacturers make alterations and design changes during the production run of a particular motorcycle of which they do not inform us. No liability can be accepted by the authors or publishers for loss, damage or injury caused by any errors in, or omissions from, the information given.

600SS (Supersport) 1994 to 1997

The smallest addition to the Supersport range, available in fully faired version only. Similar to the 750SS, with a wet clutch, no oil cooler, steel instead of aluminium swingarm, two-into-one exhaust system and a single disc front brake.

620S i.e. (Sport) 2003

New model using the engine, gearbox and fuel system from the M620 i.e. introduced the previous year. Frame, chassis and new bodywork as the 750/900 Sport models.

750SS (Supersport) 1991 to 2002

Available initially in half faired, but later also in fully faired versions. Mechanically, the 750SS is similar to its predecessor, the 750 Sport with roots which can be traced back to the 500 Pantah. It's frame components are similar to those of the 900SS but with a single front disc brake and non-adjustable forks.

From VIN 001275 the original dry clutch was replaced by a wet clutch. Improvements were made to braking in 1994 (from VIN 006007) with the fitting of a twin disc front brake, like the 900SS.

Major mechanical changes were introduced for the 1998 year with the introduction of the fuel injected 750i.e. Supersport. Like the new 900i.e. Supersport this model had completely new bodywork. A half faired version, the 750 Sport was also available. The clutch operating mechanism was moved from the clutch cover to the left-hand side of engine and the gearchange mechanism was revised.

The 750 i.e. Supersport was eventually superseded by the 800 Supersport at the end of 2002.

900SS (Supersport) 1991 to 2002

Available in Sport (half faired) or Supersport (fully faired) versions. The 904cc 900SS replaced the original 864cc engined model produced from 1976. Although using a 2-valve, air-cooled top-end, the crankcases were based on those fitted to the 6-speed 851/888 series models.

Major mechanical changes were made for the 1998 year with the introduction of the fuel injected 900i.e. Supersport. This model had Marelli IAW 1.5 fuel injection, an uprated alternator and completely new bodywork. A half faired version, the 900 Sport was also available. A final edition (FE) model was available in 1998 with the carburettor engine and old-sytle bodywork.

For 2002 two-piece cam belt covers replaced the earlier model's three-part assembly. The 900 Supersport and Sport were discontinued for 2003, giving way to the 992cc 2-valve dual-spark 1000 Supersport model and the Multi-strada.

900SL (Superlight) 1992 to 1997

Single seat version of the 900SS with carbon-fibre mudguards, clutch cover and sprocket cover.

M600 (Monster) 1994 to 2001

The M600 used the same engine as the 600SS. Frame and suspension were as the already established M750 and M900 models, but with a single disc front brake.

In 1998 modifications were made to the engine top-end and cam belt assembly, and the clutch operating mechanism was moved from the clutch cover to the left-hand side of the engine, the gearchange mechanism was revised and the alternator uprated. The choke control was resited from the top yoke to a lever on the left handlebar switch from VIN 006830. Fully electronic instruments were fitted in 2001.

M620i.e. (Monster) 2002-on

The M620i.e. was a direct replacement for the M600. Its extra displacement was gained by increasing engine stroke, the bore remained unchanged. The carburettors of the M600 were replaced by a Marelli IAW 5.9M fuel injection system. Chassis improvements amounted to improved suspension, a twin disc front brake (except for cheaper versions), different swingarm with hugger, new rear shock linkage and fully eletronic instruments. For 2004 the APTC (Adler Power Torque Plate Clutch) slipper clutch was fitted and certain models had a six-speed gearbox.

M750 (Monster) 1991 to 2002

The M750 used the same engine as the 750SS but always with a wet clutch. In 1998 modifications were made to the engine top-end and cam belt assembly, the clutch operating mechanism was moved from the clutch cover to the left-hand side of the engine, the gearchange mechanism was revised and the alternator uprated.

Fuel injection was fitted on the 2002 M750i.e. together with a modified rear suspension linkage. The model was superseded by the M800 for 2003.

M900 (Monster) 1993 to 2002

The first generation M900 used the carburettor engine fitted to the 900SS. Changes were few, apart from an uprated alternator in 1988 and the resiting of the choke control from the top yoke to the left-hand handlebar switch from VIN 009915. The 2000 M900i.e. was fitted with fuel injection. For 2002 two-piece cam belt covers replaced the three-part assembly fitted to earlier models and the rear suspension linkage was modified.

Running alongside the M900 in 2001 and 2002 was the dohc-engined 916cc (then 996cc) S4 and S4R models. The M900 finally gave way to the 992cc 2-valve dual-spark M1000 model at the end of 2002.

Engine

Type		Four-stroke 90° V-Twin			
		600 engine	**620 engine**	**750 engine**	**900 engine**
Capacity		583cc	618cc	748cc	907cc
Bore x stroke		80 x 58 mm	80 x 61.5 mm	88 x 61.5 mm	92 x 68 mm
Compression ratio		10.7:1	10.5:1	9.0:1	9.2:1
Clutch					
All 900 engines, 750SS up to VIN 001274		Dry clutch			
All other engines		Wet clutch			
Transmission		Five or six-speed constant mesh			
Final drive		Chain and sprockets			
Valve gear		Desmodromic 2-valve, belt driven cams			
Fuel system					
600SS, M600, 750/900SS/SL up to 1997, M750 up to 2001, M900 up to 1999		Mikuni BDST 38 mm CV carburettors			
750i.e. and 900i.e. Supersport and Sport		Marelli IAW 1.5M			
620i.e. Sport, M620i.e., M750i.e., M900i.e.		Marelli IAW 5.9M			
Exhaust system		Two-into-two			
Ignition system		Transistorised			

Chassis

Frame type	Steel trellis design with engine as stressed member
Fuel tank capacity (inclusive reserve capacity)	
1991 to 1997 SS and SL models	17.5 litres (4 litres)
1998 to 2001 900i.e. Supersport and Sport models	18 litres (4 litres)
620i.e. Sport, 1998 to 2002 750i.e. and 2002 900i.e. Supersport	
and Sport models	16 litres (4 litres)
1991 to 1997 M600, M750 and M900 models	18 litres (4 litres)
1998 to 2001 M600/750, 1998 and 1999 M900 models	16.5 litres (3.5 litres)
M620i.e.	14 litres (3.5 litres)
M750/900i.e.	16.5 litres (3.5 litres)
Front suspension	Showa or Marzocchi USD telescopic forks
Rear suspension	Single shock, with linkage on Monster models
Wheels	Cast alloy

	Front	**Rear**
Tyres		
620i.e. Sport, 750i.e. Sport and Supersport models	120/70-ZR17	160/60-ZR17
all other 600, 620 and 750 models	120/60-ZR17	160/60-ZR17
900 models	120/70-ZR17	170/60-ZR17

Refer to the owners handbook for approved tyre brands.

Front brake	Single or twin disc with four piston Brembo calipers
Rear brake	Single disc with two piston Brembo caliper

Dimensions

SS, SL, Sport and Supersport models

Wheelbase
  600 and 750 1991 to 1997 models . . . . .1410 mm
  620, 750 1998 to 2002 models. . . . . .1405 mm
  900 1991 to 2000 models . . . . .1410 mm
  900 2001 and 2002 models . . . . .1395 mm
Overall length . . . . .2020/2030 mm
Overall width
  750 1991 to 1993 models . . . . .710 mm
  600 and 750 1994 to 1997, 900 1991 to 1997 models . . . . .730 mm
  620, 750/900 1998 to 2002 models . . . . .780 mm
Overall height
  600, 620, 750, 2002 900 models .1110 mm
  900 1991 to 2001 models .1000/1125 mm
Seat height
  600/750/900 1991 to 1997 models . . . . .780 mm
  750 1998 to 2001 models . . . . .812 mm
  620, 2002 750 models. . . . . .815 mm
  900 1998 to 2001 models . . . . .800 mm
  900 2002 model . . . . .820 mm
Minimum ground clearance
  600 and 750 1991 to 1997, 900 1991 to 2000 models . . . . .150 mm
  620 model . . . . .110 mm
  750 1998 to 2002 models . . . . .97 mm
  900 2001 and 2002 models . . . . .105 mm
Weight (dry)
  600 model . . . . .172 kg
  620 model . . . . .182 kg
  750 1991 to 1997 models . . . . .173 to 176 kg
  750 1998 to 2002 models . . . . .183 kg (181 kg Sport)
  900 1991 to 1997 models . . . . . . .183 to 186 kg (SL model 182 kg)
  900 1998 to 2002 models . . . . .188 kg

Monster models

Wheelbase
  M600/750/900 1991 to 2001 models . . . . .1430 mm
  M620/750/900 2002-on models .1440 mm
Overall length
  1991 to 1997 models . . . . .2090 mm
  1998 to 2001 models . . . . .2080 mm
  M620/750/900 2002-on models .2100 mm

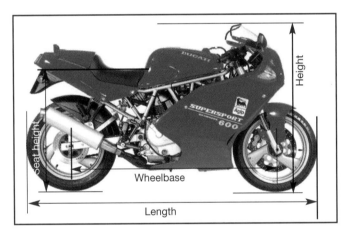

Height
Seat height
Wheelbase
Length

Monster models (continued)

Overall width
  1991 to 1997 models . . . . .770 mm
  1998 to 2001 models . . . . .800 mm
  M620/750/900 2002-on models . . . . .794 mm
Overall height (excluding mirrors)
  M600/750/900 1991 to 1997 models . . . . .1060 mm
  M600/750 1998 to 2000, M900 1998 and 1999 . . . . .1030 mm
  M600/750 2001, M900 2000 and 2001 . . . . .1050 mm
            (1130 mm M900S with cockpit fairing)
  M620/750/900 2002-on models .1058 mm
Seat height
  M600/620, 750 and 1993 to 2001 M900 . . . . .770 mm
  M900 2002 . . . . .800 mm
Minimum ground clearance
  M600/750/900 1991 to 2001 models . . . . .150 mm
  M620 model . . . . .120 mm (125 mm M620S)
  M750 2002 model . . . . .125 mm
  M900 2002 model . . . . .130 mm
Weight (dry)
  M600/620 . . . . .174 to 177 kg
  M750 . . . . .176 to 179 kg
  M900 1993 to 2001 . . . . .184 to 187 kg
  M900 2002 model . . . . .189 kg

Professional mechanics are trained in safe working procedures. However enthusiastic you may be about getting on with the job at hand, take the time to ensure that your safety is not put at risk. A moment's lack of attention can result in an accident, as can failure to observe simple precautions.

There will always be new ways of having accidents, and the following is not a comprehensive list of all dangers; it is intended rather to make you aware of the risks and to encourage a safe approach to all work you carry out on your bike.

Asbestos

● Certain friction, insulating, sealing and other products - such as brake pads, clutch linings, gaskets, etc. - contain asbestos. Extreme care must be taken to avoid inhalation of dust from such products since it is hazardous to health. If in doubt, assume that they do contain asbestos.

Fire

● Remember at all times that petrol is highly flammable. Never smoke or have any kind of naked flame around, when working on the vehicle. But the risk does not end there - a spark caused by an electrical short-circuit, by two metal surfaces contacting each other, by careless use of tools, or even by static electricity built up in your body under certain conditions, can ignite petrol vapour, which in a confined space is highly explosive. Never use petrol as a cleaning solvent. Use an approved safety solvent.

● Always disconnect the battery earth terminal before working on any part of the fuel or electrical system, and never risk spilling fuel on to a hot engine or exhaust.

● It is recommended that a fire extinguisher of a type suitable for fuel and electrical fires is kept handy in the garage or workplace at all times. Never try to extinguish a fuel or electrical fire with water.

Fumes

● Certain fumes are highly toxic and can quickly cause unconsciousness and even death if inhaled to any extent. Petrol vapour comes into this category, as do the vapours from certain solvents such as trichloro-ethylene. Any draining or pouring of such volatile fluids should be done in a well ventilated area.

● When using cleaning fluids and solvents, read the instructions carefully. Never use materials from unmarked containers - they may give off poisonous vapours.

● Never run the engine of a motor vehicle in an enclosed space such as a garage. Exhaust fumes contain carbon monoxide which is extremely poisonous; if you need to run the engine, always do so in the open air or at least have the rear of the vehicle outside the workplace.

The battery

● Never cause a spark, or allow a naked light near the vehicle's battery. It will normally be giving off a certain amount of hydrogen gas, which is highly explosive.

● Always disconnect the battery ground (earth) terminal before working on the fuel or electrical systems (except where noted).

● If possible, loosen the filler plugs or cover when charging the battery from an external source. Do not charge at an excessive rate or the battery may burst.

● Take care when topping up, cleaning or carrying the battery. The acid electrolyte, evenwhen diluted, is very corrosive and should not be allowed to contact the eyes or skin. Always wear rubber gloves and goggles or a face shield. If you ever need to prepare electrolyte yourself, always add the acid slowly to the water; never add the water to the acid.

Electricity

● When using an electric power tool, inspection light etc., always ensure that the appliance is correctly connected to its plug and that, where necessary, it is properly grounded (earthed). Do not use such appliances in damp conditions and, again, beware of creating a spark or applying excessive heat in the vicinity of fuel or fuel vapour. Also ensure that the appliances meet national safety standards.

● A severe electric shock can result from touching certain parts of the electrical system, such as the spark plug wires (HT leads), when the engine is running or being cranked, particularly if components are damp or the insulation is defective. Where an electronic ignition system is used, the secondary (HT) voltage is much higher and could prove fatal.

Remember...

✗ **Don't** start the engine without first ascertaining that the transmission is in neutral.

✗ **Don't** suddenly remove the pressure cap from a hot cooling system - cover it with a cloth and release the pressure gradually first, or you may get scalded by escaping coolant.

✗ **Don't** attempt to drain oil until you are sure it has cooled sufficiently to avoid scalding you.

✗ **Don't** grasp any part of the engine or exhaust system without first ascertaining that it is cool enough not to burn you.

✗ **Don't** allow brake fluid or antifreeze to contact the machine's paintwork or plastic components.

✗ **Don't** siphon toxic liquids such as fuel, hydraulic fluid or antifreeze by mouth, or allow them to remain on your skin.

✗ **Don't** inhale dust - it may be injurious to health (see Asbestos heading).

✗ **Don't** allow any spilled oil or grease to remain on the floor - wipe it up right away, before someone slips on it.

✗ **Don't** use ill-fitting spanners or other tools which may slip and cause injury.

✗ **Don't** lift a heavy component which may be beyond your capability - get assistance.

✗ **Don't** rush to finish a job or take unverified short cuts.

✗ **Don't** allow children or animals in or around an unattended vehicle.

✗ **Don't** inflate a tyre above the recommended pressure. Apart from overstressing the carcass, in extreme cases the tyre may blow off forcibly.

✔ **Do** ensure that the machine is supported securely at all times. This is especially important when the machine is blocked up to aid wheel or fork removal.

✔ **Do** take care when attempting to loosen a stubborn nut or bolt. It is generally better to pull on a spanner, rather than push, so that if you slip, you fall away from the machine rather than onto it.

✔ **Do** wear eye protection when using power tools such as drill, sander, bench grinder etc.

✔ **Do** use a barrier cream on your hands prior to undertaking dirty jobs - it will protect your skin from infection as well as making the dirt easier to remove afterwards; but make sure your hands aren't left slippery. Note that long-term contact with used engine oil can be a health hazard.

✔ **Do** keep loose clothing (cuffs, ties etc. and long hair) well out of the way of moving mechanical parts.

✔ **Do** remove rings, wristwatch etc., before working on the vehicle - especially the electrical system.

✔ **Do** keep your work area tidy - it is only too easy to fall over articles left lying around.

✔ **Do** exercise caution when compressing springs for removal or installation. Ensure that the tension is applied and released in a controlled manner, using suitable tools which preclude the possibility of the spring escaping violently.

✔ **Do** ensure that any lifting tackle used has a safe working load rating adequate for the job.

✔ **Do** get someone to check periodically that all is well, when working alone on the vehicle.

✔ **Do** carry out work in a logical sequence and check that everything is correctly assembled and tightened afterwards.

✔ **Do** remember that your vehicle's safety affects that of yourself and others. If in doubt on any point, get professional advice.

● If in spite of following these precautions, you are unfortunate enough to injure yourself, seek medical attention as soon as possible.

VIN (Vehicle Identification Number)

The frame serial number is stamped into the right-hand side of the steering head. The engine number is stamped into the left-hand side crankcase. Both of these numbers should be recorded and kept in a safe place so they can be furnished to law enforcement officials in the event of a theft.

The frame and engine serial numbers should also be kept in a handy place (such as with your driver's licence) so they are always available when purchasing or ordering parts for your machine.

The procedures in this manual identify the bikes by their production year, or where necessary by their VIN. Note that the production year is not necessarily the same as the year of registration.

Buying spare parts

Once you have found all the identification numbers, record them for reference when buying parts. Since the manufacturers change specifications, parts and vendors (companies that manufacture various components on the machine), providing the VIN is often the only way to be reasonably sure that you are buying the correct parts.

Whenever possible, take the worn part to the dealer so direct comparison with the new component can be made. Along the trail from the manufacturer to the parts shelf, there are numerous places that the part can end up with the wrong number or be listed incorrectly.

The two places to purchase new parts for your motorcycle – the accessory store and the franchised dealer – differ in the type of parts they carry. While dealers can obtain virtually every part for your motorcycle, the accessory dealer is usually limited to normal high wear items such as shock absorbers, tune-up parts, various engine gaskets, cables, chains, brake parts, etc. Rarely will an accessory outlet have major suspension components, cylinders, transmission gears, or cases.

Used parts can be obtained for roughly half the price of new ones, but you can't always be sure of what you're getting. Once again, take your worn part to the breaker for direct comparison.

Whether buying new, used or rebuilt parts, the best course is to deal directly with someone who specialises in parts for your particular make.

The frame number is stamped into the steering head

The engine number is stamped into the left-hand crankcase half

Engine oil level

Before you start

✔ Make sure the motorcycle is on level ground. Enlist the aid of an assistant to hold the bike upright whilst the oil level is checked.
✔ The oil level can be viewed through the sightglass in the right-hand crankcase cover – wipe any dirt off the glass to make the check easier.

Bike care:

● If you have to add oil frequently, you should check whether you have any oil leaks. If there is no sign of oil leakage from the joints and gaskets the engine could be burning oil (see *Fault Finding*).

The correct oil

● Modern, high-revving engines place great demands on their oil. It is very important that the correct oil for your bike is used.
● Always top up with a good quality oil of the specified type and viscosity and do not overfill the engine.

Oil type	Shell Advance Ultra 4 or any equivalent quality oil of SE, SF SG or higher rating
Oil viscosity	SAE 10W/40

*If you are using the motorcycle constantly in extreme conditions of heat or cold, other more suitable viscosity ranges may be used – refer to the viscosity table to select the oil best suited to your conditions.

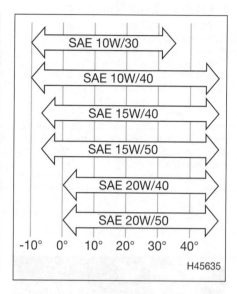

SAE 10W/30
SAE 10W/40
SAE 15W/40
SAE 15W/50
SAE 20W/40
SAE 20W/50

-10°   0°   10°   20°   30°   40°

H45635

1 Wipe the oil level sightglass in the crankcase right-hand cover.

2 With the motorcycle held vertical, the oil level should lie between the MAX and MIN lines.

3 To add oil, remove the filler cap from the front of the crankcase cover. Remove the fairing panel for access where necessary.

4 Top the engine up with the recommended oil, to bring the level up to the mid point between the MIN and MAX line.

Clutch fluid level

> **Warning: Brake and clutch hydraulic fluid can harm your eyes and damage painted surfaces, so use extreme caution when handling and pouring it and cover surrounding surfaces with rag. Do not use fluid that has been standing open for some time, as it absorbs moisture from the air which can cause a loss of clutch effectiveness.**

Before you start:

✔ Make sure you have a supply of DOT 4 hydraulic fluid.
✔ Position the bike on level ground and have an assistant hold it upright.

Bike care:

● If the fluid reservoir requires repeated topping-up this is an indication of a leak somewhere in the system, which should be investigated immediately.
● Check for signs of fluid leakage from the hydraulic hose and components – if found, rectify immediately.
● Check the operation of the clutch; if there is evidence of air in the system bleed the clutch as described in Chapter 2.

1 The clutch fluid level can be viewed through the sightglass on the square-bodied reservoir – it must lie above the MIN line (arrow).

2 The clutch fluid level can be seen through the translucent material of the remote round-bodied reservoir – it must lie between the MIN and MAX lines.

3 To top up the square-bodied clutch reservoir, remove the two screws and reservoir cover . . .

4 . . . and lift out the rubber diaphragm.

5 To top up the round-bodied clutch reservoir, unscrew the cap . . .

6 . . . then lift out the support ring and rubber diaphragm.

Suspension, steering and final drive

Suspension and steering:

● Check that the front and rear suspension operates smoothly without binding.
● Check that the suspension is adjusted as required (see Chapter 5 for details).

● Check that the steering moves smoothly from lock-to-lock.

Final drive:

● Check that the drive chain tension is correct and that the chain is adequately lubricated.
● If the chain looks dry, lubricate it – see Chapter 1.

Brake fluid levels

 Warning: Brake and clutch hydraulic fluid can harm your eyes and damage painted surfaces, so use extreme caution when handling and pouring it and cover surrounding surfaces with rag. Do not use fluid that has been standing open for some time, as it absorbs moisture from the air which can cause a dangerous loss of braking effectiveness.

Before you start:
✔ Make sure you have a supply of DOT 4 hydraulic fluid.
✔ Position the bike on level ground and have an assistant hold it upright.

Bike care:
● The fluid in the front and rear brake master cylinder reservoirs will drop slightly as the brake pads wear down.
● If any fluid reservoir requires repeated topping-up this is an indication of a leak somewhere in the system, which should be investigated immediately.

● Check for signs of fluid leakage from the hydraulic hoses and components – if found, rectify immediately.
● Check the operation of both brakes; if there is evidence of air in the system (spongy feel to lever or pedal), it must be bled as described in Chapter 6.

1 The brake fluid level can be viewed through the sightglass on the square-bodied reservoir – it must lie above the MIN line (arrow).

2 The brake fluid level can be seen through the translucent material of the remote round-bodied reservoir – it must lie between the MIN and MAX lines.

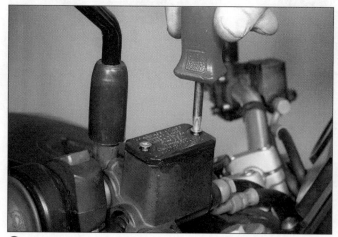

3 To top up the square-bodied front brake reservoir, remove the two screws and reservoir cover . . .

4 . . . then lift out the rubber diaphragm.

5 To top up the round-bodied front brake reservoir, remove the two screws and lift off the reservoir cover . . .

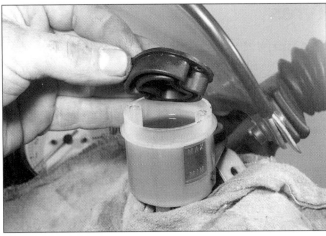

6 . . . then lift out the rubber diaphragm.

7 The rear brake fluid reservoir is located on the frame right-hand side. Unscrew the cap . . .

8 . . . lift out the support ring and rubber diaphragm to add fluid.

Legal and safety checks

Lighting and signalling:

● Take a minute to check that the headlight, tail light, brake light and turn signals all work correctly.
● Check that the horn sounds when the switch is operated.
● A working speedometer, graduated in mph, is a statutory requirement in the UK.

Safety:

● Check that the throttle grip rotates smoothly and snaps shut when released, in all steering positions.
● Check that sidestand return spring holds the stand securely up when retracted.

Fuel:

● This may seem obvious, but check that you have enough fuel to complete your journey. If you notice signs of fuel leakage – rectify the cause immediately.
● Ensure you use the correct grade unleaded fuel – see Chapter 3 Specifications.

Tyres

The correct pressures:

● Tyre pressures change with changes in air temperature and atmospheric pressure, therefore any change in the weather will affect the pressure of the tyre.

● The tyre pressures must be checked when **cold**, not immediately after riding. If the motorcycle has just been ridden the tyres will be warm and their pressures will have increased. Note that extremely low tyre pressures may cause the tyre to slip on the rim or come off. High tyre pressures will cause abnormal tread wear and unsafe handling.

● Refer to the tyre information label on the swingarm or to the machine's owners handbook for the correct tyre pressures for your model and year – if the label has been removed or you do not have a handbook either obtain one from your dealer or ask the dealer to look up the correct pressures. Note that if a different make of tyres to those specified for your model and year have been fitted it is also worth checking with the tyre manufacturer for their recommended pressure.

● Use an accurate pressure gauge. Many forecourt gauges are wildly inaccurate. If you buy your own, spend as much as you can justify on a quality gauge.

● Proper air pressure will increase tyre life and provide maximum stability and ride comfort.

Tyre care:

● Check the tyres carefully for cuts, tears, embedded nails or other sharp objects and excessive wear. Operation of the motorcycle with excessively worn tyres is extremely hazardous, as traction and handling are directly affected.

● Check the condition of the tyre valve and ensure the dust cap is in place.

● Pick out any stones or nails which may have become embedded in the tyre tread.

● If tyre damage is apparent, or unexplained loss of pressure is experienced, seek the advice of a tyre fitting specialist without delay.

Tyre tread depth:

● At the time of writing UK law requires that tread depth must be at least 1 mm over 3/4 of the tread breadth all the way around the tyre, with no bald patches. Many riders, however, consider 2 mm tread depth minimum to be a safer limit. Ducati recommend a minimum tread depth of 2 mm.

● Many tyres now incorporate wear indicators in the tread. Identify the triangular pointer or TWImark on the tyre sidewall to locate the indicator bars and replace the tyre if the tread has worn down to the bar.

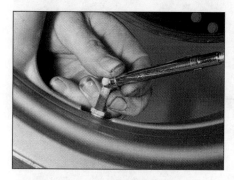

1 Check the tyre pressures when the tyres are **cold** and keep them properly inflated.

2 Measure tread depth at the centre of the tyre using a tread depth gauge.

3 Tyre tread wear indicator bar and its location marking (arrows).

Chapter 1
Routine maintenance and servicing

Contents

Air filter – cleaning 11
Battery – electrolyte level check 2
Brake – checks 14
Brake and clutch hoses – replacement 29
Brake hydraulic fluid – change 17
Cam belts – check 5
Cam belts – replacement 25
Carburettors/throttle body – synchronisation 10
Clutch hydraulic fluid – change 18
Control cables and pivot points – lubrication 15
Drive chain – check, adjustment and lubrication 1
Engine compression – check 13
Engine idle speed – check 9
Engine oil and spin-on filter – change 3
Engine oil pressure – check 12

Engine oil strainer – clean 16
Front fork oil – change 26
Fuel filter – replacement 7
Fuel system – checks 23
Nuts and bolts – tightness check 24
Rear wheel cush drive – check 22
Spark plugs – check 6
Suspension – check 20
Steering head bearings – check 19
Steering head bearings – lubrication 27
Swingarm bearings – lubrication 28
Throttle and choke cables freeplay – check 8
Valve clearances – check 4
Wheel bearings – check 21

Degrees of difficulty

Easy, suitable for novice with little experience	**Fairly easy,** suitable for beginner with some experience	**Fairly difficult,** suitable for competent DIY mechanic	**Difficult,** suitable for experienced DIY mechanic	**Very difficult,** suitable for expert DIY or professional

Spark plugs

Type
 600 and 620 models . . . .   Champion RA4HC
 750 and 900 models . . . .   Champion RA6HC
Electrode gap . . . .   0.6 mm

Engine idle speed

Carburettor models . . . .   1200 to 1300 rpm
Fuel injection models . . . .   see Section 9

Valve clearances

M620i.e., 620i.e. Sport, M750i.e., 750i.e. Supersport and Sport, M900i.e.
 Checking clearances
  Inlet opening rocker clearance . . . .   0.05 to 0.15 mm
  Inlet closing rocker clearance . . . .   0.00 to 0.20 mm
  Exhaust opening rocker clearance . . . .   0.05 to 0.15 mm
  Exhaust closing rocker clearance . . . .   0.00 to 0.20 mm
 Assembly clearances
  Inlet opening rocker clearance . . . .   0.10 to 0.15 mm
  Inlet closing rocker clearance . . . .   0.00 to 0.05 mm
  Exhaust opening rocker clearance . . . .   0.10 to 0.15 mm
  Exhaust closing rocker clearance . . . .   0.00 to 0.05 mm
900i.e. Supersport and Sport
 Checking clearances
  Inlet opening rocker clearance . . . .   0.05 to 0.12 mm
  Inlet closing rocker clearance . . . .   0.03 to 0.20 mm
  Exhaust opening rocker clearance . . . .   0.05 to 0.15 mm
  Exhaust closing rocker clearance . . . .   0.03 to 0.20 mm
 Assembly clearances
  Inlet opening rocker clearance . . . .   0.10 to 0.15 mm
  Inlet closing rocker clearance . . . .   0.10 to 0.15 mm
  Exhaust opening rocker clearance . . . .   0.00 to 0.05 mm
  Exhaust closing rocker clearance . . . .   0.00 to 0.05 mm
All other models
 Checking clearances
  Inlet opening rocker clearance . . . .   0.05 to 0.12 mm
  Inlet closing rocker clearance . . . .   0.03 to 0.20 mm
  Exhaust opening rocker clearance . . . .   0.05 to 0.15 mm
  Exhaust closing rocker clearance . . . .   0.03 to 0.20 mm
 Assembly clearances
  Inlet opening rocker clearance . . . .   0.10 to 0.12 mm
  Inlet closing rocker clearance . . . .   0.03 to 0.05 mm
  Exhaust opening rocker clearance . . . .   0.12 to 0.15 mm
  Exhaust closing rocker clearance . . . .   0.03 to 0.05 mm

Ducati specifies two different sets of valve clearances. The assembly clearances are for use during reassembly of the valve components (e.g. after cylinder head overhaul or a shim change) and the checking clearances are for use during standard service interval checks.

Oil pressure

620i.e. Sport
 Engine hot
  Between 1100 and 1300 rpm . . . .   more than 14.5 psi (1.0 Bar)
  Between 3500 and 4000 rpm . . . .   58 to 91 psi (4 to 6.3 Bar)
 Engine cold
  Between 1100 and 1300 rpm . . . .   more than 36 psi (2.5 Bar)
  Between 3500 and 4000 rpm . . . .   58 to 98 psi (4 to 6.8 Bar)
All other models
 Engine hot
  Between 1100 and 1300 rpm . . . .   21.3 psi (1.47 Bar)
  Between 3500 and 4000 rpm . . . .   57.0 psi (3.93 Bar)
 Engine cold
  Between 1100 and 1300 rpm . . . .   35.5 psi (2.45 Bar)
  Between 3500 and 4000 rpm . . . .   71.0 psi (4.90 Bar)

Cylinder compression
Standard . . . . 130 to 160 psi (9 to 11 Bar)
Minimum . . . . 116 psi (8 Bar)
Maximum difference between cylinders . . . . 29 psi (2 Bar)

Freeplay adjustments
Drive chain freeplay . . . . Refer to the label on the side of the swingarm
Front brake and clutch lever freeplay . . . . 1.0 to 1.5 mm
Throttle cable(s) . . . . 1.5 to 3.0 mm
Choke cable (lever operated type) . . . . 1.5 to 2.0 mm

Tyres
Pressures . . . . Refer to the tyre information label on the swingarm or to the machine's owners handbook
Tread depth . . . . 2 mm

Torque settings
Spark plugs . . . . 20 Nm
Engine oil drain plug . . . . 42 Nm
Rear wheel axle nut
    2003-on M620i.e. models . . . . 83 Nm
    All other models . . . . 72 Nm
Steering stem nut
    Supersport and Sport models with drilled circular nut . . . . 12 Nm
    2002-on Monster models (steering stem/bearing adjuster nut) . . . . . 30 Nm
    All other models . . . . 40 to 45 Nm
Top yoke pinch bolts
    8 mm thread . . . . 20 to 25 Nm
    10 mm thread . . . . 35 to 38 Nm

Recommended lubricants and fluids
Engine oil type . . . . Shell Advance Ultra 4 or any equivalent quality oil of SE, SF SG or higher rating
Engine oil viscosity . . . . SAE 10W/40
Engine oil capacity . . . . Approx. 3 lit (600 and 750 engines), approx. 3.5 lit (900 engine) – top up to correct mark (see *Daily (pre-ride) checks*)
Brake fluid . . . . Agip F1 Super HD DOT 4 or Shell Advance DOT 4
Fork oil . . . . see Chapter 5 Specifications
Drive chain . . . . Agip Rocol chain lube spray, aerosol chain lube suitable for O-ring chains or SAE90 gear oil
Wheel bearings . . . . High melting-point grease
Swingarm bearings . . . . Multi-purpose grease
Steering head bearings . . . . Multi-purpose grease
Cables, lever and stand pivot points . . . . Motor oil
Throttle grip . . . . Multi-purpose grease or dry film lubricant

Component locations on right-hand side

1 Fuel filter
   (location varies)
2 Idle speed screw
3 Front brake reservoir
4 Brake pads
5 Cam belt tensioners
6 Oil filler
7 Spin-on filter
8 Oil pressure switch
9 Oil filter gauze
10 Oil level sightglass
11 Oil drain plug
12 Rear brake reservoir

Component locations on left-hand side

1 Wheel bearings
2 Fork seals
3 Clutch reservoir
4 Steering head
   bearings
5 Air filter
6 Battery
7 Valves
8 Cush drive
9 Drive chain
10 Swingarm bearings
11 Spark plugs

Note: *Always perform the daily (pre-ride) checks at every maintenance interval (in addition to the procedures listed). The intervals differ according to model year – if those listed below differ from the information in your owner's manual, use those in the owner's manual.*

Daily (pre-ride) checks

☐ See *'Daily (pre-ride) checks'* at the beginning of this manual.

After the initial 600 miles (1000 km)

Note: *This check is usually performed by a Ducati dealer after the first 600 miles (1000 km) from new. Thereafter, maintenance is carried out according to the following intervals of the schedule.*

Every 600 miles (1000 km)

Carry out all the following tasks from the Daily (pre-ride) checks Section

☐ Check the engine oil level.
☐ Check the brake fluid levels and brake operation.
☐ Check the clutch fluid level and clutch operation.
☐ Check the tyre pressures, condition, and tread depth.
☐ Check for correct operation of all controls.
☐ Check the drive chain tension (Sec 1).
☐ Lubricate the drive chain (Sec 1).
☐ Check the battery electrolyte level – standard batteries (Sec 2).
☐ Check the braking system and brake pad wear (Sec 14).

Minor service

Every 3000 miles (5000 km) – 91/92/93 models
Every 4600 miles (7500 km) – 94 models
Every 6200 miles (10,000 km) – 95-on models

☐ Change the engine oil and spin-on filter (Sec 3).
☐ Check the valve clearances (Sec 4).
☐ Check the cam belts (Sec 5).
☐ Check the spark plugs (Sec 6).
☐ Replace the fuel filter (Sec 7).
☐ Check the throttle and choke cable freeplay (Sec 8)
☐ Check engine idle speed (Sec 9).
☐ Check carburettor synchronisation (carburettor models) (Sec 10).

Minor service (continued)

☐ Check the air filter (Sec 11).
☐ Check the engine oil pressure (Sec 12).
☐ Check the engine compression (Sec 13).
☐ Check the braking system and brake pad wear (Sec 14).
☐ Lubricate control cables and pivot points (Sec 15).

Major service

Every 6000 miles (10,000 km) – 91/92/93 models
Every 9300 miles (15,000 km) – 94 models
Every 12,400 miles (20,000 km) – 95-on models

Carry out all the items under the minor service, plus all of the following:

☐ Clean the engine oil strainer (Sec 16).
☐ Change the brake hydraulic fluid (Sec 17).
☐ Change the clutch hydraulic fluid (Sec 18).
☐ Check the steering head bearings for play (Sec 19).
☐ Check the front and rear suspension (Sec 20).
☐ Check the wheel bearings for play (Sec 21).
☐ Check the rear wheel cush drive for wear (Sec 22).
☐ Check the fuel system (Sec 23).
☐ Check the tightness of all nuts and bolts (Sec 24).
☐ Check throttle body synchronisation (fuel injection models) (Sec 10).

Additional maintenance

Every 12,000 miles (20,000 km) or two years – all models
☐ Replace the cam belts (Sec 25).

Every 12,000 miles (20,000 km) – 91/92/93 models
Every 14,000 miles (22,500 km) – 94 models
Every 18,500 miles (30,000 km) – 95-on models
☐ Change the front fork oil (Sec 26).

Non -scheduled maintenance

☐ Grease the steering head bearings (Sec 27)
☐ Grease the swingarm bearings (Sec 28)
☐ Replace the brake and clutch hoses (Sec 29)

1 This Chapter is designed to help the home mechanic maintain his/her motorcycle for safety, economy, long life and peak performance.

2 Deciding where to start or plug into the routine maintenance schedule depends on several factors. If the warranty period on your motorcycle has just expired, and if it has been maintained according to the warranty standards, you may want to pick up routine maintenance as it coincides with the next mileage or calendar interval. If you have owned the machine for some time but have never performed any maintenance on it, then you may want to start at the nearest interval and include some additional procedures to ensure that nothing important is overlooked. If you have just had a major engine overhaul, then you may want to start the maintenance routine from the beginning. If you have a used machine and have no knowledge of its history or maintenance record, you may desire to combine all the checks into one large service initially and then settle into the maintenance schedule prescribed.

3 Before beginning any maintenance or repair, the machine should be cleaned thoroughly, especially around the oil filter, spark plugs, valve covers, side panels, drive chain, etc. Cleaning will help ensure that dirt does not contaminate the engine and will allow you to detect wear and damage that could otherwise easily go unnoticed.

4 Certain maintenance information is sometimes printed on decals attached to the motorcycle. If the information on the decals differs from that included here, use the information on the decal.

Every 600 miles (1000 km)

1 Drive chain – check, adjustment and lubrication

Check

1 A neglected drive chain will not last long and can quickly damage the sprockets. The drive chain uses O-rings to permanently seal grease inside the links. Damaging the O-rings will allow the grease to leak out, ruining the chain.

2 If an auxiliary stand is available, use this to enable the rear wheel to be rotated easily. Remove the engine sprocket cover screws and lift the cover away (see illustration).

3 Make sure the transmission is in neutral and slowly rotate the wheel, checking for damaged rollers, loose links and pins. Also check the sprocket teeth for wear (see illustration). Install the engine sprocket cover.

Adjustment

4 To check the drive chain tension, the bike must be supported on its sidestand, without a rider seated.

5 Find the chain's tightest spot by rotating the rear wheel and feeling the amount of freeplay present on the bottom run of the chain, testing along the complete length of the chain. When the tightest spot has been found, position that point midway between the sprockets on the bottom run of the chain.

6 Measure the total up and down movement available on the bottom run of the chain midway between the sprockets (see illustration). This measurement should be as stated on the chain adjustment label stuck to the side of the swingarm (see illustration). If not, the chain must be adjusted as follows.

7 The design of chain adjuster, and therefore the method of adjustment, differs according to model.

8 On all Monster models, slacken the rear axle nut and turn the chain adjuster bolt at the end of the swingarm until chain tension is correct (see illustration). Adjust each bolt by

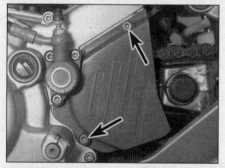

1.2 Sprocket cover is retained by two screws (arrows) on 900 engine

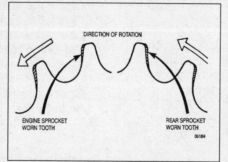

1.3 Check the sprockets for wear in the areas indicated

1.6a Chain freeplay is measured midway between the sprockets on the chain's bottom run

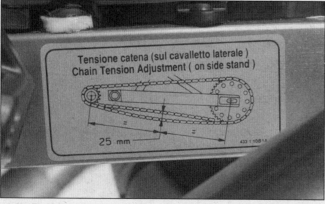

1.6b Refer to label on swingarm for chain freeplay specification

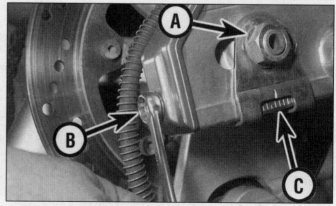

1.8 On Monster models, slacken axle nut (A) and adjust with bolts (B). Wheel alignment marks (C)

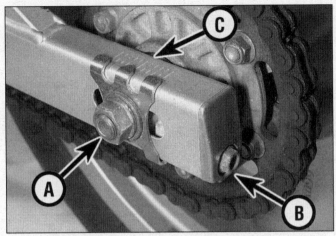

1.9 On 600SS and later 750SS models slacken axle nut (A) and adjust with bolts (B). Wheel alignment marks (C)

1.10 On 900 SS/SL and early 750 SS, slacken axle nut (A), followed by locknut (B) and make adjustment with bolt (C)

the same amount to preserve wheel alignment; check alignment by inspecting the adjuster plate pointer position in relation to the scale on the bottom edge of the swingarm. Tighten the axle nut to the specified torque setting.

9 On all 600SS, 620i.e. Sport and later 750SS, Sport and Supersport models, slacken the rear axle nut and turn the chain adjuster bolt at the end of the swingarm until chain tension is correct **(see illustration)**. Adjust each bolt by the same amount to preserve wheel alignment; check alignment by inspecting the adjuster plate pointer position in relation to the scale on the top of the swingarm. Tighten the axle nut to the specified torque.

10 On all 900SS/SL, Sport and Supersport and early 750SS models, slacken the rear axle nut and the chain adjuster locknut **(see illustration)**. Turn the adjuster bolt until chain tension is correct. Adjust each bolt by the same amount to preserve wheel alignment; check alignment by noting the adjuster block index mark in relation to the scale of the lower edge of the swingarm. Tighten the adjuster nut securely and the axle nut to the specified torque setting.

11 If the wheel alignment is suspect, a more accurate check can be made by following the procedure in Chapter 5.

12 Check that the wheel spins freely after adjustment.
13 Check the security of the rear wheel sprocket nuts **(see illustration)**. If loose, tighten them to the specified torque setting, holding them from the opposite side if necessary.

Lubrication

14 Although the chain fitted as standard equipment is of the O-ring type, grease being sealed into the internal bearing surfaces by O-rings at each end of the rollers, lubrication is still required to prevent the rollers from wearing on the sprocket teeth and to prevent the O-rings from drying up. A chain lube spray or heavy (SAE 90) gear oil is suitable for this task.
15 If an auxiliary stand is available use it to raise the rear wheel off the ground. Whilst spinning the rear wheel, spray lube onto the rollers until all are oily, then apply a small amount to the O-rings on each side.
Caution: Some propellants used in aerosols cause the O-rings to deteriorate very rapidly, so make certain that the product is marked as being suitable for use with O-ring type chains.

HAYNES HiNT *Apply oil to the top of the lower chain run – centrifugal force will work it into the chain when the bike is moving.*

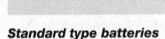
2 Battery – electrolyte level check

Standard type batteries
Caution: Be extremely careful when handling or working around the battery. The electrolyte is very caustic and an explosive gas (hydrogen) is given off when the battery is charging.

1 The battery is located under the fuel tank. Disconnect the fuel tank breather hose from its union (early SS and SL models only), release the tank front catch and raise the tank onto its prop.
2 Remove the battery as described in Chapter 8.
3 Compare the level in each cell to the UPPER and LOWER lines on the battery **(see illustration)**. If the level in any cell does not lie between these marks, remove the cell caps and top up to the upper level mark using only distilled water **(see illustration)**.
4 Check the battery for any signs of pale grey sediment at the bottom of the casing. This is caused by sulphation of the plates due to recharging at too high a rate or as a result of the battery being left discharged for long

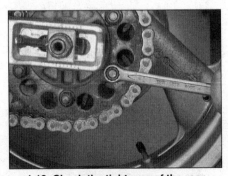
1.13 Check the tightness of the rear sprocket nuts

2.3a Electrolyte level must lie between UPPER and LOWER lines on battery case

2.3b Unscrew cell caps to add distilled water

periods. A good battery should have little or no sediment visible and its plates should be straight and pale grey or brown in colour. If sediment deposits are deep enough to reach the bottom of the plates, or if the plates are buckled and have whitish deposits on them, the battery is faulty and must be renewed. Remember that a poor battery will give rise to a large number of minor electrical faults.

5 Inspect then install the battery as described in Chapter 8.

6 If the machine is not in regular use, disconnect the battery and give it a refresher charge every month to six weeks (see Chapter 8).

Maintenance-free (MF) batteries

7 If a sealed MF (maintenance free) battery is fitted, all that should be done is to check that the terminals are clean and tight and that the casing is not damaged or leaking. See Chapter 8 for further details. **Note:** *Do not attempt to remove the battery caps to check the electrolyte level or battery specific gravity. Removal will damage the caps, resulting in electrolyte leakage and battery damage.*

8 If the machine is not in regular use, remove the battery and give it a refresher charge every month to six weeks (see Chapter 8).

 Battery terminal corrosion can be minimised by applying a layer of petroleum jelly or battery terminal grease to the terminals after the leads have been connected.

Minor service

 3 Engine oil and spin-on filter – change

⚠️ *Warning: Be careful when draining the oil, as the exhaust pipes, the engine, and the oil itself can cause severe burns.*

1 Consistent routine oil and filter changes are the single most important maintenance procedure you can perform on a motorcycle. The oil not only lubricates the internal parts of the engine and transmission, but it also acts as a coolant, a cleaner, a sealant, and a protectant. Because of these demands, the oil takes a terrific amount of abuse and should be replaced often with new oil of the recommended type and viscosity. Saving a little money on the difference in cost between a good oil and a cheap oil won't pay off if the engine is damaged.

2 Before changing the oil, warm up the engine so the oil will drain easily. On fully-faired models, remove the lower right-hand panel (see Chapter 7).

3 Put the motorcycle on its sidestand and position a clean drain tray below the engine. Unscrew the oil filler cap at the front of the crankcase right-hand cover to vent the crankcase and to act as a reminder that there is no oil in the engine.

4 Next, unscrew the oil drain plug from the underside of the right-hand crankcase half and allow the oil to flow into the drain tray **(see illustration)** – hold the motorcycle upright for a minute to allow the last drops of oil to drain. Discard the sealing washer on the drain plug as it should be replaced whenever the plug is removed. Clean any swarf off the plug magnet.

5 Position the oil drain tray so that it is below the spin-on oil filter. Unscrew the oil filter by hand or using a universal filter tool **(see illustration)** or the service tool (Pt. No. 067503210); it may be possible to use a narrow banded strap wrench. Clean the filter thread and housing on the crankcase using clean rag. Wipe off any remaining oil from the filter sealing area.

6 When the oil has completely drained, fit a new sealing washer over the drain plug **(see illustration)**. Fit the plug to the crankcase and tighten it to the torque setting specified at the beginning of the Chapter. Avoid overtightening, as damage to the threads will result.

7 Apply a smear of clean engine oil to the rubber sealing ring on the new filter, then install the filter onto the engine and tighten it by hand **(see illustrations)**. Do not overtighten the filter as the seal will be damaged and the filter will leak.

8 Refill the crankcase with oil to the proper level (see *Daily (pre-ride) checks*) and install the filler cap. Start the engine and let it run for two or three minutes (make sure that the oil pressure light extinguishes after a few seconds). Shut it off, wait a few minutes, then check the oil level – add more oil if necessary.

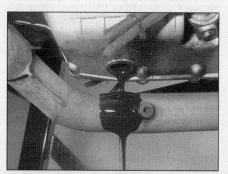

3.4 Unscrew the engine/transmission oil drain plug and allow the oil to drain fully

3.5 Removing the spin-on oil filter with a universal filter tool

3.6 Use a new sealing washer on the oil drain plug

3.7a Smear oil over the filter sealing ring . . .

3.7b . . . and tighten the filter by hand

Check that there are no oil leaks from the drain plug, spin-on filter and cartridge filter.

9 On fully-faired models, install the fairing panel (see Chapter 7).

10 The old oil drained from the engine cannot be re-used and should be disposed of properly. Check with your local refuse disposal company, disposal facility or environmental agency to see whether they will accept the used oil for recycling. Don't pour used oil into drains or onto the ground.

> **HAYNES HiNT** *Check the old oil carefully – if it is very metallic coloured, then the engine is experiencing wear from break-in (new engine) or from insufficient lubrication. If there are flakes or chips of metal in the oil, then something is drastically wrong internally and the engine will have to be disassembled for inspection and repair. If there are pieces of fibre-like material in the oil, the clutch is experiencing excessive wear and should be checked (wet clutch models).*

4 Valve clearances – check

Note: *Many owners will not be familiar with Desmodromic valve operation and may therefore prefer to entrust the work to a Ducati dealer.*

Valve clearance check

1 The engine must be completely cool for this maintenance procedure, so let the machine sit overnight before beginning.

2 Support the bike on an auxiliary stand.

3 On fully-faired models remove both fairing lower panels (see Chapter 7).

4 Remove both valve inspection covers and gaskets from the horizontal cylinder head. On machines fitted with an oil cooler, ensure that the cooler is supported with cable ties or string to prevent any strain being placed on its hoses.

5 Clearance is restricted on the vertical cylinder. Remove the battery (see Chapter 8) and its tray or support as required according to model **(see illustrations)**. On SS, SL, Sport and Supersport models remove the rear shock absorber top and bottom mounting bolts and manoeuvre the shock out of the frame **(see illustrations)** – it may be necessary to lift the rear of the machine slightly to allow the shock to clear the frame. When access if available to the valve covers, remove them with their gaskets.

6 The valve clearances must be measured with the valve closed, piston at TDC. Measure the opening and closing clearance on each valve as follows.

7 Check the closing rocker clearance first; i.e. the clearance between the rocker and closing shim **(see illustration)**. It will be necessary to hold the closing rocker down with a flat-bladed screwdriver, against valve spring pressure, to permit the clearance to be

measured. Use a feeler gauge to check the clearance and compare it with the specification. **Note:** *This clearance will be almost negligible – check though that the closing rocker shim can be rotated by finger pressure.*

8 Next check the opening rocker clearance; i.e. the clearance between the rocker and opening shim **(see illustration)**. Use a feeler gauge to check the clearance and compare it with the specifications, noting that the clearances differ for inlet and exhaust valves.

9 If any clearance is outside of the range and particularly if it exceeds the service limit, it should be adjusted by changing the size of the opening or closing rocker shim (as applicable). Take note of the exact clearance measured for use in calculating the new shim size.

Closing rocker clearance adjustment

10 First dislodge the opening rocker arm by sliding it across after removal of the spring clip **(see illustrations overleaf)**. Lift off the shim.

11 If working on the vertical cylinder, note that the valve will drop down into the combustion chamber once the wire collets are released; to prevent this, remove the spark plug and pass a length of welding rod hooked at the end, into the cylinder so that it can be held against the valve head. Press down on the closing rocker arm to relieve valve spring tension and pick out the two wire collet halves

4.5a Pull the rubber mounting pad out of the battery tray . . .

4.5b . . . for access to the vertical cylinder's inlet valve cover

4.5c On SS and SL models the rear shock absorber must be removed . . .

4.5d . . . to access the vertical cylinder's exhaust valve cover

4.7 Measuring the closing rocker clearance

4.8 Measuring the opening rocker clearance

4.10a Pick out the spring clip from the opening rocker shaft . . .

4.10b . . . move the rocker arm across and lift off the opening shim

4.11a Pick out the wire collets whilst holding the closing rocker down . . .

4.11b . . . and lift off the closing shim

4.17 Make sure the shims locate on each side of the spring clip

4.19 Measuring the opening rocker shim thickness

(see illustration). Slip the closing rocker shim off the valve (see illustration).

12 Measure the thickness of the shim with a micrometer. Note: *Due to the shim profile, you may need to have an engineering works turn up a couple of pads to fit inside the shim to enable the micrometer to make contact.*

13 If the closing rocker clearance measured was more than the standard clearance you need a thicker shim; subtract the standard clearance from the measured clearance and add this to the thickness of the existing shim to obtain the size of the new shim.

14 If the closing rocker clearance measured was less than the standard clearance you need a thinner shim; subtract the measured clearance from the standard clearance, then subtract this figure from the thickness of the existing shim to obtain the size of the new shim.

15 Replacement shims are available in various increments, ranging from 5.0 to 9.6 mm.

16 Before the shim is installed, inspect the wire collets and their groove in the valve stem. If the collets appear worn or a poor fit in the valve stem groove they must be renewed.

17 Install the new shim and hold the closing rocker arm down while the wire collets are slipped into place. Make sure they seat correctly, then install the opening rocker shim. Slide the opening valve rocker back into position. Install the spring clip, ensuring the shims locate on each side of it (see illustration).

18 Recheck the closing valve clearance. Install all disturbed components in a reverse of the removal sequence, using new gaskets on the valve covers.

Opening rocker clearance adjustment

19 To remove the opening rocker shim, use pliers to pull the spring clip from position, then move the rocker arm across in its place (see illustrations 4.10a and 4.10b). Lift off the shim. Use a micrometer to measure the thickness of the shim, noting that the post of the micrometer must sit inside the shouldered side of the shim (see illustration).

20 If the opening rocker clearance was less than the standard clearance, calculate the difference and subtract this from the size of the existing shim. For example, if the inlet valve clearance measured is 0.07 mm subtract this from the standard of 0.11 mm to obtain the correction figure. Take the thickness of the existing shim (say 3.4 mm) and subtract the correction figure (0.04 mm) to arrive at the new pad thickness of 3.36 mm.

21 In the event that the measured clearance is more than the standard, a thicker shim is required, and can be calculated by adding the difference to the existing shim size.

22 Replacement shims are available various thickness ranging from 2.0 to 5.0 or 5.6 mm depending on engine size.

23 Install the new size shim and slide the opening valve rocker back into position. Install the spring clip, making sure that the shims locate on each side of it (see illustration 4.17).

24 Recheck the opening valve clearance. Install all disturbed components in a reverse of the removal sequence, using new gaskets on the valve covers.

5 Cam belts – check

1991 to 1997 models

Note: *Setting the correct cam belt tension requires the use of the Ducati service tool (Pt. No. 88713.0748) or a spring balance. The service tool is calibrated with an index mark at the point of correct tension.*

1 On fully-faired models, remove the fairing right-hand lower panel (see Chapter 7).

2 On 600 and 750 cc engines remove the seven cam belt cover screws and remove both covers. On the 900 cc engine, it is only necessary to remove the two inspection covers from the main cam belt covers; each is secured by two screws (see illustration). Note, however that removal of the main

5.2 Cam belt tensioner can be accessed through inspection cover on 900 engine

5.3a Using the service tool to tension the cam belt. Tighten tensioner screw (arrow) to lock tensioner position

5.3b Using a spring balance to tension the cam belt

5.6a On the 900 engine, install the centre cam belt cover . . .

5.6b . . . followed by the vertical cylinder cover . . .

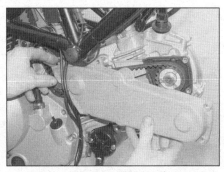

5.6c . . . and the horizontal cylinder cover

may therefore be to have belt tension set by a Ducati dealer equipped with the necessary equipment. You can, however, make a visual inspection of the belts and perform a rough check of the tension as described below.

8 On fully-faired models, remove the fairing right-hand lower panel.

9 On models with a two-piece cover arrangement, remove both cam belt covers **(see illustrations)**. On models with a three-piece cover arrangement, remove both main covers and centre cover **(see illustrations 5.6a, b and c)**.

10 Inspect each belt along its backing (flat side) and edges and check that it is not worn or damaged in any way. Check the working surface of the belt for damaged teeth, cracking between the teeth, and wear of the belt material – a shiny surface indicates extreme wear. If either belt shows signs of wear or damage, replace both belts with new ones as a pair (see Chapter 2).

11 A rough check of belt tension can be made by twisting the belt at its mid-point between the tensioner and the upper pulley. As a rule of thumb, when the belt is tensioned correctly it should just be possible to twist it by 45° with finger pressure. Any more and the belt is too slack.

12 To adjust the tension temporarily (if required), first set the valve timing so the horizontal cylinder is at TDC – remove both spark plugs to make turning the engine easier, then rotate the crankshaft so that the mark on the camshaft drive pulley aligns with the scribed line on the crankcase right-hand cover **(see illustration)**. **Note:** *To turn the*

covers will enable a full inspection of the belts as described in Step 5.

3 Have ready an Allen key to fit the tensioner bolts, then attach the hook of the service tool to the roller of the tensioner **(see illustration)**. Slacken off the tensioner bolts, then tension the belt with the service tool until the index marks on the tool align; at this exact position, tighten the tensioner bolts. **Note:** *The calibrated force of the service tool was measured and found to be 4.5 kg (10 lbs), enabling a conventional spring balance to be used (see illustration).* As a rule of thumb, when the belt is tensioned correctly it should just be possible to twist it by 45° with finger pressure. Any more than this and the belt is too slack.

4 Tension the other belt using the same procedure.

5 At the same time as belt tension is being carried out, inspect the belt for damage, wear or deterioration. Irrespective of whether the

belt is due for its scheduled renewal or not, if it shows any sign of problems, both belts must be renewed.

6 Install the belt covers and secure with their retaining screws **(see illustrations)**. Note that it is important that the covers seat correctly and are not broken, otherwise stone chips could penetrate the casing and damage the belts.

7 Install the fairing panel, where applicable.

1998-on models

Note: *Ducati specify the use of their mechanical Lowener gauge (part no. 051.2.001.1A) or Mathesis electronic belt tension tester to ensure the belts are set to the correct tension. There are two things to consider here, one is that both gauges are expensive items and will not be used all that frequently and the other is that to set belt tension on the vertical cylinder's belt using the mechanical gauge, the engine must be removed from the frame. The most cost-effective solution*

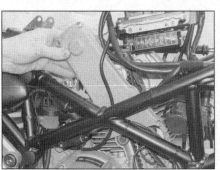

5.9a Two-piece covers – remove the vertical cylinder cover first . . .

5.9b . . . then the horizontal cover

5.12a Align the mark (A) with the line (B)

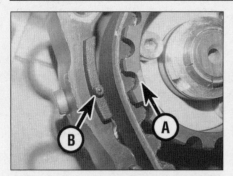

5.12b On the vertical cylinder the mark (A) aligns with the peg (B)

5.12c On the horizontal cylinder the mark (A) aligns with the gap (B)

5.13a Fit the special tools or suitable screws locating the ends in the pulley flange notches to lock them in place (arrow)

5.13b Slacken the pulley bolts (arrowed)

5.13c Tensioner bolts (arrowed)

crankshaft, position the bike on an auxiliary stand so that the rear wheel is off the ground, shift the transmission into first gear and rotate the rear wheel by hand. At this point the mark on the vertical cylinder camshaft pulley should align roughly with the peg on the belt shroud **(see illustration)**, and the mark on the horizontal pulley should align roughly with the gap between the two ridges on the cover back-piece **(see illustration)**.

13 Remove the screws from the shroud and the back-piece and replace them with either the special tools (part no. 88713.2009) or a longer screw of the same thread with its end shaped to fit in the notch in the pulley flange, thereby locking the flange and hence the camshaft in position **(see illustration)**. Slacken the three pulley bolts **(see illustration)**. Slacken the tensioner bolts and reset the tensioner so the twist is as described, then tighten the tensioner bolts

and the pulley bolts **(see illustration)**.

14 Remove the flange locking screws and replace them with the original shorter ones, then fit the belt covers. Now take the bike to a Ducati dealer to have the tension checked using the specialised equipment, and if necessary re-set. For those equipped with the Lowener gauge referred to in the note above, the correct figure for belt tension is 2.5 to 3.0 Lowener units.

6 Spark plugs – check

1 On fully-faired models, remove the fairing left-hand lower panel (see Chapter 7). Clean the area around each valve cover and plug channel to prevent any dirt falling into the combustion chamber.

2 Pull the cap off the spark plug. Using the plug spanner from the toolkit or a suitable deep socket (16 mm for the OE plug), unscrew and remove each spark plug **(see illustration)**.

3 Inspect the electrodes for wear. Both the centre and side electrodes should have square edges and the side electrode should be of uniform thickness. Look for excessive deposits and evidence of a cracked or chipped insulator around the centre electrode. Compare your spark plugs to the colour spark plug reading chart at the end of this manual. Check the threads, the washer and the ceramic insulator body for cracks and other damage.

4 If the electrodes are not excessively worn, and if the deposits can be easily removed with a wire brush, the plugs can be regapped and re-used (if no cracks or chips are visible in the insulator). If in doubt concerning the condition of the plugs, replace them with new ones, as the expense is minimal.

5 Cleaning spark plugs by sandblasting is permitted, provided you clean the plugs with a high flash-point solvent afterwards.

6 Before installing the plugs, make sure they are the correct type and heat range and check the gap between the electrodes (they are not pre-set on new plugs). For best results, use a wire-type gauge rather than a flat (feeler) gauge to check the gap. Compare the gap to that specified and adjust as necessary. If the gap must be adjusted, bend the side electrode only and be very careful not to chip or crack the insulator nose **(see illustrations)**.

6.2 Use a plug spanner or deep socket to remove the spark plugs

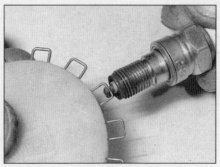

6.6a A wire type gauge is recommended to measure the spark plug electrode gap

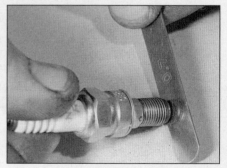

6.6b A blade type feeler gauge can also be used

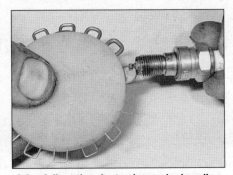

6.6c Adjust the electrode gap by bending the side electrode

Make sure the washer is in place before installing each plug.

7 Since the cylinder head is made of aluminium, which is soft and easily damaged, thread the plugs into the heads by hand. Once the plugs are finger-tight, the job can be finished with a socket. Tighten the spark plugs to the specified torque listed in this Chapter's Specifications; do not over-tighten them.

8 Reconnect the spark plug caps.

> **HAYNES HINT** *Slip a short length of hose over the end of the plug to use as a tool to thread it into place. The hose will grip the plug well enough to turn it, but will start to slip if the plug begins to cross-thread in the hole – this will prevent damaged threads and the resultant repair costs.*

7 Fuel filter – replacement

> ⚠ **Warning: Petrol is extremely flammable, so take extra precautions when you work on any part of the fuel system.** Don't smoke or allow open flames or bare light bulbs near the work area, and don't work in a garage where a natural gas-type appliance is present. If you spill any fuel on your skin, rinse it off immediately with soap and water. When you perform

any kind of work on the fuel system, wear safety glasses and have a fire extinguisher suitable for a class B type fire (flammable liquids) on hand.

SS, SL, Sport and Supersport models

1 The fuel filter is fitted inside the fuel tank on these models. It is a sealed unit, which cannot be cleaned; it must be replaced with a new one at the specified interval.

2 Perform this task when the tank is as empty as possible. Ideally the tank should be drained of all fuel.

3 Remove the front and two rear filler cap screws, and where fitted undo the inner security screw (accessed after unlocking and raising the filler cap) to free the filler cap and its surround **(see illustration)**. Plug the filler cap with a wad of rag, then fully back-off the Allen-headed grub screws from inside the filler cap housing and lift the housing and its O-ring from the tank. Note that the housing will be a tight fit in the tank due to its seals – use finger pressure via the filler hole to prise it free. Disconnect the filler cap drain hose(s) from the underside of the housing if required – alternatively you can drape the housing over the tank and lay it on some rag if enough hose is available **(see illustrations)**.

4 The filter can theoretically be removed after releasing its hose clamps, but it was found that access was very limited and removal of the complete filter and pump unit as an assembly was preferred. Note that on fuel injection models there may be residual pressure in the system. Disconnect the hose

from the fuel filter, then reach right inside the tank and manoeuvre the pump out of its clips **(see illustration)**. Lift the assembly out of the tank and rest it on rags on top of the tank – there is no need to disconnect the fuel pump wiring unless you prefer to. Disconnect the other end of the filter to free it from the pump hose.

5 Install the new filter so that the OUT marking or arrow is towards the internal metal pipe inside the tank **(see illustration)**.

6 Make a quick check of the gauze filter bag on the inlet side of the fuel pump, cleaning it if necessary. If heavily contaminated, the drained fuel should be safely disposed of and the tank cleaned with a flushing agent.

7 With the filter and pump assembly reinstalled, apply a smear of grease to the filler cap housing O-ring and make sure it is seated in its groove. Reconnect the drain hose(s) if detached and fit the housing into the fuel tank, making sure that the O-ring and upper seal remain in place. Temporarily install the filler cap to ensure that the housing is correctly aligned. Thread the grub screws into place evenly in a criss-cross sequence – this is necessary to ensure that the housing is centralised in the tank.

8 Install the filler cap and secure it with the three screws and the security screw where fitted.

9 Either install the drain plug (with new sealing washer) and install the tank as described in Chapter 4, or reconnect its fuel hose and lower it back into position (as applicable). Refill the tank with the drained fuel.

7.3a Fuel filler cap is secured by three screws (arrows)

7.3b Back off the grub screws . . .

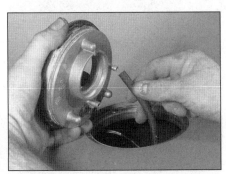

7.3c . . . to free the filler cap housing. Disconnect the drain hose

7.4 Fuel filter and pump are removed as a complete unit

7.5 Filter installed with OUT marking towards internal metal pipe

7.13 Hose clamp can be used on the fuel inlet hose to prevent fuel flow

7.14 Filter is clamped to tank underside with a single screw (arrow)

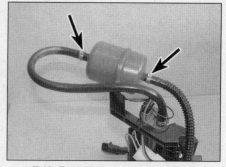

7.19 Fuel filter clamps (arrowed)

Monster models with carburettor engines

Early M900 models (up to VIN 004462)

10 The fuel filter is located forward of the right-hand side panel, and is held in a rubber mounting. Raise the fuel tank onto its prop and turn the fuel tap to the OFF position. Remove the right-hand side panel.

11 Have a rag handy to catch any fuel spills, then disconnect the two hoses from the fuel filter. Work the filter out of its rubber mounting and install the new one.

12 Reconnect the fuel pipes and secure them with their clamps. Turn the fuel tap ON and check that there are no fuel leaks. Refit all disturbed components.

Later M900 models (from VIN 004463) and all M600/750 models

13 The tank must either be drained of fuel via the drain bolt in its base, or a hose clamp applied to the fuel inlet hose to shut-off supply **(see illustration)**. If the tank is drained, remove it from the machine as described in Chapter 3 and store the fuel in a container which is suitable for petrol.

14 Have a rag handy to catch any fuel spills, then disconnect the two hoses from the fuel filter. Remove the mounting clamp screw to free the filter **(see illustration)**.

15 Reconnect the fuel pipes to the filter stubs (outlet pipe to tap connects to the angled stub of the filter) and secure them with their

clamps; if the clamps cannot be re-used replace them with new ones.

16 Refill the fuel tank with petrol, or release the hose clamp, and check that there are no leaks.

Monster models with fuel injected engines

Fuel injection models with metal fuel tank

17 Refer to Steps 1 to 9.

Fuel injection models with plastic fuel tank

18 Remove the fuel pump assembly (see Chapter 3B).

19 Have a rag handy to catch any fuel spills, then release the clamps and disconnect the two hoses from the filter – where clip type clamps are used new ones should be fitted to secure the new filter (a special tool is required to joint the clamp ends – use suitable screw-type clamps as an alternative if required) **(see illustration)**. Remove the mounting bracket screw to free the filter – note which way round the filter fits.

20 Fit the new filter, making sure it is the correct way round, and secure it to the bracket with the screw. Reconnect the fuel pipes to the filter stubs, and secure them with their clamps; if the clamps cannot be re-used replace them with new ones. Check that the arrow on the filter points in the direction of fuel flow (i.e. from the pump to the outlet on the mounting base) **(see illustration)**.

21 Install the fuel pump assembly (see Chapter 3).

8 Throttle and choke cable freeplay – check

Throttle cable(s)

1 Make sure the throttle grip rotates easily from fully closed to fully open with the front wheel turned at various angles. The grip should snap shut automatically when released.

2 If the throttle sticks, this is probably due to a cable fault. Remove the cable(s) (see Chapter 3) and lubricate it/them. Install the cable, making sure that it is correctly routed. If this fails to improve the operation of the throttle, the cable must be replaced. Note that in very rare cases the fault could lie in the carburettors or throttle bodies rather than the cable, necessitating their removal and inspection of the throttle linkage (see Chapter 3).

3 With the throttle operating smoothly, check for a small amount of freeplay at the twistgrip **(see illustration)**. The amount of freeplay can be measured and should be as given in this Chapter's Specifications. The cable(s) is/are adjustable at either the throttle grip or the carburettor/throttle body. Minor adjustments should be made at the throttle grip end **(see illustrations)**.

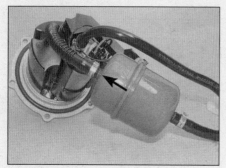

7.20 Make sure the arrow points in direction of fuel flow

8.3a Check for a small amount of freeplay in the throttle twistgrip

8.3b Cable adjuster(s) is/are located below twistgrip housing – carburettor model shown

8.4a Carburettor model throttle cables can also be adjusted at carburettor pulley (arrow)

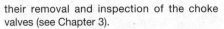

8.4b On fuel injection models slacken the locknut (arrowed) and turn the adjuster as required

8.10 Choke cable adjuster is located below left-hand handlebar switch housing

4 To adjust freeplay, slacken the locknut on the cable adjuster and rotate the adjuster until the correct amount of freeplay is obtained, then tighten the locknut against the adjuster. If all the adjustment has been taken up at the throttle grip end, re-set the adjuster to give maximum freeplay and then set the correct amount of freeplay at the adjuster(s) on the carburettor/throttle body pulley **(see illustrations)**. Slacken the locknut(s) and set the adjuster in the bracket as required, then retighten the locknut (s). Subsequent adjustments can now be made at the throttle grip.

5 After adjustment check that the throttle twistgrip operates smoothly and snaps shut quickly when released.

6 With the engine idling, turn the handlebars through the full extent of their travel. The idle speed should not change. If it does, the cable(s) may be incorrectly routed.

7 After adjustment, check the idle speed and reset if necessary.

Choke cable

8 If the choke does not operate smoothly this is probably due to a cable fault. Remove the cable as described in Chapter 3 and lubricate it. Install the cable, routing it so it takes the smoothest route possible. If this fails to improve the operation of the choke, the cable must be replaced. Note that in very rare cases the fault could lie in the carburettors/throttle bodies rather than the cable, necessitating

their removal and inspection of the choke valves (see Chapter 3).

9 There should be a very small amount of freeplay at the choke lever or knob when the choke is in the OFF position; this ensures that the choke is not in operation when the engine is running normally. If adjustment is necessary, proceed with Step 10 or 11 according to your model. On fuel injection models also check the fast idle speed as in Step 11.

10 On carburettor models, a specified freeplay is available for the lever operated choke (see Specifications) and is measured at the cable outer on the adjuster **(see illustration)**. If adjustment is necessary, slacken the locknut on the adjuster and screw the adjuster in or out to obtain the correct freeplay. No specific setting is available for the pull type choke, but adjustment can be made by repositioning the choke cable in its clamp on the carburettors.

11 On fuel injection models, with the choke lever in the fully open position make sure that the pulley cam is against the stop, and that with the engine running the speed is 2000 rpm. If not, turn the adjuster screw so that these conditions are met **(see illustration)**. Now make sure there is a small amount of freeplay as in Step 9. If necessary slacken the locknut on the cable adjuster and set the adjuster as required to provide a small amount of freeplay in the lever.

9 Engine idle speed – check

Carburettor models

1 The idle speed should be checked and adjusted before and after the carburettors are synchronised and when it is obviously too high or too low. Before adjusting the idle speed, make sure the valve clearances and spark plug gaps are correct. Also, turn the handlebars back-and-forth and see if the idle speed changes as this is done. If it does, the throttle cables may not be adjusted correctly, or may be worn out. This is a dangerous condition that can cause loss of control of the bike. Be sure to correct this problem before proceeding.

2 The engine should be at normal operating temperature, which is usually reached after 10 to 15 minutes of stop and go riding. Place the motorcycle on its stand, or hold it upright, and make sure the transmission is in neutral.

3 With the engine idling, adjust the idle speed by turning the throttle stop screw in or out until the idle speed listed in this Chapter's Specifications is obtained. The throttle stop screw is located on the underside of the carburettor assembly **(see illustration)** and can only be accessed with a long cross-point screwdriver **(see illustration)**.

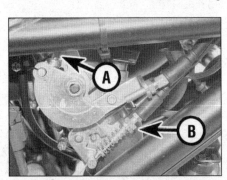

8.11 Fast idle speed adjuster screw (A); cable locknut (B) and freeplay adjuster

9.3a Idle speed adjuster (throttle stop screw) location (arrow) – carburettors removed for clarity

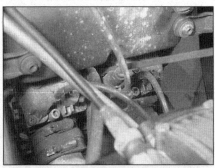

9.3b A long handled Phillips screwdriver is necessary for idle speed adjustment

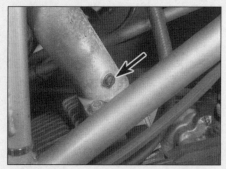

10.8 Vacuum take-off point in inlet duct (arrow)

10.11 Carburettor synchronisation screw (arrow) – carburettors removed for clarity

4 Snap the throttle open and shut a few times, then recheck the idle speed. If necessary, repeat the adjustment procedure.
5 If a smooth, steady idle can't be achieved, the fuel/air mixture may be incorrect. Refer to Chapter 3 for further carburettor information.

Fuel injection models

6 Any adjustment to the throttle bodies on models with fuel injection should be carried out by a Ducati dealer equipped with the Mathesis diagnostic tool. Using this tool a complete check and setting of the throttle bodies can be made, and this involves checking the throttle position sensor setting, the CO level from each cylinder, balancing the air flows to each cylinder, and setting the idle speed. To adjust one of these parameters without considering all of them could lead to incorrect running and CO levels that exceed permitted levels.

10 Carburettor/throttle body synchronisation – check

⚠ *Warning: Do not allow exhaust gases to build up in the work area; either perform the check outside or use an exhaust gas extraction system.*

Carburettor models

1 Carburettor synchronisation is simply the process of adjusting the carburettors so they

pass the same amount of fuel/air mixture to each cylinder. This is done by measuring the vacuum produced in each cylinder. Carburettors that are out of synchronisation will result in decreased fuel mileage, increased engine temperature, less than ideal throttle response and higher vibration levels. Before synchronising the carburettors, make sure the valve clearances are properly set.
2 To properly synchronise the carburettors, you will need some sort of vacuum gauge set-up, preferably with a gauge for each cylinder, or a manometer, which is a calibrated tube arrangement that utilises columns of mercury or steel rods to indicate engine vacuum.
3 A manometer can be purchased from a motorcycle dealer or accessory shop and should have the necessary rubber hoses supplied with it for hooking into the vacuum take-off stubs.
4 A vacuum gauge set-up can also be purchased from a dealer or mail-order specialist or fabricated from commonly available hardware and automotive vacuum gauges.
5 The manometer is the more reliable and accurate instrument, and for that reason is preferred over the vacuum gauge set-up; however, if using a mercury manometer, extra precautions must be taken during use and storage of the instrument as mercury is a liquid, and extremely toxic.
6 Due to the nature of the synchronisation procedure and the need for special instruments, most owners leave the task to a Ducati dealer.
7 Start the engine and let it run until it reaches

normal operating temperature, then shut it off.
8 Unscrew the vacuum take-off plug from the inlet duct on each cylinder and screw the vacuum take-off adapter in its place **(see illustration)**.
9 Connect the gauge hoses to the take-off adapters. Make sure there are no air leaks as false readings will result.
10 Start the engine and make sure the idle speed is as specified at the beginning of the Chapter. If it isn't, adjust it (see Section 9). If the gauges are fitted with damping adjustment, set this so that the needle flutter is just eliminated but so that they can still respond to small changes in pressure. There is no specific figure for the vacuum reading, the object it to balance the two carburettors so that there readings are the same.
11 The carburettors are adjusted by turning the synchronising screw between the carburettors, in the throttle linkage **(see illustration)**. Access to the screw is poor and requires the use of a long cross-point screwdriver. Turn the screw until the reading on each gauge is the same. **Note:** *Do not press down on the screw during adjustment, or a false reading will be obtained*. On completion, open and close the throttle quickly to settle the linkage, and recheck the gauge readings, readjusting if necessary.
12 When the adjustment is complete stop the engine, remove the vacuum gauge or manometer and install the blanking plugs, complete with their sealing washers.

Fuel Injection models

13 Any adjustment to the throttle bodies on models with fuel injection should be carried out by a Ducati dealer equipped with the Mathesis diagnostic tool. Using this tool a complete check and setting of the throttle bodies can be made, and this involves checking the throttle position sensor setting, the CO level from each cylinder, balancing the air flows to each cylinder, and setting the idle speed. To adjust one of these parameters without considering all of them could lead to incorrect running and CO levels that exceed permitted levels.

11 Air filter – clean

1 Raise the fuel tank onto its prop – there is no need to remove the tank.
2 Release the four spring hooks to free the air filter housing lid, then lift the pleated-paper air filter out of the lid **(see illustrations)**.
3 If the filter is damaged, oily or excessively dirty do not waste time cleaning it, replace it with a new one. Otherwise, use compressed air directed through the filter from the engine side to dislodge dirt and dust.
4 Wipe the inside of the air filter housing and lid clean before installing the air filter; where fitted make sure the air intake rubbers are

11.2a Release the spring hook to free the air filter housing lid

11.2b Air filter resides in housing lid

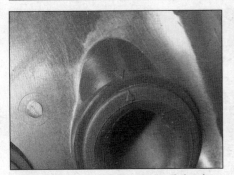

11.4 Moulded arrowheads on air intake rubbers and housing lid must align

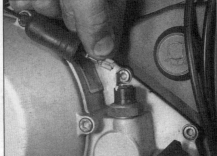

12.3a Early model oil pressure switches have a spade type terminal covered by a rubber boot . . .

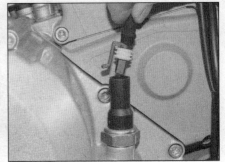

12.3b . . . while on later models the connector is of the clip type

correctly aligned **(see illustration)**. Install the filter in the lid and secure the lid with the four spring clips. Seat the fuel tank back into place.

12 Engine oil pressure – check

1 Before checking the oil pressure, check the engine oil level and top up if necessary. Two checks should be made, one with a cold engine the other with a hot engine.
2 To check the oil pressure a suitable gauge and adapter piece (which screws into the oil pressure switch thread) will be needed.
3 Disconnect the wiring from the switch and unscrew the switch from the right-hand crankcase cover **(see illustrations)**. Screw the adapter and gauge into the crankcase cover.
4 Start the engine and note the oil pressure at the engine speeds given in the Specifications for a cold engine. Stop the engine and reinstall the oil pressure switch.
5 Take the motorcycle on a short run until the engine is fully warmed up. With the engine stopped, install the pressure gauge and adapter as described in Step 3. Start the

engine and note the oil pressure at the engine speeds given in the Specifications for a hot engine. Stop the engine and remove the gauge and adapter.
6 Thread the oil pressure switch back into the crankcase cover and reconnect the wire. Slip the rubber cover into place.
7 If the oil pressure is not as specified check the oil pump and the pressure relief valve as described in Chapter 2. If they are good further internal investigation of the engine lubrication system is necessary.

13 Engine compression – check

1 A compression test will provide useful information about an engine's condition and if performed regularly, can give warning of trouble before any other symptoms become apparent.
2 Refer to the procedure under the *Fault Finding Equipment* heading in the Reference section of this Manual. The cylinder compression figure is given in the Specifications at the beginning of this Chapter.

14 Brakes – check

1 A routine general check of the brake system will ensure that any problems are discovered and remedied before the rider's safety is jeopardised.

General checks

2 Check the brake lever and pedal for loose connections, excessive play, bends, and other damage. Replace any damaged parts with new ones (see Chapter 6).
3 Measure the amount of freeplay between the front brake lever stock and its bracket and compare with that specified **(see illustration)**. If there is too little or too much freeplay make adjustment at the screw in the lever stock **(see illustration)**. Turn the adjuster clockwise to decrease freeplay and anti-clockwise to increase it. **Note:** *You may discover that the adjuster screw slot has been sealed with Araldite or similar to prevent tampering.*
4 The brake pedal height can be adjusted to suit rider preference. Make adjustment at the nut and threaded stop on the pedal underside

14.3a Measuring brake lever freeplay

14.3b Brake lever freeplay is adjusted at the screw in lever stock

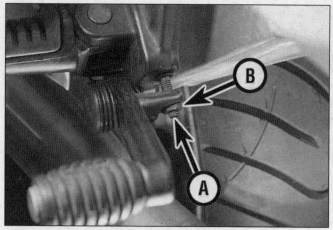

14.4a Brake pedal height adjuster screw (A) and locknut (B) – early SS/SL models

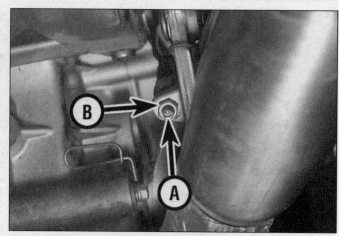

14.4b Brake pedal height adjuster screw (A) and locknut (B) – early Monster models

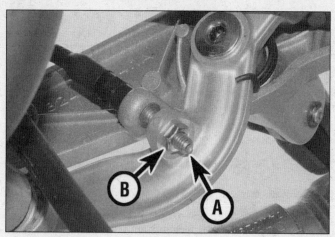

14.4c Brake pedal height adjuster screw (A) and locknut (B) – late monster models

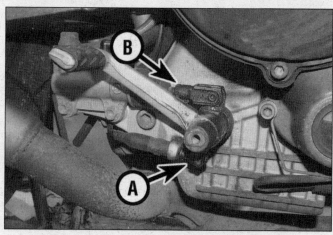

14.4d Brake pedal height adjuster screw and locknut (A), and pushrod locknut (B) – late Supersport models

(see illustrations). Check for the correct amount of freeplay (measured in terms of pushrod movement) before the brake comes into effect – Ducati advise around 2 mm. Adjustment can be made by slackening the pushrod locknut on the master cylinder clevis

and rotating the pushrod in the clevis threads (see illustration).
5 Make sure all brake fasteners are tight. Make sure the fluid level in the reservoirs is correct (see *Daily (pre-ride) checks*). Look for leaks at the hose connections and check for

cracks in the hoses. If the lever or pedal is spongy, bleed the brakes (see Chapter 6).
6 Make sure the brake light operates when the front brake lever is depressed. The front brake light switch is not adjustable. If it fails to operate properly, check it (see Chapter 8).

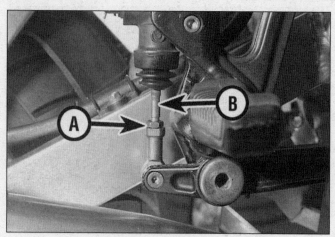

14.4e Master cylinder pushrod locknut (A) and pushrod (B) – early SS/SL models

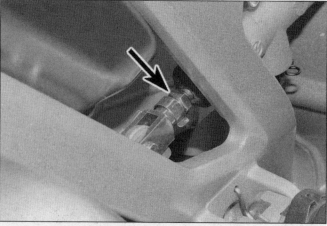

14.4f Master cylinder pushrod locknut (arrowed) and pushrod – late Monster models

14.9a Front brake pad wear can be viewed through rear of caliper

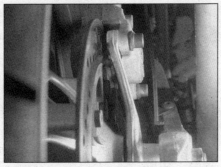

14.9b Rear brake pad wear can be viewed through caliper mouth

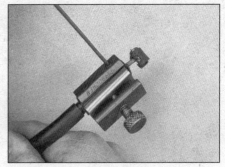

15.3 Using a pressure lubricator to oil a control cable. Make sure the tool seats around the inner cable

7 Make sure the brake light is activated just before the rear brake pedal takes effect. Early models use a pressure type switch operated by brake fluid pressure, whereas later models use a plunger type switch operated by the brake pedal stop; neither type is adjustable.

Brake pad wear check

8 The OE (original equipment) brake pads have a wear indicator groove running down the centre of the friction material (see Chapter 6). When the surrounding friction material wears down to the base of the groove, the pads must be renewed. Otherwise the thickness of the friction material is the best indication of wear – anything less than 1 mm and the pads must be replaced with new ones, though many consider 1.5 mm a safer limit.

9 The pad friction material can be viewed through the slot in the caliper without removing the caliper from the motorcycle **(see illustrations)**. If the pads are worn or there is some doubt about their condition, remove

them from the caliper for renewal or further inspection (see Chapter 6).

15 Control cables and pivot points – lubrication

1 Since the controls, cables and various other components of a motorcycle are exposed to the elements, they should be lubricated periodically to ensure safe and trouble-free operation.

2 The footrests, clutch and brake levers, brake pedal, gearchange lever linkage and sidestand pivot should be lubricated frequently. In order for the lubricant to be applied where it will do the most good, the component should be disassembled. However, if chain and cable lubricant is being used, it can be applied to the pivot joint gaps and will usually work its way into the areas where friction occurs. If motor oil or light

grease is being used, apply it sparingly as it may attract dirt (which could cause the controls to bind or wear at an accelerated rate). **Note:** *One of the best lubricants for the control lever pivots is a dry-film lubricant (available from many sources by different names). Where O-rings are fitted on the gearchange lever and rear brake pedal pivots replace them with new ones if they are damaged, deformed or deteriorated.*

3 To lubricate the cables, disconnect the relevant cable at its upper end, then lubricate the cable with a pressure adapter **(see illustration)**. See Chapter 3 for the choke and throttle cable removal procedures.

4 On models with non-electronic instruments, the speedometer and tachometer cables should be removed (see Chapter 8) and the inner cable withdrawn from the outer cable and lubricated with motor oil or cable lubricant. Do not lubricate the upper few inches of the cable as the lubricant may travel up into the meter head.

Major service

16 Engine oil strainer – clean

Note: *This operation should be combined with the engine oil and filter change under the Minor service interval.*

1 Drain the engine oil (refer to Section 3).

2 Where fitted, slip back the oil temperature sender terminal rubber cover and disconnect the wire **(see illustration)**. On early models unscrew and withdraw the strainer from the lower side of the crankcase right-hand half **(see illustration)**. On later models unscrew the strainer plug, then remove the strainer.

Note the sealing washer fitted with the strainer on early models and the plug on later models.

3 Clean the gauze in high flash-point solvent to remove all deposits which have collected **(see illustration)**. If the gauze is torn or too heavily contaminated to clean up properly, renew it. Install the gauze using a new sealing washer and tighten it securely. Where fitted,

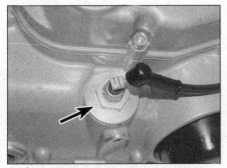

16.2a Pull back the boot and disconnect the wire. Strainer plug (arrowed)

16.2b Unscrew oil filter bolt and gauze from right-hand crankcase

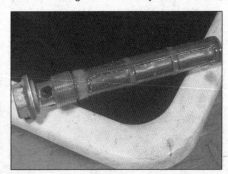

16.3 Remove all traces of swarf from the filter gauze

19.4 Checking for looseness in the steering head bearings

reconnect the oil temperature sender wire and slip its rubber cover into place.
4 Replenish the engine with fresh oil as described in Section 3.

17 Brake hydraulic fluid – change

1 The brake fluid should be replaced at the prescribed interval or whenever a master cylinder or caliper overhaul is carried out.

19.6 On Monster models remove the four bolts (arrows) to free the handlebars, noting how the choke knob locates where applicable

Refer to the brake bleeding section in Chapter 6, noting that all old fluid must be pumped from the fluid reservoir before filling with new fluid.

18 Clutch hydraulic fluid – change

1 The clutch fluid should be replaced at the prescribed interval or whenever a master cylinder or release cylinder overhaul is carried out. Refer to the clutch bleeding section in Chapter 2, noting that all old fluid must be pumped from the fluid reservoir before filling with new fluid.
2 Note that the clutch lever incorporates an adjuster set in the lever stock. Measure the amount of freeplay between the lever stock and its bracket and compare with that specified **(see illustration 14.3a)**. If there is too little or too much freeplay make adjustment at the screw in the lever stock **(see illustration 14.3b)**. Turn the adjuster clockwise to decrease freeplay and anti-clockwise to increase it. **Note:** *You may discover that the adjuster screw slot has been sealed with Araldite or similar to prevent tampering.*

19 Steering head bearings – check

1 Steering head bearings can become dented, rough or loose during normal use of the machine. In extreme cases, worn or loose steering head bearings can cause steering wobble – a condition that is potentially dangerous.

Check

2 Support the motorcycle on an auxiliary stand so that its front wheel is raised off the ground.
3 Point the front wheel straight-ahead and slowly move the handlebars from side-to-side. Any dents or roughness in the bearing races will be felt and the bars will not move smoothly and freely.
4 Next, grasp the fork sliders and try to move them forward and backward **(see illustration)**. Any looseness in the steering head bearings will be felt as front-to-rear movement of the forks. If play is felt in the bearings, adjust the steering head as follows.

Adjustment

5 Raise the fuel tank up on its prop. This will improve access to the steering head adjuster and prevent damage to the fuel tank.
6 On Monster models check the handlebar and the mating surfaces of its clamp(s) for alignment marks; if none exist, make your own to ensure the bars can be returned to their original position. Unscrew the four clamp bolts and displace the handlebars forwards, resting them on some rag **(see illustration)**. On models with a pull-type choke note how it fits.
7 On models with an adjuster nut (all except 2002-on Monster models), slacken, but do not remove, the steering stem nut, stem pinch bolt and fork pinch bolts in the top yoke **(see illustrations)**. Where the later type drilled circular steering stem nut is fitted, note that a service tool, part No. 88713.1058, is available to turn the nut. On SS/SL, Supersport and Sport models also slacken off the handlebar clamp bolts.
8 Now using a C-spanner, slacken the adjuster nut until pressure is just released, then tighten it until all freeplay is removed, yet the steering is able to move freely **(see illustration)**. The object is to set the adjuster nut so that the bearings are under a very light loading, just enough to remove any freeplay.
9 On models without an adjuster nut (2002-on Monster models), slacken, but do not

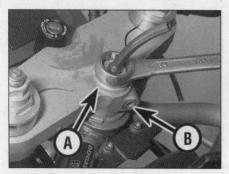

19.7a Slacken the steering stem nut (A), stem pinch bolt (B) . . .

19.7b . . . and the fork pinch bolts

19.8 Adjusting the steering head bearings with a C-spanner

remove, the steering stem pinch bolt and fork pinch bolts in the top yoke **(see illustrations)**. Slacken the steering stem/bearing adjuster nut fractionally, then tighten it to the torque setting specified at the beginning of the Chapter. Note that a service tool is available, part No. 88713.1058 to turn the nut.

Caution: Take great care not to apply excessive pressure because this will cause premature failure of the bearings.

10 If the bearings cannot be set up properly, or if there is any binding, roughness or notchiness, they will have to be removed for inspection or replacement (see Chapter 5).

11 When adjustment is complete, on models with an adjuster nut tighten the steering stem nut, and on all models tighten the stem pinch bolt and fork pinch bolts, to the correct torque setting where specified. If the handlebars were disturbed, return them to their original position (making sure on SS/SL, Supersport and Sport models that they are pressed against the yoke) and tighten their bolts, aligning the marks as appropriate **(see illustrations)**.

12 Check the bearing adjustment as described above and re-adjust if necessary.

20 Suspension – check

1 Although not included in the manufacturer's schedule, suspension checks are mentioned here to remind the rider of their importance to handling and roadholding.

Front suspension

2 While standing alongside the motorcycle, apply the front brake and push on the handlebars to compress the forks several times. See if they move up-and-down smoothly without binding. If binding is felt, the forks should be disassembled and inspected (see Chapter 5).

3 Inspect the area above the dust seal for signs of oil leakage, then carefully lever off the dust seal using a flat-bladed screwdriver and inspect the area around the fork seal **(see illustration)**. If leakage is evident, the seals must be replaced (see Chapter 5).

19.9a Steering stem pinch bolt (arrowed) . . .

19.9b . . . and fork clamp bolt (arrowed) – 2002-on Monsters

4 Check the tightness of all suspension nuts and bolts to be sure none have worked loose.

Rear suspension

5 Inspect the rear shock for fluid leakage and tightness of its mountings. If leakage is found, the shock should be replaced.

6 With the aid of an assistant to support the bike, compress the rear suspension several times. It should move up and down freely without binding. If binding is felt, the shock absorber should be removed and examined further.

7 Support the motorcycle on an auxiliary stand so that the rear wheel is off the ground. Grasp the swingarm and feel for side-to-side play and front-to-back play. Sideplay at the pivot should not exceed 0.1 mm; sideplay can be adjusted by the use of different size shims between the crankcase lugs and swingarm pivot points. There will be a certain amount of front-to-back play due to the pivot design, but if excessive, the pivot shaft and needle roller bearings housed in the crankcase lugs should be inspected for wear.

8 Swingarm pivot condition can be confirmed by removing the rear wheel and rear shock and carrying out the checks described in Step 6. If you are in any doubt about the condition of the pivot assembly, remove the swingarm for inspection (see Chapter 5). With the rear wheel and rear shock removed, you can also check that the swingarm rotates easily about its pivot, without any sign of notchiness or stiffness.

9 Check the tightness of the rear suspension mountings.

21 Wheel bearings – check

1 Support the motorcycle on an auxiliary stand so that the wheel being checked is off the ground. Check for any play in the bearings by pushing and pulling the wheel against the hub. Also rotate the wheel and check that it rotates smoothly.

2 If any play is detectable in the hub, or if the wheel does not rotate smoothly (and this is not due to brake drag), the wheel bearings must be removed and inspected for wear or damage (see Chapter 6). If the wheel does not appear to run true, refer to Chapter 6 and check runout.

3 Cast wheels are virtually maintenance free, but they should be kept clean and checked periodically for cracks and other damage. Never attempt to repair damaged cast wheels; they must be replaced with new ones. Check the tyre valve rubber for signs of damage or deterioration and have it replaced if necessary. Also, make sure the valve stem dust cap is in place and tight.

22 Rear wheel cush drive – check

1 The rubber bushes (cush drive) set in the rear wheel damp out shocks from the transmission and final drive which would

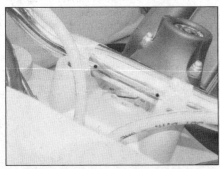
19.11a On Monsters align the clamp mating surfaces with the punch marks

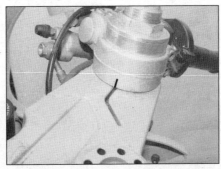
19.11b On Supersport and Sport models align the mark with the slit in the top yoke

20.3 Carefully lever the dust seal free and check for oil leakage from the fork

otherwise be transferred directly to the wheel. If the drive is harsh and play is felt, the cush drive rubbers may have worn or broken up.

2 To check, remove the rear wheel (see Chapter 6) and feel for play in the sprocket mountings – check that any play is not due to looseness of the sprocket nuts though.

3 Refer to Chapter 6 for details of cush drive rubber replacement.

23 Fuel system – checks

 Warning: Petrol (gasoline) is extremely flammable, so take extra precautions when you work on any part of the fuel system. Don't smoke or allow open flames or bare light bulbs near the work area, and don't work in a garage where a natural gas-type appliance is present. If you spill any fuel on your skin, rinse it off immediately with soap and water. When you perform any kind of work on the fuel system, wear safety glasses and have a fire extinguisher suitable for a Class B type fire (flammable liquids) on hand.

1 Disconnect the breather hose from the top of the fuel tank where fitted, release the catch and raise the fuel tank onto its prop. Check all the fuel system hoses along their entire length for signs of leakage, deterioration or damage. Replace any hoses which are cracked or deteriorated. You should also inspect the hoses with the engine running, especially on fuel injection models, as then the system is pressurised.

2 If the carburettor gaskets are leaking, the carburettors should be disassembled and rebuilt using new gaskets and seals (see Chapter 3).

3 If repeated fuel filter contamination is experienced, it is likely that the tank is contaminated. The fuel should be drained and disposed of safely. If the fuel is being contaminated by internal corrosion of the tank surfaces consider having the tank coated with a rust preventative compound.

4 On models with a tank drain plug always use a new sealing washer.

24 Nuts and bolts – tightness check

1 Since vibration of the machine tends to loosen fasteners, all nuts, bolts, screws, etc. should be periodically checked for proper tightness.

2 Pay particular attention to the following:

Spark plugs
Engine oil drain plug
Gearchange lever bolts
Footrest and stand bolts
Engine mounting bolts
Rear suspension bolts
Handlebar and yoke bolts
Front axle and clamp bolts
Rear axle bolt
Exhaust system bolts/nuts

3 If a torque wrench is available, use it along with the torque specifications at the beginning of this, or other, Chapters.

Additional maintenance

25 Cam belts – replacement

1 Refer to Chapter 2 and replace the cam belts with new ones irrespective of their apparent condition.

 Warning: Failure of a cam belt will result in extensive engine damage and likely loss of control of the motorcycle.

26 Front fork oil – change

1 Fork oil will degrade over a period of time and lose its damping qualities. The forks fitted to these machines are not fitted with drain plugs, necessitating that they be removed from the yokes and the oil drained by inverting the fork.

2 Refer to Chapter 5 for front fork removal, oil draining and refill.

Non-scheduled maintenance

27 Steering head bearings – lubrication

1 Over a period of time the grease will harden or may be washed out of the bearings by incorrect use of jet washes.

2 Disassemble the steering head for re-greasing of the bearings. Refer to Chapter 5 for details.

28 Swingarm bearings – lubrication

1 Over a period of time the grease will harden or dirt will penetrate the bearings due to failed dust seals.

2 The swingarm bearings are housing in the crankcase casting. Refer to Chapter 5 for details.

29 Brake and clutch hoses – replacement

1 The flexible brake hoses will in time deteriorate with age and must be replaced with new ones.

2 Refer to Chapters 2 (clutch) or 6 (brake) for hose removal and installation details. **Note:** *Always replace the banjo union sealing washers with new ones.*

Chapter 2
Engine, clutch and transmission

Contents

Alternator rotor, starter clutch and starter drive –
  removal, inspection and installation 14
Cam belt pulleys and drive – removal and installation 7
Cam belts – check .... see Chapter 1
Cam belts – removal and installation 6
Clutch – removal, inspection and installation
  (1991 to 1997 600 and 750 engines) 16
Clutch – removal, inspection and installation
  (1998-on 600, 620 and 750 engines) 17
Clutch – removal, inspection and installation (900 engines) 18
Clutch hydraulic fluid – change .... see Chapter 1
Clutch hydraulic system – bleeding 21
Clutch master cylinder – removal, inspection and installation 20
Clutch release cylinder – removal, inspection and installation 19
Compression – check .... see Chapter 1 and Reference
Connecting rod bearings – general information 30
Connecting rods and bearings –
  removal, inspection and installation 29
Crankcase – separating and joining 26
Crankcase and bearings – inspection 27
Crankshaft and main bearings – removal, inspection and installation ... 28
Cylinder barrels – removal, inspection and installation 11
Cylinder heads – removal and installation 8
Cylinder heads, camshafts and valves – overhaul 9
Engine/transmission unit – removal and installation 5

Gear shafts – endfloat check and overhaul 32
Gearchange mechanism (external) –
  removal, inspection and installation 15
General information 1
Idle speed – check .... see Chapter 1
Initial start-up after overhaul 34
Major engine repair – general note 4
Oil cooler and carburettor warmer kit – removal and installation ... 25
Oil pressure – check .... see Chapter 1
Oil pressure relief valve – removal, inspection and installation 24
Oil pump – removal, inspection and installation 22
Oil top-up .... see Daily (pre-ride) checks
Oil/filter change .... see Chapter 1
Operations possible with the engine in the frame 2
Operations requiring engine removal 3
Piston rings – inspection and installation 13
Pistons – removal, inspection and installation 12
Primary drive gear – removal, inspection and installation 23
Recommended running-in procedure 35
Selector drum and forks – endfloat check and overhaul 33
Spark plugs – check .... see Chapter 1
Transmission gear shafts and selector drum/forks –
  removal and installation 31
Valve clearances – check .... see Chapter 1
Valves and seats – servicing 10

Degrees of difficulty

Easy, suitable for novice with little experience	**Fairly easy,** suitable for beginner with some experience	**Fairly difficult,** suitable for competent DIY mechanic	**Difficult,** suitable for experienced DIY mechanic	**Very difficult,** suitable for expert DIY or professional 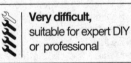

Specifications

General

Capacity	
600 engine	583 cc
620 engine	618 cc
750 engine	748 cc
900 engine	904 cc

Bore	
600 engine	80 mm
620 engine	80 mm
750 engine	88 mm
900 engine	92 mm

Stroke	
600 engine	58 mm
620 engine	61.5 mm
750 engine	61.5 mm
900 engine	68 mm

Compression ratio	
600 engine	10.7:1
620 engine	10.5:1
750 engine	9.0:1
900 engine	9.2:1
Cylinder identification	Horizontal (front cyl), Vertical (rear cyl)

Oil pump

Gear teeth clearance	0.10 mm max.
Gear-to-pump housing clearance	0.10 mm max.
Gear-to-housing cover clearance	0.07 mm max.

Valves and rockers

Valve stem runout	0.053 mm max.
Valve head runout	0.03 mm max.
Valve stem-to-guide clearance	
Standard	0.03 to 0.06 mm max.
Service limit	0.08 mm
Rocker arm-to-shaft clearance	
Standard	0.03 to 0.06 mm
Service limit	0.08 mm
Valve clearances	see Chapter 1

Cylinder bores

Piston-to-bore clearance	see below
Maximum ovality	
600, 620, 750 and 1998-on 900 engines	0.03 mm
900 engines to 1997	0.01 mm
Maximum taper	
600, 620, 750 and 1998-on 900 engines	0.03 mm
900 engines to 1997	0.015 mm

Pistons

Piston-to-bore clearance	0.025 to 0.050 mm
Service limit	0.12 mm
Piston pin-to-piston boss clearance	0.004 to 0.012 mm
Service limit	0.025 mm

Piston rings

Ring-to-groove clearance	
L-section top ring	0.15 mm max.
All square-section rings	0.10 mm max.
Ring end gap – 600 and 750 carburettor engines	
Top and second compression rings	0.30 to 0.50 mm
Service limit	1.0 mm
Oil control ring	0.25 to 0.60 mm
Service limit	1.0 mm
Ring end gap – 900 carburettor engines	
Top and second compression rings	0.20 to 0.40 mm
Service limit	0.8 mm
Oil control ring	0.20 to 0.70 mm
Service limit	1.0 mm
Ring end gap – 620i.e., 750i.e. and 900i.e. engines	
Top and second compression rings	0.20 to 0.40 mm
Service limit	0.8 mm
Oil control ring	0.30 to 0.60 mm
Service limit	1.0 mm

Clutch

Friction plate thickness	
1991 to 1997 600 and 750 engines	
Single-sided plate	3.25 mm min.
Double-sided plates	2.15 mm min.
1998-on 600 and 750 engines	
Individual plates	3.25 mm min
Complete pack	41.3 mm
2002 and 2003 620i.e. engine	
Individual plates	3.5 mm min
Complete pack	41.3 mm
2004-on 620i.e. engine	
Individual plates	3.45 mm min
Complete pack	49.3 mm
all 900 engines	2.8 mm min.

Clutch (continued)
Plain plate warpage . . . .   0.2 mm max.
Friction plate tang-to-clutch housing clearance . . . .   0.6 mm max.
Spring free length
   600 and 750 engines to 1997 . . . .   40 mm min.
   All other engines . . . .   36.5 mm min.

Crankshaft and connecting rods
Crankshaft endfloat . . . .   Nil
Connecting rod big-end sideplay . . . .   0.15 to 0.35 mm
Crankshaft big-end journal diameter (standard)
   600 and 750 engines . . . .   40.017 to 40.033 mm
   900 engine – size code A . . . .   42.006 to 42.014 mm
   900 engine – size code B . . . .   41.998 to 42.006 mm
Connecting rod bearing oil clearance
   600SS, 620 Sport and 750SS models . . . .   0.015 to 0.058 mm
   M600 and M750 models up to 1997, M900 up to 1998 . . . .   0.024 to 0.056 mm
   M600, M620i.e. and M750 1998-on . . . .   0.015 to 0.058 mm
   900SS/SL models and 1999-on M900 models . . . .   0.025 to 0.059 mm
Big-end bearing oversizes . . . .   0.25 mm, 0.50 mm
Piston pin-to-small-end bush clearance
   600 and 750 engines . . . .   0.006 to 0.028 mm
   900 engine . . . .   0.015 to 0.032 mm
   Service limit (all engines) . . . .   0.05 mm

Transmission
Gear ratios (No. of teeth)

Five-speed models
   1st gear 2.500:1 (40/16T)
   2nd gear 1.714:1 (36/21T)
   3rd gear 1.333:1 (32/24T)
   4th gear 1.074:1 (29/27T)
   5th gear 0.966:1 (28/29T)

Six-speed models
M900i.e. models
   1st gear 2.467:1 (37/15T)
   2nd gear 1.765:1 (30/17T)
   3rd gear 1.400:1 (28/20T)
   4th gear 1.181:1 (26/22T)
   5th gear 1.043:1 (24/23T)
   6th gear 0.958:1 (23/24T)

All other 900 models
   1st gear 2.467:1 (37/15T)
   2nd gear 1.765:1 (30/17T)
   3rd gear 1.350:1 (27/20T)
   4th gear 1.091:1 (24/22T)
   5th gear 0.958:1 (23/24T)
   6th gear 0.857:1 (24/28T)

M620i.e. models*
   1st gear 2.461:1 (32/13T)
   2nd gear 1.666:1 (30/18T)
   3rd gear 1.333:1 (28/21T)
   4th gear 1.130:1 (26/23T)
   5th gear 1:1 (22/22T)
   6th gear 0.923:1 (24/26T)
*M620i.e. models are fitted with either a 5-speed or 6-speed gearbox
Gearshaft endfloat . . . .   0.15 mm max.
Selector drum endfloat . . . .   0.25 mm max.
Selector fork-to-gear groove clearance . . . .   0.070 to 0.285 mm
   Service limit . . . .   0.4 mm
Selector fork groove width in gear . . . .   4.070 to 4.185 mm
Selector fork ear thickness . . . .   3.90 to 4.00 mm
Selector fork guide pin-to-drum track clearance . . . .   0.265 to 0.425 mm
   Service limit . . . .   0.6 mm
Selector fork guide pin diameter . . . .   7.665 to 7.735 mm
   Service limit . . . .   7.5 mm
Selector drum track width . . . .   8.00 to 8.09 mm
   Service limit . . . .   8.19 mm

Torque settings

Engine mounting bolts/nuts	
1991 to 2001 models	40 to 45 Nm
2002-on models.	60 Nm
Cam belt pulley nuts	
1991 to 2000 600 and 750 engines, 1991 to 2001 900 engines	
on camshafts	70 to 75 Nm
on driveshaft	60 to 65 Nm
2001-on 600 and 750 engines, 2002 900 engines	71 Nm
Cam belt driveshaft gear nut	
1991 to 2000 600 and 750 engines, 1991 to 2001 900 engines	40 to 45 Nm
2001-on 600 and 750 engines, 2002 900 engines	55 Nm
Cylinder head nuts	
1st stage	15 Nm
2nd stage	27 Nm
3rd stage*	39 ± 1 Nm
*900 engine with old type studs	42 ± 1 Nm
Alternator rotor nut	
1991 to 1997 M600, M750 and M900	157 Nm
1998 to 2001 M600, M750 and M900	186 Nm
1991 to 1993 600SS, 750SS and 900SS/SL	177 to 186 Nm
1994 to 2001 600SS, 750SS and 900SS/SL	186 Nm
All 2002-on models	190 Nm
Clutch housing bolts (900 engine and early 750 engine)	30 to 34 Nm
Clutch nut	
1991 to 1997 M600, M750 and M900	137 to 147 Nm
1998 to 2000 M600 and M750	180 Nm
2001 M600 and M750	186 Nm
1998 to 2001 M900	181.5 Nm
1991 to 2001 600SS, 750SS and 900SS/SL	180 to 190 Nm
All 2002-on engines	190 Nm
Clutch hose union bolt	17 to 20 Nm
Oil pump mounting bolts	
M8 bolts	23 to 25 Nm
M6 bolt	8 to 10 Nm
Primary drive gear nut	
1991 to 1997 M600 and M750, 1993 to 1998 M900	110 to 120 Nm
1998 to 2000 M600 and M750, 1999 M900	140 Nm
2001 M600 and M750 and 2000 to 2001 M900	186 Nm
1991 to 1998 600SS and 750SS, 1991 to 1997 900SS/SL	110 to 120 Nm
1999 to 2001 750SS and 1998 to 2001 900SS	140 Nm
All 2002-on models	190 Nm
Crankcase bolts	
M8 bolts	23 to 25 Nm
M6 bolts	8 to 10 Nm
Connecting rod big-end bolts	
First stage	20 Nm
Second stage	35 Nm
Third stage	67 Nm
Gearshaft ball bearing retainer plate screws	8 to 10 Nm

1 General information

The engine is a twin cylinder unit mounted longitudinally in the frame with the cylinders angled at 90° in an L-type configuration. The two valves per cylinder are operated by Ducati's Desmodromic system whereby each valve has an opening and closing rocker arm. Each camshaft is driven by a toothed belt from a driveshaft housed in the crankcases.

The crankcases are divided vertically, with the crankshaft running in ball bearings. The alternator, starter clutch and cam belt driveshaft gear are on the crankshaft left-hand end, and the primary drive gear and oil pump are on its right-hand end. The pistons run in plated cylinder bores.

All 900 engines and early 750 engines have a dry clutch, whereas later 750 and all 600/620 engines use a wet clutch. The clutch is hydraulically operated on all models by a lever and master cylinder on the left-hand handlebar. The clutch release cylinder is integral with the crankcase right-hand cover or clutch cover on 1991 to 1997 600 and 750 engines, whereas on all 900 engines and 1998-on 600, 620 and 750 engines the release cylinder mounts to the left-hand crankcase cover and operates the clutch via a long pushrod through the gearbox input shaft.

A six-speed gearbox is used on all 900 models and certain M620 models; all other models use a five-speed gearbox. Drive is transmitted to the rear wheel by a conventional chain and sprocket arrangement.

2 Operations possible with the engine in the frame

1 The components and assemblies listed below can be removed without having to remove the engine/transmission assembly

from the frame. If however, a number of areas require attention at the same time, removal of the engine is recommended.

    Cam belts and pulleys
    Horizontal cylinder head, barrel and piston
    Clutch
    Oil pump
    Primary gears
    Alternator and flywheel
    Starter clutch, motor and idle gear
    Gearchange external mechanism
    Oil pressure relief valve
    Cam belt driveshaft gears

3 Operations requiring engine removal

1 It is necessary to remove the engine/transmission from the frame to remove the vertical cylinder head, barrel and piston.
2 It is necessary to remove the engine/transmission assembly from the frame and separate the crankcase halves to gain access to the following components

    Transmission gear shafts
    Crankshaft and main bearings
    Connecting rods and big-end bearings
    Selector drum and forks
    Cam belt driveshaft

4 Major engine repair – general note

1 It is not always easy to determine when or if an engine should be completely overhauled, as a number of factors must be considered.
2 High mileage is not necessarily an indication that an overhaul is needed, while low mileage, on the other hand, does not preclude the need for an overhaul. Frequency of servicing is probably the single most important consideration. An engine that has regular and frequent oil and filter changes, as well as other required maintenance, will most likely give many miles of reliable service.

Conversely, a neglected engine, or one which has not been run in properly, may require an overhaul very early in its life.
3 Exhaust smoke and excessive oil consumption are both indications that piston rings and/or valve guides are in need of attention, although make sure that the fault is not due to oil leakage.
4 If the engine is making obvious knocking or rumbling noises, the connecting rod and/or main bearings are probably at fault.
5 Loss of power, rough running and high fuel consumption rates may also point to the need for an overhaul, especially if they are all present at the same time. If a complete tune-up does not remedy the situation, major mechanical work is the only solution.
6 An engine overhaul generally involves restoring the internal parts to the specifications of a new engine. The piston rings and main and connecting rod bearings are usually renewed during a major overhaul. Generally the valve seats are reground, since they are usually in less than perfect condition at this point. The end result should be a like new engine that will give as many trouble-free miles as the original.
7 Before beginning the engine overhaul, read through the related procedures to familiarise yourself with the scope and requirements of the job. Overhauling an engine is not all that difficult, but it is time consuming. Plan on the bike being tied up for a minimum of two weeks. Check on the availability of parts and make sure that any necessary special tools, equipment and supplies are obtained in advance.
8 Most work can be done with typical workshop hand tools, although a number of precision measuring tools are required for inspecting parts to determine if they must be replaced. Often a dealer will handle the inspection of parts and offer advice concerning reconditioning and replacement. As a general rule, time is the primary cost of an overhaul so it does not pay to install worn or substandard parts.
9 As a final note, to ensure maximum life and minimum trouble from a rebuilt engine, everything must be assembled with care in a spotlessly clean environment.

5 Engine/transmission unit – removal and installation

Note: *The engine cannot be removed with the motorcycle on its sidestand. An auxiliary stand, an overhead hoist, or a paddock stand on the front wheel axle will be required. Additionally, a jack will be required to support the engine/transmission unit.*

Removal of ancillaries

1 Remove the seat (see Chapter 7) and fuel tank (see Chapter 3). On fully-faired models, remove both fairing lower panels (Chapter 7).
2 Remove the battery (see Chapter 8). On models with the battery tray and its bracket bolted to the engine also remove the tray and bracket, displacing the electrical components as required **(see illustration)**.
3 Drain the engine/transmission oil and remove the spin-on filter (see Chapter 1).
4 Pull the caps off the spark plugs. Remove the air filter housing and where necessary the ignition components bracket (see Chapter 3).
5 Slacken the clip and pull the hose off the crankcase breather on the crankcase right-hand side. Remove the bolts from the crankcase breather tank(s) at the rear of the frame and lift them free, complete with their hoses **(see illustrations)**.
6 Where fitted, remove the oil cooler (see Section 25).
7 On Monster models with carburettors, make sure the fuel tap is closed (OFF) and disconnect the two fuel pipes and vacuum pipe from the vacuum fuel pump on the frame right-hand side. Remove the two screws and detach the unit from the frame.
8 Remove the carburettors or throttle bodies, according to model (see Chapter 3A or 3B). If required remove the two nuts and washers which secure each inlet duct to the cylinder heads; discard the gasket or O-ring (where fitted according to model) once the duct is free.
9 Remove the exhaust system (Chapter 3).
10 On SS and SL models unbolt the sidestand bracket from the crankcase – it is

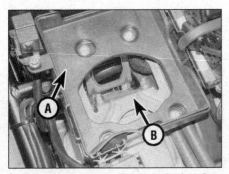

5.2 Separate the tray (A) from the bracket (B), then remove the bracket

5.5a Crankcase breather tank mountings on SS/SL models

5.5b Crankcase breather tank mounting on Monster models

5.10 Sidestand bracket is secured by two bolts (arrows) on SS/SL models

5.11a Remove the gearchange arm pinch bolt . . .

5.11b . . . and pull the arm off the gearchange shaft

secured by two bolts (see illustration). On Monster models remove the footrest bracket from each side and the sidestand bracket from the left-hand side (see Chapter 5).

11 Make a punch mark or scribe a line across the end of the gearchange shaft level with the gearchange arm split. Remove the gearchange arm pinch bolt and pull the arm off the shaft splines (see illustrations).

12 Remove the engine sprocket cover and sprocket (see Chapter 5).

13 On all models with the external clutch release cylinder on the left-hand side of the engine, have a couple of cable ties at hand before disturbing the clutch release cylinder on 900 engines. Remove its three screws and withdraw the release cylinder. Hold the piston in the body of the cylinder, place a nut or other suitable spacer against the piston, and

slip the cable ties through the mounting screw holes to secure the piston in the cylinder (see illustration). If this is not done, hydraulic pressure will allow the piston to creep out of the cylinder. Pass the release cylinder and hose up through the frame to prevent it getting in the way during engine removal. Note that it was found necessary on the bike featured in the photographs to disconnect one end of the vertical cylinder oil pipe to allow the release cylinder to pass through.

14 On early model 600 and 750 engines with the clutch release cylinder incorporated in the crankcase or clutch cover on the right-hand side of the engine, have a supply of rags at hand to catch fluid spills from the clutch hydraulic hose, then remove the hose union bolt from the right-hand crankcase cover. Place the end of the hose in a plastic bag to

prevent further fluid spills and the ingress of dirt.

15 On models equipped with a cable driven tachometer, unscrew its knurled ring and disconnect the cable from its drive on the horizontal cylinder (see illustration).

16 Trace the wiring up from the following electrical components and disconnect it at the nearest wire connector, releasing any cable ties as required and noting the routing of the wire:

- Alternator (see illustration).
- Neutral switch and rear brake light switch (see illustration).
- Oil pressure switch (see illustration).
- Sidestand switch (see illustration).
- Oil temperature sender (where fitted).
- Sensor on front cylinder valve cover (where fitted).

5.13 Clutch release cylinder piston is held in place with a nut and cable ties

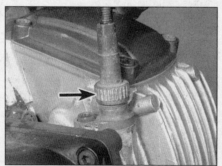

5.15 Unscrew the knurled ring (arrow) and withdraw the tachometer cable

5.16a Alternator stator coil wire connectors

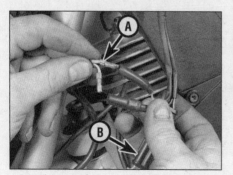

5.16b Neutral switch (A) and rear brake light switch (B) wire connectors

5.16c Disconnect the wire from the oil pressure switch

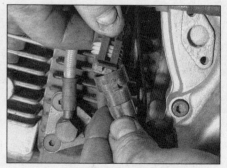

5.16d Sidestand switch wire connector

17 Peel back the rubber cover from the starter motor terminal and disconnect the cable **(see illustration)**.

18 Unbolt the engine earth cable from the rear of the crankcase **(see illustration)**.

19 Remove the rear shock absorber (see Chapter 5).

20 The engine/transmission unit is now held by its front and rear mountings and the swingarm pivot. Check around the engine that there are no other components which might hinder its removal. Remove the frame plugs from the engine mounting points on each side of the frame.

Removal of engine/transmission unit

21 The following procedure involves the rear end of the bike (rear wheel, swingarm and swingarm-mounted mudguard) being removed as an assembly, enabling the engine/transmission unit to the lowered to the ground and the front end and frame lifted off. It is advised that an assistant be on hand to steady the motorcycle and to help with manoeuvring the engine/transmission unit.

22 On early SS and SL models, remove the two rider's right-hand footrest bolts and the brake fluid reservoir bolt and tie the brake components to the swingarm **(see illustration)**. On later models remove the rear brake pedal and displace the rear master cylinder and its reservoir and tie the components to the swingarm **(see illustration)**.

5.17 Disconnect the starter motor lead

5.18 Disconnect the engine earth cable

23 Position a jack, with a block of wood on its head, under the crankcase **(see illustration)**. Do not jack it up at this point, just allow it to contact the crankcase surface.

24 Remove the pinch bolts from the pivot end of the swingarm on each side, noting that on some models the drive chain slider screw must be removed from the side of the swingarm on the left-hand side to allow the slider to be twisted out of the way. On later models (circa 1995-on) also remove the circlip from each end of the swingarm pivot.

25 Use a suitably-sized drift to tap the swingarm pivot tube out of the left-hand side. Note that Ducati produce a service tool (Pt. No. 88713.1040 or 1515) which consists of a U-shaped bracket which connects between the rear engine mounting in the frame and the swingarm, thus allowing the swingarm to

remain in position and supported whilst the engine is removed – this was not found necessary using the procedure adopted.

26 The swingarm will fall free when the pivot tube is freed and care must be taken to support it securely. Collect the thrust washers from each side of the swingarm pivot. Manoeuvre the rear wheel, rear brake components and swingarm out of the machine as a unit, and lower the engine (and frame) to the ground on the jack **(see illustration)**.

27 On models with a through-bolt and nut on the front engine mounting, counter-hold the bolt head and unscrew the nut, then withdraw the pivot bolt and washer **(see illustrations)**. On models with a bolt on each side, remove the bolt and washer from each front mounting point.

28 Unscrew the engine rear mounting bolt

5.22a Use cable ties to secure the rear brake and footrest components to the swingarm – early SS/SL models shown here

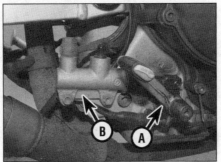
5.22b On later SS and Sport models remove the brake pedal (A) and displace the master cylinder (B) and its reservoir

5.23 Support the engine with a jack during removal

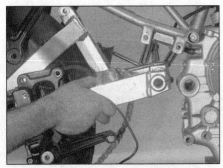
5.26 Removing the rear wheel and swingarm from the frame and engine unit

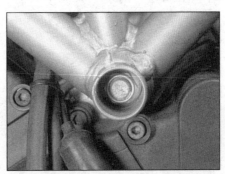
5.27a On engines supported at the front by a through-bolt, unscrew the nut . . .

5.27b . . . and remove the front mounting bolt

5.28 The engine rear mounting bolt is withdrawn from the left-hand side

5.29 Lift the frame at the rear and wheel it off the engine/transmission unit

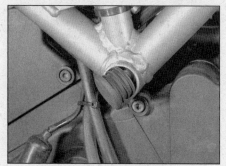

5.30a Install the plugs in the engine mounting bolt locations

5.30b Use new gaskets or O-rings (according to model) when installing the inlet ducts

and washer **(see illustration)** and withdraw it from the left-hand side.
29 With the aid of an assistant either lift the frame at the rear up and over the engine/

transmission unit, or lift the frame at the rear and manoeuvre the engine/transmission unit out from the side **(see illustration)**. Lift the engine/transmission unit onto a work bench.

6.3a Line or mark on camshaft drive pulley must align with line on crankcase cover

6.3b On 1991 to 1997 models – line on each camshaft pulley aligns with peg on belt housing (arrows)

6.3c On 1998-on models – the mark (A) aligns with the peg (B) on the vertical cylinder . . .

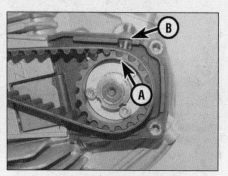

6.3d . . . and the mark (A) aligns with the gap (B) on the horizontal cylinder

Installation

30 Installation is a reverse of the removal procedure, noting the following:
● Tighten the engine mounting bolts to the specified torque.
● Install the plugs in the mounting bolt locations **(see illustration)**.
● Ensure that the wiring is routed correctly and secure it to the frame with cable ties.
● Use new gaskets or O-rings at the inlet duct joints with the cylinder heads **(see illustration)**.
● Refill the engine/transmission with oil as described in Chapter 1.
● Use new sealing washers on each side of the clutch hydraulic line union where disconnected. Tighten the union bolt to the specified torque and bleed the clutch as described in Section 21.
● Realign the matchmarks made on gearchange shaft to ensure the linkage is returned to its original position.
● Adjust the final drive chain tension as described in Chapter 1.
● Check that the clutch and rear brake work correctly before riding the motorcycle.

6 Cam belts – removal and installation

Note: *The cam belts can be removed with the engine in the frame. If the engine has already been removed, ignore the steps which do not apply.*

Removal

1 On fully-faired models, remove the fairing right-hand lower panel.
2 Remove the belt covers, manoeuvring them free of any hoses and wiring which run down the frame tubes. Note that the screws at the camshaft end of each cover locate in bushes set in the rubber belt housing and can prove difficult to slacken due to corrosion – spray them with penetrating fluid before attempting removal.
3 Before disturbing the cam belts, first check the valve timing marks and verify that they are correct. Remove both spark plugs to make turning the engine easier, then rotate the crankshaft so that the line or mark on the camshaft drive pulley aligns with the scribed line on the crankcase right-hand cover **(see illustration)**. **Note:** *To turn the crankshaft, position the bike on an auxiliary stand so that the rear wheel is off the ground, shift the transmission into first gear and rotate the rear wheel by hand.* On 1991 to 1997 models, at this point the mark on each camshaft pulley must align exactly with the peg on the belt housing **(see illustration)**. On 1998-on models, at this point the mark on the vertical cylinder camshaft pulley should align with the peg on the belt shroud **(see illustration)**, and the mark on the horizontal pulley should align with the gap between the two ridges on the cover back-piece **(see illustration)**.

6.4 Fully slacken the tensioner bolt (arrow) to allow the belt to go slack

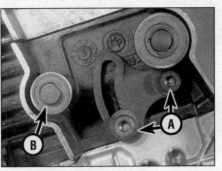

6.9 Belt tensioner bolts (A) and belt guide roller bolt (B)

6.10 Belt tensioner bearings can be withdrawn after removing circlip (arrow)

4 Use chalk to mark the belts, H for horizontal and V for the vertical cylinder and also mark an arrow on each indicating direction of rotation (both belts run anti-clockwise). Working on the horizontal cylinder first, slacken off the belt tensioner bolts and completely untension the belt **(see illustration)**. Without moving the position of either pulley, carefully manoeuvre the belt off both pulleys.
5 Perform the same operation on the vertical cylinder's belt.

Inspection

Note: *It is strongly recommended that the cam belts are replaced with new ones whenever they are disturbed, irrespective of the next service interval for this operation. The consequences of a belt failure will be* *extensive engine damage and likely loss of control of the motorcycle.*
6 Inspect each belt along its backing (flat side) and check that it is not holed (from the ingress of grit or small stones), cracked or damaged in any way. Check the edges of the belt are not torn. Check the working face of the belt for damaged teeth, cracking between the teeth and wear of the belt material – a shiny surface indicates extreme wear.
7 Check for wear of the belt teeth by fitting the belt over one of the pulleys and feeling for play between the teeth and pulley slots.
8 If either belt shows signs of wear or damage, replace both belts with new ones.
9 Check the surfaces of the belt tensioner rollers and guide rollers for damage. Also check that they revolve easily without stiffness. Each component can be unbolted from the engine casing if required **(see illustration)**.
10 The tensioner roller consists of two ball bearings which can be removed after the circlip has been freed **(see illustration)**. The guide roller must be renewed complete if it fails.

Installation

11 Make sure that the drive pulley and both camshaft pulley positions are undisturbed (see Step 3). On 1998-on models remove the screw from the shroud and the back-piece and replace it with a longer screw of the same thread with its end shaped to fit in the notch in the pulley flange, thereby locking the flange and hence the camshaft in position **(see illustration)**. Slacken the three pulley bolts **(see illustration)**. Install the vertical cylinder belt, on 1991 to 1997 models making sure that neither pulley is rotated during the process **(see illustration)** – moving the pulley just one tooth will mean that the valve timing will be incorrect. Install the horizontal cylinder belt in the same way **(see illustration)**.
Caution: Only use your hands to install the belts. Tools could damage the belt and lead to it failing in use.
12 Set cam belt tension as described in Chapter 1. On 1998-on models set the tension so the twist is maximum 45° as described in Step 11, then when all disturbed components have been refitted take the bike to a Ducati dealer to have the tension checked using the specialised equipment, and if necessary re-set.
13 Install the belt covers and secure them with their screws.
14 Where applicable, install the fairing section.

6.11a Fit the special tools or suitable screws locating the ends in the pulley flange notches to lock them in place (arrow)

6.11b Slacken the pulley bolts (arrowed)

6.11c Fit the new vertical belt over the pulleys making sure that the timing marks stay aligned

6.11d Fit the horizontal belt in the same way

| 7 | Cam belt pulleys and drive – removal and installation | |

Cam belt pulleys

Note: *All three pulleys can be removed with the engine in the frame. If the engine has already been removed, ignore the steps which do not apply.*

7.2a Either hold the pulley with an old cam belt . . .

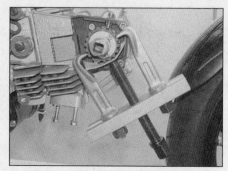

7.2b . . . or use a two-legged puller to counter-hold the pulley . . .

7.2c . . . while unscrewing the nut

Removal

1 Remove the cam belts as described in Section 6.

7.3a Remove the washer . . .

7.3c Unscrew the bolts and remove the outer plate, pulley and flange separately if required

2 Each camshaft pulley is held by a slotted nut. A Ducati service tool is available to hold the pulley whilst the nut is unscrewed.

7.3b . . . cam belt pulley, Woodruff key and plate (arrows)

7.4a Remove the cam belt driveshaft outer pulley . . .

Alternatively either the old cam belt (assuming a new one is to be fitted) can be clamped around the pulley and held with self-locking grips whilst the nut is slackened (see illustration), or a puller can be fitted onto the pulley as shown – note the use of a piece of protective card between the puller bolt and the pulley to prevent damage (see illustrations).

3 Using either the Ducati service tool or a fabricated tool to fit in the nut slots (see tool shown in illustration 7.2a), unscrew the nut then slide the washer and pulley off the shaft and retrieve the Woodruff key (see illustrations). Mark the outer face of each camshaft pulley H or V to denote their cylinder location. Where fitted also remove the plate if required. On later models the pulley assembly can be split into its component parts (outer plate, pulley and flange) by unscrewing the three bolts if required (see illustration).

4 The cam belt driveshaft pulleys are retained by a slotted nut and washer and can be removed as described above. A Woodruff key locates each pulley on the shaft and a spacer washer fits between them (see illustrations). Mark the pulleys outer and inner as a guide to installation. If you intend separating the crankcases remove the circlip from the driveshaft, where fitted (see illustration).

Installation

5 Install all components in a reverse of the removal procedure, using the marks made on dismantling to return the pulleys to their original locations. Align the slot in the pulley or

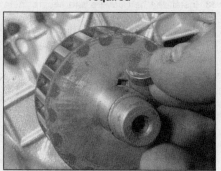

7.4b . . . Woodruff key and spacer washer . . .

7.4c . . . and the inner pulley

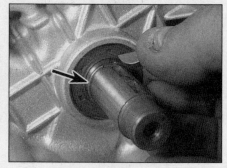

7.4d Recover the Woodruff key. Note circlip (arrow) where fitted

7.7a Hold the gear as shown while removing its nut

7.7b Extract the Woodruff key from the driveshaft keyway

7.8a Slip the drive gear off the crankshaft . . .

pulley flange (according to model) with the Woodruff key and make sure it locates correctly onto it. On later models if the pulley assembly was split into its separate components, align the cutout in the flange rim (for the locking tool), the timing mark on the pulley and the cutout in the outer plate rim **(see illustration 7.3c)**. There is no need to tighten the three bolts until the cam belts have been installed and tensioned. Use a new nut on each pulley and secure to the specified torque. When installing the cam belts make sure all timing marks are correctly aligned (see Section 6).

Cam belt drive

Note: *The drive gears can be removed with the engine in the frame. If the engine has already been removed, ignore the steps which*

do not apply. The cam belt driveshaft can only be accessed after separating the crankcases.

Removal

6 The drive gears are located on the left-hand side of the crankcase. Remove the alternator and starter clutch for access (see Section 14).
7 Flatten back the tab of the driveshaft gear nut and remove the nut, noting that the gear can be held via its two holes **(see illustration)**. Lift off the gear and retrieve the Woodruff key from the driveshaft keyway **(see illustration)**. Obtain a new lockwasher for use on installation.
8 Slide the drive gear off the end of the crankshaft and retrieve the Woodruff key from the crankshaft keyway **(see illustrations)**.

Installation

9 Make sure that the Woodruff keys are

positioned in their slots in the cam belt driveshaft and crankshaft.
10 Install the gear on the cam belt driveshaft so its dished side faces outwards. Rotate the driveshaft so that the tooth with the punch mark points directly to the crankshaft. Install a new lockwasher and tighten the nut to the specified torque **(see illustration)**. Bend a portion of the lockwasher up against a flat of the nut **(see illustration)**.
11 Install the drive gear over the Woodruff key on the crankshaft, noting that the punch mark on its outer face must align exactly with the punch mark on the cam belt driveshaft gear **(see illustration)**. If it does not, slip the gear off and rotate the crankshaft to the correct position.

7.8b . . . and remove the Woodruff key

7.10a Tighten the cam belt driveshaft gear nut to the specified torque

8 Cylinder heads – removal and installation

Note: *The horizontal cylinder head can be removed with the engine in the frame. If the engine has already been removed, ignore the steps which do not apply. The engine must be removed for vertical cylinder head removal.*

> **HAYNES HiNT** *The cylinder head nuts are likely to be difficult to slacken, particularly on the front cylinder due to its exposed location; it is advised that the nuts are sprayed with penetrating fluid first, preferably the night before.*

Removal – horizontal cylinder

1 On fully-faired models, remove the fairing lower panels (see Chapter 7).
2 Remove the oil cooler (where fitted) (see Section 25). Disconnect the wiring connector from the sensor in the horizontal head valve cover where fitted.
3 Either remove the carburettors/throttle bodies (according to model), or disconnect them from their inlet ducts adapters sufficiently to allow the inlet duct to be

7.10b Lock the nut by bending up a portion of the lock washer

7.11 Punch marks on gears must align exactly

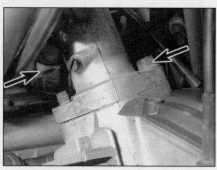

8.3 Remove the two nuts (arrows) to release the inlet ducts

8.4 Unscrew the knurled ring to release the tachometer cable

disconnected from the cylinder head (see Chapter 3). The inlet duct is retained by two nuts **(see illustration)**. Discard the gasket or O-ring (according to model) as a new one must be used on installation.

4 Where fitted unscrew the tachometer cable knurled retaining ring and withdraw the cable from its drive **(see illustration)**. Pull the plug cap off the spark plug.

5 Remove the exhaust front downpipe assembly (see Chapter 3).

6 Remove the cam belts (see Section 6).

7 Remove the four nuts and washers which retain the cylinder head on the crankcase studs **(see illustration)**. These nuts are positioned in such a way that it is impossible to attach a conventional socket to them. An open-ended spanner or a very thin ring spanner (preferably

an eight-point type) can be used to slacken them, although be very careful not to round off the corners of the nut. Removal of the camshaft bearing cap may be necessary to fit the ring spanner over the nut. **Note:** *A far better method of removal is to purchase the Ducati service tool (Pt. No. 88713.0882 or 2096 according to model) or a commercially available equivalent which can be used with a socket spanner; this also enables tightening of the nuts to the specified torque setting* **(see illustration)**. Slacken the nuts evenly in a criss-cross sequence to prevent warpage of the head.

8 Remove the cylinder head from the crankcase studs and recover the dowel and two O-rings. Note that there is no cylinder head gasket – the joint is sealed by the machined surfaces of the head and barrel.

Removal – vertical cylinder

9 Remove the engine (see Section 5).

10 Remove the cam belts (see Section 6).

11 Remove the four nuts and washers which retain the cylinder head on the crankcase studs, noting the comment in Step 7 **(see illustration)**.

12 Remove the cylinder head from the studs **(see illustration)** and recover the dowel (if loose, and noting which way round it fits) and three O-rings. Note that there is no cylinder head gasket – the joint is sealed by the machined surfaces of the head and barrel.

Installation – horizontal cylinder

13 Make sure the mating surfaces of the barrel and head are clean. Install two new O-rings and the locating dowel on the barrel with the small hole side of the dowel facing out **(see illustration)**.

14 Install the head on the barrel. Grease the threads of the studs, then install the washers, noting that where used the D-shaped washers are fitted with their flat against the casting. Install the four nuts on the studs. **Note:** *On early 900 engines, if the new type cylinder studs have been fitted, new washers and nuts should be used.*

15 Either of the service tools under Pt. No. 88713.0882 for early models or 22817.2096 for later models **(see illustration 8.7b)** can be used to tighten the nuts. If using type B note that the torque must be applied at a 90° angle to the tool **(see illustration 9.21b)**. **Note:** *It is possible to make up a copy of this tool (type B) by welding a socket (to fit the torque wrench drive) to a slim 15 mm spanner – the distance from the centre of the ring spanner to the centre of the socket measures 83 mm.*

16 Tighten the cylinder nuts to the two initial stages, then the final stage torque setting. **Note:** *On early 900 engines, if new cylinder studs have been fitted a revised torque setting should be used for the 3rd stage.*

17 Install all other components in a reverse of the removal procedure with reference to the appropriate text sections. Check the engine/transmission oil level and top up if necessary.

18 After the engine has been run for 600 miles (1000 km) the cylinder head nuts must be re-torqued to the 3rd setting.

8.7a Remove the four nuts and washers to free the horizontal cylinder head

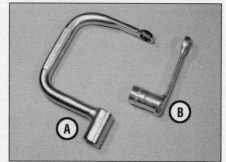

8.7b Ducati service tools for removing/installing the cylinder head nuts – version A later type, version B early type

8.11 Remove the four nuts (arrows) to free the vertical cylinder head . . .

8.12 . . . and lift the cylinder head off the barrel

8.13 Dowel and O-ring positions on horizontal cylinder (arrows)

8.19 Dowel and O-ring positions on vertical cylinder (arrows)

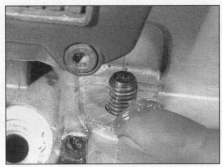

8.20a Apply grease to the cylinder head studs . . .

8.20b . . . install the washers . . .

8.20c . . . and nuts

8.21a Using the type A service tool to torque the cylinder head nuts

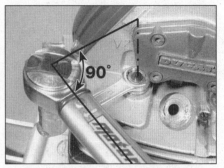

8.21b Using the type B service tool to torque the cylinder head nuts

Installation – vertical cylinder

19 Make sure the mating surfaces of the barrel and head are clean. Install three new O-rings and the locating dowel on the barrel with the small hole side of the dowel facing out (see illustration).

20 Install the head on the barrel. Grease the threads of the studs, then install the washers, noting that where used the D-shaped washers are fitted with their flat against the casting (see illustrations). Install the four nuts on the studs (see illustration. Note: On early 900 engines, if the new type cylinder studs have been fitted, new washers and nuts should be used.

21 Either of the service tools under Pt. No. 88713.0882 for early models or 22817.2096 for later models (see illustration 8.7b) can be used to tighten the nuts (see illustration). If

using type B note that the torque must be applied at a 90° angle to the tool (see illustration). Note: It is possible to make up a copy of this tool (type B) by welding a socket (to fit the torque wrench drive) to a slim 15 mm spanner – the distance from the centre of the ring spanner to the centre of the socket measures 83 mm.

22 Tighten the cylinder nuts to the two initial stages, then the final stage torque setting. Note: On early 900 engines, if new cylinder studs have been fitted a revised torque setting should be used for the 3rd stage.

23 Install the cam belts (see Section 6).

24 Install the engine in the frame (Section 5).

25 After the engine has been run for 600 miles (1000 km) the cylinder head nuts must be re-torqued to the 3rd setting.

9 Cylinder heads, camshafts and valves – overhaul

Dismantling

1 Remove the cylinder head (see Section 8).

2 Remove both valve covers and the camshaft end cover; each is secured by four bolts (see illustrations). Recover the gasket from each cover. On all except 620 engines retrieve the shim from the end of the camshaft (see illustration 9.37a).

3 On models with a cable-driven tachometer, remove the drive housing screw and manoeuvre the housing and drive gear out of the cylinder head (see illustration). On early

9.2a Remove the valve covers . . .

9.2b . . . and camshaft end cover from the cylinder head

9.3a Where a tachometer is fitted, remove the screw (arrow) and extract the drive gear

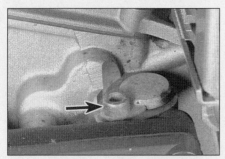

9.3b Where no tachometer is fitted, remove the screw and plate (arrow) and manoeuvre the plug out

9.4 Withdraw the spacer from the camshaft end where fitted

9.5 The pulley housing is secured by two screws

9.8 Withdraw the camshaft from the cylinder head

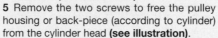

9.9a Lift the opening shim off the valve

individual valve and rocker components – in this way, no components will be inadvertently interchanged.

7 The opening (upper) rocker arm shafts must be pulled out of the head. Each shaft is drilled with a 5 mm thread to enable a service tool to be screwed into the shaft and the shaft pulled out. It was found that an M5 bolt and nut, with suitable washers, could be used to good effect as a drawbolt **(see illustration 9.11)**. As the shaft is extracted, retrieve the rocker arm, spring clip and shims from inside the cylinder head, noting their exact position. Perform the same operation on the other opening valve.

8 Withdraw the camshaft from the cylinder head, aligning it as required for smooth passage **(see illustration)** and recover its shim (not fitted on 620 engines) **(see illustration 9.31)**.

9 Lift the opening shim off the valve **(see illustration)**. Press the closing rocker arm down and retrieve the two wire collets **(see illustration)**. **Note:** *Obtain new wire collets for use on reassembly.* Slip the closing shim off the valve and withdraw the valve from the combustion chamber **(see illustrations)**.

10 The service tool (Pt. No. 88713.0143 or 2362 according to model) **(see illustration)** is essential for removing the closing rocker arms; it releases valve spring tension, enabling the rocker arm shaft to be withdrawn. Using a large flat-bladed screwdriver inserted through the other side of the cylinder head, hold the arm of the spring off the casting while the tool is positioned – this requires a degree of dexterity **(see illustration)**.

models not equipped with a tachometer, if required remove the screw and retaining plate, then manoeuvre the plug out of the cylinder head **(see illustration)**.

4 Remove the camshaft pulley (see Section 7). Remove the spacer, noting which way

round it fits **(see illustration)**.

5 Remove the two screws to free the pulley housing or back-piece (according to cylinder) from the cylinder head **(see illustration)**.

6 Before removing the valves, prepare a compartmented box in which to store the

9.9b Hold the closing rocker down and pick out the wire collets . . .

9.9c . . . lift off the closing shim . . .

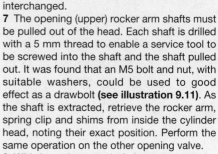

9.9d . . . and withdraw the valve from the combustion chamber

9.10a Service tool for removing the closing rocker arms

9.10b Hook the tool around the rocker arm and spring as shown

9.11 Extract the rocker arm shaft using a drawbolt tool

9.12 Always renew the valve stem seals

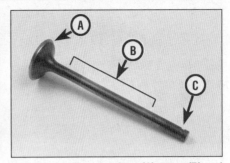

9.15 Check the valve face (A), stem (B) and wire collet groove (C) for signs of wear and damage

9.16a Insert a small hole gauge into the guide and expand it so there is a slight drag when it is pulled out . . .

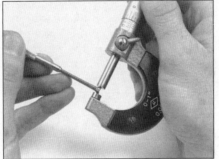

9.16b . . . then measure the hole gauge with a micrometer

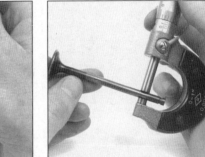

9.17 Measuring the valve stem diameter

11 With the tool correctly installed, remove the rocker arm shaft as described in Step 7 **(see illustration)**. Withdraw the rocker arm with the tool attached, then very carefully separate the components, noting their fitted order.

12 Pull the valve stem seals off the guides – new ones should be installed on reassembly **(see illustration)**.

Inspection

13 Thoroughly clean the cylinder head and remove carbon deposits from the valve heads and combustion chamber area. Inspect the head very carefully for cracks and other damage. If cracks are found, a new head will be required. Inspect the sealing surface closely, particularly if leakage has occurred at the head-to-barrel joint. If there are signs of warpage or the surface is damaged seek the advice of an engineering specialist.

14 Examine the valve seats in the combustion chamber. If they are pitted, cracked or burned, the head will require work beyond the scope of the home mechanic. Replacement valve seats are available for this engine.

15 Carefully inspect each valve face for cracks, pits and burned spots. Check the valve stem and the wire collet groove area for cracks **(see illustration)**. Rotate the valve and check for any obvious indication that it is bent – if vee blocks and a dial gauge are available, measure valve stem and head runout. Check the end of the stem for pitting and excessive wear. The presence of any of the above conditions indicates the need for valve servicing. It is advised that the wire collets are

renewed as a matter of course during a valve overhaul.

16 Clean the valve guides to remove any carbon build-up, then measure the inside diameters of the guides (at both ends and the centre of the guide) with a small hole gauge and micrometer **(see illustrations)**. These measurements, along with the valve stem diameter measurements, will enable you to compute the valve stem-to-guide clearance.

17 Measure the valve stem diameter **(see illustration)**. By subtracting the stem diameter from the valve guide bore diameter, the valve stem-to-guide clearance is obtained. If the stem-to-guide clearance is greater than that listed in the specifications, the valves and guides must be replaced as a set by a Ducati dealer.

18 Taking care to keep the valve components separate, inspect the rocker arms, rocker arm shafts and the closing rocker spring. If in any doubt about their condition replace them with

new components. Measure the rocker arm inside diameter and the shaft outside diameter (at its point of contact with the rocker arm). Subtract one from the other to obtain the rocker arm-to-shaft clearance. If in excess of the service limit the arm and shaft should be renewed.

19 Examine the camshaft lobe surfaces and the corresponding contact points on the rocker arms. All should be free from scratches, cracks or signs of excessive wear. Check the areas of the camshaft which locate in the ball bearings; there should be no sign of wear or scoring at these points. Make sure the oilways in the camshaft are clear.

20 Rotate the ball bearing in the camshaft end cap and the ball bearing(s) in the cylinder head. If the bearings feel rough or are noisy they should be renewed. On 620 engines, which only have two bearings (while all others have three) first remove the circlip securing each bearing **(see illustrations)**. The bearing

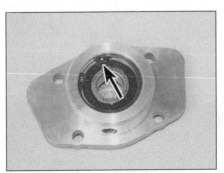

9.20a On 620 engines remove the circlip (arrowed) from the end cap bearing . . .

9.20b . . . and the bearing in the head

9.20c Ball bearing in camshaft end cap can be pulled out with a slide-hammer

9.20d Prise the oil seal out of the cylinder head

9.20e Camshaft bearing(s) set in the cylinder head

9.23 Apply the grinding compound sparingly to the valve face only

9.24a Rotate the valve grinding tool between the palms of your hands

9.24b The valve face should have a smooth unbroken appearance

in the end cap may need to be removed with a slide-hammer and bearing puller attachment **(see illustration)**. On all except 620 engines the two bearings housed in the cylinder head are separated by the tachometer gear on early models with a cable-driven tacho or a spacer on other models. Prise the oil seal out of the cylinder head **(see illustration)**. On all except 620 engines pass a long drift through the cylinder head and tap against the inner race of the (outer) bearing to drive it out of the head; move the drift around the inner race so that the bearing exits squarely **(see illustration)**. Slip the tachometer drive worm or spacer out and drift the other bearing out so that it is removed from inside the head. On 620 engines drive the bearing into the head from the outer (seal) side using a drift on the inner race.

21 Use a bearing driver or a socket which bears only on the outer race of the bearing to install it in the head or end cap. Install a new oil seal in the head. On 620 engine fit the circlips to retain the bearings **(see illustrations 9.20a and b)**.

Reassembly

22 Before installing the valves in the head, they should be ground in (lapped) to ensure a positive seal between the valves and seats. This procedure requires coarse and fine valve grinding compound and a valve grinding tool. If a grinding tool is not available, a piece of rubber or plastic hose can be slipped over the valve stem (after the valve has been installed in the guide) and used to turn the valve.

23 Apply a small amount of coarse grinding

compound to the valve face, then slip the valve into the guide **(see illustration)**. **Note:** *Make sure each valve is installed in its correct guide and be careful not to get any grinding compound on the valve stem.*

24 Attach the grinding tool (or hose) to the valve and rotate the tool between the palms of your hands. Use a back-and-forth motion (as though rubbing your hands together) rather than a circular motion (i.e. so that the valve rotates alternately clockwise and anti-clockwise rather than in one direction only). Lift the valve off the seat and turn it at regular intervals to distribute the grinding compound properly. Continue the grinding procedure until the valve face and seat contact area is of uniform width and unbroken around the entire circumference of the valve face and seat **(see illustrations)**.

25 Carefully remove the valve from the guide and wipe off all traces of grinding compound.

Use solvent to clean the valve and wipe the seat area thoroughly with a solvent soaked cloth.

26 Repeat the procedure with fine valve grinding compound, then repeat the entire procedure for the other valve.

27 Press a new valve stem oil seal on the top of the valve guide and make sure it fits fully over the guide. The black seal contained in the gasket set goes on the inlet valve and the green seal goes on the exhaust valve. **Note:** *Some earlier engines were fitted with a black inlet seal and a white exhaust seal.*

28 Install the valve spring on the closing rocker arm and attach the service tool **(see illustration)**. Pass the assembly into the cylinder head and install the rocker arm shaft partway; the threaded end of the shaft must face outwards. Slip the shim(s) into place as the rocker arm shaft is pushed fully home **(see illustrations)**. Always return the shim(s) to

9.28a Assemble the closing rocker and spring on the service tool

9.28b Insert the assembly and install the shims as the rocker arm shaft is inserted

9.28c Fit the shims on the other side of the rocker arm before pushing the shaft home

9.29 Ensure the wire collets are securely seated

9.31 Install the shim on the camshaft

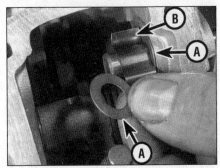
9.33a Insert the rocker arm shaft partway, then install the shim (A), spring clip (B) and shim (A) . . .

9.33b . . . install the opening rocker arm . . .

9.33c . . . and push the shaft fully home

their original locations to ensure that the rocker arm claw remains central to the valve. Remove the service tool.

29 Oil the stem of the valve and install it in its guide, twisting it slightly to assist insertion through the oil seal. Install the closing shim. Apply grease to the new wire collets to help them stay in place and hold the rocker arm down as the collets are installed in the retainer. Check that they are both properly seated **(see illustration)**.

30 Install the closing rocker for the other valve.

31 Install the camshaft, complete with its shim (not fitted on 620 engines), into the bearings in the head right-hand side **(see illustration)**. Note that the Woodruff key in the camshaft must engage the slot in the tachometer drive gear set between the bearings (where applicable).

32 At this point, check the closing rocker clearance as described in Chapter 1 (Valve clearance check).

33 Install the opening rocker arm shaft partway into the cylinder head, with its threaded end outwards. Install the shim, spring clip, shim and opening rocker arm as the shaft is pushed fully home **(see illustrations)**. Always return the shims to their original locations to ensure that the rocker arm remains central over the valve.

34 At this point, check the opening rocker clearance as described in Chapter 1.

35 Insert the rubber pulley housing or back-piece (according to cylinder) into the cylinder

head fins and press it fully into place **(see illustrations)**; secure the housing with the two screws. Install the spacer (chamfered end inwards) on the right-hand side of the camshaft

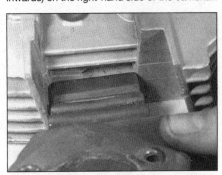
9.35a Engage the pulley housing in the cylinder head fins . . .

9.35c Install the Woodruff key in the camshaft and locate the plate over it

(see illustration 9.4). Fit the camshaft pulley as described in Section 7 **(see illustrations)**.

36 On the horizontal cylinder, where fitted install the tachometer drive gear using a new

9.35b . . . pressing it fully into place

9.35d Install the pulley and a new slotted nut

9.37a Don't forget the shim on the end of the camshaft

9.37b Use a new gasket on the camshaft end cover

O-ring at the housing joint. Secure the housing with the retaining screw. On other models and where fitted, install a new O-ring on the plug and insert it in the cylinder head. Engage the retaining plate in the plug groove and secure with the screw.

37 On all except 620 engines install the shim on the end of the camshaft and refit the end cover using a new gasket (see illustrations). Use a new gasket on each of the valve covers.

10 Valves and seats – servicing

1 Because of the complex nature of this job and the special tools and equipment required, most owners leave servicing of the valves, valve seats and valve guides to a professional.
2 The home mechanic can, however, remove the valves from the cylinder head, clean and

11.7 Cylinder barrel size code location (arrow)

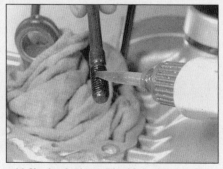

11.8b Apply thread-locking agent to the threads of the new studs

check the components for wear and grind in the valves (see Section 9). Note that replacement valve seats are available for this engine.
3 After the valve service has been performed, the head will be in like-new condition. When the head is returned, be sure to clean it again very thoroughly before installation on the engine to remove any metal particles or abrasive grit that may still be present from the valve service operations. Use compressed air, if available, to blow out all the holes and passages.

11 Cylinder barrels – removal, inspection and installation

Note: The horizontal cylinder barrel can be removed with the engine in the frame. If the engine has already been removed, ignore the steps which do not apply. The engine must be removed for vertical cylinder barrel removal.

11.8a Using a stud extractor tool to remove a broken cylinder stud

11.8c Lock two nuts together to thread the new studs into the crankcase

Removal

1 Remove the cylinder head (see Section 8).
2 Where fitted remove the oil feed pipe union bolt from the side of the barrel and recover its sealing washers – new washers should be used on installation.
3 Lift the barrel off the crankcase, tapping it gently around its mating surface with a soft-faced mallet if necessary. Pack clean rag into the crankcase mouth to prevent debris falling into the crankcase.
4 Recover the O-ring where fitted (see illustration 11.9c) and the aluminium gasket from the crankcase surface. There is a small dowel pin set in the gasket surface – if it is loose, remove it for safekeeping.

Inspection

5 The bore is highly wear resistant and should last the life of the machine. If the wear checks described below indicate that it has worn beyond its service limit or if catastrophic engine damage has occurred, the barrel must be renewed – neither reboring nor honing is possible.
6 Using telescoping gauges (see Tools and Working facilities), check the dimensions of each bore to assess the amount of wear, taper and ovality. Measure near the top (but below the level of the top piston ring at TDC), centre and bottom (level with the finned section) of the bore both parallel to and across the crankshaft axis. Calculate any differences between the measurements taken to determine any taper and ovality in the bore and compare the results to the specifications at the beginning of the Chapter. Calculate the piston-to-bore clearance as described in Section 12. If you do not have access to the precision measuring tools required, take the barrels and pistons to a Ducati dealer for assessment and advice on their condition.
7 If renewing a cylinder barrel, always quote the size code letter stamped on the sealing face at the top (see illustration) and the corresponding code letter on the piston crown (see illustration 12.3) – these should be the same.
8 If a broken cylinder stud is encountered, all four studs for that cylinder must be renewed. Note that cylinder stud breakage has been a problem on the early 900 engine and modified studs are available from Ducati dealers – the letter stamped on the end of the stud indicates the type fitted. Use a stud extractor tool to remove the studs from the crankcase (see illustration). Clean out the stud holes in the crankcase and make sure they are free of old locking compound and any cleaning fluid. Apply a few drops of suitable thread-locking compound to the threads of the new studs and screw them into position (see illustration). Use two of the old cylinder head nuts, locked together on the upper end of the stud to thread them into place (see illustration), then tighten with the stud extractor tool.

Installation

Note: The following procedure describes the installation of the barrel with the piston already

11.9a Apply a smear of sealing compound to each side of the cylinder barrel gasket

11.9b Engage the cutout in the gasket with the dowel (arrow)

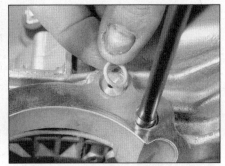

11.9c Use a new O-ring at the oilway

11.10 Smear engine oil over the cylinder bore surface

11.11 Ease the piston rings into the bore as the barrel is installed

11.12 Use a new sealing washer on each side of the oil pipe union where fitted on 900 engines

assembled on the connecting rod. If preferred, the upper section of the piston (ring area) can be fed into the bore on the bench, then assembled on the connecting rod.

9 Check that the crankcase surface is clean and that the small dowel is in place. Apply a smear of liquid gasket sealing compound to each side of the aluminium gasket and install the gasket so that its cutout engages the small dowel **(see illustrations)**. Where removed position a new O-ring around the oilway **(see illustration)**.

10 Squirt a few drops of fresh engine oil into the bore and smear it over the bore surface **(see illustration)**. Make sure that the piston ring end gaps are correctly spaced **(see illustration 13.9)** and remove any rag from the crankcase mouth.

11 Lower the barrel over the studs and very gently ease each ring into the bore using your fingertips **(see illustration)**. Seat the bore fully

onto its gasket. Hold the barrel in place and turn the crankshaft to make sure the piston moves smoothly up and down the bore.

12 Where fitted reconnect the oil feed pipe using a new sealing washer on each side of the union **(see illustration)**.

13 Install the cylinder head.

12 Pistons – removal, inspection and installation

Note: *The horizontal cylinder piston can be removed with the engine in the frame. If the engine has already been removed, ignore the steps which do not apply. The engine must be removed for vertical cylinder piston removal.*

Removal

1 Remove the cylinder barrel (Section 11).

2 Pad the crankcase mouth with clean rags to prevent anything falling in. If both pistons are being worked on, use a felt marker pen to write the cylinder identity (V or H) on the crown of each piston (or on the skirt if the piston is dirty and going to be cleaned).

3 The pistons carry markings on their crown to denote which way round they are fitted on the connecting rods. These marks are not particularly clear and the crown may require cleaning before they can be seen. Located near the valve head cutouts, the letter A denotes inlet and the letter S exhaust – there may also be another letter (A or B) at the side which denotes the piston size code **(see illustration)**. If the marks are indistinct, make your own by scribing an arrow in the crown, pointing to the front of the engine.

4 Grasp the circlip tang with needle-nose pliers and prise it out of the piston groove **(see illustrations)**. Remove the piston pin

12.3 Piston crown markings: A – inlet side, B – size code, S – exhaust side

12.4a Grasp the circlip tang with long-nose pliers . . .

12.4b . . . and remove the circlip from the piston

12.11 Measuring the piston ring-to-groove clearance

12.12 Measuring the piston diameter

12.17 Lubricate the small-end bush with engine oil

from the other side to free the piston from the connecting rod. Remove the other circlip and discard them as new ones must be used.

HAYNES HiNT *If the piston pin is a tight fit in the piston bosses, soak a rag in boiling water then wring it out and wrap it around the piston – this will expand the alloy piston sufficiently to release its grip on the pin.*

Inspection

5 Before the inspection process can be carried out, the piston must be cleaned and the old piston rings removed. Using your thumbs or a piston ring removal and installation tool, carefully remove the rings from the piston. Do not nick or gouge the piston in the process. Carefully note which way up each ring fits in its groove (there should be a mark of some description which faces up) and keep them in order according to their groove as they must be installed in their original positions if being re-used, or can be used as a guide to fitting new rings.
6 Scrape all traces of carbon from the top of the piston. A hand-held wire brush or a piece of fine emery cloth can be used once most of the deposits have been scraped away. Do not, under any circumstances, use a wire brush mounted in a drill motor to remove deposits from the piston; the piston material is soft and will be eroded away by the wire brush.
7 Use a piston ring groove cleaning tool to remove any carbon deposits from the ring

grooves. If a tool is not available, a piece broken off an old ring will do the job. Be very careful to remove only the carbon deposits. Do not remove any metal and do not nick or gouge the sides of the ring grooves.
8 Once the deposits have been removed, clean the piston with solvent and dry it thoroughly. If the cylinder identification previously marked on the piston is cleaned off, be sure to re-mark it with the correct identity. Make sure the oil return holes below the oil control ring groove are clear.
9 Carefully inspect each piston for cracks around the skirt, at the pin bosses and at the ring lands. Normal piston wear appears as even, vertical wear on the thrust surfaces of the piston and slight looseness of the top ring in its groove. If the skirt is scored or scuffed, the engine may have been suffering from overheating and/or abnormal combustion, which caused excessively high operating temperatures. The oil pump should be checked thoroughly. Also check that the circlip grooves are not damaged.
10 A hole in the piston crown, an extreme to be sure, is an indication that abnormal combustion (pre-ignition) was occurring. Burned areas at the edge of the piston crown are usually evidence of spark knock (detonation). If any of the above problems exist, the causes must be corrected or the damage will occur again.
11 Measure the piston ring-to-groove clearance by laying a new piston ring in the ring groove and slipping a feeler gauge in beside it **(see illustration)**. Check the clearance at three or four locations around the groove. If the clearance is greater than that

specified, the piston is worn and must be replaced. **Note:** *Make sure you have the correct ring for the groove.*
12 Check the piston-to-bore clearance by measuring the bore (see Section 11) and the piston diameter. Make sure each piston is matched to its correct cylinder. Measure the piston 10.0 mm up from the bottom of the skirt and at 90° to the piston pin axis **(see illustration)**. Subtract the piston diameter from the bore diameter to obtain the clearance. If it is greater than the specified figure, the piston must be renewed (Ducati recommend that the pistons in both cylinders are renewed at the same time). The plating on the cylinder bore is unlikely to wear to the same degree as the piston, but if the piston-to-bore clearance with new pistons is incorrect, the cylinder barrels must also be renewed.
13 If the pistons are to be renewed, ensure the correct size of piston is ordered. Look for the size code letter in the crown of the existing piston **(see illustration 12.3)** and in the face of the cylinder barrel **(see illustration 11.7)** and quote this when ordering new parts.
14 Apply clean engine oil to the piston pin, insert it into the piston and check for any freeplay between the two. Measure the pin external diameter and the pin bore in the piston, then subtract one from the other to arrive at the piston pin-to-piston boss clearance; compare with the specified figure.
15 Refer to Section 29 for details of the piston pin-to-small-end bush clearance check.

Installation

16 Inspect and install the piston rings (see Section 13).
17 Lubricate the piston pin and the connecting rod small-end bush with fresh engine oil **(see illustration)**.
18 Install a new circlip in one side of the piston – do not re-use old circlips. Line up the piston on its correct connecting rod, making sure the A mark faces the inlet side and the S mark faces the exhaust side for that cylinder, and insert the piston pin from the other side **(see illustration)**. Secure the pin with the other new circlip. When installing the circlips, compress them only just enough to fit them in the piston, and make sure they are properly seated in their grooves with the tang in the piston cutout **(see illustration)**.

12.18a Slide the piston pin into place . . .

12.18b . . . and secure it with the circlip – locate the circlip tang in the cutout (arrow)

13.3 Measuring piston ring end gap

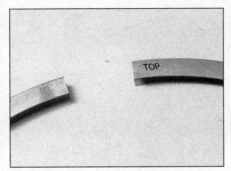

13.8a Rings are marked near their gap to denote the top surface

13.8b Install the oil ring expander . . .

13 Piston rings -
inspection and installation

Inspection

1 It is good practice to replace the piston rings when an engine is being overhauled. Before installing the new piston rings, the ring end gaps must be checked.

2 Lay out the pistons and the new ring sets so the rings will be matched with the same piston and cylinder during end gap measurement and assembly. Work on one cylinder at a time to avoid interchanging parts.

3 Insert the top ring into the bottom of the cylinder (where there is less wear) and square it up with the cylinder walls by pushing it in with the top of the piston. To measure the end gap, slip a feeler gauge between the ends of the ring and compare the measurement to the specifications at the beginning of the Chapter (see illustration).

4 If the gap is larger or smaller than specified, double check to make sure that you have the correct rings before proceeding.

5 Excess end gap is not critical unless it is greater than 1 mm. Again, double check to make sure you have the correct rings for your engine and check that the bore is not worn.

13.8c . . . and then install the side rail over it

6 Repeat the procedure for each ring that will be installed in that cylinder and then perform the same check on the other set of rings. Remember to keep the rings, pistons and cylinders matched up.

Installation

7 Once the ring end gaps have been checked install the rings on the pistons. The rings can be installed with a ring removal/installation tool, or by hand if care is taken to avoid overstressing them.

8 All rings are installed with the TOP marking or punch mark near the end gap facing up on the piston (see illustration). The different rings are identifiable by their profiles (see illustration 13.9a, b or c). The oil control ring (lowest on the piston) is installed first. It is composed of two separate components. Slip

13.8d Install the second (middle) and top compression rings

the expander into the groove, then install the side rail over it (see illustrations). Install the second compression ring in the middle groove on the piston. Finally install the top compression ring into the top groove on the piston (see illustration).

9 Check that all rings are free to rotate in their grooves, then arrange their end gaps at 120° intervals (see illustrations).

14 Alternator rotor, starter clutch and starter drive – removal, inspection and installation

Note: *The alternator and starter clutch can be removed with the engine in the frame. If the engine has already been removed, ignore the Steps which do not apply.*

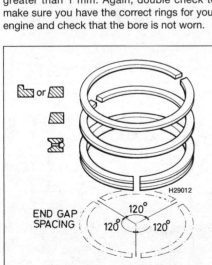

13.9a Piston ring identification (early model type) and end gap positions

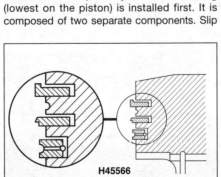

13.9b Different models (later 620/750 type shown here) have slightly different ring profiles . . .

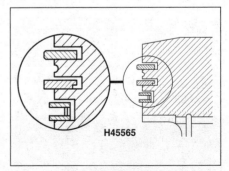

13.9c . . . check carefully, and fit new rings according to the layout of the old ones (later 900 type shown here)

14.6 Hold the oil pipe union as shown whilst the bolt is unscrewed

14.8a Remove the access cover from the crankcase left-hand cover . . .

Removal

1 On fully-faired models, remove the fairing left-hand lower panel (see Chapter 7).
2 Drain the engine oil (see Chapter 1).
3 Make a reference mark across the end of the gearchange shaft (level with the split in the clamp) and remove the pinch bolt **(see illustration 5.11a)**. Pull the gearchange linkage off the shaft **(see illustration 5.11b)**.
4 Remove the engine sprocket cover.
5 On all except early model 600 and 750 engines with the clutch release cylinder incorporated in the crankcase or clutch cover, remove the three bolts retaining the clutch release cylinder and lift the cylinder off the pushrod end **(see illustration 19.21)**. Restrain the piston in the cylinder with cable ties so

that it doesn't creep out whilst the cylinder is disconnected. Do not operate the clutch lever. Tie the release cylinder to the frame so that it is clear of the working area.
6 Also on 900 engines where fitted, remove the two oil pipe union bolts from the top of the crankcase cover **(see illustration)**. New sealing washers should be obtained for installation.
7 Trace the alternator and on later models the timing sensor wiring from the crankcase cover up to the block connector(s) and disconnect it/them. If the sidestand switch wiring runs across the crankcase left-hand cover, disconnect it at the block connector and route it clear.
8 The crankshaft left-hand end locates in a

bearing set in the crankcase cover. To enable the crankcase cover to be removed safely, without risk of breakage, the cover must be extracted using a puller, either the Ducati tool (part No. 88713.1749) or a commercially available equivalent, which bears on the crankshaft end. Remove the two screws which retain the access cover for the end of the crankshaft **(see illustration)**. Remove all the crankcase left-hand cover screws, taking note of their exact location and the location of any wire guides **(see illustration)**. Fit two suitably-sized bolts (the Ducati tool will come with these) through the puller and thread them into the access cover holes in the crankcase cover **(see illustration)**. Operate the puller centre bolt to draw the cover off the crankshaft end.
9 Where fitted peel off the cover gasket. Remove the two locating dowels if they are loose.
10 On early models locate the ignition timing markings on the pick-up coil mounting plate and record the exact position of the index lines in relation to the cast web in the crankcase **(see illustration)**. Follow the procedure in Chapter 4, Section 4, for removal of the pick-up coils, but instead of removing the coils individually remove the mounting plate complete **(see illustration)**.
11 Remove the alternator rotor nut and the Belleville washer (not fitted on early 600 and 750 engines) beneath it **(see illustration)**. To

14.8b . . . and all the cover screws (early 900 engine shown)

14.8c Use a puller to withdraw the left-hand cover

14.10a Take note of the ignition timing markings . . .

14.10b . . . before disturbing the pick-up coil plate nuts (arrows)

14.11 Unscrew the alternator rotor nut

14.12 Pick the Woodruff key out of the crankshaft keyway

14.14 Remove the circlip to withdraw the starter idle gear components

14.15 The starter motor is retained by three bolts (arrows)

do this the crankshaft must be prevented from turning using one of the following methods. The Ducati service tool (Pt. No. 88713.0710 or 2036 according to model) can be used to hold the alternator rotor steady, or if the engine is in the frame, engage a high gear and hold the rear brake on, or if one of the cylinder barrels has been removed, place a rod through the small-end eye (or place blocks of wood under the piston) and rest it on wood blocks placed across the crankcase mouth.

12 On early models with a non-integrated alternator rotor and flywheel slip the alternator rotor off the end of the crankshaft and pick the Woodruff key out of the crankshaft slot **(see illustration)**.

13 Withdraw the flywheel and starter clutch as an assembly. Remove the collar, needle roller bearing(s) and the washer from the crankshaft.

14 To remove the starter idle gear, remove the circlip and washer, then withdraw the gear and the washer beneath it **(see illustration)**.

15 The starter motor is secured by three bolts **(see illustration)**.

Inspection

16 The alternator stator coil is attached to the inside of the crankcase cover. Refer to Chapter 8 for details.

17 Examine the alternator rotor and the stator coil for signs of scuffing or damage. If the two components have come into direct contact during operation Ducati recommend that they are both renewed.

18 On early models with a non-integrated alternator rotor and flywheel check the fit of the alternator rotor on its Woodruff key and the fit of the key in the crankshaft keyway. Seek the advice of an engineering specialist if wear is discovered in these areas.

19 Hold the flywheel in one hand and with the

other, attempt to rotate the starter clutch gear **(see illustration)**. It should turn freely in one direction and lock up in the other. If it doesn't operate as described the sprag is at fault. To dismantle the starter clutch, lift the gear out of the flywheel, then where fitted remove the large circlip which retains the sprag **(see illustrations)**. Scribe a mark on the face of the sprag to ensure that it is refitted in the correct direction, then lift it out of the flywheel **(see illustration)**.

20 Inspect the sprag carefully and renew it if damaged. Also check the corresponding surface of the starter clutch gear **(see illustration)**. Examine the needle roller bearing(s) and its/their corresponding surfaces on the collar and starter clutch gear.

21 Install the sprag into the flywheel so that the previously marked side faces outwards (if installed the other way around, the clutch will lock in the wrong direction) and retain the

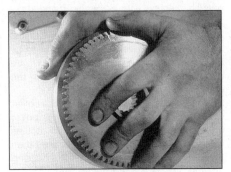

14.19a Checking the starter clutch operation

14.19b Lift the starter clutch gear out of the flywheel . . .

14.19c . . . and remove the circlip . . .

14.19d . . . to free the sprag

14.20 Examine the face (arrow) of the starter clutch gear

14.21 Ensure that all tabs of the circlip are engaged under the starter clutch body

14.23a The crankshaft end bearing locates in the left-hand cover . . .

14.23b . . . and can be drifted out of its housing if required

14.24a Prise the old gearchange shaft seal out of the cover . . .

14.24b . . . and use a socket to install the new seal into place

14.26a Install the washer over the starter idle gear shaft . . .

14.26b . . . followed by the idle gear . . .

sprag with the circlip where fitted **(see illustration)**. Install the starter clutch gear into the flywheel being careful as its boss engages the sprag.

Caution: Use only engine oil as a lubricant when assembling the starter clutch – grease will cause the clutch to malfunction.

22 Check the teeth of the starter motor, idle gear and starter clutch gear for wear, chipping or other damage.

23 Rotate the crankshaft end bearing in the crankcase cover. If it feels rough or is noisy in operation it must be renewed **(see illustration)**. Where fitted remove the circlip securing the bearing. The bearing can be drifted out from the outside of the cover **(see**

illustration); support the cover from the inside around the bearing housing to prevent damage. Install the bearing from the inside of the cover, using a socket which bears only the bearing outer race. Where removed fit the circlip into its groove.

24 The gearchange shaft oil seal should be renewed every time the crankcase cover is disturbed or if it is obviously leaking. Pry the old seal out with a flat-bladed screwdriver and use a socket to install the new seal **(see illustrations)**.

Installation

25 Install the starter motor in the crankcase using a new gasket and tighten its three bolts securely. **Note:** *The starter motor can if*

desired, be installed just before the crankcase cover.

26 Check the tightness of the starter idle gear shaft screw; if loose, remove it and apply a drop of suitable thread-locking compound to its threads then tighten it securely. Install the inner washer over the shaft, followed by the idle gear and outer washer **(see illustrations)**. Secure the idle gear with the circlip **(see illustration)**.

27 On models with a plain collar fit the collar, washer and the needle roller bearing(s) over the crankshaft **(see illustrations)**. On models with a shouldered collar, fit the bearing then the washer onto the collar with the bearing against the shouldered end, then fit the

14.26c . . . and washer . . .

14.26d . . . retain the assembly with the circlip

14.27a Slip the collar over the crankshaft . . .

14.27b . . . followed by the washer . . .

14.27c . . . and the needle roller bearing

14.27d Align the punch mark (arrow) with the crankshaft keyway when installing the flywheel

assembly onto the crankshaft with the shouldered end outermost, making sure the plain end of the collar remains in the washer, rather than being seated on it (in which case the washer will be offset from the shaft). Install the flywheel/starter clutch so that the punch mark on its boss aligns with the crankshaft keyway (see illustration). Check that the teeth of the starter clutch gear align with those of the starter idle gear as the assembly is pushed fully onto the crankshaft (see illustration).

28 On early models with a non-integrated alternator rotor and flywheel insert the Woodruff key into the crankshaft keyway and install the alternator rotor so that its slot engages the keyway (see illustration). Note: The side of the rotor which carries the DUCATI

marking faces inwards. On all except early 600 and 750 models install the Belleville washer (smeared with oil and dished side facing inwards) (see illustration). Clean all traces of old locking compound off the crankshaft threads. Apply a few drops of suitable thread-locking compound to the crankshaft threads and install the nut (see illustrations). Use the same method employed on removal to lock the crankshaft, then tighten the alternator rotor nut to the specified torque (see illustration).

29 On early models install the pick-up coil mounting plate being careful not to damage the coils on the flywheel triggers. Align the original index mark on the mounting plate with the crankcase web and secure the nuts lightly. The wiring must be reconnected as described

in Chapter 4, Section 4 and the pick-up coil air gaps checked. When all settings are correct, tighten the two mounting plate nuts securely.

30 Make sure that the mating surfaces of the cover and crankcase are clean and that all traces of old gasket or sealant (according to model) have been removed. Install the two dowels if these were removed. On models with a gasket place a new gasket one over the dowels (see illustration). On models without a gasket smear a suitable sealant onto one of the mating surfaces. If the starter motor was not installed previously, rotate the idler gear so that access is available to its right-hand screw hole and install the unit as described in Step 25.

31 Smear some grease onto the end of the crankshaft where it locates in the bearing in

14.27e Check that the starter clutch gear teeth mesh correctly with those of the idle gear

14.28a Install the alternator rotor so the DUCATI marking faces inwards, aligning its keyway with the Woodruff key (arrows)

14.28b Fit the Belleville washer (where applicable)

14.28c Apply thread-locking agent to the crankshaft threads, and install the nut

14.28d Tighten the nut to the specified torque

14.30 Install a new gasket on the crankcase

14.31 Refit the crankcase left-hand cover

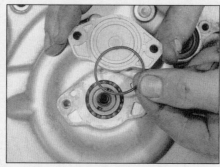

14.32 Use a new O-ring on the access cover

14.34a Use new sealing washers on each side of the oil pipe unions

14.34b Ensure that the oil pipes for the horizontal cylinder . . .

14.34c . . . and vertical cylinder are angled correctly

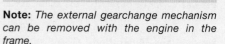

15 Gearchange mechanism (external) – removal, inspection and installation

Note: *The external gearchange mechanism can be removed with the engine in the frame.*

Removal

1 Make sure the transmission is in neutral. Remove the crankcase left-hand cover, alternator and flywheel/starter clutch assembly as described in Section 14, Steps 1 to 13. To access the stopper arm on the right-hand end of the selector drum (fitted on models from 1998 onwards) remove the clutch, referring to the Section for your model. To remove the stopper arm unscrew the bolt and remove the arm, washer and spring, noting how the roller on the arm locates against the neutral stop on the detent plate on the end of the drum, and how the spring ends locate **(see illustration)**.

2 The gearchange mechanism bracket is secured to the crankcase by two bolts. The holes in the bracket are slotted to allow for centring of the claw on installation and you are advised to make several alignment marks between the bracket and crankcase to aid installation. Remove the two bolts, then disengage the claw arm from the drum pins and lift the mechanism out of the crankcase **(see illustrations)**.

the cover. Press the crankcase cover into position with the palm of your hand, making sure that the crankshaft end slips fully into the bearing in the cover **(see illustration)**. Return all the cover screws and wire guides to their original positions and tighten them evenly and in a diagonal sequence.

32 Use a new O-ring on the small access cover and secure the cover with the two screws **(see illustration)**.

33 If disturbed, reconnect the sidestand wiring connector and secure the wiring in the guide. Reconnect the alternator wiring and where fitted the timing sensor wiring.

34 On 900 engines where fitted, use new sealing washers on each side of the oil pipe unions and tighten the union bolts securely

(see illustration). Make sure the oil pipes are routed correctly **(see illustrations)**.

35 On all except early model 600 and 750 engines with the clutch release cylinder incorporated in the crankcase or clutch cover remove the ties used to retain the clutch release cylinder piston and install the cylinder over the pushrod end. Tighten the three screws securely.

36 Install the engine sprocket cover.

37 Fit the gearchange linkage over the shaft, aligning the split in the clamp with the previously made mark on the shaft end. Tighten the linkage pinch bolt.

38 Replenish the engine/transmission oil (see Chapter 1).

39 On fully-faired models, install the fairing left-hand panel.

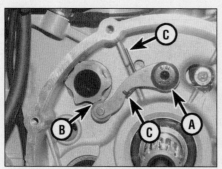

15.1 Stopper arm bolt (A). Note how the roller locates on the neutral stop (B) and how the spring ends (C) locate

15.2a Remove the two bolts (arrows) . . .

15.2b . . . to free the gearchange mechanism

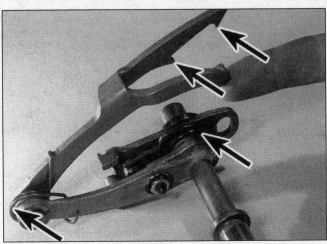

15.3 Check the claw ends and springs for wear or damage (arrows)

15.5a Checking that the gearchange arm pin is central in the mounting bracket

Inspection

3 Examine the claw ends of the gearchange mechanism at the point where they engage the drum pins **(see illustration)**. Any worn components must be renewed. Note that the drum pins can be accessed once the drum is removed from the crankcase.

4 Check the condition of the gearchange mechanism springs and renew them if necessary **(see illustration 15.3)**.

5 Measure the distance from the gearchange arm pin to the mounting bracket tabs on each side; the distance should be the same on each side of the pin **(see illustration)**. If not, slacken the adjuster locknut and turn the eccentric adjuster screw to correct the discrepancy, then tighten the locknut **(see illustration)**.

Installation

6 Install the gearchange mechanism in the crankcase and engage the claw with the drum pins. Thread the two bolts with their washers into place, align the previously-made matchmarks and secure the bolts finger-tight.
7 On models from 1998 onwards, if removed, fit the stopper arm, washer and spring onto the bolt, then install the assembly, locating to the roller on the arm in the detent on the plate on the end of the drum, and locating the spring ends correctly on the arm and against the crankcase.
8 Shift the transmission into 2nd gear. The claw ends must be equidistant from the drum pins on each side **(see illustration)**. Since it is not possible to view the pins clearly, the centring was checked by extending the claw forward and scribing a line on the crankcase level with the claw tip, then retracting the claw and making another line on the crankcase level with the claw tip **(see illustration)**. Scribe a line midway between the two claw tip markings and realign the claw tip with this mark to centralise it over the pins. When the correct position is found, tighten the two bolts securely. **Note:** *Later engines have a scribed line on the claw, enabling centring to be carried out by eye.*

15.5b Adjusting the gearchange arm pin position

9 Temporarily fit the gearchange linkage on the splined end of the shaft and check that all gears engage correctly.
10 Install the disturbed components as described in Section 14, Steps 27 to 38. On models from 1998 onwards, if removed, install the clutch, referring to the Section for your model.

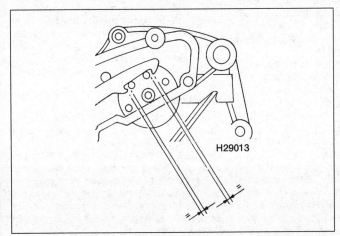

15.8a Gearchange claw must be centred over drum pins

15.8b Markings can be made on the crankcase to check claw positioning

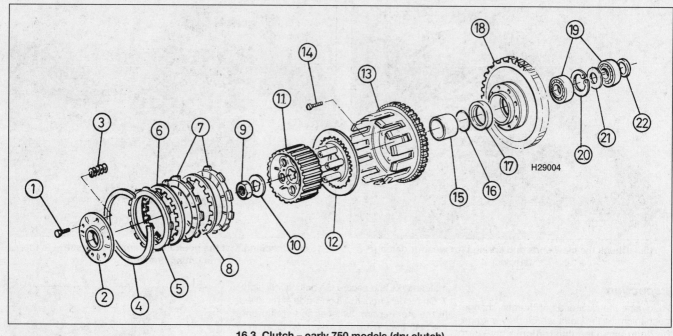

16.3 Clutch – early 750 models (dry clutch)

1 Bolts	6 Dished plain plate	12 Pressure plate
2 Spring retainer plate	7 Friction plates	13 Clutch housing
3 Springs	8 Plain plates	14 Bolts
4 Circlip	9 Clutch nut	15 Guide
5 Outer (one-sided)	10 Lock washer	16 O-ring
friction plate	11 Clutch centre	17 Oil seal

18 Driven gear
19 Bearings
20 Circlip
21 Spacer
22 Spacer

16 Clutch – removal, inspection and installation (1991 to 1997 600 and 750 engines)

Note: *The clutch can be removed with the engine in the frame. If the engine is in the frame ignore the steps which do not apply.*

750SS models up to engine VIN 001274 (i.e. those with a dry clutch).

Removal

1 Remove the fairing right-hand lower panel (see Chapter 7).

2 Remove the four screws from the clutch cover and lift the cover off the crankcase right-hand cover. The hydraulic hose can remain attached to the cover if care is taken to support the hose – do not operate the clutch lever with the cover removed.

3 Slacken the six spring retainer plate bolts evenly and in a criss-cross sequence. Withdraw the spring retainer plate and remove the six clutch springs from the posts of the clutch centre **(see illustration)**.

4 Using a couple of small flat-bladed screwdrivers, ease the large circlip out of its groove in the clutch housing. Pick the clutch plates out of the clutch housing, keeping them in order as a guide to installation.

5 Knock back the tab of the clutch nut

lockwasher with a punch. Unscrew the clutch nut from the input shaft, noting that the clutch centre must be prevented from rotating. The scissor-like tool shown in illustration 18.5 can be fabricated in the home workshop and engages the splines of the clutch centre. The Ducati service tool (Pt. No. 88713.0146) fits over the clutch centre enabling it to be held whilst the nut is slackened. Alternatively, if the engine is in the frame, the transmission can be placed in gear and the rear brake held on to prevent input shaft rotation.

6 With the clutch nut and lockwasher removed, slide the clutch centre and pressure plate off the input shaft. Discard the lockwasher and obtain a new one for use on installation.

7 Slip the guide out of the clutch housing. Undo the eight housing bolts and withdraw the housing from the driven gear boss.

8 The primary driven gear can only be accessed after the crankcase right-hand cover has been removed.

9 Drain the engine/transmission oil (see Chapter 1).

10 Disconnect the wiring from the oil pressure switch at the front of the crankcase right-hand cover. Take note of the hose routing around the front and underside of the cover, then release the hoses from their clamps. Pull the crankcase cover off and mop up any residual engine oil.

11 Pull the primary driven gear, complete

with bearings and oil seal off the input shaft.

Inspection

Note: *The plates in a dry clutch will create dust inside the casing and cover and on the clutch components. Clean off all dust using solvent, but wear an approved filtering mask in case the clutch plate material is asbestos-based.*

12 Refer to the inspection procedures for wet clutch models as below (Steps 29 to 37), plus the following.

13 The large oil seal in the crankcase right-hand cover should be renewed whenever the cover is disturbed or if there is obvious sign of failure. Using a punch, tap evenly around the rim of the seal to extract it from the casing **(see illustration 18.20a)**. Tap the new seal evenly into the casing **(see illustration 18.20b)**.

Installation

14 Refer to Steps 22 to 26 of Section 18.

15 Install the pressure plate and clutch centre over the input shaft.

16 Install a new lock washer over the input shaft and thread the clutch nut into place. Using the method employed on removal to lock the clutch centre, tighten the nut to the specified torque. Bend a portion of the lockwasher up against one of the nut flats to lock it in place.

17 Build up the clutch plates over the clutch centre, starting with a friction plate, then a

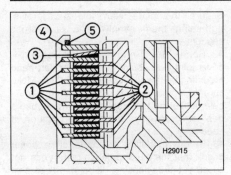

16.17 Clutch plate installation – early 750 models (dry clutch)

1 Friction plates
2 Plain plates
3 Dished plain plate
4 Outer (one-sided) friction plate
5 Circlip

plain plate and alternating them. Finally, install the dished plain plate (dished side facing into the clutch) and the single-sided friction plate (friction material facing into the clutch) **(see illustration)**. Work the large circlip into its groove in the clutch housing to retain the plates. Be careful not to deform the circlip as it is installed and make sure it is fully seated.

18 Place a spring over each of the clutch centre posts. Install the spring retainer plate and secure with the six screws, tightening them evenly in a criss-cross sequence.

19 Check that the release piston has not

eased out of its housing in the clutch cover, if necessary push it back with finger pressure. Install the clutch cover and secure with its four screws.

20 Install the fairing right-hand panel (see Chapter 7).

600SS, M600 and M750 models, and 750SS models from engine VIN 001275

Removal

21 On SS models, remove the fairing right-hand lower panel (see Chapter 7).

22 Drain the engine oil (see Chapter 1). Disconnect the wiring from the oil pressure switch at the front of the crankcase right-hand cover. Take note of the hose routing around the front and underside of the cover, then release the hoses from their clamps.

23 Have a supply of rags at hand to catch fluid spills from the clutch hydraulic hose, then remove the hose union bolt. Place the end of the hose in a plastic bag to prevent further fluid spills and the ingress of dirt.

24 Remove the ten screws from the cover and store them in a cardboard template of the cover as a guide to screw and hose clamp location. Pull the crankcase cover off the engine, if necessary tap it lightly around the periphery with a soft-faced mallet to break the gasket seal. As the cover is removed, drain off

any hydraulic fluid from the clutch release chamber and mop up any residual engine/transmission oil.

25 Slacken the six spring retainer plate bolts evenly and in a criss-cross sequence. Withdraw the spring retainer plate complete with bearing and pushrod. Remove the six clutch springs from the posts of the clutch centre **(see illustration)**.

26 Using a couple of small flat-bladed screwdrivers, ease the large circlip out of its groove in the clutch housing. Pick the clutch plates out of the clutch housing, keeping them in order as a guide to installation.

27 Knock back the tab of the clutch nut lockwasher with a punch. Unscrew the clutch nut from the input shaft, noting that the clutch centre must be prevented from rotating. The scissor-like tool shown in illustration 18.5 can be fabricated in the home workshop and engages the splines of the clutch centre. The Ducati service tool (Pt. No. 88713.0146) fits over the clutch centre enabling it to be held whilst the nut is slackened. Alternatively, if the engine is in the frame, the transmission can be placed in gear and the rear brake held on to prevent input shaft rotation.

28 With the clutch nut and lockwasher removed, slide the clutch centre and pressure plate off the input shaft. Discard the lockwasher and obtain a new one for use on installation. Withdraw the spacer and clutch

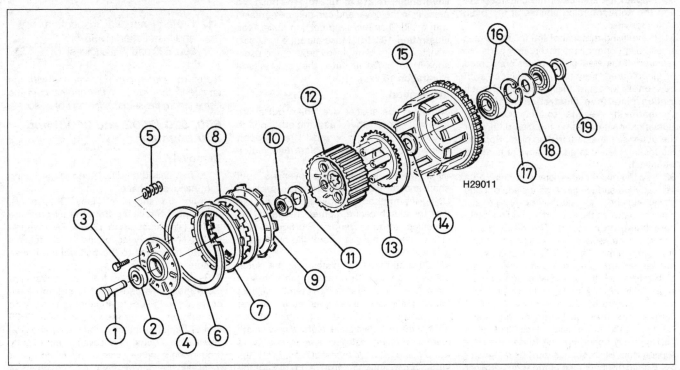

16.25 Clutch – 600 and later 750 models to end 1997 (wet clutch)

1 Pushrod
2 Bearing
3 Bolts
4 Spring retainer plate
5 Springs
6 Circlip
7 Outer (one-sided) friction plate
8 Plain plates
9 Friction plates
10 Clutch nut
11 Lock washer
12 Clutch centre
13 Pressure plate
14 Spacer
15 Clutch housing/driven gear
16 Bearings
17 Circlip
18 Spacer
19 Spacer

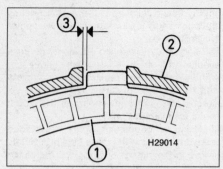

16.29 Clutch friction plate tang-to-housing slot clearance
1 Friction plate   2 Housing   3 Clearance

housing/driven gear from the shaft, followed by another spacer.

Inspection

29 Examine the slots in the housing and the tangs of the friction plates for wear **(see illustration 18.10)**. A wear pattern will develop over a period of time, and if severe will restrict clutch operation. If the slots and plate tangs are badly notched, the high spots can be filed off, but take care that this does not take the tang-to-slot clearance beyond the service limit **(see illustration)**. Measure the clearance using a feeler blade **(see illustration 17.11)**.
30 Inspect the splines of the clutch centre and the corresponding splines of the plain plates for wear.
31 If the lining material of the friction plates smells burnt or appears glazed, new parts are required. If the steel clutch plates are scored or discoloured, they must be replaced with new ones. Measure the thickness of each friction plate **(see illustration 18.13)** and compare the results to this Chapter's Specifications; note that the limit differs for the outer (single-sided) friction plate. Replace the friction plates as a set if any are near the wear limit.
32 Lay the metal plates, one at a time, on a perfectly flat surface (such as a piece of plate glass) and check for warpage by trying to slip a gauge between the flat surface and the plate **(see illustration 18.14)**. The feeler gauge should be the same thickness as the warpage limit listed in this Chapter's Specifications. Do this at several places around the plate's circumference. If the feeler gauge can be slipped under the plate, it is warped and should be replaced with a new one.
33 Measure the free length of the clutch springs with a vernier caliper **(see illustration 18.15)**. If any spring has set to less than the service limit, all six springs must be renewed.
34 Rotate the inner race of the spring retainer plate bearing. If it is noisy or feels notchy in operation renew it. The bearing can be tapped from the retainer plate using a drift. Use a socket or bearing driver which bears only on the bearing outer race to install it in the retainer plate.

35 Check the ball bearings in the primary driven gear boss. If they feel rough or are noisy when rotated they must be renewed. If the bearings are disturbed, Ducati recommend that they are renewed, together with the spacer and circlip. Pass a drift through the centre of one of the bearings to drive the other bearing out of the housing, noting that you will have to work around the inner race of the bearing to ensure its leaves the housing squarely. Once removed, withdraw the spacer and drift the other bearing out of the housing. Using circlip pliers, free the circlip from its groove.
36 Insert a new circlip into the housing groove **(see illustration 18.19a)**. Drive a new bearing into one side of the housing until it seats against the circlip – use a socket which bears only on the bearing's outer race to install it **(see illustration 18.19b)**. Place the spacer against the inner race of the bearing and drive the second new bearing in from the other side so that it seats against the other side of the circlip, sandwiching the spacer between the bearing inner races **(see illustrations 18.19c and 18.19d)**.
37 The crankshaft end bush oil seal set in cover is retained a circlip and washer. Remove the circlip and washer and pry the oil seal out with a flat-bladed screwdriver **(see illustrations 18.21a to 18.21c)**. The bush is a press fit in the cover and can only be removed with a slide-hammer type bearing puller **(see illustration 18.21d)**. Make sure the new seal is installed with correct way around and use a socket to drive it into the cover **(see illustration 18.21e)**.

Installation

38 Install the spacer over the input shaft, followed by the assembled clutch housing/driven gear. Install the spacer, followed by the pressure plate and clutch centre.
39 Install a new lock washer over the input shaft and thread the clutch nut into place. Using the method employed on removal to lock the clutch centre, tighten the nut to the specified torque. Bend a portion of the lockwasher up against one of the nut flats to lock it in place.
40 Build up the clutch plates over the clutch centre, starting with a friction plate, then a plain plate and alternating them. The last friction plate to be fitted must be the thicker one-sided plate, installed with its friction side against the last plain plate. **Note:** *If new clutch plates are being installed, smear their faces with engine oil prior to installation.* Work the large circlip into its groove in the clutch housing to retain the plates. Be careful not to deform the circlip as it is installed and make sure it is fully seated.
41 Place a spring over each of the clutch centre posts. Assembly the pushrod through the spring retainer plate and install the plate.

Secure the plate with the six screws, tightening them evenly in a criss-cross sequence.
42 Renew the O-ring at the crankcase-to-cover joint (just above the oil pump left-hand mounting bolt) **(see illustration 18.22c)**. Make sure the cover dowel is in place, then place a new gasket on the crankcase surface; use a dab of grease to hold it in position if necessary.
43 Before installing the crankcase cover check that the clutch release piston has not eased out of its housing – if so, gently press it back using finger pressure only. Install the cover and it retaining screws and hose clamps, making sure they are all returned to their original positions. Secure the hoses in the hose clamps.
44 Reconnect the clutch hydraulic hose, using new sealing washers on each side of its union. Make sure the hose is angled correctly and not kinked or strained at any point, then secure the banjo union bolt to the specified torque. Top up the clutch fluid reservoir and proceed to fill and bleed the clutch as described in Section 21.
45 Reconnect the oil pressure switch wire and slide the dust boot into place over the switch.
46 Replenish the engine oil (see Chapter 1).
47 On SS models install the fairing right-hand panel (see Chapter 7).

17 Clutch – removal, inspection and installation (1998-on 600, 620 and 750 engines)

Note: *The clutch can be removed with the engine in the frame. If the engine is in the frame ignore the steps which do not apply.*

600, 620 (2002 and 2003) and 750 engines

Removal

1 On fully-faired models, remove the fairing right-hand lower panel.
2 Drain the engine oil (see Chapter 1). Disconnect the wiring from the oil pressure switch **(see illustration 17.34)**. Remove the switch if necessary (according to your tools) if it restricts access to the bolt behind it (see Chapter 8).
3 Remove the screws from the cover and store them in a cardboard template of the cover as a guide to location, along with related components **(see illustration 17.35 and 17.58b)**. Pull the cover off the engine **(see illustration 17.58a)**, if necessary tap it lightly around the periphery with a soft-faced mallet to break the gasket seal. As the cover is removed mop up any residual engine oil. Where fitted remove and discard the gasket. Remove the dowel if it is loose **(see illustration 17.57b)**. Remove the O-ring from the oil passage and discard it as a new one should be used **(see illustration 17.57a)**.

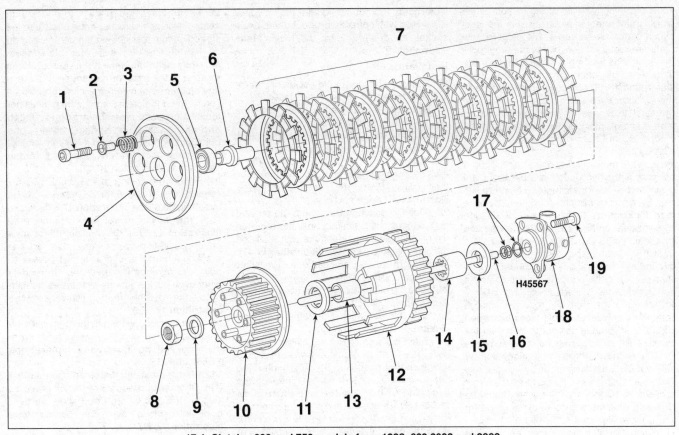

17.4 Clutch – 600 and 750 models from 1998, 620 2002 and 2003

1 Bolts	6 Pressure plate lifter	10 Clutch centre	15 Shouldered washer
2 Collars	7 Friction and plain plate	11 Thrust washer	16 Pushrod
3 Springs	assembly	12 Clutch housing	17 O-rings
4 Pressure plate	8 Clutch nut	13 Spacer	18 Release cylinder
5 Bearing	9 Lock washer	14 Bearing	19 Bolts

4 Working in a criss-cross pattern, and holding the clutch housing to prevent it turning, gradually slacken the clutch pressure plate bolts until spring pressure is released, then remove the bolts, collars, springs and the pressure plate **(see illustrations 18.32 and 31b)**. Remove the pressure plate lifter from the centre of the plate if required **(see illustration 18.31a)**. Again if required withdraw the pushrod from the shaft, noting the O-rings.

5 Remove the clutch friction and plain plates one by one, keeping them in order, and using a bent piece of wire to hook them out where necessary. Keep the plates assembled in their original order, even if you are replacing them with new ones – tie them together using a cable tie to ensure this.

6 Using a suitable drift and hammer tap the rim of the lock washer away from the clutch nut. To remove the clutch nut the transmission input shaft must be locked. This can be done in several ways. If the engine is in the frame, engage top gear and have an assistant hold the rear brake on hard with the rear tyre in firm contact with the ground.

Alternatively, the Ducati service tool (Pt. No. 88713.0146) or a commercially available equivalent can be used to stop the clutch centre from turning whilst the nut is slackened **(see illustration 18.5)**. With the shaft locked, unscrew the clutch nut, then remove the washer. If the rim of the washer is badly distorted replace it with a new one, otherwise it can reused.

7 Slide the clutch centre off the shaft **(see illustration 17.51)**.

8 Slide the thrust washer off the shaft **(see illustration 17.48)**.

9 Slide the clutch housing off the shaft – the bearing and spacer in the centre of the housing may come with it, if not slide them off the shaft afterwards **(see illustrations 17.47, 46c and b)**.

10 Slide the shouldered washer off the shaft, noting which way round it fits **(see illustration 17.46a)**.

Inspection

11 Examine the slots in the housing and the tangs of the friction plates for wear **(see illustration 18.10)**. A wear pattern will

develop over a period of time, but if severe will restrict clutch operation. If the slots and plate tangs are badly notched, the high spots can be filed off, but take care that this does not take the tang-to-slot clearance beyond the service limit **(see illustration 16.29)**. Measure the clearance using a feeler blade **(see illustration)**.

12 Inspect the splines of the clutch centre and the corresponding splines of the plain plates for wear.

17.11 Measure the tang-to-slot clearance using a feeler blade

13 If the lining material of the friction plates smells burnt or appears glazed, or if the steel clutch plates are scored or discoloured new parts are required, new plates are required – they come as a combined set. Measure the thickness of each friction plate **(see illustration 18.13)** and compare the results to this Chapter's Specifications. Also measure the total thickness of the complete set of friction and plain plates. Replace the plates as a set if any are near, on or beyond the wear limit specified.

14 Lay the metal plates, one at a time, on a perfectly flat surface (such as a piece of plate glass) and check for warpage by trying to slip a gauge between the flat surface and the plate **(see illustration 18.14)**. The feeler gauge should be the same thickness as the warpage limit listed in this Chapter's Specifications. Do this at several places around the plate's circumference. If the feeler gauge can be slipped under the plate, it is warped and a new set of plates is needed.

15 Measure the free length of the clutch springs with a vernier caliper **(see illustration 18.15)**. If any spring has set to less than the service limit, all six springs must be renewed.

16 Check the pushrod for straightness by rolling it on a flat surface or by using a dial gauge and checking its runout. If runout exceeds that specified, the pushrod must be renewed. Check the ends of the pushrod for scoring **(see illustration 18.16)**.

17 Rotate the inner race of the pressure plate bearing. If it is noisy or notchy renew it. The bearing can be tapped from the pressure plate **(see illustration 18.17)**. Use a socket or bearing driver which bears only on the bearing outer race to install it in the pressure plate.

18 Check the needle bearing in the clutch housing boss **(see illustration)**. If the bearing feels rough or noisy when rotated it must be renewed. Check the bearing spacer and the surfaces of the shaft and in the clutch housing that the bearing and spacer run on.

19 The crankshaft end bush oil seal set in the cover is retained a circlip and washer. Remove the circlip and washer and pry the oil seal out with a flat-bladed screwdriver **(see illustrations 18.21a, b and c)**. The bush is a press fit in the cover and can only be removed with a slide-hammer type bearing puller **(see**

illustration 18.21d). Make sure the new seal is installed with correct way around and use a socket to drive it into the cover **(see illustration 18.21e)**.

Installation

20 Remove all traces of old gasket or sealant from the crankcase and cover surfaces.

21 Slide the shouldered washer onto the shaft with its chamfered side facing in **(see illustration 17.46a)**. Smear the spacer (inside and out) and the needle bearing with molybdenum disulphide oil (50% molybdenum grease and 50% engine oil), then slide them onto the shaft **(see illustrations 17.46b and c)**.

22 Slide the clutch housing onto the bearing on the input shaft, making sure the teeth on the primary driven gear engage with those on the primary drive gear **(see illustration 17.47)**.

23 Slide the thrust washer onto the shaft **(see illustration 17.48)**.

24 Slide the clutch centre onto the shaft **(see illustration 17.51)**.

25 Slide the lock washer onto the shaft **(see illustration 17.52a)**. Lubricate the threads of the clutch nut with oil. Fit the clutch nut, and using the method employed on removal to lock the input shaft (see Step 6), tighten the nut to the torque setting specified at the beginning of the Chapter **(see illustration 17.52b)**. **Note:** *Check that the clutch centre rotates freely after tightening the clutch nut.* Bend the rim of the washer up against one of the flats on the nut to lock it.

26 Build up the clutch plates over the clutch centre, starting with a friction plate, then a plain plate and alternating them, making sure that if the old ones are being reused they are fitted in their correct order. **Note:** *If new clutch plates are being installed, smear their faces with engine oil prior to installation.*

27 If the pushrod was removed, fit two new O-rings into the grooves on the pushrod and smear them and the rod ends with grease **(see illustration 18.30a)**. Insert the pushrod into the input shaft (end with O-rings towards left-hand side of engine) so that its engages the piston of the release cylinder on the other side of the engine. Lubricate the pressure plate lifter and the bearing, then fit the lifter into the bearing **(see illustration 18.31a)**.

28 Fit the pressure plate into the clutch centre, aligning the mark on the plate with the slotted spring post end on the centre, and on all models making sure the plate seats correctly with its inner rim castellations locating in the slots in the centre – if there is any clearance between the clutch plates as you push on the pressure plate then it has not located properly **(see illustrations 18.31b and c)**. Fit the clutch springs, collars, and bolts and tighten the bolts evenly in a criss-cross sequence to the specified torque setting **(see illustration 18.32)**.

29 Renew the O-ring at the crankcase-to-cover joint (just above the oil pump left-hand mounting bolt) **(see illustration 17.57a)**. Make sure the cover dowel is in place **(see illustration 17.57b)**. On models fitted with a cover gasket place a new one on the crankcase surface; use a dab of grease to hold it in position if necessary. On models without a gasket smear a suitable sealant onto one of the mating surfaces **(see illustration 17.57c)**.

30 Install the cover, then fit the bolts with the guide(s), making sure they are all returned to their original positions **(see illustrations 17.58a and b)**.

31 If removed install the oil pressure switch (see Chapter 8). Reconnect the oil pressure switch wire and where fitted slide the dust boot into place over the switch **(see illustration 17.34)**.

32 Replenish the engine oil (see Chapter 1).

33 Where necessary install the fairing right-hand panel (see Chapter 7).

2004-on 620 with slipper clutch

Removal

34 Drain the engine oil (see Chapter 1). Disconnect the wiring from the oil pressure switch **(see illustration)**. Remove the switch if necessary (according to your tools) if it restricts access to the bolt behind it (see Chapter 8).

35 Remove the bolts from the cover and store them in a cardboard template of the cover as a guide to location **(see illustration)**. Note the wiring guide and spacer with the front bolt – the guide can stay around the wiring but store the spacer with its bolt and

17.18 Check the bearing and related components for wear and damage

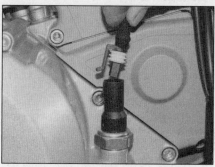

17.34 Disconnect the wiring connector from the switch – late type shown

17.35 Clutch cover bolts (arrowed)

washer (see illustration 17.58b). Pull the cover off the engine (see illustration 17.58a), if necessary tap it lightly around the periphery with a soft-faced mallet to break the gasket seal. As the cover is removed mop up any residual engine oil. Remove the dowel if it is loose (see illustration 17.57b). Remove the O-ring from the oil passage and discard it as a new one should be used (see illustration 17.57a).

36 Working in a criss-cross pattern, and holding the clutch housing to prevent it turning, gradually slacken the clutch pressure plate bolts until spring pressure is released (see illustration). Remove the bolts, washers, springs and the pressure plate (see illustrations 17.56c, b and a). Remove the pressure plate lifter from the centre of the plate if required (see illustration). Again if required withdraw the pushrod from the shaft, noting the O-rings.

37 To remove the clutch nut the transmission input shaft must be locked. Due to the fact the clutch nut is very tight conventional holding methods cannot be used. If an air wrench is available try that. Otherwise you will have to obtain either the Ducati service tools (part Nos. 88713.2532 and 88713.0137), or fabricate similar ones of your own. The first tool is one that clamps the friction and plain plates together so that the clutch holding action can be transmitted through the primary drive rather than the transmission shaft, and the second tool is one that jams the primary drive and driven gears, thus locking the clutch. You can make your own tool to clamp the plates using two strips of suitable thickness steel, with a hole drilled in each to accept bolts that then thread into the posts in the clutch centre (see illustration). By tightening the bolts the clutch hub and clutch centre are drawn together, clamping the plates. Make sure there is enough distance between the plates to fit a socket onto the nut. A tool to jam the primary gears together can be made from a suitably sized and strong piece of angled steel, cut and shaped as shown so that it locates nicely between the teeth on each gear, locking them together (see illustration). With the clutch locked, unscrew the clutch nut, then remove the washer (see illustration).

17.36a Unscrew the pressure plate bolts (arrowed) as described

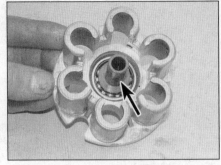
17.36b Remove the lifter piece (arrowed) from the bearing in the plate

17.37a Two holding plates can be made quite simply then bolted onto the clutch as shown

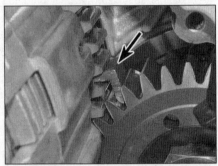
17.37b The primary gears can be jammed using a piece of suitably sized and shaped angled steel (arrowed) lodged between the gear teeth

38 Grasp the complete clutch hub/plate/centre assembly and slide it out of the clutch housing. If required remove the tools clamping the assembly together, then lift the hub and the plates off the centre, noting the springs between them and how they locate (see illustration). Separate the plates from the hub if required (see illustration). Keep the plates assembled in their original order, even if you are replacing them with new ones – tie them together using a cable tie to ensure this.

39 Slide the thrust washer off the shaft (see illustration 17.48).

40 Remove the tool jamming the primary gears together. Slide the clutch housing off the shaft – the bearing and spacer in the centre of the housing may come with it, if not

slide them off the shaft afterwards (see illustrations 17.47, 46c and b).

41 Slide the shouldered washer off the shaft, noting which way round it fits (see illustration 17.46a).

Inspection

42 Refer to Steps 11 to 19 above, plus the following.

43 Check the ribs in the clutch hub and the slots in the centre that they run in for wear and damage.

44 Check the springs that fit between the hub and the centre for sag and deflection.

Installation

45 Remove all traces of old sealant from the crankcase and cover surfaces.

17.37c With the clutch locked, unscrew the nut

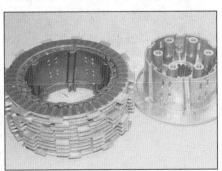
17.38a Lift the plates and hub together off the centre, noting the springs, . . .

17.38b . . . then lift the plates off the hub

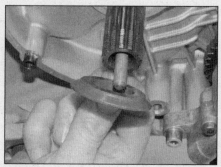

17.46a Slide the shouldered washer . . .

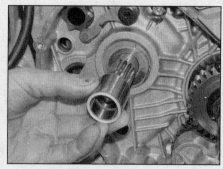

17.46b . . . the spacer . . .

17.46c . . . and the bearing onto the shaft . . .

46 Slide the shouldered washer onto the shaft with its chamfered side facing in **(see illustration)**. Smear the spacer (inside and out) and the needle bearing with molybdenum disulphide oil (50% molybdenum grease and 50% engine oil), then slide them onto the shaft **(see illustrations)**.
47 Slide the clutch housing onto the bearing on the input shaft, making sure the teeth on the primary driven gear engage with those on the primary drive gear **(see illustration)**.
48 Slide the thrust washer onto the shaft **(see illustration)**.
49 If the complete clutch hub/plate/centre assembly has not been disturbed since removal and the clamps are still in place, slide the complete assembly into the clutch housing, aligning the friction plate tabs with the slots in the housing **(see illustration 17.37a)**. Slide the clutch nut washer onto the shaft. Fit the tool to jam the primary gears together **(see illustration 17.37b)**. Lubricate the threads of the clutch nut with oil. Fit the clutch nut, and tighten it to the torque setting specified at the beginning of the Chapter **(see illustration)**. Remove the tools clamping the plates and jamming the gears. Continue from Step 55.
50 If the complete clutch hub/plate/centre assembly was dismantled, build up the clutch plates over the clutch hub, starting with a friction plate, then a plain plate and alternating them, making sure that if the old ones are being reused they are fitted in their correct order **(see illustrations)**. **Note:** *If new clutch plates are being installed, smear their faces with engine oil prior to installation.* Align the friction plate tabs as shown, noting how the outermost plate against the hub flange is positioned differently so it locates in the shallow slot in the housing when installed **(see illustration)**.
51 Slide the clutch centre onto the shaft **(see illustration)**.

17.47 . . . then fit the clutch housing . . .

17.48 . . . followed by the thrust washer

17.49 Tighten the nut to the specified torque

17.50a Fit a friction plate first . . .

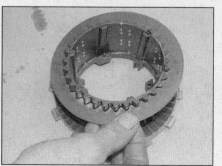

17.50b . . . then a plain plate and so on . . .

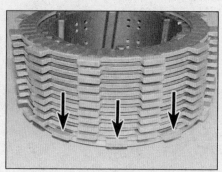

17.50c . . . then align the tabs as shown, offsetting the outermost plate tabs (arrows)

17.51 Slide the centre onto the shaft . . .

17.52a ... then fit the washer ...

17.52b ... and the nut, and tighten it finger-tight

17.53a Fit the springs onto their posts

52 Slide the clutch nut washer onto the shaft **(see illustration)**. Lubricate the threads of the clutch nut with oil. Fit the clutch nut and tighten it finger tight **(see illustration)**.
53 Fit the three springs onto the posts in the clutch centre, using grease to hold them in place – if the engine is not in the frame it is easier if the engine is turned on its side **(see illustration)**. Slide the clutch plate/hub assembly onto the centre, making sure the arrow the hub flange is aligned with the cutout in the top rim of the centre **(see illustrations)**. Locate the ribs on the hub in the slots in the centre and the friction plate tabs in the slots in the housing, and make sure the projections on the hub inner rim locate on the tops of the springs **(see illustration)**. Make sure the tab on the outermost friction plate locates in the shallow offset slot in the housing.
54 Using the method employed on removal to lock the clutch (see Step 37), tighten the nut to the torque setting specified at the beginning of the Chapter **(see illustration 17.49)**. **Note:** *Check that the clutch centre rotates freely after tightening the clutch nut.* Remove the tools clamping the plates and jamming the gears.
55 If the pushrod was removed, fit two new O-rings into the grooves on the pushrod and smear them and the rod ends with grease **(see illustration 18.30a)**. Insert the pushrod into the input shaft (end with O-rings towards left-hand side of engine) so that its engages the piston of the release cylinder on the other side of the engine.
56 Lubricate the pressure plate lifter and the

17.53b Fit the hub and plate assembly into the housing ...

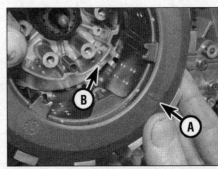

17.53c ... aligning the arrow (A) with the cutout (B) ...

17.53d ... and making sure the springs locate correctly against the hub projections

17.56a Fit the pressure plate ...

bearing, then fit the lifter into the bearing **(see illustration 17.36b)**. Fit the pressure plate into the clutch **(see illustration)**. Fit the clutch springs, washers, and bolts and tighten the bolts evenly in a criss-cross

sequence to the specified torque setting **(see illustrations)**.
57 Renew the O-ring at the crankcase-to-cover joint (just above the oil pump left-hand mounting bolt) **(see illustration)**. Make sure

17.56b ... the springs ...

17.56c ... and the bolts with their washers

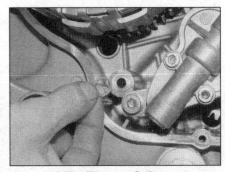

17.57a Fit a new O-ring ...

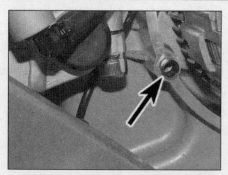

17.57b ...and make sure the dowel (arrowed) is in place

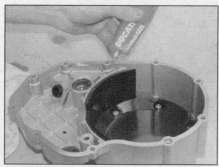

17.57c Apply some sealant to the cover

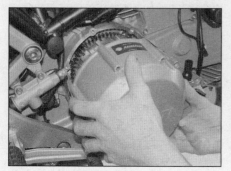

17.58a Fit the cover

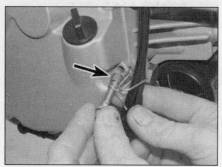

17.58b Note the spacer (arrowed) fitted with the front wiring guide

the cover dowel is in place **(see illustration)**. Smear a suitable sealant onto the cover mating surface **(see illustration)**.
58 Install the cover, then fit the bolts,

making sure they are all returned to their original positions, not forgetting the spacer and wiring guide with the front bolt **(see illustrations)**.

18.2 Clutch cover is retained by four screws

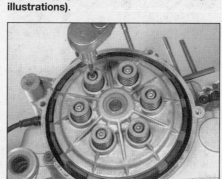

18.3 Remove the six screws to free the springs and pressure plate

18.4 Use two flat-bladed screwdrivers to extract the clutch plates

18.5 Restrain clutch centre with a holding tool while clutch nut is slackened

59 If removed install the oil pressure switch (see Chapter 8). Reconnect the oil pressure switch wire **(see illustration 17.34)**.
60 Replenish the engine oil (see Chapter 1).

18 Clutch – removal, inspection and installation (900 models)

Note: *The clutch can be removed with the engine in the frame. If the engine is in the frame ignore the steps which do not apply.*

Removal

1 On fully-faired models, remove the fairing right-hand lower panel.
2 Remove the four screws to free the clutch cover **(see illustration)**. Note that a carbon fibre cover is fitted as standard to SL models and is optional on other models – handle it with care.
3 Slacken the six pressure plate screws evenly and in a diagonal sequence **(see illustration)**. Withdraw the screws, spring retainers, springs and the pressure plate (complete with bearing and lifter piece). Slide the pushrod out of the clutch. Remove the lifter piece from the bearing, noting which way round it fits, and on 1997-on models the O-ring. Discard the O-ring if it is damaged, deformed or deteriorated and use a new one on installation.
4 Pick the clutch plates out of the clutch housing, keeping them in order as a guide to installation **(see illustration)**.
5 Unscrew the clutch nut, whilst holding the clutch centre to prevent rotation **(see illustration)**. The scissor-like tool shown can be fabricated in the home workshop and engages the splines of the clutch centre (see **Tool Tip**). The Ducati service tool (Pt. No. 88713.0146) fits over the clutch centre enabling it to be held whilst the nut is slackened. Alternatively, if the engine is in the

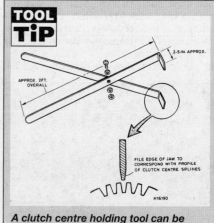

A clutch centre holding tool can be made from two strips of steel, bent over at the ends and bolted together in the middle.

18.7 Remove the eight bolts to free the clutch housing

18.8 Remove the eight bolts (arrows) to free the crankcase cover

frame, the transmission can be placed in gear and the rear brake held on to prevent input shaft rotation.

Caution: Whichever method is used to prevent clutch centre rotation, ensure that it is secure – in practice the clutch nut was found to be extremely tight.

6 With the clutch nut removed, withdraw the serrated washer, headed collar, thrust washer and O-ring. Slide the clutch centre off the input shaft.

7 Slip the guide out of the clutch housing. Undo the eight housing bolts and withdraw the housing **(see illustration)**.

8 The primary driven gear can only be accessed after the crankcase right-hand cover has been removed. Drain the engine/transmission oil (see Chapter 1). Disconnect the wiring from the oil pressure switch at the front of the crankcase right-hand cover. Take note of the hose routing around the front and underside of the cover, then release the hoses from their clamps. Remove the crankcase cover bolts **(see illustration)**, then pull off the cover and mop up any residual engine oil. Where fitted discard the gasket – a new one must be used on installation.

9 Pull the primary driven gear, complete with bearings and oil seal off the input shaft. Retrieve the spacer from the input shaft.

Inspection

Note: *The plates in a dry clutch will create dust inside the casing and cover and on the clutch components. Clean off all dust using solvent, but wear an approved filtering mask in case the clutch plate material is asbestos-based.*

10 Examine the slots in the housing and the tangs of the friction plates for wear **(see illustration)**. A wear pattern will develop over a period of time, but if severe will restrict clutch operation. If the slots and plate tangs are badly notched, the high spots can be filed off, but take care that this does not reduce the tang-to-slot clearance beyond the service

limit **(see illustration 16.29)**. Measure the clearance using a feeler blade **(see illustration 17.11)**.

11 Inspect the splines of the clutch centre and the corresponding splines of the plain plates for wear.

12 The clutch centre incorporates a cush drive type shock absorber. If play is felt between the clutch centre and its splined hub the cush drive rubbers are in need of renewal. Press the hub out of the clutch centre to access the rubber blocks. Arrange the new rubbers against the cast webs so that the vanes of the hub engage between them **(see illustration)**. Use hand pressure only to seat the hub into the clutch centre.

13 If the lining material of the friction plates smells burnt or appears glazed, new parts are required. If the steel clutch plates are scored or discoloured, they must be replaced with new ones. Measure the thickness of each friction plate **(see illustration)** and compare the results to this Chapter's Specifications. Replace the friction plates as a set if any are near the wear limit.

14 Lay the metal plates, one at a time, on a perfectly flat surface (such as a piece of plate glass) and check for warpage by trying to slip a gauge between the flat surface and the plate **(see illustration)**. The feeler gauge should be the same thickness as the warpage limit listed in this Chapter's Specifications. Do this at

18.10 Examine the clutch housing slots for wear

18.12 Cush drive rubbers correctly arranged for hub installation

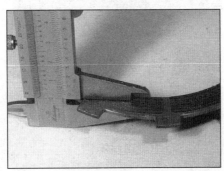

18.13 Measuring friction plate thickness

18.14 Measuring plain plate warpage

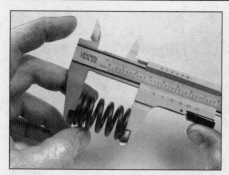

18.15 Measuring spring free length

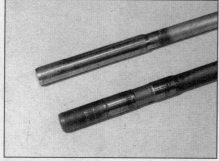

18.16 Comparison of new and worn clutch pushrods

18.17 Tap the bearing out of the pressure plate if it needs renewing

several places around the plate's circumference. If the feeler gauge can be slipped under the plate, it is warped and should be replaced with a new one.

15 Measure the free length of the clutch springs with a vernier caliper **(see illustration)**. If any spring has set to less than the service limit, all six springs must be renewed.

16 Check the pushrod for straightness by rolling it on a flat surface or by using a dial gauge and checking its runout. If runout exceeds that specified, the pushrod must be renewed. Check the ends of the pushrod for scoring **(see illustration)**.

17 Rotate the inner race of the pressure plate bearing. If it is noisy or notchy renew it. The bearing can be tapped from the pressure plate **(see illustration)**. Use a socket

or bearing driver which bears only on the bearing outer race to install it in the pressure plate.

18 Check the ball bearings in the primary driven gear boss. If they feel rough or are noisy when rotated they must be renewed. If the bearings are disturbed, Ducati recommend that they are renewed, together with the oil seal, spacer and circlip. Pry out the oil seal **(see illustration)**. Pass a drift through the centre of one of the bearings to drive the other bearing out of the housing, noting that you will have to work around the inner race of the bearing to ensure its leaves the housing squarely. Once removed, withdraw the spacer and drift the other bearing out of the housing. Using circlip pliers, free the circlip from its groove.

19 Insert a new circlip into the housing

groove, ensuring that it is fully seated in the groove **(see illustration)**. Carefully drive a new bearing into one side of the housing until it seats against the circlip – be sure to use a socket which bears only on the bearing's outer race to install it **(see illustration)**. Place the spacer against the inner race of the bearing **(see illustration)** and drive the second new bearing in from the other side so that it seats against the other side of the circlip, sandwiching the spacer between the bearing inner races **(see illustration)**. Install a new oil seal **(see illustration)**.

20 The oil seals in the crankcase right-hand cover should be renewed whenever the cover is disturbed or if there is obvious sign of failure. Using a punch, tap evenly around the rim of the large oil seal to extract it from the

18.18 Prise the oil seal out of the driven gear

18.19a Ensure that the circlip is fully seated in its groove . . .

18.19b . . . then install a bearing into one side of the driven gear . . .

18.19c . . . install the spacer . . .

18.19d . . . followed by the other bearing

18.19e Press a new oil seal into the driven gear outer face

18.20a Removing the large oil seal from the cover

18.20b Use a block of wood to ensure the new oil seal is installed squarely

18.21a Crankshaft end bush oil seal is retained by a circlip . . .

cover **(see illustration)**. Tap the new seal evenly into the cover **(see illustration)**.

21 The crankshaft end bush oil seal set in the cover is retained a circlip and washer. Remove the circlip and washer and pry the oil seal out with a flat-bladed screwdriver **(see illustrations)**. The bush is a press fit in the cover and can only be removed with a slide-hammer type bearing puller **(see illustration)**. Make sure the new seal is installed with correct way around and use a socket to drive it into the cover **(see illustration)**.

Installation

22 Install the spacer over the input shaft, followed by the primary driven gear with its clutch housing mounting bolt holes outermost – mesh the teeth of the driven gear with those of the primary drive gear **(see illustrations)**.

Renew the O-ring on the main oilway **(see illustration)**.

23 Make sure the mating surfaces of the crankcase and cover are clean and that the

18.21b . . . and washer

dowel is in place. Where a gasket was removed place a new one on the crankcase, using a dab of grease to stick it in place if necessary **(see illustration)**. On models

18.21c Pry the old oil seal out with a flat-bladed screwdriver

18.21d Crankshaft end bush

18.21e Make sure the new oil seal is installed the correct way round

18.22a Install the spacer over the input shaft . . .

18.22b . . . followed by the primary driven gear

18.22c Use a new O-ring at the oilway

18.23a Place a new gasket over the dowel (arrow)

18.23b Smear grease over the oil seal lips . . .

18.23c . . . and the driven gear boss to aid installation when fitting the cover

18.25a Install the clutch housing in the cover

18.25b Apply a thread-locking agent to the eight bolts . . .

18.25c . . . and tighten them to the specified torque

without a gasket smear a suitable sealant onto the cover mating surface **(see illustration 17.57c)**. To prevent damaging the large oil seal in the crankcase cover, smear the seal lips and the driven gear boss with grease **(see illustrations)**. Install the cover and secure it with the retaining screws, making sure that all are returned to their original positions and that the hose guides are in place.

24 Route the hoses back through the guides. Reconnect the oil pressure switch wire and slip the dust cover back into place. Replenish the engine/transmission oil (see Chapter 1).

25 Install the clutch housing over the input shaft, aligning its holes with the threaded holes in the driven gear boss **(see illustration)**. Apply a suitable thread-locking compound to the threads of the eight bolts and tighten them evenly in a cross-cross sequence to the specified torque **(see illustrations)**.

26 Fit a new O-ring into the groove inside the guide. Lubricate the O-ring with a smear of engine oil, then insert the guide (chamfered end inwards) into the clutch housing **(see illustration)**.

27 Install the clutch centre over the input shaft splines, followed by a new O-ring, the large thrust washer and headed collar; the hole in the collar must locate over the pin in the clutch centre **(see illustrations)**.

18.26 Install a new O-ring (arrow) in the guide groove and install the guide over the input shaft

18.27a Install the clutch centre on the input shaft . . .

18.27b . . . followed by a new O-ring . . .

18.27c . . . the large thrust washer . . .

18.27d . . . and headed collar – align hole and pin (arrows)

18.28a Install the serrated washer . . .

18.28b . . . and clutch nut

18.28c Hold clutch centre and tighten nut to specified torque

28 Install the serrated washer and clutch nut **(see illustrations)**. Tighten the clutch nut to the specified torque whilst holding the clutch centre in the same way as on removal **(see illustration)**.

29 Install two 2 mm thick plain plates over the clutch centre **(see illustration)**, followed by a friction plate **(see illustration)**, then the 1.5 mm plain plate (installed with its dished side facing outwards – outer face identified by a dot near the cutout on the plate periphery); install the remaining friction and 2 mm plain plates alternately, ending with a plain plate. **Note:** *The clutch plate arrangement differs on early models (circa 1991/92). If reinstalling the original plates in an early model, note that the procedure is as follows: Install the 3.5 mm thick friction plate over the clutch centre, followed by the 1.5 mm plain plate (installed with its dished side facing outwards), then the 3 mm thick friction and 2 mm plain plates alternately. If fitting new clutch plates to an early model, note that the later type arrangement described at the beginning of Step 29 will be supplied.*

30 Install two new O-rings into the grooves on the pushrod and smear them and the pushrod ends with grease **(see illustration)**. Insert the pushrod into the input shaft (end with O-rings towards left-hand side of engine) so that its engages the piston of the release cylinder on the other side of the engine **(see illustration)**.

31 Slip the lifter piece into the pressure plate bearing, on 1997-on models making sure the

O-ring is in place and using a new one if necessary, and install the pressure plate over the posts of the clutch centre **(see**

illustrations). The pressure plate must be positioned so that the hole with the slots fits over the slotted post **(see illustration)**.

18.29a Install the two thick plain plates first . . .

18.29b . . . followed by a friction plate

18.30a Install two new O-rings into the pushrod grooves . . .

18.30b . . . and install the pushrod into the input shaft

18.31a Insert the lifter piece into the pressure plate bearing . . .

18.31b . . . and install the pressure plate . . .

18.31c . . . so that hole with the slots and cast arrow fits over the post with the corresponding slots

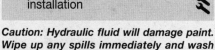

18.32 Assemble the springs, retainers and bolts

32 Install the six clutch springs, retainers and bolts, tightening them evenly in a criss-cross sequence **(see illustration)**.
33 Install the clutch cover and tighten its screws securely.

19 Clutch release cylinder – removal, inspection and installation

Caution: Hydraulic fluid will damage paint. Wipe up any spills immediately and wash the area with soap and water.

600 engines and later 750 engines (from engine VIN 001275) up to end 1997

1 The release cylinder is part of the crankcase right-hand cover, with the piston, seals and spring being housed in a bore inside the cover.
2 Remove the crankcase right-hand cover as described in Section 16, Steps 1 to 4.
3 Pick the piston and spring out of the crankcase cover. Do not resort to using levers to pry the piston out otherwise its surface will be damaged – either use a supply of compressed air directed into the union bolt

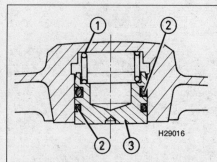

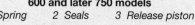

19.6 Clutch release cylinder seals – 600 and later 750 models

1 Spring   2 Seals   3 Release piston

hole or reconnect the hydraulic hose and use lever pressure to expel the piston.

⚠ *Warning: The piston may shoot out forcefully enough to cause injury. Point the piston at a pile of rags – never point the piston at yourself, including your fingers.*

4 Thoroughly clean the piston, spring and fluid passage in the cover with clean brake and clutch fluid (don't use any type of petroleum-based solvent).
5 Check the piston and bore surfaces for wear, scratches and corrosion. If the piston shows these conditions, replace it and the seals as a set. If the bore surface is damaged and cannot be renovated, the crankcase cover must be renewed.
6 Renew the piston seals as a matter of course. Install the new seals on the piston, noting that they differ in size **(see illustration)**. Fit the spring in the cover, then lubricate the piston seals with new hydraulic fluid and install the piston with its open end towards the spring. Push the piston fully into the cover bore.
7 Install the crankcase right-hand cover as described in Section 16, Steps 22 to 27.
8 Top up the clutch master cylinder and bleed the clutch (Section 21) until proper action is obtained.

Early 750 engine (up to engine VIN 001274)

9 The release cylinder is part of the clutch cover, with the piston and release mechanism being housed in a bore inside the cover.
10 Remove the fairing right-hand lower panel (see Chapter 7).
11 Have some rags at hand to catch fluid spills from the clutch hydraulic hose, then remove the hose union bolt. Place the end of the hose in a plastic bag to prevent further fluid spills and the ingress of dirt. Do not operate the clutch lever with the hose disconnected.
12 Remove the four screws to free the clutch cover. Mop up any residual hydraulic fluid from the release chamber.
13 Pry the oil seal out of position and remove the circlip from the piston **(see illustration)**. Carefully withdraw the pushrod, balls and needle bearing from the centre of the piston. Withdraw the piston and spring. Do not resort to using levers to pry the piston out otherwise its surface will be damaged – either use a supply of compressed air directed into the union bolt hole or reconnect the hydraulic hose and use lever pressure to expel the piston.

⚠ *Warning: The piston may shoot out forcefully enough to cause injury. Point the piston at a pile of rags – never point the piston at yourself, including your fingers.*

14 Check the piston and bore surfaces for wear, scratches and corrosion. If necessary, replace the piston and the seal as a set. If the bore surface is damaged and cannot be renovated, the clutch cover must be renewed.
15 Install a new seal on the piston as a matter of course. Fit the spring in the clutch cover, then lubricate the piston seal with new hydraulic fluid and install the piston with its smaller end towards the spring. Push the piston fully into the bore.
16 Using a dab of silicone grease to hold the balls in position, assemble the needle bearing, balls and pushrod into the piston. Retain them with the circlip and press in a new oil seal.
17 Mount the clutch cover back on the crankcase cover and secure with the screws. Using a new sealing washer on each side of the hydraulic hose union screw the union bolt back into place. Make sure the hose is at the correct angle and not strained at any point, then tighten the bolt to the specified torque.
18 Top up the clutch master cylinder and bleed the clutch (Section 21).
19 Refit the fairing right-hand panel (see Chapter 7).

1998-on 600, 620 and 750 engines and all 900 engines

Note: *Before overhauling the release cylinder, check the availability of replacement parts with a Ducati dealer – from 2001-on the cylinder comes as an assembly and no parts are available, with the exception of the pushrod O-ring (which is not fitted to earlier*

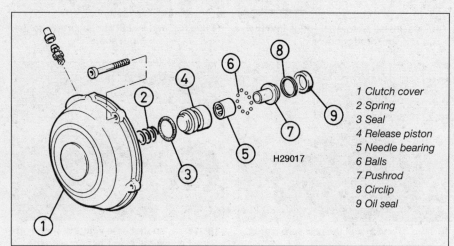

1 Clutch cover
2 Spring
3 Seal
4 Release piston
5 Needle bearing
6 Balls
7 Pushrod
8 Circlip
9 Oil seal

19.13 Clutch release cylinder components – early 750 models

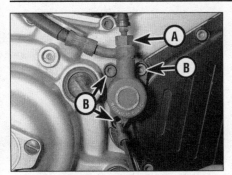

19.21 Clutch union bolt (A) and release cylinder bolts (B)

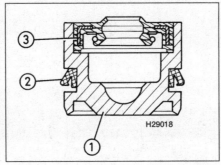

19.27 Clutch release seals – 900 models
1 Release piston 2 Fluid seal 3 Inner seal

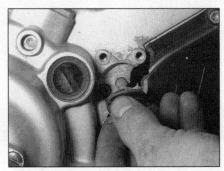

19.28 Install the gaiter on the pushrod end

models). The release cylinder for these models should not be disassembled.

Removal
20 The release cylinder is mounted on the crankcase left-hand cover, just forward of the sprocket cover.

21 If you need to detach the hydraulic hose, place a wad of rags around the union bolt to catch fluid spills, then unscrew the bolt, complete with bleed valve on later models. Place the end of the hose in a plastic bag to catch any drops of fluid and prevent the ingress of dirt. Do not operate the clutch lever whilst the hose is disconnected. Remove the three bolts and detach the release cylinder from the crankcase cover **(see illustration)**. On 2001-on models note the O-ring.

Inspection
22 Check for signs of wear and damage, and particularly for fluid leakage. If necessary, on pre-2001 models overhaul the master cylinder (see below). On 2001-on models replace the cylinder with a new one.

23 If required withdraw the pushrod from the engine, noting the O-rings. Check the pushrod for straightness by rolling it on a flat surface or by using a dial gauge and checking its runout. If runout exceeds that specified, the pushrod must be renewed. Check the ends of the pushrod for scoring **(see illustration 18.16)**. Fit two new O-rings into the grooves on the pushrod and smear them and the pushrod ends with grease **(see illustration 18.30a)**. Insert the pushrod into the engine with the O-rings on the release cylinder end.

Overhaul – pre 2001 models only
24 Pick the piston and spring out of the release cylinder. Do not resort to using levers to pry the piston out otherwise its surface will be damaged – either use a supply of compressed air directed into the union bolt hole or reconnect the hydraulic hose and use lever pressure to expel the piston.

⚠ *Warning: The piston may shoot out forcefully enough to cause injury. Point the piston at a pile of rags – never point the piston at yourself, including your fingers.*

25 Thoroughly clean the piston, spring and fluid passage in the release cylinder with clean brake and clutch fluid (don't use any type of petroleum-based solvent).

26 Check the piston and release cylinder bore for wear, scratches and corrosion. If the piston shows these conditions, replace it and the seals as a set. If the bore surface is damaged the release cylinder must be renewed.

27 Renew the piston groove seal and inner seal as a matter of course, making sure they are installed correctly **(see illustration)**. Install the spring in the release cylinder, then lubricate the piston seal with new hydraulic fluid and install the piston with its closed end towards the spring. Push the piston fully into the cover bore.

Installation
28 On pre-2001 models install the pushrod gaiter if it was removed **(see illustration)**. On 2001-on models fit the O-ring onto the master cylinder, using a new one if necessary, and smear it with grease. Install the release

cylinder over the end of the pushrod. Secure the release cylinder with the three bolts.

29 If detached, and using a new sealing washer on each side of the hose union, reconnect the hose to the release cylinder. Tighten the union bolt to the specified torque.

30 Top up the clutch master cylinder and bleed the clutch (see Section 21) until proper action is obtained.

20 Clutch master cylinder – removal, inspection and installation

Caution: Brake fluid will damage paint. Wipe up any spills immediately and wash the area with soap and water.

Removal
1 Unscrew the nut from the underside of the clutch lever pivot **(see illustration)**, then remove the pivot bolt and withdraw the clutch lever.

2 Place a rag under the master cylinder to catch any fluid spills, then remove the union bolt from the master cylinder fluid line **(see illustration)**. Tape a plastic bag over the hose end to prevent the escape of fluid and the ingress of dirt. Discard the union sealing washers – new ones should be obtained for reassembly.

3 Inspect the master cylinder clamp joint area for any sign of an alignment mark which will ensure the clamp is correctly positioned on installation; if none is found, make your own with a scribe or punch mark **(see illustration)**.

20.1 Clutch lever pivot bolt nut (arrow)

20.2 Clutch hose union bolt

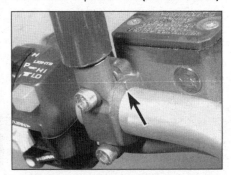

20.3 Punch mark on handlebar (arrow) aligned with clamp joint

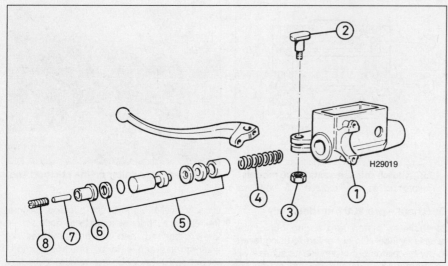

20.5 Clutch master cylinder components

1 Master cylinder/ reservoir	4 Spring	7 Pushrod
2 Lever pivot bolt	5 Piston assembly	8 Adjuster
3 Nut	6 Dust boot	

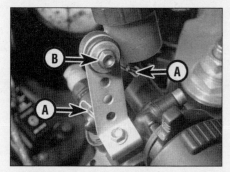

20.10 Hose clamps (A) and reservoir mounting bolt (B) on remote type reservoir

Remove the master cylinder clamp bolts and take the cylinder body (complete with fluid reservoir on the remote type) off the handlebar.

Overhaul

Note: *Before overhauling the master cylinder, check the availability of replacement parts with a Ducati dealer. If no parts are available do not disassemble it – a new one must be installed.*

21.2a Clutch bleed valve (arrow) on 600 and 750 models

20.11 Arrowhead and UP marking ensure correct fitting of clamp

4 Remove the reservoir cover/cap and rubber diaphragm and empty the brake fluid from the reservoir.
5 Remove the pushrod and rubber boot from the master cylinder bore **(see illustration)**. Using circlip pliers, remove the circlip to allow the piston, seals and spring to be withdrawn from the master cylinder bore. Take note which way around the spring is fitted.
6 Thoroughly clean all of the components in

21.2b Bleeding the clutch (900 model shown)

clean hydraulic brake and clutch fluid (don't use any type of petroleum-based solvent).
7 Check the piston and cylinder bore for wear, scratches and rust. If replacement parts are available, renew the piston seals as a matter of course. If internal parts are not available and the master cylinder is severely worn or damaged, it must be renewed as an entire assembly.
8 Install the spring in the cylinder bore in the direction noted on removal. Lubricate the piston seals with new hydraulic fluid and install the piston in the master cylinder. Secure it with the circlip, making sure it locates in its groove.
9 Install the rubber boot and pushrod.
10 On the remote type fluid reservoir, the reservoir can be detached from the master cylinder by releasing one end of its hose clamp and detaching the reservoir from its bracket **(see illustration)**.

Installation

11 Installation is the reverse of the removal steps, with the following additions:
● Align the edge of the master cylinder clamp with the previously made mark on the handlebar.
● Where so marked ensure the arrowhead next to the UP mark on the master cylinder clamp points upward **(see illustration)**.
● Use new sealing washers on each side of the hose union and tighten the union bolt to the specified torque.
● Check the clutch lever freeplay adjustment (see Chapter 1, Section 18).
● Fill and bleed the clutch hydraulic system (see Section 21).
● Operate the clutch lever and check for fluid leaks.

21 Clutch hydraulic system – bleeding

Caution: Hydraulic fluid will damage paint. Wipe up any spills immediately and wash the area with soap and water.
1 Remove the master cylinder cover/cap and diaphragm. Check that the fluid level is above the MIN marking; top it up if necessary, then set the diaphragm and cover/cap on the reservoir (but don't secure it in place).
2 Remove the cap from the bleed valve. On 600 and 750 models up to the end of 1997, the bleed valve is located next to the hose union bolt on the crankcase right-hand cover. On all other models the bleed valve is located on the release cylinder on the crankcase left-hand cover, either next to the hose union (early models) or integral with the hose union bolt (later models). Place a ring spanner over the bleed valve. Attach a rubber tube to the valve fitting and put the other end of the tube in a container **(see illustrations)**. Pour enough clean brake fluid into the container to cover the end of the tube.

22.2a Oil pump is retained by three bolts (arrows)

22.2b Manoeuvring the oil pump past primary drive gear

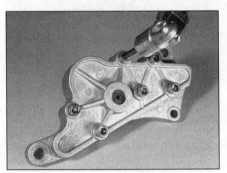

22.3a Remove the six screws . . .

22.3b . . . to free the oil pump cover

22.4a Measuring the meshed gear teeth clearance

3 Rapidly squeeze the clutch lever several times, then hold it in. With the clutch lever held in, open the bleed valve 1/4-turn with the spanner, let air and fluid escape, then tighten the valve.
4 Release the clutch lever.
5 Repeat Steps 3 and 4 until there aren't any more bubbles in the fluid flowing into the container. Replenish the master cylinder with fluid, then reinstall the diaphragm and cover/cap.

---

22 Oil pump – removal, inspection and installation

Note: *The oil pump can be removed with the engine in the frame.*

Removal

1 On all 600, 620 models and later 750 models (wet clutch models) refer to Section 16 or 17 (according to model) and remove the crankcase right-hand cover. On dry clutch models it is necessary to remove the clutch and crankcase right-hand cover to access the oil pump. Refer to Section 16 for 750 models and Section 18 for all 900 models.
2 Remove the three bolts with washers which retain the oil pump **(see illustration)**. As the pump is lifted away, tip it slightly to disengage its gear from the primary drive gear on the crankshaft **(see illustration)**. Retrieve the O-rings and dowels from the pump or crankcase.

Inspection

3 Remove the screws to free the pump cover **(see illustrations)**. Inspect the cover inner surface and check that it is not badly scored. It can be checked for distortion with a straightedge and feeler gauges.
4 Using a feeler blade (a very small set will be required), measure the clearance between the meshed gear teeth **(see illustration)**, then between the gear teeth and housing (on both gears) **(see illustration)**. Lay a straightedge across the gear housing and measure the gap between the top surface of the gears and the straightedge with feeler gauges **(see illustration)**.
5 To remove the gears from the housing, the pump gear must be removed from the driveshaft **(see illustration)**. Free the circlip,

22.4b Measuring the gear-to-housing clearance

22.4c Measuring the gear-to-housing cover clearance

22.5a Pump gear is retained by a circlip

22.5b Withdraw the driveshaft . . .

22.5c . . . and gears from the housing

22.6a Install the Woodruff key in the driveshaft . . .

22.6b . . . install the circlip (arrow) in the shaft groove and fit the gear

22.6c Install the second circlip (arrow) and the recessed washer . . .

22.6d . . . and retain them with the third circlip

washer, second circlip, gear (mark its outer face with a dab of paint as a guide to installation), Woodruff key and third circlip from the driveshaft. The driveshaft and pump gears can then be lifted out of the housing (see illustrations).

6 Assemble the pump gears in a reverse of the disassembly sequence. Locate a circlip in the lower groove of the driveshaft, then install the Woodruff key in its slot (see illustration). Fit the gear with its previously marked side outwards (it was noted on the pump shown in the photographs that the gear had a distinct line on the periphery of its inner face), aligning the gear slot with the Woodruff key (see

illustration). Secure the gear with the circlip, then fit the washer (recessed side towards the gear), followed by the circlip (see illustrations).

7 Lubricate the pump gears with fresh engine oil then install the pump cover and secure with the six screws.

Installation

8 Check that the two dowels are in place and install two new O-rings (see illustration). Angle the pump to engage its gear teeth with those of the small gear on the inside face of the primary drive gear, then seat the pump over its two dowels – make sure the O-rings remain in place.

9 Secure the pump with the two M8 and single M6 bolts, tightening them to the specified torque settings (see illustration).

10 Install the crankcase right-hand cover as described in the appropriate Section.

23 Primary drive gear – removal, inspection and installation

Note: *The primary drive gear can be removed with the engine in the frame.*

Removal

1 On all 600 models and later 750 models

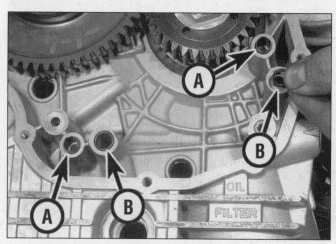

22.8 Install the two dowels (A) and two new O-rings (B)

22.9 Secure the pump with the two M8 bolts (A) and the single M6 bolt (B)

23.4a Knock back the tab of the primary drive gear lock washer . . .

23.4b . . . and remove the gear nut

23.5 Use a puller to extract the primary drive gear

(wet clutch models) refer to Section 16 or 17 (according to model) and remove the crankcase right-hand cover.

2 On dry clutch models it is necessary to remove the clutch and crankcase right-hand cover to access the primary drive gear. Refer to Section 16 for 750 models and Section 18 for all 900 models.

3 Remove the oil pump (see Section 22).

4 Knock back the tab of the primary drive gear lockwasher and undo its retaining nut **(see illustrations)**. The crankshaft must be prevented from rotating to allow the nut to be unscrewed. Either use the Ducati service tool (Pt. No. 88713.0137) which engages the holes in the face of the gear, or if either cylinder barrel is off, pass a close-fitting bar through the con-rod eye (or place supports under the piston) and rest it on wood blocks placed across the crankcase mouth. Remove the lockwasher from the shaft and discard it – a new one must be used on installation.

5 Pull the primary drive gear off the crankshaft taper with a two-legged puller. Make sure that the feet of the puller legs locate fully behind the gear and do not just contact the gear teeth **(see illustration)**. Use a soft metal pad between the centre bolt of the puller and the crankshaft end so that the crankshaft is not damaged. Tighten the puller centre bolt to draw the gear off the crankshaft.

⚠ **Warning: The primary drive gear was found to be an extremely tight fit on the crankshaft taper, necessitating the use of an hydraulic puller. Take care when carrying out this operation and stand to one side of**

the puller in case it comes off the shaft with force – if difficulty is experienced, take the machine to a Ducati dealer.

6 Once the gear is freed, extract the Woodruff key from the crankshaft.

Inspection

7 Inspect the primary drive gear teeth together with those of the primary driven gear (on the transmission input shaft). Also inspect the small oil pump drive gear teeth on the back of the primary drive gear together with those of the oil pump gear. Normal wear of the teeth will only occur after a very high mileage has been covered, but if any gear shows sign of cracks or chipped gear teeth it should be replaced.

8 Check the fit of the Woodruff key in the crankshaft and the primary drive gear slot over the Woodruff key. If the key is a loose fit and shows signs of wear replace it with a new

one. If the crankshaft slot is damaged, seek the advice of an engineering specialist.

Installation

9 Use solvent to degrease the crankshaft taper and corresponding surface of the primary drive gear. Seat the Woodruff key into its slot in the crankshaft **(see illustration)**.

10 Fit the gear over the crankshaft, aligning its slot with the Woodruff key and its teeth with those of the large driven gear **(see illustration)**. Push the gear fully home on the taper, tapping it lightly with a soft-faced mallet. Install a new lockwasher over the crankshaft, aligning its cutout with the gear slot and install the nut **(see illustration)**. Hold the crankshaft using the same method as used on removal, and tighten the primary drive gear nut to the specified torque **(see illustration)**. Bend a portion of the lockwasher against one of the nut flats **(see illustration)**.

23.9 Install the Woodruff key in the crankshaft

23.10a Install the primary drive gear over the Woodruff key . . .

23.10b . . . align the tab of the new lock washer with the gear keyway . . .

23.10c . . . then install the nut and tighten it to the specified torque

23.10d Secure the nut with the lock washer tab

24.2a Unscrew the oil pressure relief valve cap (arrow) from the crankcase

24.2b Withdraw the spring . . .

24.2c . . . and use a magnetic rod to withdraw the relief valve

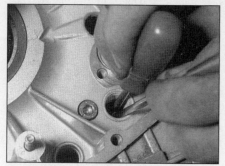

24.4 Use a screwdriver to disengage the valve from the magnetic rod

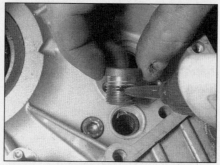

24.5 Apply thread locking agent to the relief valve cap

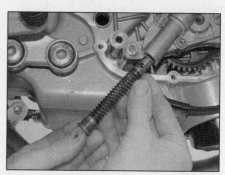

24.8 Pressure relief valve components – oil pump valve

11 Install the oil pump (see Section 22).
12 On wet clutch models install the crankcase right-hand cover (see Section 16). On dry clutch models, install the crankcase right-hand cover and clutch (refer to Section 17 for 750 models and Section 18 for 900 models).

24 Oil pressure relief valve – removal, inspection and installation

Note 1: *The oil pressure relief valve can be removed with the engine in the frame.*
Note 2: *The pressure relief valve is fitted in the left-hand side of the crankcase on engines up to the end of 1997, and from 1998-on in the oil pump casting on the right-hand side of the engine. Certain 1998 and 1999 900 engines may have a valve in both locations.*

Crankcase valve

Removal

1 Remove the crankcase left-hand cover (Section 14, Steps 1 to 9). The oil pressure relief valve is located in the bottom of the casing.
2 Unscrew the valve cap and withdraw the spring **(see illustrations)**. Using a magnetic rod if necessary, withdraw the valve from the crankcase **(see illustration)**.

Inspection

3 If the valve is clogged, wash it in high flash-

point solvent. If the valve is obviously damaged renew it.

Installation

4 Make sure the valve is the correct way around **(see illustration 24.2c)**, and insert it in the crankcase using the magnetic rod **(see illustration)**. Install the spring.
5 Clean the threads of the valve cap and apply a suitable thread-locking compound to them **(see illustration)**. Screw the cap into place and tighten it securely.
6 Install the crankcase left-hand cover as described in Section 14.

Oil pump valve

Removal

7 Follow the procedure for your model to access the oil pump (see Section 22).
8 Unscrew the valve cap and withdraw the spring and valve plunger **(see illustration)**.

Inspection

9 If the valve is clogged, wash it in high flash-point solvent. If the valve is obviously damaged renew it. Check the valve moves smoothly up and down in its bore. Check the spring for sag and deflection.

Installation

10 Lubricate the valve plunger and spring with clean oil. Clean the threads of the valve cap and apply a suitable thread-locking compound to them.
11 Make sure the valve is the correct way around **(see illustration 24.8)**, and insert it in the pump along with the spring and cap.

Screw the cap into place and tighten it securely.
12 Install the crankcase left-hand cover as described in Section 14.

25 Oil cooler and carburettor warmer kit – removal and installation

Oil cooler – 750 and 900 engines

Removal

1 On early 750SS and 900SS/SL models the oil cooler is mounted on the horizontal cylinder exhaust rocker cover **(see illustration)**. On later SS/SL models and M750 and M900 models the oil cooler is

25.1a Oil cooler mountings on SS/SL models

25.1b Oil cooler mountings on Monster models

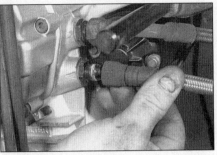

25.3 Disconnect the oil cooler feed (top) and return (bottom) hoses from their unions on the crankcase

26.6 Unscrew the neutral switch from the crankcase

mounted to the horizontal cylinder inlet rocker cover **(see illustration)**.

2 Drain the engine oil (see Chapter 1).

3 Disconnect the oil feed and return hoses from their unions on the right-hand crankcase, noting which fits where and how they are aligned **(see illustration)**. Hold the union with an open-ended spanner while the pipe gland nut is unscrewed. On later models two O-rings are fitted on each connection – discard these as new ones must be used on installation.

4 If a carburettor warmer kit is fitted, disconnect its hoses at the cooler and oil feed pipe union.

5 Remove the two screws which retain the oil cooler and withdraw it from the engine.

Installation

6 Installation is a reverse of the removal procedure. On models fitted with O-rings at the hose connections use new ones and

smear them and the threads with oil. If any of the unions are unscrewed from the crankcase or oil cooler, their sealing washers must be renewed. Replenish the engine oil on completion (see *Daily (pre-ride) checks*).

Carburettor warmer kit

7 Some machines may be fitted as standard, or as an optional extra, with a carburettor warmer kit, designed to prevent carburettor icing.

8 On 750 and 900 models, oil is routed from a union on the oil cooler feed hose to one of the carburettor float bowls, then via a short connecting hose to the other float bowl, and back to the oil cooler inlet union. On 600 models hoses route the oil directly from the feed union on the crankcases to the carburettor float bowl, then across to the other float bowl and back to the return union on the crankcase. A tap in the system allows

the warmer hose system to be isolated from the lubrication system if required.

9 If the warmer kit pipes are disturbed, ensure that any sealing washers are replaced with new ones on installation. Top up the engine oil (see *Daily (pre-ride) checks*).

26 Crankcase – separating and joining

Separating

1 Prior to crankcase separation the engine must be removed from the frame (Section 5), and the following components removed:

2 From the cylinders, remove the cam belts and pulleys (Sections 6 and 7), both cylinder heads (Section 8) and cylinder barrels (Section 11). **Note:** *The pistons can remain in place on their connecting rods if desired.*

3 From the engine left-hand side, remove the alternator, flywheel/starter clutch, starter idle gear and starter motor (Section 14), the cam belt driveshaft gears (Section 7), oil pressure relief valve (Section 24) and the gearchange external mechanism (Section 15).

4 From the engine right-hand side, remove the clutch (Section 16, 17 or 18), oil pump (Section 22), primary drive gear (Section 23) and primary driven gear – dry clutch models (Section 17 or 18).

5 Check that the engine sprocket has been removed, and that where fitted the circlip has been removed from the cam belt driveshaft.

6 Peel back its rubber sleeve and unscrew the neutral switch from the crankcase right-hand half **(see illustration)**. Recover the shim between the switch and crankcase.

7 Unscrew the selector drum detent bolt from the crankcase left-hand half and recover the washer, spring and detent ball **(see illustrations)**.

8 Before separating the crankcases feel for any endfloat in the crankshaft, both gear shafts and the selector drum **(see illustration)**. If a dial gauge is available (and if not it is best to borrow or buy one as it is a lot easier and more accurate to check endfloat this way rather than after the crankcases have been split), mount it on the crankcase and record the exact amount of endfloat **(see illustration)**. Compare this

26.7a Remove the selector drum detent bolt, washer and spring . . .

26.7b . . . and withdraw the detent ball

26.8a Feeling for any freeplay in the crankshaft bearings

26.8b Measuring gear shaft endfloat with a dial gauge

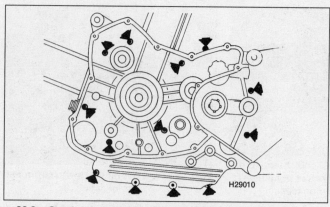

26.9a Crankcase screws – 600 and 750 engines to 1997 (later models similar)

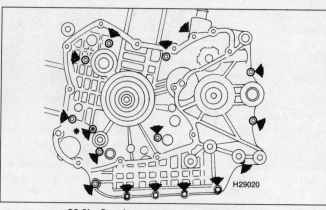

26.9b Crankcase screws – 900 engines
*Only applies to 1996-on engines

figure to that specified. If endfloat is excessive, carry out the calculation for shim size as detailed in the following sections.

9 Position the engine on its side so that the left-hand side is uppermost. Support the underside on wood blocks so that the crankshaft is not resting on the bench. Slacken the crankcase screws evenly in a diagonal sequence **(see illustrations)**. As they are removed store them in a cardboard template of the crankcase so that their positions can be identified on installation.

10 Turn the engine over so that the right-hand side is uppermost **(see illustration)**. On 2003-on 620 engines undo the two remaining screws, one above the transmission input shaft bore and the other above the cam belt driveshaft. Carefully lift the right-hand half off,

leaving all components in the left half. Remove the crankshaft, gear shafts and selector drum as described in the following sections. Lift the cam belt driveshaft out together with any shims.

11 Peel off the old gasket where fitted and discard it. Remove the two dowels if they are loose. Where fitted remove the oil passage O-ring and discard it as a new one must be used. Clean the crankcases and examine the bearings as described in the following section.

Joining

12 Install the crankshaft, gear shafts and selector drum into the left-hand crankcase half as described in the following sections. Do not omit their shims and ensure they are returned to their original locations on the shafts.

13 Install the cam belt driveshaft (with its shims where fitted) into its bearing in the left-hand crankcase **(see illustration)**.

14 Make sure that the crankcase surfaces are clean. Where removed fit a new and greased O-ring onto the oil passage. Install the two dowels and where removed position a new gasket over them **(see illustration)**. On models without a gasket apply a smear of a suitable sealant to the mating surfaces. Apply fresh engine oil to the ends of all the shafts **(see illustration)**. Lower the right-hand half into place so that it locates on the dowels and seats on the left-hand half. On 2003-on 620i.e. engines thread the right-hand screws into the crankcase, one above the transmission input shaft bore and the other above the cam belt driveshaft, and tighten them finger-tight.

15 Turn the engine over so that the left-hand side is uppermost. Install the crankcase screws in their original positions and secure them finger-tight at this stage. Working in a criss-cross sequence and starting with the larger bolts, tighten all crankcase screws a little at a time until the specified torque is reached. Note that the torque setting differs for the 8 and 6 mm bolts. Carefully cut away the section of gasket between each of the crankcase mouths.

16 Check that all shafts revolve easily. If there are any signs of stiffness, tight or rough spots, the crankcases should be split for investigation. **Note:** *If new main bearings have been fitted, they are pre-loaded during the crankcase tightening sequence. There may be*

26.10 Turn the crankcases over so that the right-hand side is uppermost

26.13 Install the cam belt driveshaft in its bearing

26.14a Place a new gasket over the crankcase dowels (arrows)

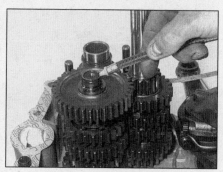

26.14b Oil all the shaft bearings . . .

26.14c . . . and install the right-hand crankcase half

some resistance felt when turning the crankshaft until the bearings bed-in. Check the gear shaft and selector drum endfloat (see Step 8). Check that all gears select by operating the selector drum cam, then return it to the neutral position.

17 Slip the selector drum detent ball into its bore in the crankcase and install the spring, washer and detent bolt.

18 Install the neutral switch with its shim and tighten it securely. Slip the rubber cover over the switch. **Note:** *The shim is essential to the correct operation of the neutral light circuit – if problems have been experienced with the light staying on or not coming on, the shim thickness may be incorrect – refer to Chapter 8 for details.*

19 Install all other assemblies in a reverse of the removal sequence.

27 Crankcase and bearings – inspection

Crankcase inspection

1 After the crankcases have been separated and all internal components removed, they should be cleaned thoroughly with solvent and dried with compressed air.

2 All traces of old gasket or sealant should be removed from the crankcase mating surfaces. Minor damage to the surfaces can be cleaned up with a fine sharpening stone or grindstone. *Caution: Be very careful not to nick or gouge the crankcase mating surfaces or oil leaks will result. Check both crankcase halves very carefully for cracks and other damage.*

3 Small cracks or holes in aluminium castings may be repaired with an epoxy resin adhesive as a temporary measure. Permanent repairs can only be effected by argon-arc welding, and only a specialist in this process is in a position to advise on the economy or practical aspect of such a repair. Alternatively, you could consider the purchase of one of the low temperature aluminium fusion welding kits. If any damage is found that can't be repaired, replace the crankcase halves as a set.

4 Damaged threads can be economically reclaimed by using a diamond section wire insert, of the Helicoil type, which is easily

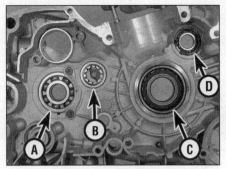

27.9a Left-hand crankcase half bearings: A – output shaft, B – input shaft, C – main, D – cam belt driveshaft

fitted after drilling and re-tapping the affected thread. Most motorcycle dealers and small engineering firms offer a service of this kind.

5 Sheared studs or screws can usually be removed with screw extractors, which consist of a tapered, left-hand thread screw of very hard steel. These are inserted into a pre-drilled hole in the stud or screw, and usually succeed in dislodging the most stubborn stud or screw. If a problem arises which seems beyond your scope, it is worth consulting a professional engineering firm before condemning an otherwise sound casing. Many of these firms advertise regularly in the motorcycle press.

6 Check that all the cylinder studs are tight in the crankcase halves. Refer to Section 11 for stud replacement.

7 The crankcase breather system is fully automatic in operation and will require no attention in normal use. If the separator unit in the top of the right-hand crankcase half is clogged with emulsified oil remove it from the crankcase and clean it thoroughly.

Crankcase bearings

8 The crankshaft main bearings can be examined as described in the next section.

9 The gear shafts locate in a ball bearing at one end and a roller bearing at the other; the inner race of the roller bearing will probably remain on the gear shaft **(see illustrations)**. If the bearings feel rough or notchy when rotated they must be renewed. Do not remove the bearings from the crankcases unless renewal is necessary. Where fitted remove the circlip, screws and washers or retaining plate securing the bearing.

10 Prise out the output shaft oil seal **(see**

27.9b Right-hand crankcase half bearings: A – cam belt driveshaft, B – main, C – input shaft, D – output shaft

illustration). Use a drift to drive the ball bearings out and check that the bearing leaves the crankcase squarely. If the bearings are a very tight fit in the housing, heat the area around the bearing for a few minutes using a heat gun so that the aluminium expands its grip on the steel bearing, then attempt removal.

11 The roller bearing outer races locate in blind holes in the crankcase and must be removed with a slide-hammer and bearing puller attachment. The inner races can be removed from the gear shafts as described in Section 32.

12 When installing new bearings in the crankcase use a socket which bears only on the outer edge of the bearing and tap it squarely into the crankcase. Use a suitable thread-locking compound on the ball bearing retaining plate and washer screws and tighten them to the specified torque. Where a bearing is secured by a circlip it is best to use a new one. Install the roller bearing inner races as described in Section 32.

13 The cam belt driveshaft runs either in a ball bearing in each crankcase half, or in a ball bearing in the left-hand crankcase and a roller bearing in the right-hand crankcase, depending on model and year. Prise out the oil seal from the left-hand crankcase, and where fitted remove the circlip before removing the bearing **(see illustration)**.

14 Drift the bearing out of the casing using a socket which bears only on the bearing outer race. Drift the bearing into the casing using a socket against its outer race and retain it with a circlip where removed, preferably using a new one. Press a new oil seal into the left-hand crankcase **(see illustration)**.

27.10 Prise out the output shaft oil seal with a large flat-bladed screwdriver

27.13 Cam belt driveshaft bearings are retained with a circlip on 900 engines

27.14 Install a new cam belt driveshaft oil seal in the left-hand crankcase

28.4a Unscrew the crankshaft oilway plugs . . .

28.4b . . . and use compressed air to clear any obstructions

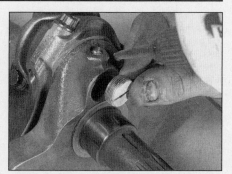

28.4c Apply a thread-locking agent to the threads of the oilway plugs

28 Crankshaft and main bearings – removal, inspection and installation

Removal

1 Separate the crankcase halves (Section 26).
2 The crankshaft will remain in the left-hand crankcase. Tap on its end with a soft-faced mallet to free it from the crankcase.
3 If required, remove the connecting rods from the crankshaft (see Section 29).

Inspection

4 Clean the crankshaft with solvent. Remove the oilway plugs from the edge and side of the crank webs, and from the left-hand end of the crankshaft, and blow through the oilways with compressed air to clear any obstructions **(see illustrations)**. A rifle-cleaning brush may also be useful to clear any stubborn blockages. Clean the threads of the oilway plugs and apply a suitable thread-locking compound to them before tightening the plugs securely **(see illustration)**.
5 Examine the main bearings; if they are scored, badly scuffed or appear to have been seized, new bearings must be installed. Always replace the main bearings as a set. If they are badly damaged, check the corresponding crankshaft journal. Evidence of extreme heat, such as discoloration, indicates that lubrication failure has occurred. Be sure to thoroughly check the oil pump and pressure relief valve as well as all oil holes and

passages before reassembling the engine. **Note**: *Ducati recommended replacing the main bearings whenever the engine is overhauled.*
6 To remove the main bearings, each casing half must be heated evenly and the bearing tapped out using a suitable drift **(see illustration)**. Either heat the casing in an oven to 100°C or immerse it in boiling water for several minutes. Whichever method is used, take care not to scald your hands when handling the casing. Tap the bearing inwards to remove it from its shouldered bush in the casing.
7 The new bearing is tapped into place using a bearing driver or large socket which bears only on the bearing outer race; contact with the bearing balls or inner race will destroy the bearing. Tap the bearing in from inside the crankcase so that it abuts the shouldered bush. Use the same method of heating the casing to aid installation of the new bearings. When the casing has cooled, check that the bearing rotates smoothly and that its outer race is a tight fit in the casing.
8 The crankshaft journals should be given a close visual examination, paying particular attention where damaged bearings have been discovered. If the journals are scored or pitted in any way a new crankshaft will be required. Note that undersizes are not available, precluding the option of re-grinding the crankshaft.

Endfloat check

9 A check of the crankshaft endfloat is

necessary whenever new main bearings are installed. **Note**: *Ducati recommended that the main bearings are renewed during an engine overhaul. They should also be renewed if the crankshaft or crankcases are renewed.*
10 Endfloat is calculated by measuring the distance between the crankcases and subtracting the length of the crankshaft. Lay a straightedge across the crankcase surface and using a depth gauge, measure the distance from the straightedge to the edge of the main bearing inner race **(see illustration)**. Do the same on the other crankcase half. Record these measurements as P1 (left-hand crankcase) and P2 (right-hand crankcase) **(see illustration)**.
11 Using a vernier gauge, measure the crankshaft across its shoulders, noting that

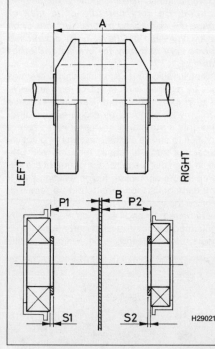

28.10b Crankshaft shim size calculation

P1 and P2 = crankcase depth
S1 and S2 = shims
A = crankshaft width across shoulders
B = gasket thickness (where appropriate)

28.6 Drifting the main bearings out of the crankcase

28.10a Measuring the crankcase depth for shim size calculation

28.11 Measuring the crankshaft width for shim size calculation

28.15 Measuring the thickness of the existing crankshaft shims

28.17a Lubricate the main bearings with engine oil

28.17b Install the shim(s) . . .

28.17c . . . and install the crankshaft in the left-hand crankcase

28.18 Install the shim(s) on the other end of the crankshaft

the shims must be removed **(see illustration)**. Record this measurement as A.

12 To calculate crankshaft endfloat, add P1 and P2 together, plus 0.3 mm to allow for the thickness of the gasket (where fitted, so do not add this on later models without a gasket), plus 0.15 mm bearing preload for models with a gasket, 0.2 mm for all other 600, 750 and 900 models, and 0.3 mm for all 620 models. **Note:** *The preload figure only applies to new bearings – never preload bearings which have been in use.* Subtract dimension A from this figure to arrive at the crankshaft shim size required. Thus, for example on a model with a gasket:

P1 + P2 + 0.3 mm (gasket allowance) + 0.15 mm (bearing pre-load) – A = total shim size required

13 In order that the crankshaft is central in the crankcases, shims should be placed on each end. Calculate the shim size for the left-hand end (S1) as follows:

P1 + 0.15 mm (half the gasket allowance) + 0.075 (half the bearing pre-load allowance) – (A ÷ 2) = shim size for left-hand end of crankshaft

14 Subtract the shim size for the left-hand end from the total shim size to arrive at the shim size for the right-hand end of the crankshaft.

15 Shim thickness can be measured with a micrometer **(see illustration)**.

Installation

16 If removed, install the connecting rods on the crankshaft (see Section 29).

17 Lubricate the main bearing in the left-hand crankcase with fresh engine oil **(see illustration)**. Ensure the shim(s) is in place and lower the crankshaft into position, making sure that the connecting rods are positioned correctly **(see illustrations)**.

18 Tap on the end of the crankshaft with a soft-faced mallet to seat the crankshaft in its

bearing. Install the shim on the right-hand end of the crankshaft **(see illustration)**.

19 Reassemble the crankcases (see Section 26). **Note:** *If new main bearings have been fitted, they are preloaded during the crankcase tightening sequence. There may be some resistance felt when turning the crankshaft until the bearings bed-in.*

29 Connecting rods and bearings – removal, inspection and installation

Note: *If the connecting rod journal is damaged or worn, two undersizes are available for regrinding of the journal. Seek the advice of a Ducati dealer if regrinding is necessary.*

Removal

1 Remove the crankshaft (see Section 28).

2 Before removing the rods from the crankshaft, measure the sideplay by inserting a feeler gauge between the two rods **(see illustration)**. In the unlikely event that sideplay is greater than specified (see Specifications at the beginning of this Chapter) the connecting rods must be renewed.

3 Using paint or a felt marker pen, mark the relevant cylinder identity on each connecting rod and bearing cap. Mark across the cap-to-connecting rod join to ensure that the cap is fitted the correct way around on reassembly.

4 Unscrew the big-end cap bolts and separate the connecting rod, cap and both bearing shells from the crankpin **(see illustration)**. Keep the rod, cap, dowels and the bearing

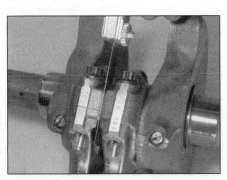

29.2 Measuring connecting rod sideplay

29.4 Removing the big-end bolts

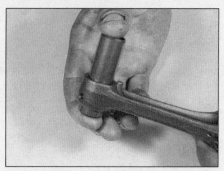

29.6a Checking for freeplay between the piston pin and small-end bush

29.6b Replacement of the small-end bush is a task for a Ducati dealer

shells together in their correct positions to ensure correct installation. **Note:** *The big-end bolts will have stretched, and must be replaced with new ones on reassembly.*

Inspection

5 Check the connecting rods for cracks and other obvious damage. Have the rods checked for twist and bend by a Ducati dealer if you are in doubt about their straightness. **Note:** *Connecting rods must be matched to the crankshaft on 900 engines as described in Step 17.*
6 Apply clean engine oil to the piston pin, insert it into the connecting rod small-end bush and check for any freeplay between the two **(see illustration)**. Measure the pin OD and the small-end bush ID at their points of contact and calculate the difference between the measurements taken to obtain the piston pin-to-small-end bush clearance. If the bush

is worn the machine should be taken to a Ducati dealer – bush renewal involves the bush being reamed to size and oilways being drilled **(see illustration)**.
7 Refer to Section 30 and examine the connecting rod bearing shells. If they are scored, badly scuffed or appear to have seized, new shells must be installed. Always replace the shells in the connecting rods as a set. If they are badly damaged, check the corresponding crankpin.
8 Evidence of extreme heat, such as discoloration, indicates that lubrication failure has occurred. Be sure to thoroughly check the oil pump and pressure relief valve as well as all oil holes and passages before reassembling the engine.

Oil clearance check

9 Whether new bearing shells are being fitted or the original ones are being re-used, the

connecting rod bearing oil clearance should be checked prior to reassembly. For some models, Ducati recommend the Plastigauge method of oil clearance measurement (see Steps 10 to 13), whereas on other models they recommend direct measurement (see Steps 14 to 15). In all cases, refer to Step 16 when the clearance has been measured.
10 Clean the backs of the bearing shells and the bearing locations in both the connecting rod and cap. Ensure the rod and cap dowels are in place. Press the bearing shells into their original locations and take care not to touch any shell's bearing surface with your fingers.
11 Cut a length of the appropriate size Plastigauge (it should be slightly shorter than the working face of the crankpin for the rod being checked). Place a strand of Plastigauge on the (cleaned) crankpin journal and fit the (clean) connecting rod, shells and cap **(see illustration)**. Make sure the cap is fitted the correct way around so the previously made markings align and tighten the big-end bolts to the specified torque (see Step 19) whilst ensuring that the connecting rod does not rotate.
12 Slacken the big-end bolts and remove the connecting rod assembly, again taking great care not to rotate the crankshaft.
13 Compare the width of the crushed Plastigauge on the crankpin to the scale printed on the Plastigauge envelope to obtain the connecting rod bearing oil clearance **(see illustration)**. Carry out the same procedure on the other connecting rod assembly. On completion carefully scrape away all traces of the Plastigauge material from the crankpin and bearing shells using a fingernail or other object which is unlikely to score the shells.
14 Assemble the connecting rod, cap, dowels and bearing shells (off the crankshaft). Tighten the big-end bolts to the specified torque setting, then using a bore micrometer, measure the ID of the bearing.
15 Using a micrometer, measure the OD of the crankshaft journal at the working face for that connecting rod. Subtract the journal diameter from the bearing diameter to obtain the oil clearance. Disassemble the connecting rod components when the check is complete. Perform the same check on the other connecting rod.
16 If the clearance is not within the specified limits, the bearing shells or crankshaft journal may be worn. Measure the crankshaft journal with a micrometer. If the journal diameter is within specification, install a set of new shells and repeat the oil clearance measurement. If the journal diameter is outside of the specification, the journal should be reground and oversize shells fitted – this type of work should be entrusted to a Ducati dealer.

Connecting rod selection

17 The connecting rods on 900 engines are available in two size selections – look for the letter A or B on the side of the rod and the corresponding size code letter on the crankshaft web **(see illustrations)**. If the rods

29.11 Lay a strip of Plastigauge on the journal, parallel to the crankshaft

29.13 Measuring the crushed Plastigauge with the scale

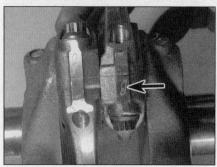

29.17a Connecting rod size code letter (arrow) . . .

29.17b . . . and crankshaft size code letter (arrow) on 900 engines

are renewed ensure that the replacement rod is of the same size code.

18 On some models each rod carries a weight code on its cap which corresponds with an identification number on the crankshaft web. Where these markings are present refer to the following table to establish the correct rod and crankshaft relationship. Both rods must have the same weight code.

Crankshaft number	Rod cap colour
01	Orange
0	Brown
1	Blue
2	Yellow
3	Green
4	Red
5	White
6	Black

Installation

Note: *New big-end bolts must be used on installation.*

19 Lubricate the bearing shells and crankpin surfaces with fresh engine oil and assemble the rod, shells and cap; make sure that the dowel pins between the rod and cap are in place. Apply a little grease to the threads and undersides of the bolt heads. Thread the bolts into place so that they are finger-tight. Assembly the rod for the other cylinder in the same way. Check that all components have been returned to their original locations using the marks made on disassembly.

20 Insert a feeler gauge between the rods and check their sideplay **(see illustration 29.2)**; ideally use a feeler gauge on each side of the rod to prevent any twist of the rod on the crankpin.

21 Leave the feeler gauges in place and tighten the big-end bolts evenly in three stages to the specified torque settings (see Specifications). Remove the feeler gauges. Check that the rods rotate smoothly and freely on the crankpin. If there are any signs of roughness or tightness, remove the rods and re-check the bearing clearance.

22 Install the crankshaft (see Section 28).

30 Connecting rod bearings – general information

1 Even though connecting rod bearings are generally replaced with new ones during the overhaul, the old bearings should be retained for close examination as they may reveal information about the condition of the engine.

2 Bearing failure occurs mainly because of lack of lubrication, the presence of dirt or other foreign particles, overloading the engine and/or corrosion. Regardless of the cause of bearing failure, it must be corrected before the engine is reassembled to prevent it recurring.

3 When examining the bearings, remove the bearings from the connecting rods and caps and lay them out on a clean surface in the same general position as their location on the crankshaft journals. This will enable you to

match any noted bearing problems with the corresponding crankshaft journal.

4 Dirt and other foreign particles get into the engine in a variety of ways. It may be left in the engine during assembly or it may pass through filters or breathers. It may get into the oil and from there into the bearings. Metal chips from machining operations and normal engine wear are often present. Abrasives are sometimes left in engine components after reconditioning operations, especially when parts are not thoroughly cleaned using the proper cleaning methods. Whatever the source, these foreign objects often end up imbedded in the soft bearing material and are easily recognised. Large particles will not imbed in the bearing and will score or gouge the bearing and journal. The best prevention for this cause of bearing failure is to clean all parts thoroughly and keep everything spotlessly clean during engine reassembly. Frequent and regular oil and filter changes are also recommended.

5 Lack of lubrication or lubrication breakdown has a number of interrelated causes. Excessive heat (which thins the oil), overloading (which squeezes the oil from the bearing face) and oil leakage or throw off (from excessive bearing clearances, worn oil pump or high engine speeds) all contribute to lubrication breakdown. Blocked oil passages will also starve a bearing and destroy it. When lack of lubrication is the cause of bearing failure, the bearing material is wiped or extruded from the steel backing of the bearing. Temperatures may increase to the point where the steel backing and the journal turn blue from overheating.

6 Riding habits can have a definite effect on bearing life. Full throttle low speed operation, or labouring the engine, puts very high loads on bearings, which tend to squeeze out the oil film. These loads cause the bearings to flex, which produces fine cracks in the bearing face (fatigue failure). Eventually the bearing material will loosen in pieces and tear away from the steel backing. Short trip riding leads to corrosion of bearings, as insufficient engine heat is produced to drive off the condensed water and corrosive gases produced. These products collect in the engine oil, forming acid and sludge. As the oil is carried to the engine bearings, the acid attacks and corrodes the bearing material.

7 Incorrect bearing installation during engine

assembly will lead to bearing failure as well. Tight fitting bearings which leave insufficient bearing oil clearances result in oil starvation. Dirt or foreign particles trapped behind a bearing insert result in high spots on the bearing which lead to failure.

8 To avoid bearing problems, clean all parts thoroughly before reassembly, double check all bearing clearance measurements and lubricate the new bearings with clean engine oil during installation.

31 Transmission gear shafts and selector drum/forks – removal and installation

Removal

1 Separate the crankcase halves (Section 26).

2 Withdraw the input shaft selector fork rod and fork. Slip the fork back on the rod for safekeeping. Withdraw the output shaft selector fork rod and manoeuvre the top selector fork out of position; the lower fork can only be removed once the output shaft has been lifted out.

3 Lift the input shaft out of the crankcase, noting that the output shaft will have to be simultaneously lifted to allow the shaft gears to disengage. Note the shim(s) on the right-hand end of the input shaft.

4 Grasp the selector drum and withdraw it from the crankcase. Recover the shims from each end of the drum. Slip the other selector fork out of the output shaft gear groove.

5 Lift the output shaft out of the crankcase. Recover the shim from its left-hand end.

Installation

Note: *Gear shaft and selector drum endfloat is controlled by shims. If the crankcases, gear shafts or selector drum have been renewed, the correct endfloat must be calculated before reassembling the crankcases.*

6 Lubricate the bearings in the left crankcase half with fresh engine oil.

7 Install the shim on the end of the output shaft and fit the shaft into its bearing **(see illustration)**. Slip the output shaft selector forks into their grooves in the gears but pivot them clear of the selector drum location in the crankcase **(see illustration)**.

31.7a Install the shim as the output shaft is inserted in the left-hand crankcase. Note the tape to protect the oil seal (arrow)

31.7b Locate the output shaft selector forks in their gear grooves

31.8 Install the shim(s) on the selector drum as it is inserted into the left-hand crankcase

31.9 Install the input shaft in the left-hand crankcase, lifting the output shaft slightly to help the gears mesh

31.10 Engage the input shaft selector fork in its gear groove and drum track, then install the fork rod

31.11a Engage the output shaft lower selector fork pin in the drum track . . .

31.11b . . . then do the same with the upper selector fork . . .

31.11c . . . and secure both forks with the rod

8 Fit the shim on the end of the selector drum and lower it into the crankcase (see illustration).
9 Install the input shaft in the crankcase, lifting the output shaft slightly to allow the gears to mesh correctly (see illustration).
10 Slip the input shaft selector fork into its gear groove and engage its pin with the drum track. Slide the selector fork rod into position (see illustration).
11 Position the pins of both output shaft selector forks in the drum tracks and install the selector fork rod (see illustrations). Install the shim on the other end of the selector drum (see illustration).
12 Install the shim(s) on the input shaft end (see illustration).
13 Check that the selector drum and both gear shafts are fully seated in their bearings and that the gears mesh correctly (see illustration).

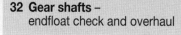

32 Gear shafts –
endfloat check and overhaul

Endfloat check

1 A check of the gear shaft endfloat is necessary if a new crankcase or new gear shaft has been fitted, or if the endfloat check in Section 26 indicates that the existing shim sizes are incorrect.
2 Endfloat can be calculated by measuring the distance between the crankcases and subtracting the length of the gear shafts. Lay a straightedge across the crankcase surface (similar to the crankshaft endfloat measurement shown in **illustration 28.10a**) and using a depth gauge, measure the distance from the

straightedge to the edge of the bearing inner race. **Note:** *The bearing inner races must be removed from the input shaft left-hand end and output shaft right-hand end and installed in their bearings. Do the same on the other crankcase half. Record these measurements as PA1 (right-hand crankcase) and PA2 (left-hand crankcase) for the input shaft and another set of measurements (PB1 and PB2) for the output shaft right and left crankcases halves* (see illustration).
3 Using a vernier gauge, measure the gear shaft from the points shown in illustration 32.2, noting that the bearing inner race and shim must be removed from the left-hand end of the input shaft and the right-hand end of the output shaft. Record this measurement as A for the input shaft and B for the output shaft. Note that the output shaft right-hand

31.11d Install the shim over the end of the selector drum

31.12 Install the shim(s) over the input shaft

31.13 The gear shafts and selector drum/forks correctly assembled

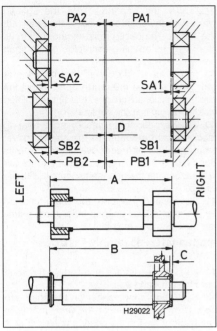

32.2 Gear shaft shim size calculation

PA1 and PA2 =
crankcase depth for input shaft
A = input shaft length
PB1 and PB2 = crankcase depth for
output shaft
B = output shaft length
SA1 and SA2 = shims for input shaft
C = output shaft spacer
SB1 and SB2 = shims for output shaft
D = gasket thickness (where appropriate)

spacer must be in place for this measurement and is represented by dimension C in the illustration.

4 To calculate the input shaft endfloat, add PA1 and PA2 together, plus 0.3 mm to allow for the thickness of the gasket (where a gasket is fitted – if no gasket is fitted, do not add this). Subtract dimension A, and 0.15 mm (prescribed endfloat) from this figure to arrive at the input shaft shim size required. Thus, for a model with a gasket:

PA1 + PA2 + 0.3 mm – A – 0.15 mm =
total shim size required (input shaft)

5 To calculate the output shaft endfloat, add PB1 and PB2 together, plus 0.3 mm to allow for the thickness of the gasket (where a gasket is fitted – if no gasket is fitted, do not add this). Subtract dimension B, and 0.15 mm (prescribed endfloat) from this figure to arrive at the output shaft shim size. Thus:

PB1 + PB2 + 0.3 mm – B – 0.15 mm =
total shim size required (output shaft)

6 In order that the gear shaft is central in the crankcases, shims should be placed on each end. Calculate the shim size for the right-hand side by subtracting 64.0 mm from PA1 or PB1 (as applicable), followed by 0.075 mm (half prescribed endfloat). Thus:

PA1 – 64.0 mm – 0.075 mm = shim size
for right-hand end of input shaft

PB1 – 64.0 mm – 0.075 mm = shim size
for right-hand end of output shaft

7 Subtract the shim size for the right-hand end from the total shim size to get the shim size for the left-hand end of the gear shaft.

Overhaul

> *When disassembling the transmission shafts, place the parts on a long rod or thread a wire through them to keep them in order and facing the proper direction. On models fitted with split needle bearings as opposed to the bearing halves illustrated, do not expand the ends too far when removing them as the cages could distort. Expand them only as much as is required to clear any ridges when sliding them off the shaft.*

Input shaft disassembly – five-gear models

8 The bearing inner race on the left-hand end of the shaft is a press fit. Use two large flat-bladed screwdrivers behind the second gear to prise the gear, shim(s) and inner race off the shaft **(see illustration 32.13)**.
9 Remove the circlip and splined washer to free the fifth gear and its bearing halves or split bearing (according to model) **(see illustration)**.
10 Remove the splined washer and circlip, followed by the third gear.
11 Remove the circlip, splined washer and fourth gear, followed by the bearing halves or split bearing (according to model).
12 Remove the thrust washer from the shaft. The first gear is integral with the input shaft.

Input shaft disassembly – six-gear models

13 The bearing inner race on the left-hand end of the shaft is a press fit. Use two large flat-bladed screwdrivers behind the second gear to prise the gear, shim(s) and inner race off the shaft **(see illustration)**.
14 Remove the circlip and splined washer to free the sixth gear and its bearing halves or split bearing (according to model).
15 Remove the splined washer and circlip, followed by the combined third/fourth gear.
16 Remove the circlip, splined washer and fifth gear, followed by the bearing halves or split bearing (according to model) and thrust washer. The first gear is integral with the input shaft.

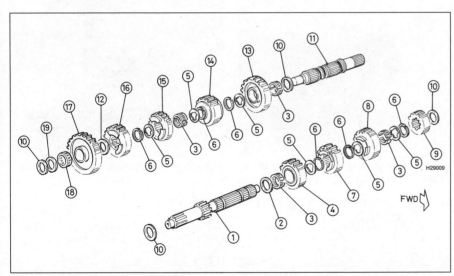

32.9 Gear shafts – five gear models

1 Input shaft	6 Circlip	13 Output second gear
2 Thrust washer	7 Input third gear	14 Output fifth gear
3 Half bearings or split bearing (according to model)	8 Input fifth gear	15 Output third gear
	9 Input second gear	16 Output fourth gear
	10 Shim (as required)	17 Output first gear
4 Input fourth gear	11 Output shaft	18 Bearing
5 Splined washer	12 Thrust washer	19 Spacer

32.13 Use levers behind the 2nd gear to draw the bearing inner race off the input shaft

32.22 Use a puller behind the 1st gear to draw the bearing inner race off the output shaft

Output shaft disassembly – five gear models

17 The bearing inner race on the right-hand end of the shaft is a press fit. Use a two-legged puller behind the first gear to draw the gear, shim(s) and inner race off the shaft **(see illustration 32.22)**. Recover the bearing and thrust washer from the shaft.
18 Withdraw the fourth gear.
19 Remove the circlip, splined washer and third gear from the shaft. Recover the bearing halves or split bearing (according to model) and splined washer.
20 Withdraw the fifth gear.
21 Remove the circlip, splined washer and second gear from the shaft. Recover the bearing halves or split bearing (according to model) and thrust washer.

Output shaft disassembly – six gear models

22 The bearing inner race on the right-hand end of the shaft is a press fit. Use a two-legged puller behind the first gear to draw the gear, shim(s) and inner race off the shaft **(see illustration)**. Recover the bearing and thrust washer from the shaft.
23 Withdraw the fifth gear.
24 Remove the circlip, splined washer and fourth gear from the shaft. Recover the bearing halves or split bearing (according to model) and splined washer(s).
25 Withdraw the third gear, its bearing halves or split bearing (according to model) and the splined washer.
26 Remove the circlip and slide off sixth gear.
27 Remove the circlip, splined washer and second gear.
28 Recover the bearing halves or split bearing (according to model) and the thrust washer.

Inspection – all engines

29 Wash all of the components in clean solvent and dry them off.
30 Check the gear teeth for cracking, chipping, pitting and other obvious wear or damage. Any pinion that is damaged as such must be replaced.
31 Inspect the dogs and the dog holes in the gears for cracks, chips, and excessive wear especially in the form of rounded edges. Make sure mating gears engage properly.

Replace the paired gears as a set if necessary.
32 Check for signs of scoring or bluing on the pinions, bushes and shaft. This could be caused by overheating due to inadequate lubrication. Check that all the oil holes and passages are clear. Replace any damaged pinions or bushes.
33 Check the circlips and thrust washers and replace any that are bent or appear weakened or worn. It is a good idea to use new circlips as a matter of course.
34 Check that each pinion moves freely on the shaft or needle roller bearing, but without undue freeplay.
35 The shaft is unlikely to sustain damage unless the engine has seized, placing an unusually high loading on the transmission, or the machine has covered a very high mileage. Check the surface of the shaft, especially where a pinion or bearing turns on it, and replace the shaft if it has scored or picked up, or if there are any cracks.
36 Examine the transmission shaft bearings as described in Section 27.

Input shaft reassembly – five gear models

37 All components are installed on the shaft from the left-hand end. Lubricate the bearings with grease prior to fitting them – in the case of the bearing halves this also helps keep them in place.
38 Slide the thrust washer on the shaft and up onto the shoulder of the first gear. Install the bearing halves or split bearing (according to model) on the shaft, then install the fourth

gear over the bearing. Slide the splined washer on the shaft and secure the gear with the circlip. The circlip must locate fully in its shaft with its opening each side of the shaft groove.
39 Install the third gear so that its selector fork groove faces the fourth gear. Install the circlip in the shaft groove. Install the splined washer up against the circlip.
40 Fit the bearing halves or split bearing (according to model) into the shaft groove, then install the fifth gear over them/it with its dogs facing the third gear. Install the splined washer against the gear and secure it with the circlip.
41 Slip second gear onto the shaft, followed by the shim(s) and bearing inner race; gently tap the inner race to seat it.

Input shaft reassembly – six gear models

42 All components are installed on the shaft from the left-hand end.
43 Slide the thrust washer on the shaft and up onto the shoulder of the first gear **(see illustration)**. Install the bearing halves or split bearing (according to model) on the shaft (see **Haynes Hint**), then install the fifth gear over the bearing so that its dogs face away from the first gear **(see illustrations)**. Slide the splined washer on the shaft and secure the gear with the circlip **(see illustrations)**. The circlip must locate fully in its shaft with its opening each side of the shaft channel **(see illustration)**.
44 Install the combined fourth/third gear with the larger (fourth) gear facing the fifth gear

32.43a Input shaft reassembly – install the thrust washer against integral 1st gear . . .

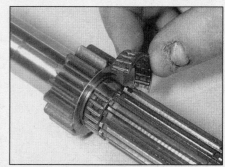

32.43b . . . locate bearing halves in their groove . . .

32.43c . . . and fit the 5th gear over the bearing

32.43d Install a splined washer on the shaft . . .

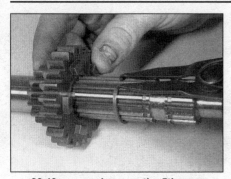

32.43e . . . and secure the 5th gear components with the circlip

32.43f Make sure the circlip opening is positioned correctly

32.44a Install the combined 4th/3rd gear on the input shaft

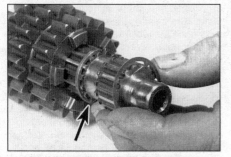

32.44b Install the circlip in its groove (arrow) and slide the splined thrust washer on the shaft

32.45a Place the bearing halves in the shaft groove . . .

32.45b . . . then position 6th gear over them

(see illustration). Install the circlip in the shaft groove, then install the splined washer up against the circlip **(see illustration)**.

45 Fit the bearing halves or split bearing (according to model) into the shaft groove, then install the sixth gear over them/it with its dogs facing the third gear **(see illustrations)**. Install the splined washer against the gear and secure it with the circlip **(see illustrations)**.

46 Slip second gear onto the shaft, followed by the shim(s) and bearing inner race; gently tap the inner race to seat it **(see illustrations)**.

Output shaft reassembly – five gear models

47 All components are installed on the shaft from the right-hand end.

48 Slide the thrust washer on the shaft and up against the shoulder. Install the bearing halves or split bearing (according to model) into the shaft and fit the second gear over them/it. Slide the splined washer up against the gear

and retain the components with the circlip.

49 Install the fifth gear with its selector groove facing away from the second gear. Install a circlip in the shaft groove.

50 Position a splined washer up against the circlip and install the bearing halves or split

32.45c Install a splined washer . . .

bearing (according to model) in the shaft. Install the third gear over the bearing. Position the splined washer up against the gear and secure the gear with the circlip.

51 Install the fourth gear over the shafts so that its selector fork groove faces the third

32.45d . . . and secure the 6th gear components with the circlip

32.46a Install 2nd gear (arrow), followed by the shim(s) . . .

32.46b . . . and bearing inner race

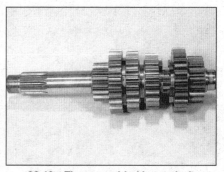

32.46c The assembled input shaft

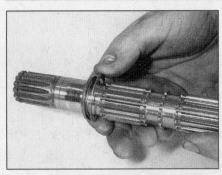

32.54a Output shaft reassembly – position the thrust washer against the shaft shoulder

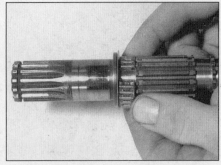

32.54b Place the bearing halves in their groove . . .

32.54c . . . slip the 2nd gear over the bearing and install the splined washer

32.54d Secure the 2nd gear components with the circlip

32.55 Install the 6th gear and position the circlip in its groove

up against the shoulder (see illustration). Install the bearing halves or split bearing (according to model) into the shaft, then fit the second gear over them/it and install the splined washer up against the gear (see illustrations). Retain the components with the circlip (see illustration).

55 Install the sixth gear with its selector groove facing away from the second gear. Install a circlip in the shaft groove (see illustration).

56 Position a splined washer up against the circlip and install the bearing halves or split bearing (according to model) in the shaft (see illustrations). Install the third gear over the bearing and position the splined washer(s) up against the gear (see illustration).

57 Install the bearing halves or split bearing (according to model) in the shaft (see illustration). Slide the fourth gear over the bearing and install the splined washer and circlip (see illustrations).

gear. Slip the thrust washer over the shaft and position the bearing on the shaft. Locate the first gear over the bearing.

52 Fit the shim(s) over the end of the shaft, followed by the bearing inner race; gently tap the inner race to seat it.

Output shaft reassembly – six gear models

53 All components are installed on the shaft from the right-hand end.

54 Slide the thrust washer on the shaft and

32.56a Position a splined washer against the circlip

32.56b Insert the bearing halves into the shaft groove . . .

32.56c . . . install the 3rd gear over the bearing, followed by the splined washer

32.57a Position the bearing halves in the shaft groove . . .

32.57b . . . install 4th gear over the bearing, followed by the splined washer

32.57c Secure the 4th gear components with the circlip

32.58a Install the 5th gear on the shaft . . .

32.58b . . . followed by the thrust washer (arrow) and bearing

32.58c Locate the 1st gear over the bearing and install the shim(s)

58 Install the fifth gear over the shaft with its selector fork groove facing the fourth gear (see illustration). Slip the thrust washer over the shaft and position the bearing on the shaft (see illustration). Locate the first gear over the bearing and fit the shim(s) over the end of the shaft (see illustration).
59 Install the bearing inner race; gently tap the inner race to seat it (see illustrations).

32.59a Install the bearing inner race

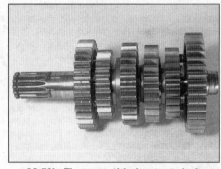

32.59b The assembled output shaft

33 Selector drum and forks – endfloat check and overhaul

Endfloat check

1 A check of the selector drum endfloat is necessary if a new drum or crankcases have been fitted, or if the existing shim size is suspected of being incorrect.
2 Endfloat is calculated by measuring the distance between the crankcases and subtracting the length of the drum shoulders. Lay a straightedge across the crankcase

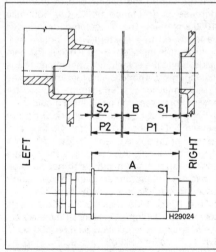

33.2 Selector drum shim size calculation

P1 and P2 = crankcase depth
S1 and S2 = shims
A = selector drum length
B = gasket thickness (where appropriate)

surface (similar to the crankshaft endfloat measurement shown in illustration 28.10a) and using a depth gauge, measure the distance from the straightedge to the edge of the drum bearing housing. Do the same on the other crankcase half. Record these measurements as P1 (right-hand crankcase) and P2 (left-hand crankcase) (see illustration).
3 Using a vernier gauge, measure the length of the selector drum across its two shoulders and record this measurement as A.
4 Add P1 and P2 together, plus 0.3 mm to allow for the thickness of the gasket (where a gasket is fitted – if no gasket is fitted, do not add this). Subtract dimension A, and 0.25 mm (prescribed endfloat) from this figure to arrive at the shim size required. Thus:

P1 + P2 + 0.3 mm – A – 0.25 mm = total shim size required

5 In order that the drum is central in the

33.7a Measuring the gear-to-fork clearance

crankcases, shims should be placed on each end. Calculate the shim size for the right-hand side by subtracting 59.0 mm from P1, followed by 0.125 mm (half prescribed endfloat). Thus:

P1 – 59.0 m – 0.125 mm = shim size for right-hand side of drum

6 Subtract the shim size for the right-hand side from the total shim size to arrive at the shim size for the left-hand side of the drum.

Overhaul

7 Inspect the selector forks for any signs of wear or damage, especially around the fork ends where they engage with the groove in the gear. Install the fork in its gear groove and use feeler gauges to measure the fork-to-gear clearance (see illustration). If outside the service limit, measure the fork groove width and fork ear thickness to determine which component is worn (see illustrations overleaf).
8 Check that the selector forks fit correctly on their rods. They should move freely with a light fit but no appreciable freeplay. Check that the fork rod holes in the crankcases are not worn or damaged.
9 The selector fork rod can be checked for trueness by rolling it along a flat surface. A bent shaft will cause difficulty in selecting gears and make the gearchange action heavy. Replace the rod if it is bent.
10 Inspect the selector drum tracks and selector fork guide pins for signs of wear or damage. If either component shows signs of wear or damage the gearshift fork(s) and drum must be replaced. Measure the selector drum

33.7b Measuring the gear fork groove width

track width and guide pin diameter and calculate the track-to-guide pin clearance (see illustrations). If outside the service limit, compare the drum track width and guide pin diameters to their service limits to determine which component is worn.

11 The change pins in the end of the drum are held in place by a spring clip. Squeeze the ears of the spring clip together to enable the change pins to be withdrawn (see illustration). When installing the pins, make sure that the spring clip locates in their grooves (see illustration).

12 Check the bearing surfaces of the selector drum and crankcase. These surfaces shouldn't suffer from wear under normal conditions.

33.10a Measuring the selector drum track width

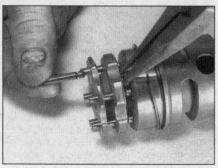

33.11a Hold the spring clip ears together while removing the change pins

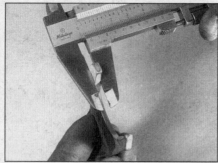

33.7c Measuring the fork ear thickness

13 If a new selector drum or crankcases are being fitted, carry out the endfloat check described above to determine shim size.

34 Initial start-up after overhaul

1 Make sure the engine oil and coolant levels are correct (see *Daily (pre-ride) checks*), then remove the spark plugs from the engine, fit them back into their caps and earth the body of each plug against the cylinder head, away from the spark plug hole.

2 Turn the ignition switch and kill switch ON, then crank the engine over with the starter

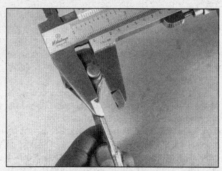

33.10b Measuring the fork guide pin diameter

33.11b Ensure spring clip engages the groove on all change pins

until the oil pressure indicator light goes off (which indicates that oil pressure exists). Turn the ignition OFF and reinstall the spark plugs.

3 Start the engine and allow it to run at a moderately fast idle until it reaches operating temperature.

 Warning: If the oil pressure indicator light doesn't go off, or if it comes on while the engine is running, stop the engine immediately.

4 Check carefully for oil leaks and make sure the transmission and controls, especially the brakes, function properly before road testing the machine. Refer to Section 35 for the recommended running-in procedure.

5 Upon completion of the road test, and after the engine has cooled down completely, recheck the engine/transmission oil level (see *Daily (pre-ride) checks*).

35 Recommended running-in procedure

1 Treat the machine gently for the first few miles to make sure oil has circulated throughout the engine and any new parts installed have started to seat.

2 Even greater care is necessary if new pistons and barrels or a new crankshaft has been installed. In the case of new pistons and barrels, the bike will have to be run in as when new. This means greater use of the transmission and a restraining hand on the throttle until at least 600 miles (1000 km) have been covered. There's no point in keeping to any set speed limit – the main idea is to keep from labouring the engine and to gradually increase performance up to the 600 mile (1000 km) mark. These recommendations can be lessened to an extent when only a new crankshaft is installed. Experience is the best guide, since it's easy to tell when an engine is running freely. The following maximum engine speed limitations, which Ducati provide for new motorcycles, can be used as a guide.

3 For the first 600 miles (1000 km) do not exceed 5500 rpm. On Monster models road speed should be kept below 70 mph (120 kph). During this time, vary the throttle position/speed and avoid harsh acceleration especially when under load. **Note:** *Don't forget to re-torque the cylinder head nuts.*

4 From 600 to 1500 miles (1000 to 2500 km) do not exceed 7000 rpm. On Monster models road speed should be kept below 90 mph (150 kph).

5 If a lubrication failure is suspected, stop the engine immediately and try to find the cause. If an engine is run without oil, even for a short period of time, severe damage will occur.

Chapter 3A
Fuel and exhaust systems – carburettor models

Contents

Air filter cleaning . . . . .see Chapter 1
Air filter housing – removal and installation 13
Carburettor overhaul – general information 5
Carburettor synchronisation . . . . .see Chapter 1
Carburettor warmer kit . . . . .see Chapter 2
Carburettors – disassembly, cleaning and inspection 7
Carburettors – reassembly, float height and fuel level check 9
Carburettors – removal and installation 6
Carburettors – separation and joining 8
Choke cable – removal and installation 11
Exhaust system – removal and installation 14
Fuel filter – replacement . . . . .see Chapter 1

Fuel pump (SS and SL models) –
    check, removal and installation . . . . .see Chapter 8
Fuel system checks . . . . .see Chapter 1
Fuel tank – cleaning and repair 3
Fuel tank and tap – removal and installation 2
General information and precautions 1
Idle fuel/air mixture adjustment – general information 4
Idle speed check . . . . .see Chapter 1
Throttle and choke cable check . . . . .see Chapter 1
Throttle cables – removal and installation 10
Vacuum fuel pump (Monsters models) – check,
    removal and installation 12

Degrees of difficulty

| Easy, suitable for novice with little experience | | Fairly easy, suitable for beginner with some experience | | Fairly difficult, suitable for competent DIY mechanic | 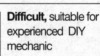 | Difficult, suitable for experienced DIY mechanic | | Very difficult, suitable for expert DIY or professional | 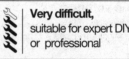 |

Specifications

Fuel
Grade	Unleaded, 95-98 RON (Research Octane Number)
Fuel tank capacity (inclusive reserve capacity)	
SS and SL models	17.5 litres (4 litres)
1991 to 1997 Monster models	18.0 litres (4 litres)
1998-on Monster models	16.5 litres (3.5 litres)

Carburettors
Type (all models)	Mikuni BDST 38 mm CV
Pilot screw setting (turns out)	Not available
Float height	see text
Idle speed	see Chapter 1
Jet sizes – 600SS model	
Main jet	132.5
Main air jet	70
Needle jet	Y-6
Jet needle	5CJ1 – 3rd notch from top
Pilot jet	37.5
Pilot air jet	60/1.4
Jet sizes – 750SS model	
Main jet	140
Main air jet	70
Needle jet	Y-6
Jet needle	5C19 – 3rd notch from top
Pilot jet	37.5
Pilot air jet	60/1.4

Carburettors (continued)

Jet sizes – 900SS and SL models

Main jet	140
Main air jet	70
Needle jet	Y-2
Jet needle	5C19 – 4th notch from top
Pilot jet	42.5
Pilot air jet	60/1.4

Jet sizes – M600 model

Main jet	132.5
Main air jet	70
Needle jet	Y-2
Jet needle	5CJ1 – 3rd notch from top
Pilot jet	
Up to end 1997	37.5
1998-on	40
Pilot air jet	Not available

Jet sizes – M750 model

Main jet	132.5
Main air jet	70
Needle jet	Y-4
Jet needle	5CJ1 – 4th notch from top
Pilot jet	
Up to end 1997	42.5
1998-on	40
Pilot air jet	Not available

Jet sizes – M900 model

Main jet	140
Main air jet	70
Needle jet	Y-2
Jet needle	5C19 – 4th notch from top
Pilot jet	40
Pilot air jet	60/1.4

Torque settings

Exhaust flange nuts	23 to 25 Nm
Handlebar clamp bolts – Monster models	22 to 27 Nm

---

1 General information and precautions

General information

The fuel system consists of the fuel tank, the fuel tap, the fuel filter, the fuel pump, the carburettors, fuel hoses and control cables. On SS and SL models the fuel filter and pump are housed inside the fuel tank.

On SS, SL and early Monsters, a screw-in type fuel tap is used. Later Monsters use a standard lever type fuel tap.

The carburettors used on all models are Mikuni CV types. On all models there is a carburettor for each cylinder. For cold starting, a choke lever mounted on the left-hand handlebar, or on the top yoke on early Monsters, operates an enrichment circuit in the carburettor. A carburettor warmer kit is available to prevent carburettor icing.

Air is drawn into the carburettors via an air filter which is housed under the fuel tank.

The exhaust system is a two-into-two design.

Many of the fuel system service procedures are considered routine maintenance items and for that reason are included in Chapter 1.

Precautions

 Warning: Petrol is extremely flammable, so take extra precautions when you work on any part of the fuel system. Don't smoke or allow open flames or bare light bulbs near the work area, and don't work in a garage where a natural gas-type appliance is present. If you spill any fuel on your skin, rinse it off immediately with soap and water. When you perform any kind of work on the fuel system, wear safety glasses and have a fire extinguisher suitable for a class B type fire (flammable liquids) on hand.

Always perform service procedures in a well-ventilated area to prevent a build-up of fumes.

Never work in a building containing a gas appliance with a pilot light, or any other form of naked flame. Ensure that there are no naked light bulbs or any sources of flame or sparks nearby.

Do not smoke (or allow anyone else to smoke) while in the vicinity of petrol or of components containing it. Remember the possible presence of vapour from these sources and move well clear before smoking.

Check all electrical equipment belonging to the house, garage or workshop where work is being undertaken (see the Safety first! section of this manual). Remember that certain electrical appliances such as drills, cutters etc. create sparks in the normal course of operation and must not be used near petrol or any component containing it. Again, remember the possible presence of fumes before using electrical equipment.

Always mop up any spilt fuel and safely dispose of the rag used.

Any stored fuel that is drained off during servicing work must be kept in sealed containers that are suitable for holding petrol, and clearly marked as such; the containers themselves should be kept in a safe place. Note that this last point applies equally to the fuel tank if it is removed from the machine; also remember to keep its cap closed at all times.

Read the Safety first! section of this manual carefully before starting work.

Owners of machines used in the US, particularly California, should note that their machines must comply at all times with Federal or State legislation governing the permissible levels of noise and of pollutants such as unburnt hydrocarbons, carbon monoxide etc. that can be emitted by those

2.1 Detach the tank breather hose from its union

2.3a Release the tank front catch

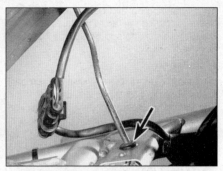

2.3b The tank prop locates in a hole in the frame (arrow) on SS/SL models

machines. All vehicles offered for sale must comply with legislation in force at the date of manufacture and must not subsequently be altered in any way which will affect their emission of noise or of pollutants.

In practice, this means that adjustments may not be made to any part of the fuel, ignition or exhaust systems by anyone who is not authorised or mechanically qualified to do so, or who does not have the tools, equipment and data necessary to properly carry out the task. Also if any part of these systems is to be replaced it must be replaced with only genuine Ducati components or by components which are approved under the relevant legislation. The machine must never be used with any part of these systems removed, modified or damaged.

2.5a Fuel tap knob (A), fuel delivery hose (B), fuel return hose (C), drain hose (D), wiring connector (E) (SS and SL model tank shown)

2 Fuel tank and tap – removal and installation

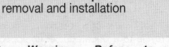

> **Warning: Refer to the precautions given in Section 1 before starting work.**

Fuel tank

Removal

1 Make sure the fuel cap is secure. On SS and SL models, detach the breather hose from its union on the top of the tank **(see illustration)**.
2 Remove the seat (see Chapter 7).
3 Release the catch securing the front of the tank to the frame, noting how it fits, then raise the tank at the front (the back of the tank is hinged on the frame) and support it on its prop **(see illustrations)**. The prop on Monster models engages the fuel tank seam.
4 Disconnect the battery negative (-ve) terminal.
5 On SS and SL models, close the fuel tap, then release the fuel delivery hose, the fuel return hose, and the drain hose clamps and detach the hoses from their unions, noting their positions and routing **(see illustration)**. Also disconnect the low fuel level sensor/fuel pump wiring. On Monsters, close the fuel tap (or turn it OFF) and disconnect the fuel hose from the carburettor side of the tap. On models with a lever type tap, unscrew the bolts securing the tap to the frame **(see illustration)**. Disconnect the low fuel level sensor wiring.

6 Remove the split pin and washer from the end of the hinge pin at the rear of the tank **(see illustration)**. Withdraw the hinge pin, then carefully lift the tank away from the machine **(see illustration)**.
7 Inspect the tank mounting rubbers, catch and hinge pin for signs of damage or deterioration and replace them if necessary. The rubbers are secured to the tank by screws.

Installation

8 Installation is the reverse of removal. Make sure the fuel pipes are correctly fitted (see Step 5) and routed and secured by their clamps.
9 With the fuel tap ON (open), check that there is no sign of fuel leakage. Check that the tank is properly seated and is not pinching any control cables or wires. Start the engine and check that there is no sign of fuel leakage, then shut if off.

Fuel tap

Removal

10 The tap should not be removed unnecessarily. If it is suspected of being faulty or is leaking it must be replaced as no method of repair is possible and no parts are available for it.
11 Remove the fuel tank (see Steps 1 to 7 above).
12 Place the tank over a container suitable and large enough for the storage of the petrol. Unscrew the drain bolt in the base of the tank and allow the fuel to drain into the container.

2.5b On later Monsters, the fuel tap is secured to the frame

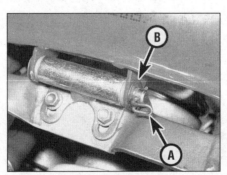

2.6a Remove the split pin (A) and washer (B) . . .

2.6b . . . then withdraw the hinge pin

13 Depending on the model, either unscrew the nut securing the tap to the tank, or release the fuel hose clamp and detach the hose, and remove the tap.

Installation

14 Installation is the reverse of removal. Make sure the fuel pipes are correctly fitted and routed and secured by their clamps. With the fuel tap ON (open), check that there is no sign of fuel leakage.

3 Fuel tank – cleaning and repair

1 All repairs to the fuel tank should be carried out by a professional who has experience in this critical and potentially dangerous work. Even after cleaning and flushing of the fuel system, explosive fumes can remain and ignite during repair of the tank.

2 If the fuel tank is removed from the bike, it should not be placed in an area where sparks or open flames could ignite the fumes coming out of the tank. Be especially careful inside garages where a natural gas-type appliance is located, because the pilot light could cause an explosion.

4 Idle fuel/air mixture adjustment – general information

1 Due to the increased emphasis on controlling motorcycle exhaust emissions,

certain governmental regulations have been formulated which directly affect the carburation of this machine. In order to comply with the regulations, the carburettors on some models are sealed so they can't be tampered with. The pilot screws on other models are accessible, but the use of an exhaust gas analyser is the only accurate way to adjust the idle fuel/air mixture and be sure the machine doesn't exceed the emissions regulations.

2 The pilot screws are set to their correct position by the manufacturer and should not be adjusted unless it is necessary to do so for a carburettor overhaul. If the screws are adjusted they should be reset to their original settings which should be recorded before any adjustment is made.

3 If the engine runs extremely rough at idle or continually stalls, and if a carburettor overhaul does not cure the problem, take the motorcycle to a Ducati dealer equipped with an exhaust gas analyser. They will be able to properly adjust the idle fuel/air mixture to achieve a smooth idle and restore low speed performance.

5 Carburettor overhaul – general information

1 Poor engine performance, hesitation, hard starting, stalling, flooding and backfiring are all signs that major carburettor maintenance may be required.

2 Keep in mind that many so-called carburettor problems are really not

carburettor problems at all, but mechanical problems within the engine or ignition system malfunctions. Try to establish for certain that the carburettors are in need of maintenance before beginning a major overhaul.

3 Check the fuel filter, the fuel hoses, the fuel pump, the intake manifold joint clamps, the air filter, the ignition system, the spark plugs and carburettor synchronisation before assuming that a carburettor overhaul is required.

4 Most carburettor problems are caused by dirt particles, varnish and other deposits which build up in and block the fuel and air passages. Also, in time, gaskets and O-rings shrink or deteriorate and cause fuel and air leaks which lead to poor performance.

5 When overhauling the carburettors, disassemble them completely and clean the parts thoroughly with a carburettor cleaning solvent and dry them with filtered, unlubricated compressed air. Blow through the fuel and air passages with compressed air to force out any dirt that may have been loosened but not removed by the solvent. Once the cleaning process is complete, reassemble the carburettor using new gaskets and O-rings.

6 Before disassembling the carburettors, make sure you have a carburettor rebuild kit (which will include all necessary O-rings and other parts), some carburettor cleaner, a supply of clean rags, some means of blowing out the carburettor passages and a clean place to work. Work on only one carburettor at a time, to avoid mixing up parts.

6 Carburettors – removal and installation

 Warning: Refer to the precautions given in Section 1 before starting work.

Removal

1 Remove the fuel tank (see Section 2).

2 Remove the air filter housing (Section 13).

3 Detach the throttle cables from the carburettors (see Section 10).

4 Detach the choke cable from the carburettors (see Section 11).

5 If fitted, unscrew the banjo bolts securing the oil warmer system feed and return pipes to the carburettor float chambers and remove the pipes. There is no need to remove the pipe connecting the float chambers unless the carburettors are to be disassembled or separated. Secure the pipes in an upright position to prevent oil spillage.

6 Pull the top breather hose from its stub on the top of each carburettor, noting which hose connects to which carburettor **(see illustration)**. Pull the bottom breather hose off its stub on the vent tank **(see illustration)**.

7 Slacken the clamps securing the carburettors to the cylinder head inlet duct adapters and ease the carburettors off the adapters, noting how they fit **(see illustrations)**. **Note:** *Keep the*

6.6a Detach the top breather hoses (arrows) from their stubs . . .

6.6b . . . and the bottom breather hose from its stub on the vent tank

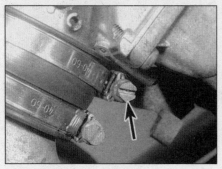

6.7a Slacken the clamp (arrow) securing each carburettor to its inlet duct adapter . . .

6.7b . . . then ease the carburettors off the adapters

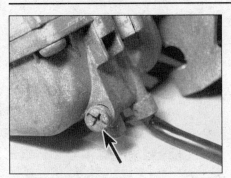

6.8 Carburettor fuel drain screw (arrow)

7.2a The carburettor top cover is secured by two screws (arrows)

7.2b Lift off the cover and remove the spring

carburettors upright to prevent fuel spillage from the float chambers and the possibility of the piston diaphragms being damaged. Remove the carburettors from the machine along with the fuel delivery hose, bottom breather hose and drain hoses.

8 Place a suitable container below the float chambers then slacken the drain screws and drain all the fuel from the carburettors **(see illustration)**. Once all the fuel has been drained, tighten the drain screws securely.

9 If necessary, release the clamps securing the inlet adapters to the cylinder head inlet ducts and remove the adapters, noting how they fit.

Installation

10 Installation is the reverse of removal, noting the following.

● Check for cracks or splits in the cylinder head inlet adapters. If they have been removed from the inlet ducts, make sure they are correctly fitted and secured by their clamps.
● Make sure the air filter housing and the cylinder head inlet adapters are fully engaged with the carburettors and their retaining clamps are securely tightened.
● Make sure all hoses are correctly routed and secured and not trapped or kinked. Where applicable, do not forget to fit the oil feed and return pipes to the bottom of the float chambers.
● Check the operation of the choke and throttle cables and adjust them as necessary (see Chapter 1).
● Check idle speed and carburettor synchronisation and adjust as necessary (see Chapter 1).

---

 7 Carburettors – disassembly, cleaning and inspection

⚠️ **Warning: Refer to the precautions given in Section 1 before starting work.**

7.3a Remove the O-ring (arrow) from the air passage

Disassembly

1 Remove the carburettors from the machine as described in the previous Section. **Note:** *Do not separate the carburettors unless absolutely necessary; each carburettor can be dismantled sufficiently for all normal cleaning and adjustments while joined to its neighbour. Dismantle the carburettors separately to avoid interchanging parts.*

2 Unscrew and remove the two top cover screws **(see illustration)**. Lift off the cover and remove the spring from inside the diaphragm assembly **(see illustration)**. Note the jet needle retainer which fits into the bottom of the spring.

3 Remove the O-ring from the air passage and discard it as a new one must be used **(see illustration)**. Carefully peel the

7.4 Push the needle up from the bottom and withdraw it from the top

7.3b Withdraw the diaphragm and piston assembly from the carburettor body

diaphragm away from its sealing groove in the carburettor and withdraw the diaphragm and piston assembly **(see illustration)**.

Caution: Do not use a sharp instrument to displace the diaphragm as it is easily damaged.

4 If necessary, push the jet needle up from the bottom of the diaphragm assembly and withdraw it from the top **(see illustration)**. Take care not to lose the clip, ring and washer and note how they fit.

5 Remove the screws securing the float chamber to the base of the carburettor and remove the float chamber **(see illustration)**. Remove the gasket and discard it as a new one must be fitted.

6 The float assembly is a push fit into the carburettor body. Carefully remove it from the

7.5 The float chamber is secured by four screws (arrows)

7.6a Carefully pull the float assembly out of the carburettor

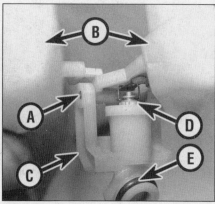

7.6b Float pin (A), float (B), float carrier (C), float needle valve (D), carrier O-ring (E)

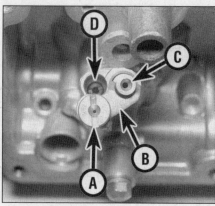

7.7 Starter jet (A), main jet retainer plate (B), main jet (C), pilot jet (D)

body, noting how it fits **(see illustration)**. Carefully withdraw the float pin, displacing it using a small punch or a nail if necessary **(see illustration)**. Remove the float from the carrier and unhook the float needle valve, noting how it fits onto the tab on the float. Discard the carrier O-ring as a new one must be used.

7 Unscrew the starter jet and remove it along with the main jet retainer plate **(see illustration)**. Remove the main jet along with its O-ring. Discard the O-ring as a new one must be used.

8 Unscrew and remove the pilot jet **(see illustration 7.7)**.

9 Unscrew the bolt securing the jet carrier to the needle jet and remove it with its collar **(see illustration)**. Carefully remove the carrier

from the carburettor body, noting how it fits **(see illustration)**. Discard the gasket as a new one must be used.

10 Note the position of the locating cut-out in the bottom of the needle jet, then push the needle jet up from the bottom and withdraw it with the piston guide through the top of the carburettor **(see illustration)**. Note which way round the guide fits into the carburettor body.

11 The pilot screw can be removed from the carburettor, but note that its setting will be disturbed (see *Haynes Hint*). Remove the pilot screw plug, then unscrew and remove the pilot screw along with its spring, washer and O-ring **(see illustration)**.

12 Remove the two screws securing the air

cut-off valve cover, noting that it is under spring pressure **(see illustration)**. Carefully release the cover and remove the spring and cut-off valve diaphragm, noting how they fit **(see illustration)**.

> **HAYNES HiNT** *To record the pilot screw's current setting, turn the screw in until it seats lightly, counting the number of turns necessary to achieve this, then fully unscrew it. On installation, the screw is simply backed out the number of turns you've recorded.*

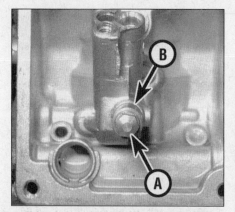

7.9a Jet carrier bolt (A) and collar (B)

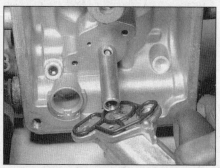

7.9b Remove the carrier and discard its gasket

7.10 Withdraw the piston guide and needle jet from the top of the carburettor

7.11 Remove the pilot screw plug to access the pilot screw (arrow)

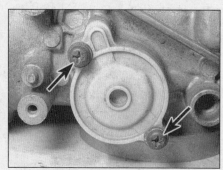

7.12a The air cut-off valve cover is secured by two screws (arrows)

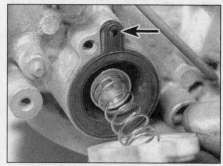

7.12b Remove the spring and valve diaphragm, noting how the hole in the tab on the diaphragm locates over the hole in the tab recess (arrow)

7.13a Remove the choke linkage bar clips (arrow)

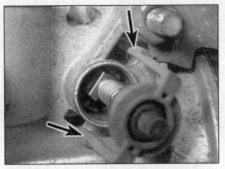

7.13b Compress the choke plunger clip ends (arrows) to release it from the carburettor

7.16 Note the air jets (arrows) in the bottom of the carburettor inlet

13 Push out the clips securing the choke linkage bar to the carburettors, noting how they fit, then remove the choke linkage bar from the plungers and the actuating slide, noting how it fits **(see illustration)**. Compress the clip ends securing the choke plunger to the carburettor body and withdraw the plunger **(see illustration)**.

Cleaning

Caution: *Use only a petroleum-based solvent for carburettor cleaning. Don't use caustic cleaners.*

14 Submerge the metal components in the solvent for approximately thirty minutes (or longer, if the directions recommend it).
15 After the carburettor has soaked long enough for the cleaner to loosen and dissolve most of the varnish and other deposits, use a brush to remove the stubborn deposits. Rinse it again, then dry it with compressed air.
16 Use a jet of compressed air to blow out all of the fuel and air passages in the main and upper body, not forgetting the air jets in the carburettor inlet **(see illustration)**.
Caution: Never clean the jets or passages with a piece of wire or a drill bit, as they will be enlarged, causing the fuel and air metering rates to be upset.

Inspection

17 Check the operation of the choke plunger. If it doesn't move smoothly, inspect the needle on the end of the choke plunger and

the plunger itself. Replace the plunger assembly if worn or bent.
18 Check the tapered portion of the pilot screw and the spring for wear or damage. Replace them if necessary.
19 Check the carburettor body, float chamber and top cover for cracks, distorted sealing surfaces and other damage. If any defects are found, replace the faulty component.
20 Check the diaphragm assembly for splits, holes and general deterioration. Holding it up to a light will help to reveal problems of this nature.
21 Insert the diaphragm assembly in the carburettor body and check that the slider moves up-and-down smoothly. Check the surface of the slider for wear. If it's worn excessively or doesn't move smoothly, replace it.
22 Check the jet needle for straightness by rolling it on a flat surface (such as a piece of glass). Replace it if it's bent or if the tip is worn.
23 Check the tip of the float needle valve and the valve seat. If either has grooves or scratches in it, or is in any way worn, the entire float assembly must be replaced as individual components are not available.
24 Operate the throttle shaft to make sure the throttle butterfly valve opens and closes smoothly. If it doesn't, replace the carburettor.
25 Check the floats for damage. This will usually be apparent by the presence of fuel inside one of the floats. If the floats are

damaged, the entire float assembly must be replaced as individual components are not available.
26 Check the air cut-off valve assembly components for wear or damage, in particular checking for splits or holes in the diaphragm, and replace any components if necessary.

---

8 Carburettors –
separation and joining

⚠ *Warning: Refer to the precautions given in Section 1 before proceeding*

Separation

1 The carburettors do not need to be separated for normal overhaul. If you need to separate them (to replace a carburettor body, for example), refer to the following procedure.
2 Remove the carburettors from the machine (see Section 6). Mark the body of each carburettor with its cylinder location to ensure that it is positioned correctly on reassembly.
3 Make a note of how the throttle return springs, linkage assembly and carburettor synchronisation springs are arranged to ensure that they are fitted correctly on reassembly **(see illustration)**. Also note the arrangement of the various hoses and their unions.
4 Push out the clips securing the choke linkage bar to the carburettors, noting how they fit, then remove the choke linkage bar from the plungers and the actuating slide, noting how it fits **(see illustration 7.13a)**.
5 Unscrew the nut on the end of the throughbolt which secures the carburettors on the inlet side just below the inlets themselves and withdraw the bolt **(see illustration)**. Unscrew the nut on the end of the throughbolt which passes through the choke actuating slide bar, then withdraw the bolt and remove the choke slide bar and the slide, noting which way round they fit and the location of the stop-clip on the end of the slide bar.
6 Note how the carburettors are joined together in the middle by two bars, and the locations of the fuel delivery and overflow hose unions, then carefully separate the

8.3 Throttle return spring, linkage assembly and synchronisation spring arrangement

8.5 Carburettor throughbolt nuts (arrows)

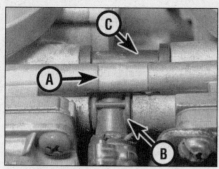

8.6 Carburettor joining bar (A), fuel delivery hose union (B), overflow hose union (C)

9.1a Install the air cut-off valve diaphragm . . .

9.1b . . . making sure the tab locates in its recess and the holes align (arrow) . . .

carburettors **(see illustration)**. Retrieve the synchronisation springs.

7 Remove the fuel hose union and its O-rings and the overflow hose union. Discard the O-rings as new ones must be used. Clean and check the condition of the filter inside the fuel hose union, and replace it if necessary.

Joining

8 Assembly is the reverse of the disassembly procedure, noting the following.

● Make sure the fuel hose union is fitted with new O-rings, and the fuel and overflow unions are correctly and securely inserted into the carburettors **(see illustration 8.6)**.

● Install the synchronisation spring after the carburettors are joined together. Make sure it is correctly and squarely seated **(see illustration 8.3)**.

● Make sure the choke slide bar and slide are fitted the correct way round, and that the tab in the middle of the choke linkage bar fits properly into its slot in the bottom of the slide, and that the slots in the arms locate correctly behind the nipple on the end of each choke plunger **(see illustrations 9.12b and 9.12c)**. Also make sure the linkage bar clips are correctly fitted with their ends located over the slide guide **(see illustration 9.12d)**.

● Check the operation of both the choke and throttle linkages ensuring that both operate smoothly and return quickly under spring pressure before installing the carburettors on the machine.

● Install the carburettors (see Section 6) and check carburettor synchronisation and idle speed (see Chapter 1).

9.1c . . . then fit the spring . . .

 9 Carburettors – reassembly and float height and fuel level check

⚠ **Warning: Refer to the precautions given in Section 1 before proceeding.**

Note: *When reassembling the carburettors, be sure to use the new O-rings, seals and other parts supplied in the rebuild kit. Do not overtighten the carburettor jets and screws as they are easily damaged.*

Note: *Ducati provide no specification for the float height, but check it using specially calibrated equipment set up in a bench-test with the carburettors removed from the bike. If the float height is suspected of being incorrect, take the assembled carburettors to a Ducati dealer for assessment and adjustment before installing them in the machine.*

9.1d . . . and the cover

1 Install the air cut-off valve diaphragm, making sure the tab locates in its recess and it is properly seated **(see illustrations)**. Fit the spring against the diaphragm, then install the cover and tighten its screws securely **(see illustrations)**.

2 Install the pilot screw (if removed) along with its spring and O-ring, turning it in until it seats lightly **(see illustration 7.11)**. Now, turn the screw out the number of turns previously recorded. Install the pilot screw plug.

3 Install the needle jet and the piston guide down through the top of the carburettor and into the body, making sure that the locating cut-out in the bottom of the needle is correctly positioned and that the piston guide is properly seated **(see illustration 7.10)**. Fit a new gasket to the base of the jet carrier, then install the carrier onto the needle jet **(see illustration)**. Fit the collar, then secure the carrier to the needle jet with the bolt **(see illustrations)**.

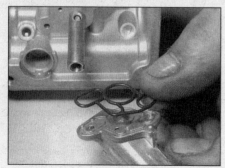

9.3a Fit a new gasket to the base of the carrier

9.3b Fit the collar over the bottom of the needle jet . . .

9.3c . . . and secure the carrier with its bolt

9.4 Install the pilot jet

9.5a Fit a new O-ring (arrow) to the base of the main jet and press it into the carrier

9.5b Fit the main jet retainer plate and secure it with the starter jet

9.8 Make sure the float chamber gasket (arrow) is properly seated in its groove

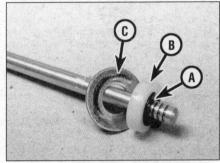
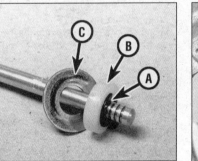

9.9 Jet needle clip (A), ring (B) and washer (C)

9.11a Make sure the needle retainer (A) is fitted into the bottom of the spring. Fit a new O-ring over the air passage (B)

4 Screw the pilot jet into the jet carrier (see illustration).

5 Fit a new O-ring to the base of the main jet and press the jet into the carrier (see illustration). Install the main jet retainer plate followed by the starter jet (see illustration).

6 Hook the float needle valve onto the float tab, then position the float assembly in the float carrier and install the pin, making sure it is secure (see illustration 7.6b). Carefully press the float assembly carrier onto the carburettor body using a new O-ring (see illustration 7.6a).

7 Ducati provide no specification for the float height, but check it using specially calibrated equipment set up in a bench-test with the carburettors removed from the bike. If the float height is suspected of being incorrect, take the carburettors, once assembled, to a

Ducati dealer for assessment and adjustment before installing them in the machine.

8 Fit a new gasket to the float chamber, making sure it is seated properly in its groove, and install the chamber on the carburettor (see illustration).

9 If removed, making sure the clip, ring and washer are correctly fitted onto the jet needle (see illustration). Install the jet needle into the diaphragm assembly (see illustration 7.4).

10 Insert the diaphragm assembly into the piston guide (see illustration 7.3b) and lightly push the piston down, ensuring the needle is correctly aligned with the needle jet. Press the diaphragm outer edge into its groove, making sure it is correctly seated. Check the diaphragm is not creased, and that the piston moves smoothly up and down in the guide.

11 Install the spring into the diaphragm assembly, making sure the jet needle retainer is fitted into the bottom of the spring (see illustration). Fit a new O-ring onto the air passage, then fit the top cover to the carburettor, and tighten its screws securely (see illustration).

12 Install the choke plunger into the carburettor body, making sure the clips locate correctly in their holes (see illustration). Fit the choke linkage bar onto the plungers and the actuating slide, making sure the tab in the middle of the linkage bar locates properly in its slot in the bottom of the slide, and that the slots in the arms locate behind the nipple on the end of each choke plunger (see illustrations).

9.11b Fit the top cover and tighten its screws securely

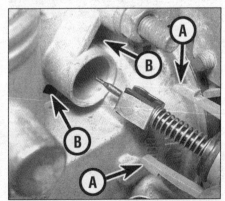

9.12a Fit the choke plunger assembly, making sure its clips (A) locate in their sockets (B)

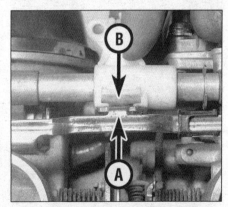

9.12b Make sure the tab on the linkage bar (A) fits into the slot in the slide (B)

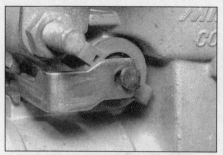

9.12c Make sure the slot in the end of each arm locates behind the nipple on each choke plunger

Secure the linkage bar in place with the clips, making sure their ends locate over the ends of the slide guide (see illustration).

13 Install the carburettors (see Section 6).

10 Throttle cables –
removal and installation

 Warning: Refer to the precautions given in Section 1 before proceeding.

Removal

1 Remove the fuel tank (see Section 2), and the air filter housing (see Section 13).
2 Slacken the locknuts securing the cable lower ends to the bracket, noting which cable fits on which arm of the bracket, and release each outer cable from the bracket (see illustration). Detach the inner cable nipples from the throttle cam. Mark each cable

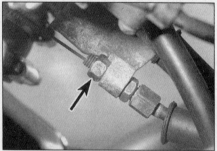

10.2 Slacken the locknut (arrowed) and remove the cable from its arm on the bracket

10.7a Fit the throttle pulley housing halves together . . .

9.12d Make sure the clips are correctly fitted with their ends located as shown (arrows)

according to its location.

3 Unscrew the two right-hand throttle pulley housing screws, and separate the two halves (see illustration). Detach the cable nipples from the pulley, then unscrew each cable retaining nut and remove each cable from the housing, noting how they fit (see illustration). Mark each cable to ensure it is connected correctly on installation.
4 Remove the cables from the machine noting the correct routing of each cable.

Installation

5 Install the cables making sure they are correctly routed. The cables must not interfere with any other component and should not be kinked or bent sharply.
6 Install the cables into the throttle pulley housing halves, making sure each cable is installed into its correct position, and tighten the retaining nuts securely. Lubricate the cable nipples with multi-purpose grease and install them into the throttle pulley.

10.3a Throttle grip pulley housing screws (arrows)

10.7b . . . and secure them with their screws

7 Fit the two halves of the housing onto the handlebar, making sure they are correctly meshed, and install the screws, tightening them securely (see illustrations).
8 Lubricate the lower cable nipples with multi-purpose grease and attach them to the carburettor throttle cam, making sure they are in their correct positions. Install the outer cable ends into the mounting bracket, making sure each cable is installed in its correct position, and tighten the locknuts securely (see illustration).
9 Operate the throttle to check that it opens and closes freely.
10 Check and adjust the throttle cable (see Chapter 1). Turn the handlebars back and forth to make sure the cable doesn't cause the steering to bind.
11 Install the air filter housing (Section 13), and the fuel tank (see Section 2).
12 Start the engine and check that the idle speed does not rise as the handlebars are turned. If it does, the throttle cable is routed incorrectly. Correct the problem before riding the motorcycle.

11 Choke cable –
removal and installation

Removal

M600 to frame VIN 006829 and M900 to frame VIN 009914

1 Remove the fuel tank (see Section 2), and the air filter housing (see Section 13).
2 Slacken the choke cable clamp screw on the top of the carburettor assembly, then

10.3b Detach the cable nipples (arrows) from their sockets in the pulley

10.8 Install the cable into the mounting bracket

11.3 The choke cable mount fits onto the steering stem nut and hooks under the handlebars

11.6a Choke cable clamp screw (arrow)

11.6b Detach the nipple from its socket in the slide

release the cable from the clamp. Detach the cable end from the actuating slide.
3 Unscrew the handlebar clamp bolts and lift the handlebars enough to release the choke knob and its support from the top yoke, noting how it fits **(see illustration)**. Withdraw the cable and knob from the support.
4 Remove the cable from the machine noting its correct routing.

All other models

5 Remove the fuel tank (see Section 2), and the air filter housing (see Section 13).
6 Slacken the choke cable clamp screw on the top of the carburettor assembly, then release the cable from the clamp **(see illustration)**. Detach the cable end from the actuating slide **(see illustration)**.
7 Note how the choke lever locates between the left-hand handlebar switch housing and the clutch master cylinder bracket **(see illustration)**, then unscrew the two switch housing screws and separate the two halves. Draw the separator away from the choke lever **(see illustration)**. Detach the cable nipple from the choke lever, then remove the cable noting how it locates in the guide **(see illustration)**.
8 Remove the cable from the machine noting its correct routing.

Installation

M600 to VIN 006829 and M900 to frame VIN 009914

9 Install the cable making sure it is correctly routed. The cable must not interfere with any other component and should not be kinked or bent sharply.
10 Install the choke knob and cable into its support, then install the assembly onto the top yoke. Mount the handlebars onto the top yoke, making sure they are central, and tighten their bolts to the torque setting specified at the beginning of the Chapter.
11 Lubricate the lower cable end nipple with multi-purpose grease. Attach the nipple to the actuating slide, then secure the outer cable end in its clamp and tighten the screw securely.
12 Check the operation of the choke cable as described in Chapter 1.
13 Install the air filter housing (Section 13), and the fuel tank (see Section 2).

All other models

14 Install the cable making sure it is correctly routed. The cable must not interfere with any other component and should not be kinked or bent sharply.
15 Lubricate the upper cable end nipple with multi-purpose grease. Install the cable in the choke lever housing and attach the nipple to the choke lever **(see illustration 11.7c)**. Tighten the cable retaining nut securely. Fit the two halves of the housing together and secure them with the screw **(see illustration 11.7b)**. Fit the switch housing onto the handlebars, making sure the pin in the lower half of the housing locates in the hole in the underside of the handlebar and that the choke lever housing is correctly positioned between the switch housing and the clutch master cylinder bracket **(see illustration 11.7a)**. Install the screws, tightening them securely.
16 Lubricate the lower cable end nipple with

multi-purpose grease. Attach the nipple to the actuating slide **(see illustration 11.6b)**, then secure the outer cable end in its clamp and tighten the screw securely **(see illustration)**.
17 Check the operation of the choke cable as described in Chapter 1.
18 Install the air filter housing (Section 13), and the fuel tank (see Section 2).

12 Vacuum fuel pump (Monster models) – check, removal and installation

Check

1 A vacuum-operated fuel pump is fitted to all Monsters. It is operated by the vacuum in the inlet duct. There is no specified method of checking the pump operation. If it is believed that insufficient fuel is being delivered to the

11.7a Note how the choke lever housing is located

11.7b Draw the separator away from the lever to expose the cable nipple

11.7c Pull the nipple out of its socket and remove the cable from its guide

11.16 Fit the cable outer end into the clamp and tighten the screw securely

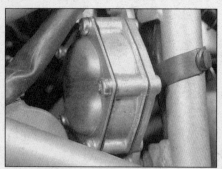

12.3 The vacuum fuel pump is secured to the frame by two bolts

13.3 Disconnect the ignition coil assembly wiring connector

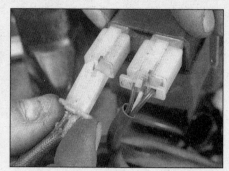

13.4 Disconnect the 2-pin wiring connector from each ignition control unit

carburettors, the pump should be taken to a Ducati dealer for assessment. There is no method of repairing the pump, nor are any individual components available for it. If the pump is faulty it must be replaced.

Removal

2 Make sure the fuel tap is closed. Release the clamps securing the fuel inlet hose, fuel outlet hose and vacuum hose to the pump, then detach the hoses, noting which fits where.
3 Unscrew the bolts securing the pump to the frame on the right-hand side of the machine, then remove the pump **(see illustration)**.

Installation

4 Installation is the reverse of removal. Make sure that all the hoses are correctly connected and secured by their clamps, and that there are no leaks when the engine is running.

13 Air filter housing – removal and installation

Removal

1 Remove the fuel tank (see Section 2).
2 Remove the battery (see Chapter 8).
3 Disconnect the ignition coil assembly wiring connector located on the right-hand side of the air filter housing **(see illustration)**.
4 Disconnect the 2-pin connector from the left-hand side of each ignition control unit **(see illustration)**.
5 Disconnect the HT leads from the spark plugs, and feed the leads through to the coils, noting their routing. Note which lead fits to which spark plug.
6 Unscrew the two bolts securing the coil and

ignition control unit assembly mounting bracket to the back of the air filter housing, then remove the assembly, noting the routing of the leads and wiring **(see illustration)**.
7 Remove the starter relay from its mounting bracket on the underside of the battery box **(see illustration)**. There is no need to disconnect its wiring or remove it from its rubber sleeve. On Monster models, displace the charging circuit fuseholder from the right-hand side of the housing **(see illustrations)**.
8 Pull the crankcase breather system hose from the left-hand side of the air filter housing **(see illustration)**.
9 Refer to Chapter 1 and remove the air filter housing lid and element.
10 Unscrew the two bolts securing the fuel tank catch bracket to the frame in front of the air filter housing and remove the bracket, noting how it fits **(see illustration)**.

13.6 The mounting bracket is secured by two bolts (arrows)

13.7a Remove the starter relay from its bracket

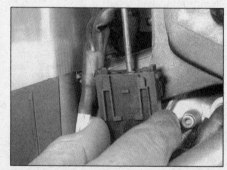

13.7b On Monster models, depress the tab on the main fuse holder . . .

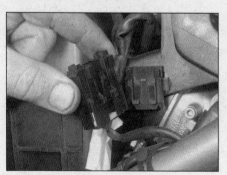

13.7c . . . and disconnect the holder from the side of the air filter housing

13.8 Remove the crankcase breather hose from the housing

13.10 Unscrew the fuel tank catch bracket mounting bolts (arrows)

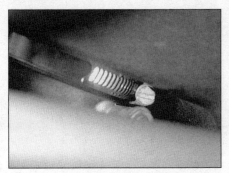

13.11 Slacken the clamp screws securing the housing to the carburettors

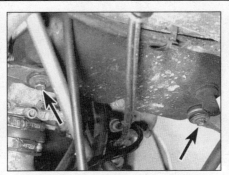

13.12a Unscrew the bolt(s) (arrows - SS model shown) on the underside at the front . . .

13.12b . . . and the bolts (arrows) on each side of the battery casing

11 Slacken the clamp screws on the underside of the air filter housing which secure the housing to the carburettor inlet ducts **(see illustration)**.

12 Unscrew the bolt(s) on the underside of the front of the housing, and the two bolts on either side of the battery box at the rear of the housing, noting the arrangement of the collars and rubber grommets. Carefully lift the housing up off the carburettors, noting how it fits **(see illustrations)**.

Installation

13 Installation is the reverse of removal. Make sure the wiring connectors and spark plug leads are securely and correctly connected. The left-hand coil HT lead is for the horizontal cylinder and the right-hand coil HT lead is for the vertical cylinder.

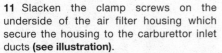

14 Exhaust system – removal and installation

⚠️ *Warning: If the engine has been running the exhaust system will be very hot. Allow the system to cool before carrying out any work.*

Silencers

Removal

1 Where fitted slacken the silencer-to-downpipe clamp bolt **(see illustration)**.
2 Unscrew and remove the silencer mounting nut and bolt, noting the arrangement of the mounting rubbers, collar(s), bush and washer, where fitted according to model and year, then carefully withdraw the silencer from the

downpipe assembly **(see illustrations)**.

Installation

3 Installation is the reverse of removal. Make sure the mounting rubbers are in good condition and correctly installed. Tighten the silencer mounting bolt securely.

Complete system

Removal

4 Where fitted remove the fairing lower panels (see Chapter 7).
5 Remove the silencers (see above).
6 Slacken the clamp securing the rear cylinder downpipe to the front cylinder downpipe assembly **(see illustration)**. On 2002-on Monster models unscrew the front cylinder downpipe assembly mounting bolt on each side **(see illustration)**.

14.1 Slacken the silencer clamp (arrowed)

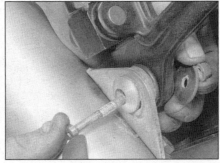

14.2a Remove the silencer mounting bolt (900SS shown) . . .

14.2b . . . and remove the silencer

14.2c Silencer mounting components - 2002-on Monsters

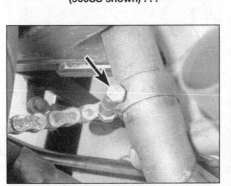

14.6a Slacken the rear cylinder downpipe clamp bolt (arrow)

14.6b Unscrew the bolt (arrowed) on each side

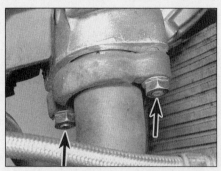

14.7 Front cylinder downpipe flange nuts (arrows)

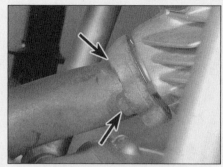

14.8 Rear cylinder downpipe flange nuts (arrows)

14.10 Fit a new gasket into each port

14.11a Fit the downpipe . . .

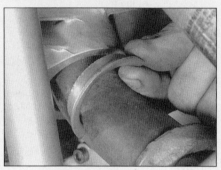

14.11b . . . the half-rings . . .

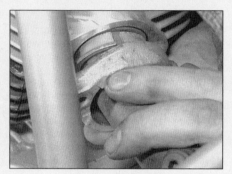

14.11c . . . the flange . . .

7 Unscrew the front downpipe flange retaining nuts from the cylinder head studs. Slide the flange off the studs and on all except 2002-on Monster models remove the half-rings, then carefully remove the front downpipe assembly **(see illustration)**. Note the collars fitted in the mounting bush on 2002-on Monster models **(see illustration 14.12a)**.

8 Unscrew the rear downpipe flange retaining nuts from the cylinder head studs **(see illustration)**. Slide the flange off the studs and remove the half-rings, then carefully remove the pipe.

9 Remove the gasket from each cylinder head and discard them as new ones must be fitted.

Installation

10 Fit a new gasket into each of the cylinder head ports with the flanged side inwards **(see illustration)**. Apply a smear of grease to the gaskets to keep them in place whilst fitting the downpipes if necessary.

11 Install the rear cylinder downpipe and support it in position, then on all except 2002-on Monsters fit the half-rings, and slide the flange onto the cylinder head studs **(see illustrations)**. Tighten the flange nuts to the torque setting specified at the beginning of the Chapter.

12 On 2002-on Monster models make sure the bush in the mounting bracket is in good condition, and fit the collar in each side **(see illustration)**. Install the front downpipe assembly, making sure the middle rear section fits correctly onto the rear cylinder downpipe **(see illustration)**. Support the assembly and on all except 2002-on Monsters fit the half-rings, then slide the flange onto the cylinder head studs **(see illustrations 14.11a, b, c and d)**. Tighten the flange nuts to the specified torque setting. Also tighten the clamp securing the rear cylinder downpipe to the front cylinder downpipe assembly.

13 Install the silencers (see above).

14 Run the engine and check the system for leaks.

15 Where necessary install the fairing panels (see Chapter 7).

14.11d . . . and secure them with the flange nuts

14.12a Fit the collar into each side of the bush

14.12b The front downpipe assembly fits over the rear cylinder downpipe

Chapter 3B
Fuel and exhaust systems – injection models

Contents

Air filter – renewal ....see Chapter 1
Air filter housing – removal and installation 5
Exhaust system – removal and installation ....see Chapter 3A
Fast idle cable – removal and installation 11
Fuel filter – removal and installation ....see Chapter 1
Fuel injection system – general information 6
Fuel injection system – testing and adjustment 7
Fuel injection system components – removal, check and installation .. 8
Fuel level warning light sensor – check and renewal ....see Chapter 8
Fuel pump – check, removal and installation 4

Fuel system – check ....see Chapter 1
Fuel tank – cleaning and repair 3
Fuel tank – removal and installation 2
General information and precautions 1
Idle speed – check ....see Chapter 1
Throttle body assembly – removal and installation 9
Throttle cable – check and adjustment ....see Chapter 1
Throttle cable – removal and installation 10
Throttle body synchronisation ....see Chapter 1

Degrees of difficulty

Easy, suitable for novice with little experience		Fairly easy, suitable for beginner with some experience		Fairly difficult, suitable for competent DIY mechanic		Difficult, suitable for experienced DIY mechanic		Very difficult, suitable for expert DIY or professional	

Specifications

Fuel

Grade	Unleaded, minimum 95 RON (Research Octane Number)

Fuel tank capacity (inclusive reserve capacity)

M620i.e.	14 litres (3.5 litres)
M750/900i.e.	16.5 litres (3.5 litres)
620i.e. Sport	16 litres (4.0 litres)
1998 to 2001 900i.e. Supersport and Sport models	18 litres (4.0 litres)
1998 to 2002 750i.e. and 2002 900 i.e. Supersport and Sport models .	16 litres (4.0 litres)

Fuel injection system data

System type

750/900i.e. Supersport and Sport models	Marelli IAW 1.5 engine management system with one injector per cylinder
620i.e. Sport and all Monster models	Marelli IAW 5.9M engine management system with one injector per cylinder
Fuel system operating pressure	3 bar
Idle speed	see Chapter 1
Timing sensor air gap	0.6 to 0.8 mm

Torque settings

Fuel pump mounting bolts (plastic tank)	10 Nm

1 General information and precautions

General information

The fuel system consists of the fuel tank, fuel pump and filter, pressure regulator, feed and return hoses and the throttle body assembly. The fuel pump supplies fuel to the injectors in the throttle body assembly, which inject the fuel into the intake tracts. The injectors are operated by the electronic control unit (ECU) using the information obtained from the various sensors it monitors (refer to Section 6 for information on the fuel injection system operation).

Precautions

⚠️ *Warning: Petrol (gasoline) is extremely flammable, so take extra precautions when you work on any part of the fuel system. Don't smoke or allow open flames or bare light bulbs near the work area, and don't work in a garage where a natural gas-type appliance is present. If you spill any fuel on your skin, rinse it off immediately with soap and water. When you perform any kind of work on the fuel system, wear safety glasses and have a fire extinguisher suitable for a class B type fire (flammable liquids) on hand.*

Residual pressure will remain in the fuel feed hoses long after the motorcycle was last used. Bear this in mind before disconnecting any fuel line.

It is vital that dirt or debris is not allowed to enter the fuel tank, the fuel hoses or the injectors whilst the hoses are disconnected. Any foreign matter in the fuel system components could result in injector damage/malfunction.

Ensure the ignition is switched off before disconnecting/reconnecting any fuel injection system wiring connector. If a connector is disconnected/reconnected with the ignition switched on, the electronic control unit (ECU) may be damaged.

Always perform service procedures in a well-ventilated area to prevent a build-up of fumes.

Never work in a building containing a gas appliance with a pilot light, or any other form of naked flame. Ensure that there are no naked light bulbs or any sources of flame or sparks nearby.

Do not smoke (or allow anyone else to smoke) while in the vicinity of petrol (gasoline) or of components containing it. Remember the possible presence of vapour from these sources and move well clear before smoking.

Check all electrical equipment belonging to the house, garage or workshop where work is being undertaken (see the Safety first! section of this manual). Remember that certain electrical appliances such as drills, cutters etc. create sparks in the normal course of operation and must not be used near petrol (gasoline) or any component containing it. Again, remember the possible presence of fumes before using electrical equipment.

Always mop up any spilt fuel and safely dispose of the rag used.

Any stored fuel that is drained off during servicing work must be kept in sealed containers that are suitable for holding petrol (gasoline), and clearly marked as such; the containers themselves should be kept in a safe place. Note that this last point applies equally to the fuel tank if it is removed from the machine; also remember to keep its filler cap closed at all times.

Read the Safety first! section of this manual carefully before starting work.

2 Fuel tank – removal and installation

⚠️ *Warning: Refer to the precautions given in Section 1 before starting work.*

Removal

1 Ensure the ignition is switched off. Make sure the fuel cap is securely closed. Remove the seat (see Chapter 7). Place some rags across the rear sub-frame.
2 Release the catch or rubber strap (according to model) securing the front of the fuel tank to the frame **(see illustrations)**.
3 Lift the front of the fuel tank pivot it all the way back until it rests on the rags on the rear sub-frame **(see illustration)**. Note that on Sport and Supersport models a support is fitted on the underside of the tank that allows it to be rested in a semi-raised position, but do not disconnect the fuel hoses while in this position unless the level of fuel is below the unions **(see illustration)**.
4 Disconnect the fuel pump assembly wiring connector **(see illustration)**.
5 Disconnect the fuel tank breather/drain hose from the Y-shaped joint, leaving the

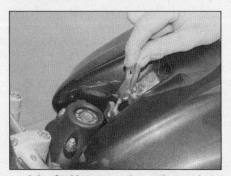
2.2a On Monsters release the catch securing the front of the tank . . .

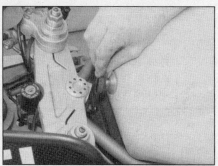
2.2b . . . on Sport and Supersport models release the rubber strap

2.3a Lay the tank back on the rear sub-frame

2.3b S and SS models have a support that locates in the frame cross-piece

2.4 Disconnect the wiring connector . . .

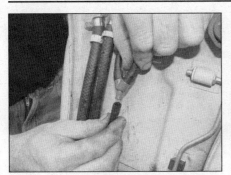

2.5 . . . and detach the breather/drain hose at the joint piece

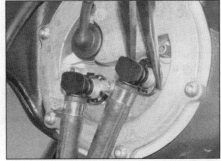

2.6 Release the connectors and detach them from the unions

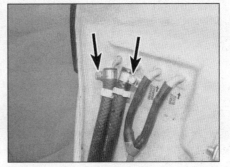

2.7 Slacken the clamp screws (arrowed) to release the hoses

individual hoses attached to the tank **(see illustration)**.

6 On models with a plastic fuel tank note the correct fitted positions of the fuel feed and return hoses. The fuel pump mounting plate outlet unions are marked 'IN' and 'OUT', so tag the hoses in a similar way to avoid confusion on installation. Release the fuel feed and return hose self-seal connectors and detach them from the unions on the tank **(see illustration)**.

All other models

7 On all other models note the correct fitted positions of the fuel feed and return hoses. The hoses should be fitted with colour-coded end-fittings; the feed hose may also have an identification mark M and the return hose an identification mark R **(see illustration)**. There should also be a label to show the correct fitting of the hoses. If the end-fittings/collars/

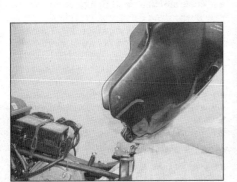

2.8a Remove the split pin . . .

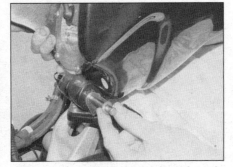

2.8b . . . then withdraw the pivot pin and remove the tank

label are not present, make identification markings to avoid confusion on installation. Position a wad of rag around the fuel hose unions, to catch any residual fuel (pressure will still be present in the fuel hoses). Use clamps or plugs on the hoses if available. Slacken the retaining clips and carefully disconnect the hoses from the fuel tank unions, whilst being prepared for fuel spillage. Either plug the fuel tank unions to prevent fuel loss or store the tank upside-down on some soft cloth once removed.

8 Withdraw the split pin from the end of the tank pivot pin **(see illustration)**. Withdraw the pivot pin then remove the tank **(see illustration)**. Note the mounting rubbers fitted with the tank.

Caution: Take care not to damage the paintwork.

9 Inspect the tank mounting rubbers for signs

of damage or deterioration and renew them if necessary. On models with quick-release fuel hoses, inspect the end fitting sealing rings for signs of damage or deterioration and renew them if necessary.

Installation

10 Prior to installation, check that the tank rear mounting bracket is securely fitted.

11 Ensure the tank mounting rubbers are correctly installed.

12 Manoeuvre the tank onto the rear sub-frame, laying it on some rag, and positioning the rear pivot in the bracket **(see illustration)**. Slide the pivot pin through and fit the split pin **(see illustrations 2.8b and a)**.

13 Reconnect the fuel hoses, using the identification markings to ensure they are correctly reconnected (see Step 6 or 7 according to model). On models with quick-release end fittings, ensure each end fitting sealing ring is in good condition and secure the hoses in position by pushing them fully in until they 'click' into position **(see illustration)**. On models without quick-release fittings, push the hoses onto their unions then secure them in position with the retaining clips **(see illustration 2.7)**.

14 Reconnect the fuel tank wiring connector then reconnect the breather/drain hose to the T-piece **(see illustrations 2.5 and 2.4)**.

15 Pivot the tank down onto the frame and secure it at the front **(see illustration 2.3a or b)**.

16 Start the engine and check that there is no sign of fuel leakage. If all is well, install the seat (see Chapter 7).

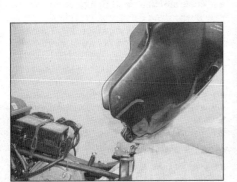

2.12 Align the pivot bore with the bracket holes

2.13 Push the connectors onto the unions until they click into place

3 Fuel tank – cleaning and repair

1 All repairs to the fuel tank should be carried out by a professional who has experience in this critical and potentially dangerous work. Even after cleaning and flushing of the fuel system, explosive fumes can remain and ignite during repair of the tank.

2 If the fuel tank is removed from the bike, it should not be placed in an area where sparks or open flames could ignite the fumes coming

out of the tank. Be especially careful inside garages where a natural gas-type appliance is located, because the pilot light could cause an explosion.

4 Fuel pump – check, removal and installation

 Warning: Refer to the precautions given in Section 1 before starting work.

Fuel pump circuit check

1 The fuel pump is located inside the fuel tank. The fuel pump runs for a few seconds when the ignition is switched ON, to pressurise the fuel system, and then cuts out until the engine is started. If the pump is thought to be faulty, first check the fuses (see Chapter 8). If they are in good condition proceed as follows.

2 Free the fuel tank from the frame (see Steps 1 to 3 of Section 2) and support it so access can be gained to the fuel tank wiring connector.

3 Ensure the ignition is switched off then disconnect the fuel tank wiring connector (see illustration 2.4) and connect the positive (+ve) lead of a voltmeter to the brown/white terminal of the connector and the negative (–ve) lead to the black terminal of the connector. Switch on the ignition switch whilst noting the reading obtained on the meter.

4 If battery voltage is present for a few seconds, the fuel pump circuit is operating correctly and the fuel pump is probably faulty.

5 If no reading is obtained, check the fuel pump circuit wiring for continuity and make sure all the connectors are free from corrosion and are securely connected. Repair/replace the wiring as necessary and clean the connectors using electrical contact cleaner. If this fails to reveal the fault, check the following components.
● Engine stop switch (see Chapter 8).
● Engine management system relays (see Section 8).
● Electronic control unit (ECU) (see Section 8).

Fuel pump check

Note: *A suitable automotive-type fuel pressure gauge will be required to check the fuel pump operating pressure.*

6 Remove the fuel pump assembly from the tank (see below). Check the pump wiring for loose or damaged terminals and check the wiring between the fuel tank connector and pump for continuity.

7 If the wiring is fine, connect a fully charged 12 volt battery to the pump wiring terminals of the connector using two auxiliary wires; connect the positive (+ve) terminal of the battery to the brown/white connector terminal and the battery negative (-ve) terminal to the black connector terminal. The pump should operate. If not, it is faulty and must be renewed.

8 If the pump operates but is thought to be

delivering an insufficient amount of fuel, first check the fuel filter is not blocked and the pipes linking the pump, filter and separator chamber are not kinked, damaged or blocked.

9 If the equipment is available, the operating pressure of the pump can be checked with the pump in place by connecting the gauge in the fuel feed line using suitable adapters and connectors (see Specifications).

Removal

Note: *Try to coincide pump removal with the tank as empty as possible. Remove and drain the tank if required.*

Models with plastic tank

10 Remove the fuel tank (see Section 2) and support it upside-down on some soft rag.

11 With the fuel tank supported upside-down, unscrew the fuel pump mounting plate retaining bolts **(see illustration)**.

12 Note the correct fitted location of the plate in relation to the tank then ease the plate out of position **(see illustration)**. Remove the sealing ring from the mounting plate and discard it **(see illustration 4.17)**; a new one must be used on installation.

Caution: Take care not to damage the paintwork.

13 Remove the filter (see Chapter 1) and the fuel level sensor if required (see Chapter 8) – these and the hoses, clips and sealing ring are the only components of the pump assembly that are available separately.

Models with metal tank

14 The fuel pump is mounted inside the fuel tank and is connected via a short piece of hose to the fuel filter. Follow the procedure detailed in Chapter 1, Section 7 – fuel filter replacement, for removal of the fuel pump as it is removed as an assembly with the filter.

Installation

Models with plastic tank

15 If removed, install the filter, using a new one if necessary (see Chapter 1), and the level sensor (see Chapter 8).

16 Check all the hoses and wiring are undamaged and are securely connected.

17 Ensure the mounting plate and tank surfaces are clean and dry, then smear the new sealing ring with grease and fit it into the groove in the pump flange **(see illustration)**.

18 Install the mounting plate assembly into the fuel tank, ensuring its 'FRONT' marking and arrow are towards the front of the tank, and aligning the bolt holes (see illustration).

19 Install the bolts and tighten them evenly and in a criss-cross sequence to the specified torque.

20 Install the fuel tank (see Section 2).

Models with metal tank

21 Installation is a reverse of the removal procedure (see Chapter 1, Section 7 – fuel filter replacement). Make sure the fuel hoses are correctly and securely fitted to the pump.

4.11 Unscrew the bolts (arrowed) . . .

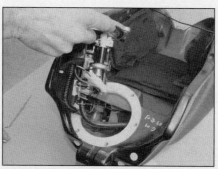

4.12 . . . and carefully withdraw the pump assembly

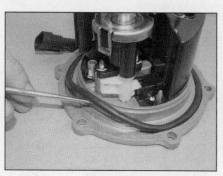

4.17 Fit a new rubber sealing ring into the groove

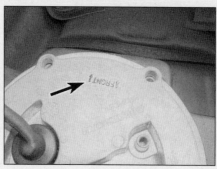

4.18 Make sure the FRONT mark and its arrow are at the front

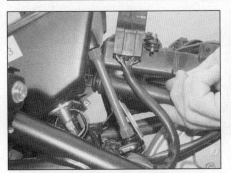

5.2a Carefully draw the breather hose out of the back of the housing . . .

5.2b . . . and the drain hose out of the front

5.3a Slacken the clamp screw (arrowed) on each duct . . .

5.3b . . . and on 2003-on models unscrew the front mounting bolt and remove the collar

5.5a Free the pegs from the grommets (arrow)

5.5b Unscrew and remove the rear peg studs

5 Air filter housing – removal and installation

Removal

M620i.e., 2002 M750/900i.e. models

1 Remove the fuel tank (see Section 2), and the air filter (see Chapter 1).
2 Pull the crankcase breather hose out of the back of the housing **(see illustrations)**.
3 Slacken the clamp screws securing the housing to the intake ducts **(see illustration)**. On 2003-on 620 models unscrew the bolt securing the front of the housing and remove the collar **(see illustration)**.
4 Pull the spark plug cap off the front cylinder.
5 Carefully lift the back of the housing to free the two pegs from their grommets, then on 2002 models lift the front to free its peg **(see illustration)**. Unscrew the rear peg studs from the housing **(see illustration)**.
6 Disconnect the front cylinder coil primary wiring connectors, then remove the housing, noting the routing of the spark plug lead **(see illustrations)**.

2000 and 2001 M900i.e., all Supersport/Sport models

7 Remove the fairing side panels (see Chapter 7). Remove the fuel tank (see Section 2), and the air filter (see Chapter 1).
8 On models with the fusebox on the end of the battery box, displace the fusebox. Remove the battery (see Chapter 8).
9 Disconnect the main loom wiring connector, the horn wiring connectors, the front cylinder injector connector, the oil temperature sensor wiring connector and the alternator wiring connector on the right-hand side of the bike **(see illustration)**. Release the wiring from its ties. Displace the relays from the electronic control unit (ECU) mounting plate, then undo the screws securing the plate and

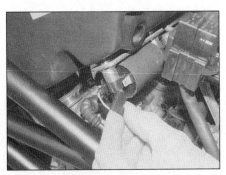

5.6a Disconnect the coil wiring connectors . . .

5.6b . . . and remove the housing

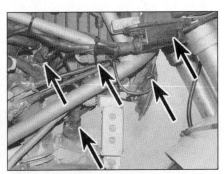

5.9a Disconnect the wiring connectors (arrowed)

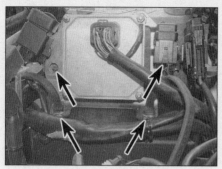

5.9b Undo the screws (arrowed) . . .

5.9c . . . and displace the electrical component mounting plate

5.11 Unscrew the bolts and displace the cooler

displace it from the back of the air filter housing – there is no need to disconnect any of the individual component wiring connectors **(see illustrations)**.

10 On 620 Sport models refer to Section 8 and remove the electronic control unit (ECU) and its mount and relays.

11 On 750 and 900 models unscrew the oil cooler mounting bolts and displace the cooler forwards **(see illustration)**.

12 Pull the crankcase breather system hose from the left-hand side of the air filter housing and the drain hose from the front **(see illustrations)**.

13 Slacken the clamp screws which secure the housing ducts to the throttle bodies ducts **(see illustration)**.

14 Unscrew the bolt(s) on the underside of the front of the housing, and the two bolts in the battery box at the rear of the housing, noting which bolt fits where, what they secure on the underside of the housing, and the arrangement of the collars and rubber grommets. Make sure all wiring and hoses are clear, then carefully lift the housing up off the throttle bodies, noting how it fits **(see illustrations)**.

Installation

M620i.e., 2002 M750/900i.e. models

15 Installation is the reverse of removal. Make sure the front cylinder spark plug lead is correctly routed. On Sport and Supersport models make sure the clips for the cover are upright when installing the housing otherwise (on some models) they don't clear the frame. Use the ring on the end of the crankcase breather hose to pull it into place, but take care not to break it – smear the hose end with oil and push it from the back as well **(see illustration)**.

2000 and 2001 M900i.e., all Supersport/Sport models

16 Installation is the reverse of removal.

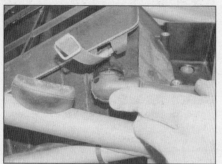

5.12a Detach the breather hose . . .

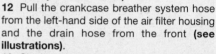

5.12b . . . and the drain hose

5.13 Slacken the clamp screw (arrowed) on each duct

5.14a Unscrew the front mounting bolts . . .

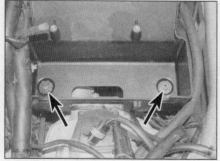

5.14b . . . and the rear mounting bolts (arrowed) . . .

5.14c . . . and remove the housing

5.15 Use the ring to pull the hose through

6 Fuel injection system – general information

1 All models are equipped with a Marelli engine management system which operates the fuel injection and ignition systems on the motorcycle. There are two different versions of the system used in the model range (see Specifications). The fuel injection side of the system functions as follows; refer to Chapter 4 for information on the ignition system.
2 The fuel pump and filter are contained in the fuel tank. On 2004-on M620i.e. models the pressure regulator is incorporated in the pump assembly. On all other models the pressure regulator is in the fuel return line from the throttle body assembly. The pump supplies fuel to the injectors in the throttle bodies, via the filter and feed hose. Excess fuel is returned to the tank via the return hose. The pressure regulator keeps the pressure in the fuel hoses constant by governing the flow of fuel back into the tank.
3 All models have a single injector per cylinder.
4 The electronic control unit (ECU) monitors signals from the following sensors:
● Throttle position sensor – informs the ECU of the throttle position, and the rate of throttle opening or closing.
● Atmospheric pressure sensor – informs the ECU of the atmospheric pressure the motorcycle is operating in.
● Air temperature sensor – informs the ECU of the ambient air temperature.
● Oil temperature sensor – informs the engine of oil temperature, which indicates engine general temperature.
● Timing sensor – informs the ECU of engine speed and crankshaft position.
5 All the above information is analysed by the ECU and based on these signals it determines the appropriate ignition and fuelling requirements for the engine. The ECU controls the fuel injector by varying its pulse width – the length of time the injector is held open – to provide a richer or weaker mixture. The mixture is constantly varied by the ECU, to provide the best setting for starting, warm-up, idle, cruising, and acceleration. The injection system is fully sequential, with each injector receiving its own operating signal from the ECU. The settings (or maps) for injection/ignition timing are stored on an EPROM which is fitted inside the ECU.
6 If there is an abnormality in any of the readings obtained from any sensor, the ECU enters its back-up mode. In this event, the ECU ignores the abnormal sensor signal, and assumes a pre-programmed value which will allow the engine to continue running (albeit at reduced efficiency). If an engine management system fault is suspected, the bike should be taken to a Ducati dealer at the earliest opportunity. A complete test of the engine management system can then be carried out,

using the Mathesis diagnostic tester which is simply plugged into the system's diagnostic connector (located underneath the seat cowling).

7 Fuel injection system – testing and adjustment

Testing

1 If a fault occurs in the system, first ensure that all the system wiring connectors are securely connected and free of corrosion. Then ensure that the fault is not due to poor maintenance – i.e. check that the air filter element is clean, that the spark plugs are in good condition and correctly gapped, that the valve clearances are correctly adjusted and the cylinder compression pressures are correct (refer to Chapter 1).
2 If these checks fail to reveal the cause of the problem, the motorcycle should be taken to a Ducati dealer for checking. They will have access to the Mathesis diagnostic tester which can be plugged into the system. The diagnostic tester will locate the fault quickly and simply. Where simple checks can be made, information is given in Section 8. The test data provided by Ducati does not enable home diagnosis.

Adjustment

3 Adjustment of CO content and injector opening timing is only possible via the Mathesis tester.

8 Fuel injection system components – removal, check and installation

Caution: Ensure the ignition is switched OFF before disconnecting and reconnecting any fuel injection system wiring connector. If a connector is disturbed with the ignition switched ON the electronic control unit (ECU) may be damaged.
Note: *To avoid unnecessary expense, if a check identifies a component as being faulty,*

8.4a Disconnect the wiring connector from the injector – Monster type shown

have your findings confirmed by a Ducati dealer before condemning the component concerned. Bear in mind that most electrical parts cannot be exchanged once purchased.

Fuel injectors

⚠️ *Warning: Refer to the precautions given in Section 1 before starting work.*
Note: *If the bike has been stored for a long period of time, Ducati recommend that a fuel additive (Tunap 231 – available from your Ducati dealer) is added to the fuel. The additive will break down any varnish or gum deposits on the injectors which may have built-up during the storage period.*

Check

1 If the engine runs, start it and allow it to idle. Check the operation of each injector using a stethoscope or sounding rod; an injector will emit a 'clicking' noise when functioning. If any injector is silent, either the injector or its wiring harness is faulty.
2 If the engine does not run, disconnect the wiring connector from each injector (see Step 4). Connect an ohmmeter across the terminals of each injector and measure its resistance. Compare the readings obtained. Ducati do not give a figure, but if each injector is different one of them may be faulty.

Removal

3 Remove the air filter housing (see Section 5) and if required (though not necessary) the throttle body assembly (see Section 9).
4 Disconnect the injector wiring connector (see illustrations). If both injectors are being removed, note the correct fitted location of each wiring connector before you disconnect them. If necessary, to avoid confusion on installation, label the connectors for identification; it is essential each one is connected to its original injector.
5 Release the hose clamps and detach the hoses from the injector (see illustration 8.4b). Note that new clamps should be used on installation.
6 Undo the retaining screw(s) and remove the injector, and on Supersport models its seat,

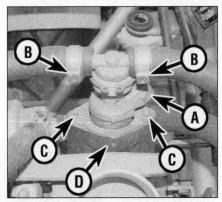

8.4b Injector wiring connector (A), hose clamps (B), mounting screws (C), and seat (D) – Supersport type

8.6a Undo the screw(s) . . .

8.6b . . . and remove the injector – Monster 620 shown

from the throttle body complete with its seals **(see illustrations)**. Handle the seals carefully; you may find that new seals are not available separately from the injectors, so if they are damaged a new injector may be necessary.

Installation

7 Ensure both seals are correctly located and lubricate them with a smear of grease.
8 Ease the injector, on Supersport models with its seat, into position in the throttle body, taking care not to damage the seals.
9 Refit the screws and tighten them. Connect the hoses and secure them using new clamps.
10 Reconnect the wiring connector to the injector. If both injectors were removed, use the marks made on removal to ensure the connectors are reconnected to the correct injector.
Caution: If the injector wiring connectors are incorrectly connected, the engine will not run.
11 Install the throttle body assembly if removed and the air filter housing.

Fuel pressure regulator

 Warning: Refer to the precautions given in Section 1 before starting work.

Check

12 If a fuel pressure gauge is available, the operation of the pressure regulator can be checked. Using a length of fuel hose and adapter, connect the gauge into the fuel hose between the tank and the throttle body then start the engine and allow it to idle. Note the pressure present in the fuel system then turn

the engine off. Compare the reading obtained to that given in the Specifications.
13 If the fuel pressure is higher than specified, check for blocked or restricted fuel hoses and passages. If all the hoses and passages are clear, the fuel pressure regulator must be faulty (check the regulator vent union is clear and unblocked before condemning it).
14 If the fuel pressure is lower than specified, first check for signs of damaged fuel hoses, including those inside the fuel tank, or a blocked fuel filter. If the hoses and filter are all in good condition, the fuel pump or pressure regulator must be faulty. Check the fuel pump as described in Section 4. If the pump performs as expected the fuel pressure regulator must be faulty.

Removal

15 On Monster models with a plastic fuel tank the pressure regulator is an integral part of the fuel pump and is not available separately. If it is faulty a new pump assembly must be installed (see Section 4).
16 On all other models the pressure regulator is fitted to the fuel pump mounting plate **(see illustration)**. Remove the air filter housing for access (see Section 5) and if required (though not necessary) the throttle body assembly (see Section 9). Fit some hose clamps to the fuel hose on each side of the regulator.
17 Note the correct fitted location of the pressure regulator vent union then, using circlip pliers, extract the regulator circlip from the mounting plate.
18 Ease the pressure regulator out from the

mounting plate along with its seals. The seals must both be renewed.

Installation

19 Remove the original seals from the pressure regulator and install the new ones. Ensure both seals are correctly located and lubricate them with a smear of engine oil to aid installation.
20 Ease the pressure regulator into position in the throttle body, taking care not to damage the seals. Ensure the vent union is correctly positioned then secure the regulator in position with the circlip.
21 Install the throttle body assembly if removed and the air filter housing.

Throttle position sensor

Note: *Checking and adjustment of the throttle position sensor requires the use of the Ducati (Mathesis) diagnostic tester. If the tester is not available, do not disturb the throttle position sensor unless absolutely necessary.*

Check

22 The throttle position sensor can only be properly checked and set up using the Mathesis tester. Refer to a Ducati dealer.

Removal

23 Remove the air filter housing (see Section 5).
24 Disconnect the wiring connector from the throttle position sensor **(see illustration)**.
25 Make alignment marks between the sensor and throttle body, then undo the retaining screws and remove the sensor **(see illustration)**.

Installation

26 Engage the sensor with the throttle valve spindle and refit its retaining screws. Align the marks made prior to removal then tighten the sensor screws and reconnect the wiring connector.
27 On completion, refit the air filter housing (see Section 5). Have the sensor checked and if necessary (and where possible) adjusted by a Ducati dealer.

Air temperature sensor

Check

28 Refer to a Ducati dealer equipped with the Mathesis tester.

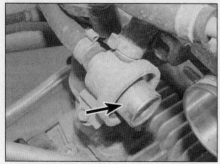

8.16 Fuel pressure regulator (arrowed)

8.24 Disconnect the wiring connector from the sensor

8.25 Throttle sensor screws (arrowed)

8.30 Air temperature/pressure sensor (arrowed) – Monsters

Removal and installation

29 On Sport and Supersport models remove the upper fairing (see Chapter 7). The air temperature sensor is mounted behind the headlight. Disconnect the sensor from its wiring connector and remove it from the bike.

30 On Monster models remove the instrument cluster (see Chapter 8). Disconnect the sensor wiring connector, then undo the mounting screw and remove the sensor **(see illustration)**.

31 Installation is the reverse of removal.

Atmospheric pressure sensor

32 On 750 and 900 Supersport models (with the 5.1 system) the AP sensor is incorporated in the ECU. Refer to a Ducati dealer equipped with the Mathesis tester.

33 On 620 Sport and all Monster models (with the 5.9 system) AP sensor is incorporated with the air temperature sensor – see Steps 28 to 31.

Timing sensor

Check

34 Refer to a Ducati dealer equipped with the Mathesis tester.

35 If the sensor is good, check the sensor air gap (see below).

36 If the air gap is correctly set then the fault must be in the wiring harness or the ECU.

Removal

37 The timing sensor is fitted to the left-hand crankcase cover **(see illustration)**. On Sport and Supersport models remove the fairing left-hand lower panel (see Chapter 7).

38 Trace the wiring back from the sensor, freeing it from all its retaining clips and ties whilst noting its correct routing, and disconnect its connector from the main wiring harness.

39 Undo the bolt and remove the sensor from the crankcase cover, complete with its O-ring and shim. Discard the O-ring; a new one must be used on installation.

Installation

40 Ensure the sensor and cover mating surfaces are clean and dry. Fit the shim to the sensor and slide on the new O-ring then ease the sensor into position.

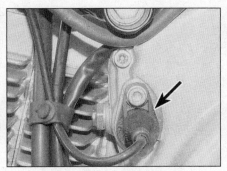

8.37 Timing sensor location

41 Clean the sensor bolt and apply a drop of fresh locking compound to its threads, then install and tighten it.

42 Check and, if necessary, adjust the sensor air gap (see Step 44).

43 Ensure the sensor wiring is correctly routed and retained by all the relevant clips and ties then reconnect its connector to the main wiring harness. Where applicable install the fairing panel (see Chapter 7).

Air gap check and adjustment

44 On Sport and Supersport models remove the fairing left-hand lower panel (see Chapter 7).

45 Unscrew the inspection plug and sealing washer from the front of the crankcase to gain access to the sensor tip. Obtain a new sealing washer for use on refitting.

46 Using feeler gauges, measure the gap between the sensor tip and the outer face of the gear. This should be 0.6 to 0.8 mm. Make sure that you are not measuring the one recessed section that forms the reference point in the gear for the sensor.

47 If the air gap is not as specified, note the measured gap then remove the sensor from the cover (see above). Measure the thickness of the shim(s) fitted to the sensor then use this to calculate the required thickness of shim(s) required to correctly set the air gap. Shims are available in various thicknesses – refer to your Ducati dealer for details. Fit the correct thickness shim(s) and a new sealing ring then install the sensor.

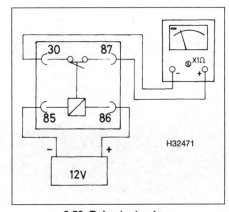

8.50 Relay test set-up

48 Once the sensor air gap is correctly set, clean the inspection plug and fit the new sealing washer. Apply a drop of locking compound to the plug threads then fit it to the crankcase and tighten it.

49 On Sport and Supersport models install the fairing panel (see Chapter 7).

Engine management system relays

Check

50 Two relays are fitted, a main relay and an injector relay. Remove the relay (see below). Connect an ohmmeter across terminals 30 and 87 of the relay **(see illustration)**. Using a battery and auxiliary wires, connect the battery positive (+ve) terminal to terminal 86 of the relay and the negative (–ve) terminal to terminal 85 of the relay and note the meter reading obtained. If the relay is operating correctly there should be continuity (zero resistance) when the battery is connected and no continuity (infinite resistance) when the battery is disconnected; the relay will be heard to 'click' as the battery is connected/disconnected. If this is not the case, renew the relay.

Removal

51 Raise the fuel tank (see Section 2). The relays are located to the rear of the air filter housing on the left-hand side **(see illustration)**.

52 Pull the relevant relay from its connector socket.

Installation

53 Plug the relay back into its socket.

54 Lower the fuel tank.

Electronic control unit (ECU)

Check

55 The electronic control unit (ECU) can only be checked using the Ducati (Mathesis) diagnostic tester (see Section 7).

Removal

56 Raise the fuel tank (see Section 2). The electronic control unit (ECU) is mounted behind the air filter housing.

57 On the 620 Sport and all Monster models, release the wiring connector catches and pull

8.51 Management system relays (arrowed)

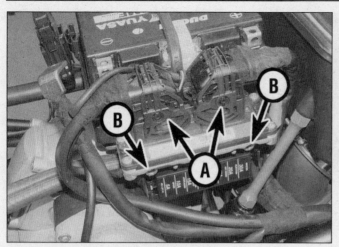

8.57 Release the catches (A) and pull the connectors off, then unscrew the bolts (B)

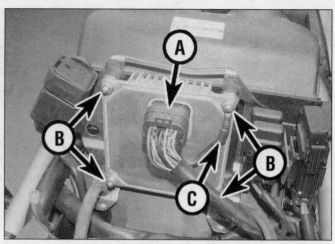

8.58 ECU wiring connector (A), mounting nuts (B) and earth wire (C) – Supersport models

the connectors off the ECU **(see illustration)**. Undo the two bolts, noting the earth cable secured by one of them. Remove the ECU, noting the collars.

58 On Supersport models, disconnect the wiring connector, then unscrew the nuts, noting the earth wire, and remove the ECU **(see illustration)**.

Installation

59 Installation is the reverse of removal. On the 620i.e. Sport and all Monster models fit the ECU with the lugs adjacent the mounting bolt holes facing out. If a new ECU has been installed, have the idle mixture set up on the Mathesis tester.

9 Throttle body assembly – removal and installation

Warning: Refer to the precautions given in Section 1 before starting work.

Removal

1 On Sport and Supersport models remove the fairing lower panels (see Chapter 8).
2 Remove the fuel tank (see Section 2).
3 Remove the air filter housing (see Section 5).
4 Disconnect the wiring connector from the

throttle position sensor and from each injector **(see illustrations 8.24 and 8.4a and b)**.
5 Detach the throttle cable and the fast idle cable (see Sections 10 and 11).
6 On models with the plastic tank slacken the clamps securing the self-seal connectors in the end of each fuel hose and carefully pull them out **(see illustration)**.
7 Slacken the retaining clips securing the throttle body assembly in the intake rubbers **(see illustration)**. Ease the throttle body assembly out of position and remove it from the bike, noting the correct routing of the fuel hoses **(see illustration)**.
8 Check each intake rubber for signs of damage or deterioration and, if necessary, renew it. The rubber is an integral part of the intake manifold; undo the retaining nuts and remove the manifold and gasket or O-ring where fitted (according to model) from the cylinder head. Discard the gasket or O-ring; a new one will be needed on installation.
Caution: Whilst the throttle body assembly is removed, tape over/plug the intake ports to prevent dirt/debris from entering the cylinder head.

Installation

9 Remove the tape/plugs from the intake ports.
10 Where necessary, ensure the cylinder

head and manifold mating surfaces are clean and dry and the manifold studs are securely fitted. If any stud is loose, remove it apply locking compound to its threads then refit it to the cylinder head and tighten it to the specified torque. Fit a new gasket or O-ring where removed, then install the manifold and tighten its nuts.
11 Lubricate the rubbers with a silicone-based spray to ease installation then ease the throttle body assembly in position **(see illustration 9.7b)**. Ensure both throttle bodies are correctly seated in the manifold rubbers then tighten the retaining clips **(see illustration 9.7a)**.
12 Route the fuel hoses correctly back up to the fuel tank. On models with the plastic tank fit the self-seal connectors back into the hoses, but do not tighten the clamps until after the hoses are connected to the tank to ensure correct alignment **(see illustration 9.6)**.
13 Connect the throttle and fast idle cables (see Sections 10 and 11). Adjust the cables as described in Chapter 1.
14 Securely reconnect the throttle position sensor and fuel injector wiring connectors **(see illustrations 8.24 and 8.4a and b)**.
15 If a new throttle body assembly has been installed, check the throttle body synchronisation, idle speed and mixture settings as described in Chapter 1.

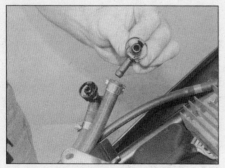

9.6 Slacken the clamps and pull the connectors out of the hoses

9.7a Slacken the clamp screw (arrowed) on each duct . . .

9.7b . . . and remove the throttle bodies

10.2a Slacken the adjuster locknut (arrowed)

10.2b Rotate the cam and free the cable end from it

10.2c Thread the adjuster out of its bracket

10.3a Undo the screws (arrowed) . . .

10.3b . . . and remove the cover

10.4 Free the cable end from the pulley and the outer cable from the housing

16 Install the air filter housing and the fuel tank (Sections 5 and 2). On models with the plastic tank tighten the clamps securing the self-seal connectors in the hose ends.
17 On Sport and Supersport models fit the fairing panels (see Chapter 7).

10 Throttle cable –
removal and installation

Warning: Refer to the precautions given in Section 1 before proceeding.

Removal

1 On Sport and Supersport models remove the fairing right-hand lower panel (see Chapter 7) to gain access to the throttle body end of the cable.
2 Pull the rubber boot up off the cable adjuster. Slacken the locknut on the cable adjuster **(see illustration)**. Turn the throttle cam round by hand to provide slack in the inner cable, then release the cable end from its socket **(see illustration)**. Unscrew the adjuster from its mounting bracket **(see illustration)**.
3 Undo the retaining screws and remove the cover from the top of the throttle twistgrip housing **(see illustrations)**.
4 Free the inner cable end from the twistgrip then slacken the locknut and unscrew the cable upper adjuster from the twistgrip housing **(see illustration)**.

5 Work along the cable, freeing it from the retaining clips and ties whilst noting its correct routing, and remove it from the bike.

Installation

6 Route the cable correctly down to the throttle bodies and secure it in position with all the relevant clips and ties.
7 Screw the upper adjuster fully into the twistgrip housing then attach the inner cable to the twistgrip **(see illustration 10.4)**. Lubricate the cable and twistgrip with multi-purpose grease then fit the cover to the housing, seating the inner cable correctly in the cover guide **(see illustration 10.3b)**. Ensure the cable is correctly routed through the guide then refit the cover retaining screws, tightening them securely **(see illustration 10.3a)**.
8 Screw the lower adjuster fully into the bracket on the throttle body and connect the inner cable end to the throttle linkage **(see illustrations 10.2c and b)**.
9 Adjust the cable as described in Chapter 1. Turn the handlebars back and forth to make sure the cable doesn't cause the steering to bind.
10 Start the engine and turn the handlebars back and forth to make sure the idle speed doesn't rise as the bars are turned. If it does, the cable is incorrectly routed and the problem must be sorted before the motorcycle is ridden.
11 On Sport and Supersport models install the fairing panel (see Chapter 7).

11 Fast idle cable –
removal and installation

⚠ *Warning: Refer to the precautions given in Section 1 before proceeding.*

Removal

1 On Sport and Supersport models remove the fairing right-hand lower panel (see Chapter 7) to gain access to the throttle body end of the cable.
2 Pull the rubber boot up off the cable adjuster. Slacken the locknut on the cable adjuster **(see illustration)**. Slacken the screw securing the cable end in the arm **(see**

11.2a Slacken the adjuster locknut (arrowed)

11.2b Slacken the screw then draw the cable end out and remove the spring

11.2c Thread the adjuster out of its bracket

illustration). Draw the cable out and remove the spring. Unscrew the adjuster from its mounting bracket (see illustration).

3 Undo the screws securing the left-hand switch housing and separate the halves.

4 On Monster models, free the inner cable from the lever and release the elbow from the housing.

5 On Sport and Supersport models, note how the choke lever locates between the left-hand handlebar switch housing and the clutch

master cylinder bracket, then unscrew the two switch housing screws and separate the two halves. Draw the separator away from the choke lever. Detach the cable nipple from the choke lever, then remove the cable noting how it locates in the guide.

6 Work along the cable, freeing it from the retaining clips and ties whilst noting its correct routing, and remove it from the bike.

Installation

7 Route the cable correctly down to the

throttle bodies and secure it in position with all the relevant clips and ties.

8 On Monster models, fit the cable elbow into the switch housing and the cable end into the lever. Lubricate the cable and lever with multi-purpose grease then fit the switch housing onto the handlebar.

9 On Sport and Supersport models, lubricate the upper cable end nipple with multi-purpose grease. Install the cable in the choke lever housing and attach the nipple to the choke lever. Tighten the cable retaining nut securely. Fit the two halves of the housing together and secure them with the screw. Fit the switch housing onto the handlebars, making sure the pin in the lower half of the housing locates in the hole in the underside of the handlebar and that the choke lever housing is correctly positioned between the switch housing and the clutch master cylinder bracket. Install the screws, tightening them securely.

10 Screw the adjuster into the bracket on the throttle body (see illustration 11.2c). Fit the spring over the cable end, then pass the cable through the hole in the arm and secure it with the screw (see illustrations and 11.2b). Set the adjuster in its bracket so that with the choke fully on the arm is against the stop on the throttle body. Tighten the locknut to secure the adjuster (see illustration 11.2a).

11 Adjust the cable as described in Chapter 1. Turn the handlebars back and forth to make sure the cable doesn't cause the steering to bind.

12 Start the engine and turn the handlebars back and forth to make sure the idle speed doesn't rise as the bars are turned. If it does, the cable is incorrectly routed and the problem must be sorted before the motorcycle is ridden.

13 On Sport and Supersport models install the fairing panel (see Chapter 7).

11.10a Fit the spring over the cable . . .

11.10b . . . then fit the cable into the arm

Chapter 4
Ignition system

Contents

Electronic control unit (fuel injection models) – check,
removal and installation . . . . .see Chapter 3B
General information 1
Ignition control units (carburettor models) – check,
removal and installation 5
Ignition (main) switch – check, removal and installation . . .see Chapter 8
Ignition HT coils – check, removal and installation 3
Ignition pick-up coil assembly (carburettor models) – check,
removal and installation 4
Ignition system – check 2
Ignition timing – general information and check 6
Immobiliser system 7
Spark plug checks . . . . .see Chapter 1
Timing sensor (fuel injection models) . . . . .see Chapter 3B

Degrees of difficulty

Easy, suitable for novice with little experience **Fairly easy,** suitable for beginner with some experience **Fairly difficult,** suitable for competent DIY mechanic **Difficult,** suitable for experienced DIY mechanic **Very difficult,** suitable for expert DIY or professional

Specifications

General information
Spark plugs . . . . see Chapter 1
Cylinder identification . . . . Horizontal (front), vertical (rear)

Ignition timing (carburettor engines)
At idle . . . . 6° BTDC
Full advance . . . . 32° BTDC

Pick-up coil (carburettor engines)
Resistance . . . . 95 to 105 ohms
Air gap . . . . 0.6 to 0.8 mm

Ignition HT coils
Carburettor engines
Primary winding resistance . . . . 3.8 to 5.2 ohms
Secondary winding resistance
  2001 M600/750 models . . . . 15.6 to 23.4 K-ohms
  All other models . . . . 10.8 to 16.2 K-ohms
Plug cap resistance . . . . 5 K-ohms
Fuel injection engines . . . . see Section 3

Torque setting
Pick-up coil screws (carburettor models) . . . . 4 to 6 Nm

1 General information

All models are fitted with a fully transistorised electronic ignition system, which due to its lack of mechanical parts is totally maintenance-free. The system on carburettor engined models comprises a trigger on the flywheel, pick-up coils, ignition control units and ignition HT coils. The system on fuel injected (i.e.) models comprises a trigger on the timing gear, a timing sensor, an electronic control unit or ECU and ignition HT coils.

On carburettor models the triggers on the flywheel, which is fitted to the left-hand end of the crankshaft, magnetically operate the pick-up coils as the crankshaft rotates. The pick-up coils send a signal to the ignition control units which then supply the ignition HT coils with the power necessary to produce a spark at the plugs. On fuel injected models a recess on the timing gear rim, representing two teeth on the gear, is used by the ECU as a marker for engine position and speed. In conjunction with the information supplied by other sensors in the system the optimum ignition timing is decided by the ECU, which then triggers the coils.

The system uses two HT coils, one for each cylinder.

The system incorporates an electronic advance system controlled by signals generated by the flywheel and the pick-up coil or timing gear and sensor, according to model.

Because of their nature, the individual ignition system components can be checked but not repaired. If ignition system troubles occur, and the faulty component can be isolated, the only cure for the problem is to replace the part with a new one. To avoid unnecessary expense, make very sure the faulty component has been positively identified before buying a replacement part.

2 Ignition system – check

Caution: The energy levels in electronic systems can be very high. On no account should the ignition be switched on whilst the plugs or plug caps are being held. Shocks from the HT circuit can be most unpleasant. Secondly, it is vital that the engine is not turned over or run with any of the plug caps removed, and that the plugs are soundly earthed when the system is checked for sparking. The ignition system components can be seriously damaged if the HT circuit becomes isolated.

1 As no means of adjustment is available, any failure of the system can be traced to failure of

a system component or a simple wiring fault. Of the two possibilities, the latter is by far the most likely. In the event of failure, check the system in a logical fashion, as described below.

2 Disconnect the HT lead from both cylinder spark plugs. Connect each lead to a spare spark plug and lay each plug on the engine with the threads contacting the engine. If necessary, hold each spark plug with an insulated tool.

⚠️ Warning: Do not remove either of the spark plugs from the engine to perform this check – atomised fuel being pumped out of the open spark plug hole could ignite, causing severe injury!

3 Having observed the above precautions, check that the kill switch is in the RUN position, turn the ignition switch ON and turn the engine over on the starter motor. If the system is in good condition a regular, fat blue spark should be evident at each plug electrode. If the spark appears thin or yellowish, or is non-existent, further investigation will be necessary. Before proceeding further, turn the ignition off and remove the key as a safety measure.

4 The ignition system must be able to produce a spark which is capable of jumping a particular size gap. Whilst Ducati do not specify the size of this gap, a healthy system should produce a spark capable of jumping at least 6 mm. A simple testing tool can be made to test the minimum gap across which the spark will jump (see Tool Tip).

5 Connect one of the spark plug HT leads from one coil to the protruding electrode on the test tool, and clip the tool to a good earth on the engine or frame. Check that the kill switch is in the RUN position, turn the ignition switch ON and turn the engine over on the starter motor. If the system is in good condition a regular, fat blue spark should be

A simple spark gap testing tool can be made from a block of wood, a large alligator clip and two nails, one of which is fashioned so that a spark plug cap or bare HT lead end can be connected to its end. Make sure the gap between the two nail ends is the same as specified.

seen to jump the gap between the nail ends. Repeat the test for the other coil. If the test results are good the entire ignition system can be considered good. If the spark appears thin or yellowish, or is non-existent, further investigation will be necessary.

6 Ignition faults can be divided into two categories, namely those where the ignition system has failed completely, and those which are due to a partial failure. The likely faults are listed below, starting with the most probable source of failure. Work through the list systematically, referring to the subsequent sections for full details of the necessary checks and tests. Note: Before checking the following items ensure that the battery is fully charged and that all fuses are in good condition.

● Loose, corroded or damaged wiring connections, broken or shorted wiring between any of the component parts of the ignition system (see Fault Finding Equipment in the Reference section).

● Faulty HT lead or spark plug cap, faulty spark plug, dirty, worn or corroded plug electrodes, or incorrect gap between electrodes.

● Faulty ignition switch or engine kill switch (see Chapter 8).

● Faulty pick-up coils or damaged flywheel triggers (carburettor engines), or faulty timing sensor (fuel injection engines).

● Faulty ignition HT coil(s).

● Faulty ignition control unit (carburettor engines) or ECU (fuel injection engines).

7 If the above checks don't reveal the cause of the problem, have the ignition system tested by a Ducati dealer.

3 Ignition HT coils – check, removal and installation

Check

1 In order to determine conclusively that the ignition coils are defective, they should be tested by a Ducati dealer equipped with the Mathesis tester.

2 However, the coils can be checked visually (for cracks and other damage) and the primary and secondary coil resistances can be measured with a multimeter. If the coils are undamaged, and if the resistance readings are as specified at the beginning of the Chapter, they are probably capable of proper operation. Note that the resistance figures given in the Specifications at the beginning of the Chapter are for carburettor models. No figures are given for fuel injection models, but the coils work in the same way, and as long as readings of the order of those given for carburettor models are obtained the coils are probably OK. When no readings are obtained at all then the coil is definitely faulty.

3 Raise or remove the fuel tank (see Chapter 3) and disconnect the battery negative (-ve)

3.3a Each ignition coil is secured by two bolts (arrows)

3.3b Ignition coils (arrowed) - fuel injected Sport and Supersport models

3.3c Vertical cylinder coil (arrowed) - fuel injected Monsters

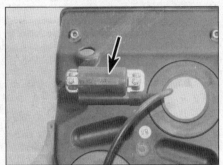

3.3d Horizontal cylinder coil (arrowed) - M620/750 and 2002 M900

lead. On all carburettor models the coils are mounted to a bracket on the air filter housing in front of the battery **(see illustration)**. The left-hand coil is for the horizontal cylinder and

the right-hand coil is for the vertical cylinder. On fuel injection Sport and Supersport models, the coils are mounted on the left-hand side of the main frame **(see illustration)**;

the front coil is for the horizontal cylinder and the rear coil is for the vertical cylinder. Remove the fairing side panel for access (see Chapter 7). On all fuel injected Monster models, the vertical cylinder coil is mounted on the left-hand side of the frame (remove the side panel for access – see Chapter 7), and the horizontal cylinder coil is mounted on the underside of the air filter housing on M620i.e., M750 and 2002 M900i.e. models or to the left-side of the frame alongside the air filter housing on 2000 and 2001 M900i.e. models **(see illustrations)**.

4 Disconnect the primary circuit electrical connectors from the coil being tested and the HT lead from the spark plug **(see illustrations)**. Mark the locations of all wires before disconnecting them.

5 Set the meter to the ohms x 1 scale and measure the resistance between the primary circuit terminals **(see illustration)**. This will give a resistance reading of the primary windings and should be consistent with the value given in the Specifications at the beginning of the Chapter.

6 To check the condition of the secondary windings, set the meter to the K-ohm scale. Unscrew the plug cap from the HT lead and connect one meter probe to the end of the HT lead and the other probe to either of the primary circuit terminals **(see illustration 3.5)**. If the reading obtained is not within the range shown in the Specifications, it is likely that the coil is defective. The plug cap resistance can be checked by measuring across the plug contact inside the cap and lead connection – compare the resistance with that specified. Screw the plug cap back on the HT lead when the checks are complete.

7 Should any of the above checks not produce the expected result, have your findings confirmed by a Ducati dealer (see Step 1). If the coil is confirmed to be faulty, it must be replaced; the coil is a sealed unit and cannot therefore be repaired. Note that the plug caps can be unscrewed from the coils and replaced separately.

Removal

8 Refer to Steps 3 and 4 above. Pull the caps off the spark plugs and feed the HT leads through to the coils, releasing them from any ties and noting their routing. On all injected Monsters except the 2000/2001 M900i.e. remove the air filter housing to access the horizontal cylinder coil nuts (see Chapter 3B).

9 Unscrew the bolts or nuts (according to model) securing the coil and remove it **(see illustrations 3.3a, b, c and d)**. On injected Sport and Supersport models if you remove the coils with the mounting brackets that mount on the frame, note the arrangement of the washer, grommets and spacers.

Installation

10 Installation is the reverse of removal. Make sure the wiring connectors and HT leads are securely connected and correctly routed.

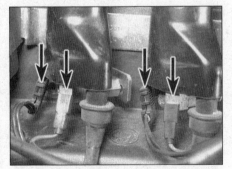

3.4a Ignition coil primary circuit electrical connectors (arrowed) - carburettor models

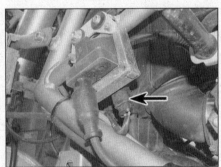

3.4b Primary circuit wiring connector (arrowed) - injected Sport and Supersport models

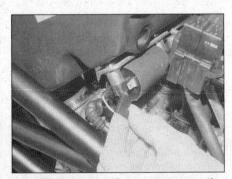

3.4c Disconnecting the connectors on the horizontal cylinder coil on injected Monsters (except 2000/1 M900)

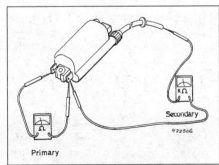

3.5 Ignition coil winding test connections

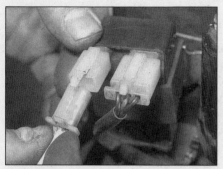

4.2 Disconnect each pick-up coil 2-pin wiring connector at its ignition control unit

4.4a Measuring the pick-up coil air gap

4.4b Pick-up coil mounting plate nuts (arrows). Adjust the position of the plate as required to set the pick-up coil air gap and the ignition timing

4 Pick-up coil assembly (carburettor models) – check, removal and installation

Check

1 Remove the fuel tank (see Chapter 3) and disconnect the battery negative (-ve) lead.

2 Trace the pick-up coil wiring back from the left-hand side crankcase cover and disconnect it at the 2-pin connector on each ignition control unit **(see illustration)**. Using a multimeter set to the ohms x 100 scale, measure between the two terminals on the pick-up coil side of each connector.

3 Compare the reading obtained with that given in the Specifications at the beginning of this Chapter. The pick-up coils must be replaced if the reading obtained differs greatly

from that given, particularly if the meter indicates a short circuit (no measurable resistance) or an open circuit (infinite, or very high resistance).

4 The pick-up coil air gap should also be checked. To do this, remove the left-hand side crankcase cover (Chapter 2, Section 14). Using a feeler gauge, measure the gap between the sensor on the pick-up coil and the trigger on the outside of the flywheel (identified as a raised plate on the outer surface of the flywheel) **(see illustration)**. Compare the measured gap with the specification listed at the beginning of the Chapter. If the gap is too big or too small, slacken the nuts securing the pick-up coil assembly mounting plate to the crankcase by just enough to allow some movement in the plate, and adjust its positioning until the air gap is as specified for each pick-up coil **(see**

illustration). **Note:** *Moving this plate can affect the ignition timing. If any adjustment in the air gap was necessary, the ignition timing should be checked and adjusted in conjunction with setting the air gap (see Section 6).*

5 With the air gap and timing both set, tighten the pick-up coil mounting plate nuts securely, making sure the plate does not move while doing so. Install the left-hand side crankcase cover (see Chapter 2, Section 14).

6 If one or both pick-up coils are thought to be faulty, first check that this is not due to a damaged or broken wire from the coil to the connector; pinched or broken wires can usually be repaired. Note that the pick-up coils are not available individually but come as a pair complete with the wiring sub-harness.

Removal

7 Remove the fuel tank (see Chapter 3) and disconnect the battery negative (-ve) lead. On SS and SL models, remove the fairing (see Chapter 7).

8 Remove the left-hand side crankcase cover (see Chapter 2, Section 14).

9 Trace the pick-up coil wiring back from the left-hand side crankcase cover and disconnect it at the 2-pin connector on each ignition control unit **(see illustration 4.2)**. Free the wiring from any clips or ties. As the wiring connectors will not fit through the wiring hole in the crankcase, it is necessary to separate the terminal pins from the connector block. Before doing this, note which pin fits into which side of the connector block to ensure correct installation.

10 Using a small flat-bladed Jeweller's screwdriver, depress the locating tongue on each terminal pin in the pick-up coil wiring connectors, and pull the pin out of the back of the connector **(see illustrations)**. Unscrew the wiring plug from the union in the crankcase and slide it off the wiring, then pull the wiring through from the inside, taking care not to snag any of the pins on the crankcase as they are easily damaged **(see illustration)**. Remove the rubber sealing grommet from inside the wiring plug union in the crankcase, accessing it from the outside of the crankcase.

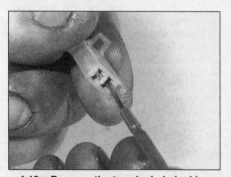

4.10a Depress the terminal pin locking tongue . . .

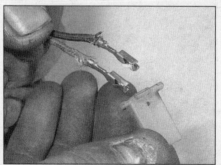

4.10b . . . and pull each pin out of the back of the connector

4.10c Unscrew the wiring plug from the union in the crankcase

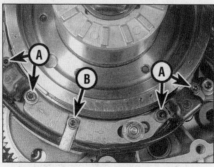

4.11 Pick-up coil screws (A), wiring clamp screw (B)

11 Remove the screws securing each pick-up coil and the wiring clamp to the pick-up coil mounting plate and remove the coil assembly **(see illustration)**.

12 Examine the flywheel triggers for signs of damage.

Installation

13 Install the pick-up coil assembly onto its mounting plate on the crankcase, and tighten the coil screws to the torque setting specified at the beginning of the Chapter **(see illustration 4.11)**. Tighten the wiring clamp bolt securely. Check the pick-up coil air gap (see Step 4).

14 Feed the wiring through the union in the crankcase and through the sealing grommet and the wiring plug. Slide the sealing grommet down the wiring and into the union in the crankcase, then screw the wiring plug into the hole and tighten it down onto the grommet so that the seal is formed.

15 Carefully install each terminal pin into its correct hole in the wiring connector, making sure it is fully inserted and secured by its locating tongue **(see illustration 4.10b)**.

16 Install the left-hand side crankcase cover (see Chapter 2, Section 14).

17 Route the wiring up to the ignition control units, and connect the red and white wire connector to the left-hand side (horizontal cylinder) ignition control unit and the black and yellow wire connector to the right-hand side (vertical cylinder) ignition control unit. Secure the wiring in its clips or ties.

18 Reconnect the battery negative (-ve) lead and install the fuel tank (see Chapter 3A). On SS and SL models, install the fairing panel (see Chapter 7).

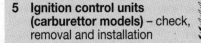

5 Ignition control units (carburettor models) – check, removal and installation

Check

1 If the tests shown in the preceding Sections have failed to isolate the cause of an ignition fault, it is likely that one or both of the ignition control units is faulty. No test details are available with which the units can be tested on home workshop equipment. Take the machine to a Ducati dealer for testing on the Mathesis diagnostic tester.

Removal

2 Remove the seat (see Chapter 7) and disconnect the battery negative (-ve) lead. The ignition control units are mounted to a bracket on the air filter housing in front of the battery **(see illustration)**. The left-hand unit is for the horizontal cylinder and the right-hand unit is for the vertical cylinder.

3 Disconnect the wiring connectors from each ignition control unit, then either withdraw the ignition control unit from its rubber sleeve,

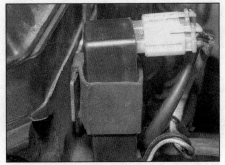

5.2 Each ignition control unit is mounted in a rubber sleeve which fits onto the bracket on the air filter housing

or remove the sleeve from its locating peg with the unit inside.

Installation

4 Installation is the reverse of removal. Make sure each connector is securely connected.

6 Ignition timing – general information and check

Note: *This procedure applies to carburettor models only. On fuel injection models no provision is made for checking the ignition timing using home equipment. If the timing is suspected of not being correct first check the timing sensor (see Chapter 3B); if that is good the system must be checked using the Mathesis tester. Take the bike to a Ducati dealer.*

General information

1 The ignition timing can be checked statically (engine off) or dynamically (engine running). A static check is only necessary if the pick-up coil mounting plate has been removed or its position relative to the flywheel altered, for example when re-setting the pick-up coil air gap (see Section 4), or if a dynamic check reveals that the timing must be adjusted. **Note:** *The timing must always be set in conjunction with setting the pick-up coil air gap, as adjustment of one can affect the other.*

2 A dynamic check (engine running) is carried

6.4 Timing mark inspection window

out using a stroboscopic lamp. The inexpensive neon lamps should be adequate in theory, but in practice may produce a pulse of such low intensity that the timing mark remains indistinct. If possible, one of the more precise xenon tube lamps should be used, powered by an external source of the appropriate voltage. **Note:** *Do not use the machine's own battery as an incorrect reading may result from stray impulses within the machine's electrical system.*

Check

Dynamic check

3 Warm the engine up to normal operating temperature then stop it. On SS and SL models, remove the fairing left-hand lower panel (see Chapter 7).

4 The timing marks on the rotor are visible through the timing mark inspection window in the left-hand side crankcase cover **(see illustration)**.

5 The timing marks for each cylinder comprise three dots, the larger one being the TDC (top dead centre) mark, the smaller dot adjacent to it being the firing point at idle, and the dot anti-clockwise from that being the firing point at full advance **(see illustration)**. The static timing mark with which these should align is a pointer inside the inspection window.

6 Connect the timing light to the horizontal cylinder HT lead as described in the manufacturer's instructions.

7 Start the engine and aim the light at the timing window.

8 With the machine idling at the specified speed, the idle timing mark should align with the static timing mark.

9 Slowly increase the engine speed whilst observing the timing mark. The timing mark should move anti-clockwise, increasing in relation to the engine speed until it reaches the full advance mark. Stop the engine and disconnect the stroboscope.

10 If the ignition timing is incorrect, or suspected of being incorrect, check and adjust it statically (see below).

Static check

11 Place the machine on an auxiliary stand so that the rear wheel is off the ground.

6.5 TDC mark (A), firing point at idle (B), firing point at full advance (C)

6.15 Flywheel pick-up coil reference marks (arrows)

12 Remove the spark plugs (see Chapter 1).

13 Select a gear and rotate the rear wheel until the engine is at TDC (top dead centre) on the horizontal cylinder, i.e. so that the TDC mark on the flywheel aligns with the static timing mark in the inspection window **(see illustration 6.4)**.

14 Remove the left-hand side crankcase cover (see Chapter 2, Section 14).

15 With the horizontal cylinder at TDC, the reference mark at the top centre of each pick-up coil should align with its reference mark on the flywheel **(see illustration)**. If the marks do not align, slacken the pick-up coil mounting plate nuts **(see illustration 4.4b)** by just enough to allow some movement in the plate, and adjust its positioning so that the reference marks are aligned. **Note:** *Moving this plate can affect the pick-up coil air gap. If any adjustment in the timing was necessary, the air gap should be checked and adjusted in conjunction with setting the timing (see Section 4).*

16 With the timing and air gap both set, tighten the pick-up coil mounting plate nuts securely, making sure the plate does not move while doing so.

17 Install the left-hand side crankcase cover (see Chapter 2, Section 14), and the spark plugs (see Chapter 1).

7 Immobiliser system

General information

1 An immobiliser system is fitted to 2002-on models as an anti-theft device. The system will only allow the machine to be started if the correct key is used to turn the ignition ON. The system consists of a transponder which is part of the ignition key, an antennae receiver which is fitted around the ignition switch, and the electronic control module (ECU).

2 When the ignition is switched ON, the ECU sends power through the receiver to the transponder. The transponder sends a coded signal back through the receiver to the ECU. If the signal sent by the transponder matches the signal stored in the ECU memory, the LED in the instrument cluster comes on and then goes off and the ECU allows the engine to be started. If the signal is not recognised the LED comes on and the injection malfunction light comes on.

3 Three keys (two black and one red) are supplied with the bike. The red key is the master key with which the system is programmed and to which the other two black keys are matched. The red key should be kept in a safe place – use the black keys only on a day-to-day basis. If the ignition lock is ever changed the transponder from the red key can be transferred to a new one. If it is lost a new ECU must be fitted. If all the keys are lost, the ECU must be replaced with a new one, so always make sure you have at least one spare key. The keys can interfere with each other so do not have more than one on your key ring. When programming keys keep others well away. You can have up to eight keys.

Programming the immobilizer

4 If any of the parts in the system (i.e. keys, antennae or ECU) are replaced, the system must be reprogrammed.

5 Make sure the battery is fully charged. Make sure the ignition is OFF for at least 30 seconds before this procedure.

6 Turn the ignition switch ON using the red key. The display will show 1-30 – how many keys have been programmed (one) and a countdown from 30 begins. Turn the key OFF before the countdown reaches zero (about 3 seconds). Within 15 seconds of this remove the red key, placing it well away from the antennae, insert a black key and turn the ignition ON. The display will be 2-30, showing the second key and the same countdown. Turn OFF and remove the key before zero. Repeat with as many black keys you are registering, then terminate the procedure by doing the red key again. When the red key is turned OFF and removed, the LED should flash. This indicates programming has been successful.

7 Within 15 seconds turn the ignition ON with the red key and leave it on for between 5 and 15 seconds (no less, no more) to allow information transfer between the decoder and the ECU. Leave the ignition OFF for a minimum of 10 seconds afterwards.

8 Check that all black keys can start the bike.

9 If at any point during the above procedure the display shows OFF, the procedure has been aborted by the system and must be started again.

10 You can check for correct programming by turning the ignition ON with the red key. If the LED flashes for 2 second pulses the immobilizer is not programmed. If it flashes for 0.7 second pulses it is programmed. If it is programmed it will then give a series of flashes indicating the number of programmed keys, including the red one.

11 If there is a fault diagnosed, the LED will flash – 1 flash indicates faulty wiring between the antennae/decoder and the ECU; 2 flashes indicates a faulty key or antennae; 3 flashes indicates the inserted key has not been recognised; four flashes indicates the ECU is programmed but not the antennae/decoder. In all the above cases the engine cannot be started.

Overriding the immobilizer

12 It is possible to start the engine if the system is faulty.

13 Turn the ignition ON, then fully open and hold open the throttle – the malfunction light should come on then turn off after 8 seconds. Release the throttle. The light should start flashing. Now enter your electronic code supplied on the code card with the bike on purchase as follows: the light will start to flash – count the number of flashes and when it equals the first number of the code, open the throttle for 2 seconds, then close it. The light should stay on for 4 seconds indicating recognition of the first number of the code. Repeat until all numbers on the code have been covered. When done the light should flash for 4 seconds, indicating the immobilizer is OFF and the engine can be started. If the light stays on, repeat the procedure. This procedure will need to be repeated every time you need to start the bike while there is a fault.

Replacement

14 To replace the antennae/decoder refer to the ignition switch removal procedure in Chapter 8.

15 To replace the ECU see Chapter 3B.

Chapter 5
Frame, suspension and final drive

Contents

Drive chain – removal, cleaning and installation 15
Drive chain and sprockets – check, adjustment
   and lubrication . . . . .see Chapter 1
Footrests and brackets – removal and installation 3
Forks – disassembly, inspection and reassembly 7
Forks – removal and installation 6
Frame – inspection and repair 2
General information 1
Handlebars – removal and installation 5
Handlebar switches . . . . .see Chapter 8
Rear shock absorber – removal, inspection and installation 10
Rear suspension linkage (Monsters only) –
   removal, inspection and installation 11

Rear wheel coupling/rubber dampers – check and
   replacement 17
Sidestand – removal and installation 4
Sprockets – check and replacement 16
Steering head bearing freeplay check and
   adjustment . . . . .see Chapter 1
Steering head bearings – inspection and replacement 9
Steering stem – removal and installation 8
Suspension – adjustments 12
Suspension checks . . . . .see Chapter 1
Swingarm bearings – check . . . . .see Chapter 1
Swingarm – inspection and bearing replacement 14
Swingarm – removal and installation 13

Degrees of difficulty

Easy, suitable for novice with little experience	Fairly easy, suitable for beginner with some experience	Fairly difficult, suitable for competent DIY mechanic	Difficult, suitable for experienced DIY mechanic	Very difficult, suitable for expert DIY or professional

Specifications

Note: *When filling the forks with fresh oil it is important to ensure that the oil level in each fork leg is the same and at the correct distance from the top of the fork tube. Oil quantities may be found to differ from those specified.*

Front forks

600SS model
  Oil level* . . . . 90 mm
  Oil capacity . . . . 390 cc
  Oil type . . . . Marzocchi Art. 550009 or SAE 7.5 fork oil

620i.e. Sport
  Oil level* . . . . 108 mm
  Oil capacity . . . . 440 cc
  Oil type . . . . Shell Advance Fork 7.5 or Donax TA
  Fork spring free length . . . . 270 mm min.

750SS model to end 1997
  Up to frame VIN 007706
    Fork type . . . . Showa GD031
    Oil level* . . . . 79.5 mm
    Oil capacity . . . . 457 cc
    Oil type . . . . Showa S.S8 or ATF SAE 10W20
    Fork spring free length . . . . 319 mm min.
  From frame VIN 007707
    Fork type . . . . Marzocchi 40USD/E
    Oil level* . . . . 90 mm
    Oil capacity . . . . 390 cc
    Oil type . . . . Marzocchi Art. 550009 or SAE 7.5 fork oil

750 i.e Sport and Supersport 1998 to 2002
  Oil level* . . . . 108 mm
  Oil capacity . . . . 528.5 to 533.5 cc
  Oil type . . . . Shell Advance Fork 7.5 or Donax TA
  Fork spring free length . . . . 270 mm min.

900SS and SL models 1991 to 1997
  Oil level* . . . . 108 mm
  Oil capacity . . . . 440 cc
  Oil type . . . . Showa S.S8 or ATF SAE 10W20
  Fork spring free length . . . . 319 mm min.

Front forks (continued)

900i.e Sport and Supersport 1998 to 2002
Oil level*	108 mm
Oil capacity	528.5 to 533.5 cc
Oil type	Shell Advance Fork 7.5 or Donax TA
Fork spring free length	270 mm min.

M600 and M750 models 1991 to 1999
Oil level*	90 mm
Oil capacity	380 cc
Oil type	Marzocchi Art. 550009 or SAE 7.5 fork oil

M600 and M750 2000 and 2001
Oil level*	80 mm
Oil capacity	440 cc
Oil type	Shell Advance Fork 7.5 or Donax TA
Fork spring free length	283 mm min.

M620i.e. 2002 and 2003, M750i.e. 2002
Oil level*	108 mm
Oil capacity	440 cc
Oil type	Shell Advance Fork 7.5 or Donax TA
Fork spring free length	270 mm min.

M620i.e. 2004-on
Oil level*	104 mm
Oil capacity	480 cc
Oil type	Shell Advance Fork 7.5 or Donax TA
Fork spring free length	270 mm min.

M900 model to end 1997
Up to frame VIN 009914**
Fork type	Showa GD041
Oil level*	79.5 mm
Oil capacity	457 cc
Oil type	Showa S.S8 or ATF SAE 10W20
Fork spring free length	319 mm min.

From frame VIN 009915
Fork type	Marzocchi 40USD/REG
Oil level*	90 mm
Oil capacity	390 cc
Oil type	Marzocchi Art. 550009 or SAE 7.5 fork oil

M900 1998 and 1999
Oil level	90 mm
Oil capacity	440 cc
Oil type	Shell Advance Fork 7.5 or Donax TA

M900i.e. 2000 to 2002
With adjustment
Oil level*	108 mm
Oil capacity	531cc
Oil type	Shell Advance Fork 7.5 or Donax TA
Fork spring free length	270 mm min.

Without adjustment
Oil level*	80 mm
Oil capacity	548cc
Oil type	Shell Advance Fork 7.5 or Donax TA
Fork spring free length	283 mm min.

* Oil level is measured from the top of the tube with the fork spring removed and the leg fully compressed.
** Ducati recommend that the oil quantity for each fork on the early M900 (with Showa forks) be increased by 30 cc to 487 cc to improve their performance.

Swingarm

Pivot pin runout limit	0.3 mm

Final drive

Chain type
600SS and 750SS 1991 to 1997	DID 520 VL2
620i.e. Sport, 750/900i.e. Sport and Supersport and 900 SS/SL	DID 520 VL4
M600 1994 to 2001 and M750 models 1991 to 2001	DID 520 VL2
M620i.e. 2002 and 2003	DID 525 VL4
M620i.e. 2004-on	DID 520 V6
M750i.e. 2002	DID 525 VL2
all M900 models	DID 520 VL4
Chain links and sprocket sizes	refer to owners manual

Torque settings
Steering stem nut
  Supersport and Sport models with drilled circular nut . . . . 12 Nm
  2002-on Monsters (steering stem/bearing adjuster nut) . . . . 30 Nm
  All other models . . . . 40 to 45 Nm
Rear shock absorber
  SS and SL, Sport and Supersport models
    Upper mounting bolt . . . . 40 to 45 Nm
    Lower mounting bolt . . . . 35 to 38 Nm
  1991 to 2001 M600, M750 and M900 models
    Upper mounting bolt . . . . 39 to 44 Nm
    Lower mounting bolt . . . . 34 to 37 Nm
  2002 and 2003 M620i.e. models
    Upper mounting bolt . . . . 43 Nm
    Lower mounting bolt . . . . 37 Nm
  2004-on M620i.e., 2002-on M750i.e. and M900i.e. models
    Upper and lower mounting bolts . . . . 42 Nm
Rear suspension linkage (Monster models only)
  1991 to 2001 M600, M750 and M900 models
    Linkage arm to frame bolt . . . . 34 to 37 Nm
    Linkage arm to linkage fork bolt . . . . 34 to 37 Nm
    Ball joint locknut to linkage fork . . . . 34 to 37 Nm
    Linkage fork to swingarm bolt . . . . 22 to 24 Nm
  M620i.e., 2002 M750i.e. and M900i.e. models
    Linkage arm to frame bolt . . . . 75 Nm
    Ball joint locknut to linkage rod . . . . 36 Nm
    Linkage rod to linkage arm bolt . . . . 42 Nm

1 General information

All models use a tubular steel trestle type frame which uses the engine as a stressed member.

Front suspension is by a pair of upside-down oil-damped telescopic forks. Forks are of Marzocchi or Showa manufacture.

At the rear, a swingarm acts on a single shock absorber. On all Monster models a three-way suspension linkage is fitted between the shock absorber and swingarm.

The drive to the rear wheel is by chain and sprockets.

2 Frame – inspection and repair

1 The frame should not require attention unless accident damage has occurred. In most cases, frame replacement is the only satisfactory remedy for such damage. A few frame specialists have the jigs and other equipment necessary for straightening the frame to the required standard of accuracy, but even then there is no simple way of assessing to what extent the frame may have been over stressed.
2 After the machine has accumulated a lot of miles, the frame should be examined closely for signs of cracking or splitting at the welded joints. Loose engine mount bolts can cause ovaling or fracturing of the mounting tabs.

Minor damage can often be repaired by welding, depending on the extent and nature of the damage.
3 Remember that a frame which is out of alignment will cause handling problems. If misalignment is suspected as the result of an accident, it will be necessary to strip the machine completely so the frame can be thoroughly checked.

3 Footrests and brackets – removal and installation

Rider's footrests
Removal
SS and SL models
1 Remove the circlip from the bottom of the

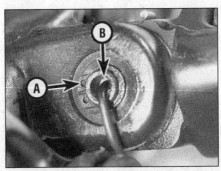

3.1a Remove the circlip (A) to release the pivot pin. Note how the brake pedal return spring end locates into the pivot pin (B)

footrest pivot pin, then withdraw the pivot pin and remove the footrest, noting how the footrest return spring is located (see illustrations). On the right-hand side footrest, note how the brake pedal return spring end locates into the bottom of the pivot pin.
2 If necessary, on some models the footrest rubber can be separated from the footrest by unscrewing the two screws on the underside of the footrest.

Monster models
3 Remove the circlip from the bottom of the footrest pivot pin, then withdraw the pivot pin and remove the footrest, noting how the return spring is located.

Installation
4 Installation is the reverse of removal. Make sure the return spring ends are correctly located.

3.1b Note how the ends of the footrest return spring locate (arrows)

3.6 The footrest rubber is secured to the footrest by two screws

3.9a Brake pedal pivot bolt (arrow)

3.9b The bracket is secured by two bolts (arrows)

Passenger footrests

Removal

SS and SL models

5 Remove the circlip from the bottom of the footrest pivot pin, then withdraw the pivot pin and remove the footrest along with the swivel plates, the spring and the detent ball, noting how they fit.

6 If necessary, on some models the footrest rubber can be separated from the footrest by unscrewing the two screws on the underside of the footrest (see illustration).

Monsters

7 Remove the circlip from the bottom of the footrest pivot pin, then withdraw the pivot pin and remove the footrest along with the swivel plates, the spring and detent balls, noting how they fit.

Installation

8 Installation is the reverse of removal. Make sure the swivel plates, spring and detent balls are correctly located.

Footrest brackets

Removal

SS and SL, Sport and Supersport models

9 On these models, each footrest has its own bracket. To remove the right-hand rider's footrest bracket, on early models unscrew the brake pedal pivot bolt and remove it along with its washer and the return spring, noting how it fits (see illustration). Unscrew the two bolts securing the rear brake master cylinder to the footrest bracket and support it so that no strain is placed on the hoses. With the exception of models with a hydraulic switch, either disconnect the brake light switch wiring at its connector and leave the switch attached to the bracket, or remove the switch (see Chapter 8). On all models unscrew the two bolts securing the footrest bracket to the frame and remove the bracket (see illustration).

10 To remove the left-hand rider's footrest bracket, unscrew the gearchange pedal pivot bolt and remove it along with its washer. Unscrew the two bolts securing the footrest bracket to the frame and remove the bracket. Where fitted note the bush and the O-rings and replace them with new ones if necessary.

11 To remove the passenger footrest brackets (except SL models), unscrew the bolt securing the silencer to the bracket, noting the arrangement of the various silencer mounting components (depending on model), then unscrew the bolts securing the bracket to the frame.

Monster models

12 On these models the rider and passenger footrests are mounted on the same bracket. To remove the right-hand bracket, unscrew the pivot bolt securing the brake pedal to the inside of the footrest bracket and remove it along with its washer and the return spring, noting how it fits. Unscrew the two bolts securing the rear brake master cylinder to the footrest bracket and support it so that no strain is placed on the hoses. Either disconnect the brake light switch wiring at its connector and leave the switch attached to the bracket, or remove the switch (see Chapter 8).

13 Unscrew the bolt securing the master cylinder reservoir to the inside of the bracket and support it in an upright position. Unscrew the bolt securing the silencer to the bracket and remove it along with its collar and washer, noting how they fit. Unscrew the bolts securing the bracket to the frame, then remove the bracket and collect the washers (see illustration). Inspect the rubber mounting dampers for damage or deterioration and replace them if necessary.

14 To remove the left-hand bracket, unscrew the gearchange pedal pivot bolt and remove it along with its washer. Where fitted note the bush and the O-rings and replace them with new ones if necessary. Unscrew the bolt securing the silencer to the bracket and remove it along with its collar and washer, noting how they fit. Unscrew the bolts securing the bracket to the frame, then remove the bracket and collect the washers (see illustration). Inspect the rubber

3.13 Footrest bracket mounting bolts on right-hand side (arrows)

3.14 Footrest bracket mounting bolts on left-hand side (arrows)

4.3 Sidestand pivot bolt (arrow)

5.4a Top yoke fork pinch bolts (arrows)

5.4b Steering stem nut (A) and pinch bolt (B)

mounting dampers for damage or deterioration and replace them if necessary.

Installation

15 Installation is the reverse of removal. Lubricate the pedal and lever pivot components with grease before assembly and replace any worn parts with new ones.

4 Sidestand – removal and installation

1 The sidestand is mounted on a bracket which is bolted onto the engine. Two extension springs, one inside the other, anchored to the bracket ensure that the stand is held in the retracted position. The sidestand incorporates a switch which illuminates a warning light in the instruments when the stand is down.

2 Support the bike on an auxiliary stand. On models with the switch incorporated in the sidestand pivot, remove the switch (see Chapter 8).

3 Free the stand springs, noting how they fit, and unscrew the pivot bolt. Withdraw the pivot bolt to free the stand from its bracket, noting the positions of the thrust washers, where fitted (see illustration). On installation apply grease to the pivot bolt shank and tighten the bolt securely. Reconnect the sidestand springs and check that they hold the stand securely up when not in use – an accident is almost certain to occur if the stand extends while the machine is in motion.

4 For check and replacement of the sidestand switch see Chapter 8.

5 Handlebars – removal and installation

SS and SL, Sport and Supersport models

Right-hand handlebar

Removal

1 Support the bike on an auxiliary stand.

2 Remove the right-hand handlebar switch housing (see Chapter 8). Unscrew the two bolts securing the front brake master cylinder assembly clamp to the handlebar and remove the assembly, noting the "UP" mark and arrowhead on the clamp face which must face up on installation. Support the assembly in an upright position so that no strain is placed on the hose.

3 Unscrew the two bolts securing the throttle pulley housing, then separate the halves and move them aside (see Chapter 3A or B, if necessary).

4 On models with the handlebars mounted below the top yoke, slacken the top yoke fork pinch bolts and the steering stem pinch bolt, then unscrew the steering stem nut and remove the top yoke (see illustrations).

5 Note the position of the handlebar on the fork, making some alignment marks if required, then slacken the handlebar clamp

bolts and slide the handlebar off the fork (see illustrations).

6 If necessary, unscrew the handlebar end-weight retaining screw, then remove the weight from the end of the handlebar and slide off the throttle twistgrip. If replacing the grip, it may be necessary to slit it using a sharp knife as it is adhered to the throttle twist.

Installation

7 Installation is the reverse of removal. On models with the handlebars mounted below the top yoke, where there are no manufacturer's alignment marks for the handlebars relative to the fork and the top yoke, they can be positioned according to rider's preference, within the obvious limits. On models with the handlebars mounted above the top yoke align the mark on the clamp with the slit in the yoke (see illustration). If removed, apply a smear of grease to the inside of the throttle twist and a suitable non-permanent locking compound to the handlebar end-weight retaining screw. If a new grip is being fitted, secure it to the throttle twist using a suitable adhesive. On models with the handlebars mounted below the top yoke tighten the steering stem nut to the torque setting specified at the beginning of the Chapter. Make sure the front brake master cylinder assembly clamp is installed with its "UP" mark and arrowhead facing up.

Left-hand handlebar

Removal

8 Support the bike on an auxiliary stand.

9 Remove the left-hand handlebar switch

5.5a Handlebar clamp bolts (arrowed - handlebars below top yoke)

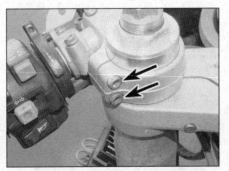

5.5b Handlebar clamp bolts (arrowed - handlebars above top yoke)

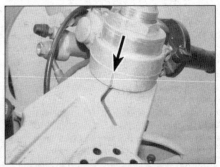

5.7 Align the mark (arrowed) with the slit in the yoke

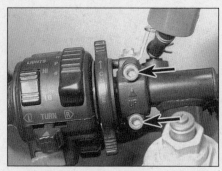

5.9 The clutch lever/master cylinder assembly clamp is secured by two bolts (arrows)

5.20 Handlebar clamp bolts (arrows) on Monster models (double clamp type shown)

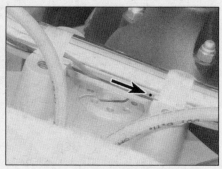

5.22 Where present, align the punch mark (arrowed) with the clamp mating surface

housing (see Chapter 8). Unscrew the two bolts securing the clutch lever/master cylinder assembly clamp to the handlebar and remove the assembly, noting the "UP" mark and arrowhead on the clamp face which must face up on installation (see illustration). Support the assembly in an upright position so that no strain is placed on the hose.

10 Detach the choke cable (see Chapter 3A).
11 On models with the handlebars mounted below the top yoke, slacken the top yoke fork pinch bolts and the steering stem pinch bolt, then unscrew the steering stem nut and remove the top yoke (see illustrations 5.4a and 5.4b).
12 Note the position of the handlebar on the fork, making some alignment marks if required, then slacken the handlebar clamp bolts and slide the handlebar off the fork (see illustration 5.5a or b).
13 If necessary, unscrew the handlebar end-weight retaining screw, then remove the weight from the end of the handlebar. If replacing the grip, it may be necessary to slit it using a sharp knife as it is adhered to the handlebar. The choke lever housing can now be slid off the handlebar if required.

Installation
14 Installation is the reverse of removal. On models with the handlebars mounted below the top yoke, where there are no manufacturer's alignment marks for the handlebars relative to the fork and the top yoke, they can be positioned according to rider's preference, within the obvious limits. On models with the handlebars mounted above the top yoke align the mark on the clamp with the slit in the yoke (see illustration 5.7). If removed, do not forget to install the choke lever housing on the handlebar. If removed, apply a suitable non-permanent locking compound to the handlebar end-weight retaining screw. If a new grip is being fitted, secure it to the handlebar using a suitable adhesive. On models with the handlebars mounted below the top yoke tighten the steering stem nut to the torque setting specified at the beginning of the Chapter. Make sure the clutch lever/master cylinder assembly clamp is installed with its "UP" mark and arrowhead facing up.

Monster models

Removal

Note: *If required, the handlebars can be displaced for access to the fork top bolts or the top yoke without removing the switch and cable housings, the front brake master cylinder assembly and the clutch lever/master cylinder assembly.*

15 Remove both left- and right-hand handlebar switches (see Chapter 8).
16 Unscrew the two bolts securing the front brake master cylinder assembly clamp to the handlebar and remove the assembly. Support the assembly in an upright position and so that no strain is placed on the hose.
17 Unscrew the two bolts securing the clutch lever/master cylinder assembly clamp to the handlebar and remove the assembly.
18 Unscrew the two bolts securing the throttle pulley housing, then separate the halves and move them aside (see Chapter 3A or B if necessary).
19 On models with a choke lever (as opposed to a knob), detach the cable (see Chapter 3A or B).
20 Note which side of the clamp any gap between the mating surface exists so they can be installed the same. Prise out the caps from the bolts securing the handlebar clamp(s) to the top yoke, then unscrew the bolts and remove the clamp(s) and the handlebars (see illustration).
21 If necessary, unscrew the handlebar end-weight retaining screws, then remove the weights from the end of the handlebars. If replacing the grips, it may be necessary to slit them using a sharp knife as they are adhered to the throttle twist (right-hand) and the handlebar (left-hand). Where applicable, the choke lever housing can now be slid off the handlebar if required.

Installation

22 Installation is the reverse of removal. Where applicable, do not forget to slide the choke lever housing onto the handlebars, if removed. Align the handlebars so that the ridges are central in the clamp mounts and with the punch mark (where present) aligned with the clamp mating surfaces (see

illustration). Fit the clamp(s) with the arrow or mark (where marked) facing forward, and with any gap positioned as before. Tighten the bolt on the closed side of the clamp first.
23 If removed, apply a suitable non-permanent locking compound to the handlebar end-weight retaining screws. If new grips are being fitted, secure them using a suitable adhesive. Make sure the front brake master cylinder and clutch lever/master cylinder assembly clamps are installed so that the dot on the handlebar aligns with the clamp joint.

6 Forks – removal and installation

Removal

1 Remove the front wheel (see Chapter 6).
2 Remove the front mudguard (Chapter 7).
3 Where fitted, although not strictly necessary, it is advisable to remove the fairing to improve access and to avoid the possibility of damaging it (see Chapter 7).
4 On SS and SL, Sport and Supersport models, slacken the handlebar clamp bolts, and note the position of the handlebars and how they align (see illustration 5.5a or b).
5 Slacken, but do not remove, the fork pinch bolts in the top yoke (see illustration – Monster models) (see illustration 5.4a – SS/SL models).

6.5 Top yoke fork pinch bolts on Monster models

6.7a Measure the height of the forks above the top yoke so they can be installed in the same position

6.7b Bottom yoke fork pinch bolts (arrows)

6.8 On SS and SL models, make sure the forks pass through the handlebar clamps

6 If the forks are to be disassembled, slacken the fork top bolts now.

7 Note the position of the top of the fork tubes relative to the top yoke, using a ruler to measure the distance between them, so that they are installed in the same position **(see illustration)**. Slacken but do not remove the fork clamp bolts in the bottom yoke, and remove the forks by twisting them and pulling them downwards **(see illustration)**.

 HAYNES HINT *If the fork legs are seized in the yokes, spray the area with penetrating oil and allow time for it to soak in before trying again.*

Installation

8 Remove all traces of corrosion from the fork tubes and the yokes and slide the forks back into place, making sure they pass through the handlebar clamps on SS and SL models **(see illustration)**. Align the forks with the top yoke as noted on removal **(see illustration 6.7a)**.

9 Tighten the bottom yoke fork pinch bolts securely **(see illustration)**. If the fork legs have been dismantled, tighten the fork tube top bolts. Now tighten the top yoke fork pinch bolts securely **(see illustration 5.4a or 6.5)**.

10 On SS and SL, Sport and Supersport models, tighten the handlebar clamp bolts, making sure the handlebars are positioned as noted on removal **(see illustration 5.5a or b and 5.7)**.

6.9 Tighten the bottom yoke pinch bolts securely

11 Install the front mudguard (see Chapter 7), and the front wheel (see Chapter 6).

12 Where fitted install the fairing, if removed (see Chapter 7).

13 Check the operation of the front forks and brake before taking the machine out on the road.

7 Forks – disassembly, inspection and reassembly

1991 to 1997 900SS/SL (inc. 1998 900SS FE), Early 750SS to frame VIN 007706, early M900 to frame VIN 009914 (Showa forks)

Note: *It is advisable to measure the fork oil level before the forks are dismantled and also to drain the oil into a measuring jug in order that the quantity can be recorded for refilling. Specifications are given at the beginning of this Chapter for oil quantity and level although these may be found to differ from that measured.*

Disassembly

1 Always dismantle the fork legs separately to avoid interchanging parts and thus causing an accelerated rate of wear. Store all components in separate, clearly marked containers **(see illustration)**.

2 Before dismantling the fork, it is advised

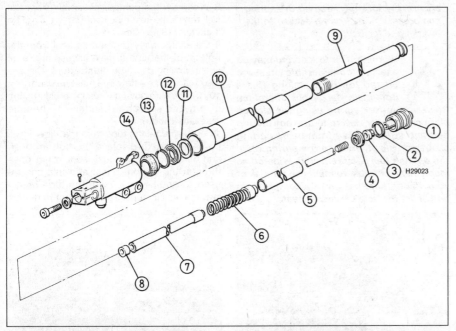

7.1 Front fork components – 750SS to frame VIN 007706 and M900 to frame VIN 009914

1 Top bolt	*6 Spring*	*11 Oil seal washer*
2 Seat rubber	*7 Damper rod*	*12 Oil seal*
3 Locknut	*8 Damper rod seat*	*13 Retaining clip*
4 Slider	*9 Fork slider*	*14 Dust seal*
5 Spring sleeve	*10 Fork tube*	

7.2a Remove one of the axle clamp bolts . . .

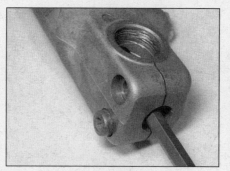

7.2b . . . to allow the damper rod bolt to be unscrewed

7.3 Unscrew the fork top bolt

that the damper assembly bolt be slackened at this stage. To access the bolt, remove one of the axle clamp bolts **(see illustration)**. Compress the fork tube in the slider so that the spring exerts maximum pressure on the damper head, then have an assistant slacken the damper bolt in the base of the fork slider **(see illustration)**. Also set the damper adjusters to the minimum setting (Section 12).

3 If the fork top bolt was not slackened with the fork in situ, carefully clamp the fork tube in a vice, taking care not to overtighten or score its surface, then slacken the fork top bolt **(see illustration)**. Unscrew the fork top bolt from the top of the fork tube.

4 Hold the fork vertical and slide the fork tube down onto the slider (wrap a rag around the sleeve on the top of the spring and the top of the tube to minimise oil spillage) while, with the aid of an assistant if necessary, keeping the damper rod and top bolt fully extended. It is now necessary to compress the spring in order to access the locknut below the top bolt. Ducati provide two special tools (Pt. Nos. 887131036 and 887130957) to make this easier. One is a handle which fits around the spring sleeve and enables the spring to be compressed easily, and the other is a slotted plate which fits onto the damper rod immediately below the locknut and acts as a spring seat. If the special tools are not available, a slotted plate can be easily fabricated by cutting a slot into a large steel washer (see **Tool Tip**), and the spring can be compressed using two screwdrivers inserted into the holes in the top of the spring collar.

A spring restraint can be easily made by cutting a slot the width of the damper rod in a large steel washer. The slotted plate fits around the damper rod immediately below the locknut. The pressure of the spring against the plate butts the plate against the locknut, keeping the spring compressed and allowing access to the locknut and top bolt.

⚠ *Warning: The fork spring may be exerting considerable pressure on the top bolt, making this a potentially dangerous operation. Restrain the fork spring using the slotted plate or a similar device to prevent the top bolt and spring sleeve from being sprung clear, and slowly release the spring once the top bolt has been removed. Wipe off as much oil as possible to minimise the risk of your hands slipping on oily components and enlist the help of an assistant.*

Counter-hold the locknut immediately below the top bolt with a spanner and unscrew the top bolt **(see illustration)**. Compress the spring to enable the restraining plate to be removed, then carefully release the spring.

5 Withdraw the spring sleeve and the spring, noting how they fit. Remove the washer (where fitted), the seat rubber and the slider from the top of the sleeve, noting how they fit.

6 Invert the fork leg over a suitable container and pump the fork and damper rod vigorously to expel as much fork oil as possible.

7 Remove the previously slackened damper assembly bolt and its copper sealing washer from the bottom of the slider. Discard the sealing washer as a new one must be used on reassembly. If the damper bolt was not slackened before dismantling the fork, it may be necessary to secure the damper to prevent it from turning.

8 Withdraw the damper assembly from the fork tube – the seat may come with it, if not tip it out later (Step 13).

9 Carefully prise out the dust seal from the bottom of the tube to gain access to the oil seal retaining clip **(see illustration)**. Discard the dust seal as a new one must be used.

10 Carefully remove the retaining clip, taking care not to scratch the surface of the tube **(see illustration)**.

11 To separate the tube from the slider it will be necessary to displace the bottom bush and oil seal. The top bush should not pass through the bottom bush, and this can be used to good effect. Push the tube gently inwards until it stops. Take care not to do this

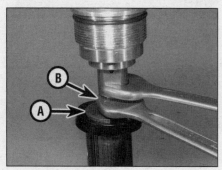

7.4 With the spring restraint (A) in place, counter-hold the locknut (B) and unscrew the top bolt from the damper rod

7.9 Prise off the dust seal . . .

7.10 . . . then lever out the retaining clip using a flat-bladed screwdriver

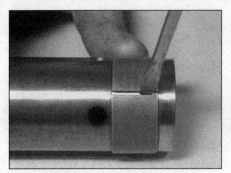

7.12a Carefully lever apart the ends of the top bush and remove it from the slider

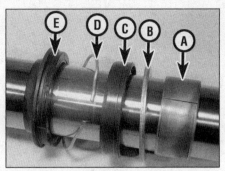

7.12b Bottom bush (A), oil seal washer (B), oil seal (C), retaining clip (D), dust seal (E)

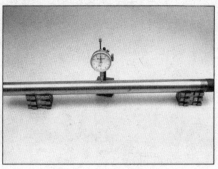

7.15 Check the fork slider for runout using V-blocks and a dial gauge

forcibly. Then pull the tube sharply outwards until the top bush strikes the bottom bush. Repeat this operation until the bottom bush and oil seal are tapped out of the slider.

12 With the tube and slider separated, remove the top bush from the slider by carefully levering its ends apart using a screwdriver **(see illustration)**. Slide the bottom bush, the oil seal washer, the oil seal, the retaining clip and the dust seal off the slider, noting which way up they fit **(see illustration)**. Discard the oil seal and the dust seal as new ones must be used.

13 If the damper assembly seat didn't come out with the damper assembly, tip it out of the slider, noting which way up it fits.

Inspection

14 Clean all parts in solvent and blow them dry with compressed air, if available. Check the fork slider for score marks, scratches, flaking of the chrome finish and excessive or abnormal wear. Look for dents in the tube and replace the tube in both forks if any are found. Check the fork seal seat for nicks, gouges and scratches. If damage is evident, leaks will occur. Also check the oil seal washer for damage and distortion, and replace it if necessary.

15 Check the fork slider for runout using V-blocks and a dial gauge. If the runout exceed 0.1 mm In the middle of the tube replace it with a new one **(see illustration)**.

 Warning: If the slider is bent, it should not be straightened; replace it with a new one.

16 Check the spring for cracks and other damage. Measure the spring free length and compare the measurement to the

specifications at the beginning of the Chapter. If it is defective or sagged below the service limit, replace the springs in both forks with new ones. Never replace only one spring.

17 Examine the working surfaces of the two bushes; if worn or scuffed they must be replaced.

18 Check all of the damper assembly components for damage and wear, and replace any that are defective.

Reassembly

19 Wrap some insulating tape over the ridges on the end of the fork slider to protect the lips of the new oil seal as it is installed. Apply a smear of the specified clean fork oil to the lips of the oil seal and the inner surface of each bush, then slide the new dust seal, the retaining clip, the oil seal, the oil seal washer and the bottom bush onto the fork slider, making sure that the marked side of the oil seal faces the

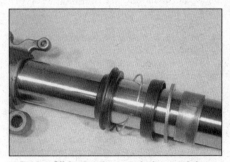

7.19a Slide the dust seal, the retaining clip, the oil seal, the oil seal washer and the bottom bush onto the slider as shown

dust seal **(see illustration)**. Remove the insulating tape and fit the top bush into its recess in the slider **(see illustration)**.

20 Apply a smear of the specified clean fork oil to the outer surface of each bush, then carefully insert the slider fully into the fork tube **(see illustration)**.

21 Support the fork upside down, then press the bottom bush squarely into its recess in the fork tube as far as possible **(see illustration)**. Slide the oil seal washer on top of the bush, and keep the oil seal, the retaining clip and the dust seal out of the way by sliding them up the slider. If necessary, tape them to the slider to prevent them from falling down and interfering as the bush is drifted into place.

22 Using either the special service tool (Pt. No. 887130960) or a suitable drift, carefully drive the bottom bush fully into its recess using the oil seal washer to prevent damaging the edges of the bush **(see illustration)**. Make

7.19b Make sure the top bush seats properly in its recess

7.20 Fit the slider into the bottom of the fork tube

7.21 Make sure the bottom bush enters the fork tube squarely

7.22 Drive the bush into place using a suitable drift

7.23 Drive the oil seal into the bottom of the tube . . .

7.24a . . . and fit its retaining clip, making sure it is properly seated . . .

7.24b . . . then press the dust seal into place

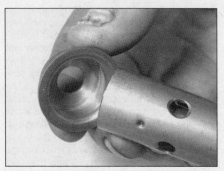

7.25a Fit the damper rod seat onto the end of the damper rod

7.25b Use a new sealing washer on the damper rod bolt

7.26a Pour the specified quantity and type of oil into the top of the tube

sure the bush enters the recess squarely, and take care not to scratch or gouge the slider (it is best to make sure that the fork slider is pushed fully into the tube so that any accidental scratching is confined to the area

7.26b Measure the oil level with the fork held vertical

that does not affect the oil seal).

23 When the bush is seated fully and squarely in its recess in the tube, (remove the washer to check, wipe the recess clean, then reinstall the washer), drive the oil seal into place as described in Step 22 until the retaining clip groove is visible above the seal **(see illustration)**.

24 Once the oil seal is correctly seated, fit the retaining clip, making sure it is correctly located in its groove, then press the dust seal into position **(see illustrations)**.

25 Install the damper assembly seat onto the bottom of the damper assembly, then insert the damper into the top of the fork tube and down through the slider until it seats on the bottom of the slider **(see illustration)**. Fit a new copper sealing washer to the damper assembly bolt and apply a few drops of a suitable non-permanent thread locking compound, then install the bolt into the

bottom of the slider and tighten it securely **(see illustration)**. Install the removed axle clamp bolt, but do not tighten it.

26 Slowly pour in half the specified quantity and grade of fork oil, and pump the damper rod at least ten times to distribute the oil evenly, then pour in the rest of the oil **(see illustration)**. Now measure the oil level. Fully compress the fork tube and the damper and measure the fork oil level from the top of the tube **(see illustration)**. Add or subtract fork oil until the oil is at the level quoted in the Specifications Section – the level not the quantity is the more accurate Specification, as long as all the oil has been distributed and all air expelled.

27 Install the slider, the seat rubber and the washer (where fitted) into the top of the spring sleeve **(see illustrations)**. Withdraw the damper rod as far as possible out of the fork tube, and keep it extended using the aid of an

7.27a Fit the slider into the top of the spring sleeve . . .

7.27b . . . followed by the seat rubber . . .

7.27c . . . and the washer

7.27d Fit the spring into the tube . . .

7.27e . . . followed by the spring sleeve

7.29a Keeping the spring compressed, thread the locknut onto the damper rod

assistant and a piece of wire tied around it to hold it. Install the spring with its tapered end upwards into the fork tube, then install the spring sleeve **(see illustration)**.

28 On 900SS/SL models adjust the rebound damping adjuster screw in the middle of the top bolt so that it projects 1.5 mm above the top of the bolt.

29 Compress the spring using the method described in Step 4 and fit the spring restraint, then thread the locknut on the damper rod as far down the rod as possible **(see illustration)**.

 Warning: This is a potentially dangerous operation and should be performed with care, using an assistant if necessary. Wipe off any excess oil before starting to prevent the possibility of slipping.

Fit a new O-ring to the fork top bolt. Keeping the spring compressed, thread the top bolt onto the damper rod as far as it will go, then, counter-holding the top bolt, tighten the locknut securely against **(see illustration)**. Compress the spring to enable the restraining plate and holding wire to be removed, then carefully release the spring.

30 Apply a smear of the specified clean oil to the top bolt O-ring. Fully extend the fork slider, then press down on the top bolt to compress the spring and thread the bolt into the fork tube.

Note: *The top bolt can be tightened at this stage if the tube is held between the padded jaws of a vice, but do not risk distorting the tube by doing so. A better method is to tighten the top bolt when the fork has been installed in the bike and is securely held in the yokes.*

7.29b Fit a new O-ring onto the top bolt and thread it onto the damper rod

 *Warning: It will be necessary to compress the spring by pressing it down using the top bolt to engage the threads of the top bolt with the fork tube. This is a potentially dangerous operation and should be performed with care, using an assistant if necessary. Wipe off any excess oil before starting to prevent the possibility of slipping.* Keep the fork tube fully extended whilst pressing on the spring. Screw the top bolt carefully into the fork tube making sure it is not cross-threaded.

31 Install the forks as described in Section 6.

600SS, early 750SS from frame VIN 007707, 1991 to 1999 M600 and 750, 1998 and 1999 M900 (Marzocchi forks)

Note: *It is advisable to measure the fork oil level before the forks are dismantled and also to drain the oil into a measuring jug in order*

that the quantity can be recorded for refilling. Specifications are given at the beginning of this Chapter for oil quantity and level although these may be found to differ from that measured.

Disassembly

32 Always dismantle the fork legs separately to avoid interchanging parts and thus causing an accelerated rate of wear. Store all components in separate, clearly marked containers **(see illustration)**.

33 If the fork top bolt was not slackened with the fork in situ, carefully clamp the fork tube in a vice, taking care not to overtighten or score its surface, then slacken the fork top bolt. Unscrew the fork top bolt from the top of the fork tube.

34 Hold the fork vertical and slide the fork tube down onto the slider (wrap a rag around the sleeve on the top of the spring and the top of the tube to minimise oil spillage) while, with

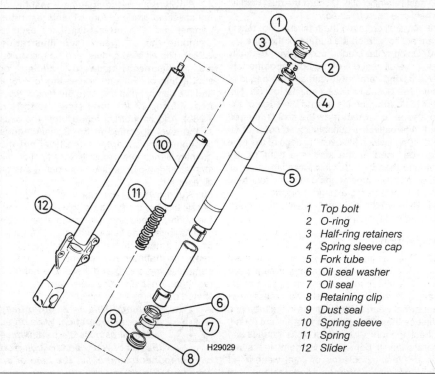

1 Top bolt
2 O-ring
3 Half-ring retainers
4 Spring sleeve cap
5 Fork tube
6 Oil seal washer
7 Oil seal
8 Retaining clip
9 Dust seal
10 Spring sleeve
11 Spring
12 Slider

7.32 Front fork components – 600SS, 750SS from frame VIN 007707, M600 and M750

the aid of an assistant if necessary, keeping the damper rod fully extended. It is now necessary to compress the spring whilst keeping the damper rod extended in order to release the two half-ring spring retainers. Ducati provide a special tool (Pt. No. 887131151) to make this easier. The tool is basically a rod, threaded on one end, which screws into the top of the damper rod and acts as a handle for keeping the damper rod extended while the spring is compressed. If the special tool is not available, a suitable bolt can be used instead.

 Warning: The fork spring may be exerting considerable pressure on the half-ring retainers, making this a potentially dangerous operation. Wipe off as much oil as possible to minimise the risk of your hands slipping on oily components and enlist the help of an assistant. Slowly release the spring once the retainers have been removed.

Compress the spring to enable the retainers to be removed, then carefully release the spring. Unscrew the special tool or bolt from the end of the damper rod.

35 Withdraw the spring sleeve cap, the spring sleeve and the spring, noting how they fit.

36 Invert the fork leg over a suitable container and pump the fork and damper rod vigorously to expel as much fork oil as possible.

37 Withdraw the fork slider assembly from the fork tube.

38 Carefully prise out the dust seal from the bottom of the fork tube to gain access to the oil seal retaining clip. Discard the dust seal as a new one must be used.

39 Carefully remove the retaining clip, taking care not to scratch the surface of the tube.

40 Using a flat-bladed screwdriver, carefully lever the oil seal out of the bottom of the fork tube, taking care not to damage the edges of the tube. Ducati provide a special tool (Pt. No. 887131152) which fits around the edge of the fork tube to protect it as the seal is levered out. Alternatively a suitable lipped collar or an old oil seal which fits over the edge of the tube can be used. If the seal is a tight fit, try rotating the fork tube whilst levering the seal. Alternatively, immerse the end of the fork tube in very hot water to expand it slightly.

41 Remove the oil seal washer, noting which way up it fits.

Inspection

42 Clean all parts in solvent and blow them dry with compressed air, if available. Check the fork slider for score marks, scratches, flaking of the chrome finish and excessive or abnormal wear. Look for dents in the tube and replace the tube in both forks if any are found. Check the fork seal seat for nicks, gouges and scratches. If damage is evident, leaks will occur. Also check the oil seal washer for damage and distortion, and replace it if necessary.

43 If the fork slider is suspected of being bent, it can be checked for runout using V-blocks and a dial gauge **(see illustration 7.15)**. No service limit is provided by the manufacturer – seek the advice of a Ducati dealer if in doubt about its condition.

 Warning: If the slider is bent, it should not be straightened; replace it with a new one.

44 Check the spring for cracks and other damage. If it is defective or sagged, replace the springs in both forks with new ones. Never replace only one spring.

Reassembly

45 Install the oil seal washer with its lipped side facing out, into the bottom of the fork tube.

46 Install the new oil seal, with its marked side facing out, into the bottom of the fork tube, and drive it fully into place until the retaining clip groove is visible above the seal. Ducati provide a special tool (Pt. No. 887131153) for installing the seal, or alternatively use a seal driver or other suitable drift (such as a large socket) which bears only on the outer edge of the seal.

47 Once the oil seal is correctly seated, fit the retaining clip, making sure it is correctly located in its groove.

48 Fit the dust seal onto the fork slider assembly, making sure it is the right way up, then lubricate the slider and dust seal with the specified clean fork oil and insert it into the fork tube. Compress the slider fully into the tube, then press the dust seal into the bottom of the tube.

49 Slowly pour in the specified quantity of the specified grade of fork oil, and pump the damper and tube at least ten times each to distribute the oil evenly **(see illustration 7.26a)**. The oil level should also be measured and adjustment made by adding or subtracting oil. Fully compress the fork tube and the damper and measure the fork oil level from the top of the tube **(see illustration 7.26b)**. Add or subtract fork oil until the oil is at the level specified in the Specifications Section of this Chapter – the level not the quantity is the more accurate Specification, as long as all the oil has been distributed and all air expelled.

50 Withdraw the damper rod as far as possible out of the fork tube. Install the spring, the spring sleeve and the spring sleeve cap with its lipped side facing out.

51 Using the method described in Step 34 to keep the damper rod extended, carefully compress the spring and install the half-ring retainers, making sure they are properly seated before releasing the spring.

 Warning: This is a potentially dangerous operation. Wipe off as much oil as possible to minimise the risk of your hands slipping on oily components and enlist the help of an assistant. Slowly release the spring once the retainers have been installed.

52 Apply a smear of the specified clean oil to the top bolt O-ring. Fully extend the fork slider, then press down on the top bolt to compress the spring and thread the bolt into the fork tube. **Note:** *The top bolt can be tightened to the specified torque setting at this stage if the tube is held between the padded jaws of a vice, but do not risk distorting the tube by doing so. A better method is to tighten the top bolt when the fork has been installed in the bike and is securely held in the yokes.*

 Warning: It will be necessary to compress the spring by pressing it down using the top bolt to engage the threads of the top bolt with the fork tube. This is a potentially dangerous operation and should be performed with care, using an assistant if necessary. Wipe off any excess oil before starting to prevent the possibility of slipping. Keep the fork tube fully extended whilst pressing on the spring. Screw the top bolt carefully into the fork tube making sure it is not cross-threaded.

53 Install the forks as described in Section 6.

Early M900 from frame VIN 009915 to end 1997 (Marzocchi forks)

Note: *It is advisable to measure the fork oil level before the forks are dismantled and also to drain the oil into a measuring jug in order that the quantity can be recorded for refilling. Specifications are given at the beginning of this Chapter for oil quantity and level although these may be found to differ from that measured.*

Disassembly

54 Always dismantle the fork legs separately to avoid interchanging parts and thus causing an accelerated rate of wear. Store all components in separate, clearly marked containers **(see illustration)**.

55 If the fork top bolt was not slackened with the fork in situ, carefully clamp the fork tube in a vice, taking care not to overtighten or score its surface, then slacken the fork top bolt. Unscrew the fork top bolt from the top of the fork tube.

56 Hold the flats of the damper rod locknut with an open-ended spanner and unscrew the top bolt from the damper rod.

57 Hold the fork vertical and slide the fork tube down onto the slider (wrap a rag around the collar on the top of the spring and the top of the tube to minimise oil spillage) while, with the aid of an assistant if necessary, keeping the damper rod fully extended. It is now necessary to compress the spring whilst keeping the damper rod extended in order to release the slotted spring retainer. Compress the spring to enable the retainer to be removed, then carefully release the spring.

 Warning: The fork spring may be exerting considerable pressure on the retainer, making this a potentially dangerous operation.

Wipe off as much oil as possible to minimise the risk of your hands slipping on oily components and enlist the help of an assistant. Slowly release the spring once the retainer has been removed.

58 Withdraw the spring sleeve cap, the spring sleeve and the spring, noting how they fit.

59 Invert the fork leg over a suitable container and pump the fork and damper rod vigorously to expel as much fork oil as possible.

60 Withdraw the fork slider assembly from the fork tube.

61 Slacken off the grub screw in the side of the slider a few turns. Remove the damper rod bolt and its copper sealing washer from the bottom of the slider. Discard the sealing washer as a new one must be used on reassembly.

62 Withdraw the damper rod from the fork tube.

63 Carefully prise out the dust seal from the bottom of the fork tube to gain access to the oil seal retaining clip. Discard the dust seal as a new one must be used.

64 Carefully remove the retaining clip, taking care not to scratch the surface of the tube.

65 Using a flat-bladed screwdriver, carefully lever the oil seal out of the bottom of the fork tube, taking care not to damage the edges of the tube. Ducati provide a special tool (Pt. No. 887131152) which fits around the edge of the fork tube to protect it as the seal is levered out. Alternatively a suitable lipped collar or an old oil seal which fits over the edge of the tube can be used. If the seal is a tight fit, try rotating the fork tube whilst levering the seal. Alternatively, immerse the end of the fork tube in very hot water to expand it slightly.

66 Remove the oil seal washer, noting which way up it fits.

Inspection

67 Clean all parts in solvent and blow them dry with compressed air, if available. Check the fork slider for score marks, scratches, flaking of the chrome finish and excessive or abnormal wear. Look for dents in the tube and replace the tube in both forks if any are found. Check the fork seal seat for nicks, gouges and scratches. If damage is evident, leaks will occur. Also check the oil seal washer for damage and distortion, and replace it if necessary.

68 If the fork slider is suspected of being bent, it can be checked for runout using V-blocks and a dial gauge **(see illustration 7.15)**. No service limit is provided by the manufacturer – seek the advice of a Ducati dealer if in doubt about its condition.

⚠️ *Warning: If the slider is bent, it should not be straightened; replace it with a new one.*

69 Check the spring for cracks and other damage. If it is defective or sagged, replace the springs in both forks with new ones. Never replace only one spring.

70 Check all the damper rod assembly components for damage and wear, and replace any that are defective.

Reassembly

71 Install the oil seal washer with its lipped side facing out, into the bottom of the fork tube.

72 Install the new oil seal, with its marked side facing out, into the bottom of the fork tube, and drive it fully into place until the retaining clip groove is visible above the seal. Ducati provide a special tool (Pt. No. 887131153) for installing the seal, or alternatively use a seal driver or other suitable drift (such as a large socket) which bears only on the outer edge of the seal.

73 Once the oil seal is correctly seated, fit the retaining clip, making sure it is correctly located in its groove.

74 Insert the damper rod into the top of the fork slider until it seats on the bottom. Fit a new copper sealing washer to the damper assembly bolt and apply a few drops of a suitable non-permanent thread locking compound, then install the bolt into the bottom of the slider and tighten securely. Tighten the grub screw in the side of the slider.

75 Fit the dust seal onto the fork slider assembly, making sure it is the right way up, then lubricate the slider and dust seal with the specified clean fork oil and insert it into the fork tube. Compress the slider fully into the tube, then press the dust seal into the bottom of the tube.

76 Slowly pour in the specified quantity of the specified grade of fork oil, and pump the damper and tube at least ten times each to distribute the oil evenly **(see illustration 7.26a)**. The oil level should also be measured and adjustment made by adding or subtracting oil. Fully compress the fork tube and the damper and measure the fork oil level from the top of the tube **(see illus-**

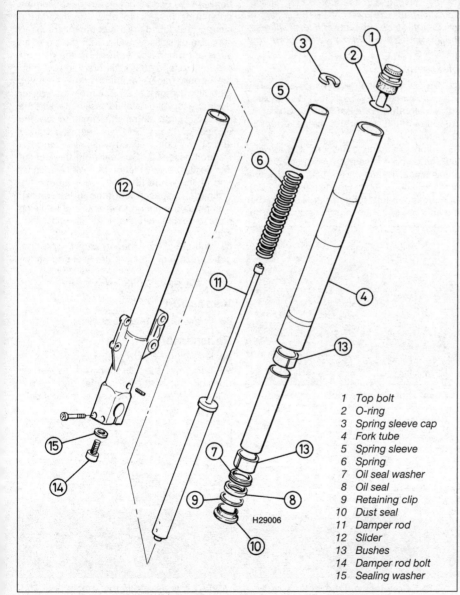

1 Top bolt
2 O-ring
3 Spring sleeve cap
4 Fork tube
5 Spring sleeve
6 Spring
7 Oil seal washer
8 Oil seal
9 Retaining clip
10 Dust seal
11 Damper rod
12 Slider
13 Bushes
14 Damper rod bolt
15 Sealing washer

H29006

7.54 Front fork components – M900 from frame VIN 009915

tration 7.26b). Add or subtract fork oil until the oil is at the level specified in the Specifications Section of this Chapter – the level not the quantity is the more accurate Specification, as long as all the oil has been distributed and all air expelled..

77 Withdraw the damper rod as far as possible out of the fork tube. Install the spring, the spring sleeve and the spring sleeve cap with its lipped side facing out.

78 Hold the damper rod extended, then carefully compress the spring sleeve and install the slotted spring retainer, making sure it is properly seated beneath the nut before releasing the spring.

 Warning: This is a potentially dangerous operation. Wipe off as much oil as possible to minimise the risk of your hands slipping on oily components and enlist the help of an assistant. Slowly release the spring once the retainer has been installed.

79 Hold the damper rod nut with an open-ended spanner and thread the top bolt on the damper rod, tightening it securely.

80 Apply a smear of the specified clean oil to the top bolt O-ring. Fully extend the fork slider, then press down on the top bolt to compress the spring and thread the bolt into the fork tube. **Note:** *The top bolt can be tightened to the specified torque setting at this stage if the tube is held between the padded jaws of a vice, but do not risk distorting the tube by doing so. A better method is to tighten the top bolt when the fork has been installed in the bike and is securely held in the yokes.*

7.84 Unscrew the top bolt

7.85b . . . and how they fit

 Warning: It will be necessary to compress the spring by pressing it down using the top bolt to engage the threads of the top bolt with the fork tube. This is a potentially dangerous operation and should be performed with care, using an assistant if necessary. Wipe off any excess oil before starting to prevent the possibility of slipping. Keep the fork tube fully extended whilst pressing on the spring. Screw the top bolt carefully into the fork tube making sure it is not cross-threaded.

81 Install the forks as described in Section 6.

M900i.e. (with adjustment) and 1998 to 2002 900i.e. Supersport

Note: *It is advisable to measure the fork oil level before the forks are dismantled and also to drain the oil into a measuring jug in order that the quantity can be recorded for refilling. Specifications are given at the beginning of this Chapter for oil quantity and level although these may be found to differ from that measured.*

Disassembly

82 Always dismantle the fork legs separately to avoid interchanging parts and thus causing an accelerated rate of wear. Store all components in separate, clearly marked containers.

83 Before dismantling the fork, it is advised that the damper assembly bolt be slackened at this stage. To access the bolt, remove one of the axle clamp bolts **(see illustration 7.2a)**. Compress the fork tube in the slider so that the spring exerts maximum pressure on the

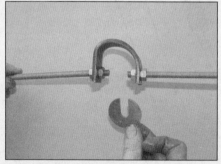

7.85a These are the tools we made . . .

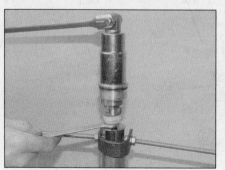

7.85c Counter-hold the locknut and unscrew the top bolt assembly . . .

damper head, then have an assistant slacken the damper bolt in the base of the fork slider **(see illustration 7.2b)**.

84 If the fork top bolt was not slackened with the fork in situ, carefully clamp the fork tube in a vice, taking care not to overtighten or score its surface, then slacken the fork top bolt **(see illustration)**. Unscrew the fork top bolt from the top of the fork tube.

85 It is now necessary to compress the spring in order to access the locknut below the top bolt. Obtain either the Ducati service tool set (Pt. Nos. 887131036 and 887130957), or construct home-made equivalents from a piece of steel strap bent into a U-shape and some threaded rod and nuts (for the holding tool) and a washer with a slot cut into it to the middle (the retaining plate) **(see illustration)**. Either place the fork upright on the floor or carefully clamp the brake caliper lugs between the padded jaws of a vice. Slide the outer tube fully down onto the inner tube (wrap a rag around the top of the outer tube to minimise oil spillage) while, with the aid of an assistant if necessary, keeping the damper rod fully extended. Fit the holding tool onto the upper spacer, locating it into the holes **(see illustration)**. Push down on the spacer using the tool and have an assistant insert the retaining plate under the locknut on the damper cartridge. This will keep the spacer and spring compressed while removing the top bolt assembly. Counter-hold the locknut immediately below the top bolt with a spanner and unscrew the top bolt, and remove the washer and spacer seat **(see illustrations)**. Compress the spring to enable the retaining plate to be removed, then carefully release the spring.

86 Withdraw the spacer and the spring, noting how they fit. Note the seal ring on the spacer.

87 Follow Steps 9 through to 13 above.

Inspection

88 Follow Steps 14 to 18 above.

Reassembly

89 Follow Steps 19 to 26 above.

90 Withdraw the damper rod as far as possible out of the fork tube, and keep it extended. Make sure the seal ring is correctly

7.85d . . . and remove the spacer seat and washer

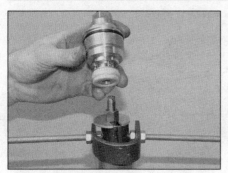

7.92 Thread the top bolt assembly onto the rod

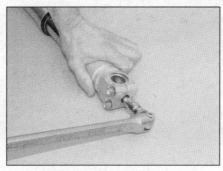

7.96 Slacken the damper rod bolt

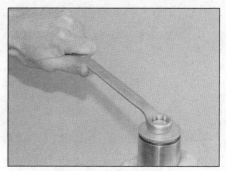

7.97 Unscrew the top bolt

fitted on the spacer. Install the spring with its tapered end upwards into the fork tube, then install the spacer.

91 Compress the spring using the method described in Step 85 and fit the retainer plate.

92 Fit a new O-ring to the fork top bolt. Fit the washer and spacer seat with the top bolt **(see illustration 7.85d)**, then thread the top bolt onto the damper rod as far as it will go **(see illustration)**. Counter-holding the top bolt, tighten the locknut securely against it **(see illustration 7.85c)**. Compress the spring to enable the retaining plate to be removed, then carefully release the spring.

93 Apply a smear of the specified clean oil to the top bolt O-ring. Fully extend the fork slider, then thread the top bolt into the fork tube making sure it is not cross-threaded **(see illustration 7.84)**. Note: *The top bolt can be tightened at this stage if the tube is held between the padded jaws of a vice, but do not risk distorting the tube by doing so. A better method is to tighten the top bolt when the fork has been installed in the bike and is securely held in the yokes.*

94 Install the forks as described in Section 6.

M620i.e., 2002 M750i.e., 620i.e. Sport, 750i.e. Sport and 900i.e. Sport

Note: *It is advisable to measure the fork oil level before the forks are dismantled and also to drain the oil into a measuring jug in order that the quantity can be recorded for refilling. Specifications are given at the beginning of* this Chapter for oil quantity and level although these may be found to differ from that measured.

Disassembly

95 Always dismantle the fork legs separately to avoid interchanging parts and thus causing an accelerated rate of wear. Store all components in separate, clearly marked containers.

96 Before dismantling the fork, it is advised that the damper assembly bolt be slackened at this stage. Compress the fork tube in the slider so that the spring exerts maximum pressure on the damper head, then have an assistant slacken then lightly retighten the damper bolt in the base of the fork slider **(see illustration)**.

97 If the fork top bolt was not slackened with the fork in situ, carefully clamp the fork tube in a vice, taking care not to overtighten or score its surface, then slacken the fork top bolt **(see illustration)**. Unscrew the fork top bolt from the top of the fork tube.

98 Counter-hold the locknut immediately below the top bolt with a spanner and unscrew the top bolt **(see illustration)**. Compress the spring to enable the retaining plate to be removed, then carefully release the spring and remove it **(see illustrations)**.

99 Invert the fork leg over a suitable container and pump the fork and damper rod vigorously to expel as much fork oil as possible **(see illustration)**. While the fork is tipped over to expel the oil, remove the spring spacer **(see illustration)**.

100 Remove the previously slackened damper assembly bolt and its copper sealing

7.98a Counter-hold the locknut and unscrew the top bolt assembly

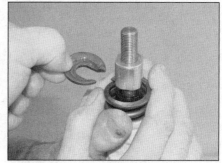

7.98b Remove the retaining plate . . .

7.98c . . . and the spring

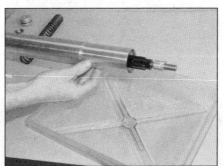

7.99a Tip and pump the oil out of the fork . . .

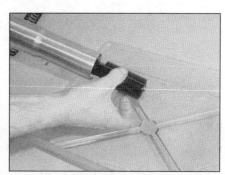

7.99b . . . removing the spacer as you do

7.100 Unscrew and remove the damper bolt . . .

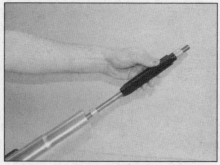

7.101 . . . then withdraw the damper assembly

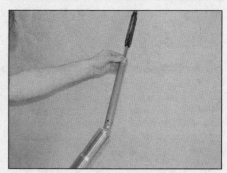

7.105 Slide the damper assembly into the fork

washer from the bottom of the slider **(see illustration)**. Discard the sealing washer as a new one must be used on reassembly. If the damper bolt was not slackened before dismantling the fork, it may be necessary to secure the damper to prevent it from turning.

101 Withdraw the damper assembly from the fork tube **(see illustration)**.

102 Follow Steps 9 through to 13 above.

Inspection

103 Follow Steps 14 to 18 above.

Reassembly

104 Follow Steps 19 to 24 above.

105 Insert the damper assembly into the top of the fork tube and down through the slider until it seats on the bottom of the slider **(see illustration)**. Fit a new copper sealing washer to the damper assembly bolt and apply a few drops of a suitable non-permanent thread

locking compound, then install the bolt into the bottom of the slider and tighten it securely **(see illustration 7.100)**.

106 Slowly pour in half the specified quantity and grade of fork oil, and pump the damper rod at least ten times to distribute the oil evenly, then pour in the rest of the oil **(see illustration)**. Now measure the oil level. Fully compress the fork tube and the damper and measure the fork oil level from the top of the tube **(see illustration)**. Add or subtract fork oil until the oil is at the level quoted in the Specifications Section – the level not the quantity is the more accurate Specification, as long as all the oil has been distributed and all air expelled.

107 Withdraw the damper rod as far as possible out of the fork tube, and keep it extended. Insert the spacer into the fork tube, then fit the spring with the closer wound coils at the top **(see illustrations)**.

108 Compress the spring and fit the retainer plate **(see illustration 7.98b)**. Make sure the locknut is tight against the damper assembly.

109 Fit a new O-ring to the fork top bolt. Thread the top bolt onto the damper rod as far as it will go. Counter-holding the locknut, tighten the top bolt securely against it **(see illustration 7.98a)**. Compress the spring to enable the retaining plate to be removed, then carefully release the spring.

110 Apply a smear of the specified clean oil to the top bolt O-ring. Fully extend the fork slider, then thread the top bolt into the fork tube making sure it is not cross-threaded **(see illustration 7.97)**. *Note: The top bolt can be tightened at this stage if the tube is held between the padded jaws of a vice, but do not risk distorting the tube by doing so. A better method is to tighten the top bolt when the fork has been installed in the bike and is securely held in the yokes.*

111 Install the forks as described in Section 6.

2000 to 2001 M600 and 750, 2000 to 2002 M900i.e. (without adjustment), 1998 to 2002 750i.e. Supersport

Note: *It is advisable to measure the fork oil level before the forks are dismantled and also to drain the oil into a measuring jug in order that the quantity can be recorded for refilling. Specifications are given at the beginning of this Chapter for oil quantity and level although these may be found to differ from that measured.*

Disassembly

112 Always dismantle the fork legs separately to avoid interchanging parts and thus causing an accelerated rate of wear. Store all components in separate, clearly marked containers.

113 Before dismantling the fork, it is advised that the damper assembly bolt be slackened at this stage. Compress the fork tube in the slider so that the spring exerts maximum pressure on the damper head, then have an assistant slacken the damper bolt in the base of the fork slider **(see illustration 7.96)**.

114 If the fork top bolt was not slackened with the fork in situ, carefully clamp the fork tube in a vice, taking care not to overtighten or score its surface, then slacken the fork top

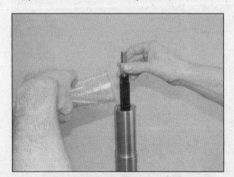

7.106a Pour the specified quantity and type of oil into the top of the tube

7.106b Measure the oil level with the fork held vertical

7.107a Install the spacer . . .

7.107b . . . followed by the spring

8.3a The brake hose union is secured to the frame by two bolts

8.3b The turn signal mount is held to the top yoke by a single bolt

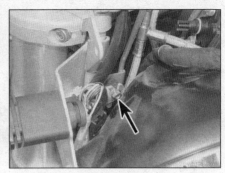

8.3c Unscrew the bolt on the right (arrowed) from the top . . .

8.3d . . . and the bolt on the left from the underside . . .

8.3e . . . and lift the bracket off the studs

bolt **(see illustration 7.97)**. Unscrew the fork top bolt from the top of the fork tube.

115 Counter-hold the top bolt and slacken the locknut immediately below it, then seat it back against the top bolt, not so that it is tight but so its position can be recorded. Now thread the top bolt off the rod. Measure the distance between the top of the locknut and the top of the damper rod and record It so the nut can be set In the same position on reassembly. Thread the locknut off the rod, then remove the spacer seat, the spacer, the spring seat (which will probably be In the bottom of the spacer) and the spring, noting which way up all components fit.

116 Follow Steps 6 through to 13 above.

Inspection

117 Follow Steps 14 to 18 above.

Reassembly

118 Follow Steps 19 to 26 above.

119 Withdraw the damper rod as far as possible out of the fork tube, and keep it extended. If removed fit the long shoulder of the spring seat into the bottom end of the spacer (the end with the indent). Install the spring with its tapered end upwards into the fork tube, then install the spacer, followed by the spacer seat.

120 Carefully compress the spring and thread the nut, rounded end facing down, onto the damper rod and set it to the distance recorded before it was removed.

121 Fit a new O-ring to the fork top bolt. Thread the top bolt onto the damper rod and seat it on the locknut. Counter-holding the locknut, tighten the top bolt securely against it.

122 Apply a smear of the specified clean oil to the top bolt O-ring. Fully extend the fork slider, then thread the top bolt into the fork tube making sure it is not cross-threaded **(see illustration 7.84)**. Note: *The top bolt can be tightened at this stage if the tube is held between the padded jaws of a vice, but do not risk distorting the tube by doing so. A better method is to tighten the top bolt when the fork has been installed in the bike and is securely held in the yokes.*

123 Install the forks as described in Section 6.

---

8 Steering stem – removal and installation

Caution: Although not strictly necessary, before removing the steering stem it is recommended that the fuel tank be removed or raised up on its prop. This will prevent accidental damage to the paintwork.

Removal

1 Where fitted remove the fairing (see Chapter 7).

2 Remove the front forks (see Section 6).

3 On Monster models, where necessary, displace the instrument cluster, headlight bracket, handlebars, brake hose union, and turn signals from the top yoke and move them aside. There should be no need to disconnect

8.4a Bottom yoke brake hose clamp – 900SS shown

any wiring, cables or hoses **(see illustrations)**. On later Monster models, unscrew the two bracket bolts and lift the bracket off the instrument cluster studs in the top yoke **(see illustrations)**.

4 Unscrew the bolt(s) securing the brake hose clamp and the speedometer cable clamp (where fitted) to the bottom yoke **(see illustration)**. On Monster models the clamp is formed by the base of the headlight bracket; removal of the bolts releases the headlight assembly, which should then be supported **(see illustration)**.

5 On SS and SL models, if the top yoke is to be removed from the bike altogether, trace the ignition switch wiring, noting its routing and releasing it from any clips or ties, and disconnect it at its connector.

6 Slacken the steering stem pinch bolt, then on all except 2002-on Monster models

8.4b The brake hose(s) and speedometer cable are secured by the base of the headlight bracket. Unscrew the two bolts to release them from the yoke

8.6a A special tool is required to slacken the circular type nut (arrowed) used on later models

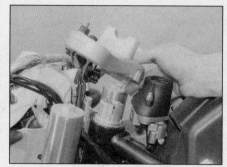

8.6b Lift the top yoke off the steering stem

8.7 Commercially available tools as shown are available for such nuts

remove the steering stem nut, with its washer where fitted (see illustration 5.4b). On later models with the drilled circular nut a peg spanner is needed to slacken the nut (see illustration) – Ducati can provide the tool, part No. 88713.1058, or you may be able to purchase a universal multi-fit peg tool from a good supplier of automotive tools (see illustration 8.7). Lift the top yoke off the steering stem (see illustration).

7 Supporting the bottom yoke, on all except 2002-on Monster models unscrew and remove the adjuster nut using a C-spanner. On 2002-on Monsters unscrew the steering stem nut/adjuster nut using the Ducati tool, part No. 88713.1058 or you may be able to purchase a universal multi-fit peg tool from a good supplier of automotive tools as shown (see illustration). On all models remove the bearing cover.

8 Gently lower the bottom yoke and steering stem out of the frame.

9 Remove the upper bearing from the top of the steering head. Remove all traces of old grease from the bearings and races and check them for wear or damage as described in Section 9. Note: Do not attempt to remove the outer races from the frame or the lower bearing from the steering stem unless they are to be replaced.

Installation

10 Smear a liberal quantity of grease on the bearing races in the frame. Work the grease well into both the upper and lower bearings.

11 Carefully lift the steering stem/bottom

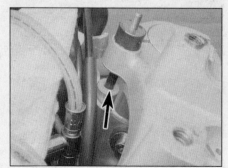

8.12 Make sure the studs in the yoke locate in the holes in the bracket (arrow)

yoke up through the frame. Install the upper bearing in the top of the steering head. Install the bearing cover and thread the adjuster nut, or on 2002-on Monsters the steering stem nut/adjuster nut (see Step 7), on the steering stem. Tighten the adjuster nut until all play is taken out of the bearings. Adjust the bearings as described in Chapter 1 after the installation procedure is complete.

Caution: Take great care not to apply excessive pressure because this will cause premature failure of the bearings.

12 Install the top yoke onto the steering stem, on later Monsters making sure it locates correctly (see illustration). Install the washer (where fitted) and steering stem nut (except 2002-on Monsters) and tighten it finger-tight at this stage. Temporarily install one of the forks to align the top and bottom yokes, and secure it by tightening the bottom yoke clamp bolts only.

13 Tighten the steering stem nut to the specified torque setting. On SS and SL models, if disconnected, reconnect the ignition switch wiring connector and secure it with the clips and ties, making sure it is correctly routed.

14 Install the fork legs (see Section 6).

15 Install the brake hose clamp on the

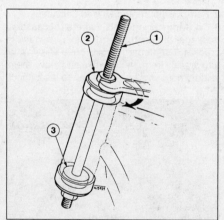

9.6 Drawbolt arrangement for fitting steering head bearing races
1 Long bolt or threaded bar
2 Thick washer
3 Guide for lower race

bottom yoke. On Monsters, make sure the headlight bracket is correctly mounted and that the speedometer cable is installed behind the clamp as well as the brake hose(s).

16 On Monsters, where necessary according to year and model, install the headlight bracket, instrument cluster, handlebars, brake hose union, and turn signals.

17 Where removed install the fairing (see Chapter 7).

18 Carry out a check of the steering head bearing freeplay as described in Chapter 1, and if necessary re-adjust.

9 Steering head bearings – inspection and replacement

Inspection

1 Remove the steering stem as described in Section 8.

2 Remove all traces of old grease from the bearings and races and check them for wear or damage.

3 The races should be polished and free from indentations. Inspect the bearing rollers (tapered roller type bearing) or bearing balls (2002-on Monster models) for signs of wear, damage or discoloration, and examine the bearing roller/ball retainer cage for signs of cracks or splits. Spin the bearings by hand. They should spin freely and smoothly. If there are any signs of wear on any of the above components both upper and lower bearing assemblies must be replaced as a set.

Replacement

4 The races are an interference fit in the steering head and can be tapped from position with a suitable drift. Tap firmly and evenly around each race to ensure that it is driven out squarely. It may prove advantageous to curve the end of the drift slightly to improve access.

5 Alternatively, the races can be removed using a slide-hammer type bearing extractor; these can often be hired from tool shops.

6 The new races can be pressed into the head using a drawbolt arrangement (see illustration), or by using a large diameter

tubular drift which bears only on the outer edge of the race. Ensure that the drawbolt washer or drift (as applicable) bears only on the outer edge of the race and does not contact the working surface. Alternatively, have the races installed by a Ducati dealer.

 Installation of new head bearing races is made much easier if the races are left overnight in the freezer. This causes them to contract slightly making them a looser fit.

7 To remove the lower bearing from the steering stem, use two screwdrivers placed on opposite sides of the race to work it free. If the bearing is firmly in place it will be necessary to use a bearing puller, or in extreme circumstances to split the bearing's inner section.

8 Fit the new lower bearing onto the steering stem, noting that the washer must first be in place on the stem. A length of tubing with an internal diameter slightly larger than the steering stem will be needed to tap the new bearing into position. Ensure that the drift bears only on the inner edge of the bearing and does not contact the rollers.

9 Install the steering stem as described in Section 8.

10 Rear shock absorber – removal, inspection and installation

Removal

SS and SL, Sport and Supersport models

1 Support the machine securely in an upright position using an auxiliary stand. Place a support under the rear wheel so that it is just supported, but so that there is no pressure on the shock absorber.

2 Remove the fuel tank (see Chapter 3), and to prevent the possibility of damage the side panels (see Chapter 7). Slacken the clamps securing the hoses to the crankcase breather

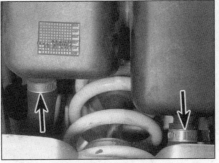

10.2a Slacken the clamps (arrows) and detach the hoses

tank assembly and detach the hoses (see illustration). Unscrew the two bolts securing the vent tank assembly to the frame and remove it (see illustration). On models with a remote reservoir free it from its holder.

3 Unscrew the shock absorber lower mounting bolt nut, then withdraw the bolt and collect the washers (see illustration).

4 Support the shock absorber and unscrew the upper mounting bolt, noting the washers (see illustration). Withdraw the bolt and manoeuvre the shock absorber out through the top of the frame. Check the condition of the O-rings that fit against the top mounting and replace them if necessary (see illustration).

1991 to 2001 Monster models

5 Support the machine securely in an upright

10.2b The crankcase breather tank assembly is secured by two bolts (arrow)

position using an auxiliary stand. Place a support under the rear wheel so that it is just supported, but so that there is no pressure on the shock absorber.

6 Remove the fuel tank (see Chapter 3), and the side panels (see Chapter 7). Slacken the clamps securing the hoses to the crankcase breather tank, then unscrew the two tank mounting bolts and remove the tank (see illustrations). On models with a remote reservoir free it from its holder.

7 Unscrew the shock absorber lower mounting bolt nut, accessing it via the hole in the right-hand side of the swingarm, then withdraw the bolt and collect the washer(s) (a special plate washer is fitted to early M600 and all M900 models).

8 Support the shock absorber and unscrew

10.3 Rear shock absorber lower mounting bolt (arrow)

10.4a Rear shock absorber upper mounting bolt (arrow)

10.4b Replace the top mounting O-rings if necessary

10.6a Clamp securing hose to crankcase breather tank

10.6b The tank is secured to the frame by two bolts (rear bolt shown)

10.8 Shock absorber top mounting bolt

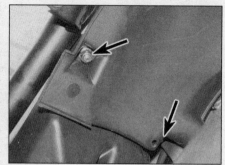

10.10a Unscrew the nuts (arrowed) on the underside . . .

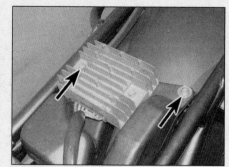

10.10b . . . and the bolts (arrowed) on top . . .

the upper mounting bolt **(see illustration)**. Withdraw the bolt and manoeuvre the shock absorber out through the top of the frame.

2002-on Monster models

9 Support the machine securely in an upright position using an auxiliary stand. Place a support under the rear wheel so that it is just supported, but so that there is no pressure on the shock absorber.
10 Remove the seat (see Chapter 7). Slacken the clamps securing the hoses to the crankcase breather tank, then unscrew the tank mounting bolts and nuts and remove the tank, disconnecting the regulator/rectifier wiring connectors when accessible **(see illustrations)**.
11 Displace the master cylinder from the

frame and detach the brake pedal from the master cylinder pushrod **(see illustrations)**. On models with a remote reservoir free it from its holder.
12 Unscrew the shock absorber lower mounting bolt nut, accessing it via the hole in the right-hand side of the swingarm, then withdraw the bolt **(see illustration)**. Note that the bolt threads into a captive nut in the swingarm which will no longer be held, and that the bottom end of the linkage rod is now free, and that there is a collar on each side of the ball joint in the end of the rod that could fall out **(see illustrations 11.13b and 16b)**. Remove them all for safekeeping if required.
13 Support the shock absorber and unscrew the upper mounting bolt **(see illustration)**.

Withdraw the bolt and manoeuvre the shock absorber out through the top of the frame.

Inspection

14 Inspect the shock absorber for obvious physical damage and the coil spring for looseness, cracks or signs of fatigue.
15 Inspect the damper rod for signs of bending, pitting and oil leakage.
16 Inspect the pivot hardware at the top and bottom of the shock for wear or damage.
17 If the shock absorber is in any way damaged or worn, on some models it can be disassembled and the damaged or worn components replaced, while on others a new unit must be installed. It is advised that the unit is taken to a Ducati dealer or suspension specialist for assessment.

Installation

18 Installation is the reverse of removal, noting the following.
● Apply multi-purpose lithium grease to the pivot points.
● Install the upper mounting bolt first, but do not tighten it until the lower bolt is installed.
● Tighten the mounting bolts to the torque setting specified at the beginning of the Chapter.
● If the shock absorber has been disassembled, adjust the settings as required (see Section 12).
● Check the operation of the rear suspension before taking the machine on the road.

10.10c . . . then displace the tank and disconnect the wiring connectors (arrowed)

10.11a Unscrew the bolts (arrowed) . . .

10.11b . . . then release the clip and pull out the clevis pin to detach the pedal . . .

10.12 Unscrew the bolt (arrowed)

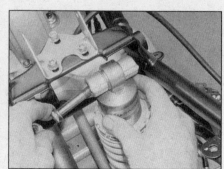

10.13 Unscrew the top bolt and remove the shock absorber

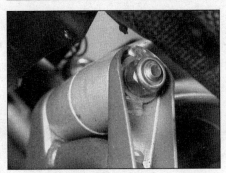

11.6 Linkage arm-to-linkage fork nut

11.7 Linkage fork-to-swingarm ball joint nut

11.10 Remove the linkage rod-to-arm bolt

11 Rear suspension linkage (Monster models) – removal, inspection and installation

Removal

1991 to 2001 models

1 Support the machine securely in an upright position using an auxiliary stand. Place a support under the rear wheel so that it is just supported, but so that there is no pressure on the shock absorber.
2 Remove the seat (see Chapter 7).
3 Slacken the clamps securing the hoses to the crankcase breather tank, then unscrew the two tank mounting bolts and remove the tank (see illustrations 10.6a and 10.6b).
4 Unscrew the nut and withdraw the bolt securing the linkage arm to the top of the shock absorber (see illustration 10.8).
5 Unscrew the nut and withdraw the bolt securing the linkage arm to the frame.
6 Unscrew the nut and withdraw the bolt securing the linkage arm to the linkage fork, then manoeuvre the linkage arm out of the frame, noting how it fits (see illustration).
7 Unscrew the nuts and withdraw the bolts securing the linkage fork to the swingarm and remove the fork (see illustration).

2002-on models

8 Remove the seat (see Chapter 7). Slacken the clamps securing the hoses to the crankcase breather tank, then unscrew the tank mounting bolts and nuts and remove the tank, disconnecting the regulator/rectifier wiring connectors when accessible (see illustrations 10.10a, b and c).
9 Displace the master cylinder from the frame and detach the brake pedal from the master cylinder pushrod (see illustrations 10.11a and b).
10 Unscrew and withdraw the bolt securing the linkage rod to the linkage arm (see illustration).
11 Unscrew and withdraw the bolt securing the linkage arm to the top of the shock absorber (see illustration 10.13).
12 Remove the blanking plug from the frame (see illustration). Unscrew and withdraw the bolt securing the linkage arm to the frame, noting the washer, and remove the linkage arm (see illustration). Remove the bolt's sleeve nut and spacer from its bore.
13 Unscrew the linkage rod/shock absorber lower mounting bolt, accessing it via the hole in the right-hand side of the swingarm, then partially withdraw the bolt, leaving the shock absorber still supported by it (see illustration 10.12). Remove the rod, taking care not to let the ball joint collars drop out (see illustration). Note that the bolt threads into a captive nut in the swingarm which will no longer be held (see illustration).

11.12a Remove the blanking plug to access the bolt head . . .

11.12b . . . then unscrew the bolt and remove the arm

11.13a Remove the linkage rod

11.13b Linkage rod/shock absorber captive nut (arrowed)

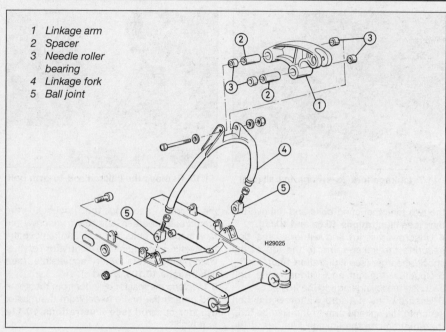

1 Linkage arm
2 Spacer
3 Needle roller bearing
4 Linkage fork
5 Ball joint

H29025

11.14 Suspension linkage components - models to end 2001

Inspection

14 Thoroughly clean all components, removing all traces of dirt, corrosion and grease **(see illustration)**.

15 Inspect all components closely, looking for obvious signs of wear such as heavy scoring, or for damage such as cracks or distortion.

16 Withdraw the spacer(s) from the bearings **(see illustration)**. On 2002-on models remove the collars from the ball joints **(see illustration)**. Check the condition of the needle roller bearings in the linkage arm and of the ball joints on each end of the linkage fork or rod (according to model), referring to Tools and Workshop Tips for information **(see illustration)**. On 2002-on models make sure the seals on each side of the bearings in the linkage arm are in good condition. Lever the old ones out and replace them with new ones if necessary – you will have to remove them before replacing the bearings if that is being done. Do not reuse old seals with new bearings.

17 Worn bearings can be drifted out of their bores, but note that removal will destroy them; new bearings should be obtained before work commences. The new bearings should be pressed or drawn into their bores rather than driven into position. In the absence of a press, a suitable drawbolt arrangement can be made up as described below.

18 It will be necessary to obtain a long bolt or a length of threaded rod from a local engineering works or some other supplier. The bolt or rod should be about one inch longer than the combined width of the linkage arm and one bearing. Also required are suitable nuts and two large and robust washers having a larger outside diameter than the bearing housing. In the case of the threaded rod, fit one nut to one end of the rod and stake it in place for convenience.

19 Fit one of the washers over the bolt or rod so that it rests against the head, then pass the assembly through the relevant bore. Over the projecting end place the bearing, which should be greased to ease installation, followed by the remaining washer and nut.

20 Holding the bearing to ensure that it is kept square, slowly tighten the nut so that the bearing is drawn into its bore.

21 Once it is fully home, remove the drawbolt arrangement and, if necessary, repeat the procedure to fit the other bearings. Do not forget to install the spacer in between the bearings.

22 If you want to replace the ball joints on the end of the linkage fork or rod (according to model), first note how far they are threaded into the fork or rod so the new ones can be set to the same position – discrepancies will result in a changed, and on forked models possibly an uneven, ride height. To replace the ball joints, slacken the locknut, then unscrew the joint and remove it from the end of the fork or rod. On installation, make sure that each ball joint is set to the same position as on removal, and that on forked models they are exactly even, then tighten the locknuts securely.

23 Lubricate the needle roller bearings, the spacer(s), the seals (2002-on models), the ball joints and the pivot bolts with molybdenum disulphide grease.

Installation

24 Installation is the reverse of removal, noting the following.

● Apply multi-purpose lithium grease to the pivot points (see Step 23).

● On models to end 2001 do not forget to install the washers on the linkage arm-to-shock absorber bolt and linkage arm-to-linkage fork bolt.

● On 2002-on models, when installing the linkage arm, locate it between its frame mounts, then slide the bolt through, then fit the spacer onto the bolt and thread the sleeve nut on. Make sure the collars are fitted on each side of each ball joint in the linkage rod. Attach the linkage rod to the arm before the shock absorber and tighten the bolt to the specified torque by raising the arm, otherwise it is difficult to get a torque wrench on the bolt.

● With the exception of the rod-to-arm bolt, do not fully tighten any of the bolts until they have all been installed.

● Tighten the bolts to the torque settings specified at the beginning of the Chapter.

● Check the operation of the rear suspension before taking the machine on the road.

11.16a Withdraw the spacer(s) from the arm . . .

11.16b . . . and the collars from the rod (2002-on models)

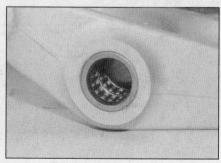

11.16c Check the bearings in the arm as described

12 Suspension – adjustments

Front forks – 900SS and SL, 900i.e. Supersport and M900 (inc. Special) models

Caution: Always ensure that both front fork settings are the same. Uneven settings will upset the handling of the machine and could cause it to become unstable.

Spring preload

1 The front fork spring preload adjuster is located in the centre of each fork top bolt and is adjusted using a suitable spanner (see illustration).

2 The amount of preload is indicated by distance between the top of the adjuster nut and the top of the top bolt. The distance ranges from 10 to 25 mm. To set the preload to the standard amount, turn the adjuster until the distance is 18 mm.

3 To reduce the preload (i.e. soften the ride), rotate the adjuster anti-clockwise.

4 To increase the preload (i.e. stiffen the ride), rotate the adjuster clockwise.

5 Always ensure both adjusters are set to the same position.

Rebound damping

6 The rebound damping adjuster is situated in the centre of the preload adjuster and is adjusted using a flat-bladed screwdriver (see illustration 12.1).

7 Damping positions are identified by counting the number of clicks emitted by the adjuster when it is turned. There are fourteen damping positions.

8 The standard setting recommended is four clicks (900SS/SL) or seven clicks (900i.e. Supersport) or six clicks (M900i.e.) anti-clockwise from the maximum damping setting. The maximum setting is when the adjuster is turned fully clockwise.

9 To establish the present setting, turn one of the adjusters fully clockwise whilst counting the number of clicks emitted, then rotate it back to its original position. Repeat the procedure on the other adjuster to ensure both are set in the same position.

10 To reduce the rebound damping, turn the adjuster anti-clockwise.

11 To increase the rebound damping, turn the adjuster clockwise.

12 Always ensure both adjusters are set to the same position.

Compression damping

13 The compression damping adjuster is situated at the bottom of each fork slider and is adjusted using a flat-bladed screwdriver, on 900i.e. models via the hole in the wheel axle (see illustration).

14 Damping positions are indicated by counting the number of clicks emitted by the adjuster when it is turned. There are fourteen

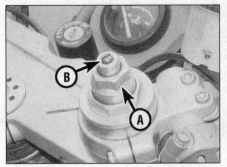

12.1 Front fork pre-load adjuster (A) and rebound damping adjuster (B)

damping positions on 900SS/SL models and sixteen on 900i.e. Supersport and M900i.e. models.

15 The standard setting recommended is six clicks (900SS/SL and M900i.e.) or eleven clicks (900i.e. Supersport) anti-clockwise from the maximum damping setting. The maximum setting is when the adjuster is turned fully clockwise.

16 To establish the present setting, rotate one of the adjusters fully clockwise whilst counting the number of clicks emitted, then rotate it back to its original position. Repeat the procedure on the other adjuster to ensure both are set in the same position.

17 To reduce the compression damping, turn the adjuster anti-clockwise. To increase the compression damping, turn the adjuster clockwise.

18 Always ensure both adjusters are set to the same position.

Front forks – M900 model from frame VIN 009915 to end 1997

Rebound and compression damping

19 The rebound damping adjuster is situated on the right-hand fork top bolt and the compression damping adjuster on the left-hand fork top bolt. Each adjuster position is identified by clicks.

20 Turn the adjuster clockwise to increase damping and anti-clockwise to reduce damping. The standard setting for compression and rebound damping is seven clicks out from the fully clockwise position.

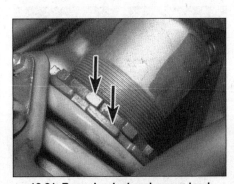

12.21 Rear shock absorber pre-load adjuster rings (arrows)

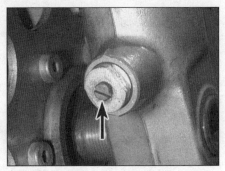

12.13 Front fork compression damping adjuster (arrow) - 900SS/SL

Rear shock absorber – SS and SL, Sport and Supersport models

Spring pre-load

21 The rear shock absorber spring preload adjuster is in the form of two locking rings threaded to the body of the shock absorber (see illustration).

22 To increase the amount of pre-load, slacken the lock ring, turn the adjuster ring by the required amount so the spring is compressed, then tighten the lock ring against the adjuster ring.

23 To decrease the amount of pre-load, slacken the top lock ring, turn the adjuster ring by the required amount so the spring extends, then tighten the lock ring against the adjuster ring.

24 On 600SS models 14 mm of preload is recommended. Ducati do not provide a standard setting for 750 and 900 SS/SL models – if in doubt, consult a Ducati dealer. On 620i.e. Sport, 750i.e. Supersport and Sport and 900i.e. Sport models the standard setting is with a spring length of 177 mm; on 900i.e. Supersport models the standard setting is 160 mm.

Rebound damping

25 The rear shock absorber rebound damping adjuster is situated at the base of the shock absorber and is adjusted by using a flat-bladed screwdriver (see illustration). On 900i.e. Supersport models with an Ohlins shock, turn the upper knurled ring to make adjustment.

12.25 Rear shock absorber rebound damping adjuster (arrow)

26 To increase the rebound damping, turn the adjuster clockwise.

27 To reduce the rebound damping, turn the adjuster anti-clockwise.

28 The standard setting is six clicks (600SS, 750i.e. Sport and 900i.e. Sport), eight clicks (620i.e. Sport and 750i.e. Supersport), or ten clicks (900i.e. Supersport) back from fully clockwise. Ducati do not provide a standard setting for 750SS and 900SS/SL models – if in doubt, consult a Ducati dealer.

Compression damping

29 The rear shock absorber compression damping adjuster is situated at the top of the shock absorber reservoir and is adjusted using a flat-bladed screwdriver on Showa units, or by turning the knurled adjuster knob on Sachs-Boge units **(see illustration)**.

30 To increase the rebound damping, turn the adjuster clockwise.

31 To reduce the rebound damping, turn the adjuster anti-clockwise.

32 The standard setting is twenty-five clicks (600SS, 750i.e. Sport and 900 i.e. Sport), eighteen clicks (620 i.e. Sport and 750 i.e. Supersport), or fourteen clicks (900 i.e. Supersport) back from fully clockwise. Ducati do not provide a standard setting for 750SS and 900SS/SL models – if in doubt, consult a Ducati dealer.

Ride-height

33 On 900i.e. Supersport models with an Ohlins shock absorber, the ride-height can be adjusted without affecting pre-load.

34 Slacken the locknut on the base of the shock absorber, then turn the adjuster nut as required to extend or reduce the length of the rod. Tighten the locknut against the adjuster on completion.

Rear shock absorber – Monster models

35 The rear shock absorber is adjustable for spring pre-load and rebound damping.

Spring pre-load

36 The rear shock absorber spring preload adjuster is in the form of two locking rings threaded to the body of the shock absorber.

37 To increase the amount of pre-load, slacken the lock ring, turn the adjuster ring by the required amount so the spring is compressed, then tighten the lock ring against the adjuster ring.

38 To decrease the amount of pre-load, slacken the lock ring, turn the adjuster ring by the required amount so the spring extends, then tighten the lock ring against the adjuster ring.

39 Ducati recommend a pre-load of 20 mm or a spring set length of 165 mm.

Rebound damping

40 The rear suspension rebound damping adjuster is situated at the base of the shock

12.29 Rear shock absorber compression damping adjuster (arrow)

absorber and is adjusted using a flat-bladed screwdriver.

41 Damping positions are indicated by counting the number of clicks when it is turned. There are fifteen damping positions.

42 The standard setting is eight clicks anti-clockwise from the maximum damping setting. The maximum setting is when the adjuster is turned fully clockwise.

43 To establish the present setting, rotate the adjuster fully clockwise whilst counting the number of clicks, then rotate it back to its original position.

44 To reduce the rebound damping, turn the adjuster anti-clockwise.

45 To increase the rebound damping, turn the adjuster clockwise.

13 Swingarm – removal and installation

Removal

Note: *Before removing the swingarm, it is advisable to perform the swingarm checks described in Chapter 1.*

SS and SL, Supersport and Sport models

1 Remove the rear wheel (see Chapter 6). On models with a torque arm between the swingarm and caliper bracket, detach the arm

13.5 The chain slider is secured by two bolts (arrows) - later Supersport and Sport slider differs

13.2 Remove the brake hose clamp

from either or both components as required.

2 Remove the brake hose clamp from the swingarm **(see illustration)**. Support the caliper so that no strain is placed on the hose.

3 Support the swingarm and remove the rear shock absorber lower mounting bolt (see Section 10 if necessary).

4 If the swingarm and chain need to be separated, remove the chain (see Section 15). Otherwise, remove the front sprocket (see Section 16). Because the chain passes through the bridge on the swingarm, it cannot be separated from the swingarm unless it is split, and will therefore come away with the swingarm. It is not recommended to split the chain unless necessary.

5 Unscrew the bolts securing the chain slider to the front of the swingarm and remove it **(see illustration)**. Check the condition of the slider and replace it if it is worn or damaged.

6 Before removing the swingarm it is advisable to re-check for play either in the bearings or pivot pin (twist), or in the shim(s) between the swingarm and the engine (side-to-side). Any problems which may have been masked with the wheel and shock absorber in place are highlighted with these components removed.

7 Prise off the swingarm pivot pin caps on both sides of the swingarm pivot **(see illustration)**.

8 Slacken the swingarm pivot pin clamp bolt on the bottom of each side of the swingarm

13.7 Remove the swingarm pivot caps

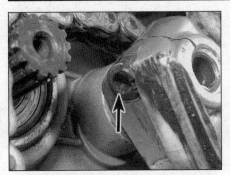

13.8 Slacken each swingarm pivot clamp bolt (arrow)

13.9 Recover the shims as you remove the swingarm

13.23 Do not forget to install the swingarm shims

(see illustration). On later models, remove the circlip from one side of the swingarm pivot pin.

9 With the aid of an assistant to support the swingarm if necessary, drift the pivot pin out from one side of the swingarm (the side on which the circlip was removed, where fitted), then manoeuvre the swingarm out of the rear of the machine. Recover the shim(s) that fit on the inside of the swingarm mounts **(see illustration).** Note that Ducati recommend that the pivot pin without circlips fitted to earlier models be replaced with the pivot pin with circlips fitted to later models; it is also necessary to replace the pivot pin caps – refer to a Ducati dealer for advice on the parts required.

10 If necessary, remove the rear mudguard from the swingarm (see Chapter 7).

11 Inspect all components for wear or damage (see Section 14).

Monster models

12 Remove the rear wheel (see Chapter 6).

13 Remove the brake hose clamp from the swingarm. Support the caliper so that no strain is placed on the hose.

14 Remove the exhaust system (see Chapter 3).

15 Support the swingarm and remove the rear shock absorber lower mounting bolt and on pre-2002 models the bolts securing the linkage fork ball joints to the swingarm (see Sections 10 and 11).

16 Unscrew the bolts securing the chain slider to the front of the swingarm and remove it. Check the condition of the slider and replace it if it is worn or damaged.

17 Before removing the swingarm it is advisable to re-check for play either in the bearings or pivot pin (twist), or in the shim(s) between the swingarm and the engine (side-to-side). Any problems which may have been masked with the wheel and shock absorber in place (see Chapter 1) are highlighted with these components removed.

18 Prise off the swingarm pivot pin caps on both sides of the swingarm.

19 Slacken the swingarm pivot pin clamp bolt on each side of the swingarm. On later models, remove the circlip from one side of the swingarm pivot pin.

20 With the aid of an assistant to support the swingarm if necessary, drift the pivot pin out

from one side of the swingarm (the side on which the circlip was removed, where fitted), then manoeuvre the swingarm out of the rear of the machine. Recover the shim(s) that fit on the inside of the swingarm mounts. Note that Ducati recommend that the pivot pin without circlips fitted to earlier models be replaced with the pivot pin with circlips fitted to later models; it is also necessary to replace the pivot pin caps – refer to a Ducati dealer for advice on the parts required.

21 If necessary, remove the rear mudguard from the swingarm (see Chapter 7).

22 Inspect all components for wear or damage (see Section 14).

Installation

23 Installation is the reverse of removal, noting the following.

● Ducati recommend that the pivot pin without circlips fitted to earlier models be replaced with the pivot pin with circlips fitted to earlier models. See Step 9 or 20.

● Lubricate the bearings, the pivot pin and the shock absorber pivots with molybdenum disulphide grease.

● Do not forget to fit the shim(s) on the inside of the swingarm mounts, or if only one 0.1 mm shim is needed fitting it on the right-hand side, using extra ones as necessary to eliminate excessive side play (see Section 14) **(see illustration).** If unequal shimming is required on each side, fit the largest shim(s) on the right-hand side.

● Tighten the shock absorber and linkage bolts (Monster only) to the torque settings specified at the beginning of the Chapter.

● Tighten the swingarm pivot pin clamp bolts to the torque setting specified at the beginning of the Chapter.

● Check the operation of the rear suspension before taking the machine on the road.

14 Swingarm – inspection and bearing replacement

Inspection

1 Thoroughly clean all components, removing all traces of dirt, corrosion and grease. Inspect all components closely, looking for

obvious signs of wear such as heavy scoring, and cracks or distortion due to accident damage. Any damaged or worn component must be replaced.

2 Check the swingarm pivot pin for runout using V-blocks and a dial gauge and compare the reading to the limit in the specifications at the beginning of the Chapter. Also take several measurements along the length of the pivot pin using a vernier caliper to determine whether there is any wear in the area of contact with the bearings. If the swingarm checks made earlier revealed any play in the swingarm bearings in the form of twist rather than side-to-side play, this could arise either due to wear of the pivot pin or due to wear in the bearings. It is more likely that the wear will occur in the pin, in which case it must be replaced. If the pin is good, then examine the bearings.

3 If the swingarm checks in Chapter 1 revealed any side-to-side play, or endfloat, in the swingarm pivot, then extra shims must be used when installing the swingarm to negate this. Replacement shims are available in 0.1 mm or 0.2 mm sizes. Use as many shims as required to reduce the side-to-side play to a maximum of 0.1 mm, but note that the swingarm should not be a tight fit and must be able to pivot freely. If only one 0.1 mm shim is required, fit it on the right-hand side. If unequal shimming is required on each side, fit the largest shim(s) on the right-hand side.

4 The swingarm bearings are housed in the engine casing. Lever out the seals with a screwdriver and check the condition of the bearings **(see illustrations).** If they are worn

14.4a Lever out the seals using a flat-bladed screwdriver

14.4b Swingarm bearings are of the needle roller type

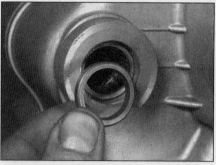

14.6 Use new seals if the bearings have been replaced or if the old ones are worn

16.1 Front sprocket cover

or loose, or feel rough or pitted, they must be replaced. Note that removal of the bearings will damage them and necessitate replacement. Also check the condition of the seals and replace them if necessary.

Bearing replacement

5 The swingarm bearings are housed in the crankcases. Each crankcase half houses a seal on the outside, two needle roller bearings and a seal and retaining circlip on the inside. Lever out the seals with a screwdriver to access the bearings (see illustration 14.4a).
6 Worn bearings can be drifted or pulled out of their bores, but note that removal will destroy them; new bearings should be obtained before work commences. The new bearings should be pressed or drawn into their bores rather than driven into position. In the absence of a press, a suitable drawbolt arrangement can be made up as described in Section 11 of this Chapter. Otherwise the bearings must be replaced by a Ducati dealer. If the bearings are replaced, also fit new seals (see illustration).

15 Drive chain – removal, cleaning and installation

Removal

SS and SL models

Note: *The original equipment drive chain fitted to all models has a staked-type master (soft) link which can be disassembled using one of several commercially-available drive chain cutting/staking tools. Such chains can be recognised by the soft link side plate's identification marks (and usually its different colour), as well as by the staked ends of the link's two pins which look as if they have been deeply centre-punched, instead of peened over as with all the other pins.*

⚠️ *Warning: NEVER install a drive chain which uses a spring clip-type master (split) link. Use ONLY the correct service tools to secure the staked-type of soft link – if you do not have access to such tools, have the chain replaced by a Ducati dealer to be sure of having it securely installed. Refer to Tools and Workshop Tips in*

the Reference section for details of using a chain splitting and riveting tool.
1 Locate the master (split) link in a suitable position to work on by rotating the back wheel.
2 Slacken the drive chain as described in Chapter 1.
3 Split the chain at the soft link using the chain splitter, following the manufacturer's operating instructions. Remove the front sprocket cover (see Section 16). Slip the chain off the sprockets, noting its routing through the swingarm.

Monster models

4 Support the machine securely in an upright position using an auxiliary stand so that the rear wheel is just on the ground, but so that there is no pressure on the shock absorber.
5 On 1991 to 2001 models, unscrew the bolts securing the suspension linkage fork to the swingarm (see illustration 11.7). Swing the fork backwards to provide room for the chain to pass between it and the swingarm. Raise the height of the auxiliary stand if necessary.
6 Unscrew the bolts securing the front sprocket cover and remove the cover.
7 Slacken the drive chain as described in Chapter 1.
8 Remove the front sprocket (see Section 16). Slip the chain off the sprockets and remove it from the machine.

Cleaning

9 Soak the chain in kerosene (paraffin) for approximately five or six minutes.
Caution: Don't use gasoline (petrol), solvent or other cleaning fluids. Don't use high-pressure water.
10 Remove the chain, wipe it off, then blow dry it with compressed air immediately. The entire process shouldn't take longer than ten minutes – if it does, the O-rings in the chain rollers could be damaged.

Installation

SS and SL models

11 Install the drive chain through the swingarm sections and around the front sprocket, leaving the two ends in a convenient position to work on.
12 Install the new master (soft) link from the inside with the four O-rings correctly located

between the link plates. Install the new side plate with its identification marks facing out. Stake the new link using the drive chain cutting/staking tool, following carefully the instructions of both the chain manufacturer and the tool manufacturer. DO NOT re-use old master (split) link components.
13 After staking, check the master (split) link and stakes for any signs of cracking. If there is any evidence of cracking, the master (split) link, O-rings and side plate must be replaced.
14 Install the front sprocket cover.
15 On completion adjust and lubricate the chain following the procedures described in Chapter 1.

Monster models

16 Install the chain around the rear sprocket.
17 Install the chain around the front sprocket, then install the front sprocket (see Section 16).
18 Install the front sprocket cover.
19 On 1991 to 2001 models, align the suspension linkage fork ends with their mounts on the swingarm, then install the bolts and tighten them to the torque setting specified at the beginning of the Chapter.
20 On completion adjust and lubricate the chain following the procedures described in Chapter 1.

16 Sprockets – check and replacement

Check

1 Unscrew the bolts securing the front sprocket cover and remove the cover (see illustration).
2 Check the wear pattern on both sprockets (see Chapter 1). If the sprocket teeth are worn excessively, replace the chain and both sprockets as a set. Whenever the drive chain is inspected, the sprockets should be inspected also. If you are replacing the chain, replace the sprockets as well.
3 Adjust and lubricate the chain following the procedures described in Chapter 1.

Replacement

Front sprocket

4 Unscrew the bolts securing the front

16.6a The sprocket retaining plate is secured by two bolts (arrows)

16.6b Rotate the plate so that its teeth align with the grooves, then draw it off the shaft

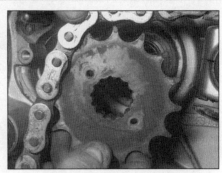

16.8a Fit the chain around the sprocket then slide them onto the shaft

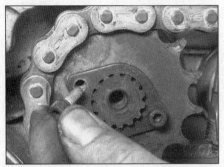

16.8b Install the retaining plate bolts and tighten them securely

16.11 The sprocket is secured to the coupling by six nuts (arrows)

14 Install the rear wheel (see Chapter 6).
15 Adjust and lubricate the chain following the procedures described in Chapter 1.

17 Rear wheel coupling/rubber dampers – check and replacement

1 Remove the rear wheel (see Chapter 6), then remove the rear sprocket from the coupling (see Section 16).
2 Grasp the sprocket coupling and lift it out of the wheel, noting how it fits **(see illustration)**.
3 Inspect all the drive pins on the back of the coupling flange for wear or damage **(see illustration)**. Check that each pin is tightly and securely screwed into the flange. If any of the pins are loose, remove them completely, then apply a suitable non-permanent thread locking compound to the threads and tighten them securely.
4 Check the rubber dampers in the wheel hub for looseness, wear, damage and deterioration, and replace them as necessary **(see illustration)**. The dampers must be drawn out of the hub, using an internal puller if required. Make sure the new dampers are inserted fully and squarely into the hub.
5 Fit the coupling into the dampers and check for any looseness or freeplay between the drive pins and the dampers. If any is found, and all the drive pins and dampers are tight, then wear has occurred between the drive pins and their bores in the dampers, and both sets of components must be replaced.
6 Installation is the reverse of removal.

sprocket cover and remove the cover **(see illustration 16.1)**.
5 Shift the transmission into gear and have an assistant sit on the seat and apply the rear brake hard. This effectively locks the sprockets which allows the sprocket retaining plate bolts to be slackened without the sprocket rotating.
6 Unscrew the two bolts securing the sprocket retaining plate, then rotate the plate slightly in its groove until its teeth align with the spline grooves on the shaft and remove the plate, noting how it fits **(see illustrations)**.
7 Slide the sprocket and chain off the shaft, then slip the sprocket out of the chain. If the chain is too tight to allow the sprocket to be slid off the shaft, slacken the chain adjusters to provide some freeplay (see Chapter 1).
8 Engage the new sprocket with the chain and slide it on the shaft **(see illustration)**. Slide the retaining plate onto the shaft and align it in its

groove, then align its bolt holes with those in the sprocket. Install the bolts, then shift the transmission into gear and have an assistant sit on the seat and apply the rear brake hard, and tighten the bolts securely **(see illustration)**.
9 Install the sprocket cover. Adjust and lubricate the chain following the procedures described in Chapter 1.

Rear sprocket
10 Remove the rear wheel (see Chapter 6).
11 Unscrew the nuts securing the sprocket to the wheel coupling, then remove the sprocket, noting which way round it fits **(see illustration)**.
12 Before installing the new rear sprocket, check the wheel coupling and damper assembly components (see Section 17).
13 Install the sprocket onto the coupling, then apply a suitable non-permanent thread locking compound to the stud threads and tighten the sprocket nuts securely.

17.2 Lift the coupling out of the wheel

17.3 Check each drive pin (arrows) for looseness, wear and damage

17.4 Check each rubber damper (arrows) for looseness, wear, damage and deterioration

Notes

Chapter 6
Brakes, wheels and tyres

Contents

Brake fluid level check . . . . .see Daily (pre-ride) checks
Brake light switches check and replacement . . . . .see Chapter 8
Brake pad wear check . . . . .see Chapter 1
Brake hoses and unions – inspection and replacement 10
Brake system bleeding 11
Brake system check . . . . .see Chapter 1
Front brake caliper(s) – removal, overhaul and installation 3
Front brake disc – inspection, removal and installation 4
Front brake master cylinder – removal, overhaul and installation . . . 5
Front brake pads – replacement 2
Front wheel – removal and installation 14

General information 1
Rear brake caliper – removal, overhaul and installation 7
Rear brake disc – inspection, removal and installation 8
Rear brake master cylinder – removal, overhaul and installation . . . 9
Rear brake pads – replacement 6
Rear wheel – removal and installation 15
Tyres – general information and fitting 17
Wheel bearing check . . . . .see Chapter 1
Wheel bearings – removal, inspection and installation 16
Wheels – alignment check 13
Wheels – inspection and repair 12

Degrees of difficulty

Easy, suitable for novice with little experience	**Fairly easy,** suitable for beginner with some experience	**Fairly difficult,** suitable for competent DIY mechanic	**Difficult,** suitable for experienced DIY mechanic	**Very difficult,** suitable for expert DIY or professional

Specifications

Brakes

Brake fluid type . . . . DOT 4 (AGIP F1 Super HD or Shell Advance)
Disc minimum thickness (front)
  900SL
    Standard . . . . 4.4 to 4.6 mm
    Service limit . . . . 3.5 mm
  All other models
    Standard . . . . 3.9 to 4.1 mm
    Service limit . . . . 3.6 mm
Disc minimum thickness (rear)
  Standard . . . . 3.9 to 4.1 mm
  Service limit . . . . 3.6 mm
Disc maximum runout (front and rear, all models) . . . . 0.3 mm

Wheels

Maximum wheel runout (front and rear)
  Axial (side-to-side) . . . . 2.0 mm
  Radial (out-of-round) . . . . 2.0 mm
Maximum axle runout . . . . 0.2 mm

Tyres

Tyre pressures . . . . Refer to the tyre information label on the swingarm or the machine's owners handbook

Tyre sizes (620i.e. Sport, 750i.e. Sport and Supersport models)*
  Front 120/70-ZR17
  Rear 160/60-ZR17
Tyre sizes (600SS, 750SS, M600, M620 and M750 models)*
  Front 120/60-ZR17
  Rear 160/60-ZR17
Tyre sizes (all 900 models)*
  Front 120/70-ZR17
  Rear 170/60-ZR17

*Refer to the owners handbook for approved tyre brands.

Torque settings

Front brake caliper mounting bolts
    Single pad pin caliper (early models) . . . .   35 to 38 Nm
    Double pad pin caliper (later models) . . . .   43 Nm
Rear brake caliper mounting bolts . . . .   23 to 25 Nm
Brake caliper joining bolts . . . .   33 Nm
Disc mounting bolts . . . .   25 Nm
Brake hose banjo bolts . . . .   17 to 20 Nm
Front axle
    Early style (threading into fork) . . . .   70 to 76 Nm
    Later style (with securing nut) . . . .   63 Nm
Front axle clamp bolts . . . .   20 to 25 Nm
Rear axle nut(s)
    16 mm type . . . .   70 to 76 Nm
    25 mm type . . . .   83 Nm

1 General information

All models covered in this manual are fitted with cast alloy wheels designed for tubeless tyres only.

Both front and rear brakes are hydraulically operated disc brakes, the front having either a single or twin calipers with four opposed pistons. On all models the rear has a single caliper with two opposed pistons.

Caution: Disc brake components rarely require disassembly. Do not disassemble components unless absolutely necessary. If a hydraulic brake line is loosened, the entire system must be disassembled, drained, cleaned and then properly filled and bled upon reassembly. Do not use solvents on internal brake components. Solvents will cause the seals to swell and distort. Use only clean brake fluid or denatured alcohol for cleaning. Use care when working with brake fluid as it can injure your eyes and it will damage painted surfaces and plastic parts.

2 Front brake pads – replacement

Warning: The dust created by the brake system may contain asbestos, which is harmful to your health. Never blow it out with compressed air and don't inhale any of it. An approved filtering mask should be worn when working on the brakes.

1 Remove the R-pin(s) from the pad pin(s), then withdraw the pad pin(s) from the caliper, using a drift from the inside to dislodge it/them if necessary **(see illustrations)**. Note how the pin(s) fit(s) in relation to the spring as you remove it.

2 Remove the pad spring, noting how it fits, then withdraw the pads from the caliper, noting how they fit **(see illustrations)**.

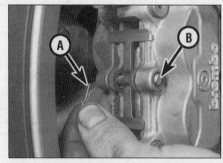
2.1a Remove the R-pin (A), followed by the pad pin (B) - single pin type

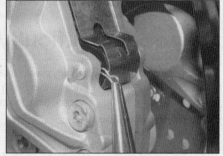
2.1b Remove the R-pins . . .

2.1c . . . then withdraw the pad pins - double pin type

2.2a Remove the pad spring . . .

2.2b . . . followed by the pads - single pin type

2.2c Remove the pad spring . . .

2.2d . . . followed by the pads - double pin type

3 Inspect the surface of each pad for contamination and check that the friction material has not worn beyond its wear limit. If either pad is worn down to, or beyond, the wear groove (i.e. the groove(s) are no longer visible), or the thickness of the material is 1mm or less, is fouled with oil or grease, or heavily scored or damaged by dirt and debris, both pads must be replaced as a set **(see illustration)**. **Note:** *Non original pads (such as shown in illustration 2.2b) may have a step or wear line in the pad material which indicates the service limit – check with the pad manufacturer or supplier for clarification.* Note that it is not possible to degrease the friction material; if the pads are contaminated in any way they must be replaced.

4 If the pads are in good condition clean them carefully, using a fine wire brush which is completely free of oil and grease to remove all traces of road dirt and corrosion. Using a pointed instrument, clean out the grooves in the friction material and dig out any embedded particles of foreign matter.

5 Check the condition of the brake disc (see Section 4).

6 Remove all traces of corrosion from the pad pin. Inspect the pin for signs of damage and replace if necessary.

7 Push the pistons as far back into the caliper as possible using hand pressure only. Due to the increased friction material thickness of new pads, it may be necessary to remove the master cylinder reservoir cover and diaphragm and siphon out some fluid.

8 Smear the backs of the pads and the shank of the pad pin with copper-based grease, making sure that none gets on the front or sides of the pads.

9 Installation of the pads and pad pin(s) is the reverse of removal. Insert the pads into the caliper so that the friction material of each pad is facing the disc. Make sure the pad spring is correctly positioned with its arrow facing out and pointing in the direction of rotation of the wheel **(see illustration)**. Align

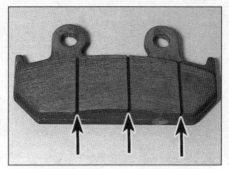

2.3 Brake pads must be replaced when the wear grooves (arrows) are no longer visible (typical pad design shown)

the hole(s) in each pad with those in the caliper, then install the pad pin(s), making sure it/they pass(es) correctly through the spring so it is held. Tap the pad pin using a drift and small hammer to make sure it is fully seated, then secure it with the R-pin(s).

10 Top up the master cylinder reservoir if necessary (see *Daily (pre-ride) checks*), and replace the reservoir cover and diaphragm if removed.

11 Operate the brake lever several times to bring the pads into contact with the disc. Check the master cylinder fluid level and the operation of the brake before riding the motorcycle.

---

3 Front brake caliper(s) – removal, overhaul and installation

⚠️ *Warning: If a caliper indicates the need for an overhaul (usually due to leaking fluid or sticky operation), all old brake fluid should be flushed from the system. Also, the dust created by the brake system may contain asbestos, which is harmful to your*

health. Never blow it out with compressed air and don't inhale any of it. An approved filtering mask should be worn when working on the brakes. Do not, under any circumstances, use petroleum-based solvents to clean brake parts. Use clean brake fluid, brake cleaner or denatured alcohol only.

Note: *Ducati do not recommend that the calipers are disassembled for overhaul or replacement of worn or damaged components, consequently replacement parts and seals (essential for rebuilding the caliper) may not be available. Check first with dealers, local parts stockists and other suppliers before disassembling the calipers to check on the availability of parts. If your caliper is worn or damaged and no parts are available, the only alternative is to fit a new caliper.*

Removal

1 Remove the brake hose banjo bolt, noting its position on the caliper and separate the hose from the caliper **(see illustration)**. Plug the hose end or wrap a plastic bag tightly around it to minimise fluid loss and prevent dirt entering the system. Discard the sealing washers as new ones must be used on installation. **Note:** *If you are planning to overhaul the caliper and don't have a source of compressed air to blow out the pistons, just loosen the banjo bolt at this stage and retighten it lightly. The bike's hydraulic system can then be used to ease the pistons out of their bores once the pads have been removed. Disconnect the hose once the pistons have been sufficiently displaced.*

2 Unscrew the caliper mounting bolts, noting the order of the washers, and slide the caliper away from the disc **(see illustration 3.1)**. Note the speedometer cable guide secured by the top bolt on the left-hand caliper. Remove the brake pads as described in Section 2.

Overhaul

3 Clean the exterior of the caliper with

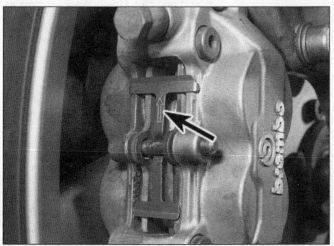

2.9 The arrow on the pad spring (arrow) must point in the direction of wheel rotation

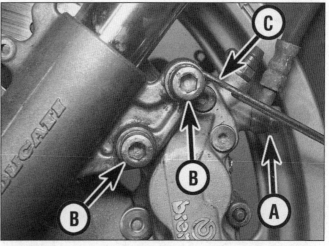

3.1 Brake hose banjo bolt (A), caliper mounting bolts (B), cable guide (C)

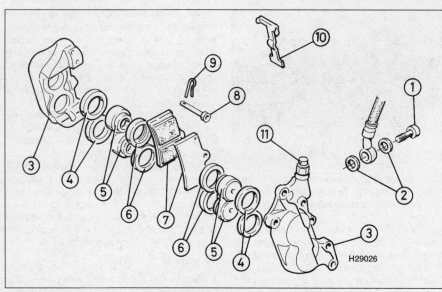

3.3 Front brake caliper components

1 Brake hose banjo bolt	5 Piston	9 R-pin
2 Sealing washer	6 Dust seal	10 Pad spring
3 Caliper body	7 Brake pads	11 Bleed valve and cover
4 Piston seal	8 Pad pin	

caliper is in bad shape the master cylinder should also be checked.

10 Lubricate the new piston seals with clean brake fluid and install them in their grooves in the caliper bores. Note that two sizes of bore and piston are used in some calipers and care must therefore be taken when installing the new seals to ensure that the correct size seals are fitted to the correct bores. The same care must be taken when fitting the new dust seals and the pistons.

11 Lubricate the new dust seals with clean brake fluid and install them in their grooves in the caliper bores.

12 Lubricate the pistons with clean brake fluid and install them closed-end first into the caliper bores. Using your thumbs, push the pistons all the way in, making sure they enter the bore squarely.

13 Lubricate the new caliper seals and install them into one half of the caliper body.

14 Join the two halves of the caliper body together, making sure that the new caliper seals are correctly seated in their recesses.

15 Apply a thread-locking compound to the four caliper assembly bolts, then install them in the caliper body and tighten them to the specified torque setting.

denatured alcohol or brake system cleaner **(see illustration)**.

4 Ease the pistons partially out of their bores in the caliper body, either by hydraulic pressure from the front brake lever, or by using compressed air directed into the fluid inlet. Place a wad of rag between the opposed pistons and make sure that they do not touch. Use only low pressure to ease the pistons partially out and make sure all four pistons are moved at the same time.

 Warning: Never place your fingers in front of the pistons in an attempt to catch or protect them when applying compressed air, as serious injury could result.

5 Unscrew the four caliper body bolts and separate the caliper into its two halves. Fully extract the pistons from their bores, having marked their heads and caliper body with a felt marker to ensure that the pistons can be

matched to their original bores on reassembly. Extract and discard the caliper seals as new ones must be used.

6 Using a wooden or plastic tool, remove the dust seals from the caliper bores and discard them. New seals must be used on installation. If a metal tool is being used, take great care not to damage the caliper bores.

7 Remove and discard the piston seals in the same way.

8 Clean the pistons and bores with denatured alcohol, clean brake fluid or brake system cleaner. If compressed air is available, use it to dry the parts thoroughly (make sure it's filtered and unlubricated).

Caution: Do not, under any circumstances, use a petroleum-based solvent to clean brake parts.

9 Inspect the caliper bores and pistons for signs of corrosion, nicks and burrs and loss of plating. If surface defects are present, the caliper assembly must be replaced. If the

Installation

16 Install the brake pads (see Section 2).

17 Install the caliper on the brake disc making sure the pads sit squarely over the disc, then install the caliper mounting bolts and washers and tighten them to the torque setting specified at the beginning of the Chapter **(see illustrations)**. Do not forget to secure the speedometer cable guide with the top bolt on the left-hand side caliper.

18 Connect the brake hose to the caliper, using a new sealing washer on each side of the fitting. Tighten the banjo bolt to the torque setting specified at the beginning of the Chapter.

19 Fill the master cylinder with the recommended brake fluid (see *Daily (pre-ride) checks*) and bleed the hydraulic system as described in Section 11.

20 Check for leaks and thoroughly test the operation of the brake before riding the motorcycle.

4 Front brake disc – inspection, removal and installation

Inspection

1 Visually inspect the surface of the disc for score marks and other damage. Light scratches are normal after use and won't affect brake operation, but deep grooves and heavy score marks will reduce braking efficiency and accelerate pad wear. If a disc is badly grooved it must be machined or replaced.

2 To check disc runout, position the bike on

3.17a Mount the caliper onto the disc

3.17b Do not forget to install the cable guide (arrow) on the upper mounting bolt on the left-hand side caliper

4.2 Set up a dial indicator to contact the brake disc, then rotate the wheel to check for runout

4.3 Using a micrometer to measure disc thickness

4.5 The disc is secured to the wheel by six bolts (arrows)

an auxiliary stand and support it so that the front wheel is raised off the ground. Mount a dial indicator to a fork leg, with the plunger on the indicator touching the surface of the disc about 10 mm (1/2 inch) from the outer edge **(see illustration)**. Rotate the wheel and watch the indicator needle, comparing the reading with the limit listed in the Specifications at the beginning of the Chapter. If the runout is greater than the service limit, check the wheel bearings for play (see Chapter 1). If the bearings are worn, replace them (see Section 16) and repeat this check. If the disc runout is still excessive, it will have to be replaced, although machining by a competent engineering shop may be possible.

3 The disc must not be machined or allowed to wear down to a thickness less than the service limit as listed in this Chapter's Specifications. The thickness of the disc can be checked with a micrometer **(see illustration)**. If the thickness of the disc is less than the service limit, it must be replaced.

Removal

4 Remove the wheel (see Section 14).
Caution: Do not lay the wheel down and allow it to rest on either disc – the disc could become warped. Set the wheel on wood blocks so the disc doesn't support the weight of the wheel.

5 Mark the relationship of the disc to the wheel, so it can be installed in the same position. Unscrew the disc retaining bolts, loosening them a little at a time in a criss-cross pattern to avoid distorting the disc, then remove the disc from the wheel **(see illustration)**.

Installation

6 Install the disc on the wheel, aligning the previously applied matchmarks if you're reinstalling the original disc.
7 Apply a suitable non-permanent thread locking compound to the disc mounting bolt threads, then install the bolts and tighten them in a criss-cross pattern evenly and progressively to the torque setting specified at the beginning of the Chapter. Clean off all grease from the brake disc(s) using acetone or brake system cleaner. If a new brake disc has

been installed, remove any protective coating from its working surfaces.
8 Install the wheel (see Section 14).
9 Operate the brake lever several times to bring the pads into contact with the disc. Check the operation of the brakes carefully before riding the bike.

5 Front brake master cylinder – removal, overhaul and installation

Note: *Ducati do not recommend that the master cylinder is disassembled for overhaul or replacement of worn or damaged components, consequently replacement parts and seals (essential for rebuilding the master cylinder) may not be available. Check first with dealers, local parts stockists and other suppliers before disassembling the master cylinder to check on the availability of parts. If the master cylinder is worn or damaged and no parts are available, the only alternative is to fit a new master cylinder.*

1 If the master cylinder is leaking fluid, or if the lever does not produce a firm feel when the brake is applied, and bleeding the brakes does not help (see Section 11), and the hydraulic hoses are all in good condition, then master cylinder overhaul is recommended.
2 Before disassembling the master cylinder, read through the entire procedure and make sure that you have the correct rebuild kit (see **Note** above). Also, you will need some new, clean

brake fluid of the recommended type, some clean rags and internal circlip pliers. **Note:** *To prevent damage to the paint from spilled brake fluid, always cover the fuel tank or raise it up on its prop when working on the master cylinder.*
Caution: Disassembly, overhaul and reassembly of the brake master cylinder must be done in a spotlessly clean work area to avoid contamination and possible failure of the brake hydraulic system components.

Removal

3 On Monster models, if required, remove the rear view mirror (see Chapter 7).
4 On models fitted with an integral master cylinder and reservoir, loosen, but do not remove, the screws holding the reservoir cover in place.
5 Trace the brake light switch wiring back from the switch and disconnect it at its connector.
6 Remove the locknut from the underside of the brake lever pivot bolt, then unscrew the bolt and remove the brake lever **(see illustration)**.
7 Unscrew the banjo bolt and separate the brake hose(s) from the master cylinder, noting the arrangement of the washers and the spacer on models with dual front brakes and the alignment of the hose(s) **(see illustration)**. Discard the sealing washers as these must be replaced with new ones. Wrap the end of the hose(s) in a clean rag and either suspend in an upright position or bend down carefully and place the open end in a clean container. The

5.6 Brake lever pivot bolt locknut (arrow)

5.7 Brake hose banjo bolt arrangement on dual front brake models

5.8 The master cylinder assembly clamp is secured by two bolts (arrows)

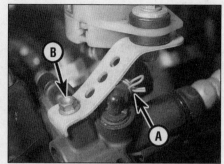

5.9 Reservoir hose clamp (A) and reservoir mounting bolt (B)

objective is to prevent excessive loss of brake fluid, fluid spills and system contamination.

8 Remove the master cylinder mounting bolts to free the clamp, then lift the master cylinder and reservoir away from the handlebar **(see illustration)**.

Caution: Do not tip the master cylinder upside down or brake fluid will run out.

9 On models with a separate reservoir, if required separate the reservoir from the master cylinder by releasing the hose clamp and detaching the hose, then unscrew the bolt securing the reservoir **(see illustration)**.

Overhaul

10 Remove the reservoir cover and the rubber diaphragm **(see illustration)**. Drain the brake fluid from the reservoir into a suitable container. Wipe any remaining fluid out of the reservoir with a clean rag.

11 Unscrew the nuts securing the brake light switch to the bottom of the master cylinder and remove the switch **(see illustration)**.

12 Carefully remove the dust boot from the end of the piston.

13 Using circlip pliers, remove the circlip and slide out the piston assembly and the spring, noting how they fit. Lay the parts out in the

proper order to prevent confusion during reassembly.

14 Clean all parts with clean brake fluid or denatured alcohol. If compressed air is available, use it to dry the parts thoroughly (make sure it's filtered and unlubricated).

Caution: Do not, under any circumstances, use a petroleum-based solvent to clean brake parts.

15 Check the master cylinder bore for corrosion, scratches, nicks and score marks. If damage or wear is evident, the master cylinder must be replaced with a new one. If the master cylinder is in poor condition, then the caliper(s) should be checked as well. Check that the fluid inlet and outlet ports in the master cylinder are clear.

16 Install the spring in the master cylinder bore.

17 Install new seals on the piston. Lubricate the piston components with clean hydraulic fluid and install the assembly into the master cylinder, making sure all the components are the correct way round. Make sure the lips on the cup seals do not turn inside out when they are slipped into the bore. Depress the piston and install the new circlip, making sure that it locates in the master cylinder groove.

18 Install the rubber dust boot, making sure the lip is seated correctly in the piston groove.

19 Install the brake light switch **(see illustration 5.11)**.

20 Inspect the reservoir cover rubber diaphragm and replace if damaged or deteriorated. On models with a separate reservoir, inspect the reservoir hose for cracks or splits and replace if necessary.

Installation

21 On models with a separate reservoir, if removed install the reservoir onto its mount and attach the hose, securing it with its clamp **(see illustration 5.9)**.

22 Attach the master cylinder to the handlebar. Fit the clamp with its "UP" mark and arrowhead pointing upwards on SS/SL models, or with its mirror mounting upwards on Monster models; tighten the upper bolt first then the lower bolt **(see illustration 5.8)**.

23 Connect the brake hose(s) to the master cylinder, using new sealing washers on each side of the union, and aligning the hose(s) as noted on removal **(see illustration 5.7)**. Tighten the banjo bolt to the torque setting specified at the beginning of this Chapter.

24 Install the brake lever into its bracket and secure it with its pivot bolt.

25 Connect the brake light switch wiring. On Monsters, if removed install the rear view mirror (see Chapter 7).

26 Fill the fluid reservoir with the specified brake fluid as described in Daily (pre-ride) checks. Refer to Section 11 of this Chapter and bleed the air from the system.

27 Fit the rubber diaphragm, making sure it is correctly seated, and the cover, onto the master cylinder reservoir.

6 Rear brake pads –
replacement

> **Warning: The dust created by the brake system may contain asbestos, which is harmful to your health. Never blow it out with compressed air and don't inhale any of it. An approved filtering mask should be worn when working on the brakes.**

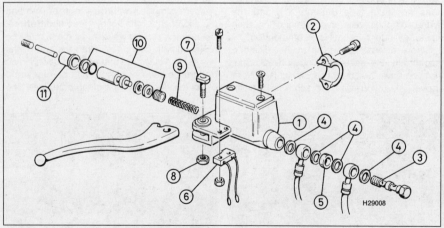

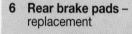

5.10 Front brake master cylinder components

1 Reservoir/master cylinder	5 Spacer	9 Spring
2 Clamp	6 Brake light switch	10 Piston and seal
3 Brake hose banjo bolt	7 Brake lever pivot bolt	assembly
4 Sealing washers	8 Locknut	11 Rubber boot

5.11 The front brake switch is secured by two small nuts (arrows)

6.1 Withdraw the pad pin using a pair of pliers

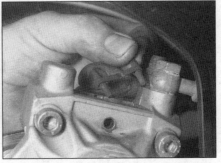

6.2a Remove the pad spring . . .

6.2b . . . then withdraw the pads from the caliper

1 Withdraw the pad pin from the caliper, using a drift from the inside to dislodge it if necessary **(see illustration)**. Note how the pin fits in relation to the spring as you remove it.
2 Remove the pad spring, then withdraw the pads from the caliper, noting how they fit **(see illustrations)**.
3 Inspect the surface of each pad for contamination and check that the friction material has not worn beyond its wear limit. If either pad is worn down to, or beyond, the wear groove (i.e. the groove is no longer visible), fouled with oil or grease, or heavily scored or damaged by dirt and debris, both pads must be replaced as a set **(see illustration 2.3)**. Note: *Non original pads (such as shown in illustration 6.2b) may have a step or wear line in the pad material which indicates the service limit – check with the pad manufacturer or supplier for clarification.* Note that it is not possible to degrease the friction material; if the pads are contaminated in any way they must be replaced.
4 If the pads are in good condition clean them carefully, using a fine wire brush which is completely free of oil and grease to remove all traces of road dirt and corrosion. Using a pointed instrument, clean out the groove in the friction material and dig out any embedded particles of foreign matter.
5 Check the condition of the brake disc (see Section 8).
6 Remove all traces of corrosion from the pad pin. Inspect the pin for signs of damage and replace it if necessary.
7 Push the pistons as far back into the caliper as possible using hand pressure only. Due to

the increased friction material thickness of new pads, it may be necessary to remove the master cylinder reservoir cover and diaphragm and siphon out some fluid.
8 Smear the backs of the pads and the shank of the pad pin with copper-based grease, making sure that none gets on the front or sides of the pads.
9 Installation of the pads and pad pin is the reverse of removal. Make sure the pad spring is correctly positioned **(see illustration 6.2a)**. Insert the pads into the caliper so that the friction material of each pad is facing the disc. Align the hole in each pad with those in the caliper, then install the pad pin **(see illustration)**. Tap the pad pin using a drift and small hammer to make sure it is fully seated.
10 Top up the master cylinder reservoir if necessary (see *Daily (pre-ride) checks*), and replace the reservoir cover and diaphragm if removed.
11 Operate the brake pedal several times to bring the pads into contact with the disc. Check the master cylinder fluid level and the operation of the brake before riding the motorcycle.

7 Rear brake caliper – removal, overhaul and installation

⚠ *Warning: If a caliper indicates the need for an overhaul (usually due to leaking fluid or sticky operation), all old brake fluid should be flushed from the system. Also, the dust created by the brake system may contain asbestos, which is harmful to your health.*

Never blow it out with compressed air and don't inhale any of it. An approved filtering mask should be worn when working on the brakes. Do not, under any circumstances, use petroleum-based solvents to clean brake parts. Use clean brake fluid, brake cleaner or denatured alcohol only.
Note: *Ducati do not recommend that the caliper is disassembled for overhaul or replacement of worn or damaged components, consequently replacement parts and seals (essential for rebuilding the caliper) may not be available. Check first with dealers, local parts stockists and other suppliers before disassembling the caliper to check on the availability of parts. If your caliper is worn or damaged and no parts are available, the only alternative is to fit a new caliper.*

Removal

1 Remove the brake hose banjo bolt, noting its position on the caliper, and separate the hose from the caliper **(see illustration)**. Plug the hose end or wrap a plastic bag tightly around it to minimise fluid loss and prevent dirt entering the system. Discard the sealing washers as new ones must be used on installation. **Note:** *If you are planning to overhaul the caliper and don't have a source of compressed air to blow out the pistons, just loosen the banjo bolt at this stage and retighten it lightly. The bike's hydraulic system can then be used to ease the pistons out of the body once the pads have been removed. Disconnect the hose once the pistons have been sufficiently displaced.*
2 Unscrew the caliper mounting bolts, and slide the caliper away from the disc **(see illustration)**. Remove the brake pads as

6.9 Fit the pad pin through the holes in the caliper and the top of each pad

7.1 Brake hose banjo bolt (arrow)

7.2 Rear brake caliper mounting bolts (arrows)

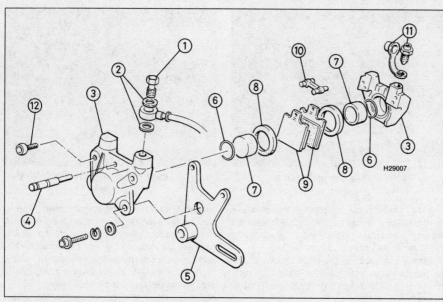

7.3 Rear brake caliper components

1 Brake hose banjo bolt	5 Caliper mounting bracket	9 Brake pads
2 Sealing washer	6 Piston seal	10 Pad spring
3 Caliper halves	7 Piston	11 Bleed valve and cover
4 Pad pin	8 Dust seal	12 Caliper joining bolts

9 Thoroughly inspect the caliper bores and pistons for any signs of corrosion, nicks and burrs and loss of plating. If any surface defects are present, the caliper assembly must be replaced. If the caliper is in bad shape the master cylinder should also be checked.

10 Lubricate the new piston seals with clean brake fluid and install them in their grooves in the caliper bores.

11 Lubricate the new dust seals with clean brake fluid and install them in their grooves in the caliper bores.

12 Lubricate the pistons with clean brake fluid and install them closed-end first into the caliper bores. Using your thumbs, push the pistons all the way in, making sure they enter the bore squarely.

13 Lubricate the new caliper seals and install them into one half of the caliper body.

14 Join the two halves of the caliper body together, making sure that the new caliper seals are correctly seated in their recesses.

15 Apply a thread-locking compound to the two caliper assembly bolts, then install them in the caliper body and tighten them to the specified torque setting.

Installation

16 Install the brake pads as described in Section 6.

17 Install the caliper on the brake disc, making sure the pads sit squarely either side of the disc, then install the caliper mounting bolts and tighten them to the torque setting specified at the beginning of the Chapter **(see illustrations)**. Do not forget to install the brake torque arm (where applicable).

18 Connect the brake hose to the caliper using new sealing washers on each side of the fitting. Position the hose as noted on removal **(see illustration 7.1)**. Tighten the banjo bolt to the torque setting specified at the beginning of the Chapter.

19 Fill the master cylinder with the recommended brake fluid (see *Daily (pre-ride) checks*) and bleed the hydraulic system as described in Section 11.

20 Check for leaks and thoroughly test the operation of the brake before riding the motorcycle.

described in Section 6. Where fitted, note the fitting of the brake torque arm.

Overhaul

3 Clean the exterior of the caliper with denatured alcohol or brake system cleaner **(see illustration)**.

4 Ease the pistons partially out of their bores in the caliper body, either by hydraulic pressure from the rear brake pedal, or by using compressed air directed into the fluid inlet. Place a wad of rag between the pistons and make sure that they do not touch. Use only low pressure to ease the pistons partially out and make sure both pistons are moved at the same time.

⚠ *Warning: Never place your fingers in front of the pistons in an attempt to catch or protect them when applying compressed air, as serious injury could result.*

5 Unscrew the two caliper body bolts and

separate the caliper into its two halves. Fully extract the pistons from their bores, having marked their heads and caliper body with a felt marker to ensure that the pistons can be matched to their original bores on reassembly. Extract and discard the caliper seals as new ones must be used.

6 Using a wooden or plastic tool, remove the dust seals from the caliper bores and discard them. New seals must be used on installation. If a metal tool is being used, take great care not to damage the caliper bores.

7 Remove and discard the piston seals in the same way.

8 Clean the pistons and bores with denatured alcohol, clean brake fluid or brake system cleaner. If compressed air is available, use it to dry the parts thoroughly (make sure it's filtered and unlubricated).

Caution: Do not, under any circumstances, use a petroleum-based solvent to clean brake parts.

8 Rear brake disc – inspection, removal and installation

Inspection

1 Refer to Section 4 of this Chapter, noting that the dial indicator should be attached to the swingarm.

Removal

2 Remove the rear wheel (see Section 15).

3 Mark the relationship of the disc to the wheel so it can be installed in the same position. Unscrew the disc retaining bolts,

7.17a Mount the caliper onto the disc . . .

7.17b . . . and secure it with the two mounting bolts

8.3 The rear disc is secured to the wheel by six bolts (arrows)

9.4 Brake hose banjo bolt (A), reservoir hose clamp and elbow (B)

9.5a Pushrod ball joint-to-brake pedal bolt (arrow)

loosening them a little at a time in a criss-cross pattern to avoid distorting the disc, and remove the disc (see illustration).

Installation

4 Position the disc on the wheel, aligning the previously applied matchmarks if you're reinstalling the original disc.

5 Apply a suitable non-permanent thread locking compound to the disc mounting bolts, then install the bolts and tighten them in a criss-cross pattern evenly and progressively to the torque setting specified at the beginning of this Chapter. Clean off all grease from the brake disc using acetone or brake system cleaner. If a new brake disc has been installed, remove any protective coating from its working surfaces.

6 Install the rear wheel (see Section 15).

7 Operate the brake pedal several times to bring the pads into contact with the disc. Check the operation of the brake carefully before riding the motorcycle.

9 Rear brake master cylinder – removal, overhaul and installation

Note: *Ducati do not recommend that the master cylinder is disassembled for overhaul or replacement of worn or damaged components, consequently replacement parts and seals (essential for rebuilding the master cylinder) may not be available. Check first with dealers, local parts stockists and other suppliers before disassembling the master cylinder to check on the availability of parts. If the master cylinder is worn or damaged and no parts are available, the only alternative is to fit a new master cylinder.*

1 If the master cylinder is leaking fluid, or if the pedal does not produce a firm feel when the brake is applied, and bleeding the brakes does not help (see Section 11), and the hydraulic hoses are all in good condition, then master cylinder overhaul is recommended.

2 Before disassembling the master cylinder, read through the entire procedure and make sure that you have the correct rebuild kit (see *Note* above). Also, you will need some new, clean brake fluid of the recommended type, some clean rags and internal circlip pliers.

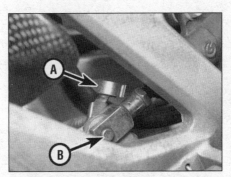

9.5b Release the clip (A) from the pushrod; push the pin (B) through from the outside

Caution: Disassembly, overhaul and reassembly of the brake master cylinder must be done in a spotlessly clean work area to avoid contamination and possible failure of the brake hydraulic system components.

Removal

3 On early 750SS and 900SS models with a pressure type brake switch, disconnect the wiring connectors from the switch terminals.

4 Unscrew the brake hose banjo bolt (brake switch on early 750SS and 900SS models) and separate the brake hose from the master cylinder (see illustration). Note the alignment of the hose union. Discard the two sealing washers as these must be replaced with new ones. Wrap the end of the hose in a clean rag and suspend the hose in an upright position or bend it down carefully and place the open

9.6b Master cylinder mounting bolts on Monsters

9.6a Master cylinder mounting bolts (arrows) on early style SS/SL models

end in a clean container. The objective is to prevent excessive loss of brake fluid, fluid spills and system contamination.

5 On early style SS and SL models, unscrew the nut from the bolt securing the brake pedal to the master cylinder pushrod ball joint (see illustration). Withdraw the bolt and separate the pedal from the pushrod. On Monsters and some later style Sport and Supersport models, remove the clip from the pushrod, then push the pin through from the outside and remove the clip/pin, noting how it fits (see illustration). On other later style Sport and Supersport models remove the circlip from the pivot and withdraw the pivot.

6 Unscrew the two bolts securing the master cylinder to the footrest bracket (see illustrations).

7 Remove the bolt securing the master cylinder reservoir to the frame (on SS/SL,

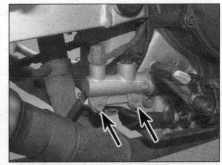

9.6c Master cylinder mounting bolts (arrows) on later style SS/SL models

9.7 The reservoir is secured to the frame by a single bolt (early style SS/SL shown)

Sport and Supersport models) or to the back of the footrest bracket (on Monsters), then remove the reservoir cover and pour the fluid into a container **(see illustration)**.

8 Separate the fluid reservoir hose from the elbow on the master cylinder by releasing the hose clamp **(see illustration 9.4)**.

Overhaul

9 If necessary, slacken the ball joint or clevis locknut, then unscrew the ball joint or clevis with its locknut and remove them from the pushrod **(see illustration)**. Note the position of the ball joint or clevis on the pushrod before removing it so it can be installed in the same position.

10 Dislodge the rubber dust boot from the base of the master cylinder to reveal the pushrod retaining circlip.

11 Depress the pushrod and, using circlip pliers, remove the circlip. Slide out the piston assembly and spring. If they are difficult to remove, apply low pressure compressed air to the fluid outlet. Lay the parts out in the proper order to prevent confusion during reassembly.

12 Clean all of the parts with clean brake fluid or denatured alcohol. If compressed air is available, use it to dry the parts thoroughly (make sure it's filtered and unlubricated). **Caution: Do not, under any circumstances, use a petroleum-based solvent to clean brake parts.**

13 Check the master cylinder bore for corrosion, scratches, nicks and score marks. If the necessary measuring equipment is available, compare the dimensions of the piston and bore to those given in the Specifications Section of this Chapter. If damage is evident, the master cylinder must be replaced with a new one. If the master cylinder is in poor condition, then the caliper should be checked as well.

14 Inspect the reservoir hose for cracks or splits and replace if necessary.

15 Install the spring in the master cylinder bore.

16 Install new seals on the piston. Lubricate the piston assembly components with clean hydraulic fluid and install the assembly into the master cylinder, making sure all the components are the correct way round. Make sure the lips on the cup seals do not turn inside out when they are slipped into the bore.

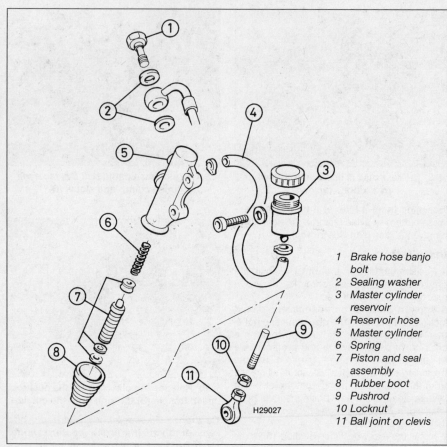

1 Brake hose banjo bolt
2 Sealing washer
3 Master cylinder reservoir
4 Reservoir hose
5 Master cylinder
6 Spring
7 Piston and seal assembly
8 Rubber boot
9 Pushrod
10 Locknut
11 Ball joint or clevis

9.9 Rear brake master cylinder components

17 Install and depress the pushrod, then install a new circlip, making sure it is properly seated in the groove.

18 Install the rubber dust boot, making sure the lip is seated properly in the groove.

Installation

19 Install the master cylinder onto the frame or footrest bracket (as applicable) and tighten the mounting bolts securely.

20 Install the master cylinder reservoir and tighten its bolt securely. Fit the reservoir hose onto the master cylinder, making sure that it is securely connected, correctly routed and secured by clamps at each end **(see illustration 9.4)**. If the clamps have weakened, use new ones.

21 Connect the brake hose banjo bolt (brake switch on early 750SS and 900SS models) to the master cylinder, using a new sealing washer on each side of the banjo union. Ensure that the hose is positioned as noted on removal **(see illustration 9.4)** and tighten the banjo bolt to the specified torque setting. On early 750SS and 900SS models, connect the brake light switch wiring.

22 If removed, install the ball joint or clevis and its locknut onto the master cylinder pushrod end. Position the ball joint or clevis as noted on removal, then tighten the locknut against it to secure it.

23 Align the brake pedal with the master cylinder pushrod ball joint or clevis and slide in the bolt or clevis pin **(see illustration 9.5a or 9.5b)**. Secure the bolt with its nut or secure the clip to the pushrod **(see illustration)**.

24 Fill the fluid reservoir with the specified fluid (see *Daily (pre-ride) checks*) and bleed the system following the procedure in Section 11.

25 Check the brake pedal height and freeplay as described in Chapter 1, Section 14.

26 Check the operation of the rear brake carefully before riding the motorcycle.

9.23 Secure the clip around the clevis to lock the pin in place on Monsters

10 Brake hoses and unions –
inspection and replacement

Inspection

1 Brake hose condition should be checked regularly (see Chapter 1).
2 Twist and flex the rubber hoses while looking for cracks, bulges and seeping fluid. Check extra carefully around the areas where the hoses connect with the banjo fittings, as these are common areas for hose failure.
3 Inspect the metal banjo union fittings connected to the brake hoses. If the fittings are rusted, scratched or cracked, replace them.

Replacement

4 The brake hoses have banjo union fittings on each end. Cover the surrounding area with plenty of rags and unscrew the banjo bolt on each end of the hose, noting the alignment of the hose and its routing before removing it. Detach the hose from any clips that may be present and remove the hose. Discard the sealing washers.
5 Position the new hose, making sure it isn't twisted or otherwise strained, then align and route it as noted on removal. Install the banjo bolts, using new sealing washers on both sides of the unions, and tighten them to the torque setting specified at the beginning of the Chapter. Make sure they are correctly aligned and routed clear of all moving components.
6 Flush the old brake fluid from the system, refill with the recommended fluid (see *Daily (pre-ride) checks*) and bleed the air from the system (see Section 11). Check the operation of the brakes carefully before riding the motorcycle.

11 Brake system bleeding

1 Bleeding the brakes is simply the process of removing all the air bubbles from the brake fluid reservoirs, the hoses and the brake calipers. Bleeding is necessary whenever a brake system hydraulic connection is loosened, when a component or hose is replaced, or when the master cylinder or caliper is overhauled. Leaks in the system may also allow air to enter, but leaking brake fluid will reveal their presence and warn you of the need for repair.
2 To bleed the brakes, you will need some new, clean DOT 4 brake fluid, a length of clear vinyl or plastic tubing, a small container partially filled with clean brake fluid, some rags and a spanner to fit the brake caliper bleed valves.
3 Cover the fuel tank and other painted components to prevent damage in the event that brake fluid is spilled.
4 On models fitted with an underslung rear

11.6 Brake caliper bleed valve (arrow)

brake caliper, remove the caliper (but do not detach the brake hose) and position it in an upright position before bleeding (Section 7).
5 Remove the reservoir cap/cover and diaphragm and slowly pump the brake lever or pedal a few times, until no air bubbles can be seen floating up from the holes in the bottom of the reservoir. Doing this bleeds the air from the master cylinder end of the line. Loosely refit the reservoir cap/cover.
6 Pull the dust cap off the bleed valve **(see illustration)**. Attach one end of the clear vinyl or plastic tubing to the bleed valve and submerge the other end in the brake fluid in the container.
7 Remove the reservoir cap/cover and check the fluid level. Do not allow the fluid level to drop below the MIN mark during the bleeding process.
8 Carefully pump the brake lever or pedal three or four times and hold it in (front) or down (rear) while opening the caliper bleed valve. When the valve is opened, brake fluid will flow out of the caliper into the clear tubing and the lever will move toward the handlebar or the pedal will move down.
9 Retighten the bleed valve, then release the brake lever or pedal gradually. Repeat the process until no air bubbles are visible in the brake fluid leaving the caliper and the lever or pedal is firm when applied. Disconnect the bleeding equipment and install the dust cap on the bleed valve.
10 Check the fluid level (see *Daily (pre-ride) checks*). Install the diaphragm and cap/cover assembly, wipe up any spilled brake fluid and check the entire system for leaks.

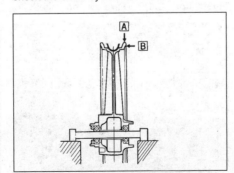

12.2 Check the wheel for radial (out-of-round) runout (A) and axial (side-to-side) runout (B)

HAYNES HiNT *If it's not possible to produce a firm feel to the lever or pedal the fluid my be aerated. Let the brake fluid in the system stabilise for a few hours and then repeat the procedure when the tiny bubbles in the system have settled out.*

12 Wheels – inspection and repair

1 In order to carry out a proper inspection of the wheels, it is necessary to support the bike upright so that the wheel being inspected is raised off the ground. Position the motorcycle on an auxiliary stand. Clean the wheels thoroughly to remove mud and dirt that may interfere with the inspection procedure or mask defects. Make a general check of the wheels and tyres as described in Chapter 1 and *Daily (pre-ride) checks*.
2 Attach a dial indicator to the fork slider or the swingarm and position its stem against the side of the rim **(see illustration)**. Spin the wheel slowly and check the axial (side-to-side) runout of the rim. In order to accurately check radial (out of round) runout with the dial indicator, the wheel would have to be removed from the machine, and the tyre from the wheel. With the axle clamped in a vice and the dial indicator positioned on the top of the rim, the wheel can be rotated to check the runout.
3 An easier, though slightly less accurate, method is to attach a stiff wire pointer to the fork slider or the swingarm and position the end a fraction of an inch from the wheel (where the wheel and tyre join). If the wheel is true, the distance from the pointer to the rim will be constant as the wheel is rotated. **Note:** *If wheel runout is excessive, check the wheel bearings very carefully before replacing the wheel.*
4 The wheels should also be visually inspected for cracks, flat spots on the rim and other damage. Look very closely for dents in the area where the tyre bead contacts the rim. Dents in this area may prevent complete sealing of the tyre against the rim, which leads to deflation of the tyre over a period of time. If damage is evident, or if runout in either direction is excessive, the wheel will have to be replaced with a new one. Never attempt to repair a damaged cast alloy wheel.

13 Wheels – alignment check

1 Misalignment of the wheels, which may be due to a cocked rear wheel or a bent frame or fork yokes, can cause strange and possibly serious handling problems. If the frame or

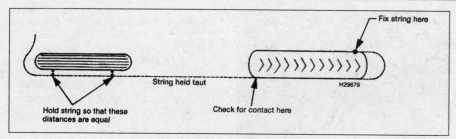

13.6 Wheel alignment check using string

yokes are at fault, repair by a frame specialist or replacement with new parts are the only alternatives.

2 To check the alignment you will need an assistant, a length of string or a perfectly straight piece of wood and a ruler. A plumb bob or other suitable weight will also be required.

3 In order to make a proper check of the wheels it is necessary to support the bike in an upright position, using an auxiliary stand. Measure the width of both tyres at their widest points. Subtract the smaller measurement from the larger measurement, then divide the difference by two. The result is the amount of offset that should exist between the front and rear tyres on both sides.

4 If a string is used, have your assistant hold one end of it about halfway between the floor and the rear axle, touching the rear sidewall of the tyre.

5 Run the other end of the string forward and pull it tight so that it is roughly parallel to the floor. Slowly bring the string into contact with the front sidewall of the rear tyre, then turn the front wheel until it is parallel with the string. Measure the distance from the front tyre sidewall to the string.

6 Repeat the procedure on the other side of the motorcycle. The distance from the front tyre sidewall to the string should be equal on both sides (see illustration).

7 As was previously pointed out, a perfectly straight length of wood may be substituted for the string (see illustration). The procedure is the same.

8 If the distance between the string and tyre is greater on one side, or if the rear wheel appears to be cocked, refer to Chapter 1, Section 20 and make sure swingarm sideplay is not excessive.

9 If the front-to-back alignment is correct, the wheels still may be out of alignment vertically.

10 Using the plumb bob, or other suitable weight, and a length of string, check the rear wheel to make sure it is vertical. To do this, hold the string against the tyre upper sidewall and allow the weight to settle just off the floor. When the string touches both the upper and lower tyre sidewalls and is perfectly straight, the wheel is vertical. If it is not, place thin spacers under one leg of the auxiliary stand.

11 Once the rear wheel is vertical, check the front wheel in the same manner. If both wheels are not perfectly vertical, the frame and/or major suspension components are bent.

14 Front wheel – removal and installation

Removal

1 Position the motorcycle on an auxiliary stand and support it under the crankcase (fairings removed where applicable) so that the front wheel is off the ground. Always make sure the motorcycle is properly supported.

2 On models with a cable driven speedometer, unscrew the knurled ring securing the cable to the speedometer drive housing on the left side of the wheel hub and detach the cable. If the ring has become corroded and will not come undone, the cable can be left attached to the drive housing, which can then be detached from the wheel on removal.

3 Remove the brake caliper mounting bolts and slide the caliper(s) off the disc (see illustration 3.1). There is no need to

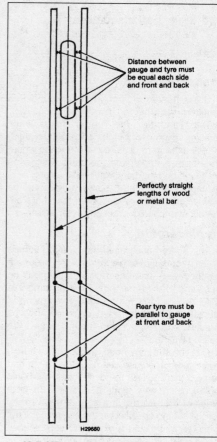

13.7 Wheel alignment check using a straight-edge

disconnect the brake hose from the caliper(s). Support the caliper(s) with a piece of wire or a bungee cord so that no strain is placed on its hydraulic hose.

4 On models with an axle bolt that threads into the left-hand fork, slacken the axle clamp bolts on the bottom of the right fork, then unscrew the axle (see illustration). On models with a nut on the left-hand end of the axle, unscrew the nut, then slacken the axle clamp bolts in the bottom of each fork (see illustration).

5 Support the wheel, then withdraw the axle from the right-hand side and carefully lower the wheel (see illustration). Note: Do not

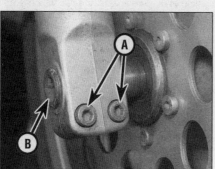

14.4a Axle clamp bolts (A), axle (B)

14.4b Axle nut (A), axle clamp bolts (B)

14.5 Withdraw the axle from the right

14.6 Speedometer drive housing (A) and driveplate (B)

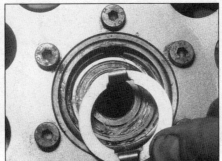

14.9 Fit the driveplate into the wheel hub

14.10 Fit the spacer between the wheel and the fork

operate the front brake lever with the caliper(s) removed.

6 On models with a cable driven speedometer remove the speedometer drive housing and the driveplate from the left-hand side of the wheel, noting how they fit **(see illustration)**. On other models remove the spacer **(see illustration 14.10)**.

Caution: Don't lay the wheel down and allow it to rest on either disc – the disc could become warped. Set the wheel on wood blocks so the disc doesn't support the weight of the wheel.

7 Check the axle for straightness by rolling it on a flat surface such as a piece of plate glass (first wipe off all old grease and remove any corrosion using fine emery cloth). If the equipment is available, place the axle in V-blocks and measure the runout using a dial indicator. If the axle is bent or the runout exceeds the limit specified at the beginning of the Chapter, replace it.

8 Check the condition of the wheel bearings (see Section 16).

Installation

9 On models with a cable driven speedometer apply a smear of lithium-based grease to the speedometer drive components. Fit the speedometer driveplate into the wheel, making sure its locating tangs are correctly located in the slots in the wheel hub and the drive tabs face out **(see illustration)**. Fit the drive housing, aligning its drive gear slots with the driveplate tabs **(see illustration 14.6)**.

10 Manoeuvre the wheel into position. Apply

a thin coat of grease to the axle. On models without a speedo cable lubricate the spacer with grease and fit it into the seal in the left-hand side of the wheel **(see illustration)**.

11 Lift the wheel into position, then install the axle from the right-hand side **(see illustration)**. On models with the axle bolt engage its threads with those of the bush in the bottom of the left-hand fork. On models with a cable speedometer make sure the speedometer drive housing is positioned so that its cable socket faces horizontally back. On models with an axle nut, align the axle head so its notches face up and down, in line with those in the fork, then thread the nut onto the axle **(see illustrations)**. Tighten the axle bolt or nut to the torque setting specified at the beginning of the Chapter **(see illustration)**. On models with a nut, counter-hold the axle using a screwdriver or other rod

through the holes via the bottom of the fork **(see illustration)**.

12 Install the brake caliper(s) making sure the pads sit squarely on either side of the disc **(see illustration 7.17a)**. Fit the caliper mounting bolts and tighten them to the torque setting specified at the beginning of the Chapter **(see illustration 7.17b)**.

13 If removed from the speedometer drive housing, pass the speedometer cable through its guide on the brake caliper, then connect the cable to the drive housing. Align the slot in the cable end with the drive tab, and securely tighten its knurled ring.

14 Apply the front brake a few times to bring the pads back into contact with the disc(s). Move the motorcycle off the auxiliary stand and support, then apply the front brake and pump the front forks a few times to settle all components in position.

14.11a Slide the axle in from the right

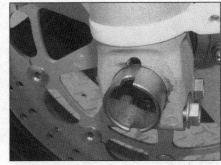

14.11b Align the axle head as shown . . .

14.11c . . . then fit the nut

14.11d Tighten the axle to the specified torque setting

14.11e Counter-hold the axle using a rod through the holes

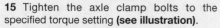

14.15 Tighten the axle clamp bolts to the specified torque setting

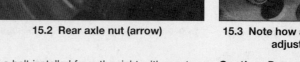

15.2 Rear axle nut (arrow)

15.3 Note how axle passes through chain adjuster block (arrow)

15 Tighten the axle clamp bolts to the specified torque setting **(see illustration)**.
16 Check for correct operation of the front brake before riding the motorcycle.

15 Rear wheel –
removal and installation

Removal

1 Position the motorcycle on an auxiliary stand so that it is upright and the rear wheel is off the ground. Always make sure the bike is properly supported.
2 Unscrew the nut on the end of the rear axle **(see illustration)**. Note that on some models the axle is in the form of a rod with a nut on each end, either of which can be unscrewed, whilst on other models the axle is in the form

of a bolt installed from the right with a nut on the left-hand end, in which case it is the nut which must be unscrewed from the bolt.
3 Support the wheel then withdraw the axle and lower the wheel to the ground. Note how the axle passes through the chain adjuster blocks in the swingarm **(see illustration)** and the wheel alignment plates (where applicable). Manoeuvre the brake caliper mounting assembly as necessary to allow axle removal, noting how (on most models) the slot in the caliper mounting plate locates over the lug on the swingarm. Support the caliper assembly so that no strain is placed on the hose, and where fitted, the speed sensor wiring.
4 Disengage the chain from the sprocket and remove the wheel from the swingarm **(see illustration)**. Remove the spacer from the left-hand side of the wheel, noting which way round it fits **(see illustration)**.

Caution: Do not lay the wheel down and allow it to rest on the disc or the sprocket – they could become warped. Set the wheel on wood blocks so the disc or the sprocket doesn't support the weight of the wheel. Do not operate the brake pedal with the wheel removed.
5 Check the axle for straightness by rolling it on a flat surface such as a piece of plate glass (if the axle is corroded, first remove the corrosion with fine emery cloth). If the equipment is available, place the axle in V-blocks and measure the runout using a dial indicator. If the axle is bent or the runout exceeds the limit specified at the beginning of the Chapter, replace it.
6 Check the condition of the wheel bearings (see Section 16).

Installation

7 Install the spacer, with its angled side facing inwards, into the left-hand side of the wheel **(see illustration 15.4b)**.
8 Apply a thin coat of grease to the axle.
9 Engage the drive chain with the sprocket and lift the wheel into position. Make sure the spacer remains in the wheel and the disc fits correctly in the caliper, with the brake pads sitting squarely on each side of the disc. Make sure the slot in the caliper mounting bracket is correctly located over the lug on the swingarm **(see illustration)**.
10 Slide the axle into position, making sure it passes through each chain adjuster block and the caliper mounting bracket, and fit the axle nut; secure the nut finger-tight at this stage **(see illustrations)**. If it is difficult to insert the

15.4a Disengage the chain from the sprocket

15.4b Note which way round the spacer fits

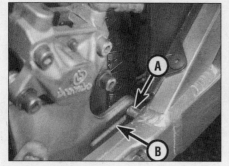

15.9 Locate the lug on the swingarm (A) in the slot in the caliper bracket (B)

15.10a Install the axle into the wheel . . .

15.10b . . . not forgetting the chain adjuster blocks . . .

15.10c ... and fit the axle nut

axle due to the tension of the drive chain, slacken the chain adjusters (see Chapter 1).

11 Remove the auxiliary stand.

12 Adjust the chain slack as described in Chapter 1.

13 Tighten the axle nut to the torque setting specified at the beginning of the Chapter, counter-holding the nut or axle head on the other side of the wheel if necessary.

14 Operate the brake pedal several times to bring the pads into contact with the disc. Check the operation of the rear brake carefully before riding the bike. On models with a speed sensor check the sensor air gap (see Chapter 8, Section 15).

16 Wheel bearings – removal, inspection and installation

Front wheel bearings

Note: *Always replace the wheel bearings in pairs. Never replace the bearings individually. Avoid using a high pressure cleaner on the wheel bearing area.*

1 Remove the front wheel (see Section 14).

2 Set the wheel on blocks so as not to allow the weight of the wheel to rest on the brake disc. The bearing spacer in the wheel has a notch in one end **(see illustrations)**. Lay the wheel down so that the notch faces upwards.

3 Using a metal rod (preferably a brass drift

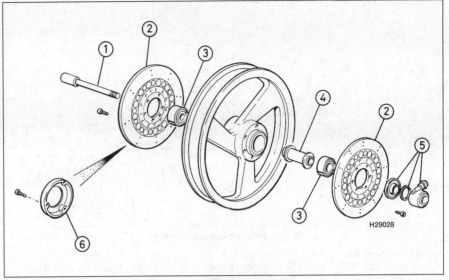

16.2a Front wheel components

1 Axle	5 Speedometer drive gear
2 Disc	components (replaced by single
3 Bearing	spacer on non-cable models)
4 Bearing spacer	6 Cover (single disc models)

punch) inserted through the centre of the upper bearing so that it locates in the notch in the bearing spacer, drive the lower bearing out of the wheel **(see illustration)**. The bearing spacer will also come out.

4 Lay the wheel on its other side so that the remaining bearing faces down, then install the bearing spacer back into the wheel so the notch in its end faces up. Drive the bearing out of the wheel using the same technique as above.

5 If the bearings are of the unsealed type or are only sealed on one side, clean them with a high flash-point solvent (one which won't leave any residue) and blow them dry with compressed air (don't let the bearings spin as you dry them). Apply a few drops of oil to the bearing. **Note:** *If the bearing is sealed on both sides don't attempt to clean it.*

6 Hold the outer race of the bearing and rotate the inner race – if the bearing doesn't turn smoothly, has rough spots or is noisy, replace it with a new one.

7 If the bearing is good and can be re-used, wash it in solvent once again and dry it, then pack the bearing with high-quality lithium-based grease.

8 Thoroughly clean the hub area of the wheel. Install the left-hand side bearing into its recess in the hub, with the marked or sealed side facing outwards. Using a bearing driver or a socket large enough to contact the outer race of the bearing, drive it in squarely until it's completely seated **(see illustration)**.

9 Turn the wheel over and install the bearing spacer. Drive the right-hand side bearing into place as described above.

10 Clean off all grease from the brake disc(s) using acetone or brake system cleaner then install the wheel as described in Section 14.

Rear wheel bearings

11 Remove the rear wheel (see Section 15). Lift the rear sprocket and sprocket coupling

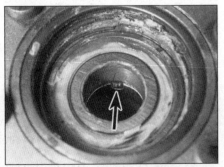

16.2b Use the notch in the spacer (arrow) as a location for the drift ...

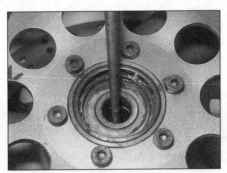

16.3 ... and drive out the bearing

16.8 Drive the bearing in squarely using a bearing driver or socket

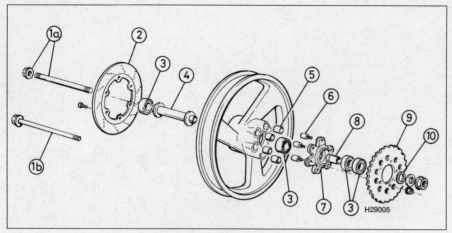

16.11a Rear wheel components

1a Axle (900 models)
1b Axle (early 600/750 models)
2 Disc
3 Bearing
4 Bearing spacer
5 Rubber dampers
6 Drive pins
7 Sprocket coupling
8 Spacer
9 Rear sprocket
10 Circlip

assembly out of the wheel, noting how it fits **(see illustrations)**.

12 Set the wheel on blocks so as not to allow the weight of the wheel to rest on the brake disc. The bearing spacer in the wheel has a notch in one end. Lay the wheel down so that the notch faces upwards **(see illustration 16.2b)**.

13 Using a metal rod (preferably a brass drift punch) inserted through the centre of the upper bearing so that it locates in the notch in the bearing spacer, drive the lower bearing

out of the wheel **(see illustration 16.3)**. The bearing spacer will also come out.

14 Lay the wheel on its other side so that the remaining bearing faces down, then install the bearing spacer back into the wheel so that the notch in its end faces up. Drive the bearing out of the wheel using the same technique as above.

15 If the bearings are of the unsealed type or are only sealed on one side, clean them with a high flash-point solvent (one which won't

16.11b Lift the sprocket coupling out of the wheel

leave any residue) and blow them dry with compressed air (don't let the bearings spin as you dry them). Apply a few drops of oil to the bearing. **Note:** *If the bearing is sealed on both sides don't attempt to clean it.*

16 Hold the outer race of the bearing and rotate the inner race – if the bearing doesn't turn smoothly, has rough spots or is noisy, replace it with a new one.

17 If the bearing is good and can be re-used, wash it in solvent once again and dry it, then pack the bearing with high-quality lithium-based grease.

18 Thoroughly clean the hub area of the wheel. Install the left-hand side bearing into its recess in the hub, with the marked or sealed side facing outwards **(see illustration)**. Using a bearing driver or a socket large enough to contact the outer race of the bearing, drive it in squarely until it's completely seated **(see illustration)**.

19 Turn the wheel over and install the bearing spacer. Drive the right hand side bearing into place as described above.

20 Clean off all grease from the brake disc using acetone or brake system cleaner. Install the rear sprocket and sprocket coupling assembly onto the wheel, then install the wheel (see Section 15).

Sprocket coupling bearing

21 Remove the rear wheel (see Section 15). Lift the sprocket and sprocket coupling assembly out of the wheel, noting how it fits **(see illustration 16.11b)**.

22 Remove the spacer from the inside of the coupling bearing **(see illustration)**. Using a pair of internal circlip pliers, remove the circlip from the outer side of the coupling **(see illustration)**.

23 Support the coupling on blocks of wood and drive the bearings out from the inside with a bearing driver or socket large enough to contact the outer race of the bearings.

24 If the bearings are of the unsealed type or are only sealed on one side, clean them with a high flash-point solvent (one which won't leave any residue) and blow them dry with compressed air (don't let the bearings spin as you dry them). Apply a few drops of oil to the bearing. **Note:** *If the bearing is sealed on both sides don't attempt to clean it.*

16.18a Fit the bearing into the wheel . . .

16.18b . . . and drive it in squarely using a bearing driver or socket

16.22a Remove the spacer from the inside . . .

16.22b . . . and the circlip from the outside of the coupling

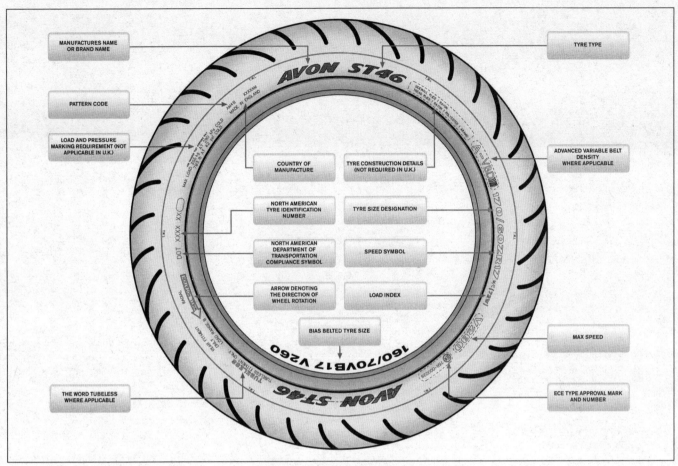

17.3 Common tyre sidewall markings

25 Hold the outer race of the bearing and rotate the inner race – if the bearing doesn't turn smoothly, has rough spots or is noisy, replace it with anew one.

26 If the bearing is good and can be re-used, wash it in solvent once again and dry it, then pack the bearing with high-quality lithium-based grease.

27 Thoroughly clean the bearing recess then install the bearings into the recess in the coupling, with the marked or sealed side on the inner bearing facing the wheel, and the marked or sealed side on the outer bearing facing out. Using a bearing driver or a socket large enough to contact the outer race of the bearings, drive them in one at a time until they are completely seated.

28 Install the circlip into the outer side of the coupling, making sure it is properly seated in its groove **(see illustration 16.22b)**. Install the

spacer into the inside of the coupling **(see illustration 16.22a)**.

29 Clean off all grease from the brake disc using acetone or brake system cleaner. Install the rear sprocket and sprocket coupling assembly onto the wheel, then install the wheel (see Section 15).

17 Tyres – general information and fitting

General information

1 The wheels fitted to all models are designed to take tubeless tyres only.

2 Refer to the Daily (pre-ride) checks listed at the beginning of this manual for tyre maintenance.

Fitting new tyres

3 When selecting new tyres, refer to the tyre information and the tyre options listed in the owners handbook. Ensure that front and rear tyre types are compatible, the correct size and correct speed rating; if necessary seek advice from a Ducati dealer or tyre fitting specialist **(see illustration)**.

4 It is recommended that tyres are fitted by a motorcycle tyre specialist rather than attempted in the home workshop. This is particularly relevant in the case of tubeless tyres because the force required to break the seal between the wheel rim and tyre bead is substantial, and is usually beyond the capabilities of an individual working with normal tyre levers. Additionally, the specialist will be able to balance the wheels after tyre fitting.

Chapter 7
Fairing and bodywork

Contents

Fairing panels – removal and installation 2
Fairing stay (1991 to 1997 SS and SL models) – removal
   and installation 4
Front mudguard – removal and installation 7
General information 1

Rear mudguard – removal and installation 8
Rear view mirrors – removal and installation 6
Seat – removal and installation 9
Side panels – removal and installation 5
Windshield – removal and installation 3

Degrees of difficulty

Easy, suitable for novice with little experience	**Fairly easy,** suitable for beginner with some experience	**Fairly difficult,** suitable for competent DIY mechanic	**Difficult,** suitable for experienced DIY mechanic	**Very difficult,** suitable for expert DIY or professional

1 General information

This Chapter covers the procedures necessary to remove and install the body parts. Since many service and repair operations on these motorcycles require the removal of the body parts, the procedures are grouped here and referred to from other Chapters.

In the case of damage to the body parts, it is usually necessary to remove the broken component and replace it with a new (or used) one. The material that the body panels are composed of doesn't lend itself to conventional repair techniques. There are however some shops that specialise in "plastic welding", so it may be worthwhile seeking the advice of one of these specialists before consigning an expensive component to the bin.

When attempting to remove any body panel, first study it closely, noting any fasteners and associated fittings, to be sure of returning everything to its correct place on installation. In some cases the aid of an assistant will be required when removing panels, to help avoid the risk of damage to paintwork. Once the evident fasteners have been removed, try to withdraw the panel as described but DO NOT FORCE IT – if it will not release, check that all fasteners have been removed and try again. Where a panel engages another by means of tabs, be careful not to break the tab or its mating slot or to damage the paintwork. Remember that a few moments of patience at this stage will save you a lot of money in replacing broken fairing panels!

When installing a body panel, first study it closely, noting any fasteners and associated fittings removed with it, to be sure of returning everything to its correct place. Check that all fasteners are in good condition, including all trim nuts or clips and damping/rubber mounts; any of these must be replaced if faulty before the panel is reassembled. Check also that all mounting brackets are straight and repair or replace them if necessary before attempting to install the panel. Where assistance was required to remove a panel, make sure your assistant is on hand to install it.

Carefully settle the panel in place, following the instructions provided, and check that it engages correctly with its partners (where applicable) before tightening any of the fasteners. Where a panel engages another by means of tabs, be careful not to break the tab or its mating slot. Note that a small amount of lubricant (liquid soap or similar) applied to the mounting rubbers of the side panels will assist the panel retaining pegs to engage without the need for undue pressure.

Tighten the fasteners securely, but be careful not to overtighten any of them or the panel may break (not always immediately) due to the uneven stress.

2.2 Main fairing fasteners (A), lower fairing panel fasteners (B)

2.3 Note how the edge of the fairing panel locates under the edge of the main fairing

2.6 Lower fairing panel bottom fasteners

2 Fairing panels –
removed and installation

Early style SS/SL models (1991-97)

Main fairing

1 Remove the rear view mirrors (refer to Section 6).
2 Unscrew the fasteners securing the main fairing to each lower panel (see illustration).
3 Carefully draw the main fairing forward until it is clear of the headlight. Note how the lower fairing panels engage with the main fairing (see illustration).
4 Installation is the reverse of removal. Make

sure the fairing fits correctly over the headlight and its foam surround, and that the fasteners are correctly and securely fitted.

Lower fairing panels

5 Disconnect the turn signal wiring connectors from the back of the turn signal assembly in the panel being removed.
6 Unscrew the two fasteners securing the bottom of each panel to the other, noting the arrangement of the fasteners and how the panels fit together (see illustration).
7 Unscrew the two fasteners securing the panel to the main fairing (see illustration 2.2).
8 Support the panel, then unscrew the remaining two fasteners securing the panel to the frame and the main fairing stay (see illustration 2.2). Carefully remove the panel, noting how it fits.

9 Installation is the reverse of removal. Make sure the panels fit correctly together at the bottom (see illustration), and to the main fairing at the top, and that the fasteners are correctly and securely fitted (see illustration).

Late style Sport and Supersport models (1998-on)

Main fairing

Note: If you intend to remove the lower fairing panels as well, do so first, then ignore the instructions which do not apply.
10 Remove the rear view mirrors (refer to Section 6).
11 Unscrew the fasteners securing the main fairing to each lower panel (see illustration 2.15). Carefully pull the side of each lower panel away, then unscrew the fasteners securing the fairing to the bracket (see illustration).
12 Carefully draw the main fairing forward until it is clear of the headlight, noting how the pin locates (see illustration).
13 Installation is the reverse of removal. Make sure the fairing fits correctly over the headlight and its surround, and that the pin locates in its hole (see illustration).

Lower fairing panels

14 On fully faired models, unscrew the fasteners securing the bottom of each panel to the other, noting the arrangement of the fasteners and how the panels fit together (see illustration 2.15).
15 Unscrew the fasteners securing the panel

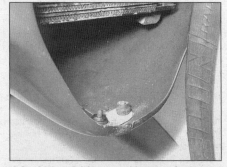

2.9a Lower fairing panel bottom fasteners are secured by captive nuts on the inside

2.9b The front lower fairing panel bolt mounts to the fairing stay as shown

2.11 Undo the screws (arrowed) securing each side to the bracket

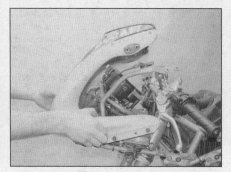

2.12 Carefully remove the main fairing

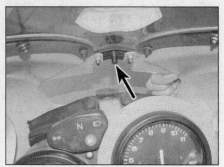

2.13 Make sure the pin (arrowed) locates correctly

2.15 Fairing panel fasteners (arrowed)

2.16a Displace the panel . . .

to the main fairing and the frame (see illustration).

16 Carefully displace the panel, and disconnect the turn signal wiring connectors when accessible (see illustrations).

17 Installation is the reverse of removal.

Monster models

18 To remove the cockpit fairing where fitted, when unscrewing the bolt on each side counter-hold the nut on the inside and unscrew the bolt from the outside (see illustration). Note how the slot in the fairing inner section locates over the rubber grommet (see illustration).

2.16b . . . and disconnect the wiring connectors

2.18a Counter-hold the nuts while unscrewing the bolts

| 3 | Windshield (SS/SL, Supersport and Sport models only) – removal and installation |

Removal

1 Remove the fasteners securing the

windshield to the main fairing assembly, noting how they fit, then lift the windshield away from the bike (see illustration).

Installation

2 Installation is a reverse of removal. Make sure the fasteners are correctly and securely fitted.

| 4 | Fairing stay (1991 to 1997 SS and SL models) – removal and installation |

Removal

1 Remove the main fairing and the lower fairing panels (see Section 2).

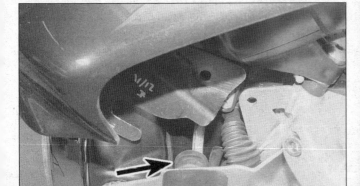

2.18b Note how the slot locates over the grommet (arrowed)

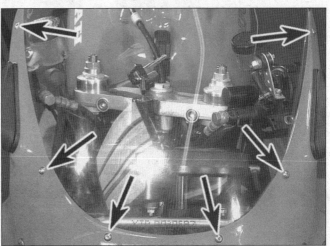

3.1 The windshield is secured by six fasteners (arrows) - early style shown

2 Remove the headlight (Chapter 8).
3 Remove the instrument cluster (Chapter 8).
4 Note the routing of all the wiring and cables, and release them from any clips or ties, noting their positions.
5 Unscrew the two bolts securing the fairing stay to the frame, and the two bolts securing the stay to the headstock, then carefully remove the stay, taking care not to snag any wiring **(see illustrations)**.

Installation

6 Installation is the reverse of removal. Make sure all wiring and cables are correctly routed and secured with ties and clips as required.

4.5a The fairing stay is mounted to the frame . . .

4.5b . . . and to the steering head

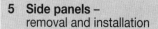

5   Side panels –
removal and installation

Removal

1991 to 1997 SS models

1 Remove the seat (see Section 9).
2 The side panels are secured by two bolts at the front, and by a lug on the bottom of the grab-rail which locates into a rubber grommet **(see illustrations)**. Unscrew the two bolts, then gently draw the panel backwards to release it from the lug. Do not force or bend the panel while removing it.

900SL model

3 On this model, the side panels are integral with the seat. See Section 9 for removal and installation.

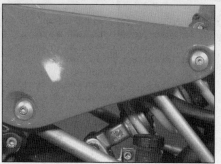

5.2a The side panel is secured by two bolts at the front . . .

5.2b . . . and by a lug on the grab-rail at the back

1998-on Sport and Supersport models

4 Remove the seat (see Section 9).
5 Undo the two screws, then gently draw the panel away to release the lug from the grommet **(see illustrations)**.

Monster models

6 Remove the seat (see Section 9).
7 Undo the two screws securing the side panel to the frame, then carefully remove the panel, noting how it fits **(see illustration)**.

Installation

8 Installation is the reverse of removal.

6   Rear view mirrors –
removal and installation

Removal

1991 to 1997 SS and SL models

1 Peel back the rubber boot at the base of each mirror to access the mounting bolts **(see illustration)**. Unscrew the two bolts and remove the mirror, noting how it fits. The nuts are captive in the end of the fairing stay **(see illustration)**.

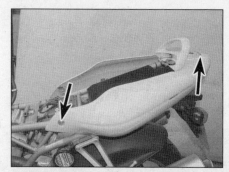

5.5a Undo the screws (arrowed) . . .

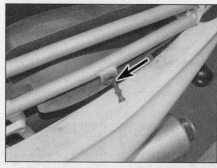

5.5b . . . and release the peg from the grommet (arrow)

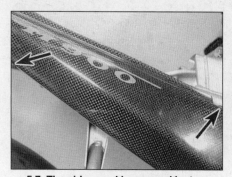

5.7 The side panel is secured by two screws (arrows)

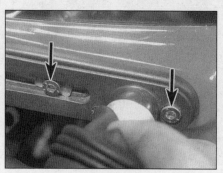

6.1a The mirror is secured by two bolts (arrows) . . .

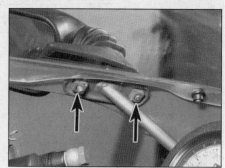

6.1b . . . which thread into captive nuts (arrows)

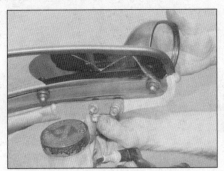

6.2a Unscrew the nuts on the inside . . .

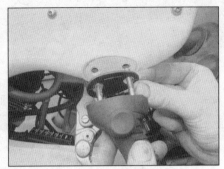

6.2b . . . and remove the mirror

6.3 The mirrors screw into the top of each master cylinder clamp

1998-on Sport and Supersport models

2 Unscrew the two nuts on the inside and draw the mirror off the fairing, noting the damper pad (see illustrations).

Monster models

3 Draw the rubber boot up the mirror stem (where fitted), then unscrew the mirror from its mounting on the handlebar, using a suitable spanner on the lower nut to initially slacken it (see illustration).

Installation

SS, SL, Sport and Supersport models

4 Installation is the reverse of removal.

Monster models

5 Install the mirror into its mounting and screw it in until it is fully home. If the position of the mirror is not as required, counter-hold

the lower nut on the stem and slacken the top nut. Adjust the mirror as required, then tighten the top nut whilst counter-holding the mirror.

---

7 Front mudguard – removal and installation

Removal

1 Unscrew the two bolts securing each side of the mudguard to the front fork, then carefully remove the mudguard (see illustration). On later models note the bands which hold the mudguard and how they locate in the grooves in the forks (see illustrations).

Installation

2 Installation is the reverse of removal.

---

8 Rear mudguard – removal and installation

Removal

1 Remove the screws securing the rear mudguard to the swingarm (see illustration). On SS, SL, Sport and Supersport models, also remove the screw securing the mudguard to the chainguard (see illustration). On Monster models, note the position of the brake hose bracket.

2 Manoeuvre the mudguard out of the back of the machine, noting how it fits.

Installation

3 Installation is the reverse of removal. On Monster models, make sure the brake hose bracket is correctly positioned.

---

9 Seat – removal and installation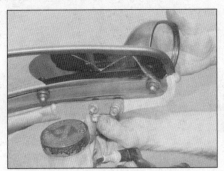

Removal

SS, Sport, Supersport and Monster models

1 Insert the ignition key into the seat lock. On SS, Sport, Supersport and later Monsters, turn the key clockwise to unlock the seat, whilst on early Monsters pull the lever under the lock upwards to release the lock.

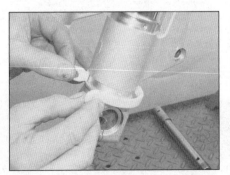

7.1a Unscrew the two bolts (arrows) to free the front mudguard - early style shown

7.1b Later models mudguard bolts (arrowed) . . .

8.1a The rear mudguard is secured to the swingarm (arrows) . . .

8.1b . . . and on SS/SL models also to the chainguard (arrow)

(Bottom-left image caption:)

7.1c . . . thread into bands which locate in grooves in the fork

9.3 The rear cowl is secured to the seat by two bolts (arrows) on Monsters

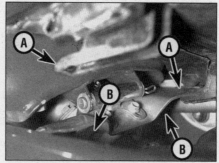

9.5a The tabs on the seat (A) locate under the tank bracket (B)

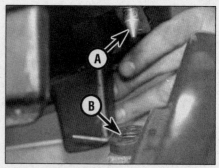

9.5b Locate the stud (A) into the latch (B) and push the seat down to engage it

2 Lift the rear of the seat and draw it back and away from the bike. Note how the tabs at the front of the seat locate under the tank mounting bracket, and how the seat locates onto the frame rail.

3 On Monsters, if required the seat can be separated from the rear cowl by unscrewing the bolts on the underside of the seat securing the two together **(see illustration)**.

900SL model

4 On these models, the seat is integral with

the side panel/rear cowl unit, and is removed as one assembly. Unscrew the two bolts on each side panel, then carefully lift the assembly away, noting how it fits. If required, unscrew the bolts securing the seat pads and separate them from the unit.

Installation

SS, Sport, Supersport and Monster models

5 Locate the tabs at the front of the seat

under the fuel tank mounting bracket **(see illustration)**. Align the seat at the rear and push down on it to engage the latch **(see illustration)**.

900SL model

6 Installation is the reverse of removal.

10 Passenger grab-rail (SS, Sport and Supersport models) – removal and installation

Removal

1 Remove the seat (see Section 9).
2 Remove the side panels (see Section 5).
3 On 1991 to 1997 SS models, unscrew the two bolts on each side of the grab-rail securing it to the frame and remove the grab-rail **(see illustration)**. On 1998-on Sport and Supersport models the grab-rail is combined with the tail light mounting and seat lock; four bolts retain the grab-rail to the frame **(see illustration)**.

Installation

4 Installation is the reverse of removal.

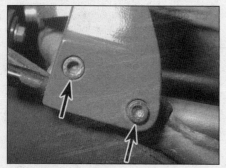

10.3a The grab-rail is secured by two bolts (arrows) on each side - SS models . . .

10.3b . . . and 1998-on Sport/Supersport models

Chapter 8
Electrical system

Contents

Alternator – removal and installation 33
Alternator stator coils – check 34
Battery – charging 4
Battery – removal, installation and inspection 3
Brake light switches – check and replacement 14
Charging system – leakage and output test 32
Charging system testing – general information and precautions . . . 31
Electrical fault finding 2
Fuel pump (SS and SL carburettor models only) –
   check, removal and installation 27
Fuel pump (fuel injection models) . . . . .see Chapter 3B
Fuses – check and replacement 5
General information 1
General relay (carburettor models) – check and replacement 24
Handlebar switches – check 20
Handlebar switches – removal and installation 21
Headlight assembly – removal, installation and beam height 8
Headlight bulb and sidelight bulb – replacement 7
Horn – check and replacement 25
Ignition (main) switch – check, removal and installation 19
Ignition system components .see Chapter 4
Instrument and warning light bulbs – replacement 17
Instrument cluster and speedometer/tachometer cables –
   removal and installation 15
Instruments – check and replacement 16
Lighting system – check 6
Low fuel level sensor – check and replacement 26
Main and injection relays (fuel injection models) . . . . . .see Chapter 3B
Neutral switch – check and replacement 22
Oil pressure switch – check and replacement 18
Regulator/rectifier unit – check and replacement 35
Sidestand switch – check and replacement 23
Starter motor – disassembly, inspection and reassembly 30
Starter motor – removal and installation 29
Starter relay – check and replacement 28
Tail light assembly and licence plate assembly –
   removal and installation 10
Tail light bulb and licence plate bulb – replacement 9
Turn signal assemblies – removal and installation 12
Turn signal bulbs – replacement 11
Turn signal circuit – check 13

Degrees of difficulty

Easy, suitable for novice with little experience	**Fairly easy,** suitable for beginner with some experience	**Fairly difficult,** suitable for competent DIY mechanic	**Difficult,** suitable for experienced DIY mechanic	**Very difficult,** suitable for expert DIY or professional

Specifications

Battery

Standard (fillable) battery	
Capacity	12V, 16Ah
Model	YB16AL-A2
Specific gravity	1.260
Maintenance-free battery	
Capacity	12V, 10 Ah
Model	YT12B-BS (MF)

Alternator

Output	
1991 to 1997 600 and 750 engines	300 W
1998-on 600, 620 and 750 engines	520 W
1991 and 1992 900 engines	300 W
1993 to 1997 900 engines	350 W
1998 to 2002 900 engines	520 W
Stator coil resistance – 1991 to 1997 models with 2-wire stator	0.2 to 0.4 ohm

Fuses

Circuit fuses (fusebox) . . . . see fusebox lid and wiring diagrams
Charging circuit fuse . . . . 30A or 40 A (according to model - see wiring diagrams)

Bulbs

Headlight . . . . 60/55W H4 halogen
Sidelight 5W
Brake/tail light 21/5W
Licence plate light (Monster models only) 5W
Turn signal lights 10W
Instrument illumination lights 2W, 3W*
Instrument warning lights 1.2W, 2W*
*LEDs on 2002 M750/900i.e., M620i.e. and 620i.e. Sport models

Torque settings

Oil pressure switch . . . . 18 to 20 Nm
Starter motor mounting bolts . . . . 10 Nm
Alternator stator coil bolts . . . . 10 Nm

1 General information

All models have a battery-fed 12-volt electrical system charged by an alternator unit mounted on the left-hand end of the crankshaft, and a regulator/rectifier unit. The single phase two-wire alternator fitted to early models was replaced by a three-wire three phase alternator in 1998.

The regulator maintains the charging system output within the specified range to prevent overcharging, and the rectifier converts the ac (alternating current) output of the alternator to dc (direct current) to power the lights and other components and to charge the battery.

The starter motor is mounted underneath the horizontal cylinder. The starting system includes the motor, the battery, the relay and the various wires and switches.

The wiring system includes a general relay which affects all circuits wired through the fusebox.

Note: *Keep in mind that electrical parts, once purchased, cannot be returned. To avoid unnecessary expense, make very sure the faulty component has been positively identified before buying a replacement part.*

2 Electrical fault finding

 Warning: To prevent the risk of short circuits, the ignition (main) switch must always be "OFF" and the battery negative (-ve) terminal should be disconnected before any of the bike's other electrical components are disturbed. Don't forget to reconnect the terminal securely once work is finished or if battery power is needed for circuit testing.

1 A typical electrical circuit consists of an electrical component, the switches, relays, etc. related to that component and the wiring and connectors that hook the component to both the battery and the frame. To aid in locating a problem in any electrical circuit, refer to the wiring diagrams at the end of this Chapter.

2 Before tackling any troublesome electrical circuit, first study the wiring diagrams (see end of Chapter) thoroughly to get a complete picture of what makes up that individual circuit. Trouble spots, for instance, can often be narrowed down by noting if other components related to that circuit are operating properly or not. If several components or circuits fail at one time, chances are the fault lies in the fuse, general relay or earth connection, as several circuits often are routed through the same fuse, relay and earth connections.

3 Electrical problems often stem from simple causes, such as loose or corroded connections or a blown fuse. Prior to any electrical fault finding, always visually check the condition of the fuse, wires and connections in the problem circuit. Intermittent failures can be especially frustrating, since you can't always duplicate the failure when it's convenient to test. In such situations, a good practice is to clean all connections in the affected circuit, whether or not they appear to be good. All of the connections and wires should also be wiggled to check for looseness which can cause intermittent failure.

4 If testing instruments are going to be utilised, use the wiring diagram to plan where you will make the necessary connections in order to accurately pinpoint the trouble spot.

5 The basic tools needed for electrical fault finding include a battery and bulb test circuit, a continuity tester, test light and a jumper wire. For more extensive checks, a multimeter capable of measuring ohms, volts and amps will be required. Full details on the use of this test equipment are given in *Fault Finding Equipment* in the Reference section at the end of this manual.

3 Battery – removal, installation and inspection

Caution: Be extremely careful when handling or working around the battery. The electrolyte is very caustic and an explosive gas (hydrogen) is given off when the battery is charging.

Removal and installation

1 Raise or remove the fuel tank (see Chapter 3A or B). Pull back the terminal covers and disconnect the leads from the battery, disconnecting the negative (-ve) terminal first **(see illustrations)**. Release the rubber

3.1a Pull back the cover to expose the terminal screw

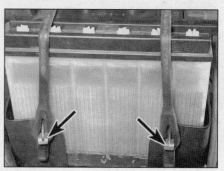

3.1b Release the rubber retaining straps from their hooks (arrows) . . .

3.1c . . . and disconnect the vent hose

3.1d Lift the battery out of its case

3.1e On later Monster models the MF battery is held by a single strap . . .

3.1f . . . and lies flat on its tray

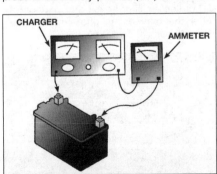
3.2 Connect the positive (+ve) terminal first on installation

strap(s) securing the battery in its tray and where fitted disconnect the vent hose from its union on the side of the battery, then lift the battery out (see illustrations).

2 On installation, clean the battery terminals and lead ends with a wire brush or knife and emery paper. Reconnect the leads, connecting the positive (+ve) terminal first, then fit the insulating covers over the terminals (see illustration). Fit the battery straps and reconnect the vent hose, then install the fuel tank.

HAYNES HiNT *Battery corrosion can be kept to a minimum by applying a layer of petroleum jelly to the terminals after the cables have been connected.*

Inspection

3 In addition to the procedures detailed in Chapter 1, the following checks should be regularly performed.

4 Check the battery terminals and leads for tightness and corrosion. If corrosion is evident, disconnect the leads from the battery, disconnecting the negative (-ve) terminal first, and clean the terminals and lead ends with a wire brush or knife and emery paper. Reconnect the leads, connecting the negative (-ve) terminal last, and apply a thin coat of petroleum jelly to the connections to slow further corrosion.

5 The battery case should be kept clean to prevent current leakage, which can discharge the battery over a period of time (especially when it sits unused). Wash the outside of the case with a solution of baking soda and water. Rinse the battery thoroughly, then dry it.

6 Look for cracks in the case and replace the battery if any are found. If acid has been spilled on the frame or battery holder, neutralise it with a baking soda and water solution, dry it thoroughly, then touch up any damaged paint. Make sure the battery vent tube is routed correctly and is not kinked or pinched.

7 If the motorcycle sits unused for long periods of time, disconnect the cables from the battery terminals, negative (-ve) terminal first. Refer to Section 4 and charge the battery once every month to six weeks.

8 The condition of the battery can be assessed by measuring the voltage present at the battery terminals. Connect the voltmeter positive (+ve) probe to the battery positive (+ve) terminal and

the negative (-ve) probe to the battery negative (-ve) terminal. When fully charged there should be approximately 13 volts present. If the voltage falls below 12.3 volts (standard fillable battery) or 12.6 volts (maintenance-free battery) it must be removed, disconnecting the negative (-ve) terminal first, and recharged as described below in Section 4.

9 If a standard (fillable) battery is fitted you can carry out a specific gravity to assess the condition of the battery – refer to *Fault Finding Equipment* in the Reference section of this Manual.

4 Battery – charging

Caution: Be extremely careful when handling or working around the battery. The electrolyte is very caustic and an explosive gas (hydrogen) is given off when the battery is charging.

1 Remove the battery (see Section 3).

2 The standard fillable battery should be charged at a maximum rate of 1.5 amps and the maintenance-free battery at 1 amp, for 5 to 10 hours. Exceeding this figure can cause the battery to overheat, buckling the plates and rendering it useless. Few owners will have access to an expensive current controlled charger, so if a normal domestic charger is used check that after a possible initial peak, the charge rate falls to a safe level (see illustration). If the battery becomes hot during charging stop. Further charging will cause damage. Note: *In emergencies the battery can be charged at a higher rate of for a period of 1 hour. However, this is not recommended and the low amp charge is by far the safer method of charging the battery.*

3 The maintenance-free battery

4 If the recharged battery discharges rapidly if left disconnected it is likely that an internal short caused by physical damage or sulphation has occurred. A new battery will be required. A sound item will tend to lose its charge at about 1% per day.

5 Install the battery (see Section 3).

6 If the motorcycle sits unused for long periods of time, charge the battery once every month to six weeks and leave it disconnected.

CHARGER   AMMETER

4.2 If the charger doesn't have an ammeter built in, connect one in series as shown. DO NOT connect the ammeter between the battery terminals or it will be ruined

5.1a Circuit fusebox – SS and SL models

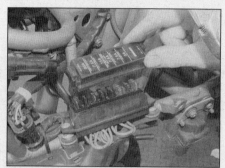

5.1b Fusebox – 900i.e. circa 2000

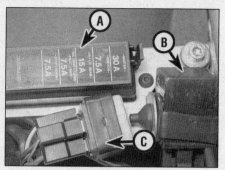

5.1c Circuit fusebox (A), turn signal relay (B), general relay (C) – early Monsters

5.1d Fusebox (arrowed) – later monsters

5.1e Charging circuit fuse – early SS and SL models

5.1f Charging circuit fuse – early Monsters

5.1g Charging circuit fuse location – later Monsters

5.1h Charging circuit fuse location – later Supersports and Sports

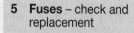

5 Fuses – check and replacement

1 Most circuits are protected by fuses of different ratings. All circuit fuses are located in the fusebox. On SS, SL, Sport and Supersport models, the fusebox is situated on the left-hand side of the instrument cluster up to approximately 2000, and on the left-hand end of the battery under the fuel tank thereafter **(see illustrations)**. On Monster models the fusebox is under the seat on carburettor-engined models and on the right-hand side of the battery below the ECU on injected models **(see illustrations)**. On all models an additional 30 or 40 A (according to year) fuse is incorporated in the charging circuit, and is located behind the right-hand

side of the fairing on early SS and SL models, and on the air filter housing or battery tray under the tank on all other models **(see illustrations)**.

2 To gain access to the fuses, unclip the fusebox lid **(see illustration)**. The fuses are labelled for easy identification.

3 The fuses can be removed and checked visually. If you can't pull the fuse out with your fingertips, use a pair of needle-nose pliers. A blown fuse is easily identified by a break in the element **(see illustration)**. Each fuse is clearly marked with its rating and must only be replaced by a fuse of the correct rating. One spare fuse of each rating is included in the circuit fusebox.

Caution: Never put in a fuse of a higher rating or bridge the terminals with any other substitute, however temporary it may be. Serious damage may be done to the circuit, or a fire may start. If the spare fuses are used, always replace them so that a spare fuse of each rating is carried on the bike at all times.

5.2 Unclip the fusebox lid to access the fuses

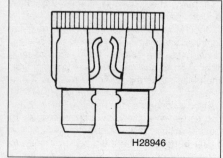

5.3 A blown fuse (plug-in type) can be identified by a break in its element

4 If a fuse blows, be sure to check the wiring circuit very carefully for evidence of a short-circuit. Look for bare wires and chafed, melted or burned insulation. If a fuse is replaced before the cause is located, the new fuse will blow immediately.

5 Occasionally a fuse will blow or cause an open-circuit for no obvious reason. Corrosion of the fuse ends and fusebox terminals may occur and cause poor fuse contact. If this happens, remove the corrosion with a wire brush or emery paper, then spray the fuse end and terminals with electrical contact cleaner.

6 Lighting system – check

1 The battery provides power for operation of the headlight, tail light, brake light and instrument cluster lights. If none of the lights operate, always check the fuse (Section 5) and general relay (see Section 24) and battery voltage before proceeding. Low battery voltage indicates either a faulty battery or a defective charging system. Refer to Section 3 for battery checks and Sections 31 and 32 for charging system tests.

Headlight

2 If the headlight fails to work, first check the fuse with the key "ON" (see Section 5) and the bulb, then unplug the electrical connector for the headlight (see Section 7) and use jumper wires to connect the bulb directly to the battery terminals. If the light comes on, the problem lies in the wiring or one of the switches in the circuit. Refer to Section 20 for the switch testing procedures, and also the wiring diagrams at the end of this Chapter.

Tail light

3 If the tail light fails to work, check the bulb and the bulb terminals first, then the fuses, then check for battery voltage at the tail light electrical connector. If voltage is present, check the earth circuit for an open or poor connection.

4 If no voltage is indicated, check the wiring between the tail light and the ignition switch, then check the switch. Also check the lighting switch.

Brake light

5 See Section 14 for the brake light switch checking procedure.

Neutral indicator light

6 If the neutral light fails to operate when the transmission is in neutral, check the fuses and the bulb (see Sections 5 and 17). If they are in good condition, check for battery voltage at the connector attached to the neutral switch at the back of the engine on the right-hand side. If battery voltage is present, refer to Section 22 for the neutral switch check and replacement procedures.

7 If no voltage is indicated, check the wiring between the switch and the bulb for open-circuits and poor connections.

Oil pressure warning light

8 See Section 18 for the oil pressure switch check.

7 Headlight bulb and sidelight bulb – replacement

Note: *The headlight bulb is of the quartz-halogen type. Do not touch the bulb glass as skin acids will shorten the bulb's service life. If the bulb is accidentally touched, it should be wiped carefully when cold with a rag soaked in methylated spirit and dried before fitting.*

⚠️ **Warning: Allow the bulb time to cool before removing it if the headlight has just been on.**

Headlight

SS/SL, Sport and Supersport models

1 The headlight bulb can be accessed from the back of the housing. If access is too restricted, remove the main fairing (see Chapter 7).

2 Remove the rubber dust cover and disconnect the headlight wiring connector, noting how it fits **(see illustration)**.

3 Release the bulb retainer, noting how it fits, then remove the bulb **(see illustrations)**.

4 Fit the new bulb, bearing in mind the information in the **Note** above. Make sure the tabs on the bulb fit correctly in the slots in the bulb housing, and secure it in position with the retainer.

5 Connect the wiring connector, then install the dust cover, making sure it is correctly seated **(see illustration)**.

6 Check the operation of the headlight, then install the main fairing if removed.

Monster models

7 Slacken the screw securing the headlight rim to the headlight shell, and ease the rim out of the shell **(see illustration)**.

8 Disconnect the wire connectors from the

7.2 Pull back the cover to access the connector

7.3a Remove the retainer to release the bulb . . .

7.3b . . . then remove the bulb

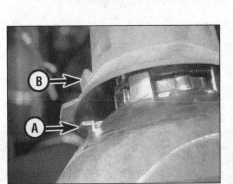

7.5 The tab (A) on the headlight locates into the pocket (B) in the cover to secure it

7.7 Slacken the single screw at the bottom of the headlight rim

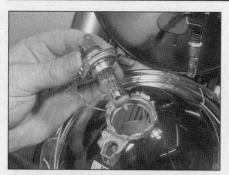

7.9 Release the bulb retainer and lift out the headlight bulb

7.10 Ensure the tangs of the bulb retainer are correctly engaged in the hooks

7.15a Remove the bulbholder from the headlight . . .

7.15b . . . and remove the bulb from the holder – early style models

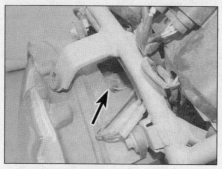
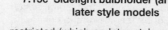
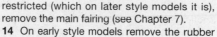
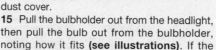

7.15c Sidelight bulbholder (arrowed) – later style models

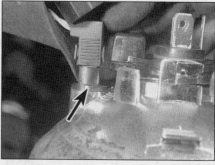

7.16 The tab (arrowed) locates in the slot in the bulbholder

headlight. Slip the sidelight bulbholder out of the headlight (see illustration 7.20).

9 Release the bulb retainer, noting how it fits, then remove the bulb (see illustration).

10 Fit the new bulb, bearing in mind the information in the **Note** above. Make sure the tabs on the bulb fit correctly in the slots in the bulb housing, and secure it in position with the retainer (see illustration).

11 Connect the wire connectors and install the sidelight bulbholder

12 Check the operation of the headlight, then locate the top edge of the rim on the shell lug and clip the rim into place at the bottom of the shell; tighten the screw to secure the rim.

Sidelight

SS/SL, Sport and Supersport models

13 The sidelight bulb can be accessed from the back of the housing. If access is too

restricted (which on later style models it is), remove the main fairing (see Chapter 7).

14 On early style models remove the rubber dust cover.

15 Pull the bulbholder out from the headlight, then pull the bulb out from the bulbholder, noting how it fits (see illustrations). If the socket contacts are dirty or corroded, they should be scraped clean and sprayed with electrical contact cleaner before the new bulb is installed.

16 Install the new bulb in the bulbholder, then press the bulbholder back into the headlight, on early style models making sure the tabs locate in the recesses in the bulbholder (see illustration).

17 Install the dust cover, making sure it is correctly seated (see illustration 7.5).

18 Check the operation of the sidelight, then install the main fairing if removed.

Monster models

19 Slacken the screw securing the headlight rim to the headlight shell, and ease the rim out of the shell (see illustration 7.7).

20 Pull the sidelight bulbholder out from the headlight (see illustration). The bulb can be removed by twisting it anti-clockwise. If the socket contacts are dirty or corroded, they should be scraped clean and sprayed with electrical contact cleaner before the new bulb is installed.

21 Install the new bulb in the bulbholder, then press the bulbholder back into the headlight.

22 Check the operation of the sidelight, then locate the top edge of the rim on the shell lug and clip the rim into place at the bottom of the shell; tighten the screw to secure the rim.

8 Headlight assembly – removal, installation and beam height

Removal

SS/SL, Sport and Supersport models

1 Remove the main fairing (see Chapter 7). On early style models remove the foam surround from around the headlight (see illustration).

2 Remove the rubber dust cover, then disconnect the wiring connector from the headlight bulb and pull the sidelight bulbholder out of the headlight (see illustrations 7.2 and 7.15a and c).

7.20 Sidelight bulbholder removal on Monster models

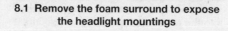

8.1 Remove the foam surround to expose the headlight mountings

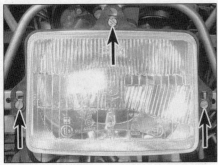

8.3a Headlight mountings (arrows)

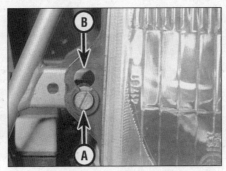

8.3b Press down on the headlight so that the screwhead (A) can pass through the hole (B)

8.3c . . . and withdraw the headlight assembly

8.4 Headlight mounting bolts on left side

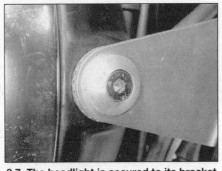

8.7 The headlight is secured to its bracket by a bolt on each side

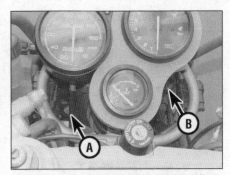

8.13 Vertical adjuster (A), horizontal adjuster (B) – later style Supersport and Sport models

3 On early style models the headlight is secured to the fairing stay by three screws which fit into the mounting sockets in the headlight rim (see illustration). To remove the headlight, carefully press down on it so that the screw shafts are released from the clips, then draw the headlight forward so that the mounting screw heads can pass through the holes above the clips (see illustrations).
4 On later style models unscrew the four bolts securing the headlight and draw it forwards off the front frame (see illustration).

Monster models

5 Slacken the screw securing the headlight rim to the headlight shell, and ease the rim out of the shell (see illustration 7.7).
6 Disconnect the wire connectors from the headlight and sidelight.
7 To remove the headlight shell unscrew the bolts securing the shell to the brackets and remove the shell (see illustration). If necessary, unscrew the bolts securing the brackets to the frame and remove the brackets.

Installation

SS/SL, Sport and Supersport models

8 On early style models align the headlight so that the three mounting screw heads pass through the hole of each mounting point on the headlight rim. Carefully push the headlight upwards so that the screw shafts are pressed into the clips below each hole.
9 The rest of the installation procedure, and

that for later style models, is the reverse of removal. Make sure all the wiring is correctly connected and secured. Check the operation of the headlight and sidelight. Check the headlight aim.

Monster models

10 Installation is the reverse of removal. Make sure all the wiring is correctly connected and secured. Check the operation of the headlight and sidelight. Check the headlight aim.

Beam height

11 Check beam height in accordance with local laws. For UK models, refer to *MOT Test Checks* in the Reference section of this Manual.
12 On early style SS and SL models remove the main fairing for access to the headlight unit adjusters (which double as the headlight mounting screws) (see illustration 8.3a). Vertical adjustment can be made by turning the mounting screw at the top of the headlight, and horizontal adjustment by the screw on each side of the headlight.
13 On later style Sport and Supersport models vertical adjustment is made by turning the adjuster screw on the bottom left-hand side of the headlight housing – turn the screw clockwise to lower the beam and anti-clockwise to raise it (see illustration). Horizontal adjustment is made by turning the adjuster screw on the top right-hand side of the headlight housing – turn the screw clockwise to move the beam to the right and anti-clockwise to move it to the left.

14 On Monster models vertical adjustment can be made by slackening the two shell mounting bolts (see illustration 8.7) and rotating the shell in the brackets. Tighten the bolts when the height is correct. No horizontal adjustment is possible.

9 Tail light bulb and licence plate bulb – replacement

Tail light bulb

1 Unscrew the two screws securing the tail light lens and remove the lens from the tail light assembly.
2 Push the bulb into the holder and twist it anti-clockwise to remove it (see illustration).

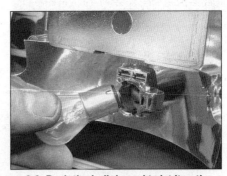

9.2 Push the bulb in and twist it anti-clockwise to release it

9.3 Fit the lens onto the tail light

9.4 Pull the bulbholder out of the light assembly

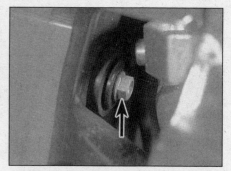

10.3a On early style SS and SL, a nut on each side of tail light (arrow) secures it to the frame

3 Unscrew the nuts securing the tail light and carefully withdraw it out **(see illustrations)**. Note the fitting of any collars and rubber grommets.

Installation

4 Installation is the reverse of removal. Check the operation of the tail light and the brake light and secure the wiring with the clips or ties.

Licence plate light assembly (where fitted)

Removal

5 Pull the bulbholder out of the back of the light **(see illustration 9.4)**.
6 Unscrew the two nuts securing the licence plate light and remove it from the back of the bike **(see illustration)**.

Installation

7 Installation is the reverse of removal. Check the operation of the licence plate light.

10.3b On Monsters, the tail light assembly is secured by two nuts (arrows)

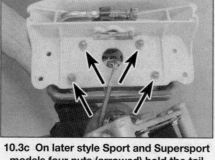

10.3c On later style Sport and Supersport models four nuts (arrowed) hold the tail light to the grab-rail assembly (shown displaced for clarity)

Check the socket terminals for corrosion and clean them if necessary. Line up the pins of the new bulb with the slots in the socket, then push the bulb in and turn it clockwise until it locks into place. **Note:** *The pins on the bulb are offset so it can only be installed one way. It is a good idea to use a paper towel or dry cloth when handling the new bulb to prevent injury if the bulb should break and to increase bulb life.*
3 Install the lens onto the tail light and secure it with its screws **(see illustration)**. Take care not to overtighten the screws as the lens is easily cracked.

Licence plate bulb (where fitted)

4 Pull the bulbholder out from the back of the licence plate light, accessing it from inside the mudguard or from behind the light housing on later Monster models **(see illustration)**.
5 Push the bulb into the holder and twist it anti-clockwise to remove it. Check the socket terminals for corrosion and clean them if necessary. Line up the pins of the new bulb with the slots in the socket, then push the bulb in and turn it clockwise until it locks into place. **Note:** *The pins on the bulb are offset so it can only be installed one way. It is a good idea to use a paper towel or dry cloth when handling the new bulb to prevent injury if the bulb should break and to increase bulb life.*
6 Push the bulbholder back into the light unit.

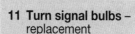

10 Tail light assembly and licence plate light assembly – removal and installation

Tail light assembly

Removal

1 Remove the seat and, on SS, Sport and Supersport models also remove the side panels (see Chapter 7). On later style Sport and Supersport models unscrew the bolts securing the tail light and grab-rail assembly to the rear sub-frame.
2 Trace the tail light wiring back from the assembly and disconnect it at the connector. Release the wiring from any clips or ties.

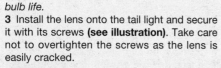

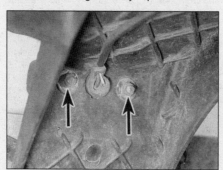

10.6 The licence plate light is secured to the mudguard by two nuts (arrows)

11 Turn signal bulbs – replacement

Front (1991 to 1997 SS and SL models)

1 Unscrew the turn signal assembly retaining screw and remove the assembly from the fairing panel, noting how it fits **(see illustration)**.

11.1 The front turn signal lens is secured to the fairing panel by a single screw (arrow)

11.2 Twist the bulbholder anti-clockwise to release it from the lens

11.3 To release the bulb from its holder gently push it in and twist it anti-clockwise

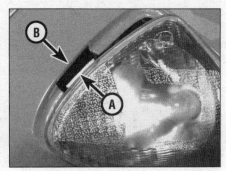

11.4 Locate the tab (A) in the cut-out (B)

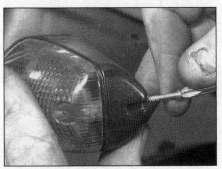

11.5 The lens is secured to the cover by a single screw

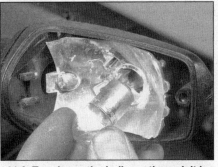

11.6 To release the bulb gently push it in and twist it anti-clockwise

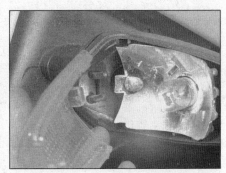

11.7 Engage the lens tab in the cutout when installing the lens

2 Twist the bulbholder anti-clockwise to release it from the casing (see illustration).
3 Push the bulb into the holder and twist it anti-clockwise to remove it (see illustration). Check the socket terminals for corrosion and clean them if necessary. Line up the pins of the new bulb with the slots in the socket, then push the bulb in and turn it clockwise until it locks into place. Note: It is a good idea to use a paper towel or dry cloth when handling the new bulb to prevent injury if the bulb should break and to increase bulb life.
4 Install the bulbholder back into the casing, and the assembly back into the fairing, locating the tab on the casing in the cut-out in the fairing, and tighten the retaining screw (see illustration). Take care not to overtighten the screw as the assembly is easily cracked.

> **HAYNES HiNT**
> If the socket contacts are dirty or corroded, scrape them clean and spray with electrical contact cleaner before a new bulb is installed.

Front and rear (all other models)

5 Unscrew the turn signal lens retaining screw from the turn signal cover and remove the lens assembly, noting how and which way round it fits (see illustration).

6 Push the bulb into the holder and twist it anti-clockwise to remove it (see illustration). Check the socket terminals for corrosion and clean them if necessary. Line up the pins of the new bulb with the slots in the socket, then push the bulb in and turn it clockwise until it locks into place. Note: It is a good idea to use a paper towel or dry cloth when handling the new bulb to prevent injury if the bulb should break and to increase bulb life.
7 Install the lens back onto the cover and tighten the retaining screw (see illustration). Take care not to overtighten the screw as the assembly is easily cracked.

12 Turn signal assemblies –
removal and installation

Front

Removal – SS/SL, Sport and Supersport models

1 On 1991 to 1997 SS and SL models, unscrew the turn signal assembly retaining screw and remove the assembly from the fairing panel, noting how it fits (see illustration 11.1). Disconnect the wiring connectors from the back of the bulbholder (see illustration).

2 On 1998-on Supersport and Sport models, remove the lower fairing panel (see Chapter 7), then undo the nut and remove the bolt securing the turn signal, then remove the signal, noting how it fits.

Removal – Monster models

3 Trace the turn signal wiring back from the turn signal and disconnect it at the connectors. Pull the wiring through to the turn signal mounting, noting its routing.
4 Unscrew the bolt securing the assembly to the support and ease the turn signal off, taking care not to snag the wiring as you draw

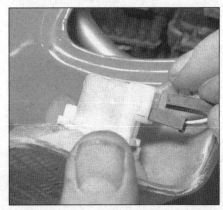

12.1 Disconnect the turn signal wiring connectors

12.4a A single bolt secures the turn signal to its support on early models

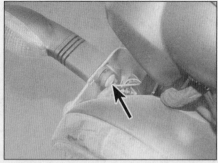

12.4b Turn signal bolt (arrowed) later models

it through **(see illustrations)**. Note how the pin on the end of the turn signal fits into the hole in the support.

5 On early models to remove the turn signal assembly and its support as a unit, unscrew the bolt securing the assembly to the top yoke, then remove the complete assembly. Note the arrangement of the rubber grommet and collar and how the pin on the back of the support fits into the hole in the top yoke.

Installation – all models

6 Installation is the reverse of removal. Make sure the wiring is correctly routed and securely connected. Check the operation of the turn signals.

Rear

Removal – SS/SL, Sport and Supersport models

7 Remove the seat (see Chapter 7). Trace the turn signal wiring back from the turn signal and disconnect it at the connectors. Pull the wiring through to the turn signal mounting, releasing it from any clips or ties and noting its routing.

8 Unscrew the nut on the inside of the mudguard and remove the turn signal, noting how it fits and taking care not to snag the wiring as you draw it through the mounting hole **(see illustration)**.

Removal – Monster models

9 Remove the seat (see Chapter 7). Trace the turn signal wiring back from the turn signal and disconnect it at the connectors. Pull the wiring through to the turn signal mounting, noting its routing.

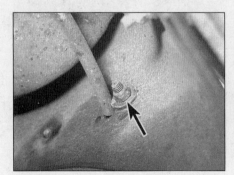

12.8 The turn signal is secured by a nut on the inside of the mudguard (arrow)

10 Unscrew the bolt securing the turn signal to the mudguard and remove the signal, taking care not to snag the wiring as you draw it through. Note how the pin on the end of the turn signal fits into the hole in the support.

Installation – all models

11 Installation is the reverse of removal. Make sure the wiring is correctly routed and securely connected. Check the operation of the turn signals.

13 Turn signal circuit – check

1 The battery provides power for operation of the turn signal lights, so if they do not operate, always check the battery voltage first (see *Fault Finding Equipment* in the Reference section). Low battery voltage indicates either a faulty battery or a defective charging system. Refer to Section 3 for battery checks and Sections 31 and 32 for charging system tests. Also, check the fuses (see Section 5) and the switch (see Section 21).

2 Most turn signal problems are the result of a burned out bulb or corroded socket. This is especially true when the turn signals function properly in one direction, but fail to flash in the other direction. Check the bulbs and the sockets (see Section 11).

3 If the bulbs and sockets are good, check for power at the turn signal relay (where fitted) with the ignition ON. Turn the ignition OFF when the check is complete.

14.6 The brake light switch is secured by two nuts (arrow) on its underside

4 If no power was present at the relay, check the wiring from the fuse to the general relay for continuity.

5 If power was present at the relay, using the appropriate wiring diagram at the end of this Chapter, check the wiring between the relay, turn signal switch and turn signal lights for continuity. If the wiring and switch are sound, replace the relay with a new one.

14 Brake light switches – check and replacement

Circuit check

1 Before checking any electrical circuit, check the bulb (see Section 9) and fuses (see Section 5).

2 Trace the brake switch wiring back from the switch and disconnect it at its connector (on early 750SS and 900SS models disconnect the wiring connectors from the switch terminals on the rear brake switch). Using a meter or test light connected to a good earth and with the ignition switched ON, check for voltage at the wire on the supply side of the brake light switch wiring connector. If there's no voltage present, check the wire between the switch and the fusebox (see the *wiring diagrams* at the end of this Chapter).

3 If voltage is available, check for continuity between the wiring connector terminals on the switch side. With the brake lever or pedal applied, there should be continuity (zero resistance). With the brake lever or pedal released, there should be no continuity (infinite resistance).

4 If the switch is good, check the wiring between the switch and the brake light (see the *wiring diagrams* at the end of this Chapter).

Switch replacement

Front brake lever switch

5 Trace the brake switch wiring back from the switch and disconnect it at its connector.

6 Unscrew the two nuts on the underside of the switch and detach the switch from the bottom of the front brake master cylinder **(see illustration)**.

7 Installation is the reverse of removal.

Rear brake pedal switch – 750SS to frame VIN 001364 and 900SS to frame VIN 002305

Caution: The rear brake switch on these models is of the pressure type and screws into the master cylinder, doubling as the brake hose banjo bolt. Take care to protect the surrounding components from contact with brake fluid when the switch is removed.

8 Disconnect the wiring from the switch.

9 Wrap a rag around the master cylinder to catch any brake fluid that escapes, then

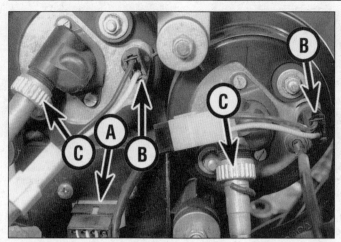

15.2 Disconnect the wiring connector (A), pull out the bulbholders (B) and unscrew the cable retaining rings (C)

15.5 The instrument cluster is secured by three nuts (arrows)

unscrew the switch from the cylinder. Wrap a plastic bag around the end of the brake hose and support it in an upright position to minimise the loss of fluid. Discard the sealing washers as new ones must be used. Do not operate the brake pedal with the switch removed.

10 Fit new sealing washers on each side of the brake hose union, then install the switch and tighten it securely. Bleed the hydraulic system as described in Chapter 6, and check for any signs of leakage and for the correct operation of the brake before taking the bike out on the road.

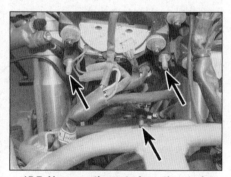

15.7 Unscrew the nuts from the studs (arrowed) and displace the cluster . . .

Rear brake pedal switch – all other models

11 The switch is mounted to the back of the right-hand footrest bracket. Trace the wiring back from the switch and disconnect it at the connector.
12 Unscrew the switch and remove it from the bracket.
13 Installation is the reverse of removal.

15 Instrument cluster and speedometer/tachometer cables – removal and installation

Instrument cluster

Removal – 1991 to 1997 SS and SL models

1 Remove the main fairing (see Chapter 7).
2 Disconnect the instrument cluster wiring connector, and pull out the bulbholders from their sockets **(see illustration)**.
3 Where fitted unscrew the speedometer cable and tachometer cable retaining rings from the rear of the instrument cluster and detach the cables **(see illustration 15.2)**.
4 Unscrew the lockring securing the trip odometer knob to the panel on the left-hand side of the instrument cluster, then feed the

trip cable through to the speedometer, noting its routing.
5 Unscrew the three nuts securing the instrument cluster to the fairing stay and lift the assembly off the stay **(see illustration)**.

Removal – 620i.e. Sport, 1998-on 750 and 900 Sport and Supersport models

6 Remove the main fairing (see Chapter 7).
7 Unscrew the three nuts securing the instrument cluster to the front frame and lift it off **(see illustration)**.
8 Disconnect the instrument cluster wiring connector.
9 On 750 and 900 models detach the speedometer cable **(see illustration)**.

Removal – M620i.e., 2001-on M600/750, 2000-on M900 models

10 Where applicable, detach the speedometer cable.
11 Unscrew the two bolts securing the instrument cluster to the top yoke and displace it, then disconnect the wiring connector **(see illustrations)**.

Removal – 1991 to 2000 M600/750, 1993 to 1999 M900 models

12 Disconnect the instrument cluster wiring connector, and pull the bulbholder out of its socket.
13 Unscrew the speedometer cable retaining

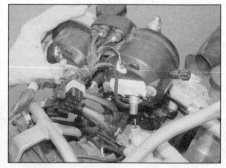

15.9 . . . then disconnect the wiring connector and detach the speedo cable

15.11a Unscrew the bolts (arrowed) . . .

15.11b . . . then displace the cluster and disconnect the wiring connector

15.15 The instrument cluster is secured to the top yoke by two bolts (arrows)

15.17a Unscrew the speedometer cable retaining ring (arrow)

15.17b On Monsters, the cable retaining ring is covered by a rubber boot

ring from the rear of the instrument cluster and detach the cable **(see illustration 15.17b)**.

14 Remove the screw in the centre of the trip odometer knob on the left-hand side of the instrument cluster, then remove the knob from the speedometer.

15 Unscrew the two bolts securing the instrument cluster to the top yoke and carefully lift the assembly off the yoke **(see illustration)**.

Installation – all models

16 Installation is the reverse of removal. Make sure that the drive cables (where fitted), and wiring are correctly routed and secured.

Speedometer cable

Removal

17 Unscrew the speedometer cable retaining

ring from the rear of the instrument cluster and detach the cable **(see illustrations)**.

18 Unscrew the speedometer cable retaining ring from the rear of the drive housing on the left-hand side of the front wheel.

19 Withdraw the cable from the guides on the brake caliper and bottom yoke (Monsters only) and remove it from the bike, noting its correct routing.

Installation

20 Installation is the reverse of removal. Check that the cable doesn't restrict steering movement or interfere with other components.

Tachometer cable – Early style SS and SL models only

Removal

21 Unscrew the tachometer cable retaining

ring from rear of the instrument cluster and detach the cable **(see illustrations)**.

22 Unscrew the tachometer cable retaining ring from the top right-hand side of the horizontal cylinder.

23 Withdraw the cable and remove it from the bike, noting its correct routing.

Installation

24 Installation is the reverse of removal. Check that the cable doesn't restrict steering movement or interfere with other components.

Speed sensor – M620i.e., 620i.e. Sport, M750i.e., 2002 M900i.e.

Air gap check

25 Using a feeler gauge, check that the gap between the sensor tip and a brake disc bolt head is 0.6 to 2.2 mm **(see illustration)**.

Removal and installation

26 Unscrew the bolt securing the sensor and remove it from the caliper bracket along with its spacer **(see illustrations)**.

27 Installation is the reverse of removal.

15.21a Unscrew the tachometer cable retaining ring (arrow) . . .

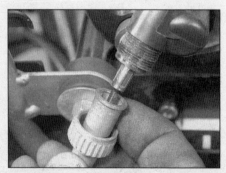

15.21b . . . and withdraw the cable

16 Instruments – check and replacement

Check

1 Special equipment is required to properly check the operation of the instruments. If believed to be faulty, take the motorcycle to a Ducati dealer for assessment. First make sure the fault is not due to a faulty speedometer or tachometer cable (where fitted), or faulty, loose or corroded wiring to the instruments or connectors on them. On models with an electronic speedometer, check the wire connections to the speed sensor fitted in the rear brake caliper bracket and check the sensor air gap (see Section 15).

Replacement

Note 1: *On 2002 M750/900i.e and all M620i.e. and 620i.e. Sport models the instrument cluster is supplied as a unit and no individual components are available for it.*

15.25 Checking the speed sensor air gap

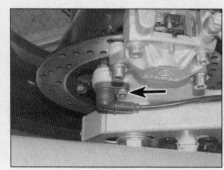

15.26 Speed sensor mounting bolt (arrowed)

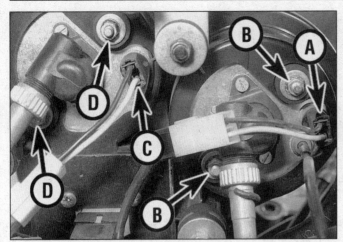

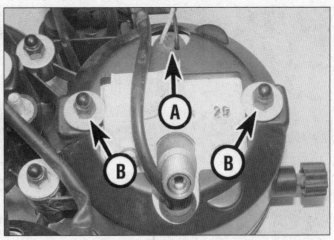

16.2a Speedometer bulb (A), speedometer retaining nuts (B), tachometer bulb (C), tachometer retaining nuts (D) – early SS/SL type

16.2b Speedometer bulb (A) and retaining nuts (B) – later style

Note 2: *For best access to the individual instruments remove the fairing and/or instrument cluster as required according to model. If you do so, ignore any Steps below which do not apply.*

Speedometer

SS/SL, Sport (except 620i.e.) and Supersport models

2 Pull the bulbholder(s) out of the socket(s) **(see illustrations)**.

3 Unscrew the speedometer cable retaining ring from the rear of the instrument cluster and detach the cable **(see illustration 15.17a)**.

4 On early models unscrew the lockring securing the trip odometer knob to the panel on the left-hand side of the instrument cluster, then feed the trip cable through to the speedometer, noting its routing. On later models undo the screw in the middle of the trip knob and remove the knob **(see illustration)**.

5 Unscrew the nuts on the back of the speedometer and withdraw the speedometer through the front of the instrument cluster **(see illustration 16.2a or b)**. Note the arrangement of the washer, spacer (where fitted) and rubber grommet.

6 Install the speedometer by reversing the removal sequence.

1991 to 2000 M600/750, 1993 to 1999 M900 models

7 Unscrew the speedometer cable retaining ring from the rear of the instrument cluster and detach the cable **(see illustration 15.17b)**.

8 Remove the screw in the centre of the trip odometer knob on the left-hand side of the instrument cluster, then remove the knob from the speedometer.

9 Unscrew the two nuts on the back of the speedometer **(see illustration)**. Carefully withdraw the speedometer through the front of the instrument cluster and remove the bulbholders from their sockets as they become accessible. Note the arrangement of the washer and rubber grommet.

10 Install the speedometer by reversing the removal sequence.

2001 M600/750, 2000 and 2001 M900i.e.

11 Undo the screw in the middle of the trip knob and remove the knob **(see illustration 16.4)**.

12 Unscrew the nuts on the back of the instrument cluster. Displace the rear cover, then pull the relevant bulbholder(s) out of the instrument and remove the instrument. Note the rubber grommet.

13 Install the speedometer by reversing the removal sequence.

Tachometer

SS/SL, Sport (except 620i.e.) and Supersport models

14 Pull the bulbholder(s) out of the socket(s) **(see illustration 16.2a)**, and disconnect any wiring connectors **(see illustration)**.

15 Where fitted unscrew the tachometer cable retaining ring from the rear of the instrument cluster and detach the cable **(see illustrations 15.21a and b)**.

16 Unscrew the nuts on the back of the tachometer and withdraw the tachometer through the front of the instrument cluster **(see illustration 16.2a or 16.14)**. Note the arrangement of the washer, spacer (where fitted) and rubber grommet.

17 Install the tachometer by reversing the removal sequence.

2001 M600/750, 2000 and 2001 M900i.e.

18 See Steps 11 to 13 above.

16.4 Undo the small screw (arrowed) and remove the knob

16.9 The speedometer is secured by two nuts

16.14 Disconnect the wiring connectors where necessary

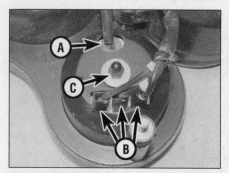

16.19 Bulbholder (A), wiring connectors (B) and retaining nut (C) – later style

17.1a Pull the bulbholder out of its socket . . .

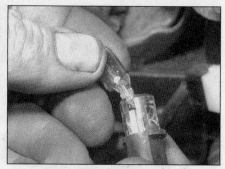

17.1b . . . and the bulb out of the bulbholder

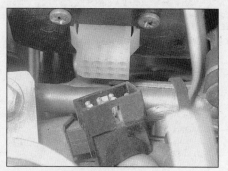

17.3 Disconnect the instrument cluster wiring connector . . .

Oil temperature gauge (SS/SL, Sport and Supersport where fitted)

19 Pull the bulbholder out of its socket (see illustration).

17.4a . . . then unscrew the two screws (arrows) . . .

17.5 Instrument cluster warning light panel

16 Disconnect the temperature gauge wiring.
17 Unscrew the nut on the back of the temperature gauge and withdraw the gauge through the front of the instrument cluster. Note the arrangement of the washer, spacer (where fitted) and rubber grommet.
18 Install the gauge by reversing the removal sequence.

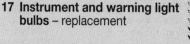

17 Instrument and warning light bulbs – replacement

1991 to 1997 600SS, 750SS and 900SS/SL models

Instrument bulbs

1 Pull the relevant bulbholder out of the back

17.4b . . . and withdraw the panel

17.10 Unscrew the nut to release the warning light panel

of the cluster (see illustration). Gently pull the bulb out of the bulbholder (see illustration). If the socket contacts are dirty or corroded, scrape them clean and spray with electrical contact cleaner before a new bulb is installed.
2 Carefully push the new bulb into position, then push the bulbholder back into the rear of the cluster.

Warning light bulbs

3 Disconnect the instrument cluster wiring connector from the back of the cluster (see illustration).
4 Remove the two screws securing the warning light panel to the cluster, then carefully withdraw the panel from the cluster (see illustrations).
5 Pull the relevant bulb out of its holder in the panel (see illustration). If the socket contacts are dirty or corroded, scrape them clean and spray with electrical contact cleaner before a new bulb is installed.
6 Carefully push the new bulb into its holder, then install the panel into the cluster and secure it with its screws. Connect the wiring connector.

1991 to 2000 M600/750, 1993 to 1999 M900 models

Instrument bulbs

7 Remove the speedometer (see Section 16).
8 Gently pull the bulb out of the bulbholder. If the socket contacts are dirty or corroded, scrape them clean and spray with electrical contact cleaner before a new bulb is installed.
9 Carefully push the new bulb into the bulbholder, then install the speedometer (see Section 16).

Warning light bulbs

10 Unscrew the nut, washer and grommet on the back of the instrument cluster which secures the warning light panel to the cluster (see illustration). Withdraw the panel from the top of the cluster.
11 Pull the relevant bulbholder out of the back of the panel, then gently pull the bulb out

17.11 Bulbholders are a push fit in warning light panel

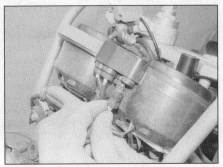

17.16a Pull out the bulbholder . . .

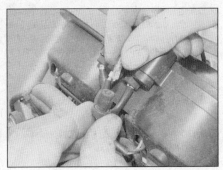

17.16b . . . then remove the bulb

of the holder **(see illustration)**. If the socket contacts are dirty or corroded, scrape them clean and spray with electrical contact cleaner before a new bulb is installed.

12 Carefully push the new bulb into its holder, then install the holder into the panel, and the panel into the cluster. Secure the panel with the grommet, washer and nut.

1998 to 2002 750/900SS, Sport and Supersport models

Instrument bulbs

13 Displace the instrument cluster (see Section 15). Pull the relevant bulbholder out of the back of the cluster **(see illustration 16.2b, 14, or 19)**. Gently pull the bulb out of the bulbholder. If the socket contacts are dirty or corroded, scrape them clean and spray with electrical contact cleaner before a new bulb is installed.

14 Carefully push the new bulb into position, then push the bulbholder back into the rear of the cluster.

Warning light bulbs

15 Remove the fairing (see Chapter 7).

16 Pull the relevant bulbholder out of the panel then remove the bulb **(see illustrations)**. If the socket contacts are dirty or corroded, scrape them clean and spray with electrical contact cleaner before a new bulb is installed.

17 Carefully push the new bulb into its holder, then push the bulbholder back into the rear of the panel.

2001 M600/750, 2000 and 2001 M900i.e.

18 Undo the screw in the middle of the trip knob and remove the knob **(see illustration 16.4)**.

19 Displace the instrument cluster (see Section 15). Unscrew the nuts on the back of the instrument cluster. Displace the rear cover, then pull the relevant bulbholder(s) out of the instrument.

20 Install the bulb by reversing the removal sequence.

2002 M750/900i.e, M620i.e. and 620i.e. Sport models

21 All lights are LED's which are not available individually. If one fails a new instrument cluster must be installed.

---

18 Oil pressure switch – check and replacement

Check

1 The oil pressure warning light should come on when the ignition (main) switch is turned ON and extinguish a few seconds after the engine is started. If the oil pressure light comes on whilst the engine is running, stop the engine immediately and carry out an oil pressure check as described in Chapter 2.

2 If the oil pressure warning light does not come on when the ignition is turned on, check the bulb (see Section 17) and fuses (see Section 5).

3 The oil pressure switch is screwed into the right-hand side of the crankcase adjacent to the oil filler cap **(see illustration)**. Pull back the rubber cover (where fitted) and detach the wiring connector from the switch **(see illustration)**. With the ignition switched ON, ground (earth) the wire on the crankcase and check that the warning light comes on. If the light comes on, the switch is defective and must be replaced.

4 If the light still does not come on, check for voltage at the wire terminal using a test light. If there is no voltage present, check the wire between the switch, the instrument cluster and fusebox for continuity (see the *wiring diagrams* at the end of this Chapter).

5 If the warning light comes on whilst the engine is running, yet the oil pressure is satisfactory, remove the wire from the oil

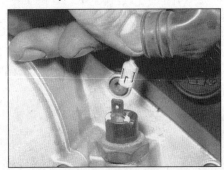

18.3a Early style oil pressure switch connector

pressure switch. With the wire detached and the ignition switched ON the light should be out. If it is illuminated, the wire between the switch and instrument cluster must be earthed at some point. If the wiring is good, the switch must be assumed faulty and replaced.

Replacement

6 The oil pressure switch is screwed into the right-hand side of the crankcase adjacent to the oil filler cap. Pull back the rubber cover (where fitted) and detach the wiring connector from the switch.

7 Unscrew the switch and withdraw it from the crankcase. Discard the sealing washer as a new one must be used.

8 Clean the threads of the switch and fit a new sealing washer to it.

9 Install the switch into the crankcase and tighten it to the torque setting specified at the beginning of the Chapter.

10 Connect the wiring and check the operation of the switch (see Steps 1 to 5 above). Cover the terminal with the rubber cover.

---

19 Ignition (main) switch – check, removal and installation

Check

Note: *Disconnect the battery negative (-ve) lead before working on the ignition switch.*

1 Trace the ignition (main) switch wiring back from the base of the switch and disconnect it at the connector.

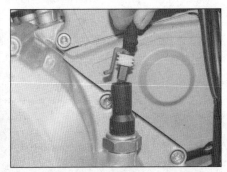

18.3b Later style oil pressure switch connector

2 Using an ohmmeter or a continuity tester, check the continuity of the terminal pairs (see the *wiring diagrams* at the end of this Chapter). Continuity should exist between the terminals connected by a solid line on the diagram when the switch is in the indicated position.

3 If the switch fails any of the tests, replace it.

Removal and installation – SS, SL, Sport and Supersport models

4 The ignition switch is secured to the underside of the top yoke by two bolts. Certain models are fitted with special security bolts which will require careful extraction; in this case it is recommended that the top yoke is removed (see Chapter 5, Section 8) and taken to a Ducati dealer for extraction of the bolts. Where conventional bolts are used, disconnect the switch wiring connector and remove the two bolts to free the switch from the top yoke. Remove the fairing for improved access if necessary (see Chapter 7).

5 On models fitted with an immobilizer, disconnect the antennae wiring connector and the main ignition switch connector, freeing the wiring from any ties. Remove the two bolts from the underside of the switch assembly and detach it from the top yoke. Slip the cover off the switch body and carefully withdraw the antennae ring from inside the cover.

6 Installation is a reverse of the removal procedure. Apply threadlock to all nuts/bolts on installation. On models with an immobilizer also apply some threadlock to the locating pins in the cover, and make sure it locates correctly onto the antennae.

Removal and installation – Monster models

7 The ignition switch is mounted to the frame by two Allen bolts. Raise the fuel tank and disconnect the battery negative (-ve) lead. Trace the wiring from the ignition switch to its block connector and disconnect it. Remove the two bolts from the top of the switch to free the top cover, then remove the two bolts from

the underside of the switch to free it from the frame.

8 On models fitted with an immobilizer, disconnect the antennae wiring connector and the main ignition switch wiring connector and free the wiring from its ties. Unscrew the nuts securing the switch cover and remove it, then remove the antennae ring, noting how it fits and the routing of its wiring. Remove the two special bolts securing the switch, then remove the plate and the switch from the frame.

9 Installation is a reverse of the removal procedure. Apply threadlock to all nuts/bolts on installation. On models with an immobilizer also apply some threadlock to the locating pins in the cover, and make sure it locates correctly onto the antennae.

20 Handlebar switches – check

1 Generally speaking, the switches are reliable and trouble-free. Most troubles, when they do occur, are caused by dirty or corroded contacts, but wear and breakage of internal parts is a possibility that should not be overlooked. If breakage does occur, the entire switch and related wiring harness will have to be replaced with a new one, since individual parts are not available.

2 The switches can be checked for continuity using an ohmmeter or a continuity test light. Always disconnect the battery negative (-ve) lead, which will prevent the possibility of a short circuit, before making the checks.

3 Trace the wiring of the relevant switch back to its connector(s) and disconnect it.

4 Using the ohmmeter or test light, check for continuity between the terminals of the switch harness with the switch in the various positions (i.e. switch off – no continuity, switch on – continuity) (see the *wiring diagrams* at the end of this Chapter).

5 If the continuity check indicates that a problem exists, refer to Section 21, remove the switch and spray the switch contacts with electrical contact cleaner. If they are accessible, the contacts can

be scraped clean with a knife or polished with crocus cloth. If switch components are damaged or broken, it will be obvious when the switch is disassembled.

21 Handlebar switches – removal and installation

Right-hand handlebar switch

Removal

1 If the switch is to be removed from the bike, rather than just displaced from the handlebar, trace the wiring harness back from the switch and disconnect it at the wiring connector. Work back along the harness, freeing it from all the relevant clips and ties, whilst noting its correct routing.

2 Unscrew the switch retaining screws on the underside of the switch and remove the switch from the handlebar, noting how it fits **(see illustration)**.

Installation

3 Installation is the reverse of removal. Make sure the locating pin in the lower half of the switch fits into hole in the underside of the handlebar **(see illustration 21.6)**.

Left-hand handlebar switch

Removal

4 If the switch is to be removed from the bike, rather than just displaced from the handlebar, trace the wiring harness back from the switch and disconnect it at the wiring connector. Work back along the harness, freeing it from all the relevant clips and ties, whilst noting its correct routing.

5 Unscrew the switch retaining screws on the underside of the switch and remove the switch from the handlebar, noting how it fits **(see illustration)**.

Installation

6 Installation is the reverse of removal. Make sure the locating pin in the lower half of the switch fits into hole in the underside of the handlebar **(see illustration)**.

21.2 The screws are on the underside of the right-hand handlebar switch (arrow)

21.5 The screws are on the underside of the left-hand handlebar switch

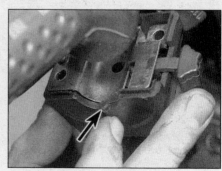

21.6 The pin (arrow) locates in the hole in the underside of the handlebar

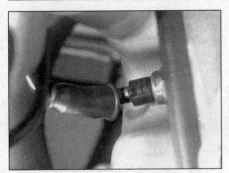

22.2 Pull back the rubber boot on the switch to access the wiring connector

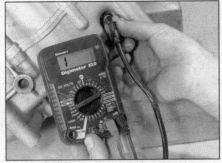

22.7 Checking the neutral switch set-up with a multimeter – infinite resistance is indicated when switch opens

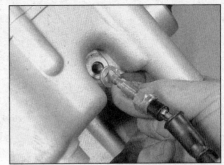

22.9 Unscrew the neutral switch from the crankcase and remove the shim

22 Neutral switch – check and replacement

Check

1 Before checking the switch, check the bulb (see Section 17) and fuses (see Section 5).
2 The neutral switch is screwed into the back of the crankcase on the right-hand side **(see illustration)**. Trace the wiring back from the switch and disconnect it at its connector. Using a meter or test light connected to a good earth and with the ignition switched "ON", check for voltage on the supply side of the wiring connector. If there's no voltage present, check the wire between the switch and the fusebox (see the *wiring diagrams* at the end of this Chapter).
3 If voltage is available, check for continuity between the wiring connector terminals on the switch side. With the gearbox in neutral, there should be continuity (zero resistance). With any gear selected, there should be no continuity (infinite resistance).
4 If the switch is good, check the wire between the switch and the neutral light for continuity (see the *wiring diagrams* at the end of this Chapter).
5 The successful operation of the neutral switch also depends on its plunger being the correct distance from the trigger on the selector drum. Since crankcase thicknesses may vary from model-to-model, a shim is used between the neutral switch and the

crankcase surface to ensure that the switch is set to the correct height. If problems are experienced with the neutral light staying on when the transmission is in gear, or the light not coming on when in neutral, check the neutral switch set-up as described in Step 6 or 7.
6 Shift the transmission into neutral. Turn the ignition ON – the neutral light should be ON. Now unscrew the switch and note the position where the neutral light goes out; this should occur between a half turn and a whole turn of the switch. If the light goes out before a half turn of the switch the shim must be replaced with a thinner one. If the light goes out after a whole turn of the switch the shim must be replaced with a thicker one. Replacement shims are available in 1 mm, 1.5 mm and 2 mm thicknesses.
7 If checking the switch set-up with a continuity tester, shift the transmission into neutral, then trace the wiring up from the switch and disconnect the two switch wires at the connector. Connect a continuity tester across the two wires on the switch side of the connector. The tester should indicate continuity (0 ohms). Now unscrew the switch and note the position where the tester indicates no continuity (infinite resistance); this should occur between a half turn and a whole turn of the switch **(see illustration)**. If no continuity (switch opens) occurs before a half turn, the shim should be replaced with a thinner one. If no continuity occurs after a whole turn of the switch the shim should be replaced with a thicker one. Replacement

shims are available in 1 mm, 1.5 mm and 2 mm thicknesses.

Replacement

8 The neutral switch is screwed into the back of the crankcase on the right-hand side **(see illustration 22.2)**. Trace the wiring back from the switch and disconnect it at its connector.
9 Unscrew the switch from the crankcase and remove it along with its shim **(see illustration)**.
10 Install the switch and tighten it securely. Slip the rubber cover back over the switch.
11 Reconnect the wiring and check the operation of the neutral light.

23 Sidestand switch – check and replacement

Check

1 The sidestand switch is mounted on the sidestand or its bracket (according to year) on the left-hand side of the engine **(see illustrations)**. A warning light on the instrument cluster indicates when the sidestand is down. Before checking the electrical circuit, check the bulb (see Section 17) and fuse (see Section 5).
2 Trace the wiring back from the switch and disconnect it at the connector.
3 Check the operation of the switch using an ohmmeter or continuity test light. Connect the meter to the terminals on the switch side of the connector. With the sidestand down there should be continuity (zero resistance) between the terminals, and with the stand up there should be no continuity (infinite resistance).
4 If the switch does not perform as expected, it is defective and must be replaced. Check first that the fault is not caused by the ingress of road dirt; spray the switch with a water dispersant aerosol.
5 If the switch is good, check the wiring between the switch and the instrument cluster (see the *wiring diagrams* at the end of this book).

23.1a Sidestand switch (arrowed) – early style

23.1b Sidestand switch (arrowed) – later style

Replacement

6 The sidestand switch is mounted on the sidestand or its bracket (according to year) on the left-hand side of the engine **(see illustration 23.1a or b)**. Trace the wiring back from the switch and disconnect it at the connector.

7 Work back along the switch wiring, freeing it from any relevant retaining clips and ties, noting its correct routing.

8 To remove the old style 'plunger type' switch, unscrew the switch and remove it from the bracket, noting how it fits **(see illustration 23.1a)**.

8 To remove the new style 'rotary type' switch, unscrew the switch bolt and remove it from the stand, noting how it fits **(see illustration 23.1b)**.

9 Fit the new switch, making sure it is secure.

10 Make sure the wiring is correctly routed up to the connector and retained by all the necessary clips and ties.

11 Reconnect the wiring connector and check the operation of the sidestand switch.

---

24 General relay (carburettor models) – check and replacement

Check

1 The relay is mounted on the inside of the right-hand side of the main fairing on SS and SL models, and under the seat on Monster models **(see illustration 5.1c)**. It acts as a switch for all circuits connected via the fusebox (see *wiring diagrams* at the end of this Chapter). If all these circuits fail at the same time, the relay should be inspected before the individual components in the circuits involved.

2 When the ignition is switched ON, the relay should be heard to click. If it doesn't, first check the 30A main fuse in the fusebox, then check for voltage at the white/red wire (SS/SL models) or orange/blue wire (Monster models) from terminal 85 on the relay. If no voltage is present, check the wires between the relay's terminal 85 and the ignition switch, and between the ignition switch and the main 30A fuse (see *wiring diagrams* at the end of this Chapter). If voltage is present and the relay

doesn't click, it is faulty and must be replaced.

3 If the relay clicks, turn the ignition OFF and remove the relay from the machine as described below. Connect an ohmmeter across terminals 30 and 87 of the relay. Connect a fully-charged 12 volt battery (the machine's battery will do) across terminals 86 and 85 of the relay; the wire from the battery positive terminal goes to the relay 85 terminal, and the wire from its negative terminal goes to the relay 86 terminal. With battery voltage applied, continuity should be shown on the ohmmeter. If no continuity (infinite resistance) is shown, the relay is faulty and must be replaced.

Replacement

Note: *Disconnect the battery negative (-ve) lead before removing the relay.*

4 The relay is mounted on the inside of the right-hand side of the main fairing on SS and SL models, and under the seat on Monsters.

5 Make a note of which wires fit on which terminals (they are numbered), then disconnect the wiring and remove the relay from its sleeve.

6 Install the new relay and connect the wiring as noted on removal (see also *wiring diagrams* at the end of this Chapter).

---

25 Horn – check and replacement

Check

1 The horn is mounted at the front of the bike **(see illustration 25.4)**.

2 Unplug the wiring connectors from the horn **(see illustration)**. Using two jumper wires, apply battery voltage directly to the terminals on the horn. If the horn sounds, first check the fuse (see Section 5), then check the switch (see Section 21) and the wiring between the switch and the horn (see the *wiring diagrams* at the end of this Chapter).

3 If the horn doesn't sound, replace it.

Replacement

4 The horn is mounted at the front of the bike **(see illustration)**.

5 Unplug the wiring connectors from the horn

(see illustration 25.2), then unscrew the bolt securing the horn to its mounting bracket and remove it from the bike.

6 Install the horn and securely tighten the bolt, then connect the wiring connectors.

---

26 Low fuel level sensor – check and replacement

⚠️ *Warning: Petrol (gasoline) is extremely flammable, so take extra pre-cautions when you work on any part of the fuel system. Don't smoke or allow open flames or bare light bulbs near the work area, and don't work in a garage where a natural gas-type appliance is present. If you spill any fuel on your skin, rinse it off immediately with soap and water. When you perform any kind of work on the fuel system, wear safety glasses and have a fire extinguisher suitable for a class B type fire (flammable liquids) on hand.*

Check

Models with a plastic tank

1 The level sensor on these models is an integral component of the fuel pump – see Chapter 3B. No test details are provided.

All other models

2 If the low fuel level warning light has not come on and the tank consequently runs dry, check the fuses and the bulb (see Sections 5 and 17). If the fuses and bulb are in good condition, check for battery voltage at the sensor connector supply wires with the ignition ON, referring to the Wiring Diagrams at the end of the Chapter **(see illustration)**.

3 If no voltage is indicated, check the wiring to the sensor connector for open-circuits and poor connections (see the *wiring diagrams* at the end of this Chapter).

4 If voltage is present at the connector, the sensor is faulty and must be replaced.

Replacement

Models with a plastic tank

5 The level sensor on these models is an integral component of the fuel pump – see Chapter 3B.

25.2 Disconnect the horn wiring connectors

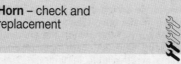

25.4 The horn is secured by a single bolt (arrow)

26.2 Low fuel level sensor wiring connector

All other models

6 Drain and remove the fuel tank (see Chapter 3). Access the fuel pump (see Section 27 for carburettor models and Chapter 3B for fuel injection models) and disconnect the wiring from it.

7 Unscrew the sensor from the base of the tank and withdraw it. Discard the sealing washer as a new one must be used.

8 Install the sensor by reversing the removal process, using a new gasket.

27 Fuel pump (SS and SL carburettor models only) – check, removal and installation

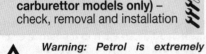

> **Warning:** *Petrol is extremely flammable, so take extra precautions when you work on any part of the fuel system. Don't smoke or allow open flames or bare light bulbs near the work area, and don't work in a garage where a natural gas-type appliance is present. If you spill any fuel on your skin, rinse it off immediately with soap and water. When you perform any kind of work on the fuel system, wear safety glasses and have a fire extinguisher suitable for a class B type fire (flammable liquids) on hand.*

Check

1 The fuel pump is located inside the fuel tank.

2 It should be possible to hear the fuel pump running whenever the ignition is switched ON – place your ear close beside the tank. If you can't hear anything, check the circuit fuse (see Section 5).

3 If the fuse is good, disconnect the fuel tank wiring connector and check for battery voltage at the red/black wire on the supply side of the connector. If no voltage is present, check the wiring between the pump and the fusebox, and between the fusebox and the general relay (see the *wiring diagrams* at the end of this Chapter).

4 If voltage is present, remove the pump from the tank (see below) and check it for loose or corroded terminals.

5 If the pump still does not work, using a fully charged 12 volt battery and two insulated jumper wires, connect the positive (+) terminal of the battery to the pump's red/black

terminal, and the negative (-) terminal of the battery to the pump's other terminal **(see illustration)**. The pump should operate. If the pump does not operate it must be replaced.

6 If the pump operates but is thought to be delivering an insufficient amount of fuel, first check the fuel tank breather and the condition of the filters and the pipes inside the tank, and the pipes between the tank and the carburettors (see Chapter 3). Check carefully for signs of kinked, trapped, pinched or blocked pipes. Also check the fuel tap.

Removal

7 The fuel pump is mounted inside the fuel tank and is connected via a short piece of hose to the fuel filter. Follow the procedure detailed in Chapter 1, Section 7 – fuel filter replacement, for removal of the fuel pump as it is removed as an assembly with the filter.

Installation

8 Installation is a reverse of the removal procedure (see Chapter 1, Section 7 – fuel filter replacement). Make sure the fuel hoses are correctly and securely fitted to the pump.

28 Starter relay – check and replacement

Check

1 If the starter circuit is faulty, first check the fuses (see Section 5).

2 The starter relay is mounted in a rubber sleeve which fits onto a bracket under the air filter housing on the right-hand side **(see illustrations)**. With the ignition switch ON, the engine kill switch in RUN and the transmission in neutral, press the starter switch. The relay should be heard to click.

3 If the relay doesn't click, switch off the ignition and remove the relay as described below; test it as follows.

4 Set a multimeter to the ohms x 1 scale and connect it across the relay's starter motor and battery lead terminals. Using a fully-charged 12 volt battery and two insulated jumper wires, connect the positive (+ve) terminal of the battery to the supply wire terminal pin on the relay, and the negative (-ve) terminal to the

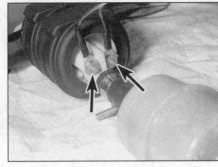

27.5 Fuel pump terminals (arrows)

other terminal pin on the relay. At this point the relay should click and the multimeter read 0 ohms (continuity). If this is the case the relay is proved good. If the relay does not click when battery voltage is applied and indicates no continuity (infinite resistance) across its terminals, it is faulty and must be replaced.

5 If the relay is good, check for battery voltage at the red/blue (or red/green) wire when the starter button is pressed and the ignition is ON. Check the other components in the starter circuit as described in the relevant sections of this Chapter. If all components are good, check the wiring between the various components (see the *wiring diagrams* at the end of this book).

Replacement

6 The starter relay is mounted in a rubber sleeve which fits onto a bracket on the bottom of the right-hand side of the air filter housing **(see illustration 28.2a or b)**. Where fitted remove the fairing right-hand lower panel for improved access (see Chapter 7).

7 Raise the fuel tank and disconnect the battery terminals, remembering to disconnect the negative (-ve) terminal first.

8 Disconnect the relay wiring connector, then unscrew the two nuts securing the starter motor and battery leads to the relay and detach the leads **(see illustration)**. Remove the relay with its rubber sleeve from its mounting lugs on the air filter housing **(see illustration 28.2a)**.

9 Installation is the reverse of removal ensuring the terminal screws are securely tightened. Connect the negative (-ve) lead last when reconnecting the battery.

28.2a Starter motor relay – style fitted to most models

28.2b Starter motor relay (arrowed) – style fitted to late Monster models

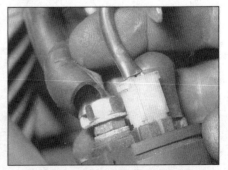

28.8 Starter relay terminals and wire connector

29.3 Starter motor terminal

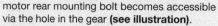

29.5 Starter motor mounting bolts (arrows). Note access to the rear bolt is via the hole in the idle gear

29.8 Install the starter motor using a new gasket

29 Starter motor – removal and installation

Removal

1 Disconnect the fuel tank breather hose from its union (SS/SL models), then release the fuel tank front catch and raise it onto its prop. Disconnect the battery negative (-ve) lead.
2 Where fitted, remove the left-hand side lower fairing panel (see Chapter 7).
3 The starter motor is mounted to the front of the engine below the horizontal cylinder. Peel back the rubber cover on the wiring terminal and unscrew the nut securing the starter cable to the motor (see illustration).
4 Remove the left-hand side crankcase cover (see Chapter 2, Section 14).
5 Rotate the starter idle gear until the starter

motor rear mounting bolt becomes accessible via the hole in the gear (see illustration).
6 Unscrew the three starter motor mounting bolts and slide the starter motor out of the crankcase.
7 Remove the gasket on the end of the starter motor and discard it – a new one must be used.

Installation

8 Install a new gasket onto the end of the starter motor making sure the bolt holes are correctly aligned (see illustration).
9 Manoeuvre the motor into position and slide it into the crankcase. Ensure that the starter motor teeth mesh correctly with those of the starter idle gear.
10 Rotate the starter idle gear until the starter motor rear mounting bolt hole becomes accessible via the hole in the gear (see illustration 29.5). Apply a suitable non-permanent thread-locking compound to the

threads of the mounting bolts, then install them and tighten them to the torque setting specified at the beginning of the Chapter.
11 Install the left-hand side crankcase cover (see Chapter 2, Section 14).
12 Connect the starter motor cable, and secure it with the spring washer and retaining nut. Make sure the rubber cover is correctly seated over the terminal.
13 Where fitted, install the left-hand side lower fairing panel (see Chapter 7).
14 Connect the battery negative (-ve) lead, then lower the tank and secure it with its catch. Connect the fuel tank breather hose on SS and SL models.

30 Starter motor – disassembly, inspection and reassembly

Disassembly

1 Remove the starter motor (see Section 27).
2 If no alignment marks are visible between the main housing and the end covers, make your own (see illustration).
3 Remove the circlip from the front end of the shaft and slide the drive pinion off the shaft (see illustration).
4 Unscrew the two long bolts then remove the right-hand end cover from the motor along with its sealing O-ring and the brushplate assembly (see illustrations). Remove the shim from the armature noting its correct fitted position.
5 Remove the main housing (see illustration).
6 Wrap insulating tape around the splines of the

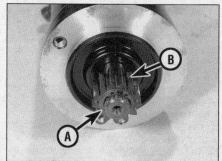

30.2 Make alignment marks (arrows) across each end cover joint

30.3 Remove the circlip (A) and slide the pinion (B) off the shaft

30.4a Unscrew the two bolts (arrows) . . .

30.4b . . . and remove right-hand end cover

30.5 Remove the main housing

30.6 Remove the left-hand end cover

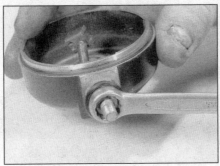

30.7 Unscrew the nut and remove the terminal bolt from the right-hand cover

30.8 Displace the brush springs and remove the brushes

shaft – this will protect the oil seal from damage by the splines as the left-hand end cover is removed. Remove the end cover from the motor along with its sealing O-ring **(see illustration)**.
7 Noting the correct fitted location of each component, unscrew the nut from the terminal bolt on the right-hand end cover and remove the insulating washer and the rubber O-ring **(see illustration)**. Withdraw the terminal bolt and brushplate assembly from the cover.
8 Lift each brush spring end onto the top of each brush holder and slide the brushes out from their holders **(see illustration)**.

 HAYNES HiNT *Lifting the end of the brush spring so that it is against the top of the brush holder and not pressing into the brush holder makes it much easier to install the brushes on reassembly.*

Inspection

Note: *No internal replacement parts are available from Ducati for the starter motor. If the following checks reveal a worn or faulty internal component, seek the advice of a Ducati dealer or auto electrical specialist before buying a new starter motor.*

9 The parts of the starter motor that are most likely to require attention are the brushes. Ducati do not provide service limit specifications for the length of the brushes. If the brushes are not worn excessively, nor cracked, chipped, or otherwise damaged, they may be re-used **(see illustration)**.
10 Inspect the commutator bars on the

armature for scoring, scratches and discoloration. The commutator can be cleaned and polished with crocus cloth, but do not use sandpaper or emery paper. After cleaning, wipe away any residue with a cloth soaked in electrical system cleaner or denatured alcohol.
11 Using an ohmmeter or a continuity test light, check for continuity between the commutator bars **(see illustration)**. Continuity should exist between each bar and all of the others. Also, check for continuity between the commutator bars and the armature shaft **(see illustration)**. There should be no continuity (infinite resistance) between the commutator and the shaft. If the checks indicate otherwise, the armature is defective.
12 Check for continuity between each brush and the terminal bolt. There should be continuity (zero resistance). Check for continuity between the terminal bolt and the housing (when assembled). There should be no continuity (infinite resistance).

13 Check the starter drive pinion for worn, cracked, chipped and broken teeth. If the gear is damaged or worn, replace the pinion.
14 Inspect the end covers for signs of cracks or wear. Inspect the magnets in the main housing and the housing itself for cracks.
15 Inspect the insulating washer, O-rings and left-hand cover oil seal for signs of damage and replace if necessary.

Reassembly

16 Fit the sealing O-ring to the left-hand end cover and carefully slide the end cover into position **(see illustration)**. Remove the protective insulating tape from the shaft.
17 Fit the main housing over the armature, aligning the marks made on removal **(see illustration 30.5)**.
18 Ensure that the rubber insulating grommet is in place on the terminal bolt, then insert the bolt through the right-hand cover **(see illustrations)**. Fit the O-ring and the insulating

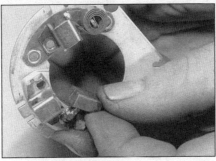

30.9 Inspect the brushes for wear and damage

30.11a Continuity should exist between the commutator bars

30.11b There should be no continuity between the commutator bars and the armature shaft

30.16 Make sure the sealing ring is fitted on the cover

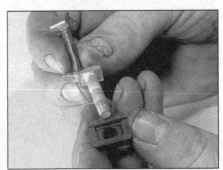

30.18a Fit the insulating grommet onto the terminal bolt . . .

30.18b . . . then fit the bolt into the right-hand cover

30.18c Fit the O-ring (arrow) and the insulating washer . . .

30.18d . . . and secure the assembly with the nut

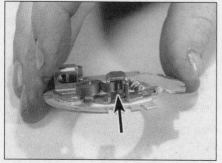

30.19a Fit the brushes and position the spring ends as shown (arrow)

30.19b Fit the brushplate into the right-hand cover

30.19c Make sure the sealing ring is fitted on the cover

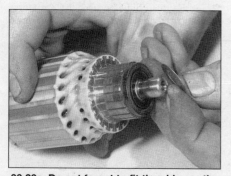

30.20a Do not forget to fit the shim on the armature shaft

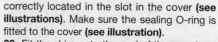

30.20b Manipulate the brushes onto the commutator bars as the cover is fitted

illustrations). As it is inserted, locate the brushes on the commutator bars. Check that each brush is securely pressed against the commutator by its spring and is free to move easily in its holder.

21 Check the marks made on removal are correctly aligned then fit the long bolts and tighten them securely (see illustration).

22 Slide the drive pinion onto the front of the shaft and secure it in place with the circlip, making sure it is correctly seated in its groove (see illustrations).

23 Install the starter motor (see Section 27).

31 Charging system testing – general information and precautions

1 If the performance of the charging system is suspect, the system as a whole should be

washer and secure them in place with the nut (see illustrations)

19 Lift the brush springs on the brushplate and slide the brushes back into position in their holders, then install the brushplate assembly in the right-hand end cover making sure its tab is

correctly located in the slot in the cover (see illustrations). Make sure the sealing O-ring is fitted to the cover (see illustration).

20 Fit the shim onto the end of the armature, then fit the right-hand end cover, taking care not to damage the brushes (see

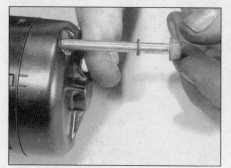

30.21 Make sure the sealing washer is installed with each long bolt

30.22a Fit the pinion onto the shaft . . .

30.22b . . . and secure it with the circlip

checked first, followed by testing of the individual components. **Note:** *Before beginning the checks, make sure the battery is fully charged and that all system connections are clean and tight.*

2 Checking the output of the charging system and the performance of the various components within the charging system requires the use of a multimeter (with voltage, current and resistance checking facilities).

3 When making the checks, follow the procedures carefully to prevent incorrect connections or short circuits, as irreparable damage to electrical system components may result if short circuits occur.

4 If a multimeter is not available, the job of checking the charging system should be left to a Ducati dealer.

5 Note that with the exception of early 900 models, all engines with two-wire alternators are fitted with uprated regulator/rectifier and alternator units. If replacement of either of these components is necessary, quote your engine and frame number to the dealer in order that the correct unit is supplied for your machine. Uprated units can be fitted to early 900 models, but note that both components must be replaced. An uprated regulator/rectifier should not be used with an original alternator, and vice versa. The uprated regulator/rectifier unit is identified by the number 343637 stamped into its casing. The uprated alternator is identified by a blue mark on both the rotor and stator coils.

32 Charging system – leakage and output test

1 If the charging system of the machine is thought to be faulty, disconnect the fuel tank breather hose from its union (SS and SL models), then release the fuel tank front catch and raise it onto its prop. Perform the following checks.

Leakage test

2 Turn the ignition switch OFF and disconnect the lead from the battery negative (-ve) terminal.
3 Set the multimeter to the mA (milli Amps) function and connect its negative (-ve) probe

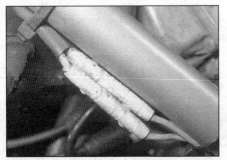

33.3 Alternator wiring connectors – early models

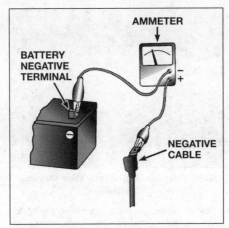

32.3 Checking the charging system leakage rate. Connect the meter as shown

to the battery negative (-ve) terminal, and positive (+ve) probe to the disconnected negative (-ve) lead **(see illustration)**. With the meter connected like this the reading should not exceed 0.1 mA.

4 If the reading exceeds the specified amount it is likely that there is a short circuit in the wiring, although if an alarm is fitted remember to take its current draw into account. Thoroughly check the wiring between the various components (see the *wiring diagrams* at the end of this book).

5 If the reading is below the specified amount, the leakage rate is satisfactory. Disconnect the meter and connect the negative (-ve) lead to the battery, tightening it securely. Check the alternator output as described below.

Output test

6 Start the engine and warm it up to normal operating temperature.

7 Allow the engine to idle and connect a multimeter set to the 0-20 volts dc scale (voltmeter) across the terminals of the battery (positive (+ve) lead to battery positive (+ve) terminal, negative (-ve) lead to battery negative (-ve) terminal). Slowly increase the engine speed to 3000 rpm and note the reading obtained. At this speed the voltage should be around 13.5 to 15.5 volts. If the voltage is below this it will be necessary to check the alternator and regulator as described in the

33.6 The stator coil assembly bolts (arrowed). Early model type shown – later models have three bolts

following Sections. **Note:** *Occasionally the condition may arise where the charging voltage is excessive. This condition is almost certainly due to a faulty regulator/rectifier which should be tested as described in Section 35.*

> **HAYNES HINT** *Clues to a faulty regulator are constantly blowing bulbs, with brightness varying considerably with engine speed, and battery overheating, necessitating frequent topping up of the electrolyte level.*

33 Alternator – removal and installation

Removal

1 Raise fuel tank. Disconnect the battery negative (-ve) lead.
2 Where fitted, remove the left-hand side lower fairing panel (see Chapter 7).
3 Trace the alternator wiring back from the left-hand side crankcase cover, releasing it from any clips or ties, and disconnect it at the connector(s) **(see illustration)**.
4 Remove the left-hand side crankcase cover and alternator rotor (see Chapter 2, Section 14).
5 To remove the stator from the crankcase cover, on older models the stator wiring must be drawn through the hole in the crankcase cover. Unscrew the wiring plug from the union on the outside of the crankcase and slide it off the wiring, then pull the wiring through from the inside, taking care not to snag the connectors on the crankcase as they are easily damaged. Remove the rubber sealing grommet from inside the wiring plug union in the crankcase, accessing it from the outside of the crankcase. On later models free the wiring grommet from its cutout.
6 Unscrew the bolts securing the stator, then remove the assembly from the cover **(see illustration)**.

Installation

7 Install the alternator rotor (see Chapter 2, Section 14).
8 Install the stator into the cover, aligning the wiring with the hole in the cover. Apply some suitable non-permanent thread-locking compound to the stator bolt threads, then install the bolts and tighten them to the torque setting specified at the beginning of the Chapter.
9 Feed the wiring through its union in the crankcase and through the sealing grommet and the wiring plug. Slide the sealing grommet down the wiring and into the union in the crankcase, then screw the wiring plug into the union and tighten it down onto the grommet so that the seal is formed.
10 Install the left-hand side crankcase cover (see Chapter 2, Section 14). Connect the alternator wiring and secure it with any clips or ties **(see illustration 33.3)**.

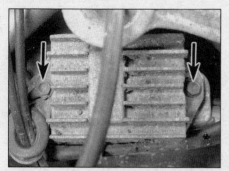

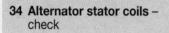

35.6a The regulator/rectifier is secured by two bolts (arrows)

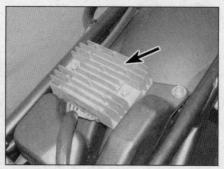

35.6b Regulator/rectifier – later Monster models

35.6c Regulator/rectifier – later style Sport and Supersport models

34 Alternator stator coils – check

1 Where fitted, remove the left-hand side lower fairing panel.

2 Trace the wiring back from the alternator and disconnect it at the connector(s) (see illustration 33.3).

3 On early models with a two-wire alternator, using a multimeter set to the ohms x 1 (ohmmeter) scale measure the resistance between the two yellow wires on the alternator side of the connectors, then check for continuity between each terminal and earth. If the stator coil windings are in good condition the resistance reading should be within the range shown in the Specifications at the start of this Chapter and there should be no continuity (infinite resistance) between each terminal and earth. If not, the alternator stator coil assembly is at fault and should be replaced. Note: *Before condemning the stator coils, check the fault is not due to damaged wiring between the connector and coils.*

4 On 1998-on models with a three-wire alternator, using a multimeter set to the ohms x 1 (ohmmeter) scale measure the resistance between each pair of yellow wires on the alternator side of the connectors, thereby taking three reading in all, then check for continuity between each terminal and earth. If the stator coil windings are in good condition the resistance reading should be the same for each (no specific value is specified) and there should be no continuity (infinite resistance) between each terminal and earth. If not, the alternator stator coil assembly is at fault and should be

replaced. Note: *Before condemning the stator coils, check the fault is not due to damaged wiring between the connector and coils.*

35 Regulator/rectifier unit – check and replacement

Check

1 Clues to a faulty regulator are constantly blowing bulbs, with brightness varying considerably with engine speed, and battery overheating, necessitating frequent topping up of the electrolyte level. If this is the case, carry out a charging system output test (see Section 32). Also carry out an alternator stator coil check (see Section 34). The test details given below apply to 1991 to 1997 models with a two-wire alternator. No test details are available for 1998-on models fitted with a three-wire alternator; testing can only be carried out with the Mathesis tester although nothing can be lost by initially checking the wiring and connectors to the unit.

2 The regulator/rectifier unit is mounted to the underside of the frame, behind the steering stem, on most models, or on later Monster models under the seat (see illustration 35.6a, b or c). Trace the wiring back from the unit and disconnect it at the connectors. If access is restricted by the fairing panels (where fitted), remove them as required (see Chapter 7).

3 Switch the ignition ON. Using a multimeter set to the 0 – 20 volts dc scale, connect the meter positive (+ve) probe to the red/black terminal on the supply side of the connector and the negative (-ve) probe to earth. Full

battery voltage should be present. Switch the ignition switch OFF.

4 If the above checks do not provide the expected results check the wiring between the battery, regulator/rectifier and alternator (see the *wiring diagrams* at the end of this book).

5 If the wiring checks out, the regulator/rectifier unit is probably faulty. To further check the unit, use a multimeter set to the appropriate resistance scale to check the terminals of the regulator/rectifier shown in the table below. If the readings do not compare closely with those shown in the table the regulator/rectifier unit can be considered faulty. Note: *The use of certain multimeters could lead to false readings being obtained. Therefore, if the above check shows the regulator/rectifier unit to be faulty take the unit to a Ducati dealer for confirmation of its condition before replacing it.*

Replacement

6 The regulator/rectifier unit is mounted to the underside of the frame, behind the steering stem (see illustrations). Trace the wiring back from the unit and disconnect it at the connectors. If access is restricted by the fairing panels (where fitted), remove them as required.

7 Unscrew the two bolts securing the unit and its mounting plate (where fitted) to the frame and remove it/them. Note: *Ducati recommend that the rubber washers fitted to early models be replaced with the steel washers fitted to later models as they improve the heat transfer of the unit.*

8 Install the new unit and its mounting plate where fitted and tighten its bolts. Connect the wiring at the connectors.

9 Install any removed fairing panels (see Chapter 7).

Test table – 1991 to 1997 models with two-wire alternator						
+ −	Yellow 1	Yellow 2	Red	White	Black	Earth
Yellow 1	-	> 2 M ohm	> 100 K ohm	> 2 M ohm	> 2 M ohm	> 2 M ohm
Yellow 2	> 2 M ohm	-	> 100 K ohm	> 2 M ohm	> 2 M ohm	> 2 M ohm
Red	> 100 K ohm	> 100 K ohm	-	> 2 M ohm	> 2 M ohm	> 2 M ohm
White	> 2 M ohm	> 2 M ohm	> 2 M ohm	-	> 2 M ohm	> 2 M ohm
Black	> 2 M ohm	> 2 M ohm	> 2 M ohm	> 2 M ohm	-	> 2 M ohm
Earth	> 2 M ohm	> 2 M ohm	> 2 M ohm	> 2 M ohm	> 2 M ohm	-

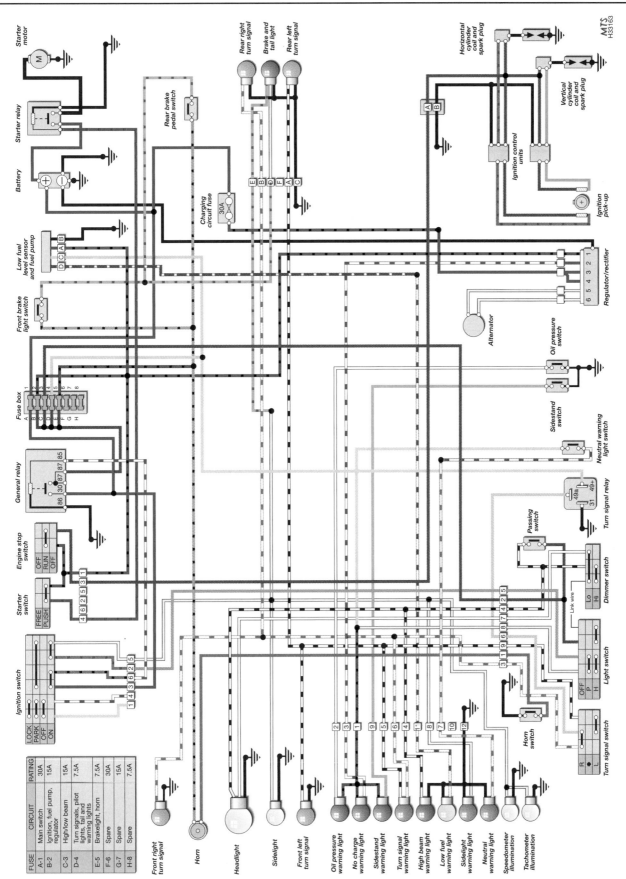

600SS, 750SS and 900SS/SL models 1991-93

FUSE	CIRCUIT	RATING
A-1	Main switch	30A
B-2	Ignition, fuel pump, regulator	15A
C-3	High/low beam	15A
D-4	Turn signals, pilot lights, tail and warning lights	7.5A
E-5	Brakelight, horn	7.5A
F-6	Spare	30A
G-7	Spare	15A
H-8	Spare	7.5A

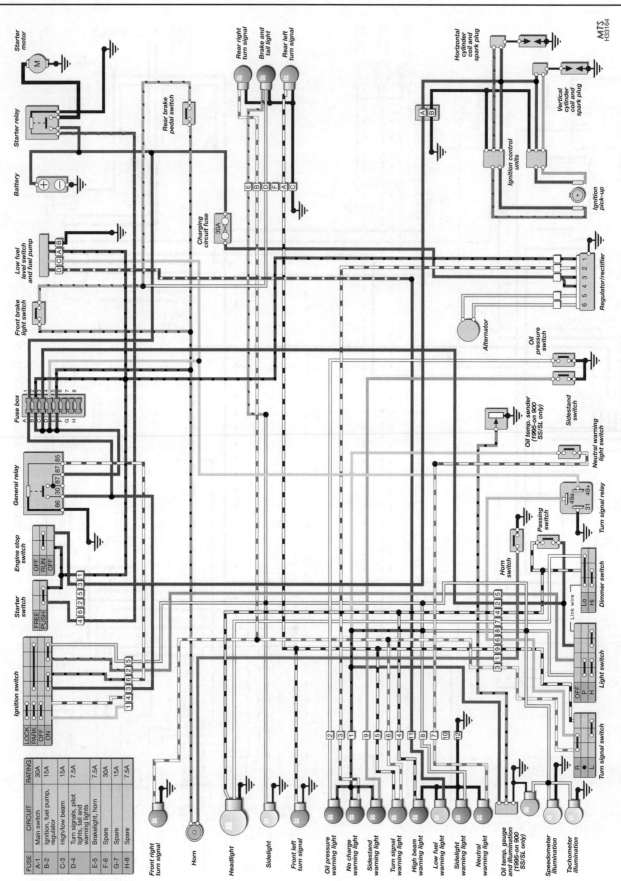

600SS, 750SS and 900SS/SL models 1994-97

FUSE	CIRCUIT	RATING
A-1	Main switch	30A
B-2	Ignition, fuel pump, regulator	15A
C-3	High/low beam	15A
D-4	Turn signals, pilot lights, tail and warning lights	7.5A
E-5	Brakelight, horn	7.5A
F-6	Spare	30A
G-7	Spare	15A
H-8	Spare	7.5A

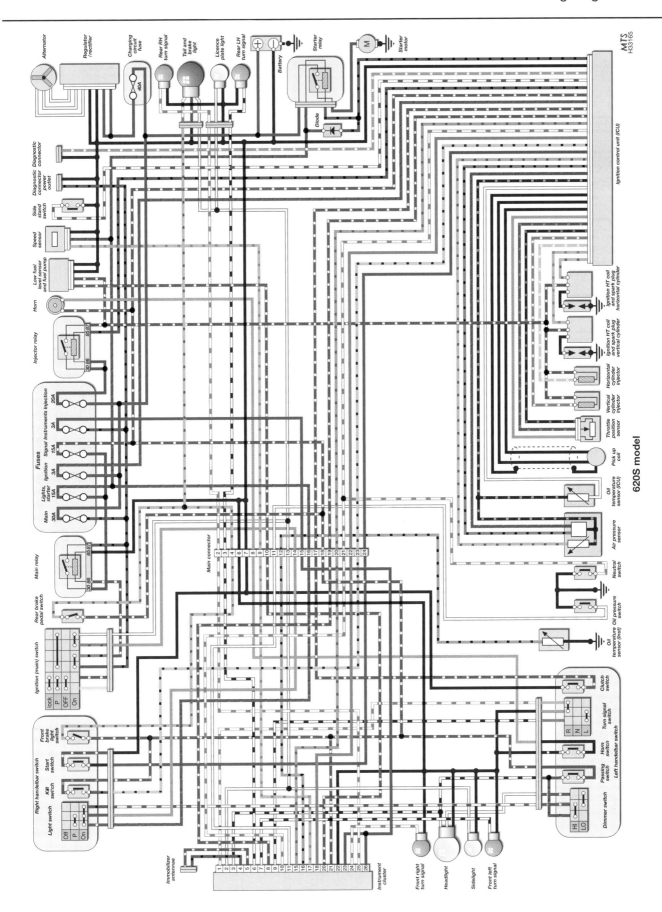

620S model

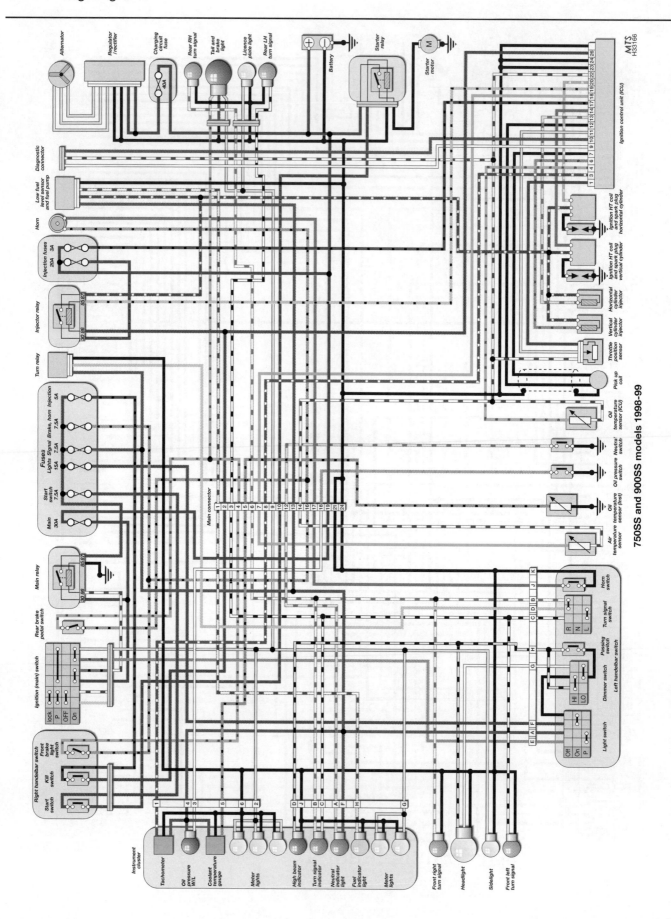

750SS and 900SS models 1998-99

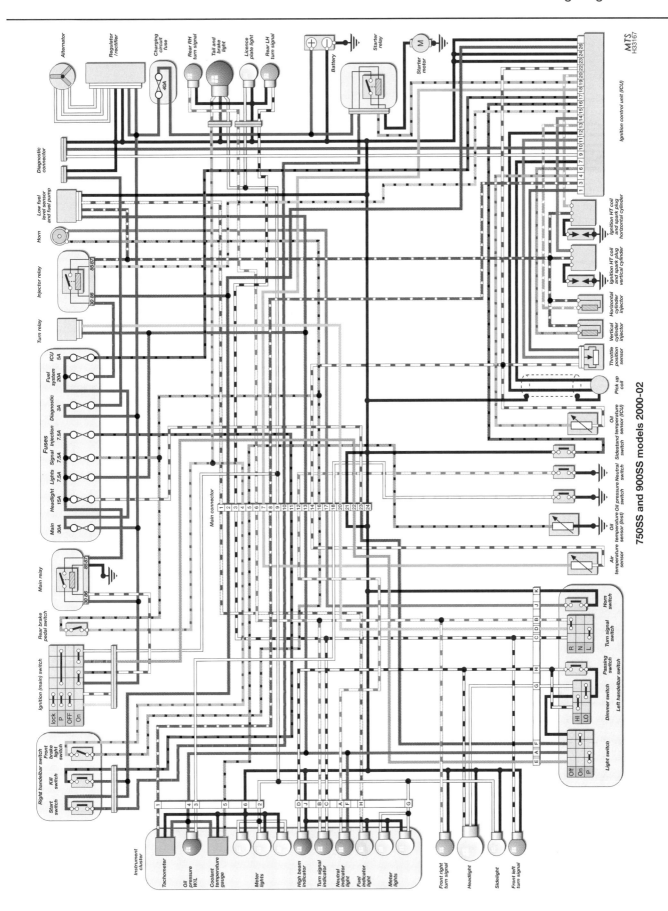

750SS and 900SS models 2000-02

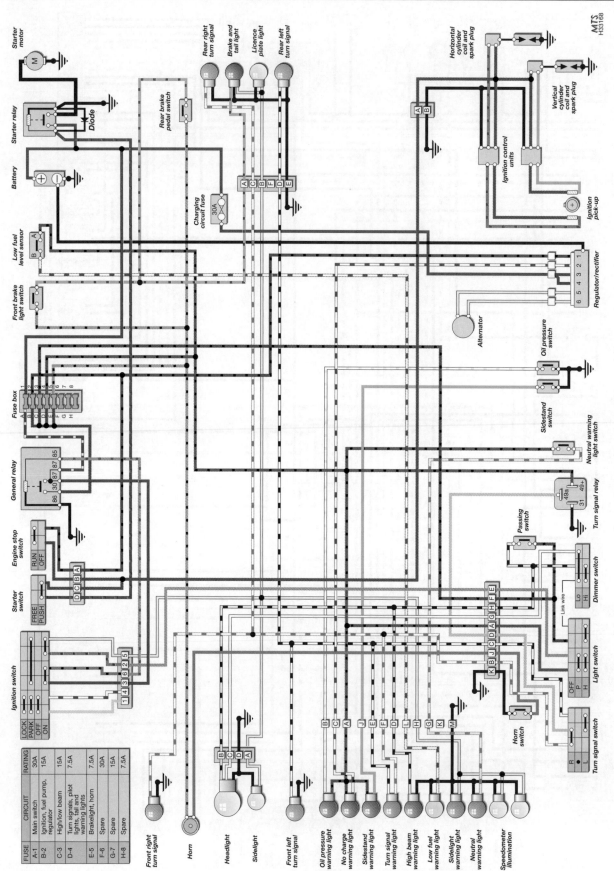

M600, M750 and M900 models 1991-97

FUSE	CIRCUIT	RATING
A-1	Main switch	30A
B-2	Ignition, fuel pump, regulator	15A
C-3	High/low beam	15A
D-4	Turn signals, pilot lights, tail and warning lights	7.5A
E-5	Brakelight, horn	7.5A
F-6	Spare	30A
G-7	Spare	15A
H-8	Spare	7.5A

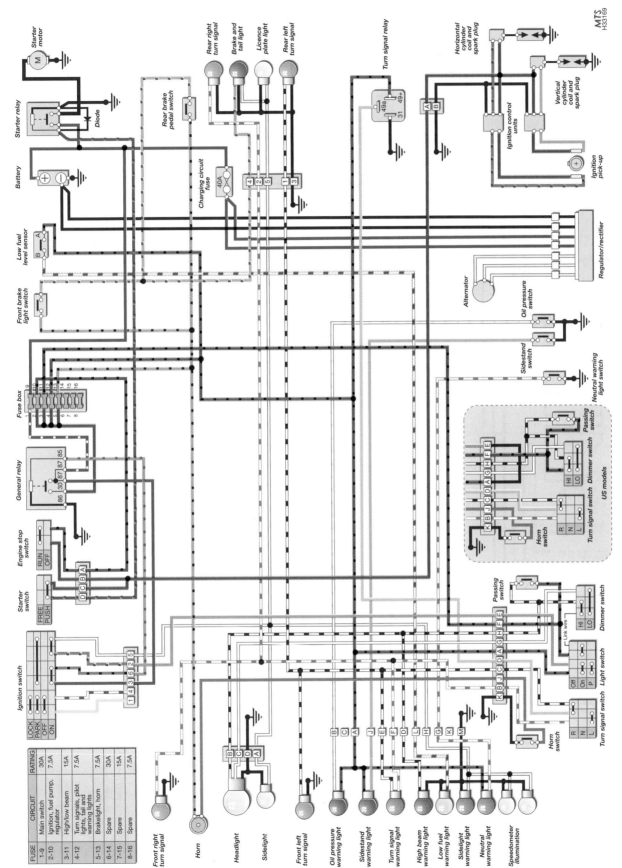

MTS
H33169

M600, M750 and M900 models 1998-99

FUSE	CIRCUIT	RATING
1-9	Main switch	30A
2-10	Ignition, fuel pump, regulator	7.5A
3-11	High/low beam	15A
4-12	Turn signals, pilot lights, tail and warning lights	7.5A
5-13	Brakelight, horn	30A
6-14	Spare	15A
7-15	Spare	7.5A
8-16	Spare	

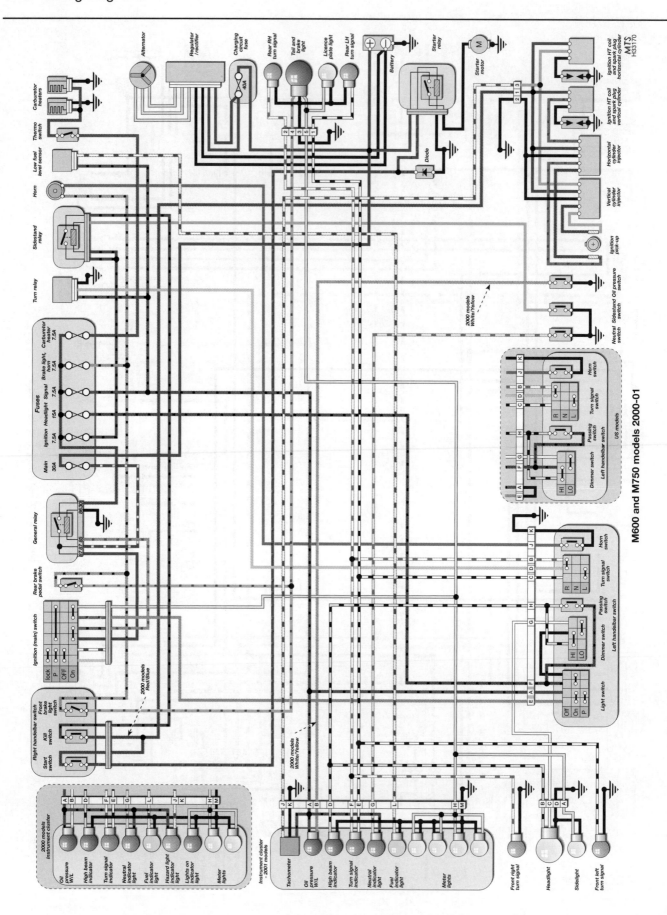

M600 and M750 models 2000-01

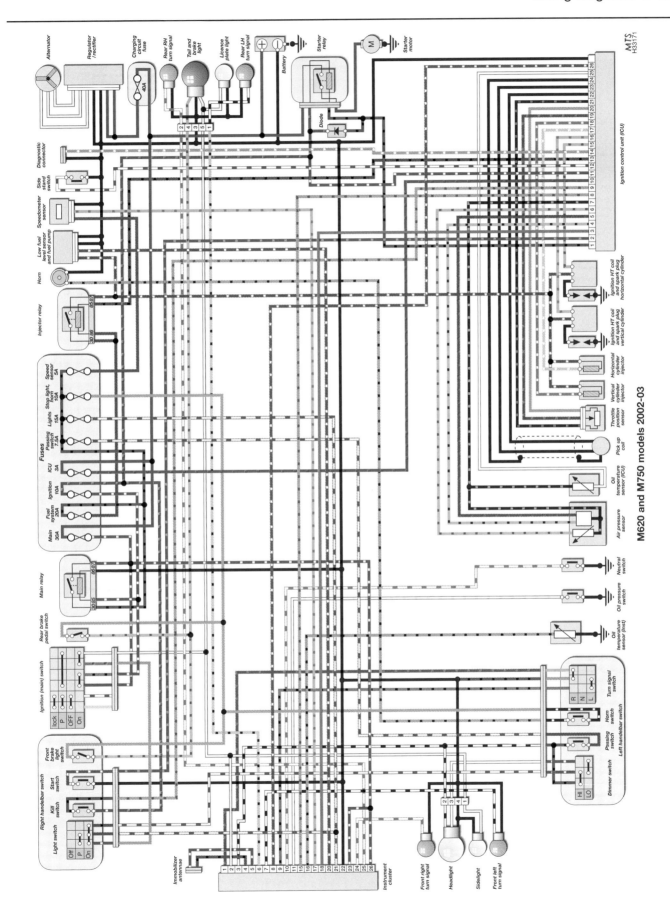

M620 and M750 models 2002-03

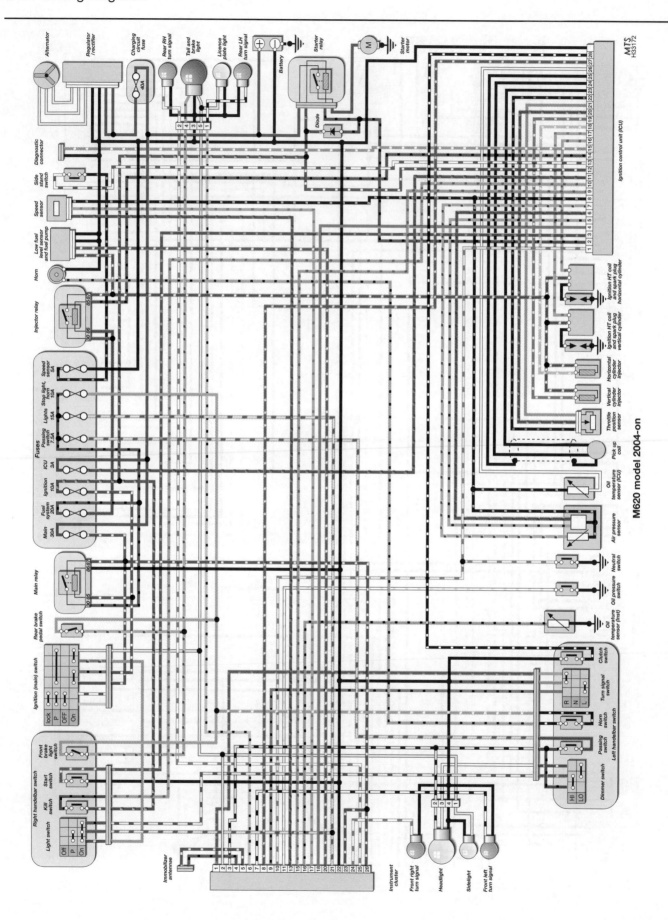

M620 model 2004-on

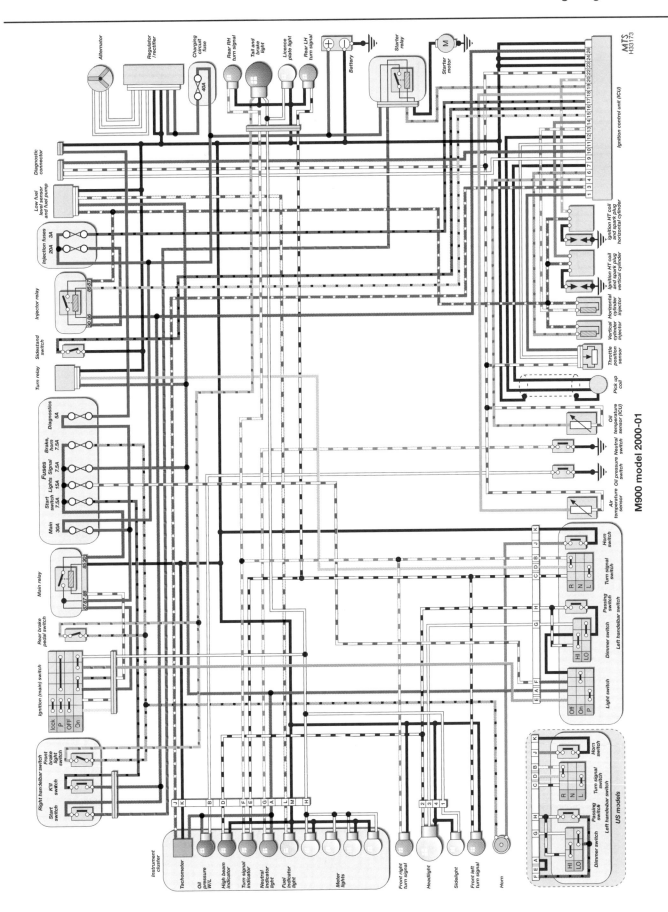

M900 model 2000-01

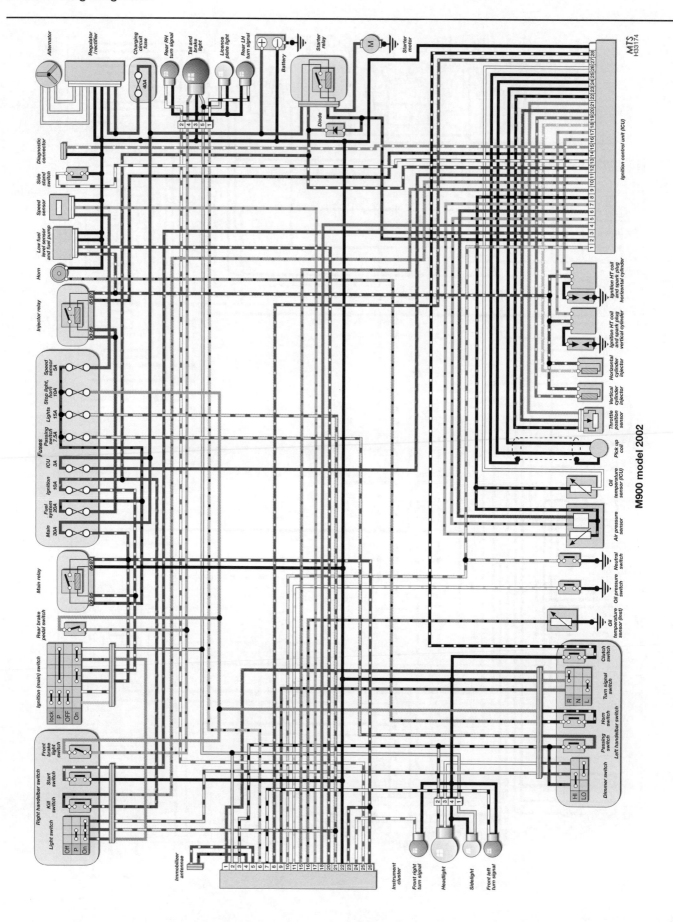

M900 model 2002

Reference

Tools and Workshop Tips REF•2

● Building up a tool kit and equipping your workshop ● Using tools ● Understanding bearing, seal, fastener and chain sizes and markings ● Repair techniques

Security REF•20

● Locks and chains ● U-locks ● Disc locks ● Alarms and immobilisers ● Security marking systems ● Tips on how to prevent bike theft

Lubricants and fluids REF•23

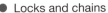

● Engine oils ● Transmission (gear) oils ● Coolant/anti-freeze ● Fork oils and suspension fluids ● Brake/clutch fluids ● Spray lubes, degreasers and solvents

Conversion Factors REF•26

34 Nm x 0.738
= 25 lbf ft

● Formulae for conversion of the metric (SI) units used throughout the manual into Imperial measures

MOT Test Checks REF•27

● A guide to the UK MOT test ● Which items are tested ● How to prepare your motorcycle for the test and perform a pre-test check

Storage REF•32

● How to prepare your motorcycle for going into storage and protect essential systems ● How to get the motorcycle back on the road

Fault Finding REF•35

● Common faults and their likely causes ● How to check engine cylinder compression ● How to make electrical tests and use test meters

Index REF•48

Buying tools

A toolkit is a fundamental requirement for servicing and repairing a motorcycle. Although there will be an initial expense in building up enough tools for servicing, this will soon be offset by the savings made by doing the job yourself. As experience and confidence grow, additional tools can be added to enable the repair and overhaul of the motorcycle. Many of the specialist tools are expensive and not often used so it may be preferable to hire them, or for a group of friends or motorcycle club to join in the purchase.

As a rule, it is better to buy more expensive, good quality tools. Cheaper tools are likely to wear out faster and need to be renewed more often, nullifying the original saving.

> ⚠️ **Warning: To avoid the risk of a poor quality tool breaking in use, causing injury or damage to the component being worked on, always aim to purchase tools which meet the relevant national safety standards.**

The following lists of tools do not represent the manufacturer's service tools, but serve as a guide to help the owner decide which tools are needed for this level of work. In addition, items such as an electric drill, hacksaw, files, soldering iron and a workbench equipped with a vice, may be needed. Although not classed as tools, a selection of bolts, screws, nuts, washers and pieces of tubing always come in useful.

For more information about tools, refer to the Haynes *Motorcycle Workshop Practice TechBook* (Bk. No. 3470).

Manufacturer's service tools

Inevitably certain tasks require the use of a service tool. Where possible an alternative tool or method of approach is recommended, but sometimes there is no option if personal injury or damage to the component is to be avoided. Where required, service tools are referred to in the relevant procedure.

Service tools can usually only be purchased from a motorcycle dealer and are identified by a part number. Some of the commonly-used tools, such as rotor pullers, are available in aftermarket form from mail-order motorcycle tool and accessory suppliers.

Maintenance and minor repair tools

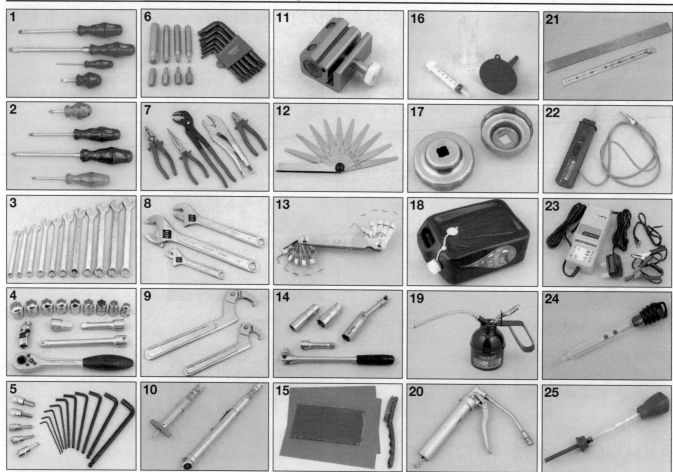

1 Set of flat-bladed screwdrivers
2 Set of Phillips head screwdrivers
3 Combination open-end and ring spanners
4 Socket set (3/8 inch or 1/2 inch drive)
5 Set of Allen keys or bits

6 Set of Torx keys or bits
7 Pliers, cutters and self-locking grips (Mole grips)
8 Adjustable spanners
9 C-spanners
10 Tread depth gauge and tyre pressure gauge

11 Cable oiler clamp
12 Feeler gauges
13 Spark plug gap measuring tool
14 Spark plug spanner or deep plug sockets
15 Wire brush and emery paper

16 Calibrated syringe, measuring vessel and funnel
17 Oil filter adapters
18 Oil drainer can or tray
19 Pump type oil can
20 Grease gun

21 Straight-edge and steel rule
22 Continuity tester
23 Battery charger
24 Hydrometer (for battery specific gravity check)
25 Anti-freeze tester (for liquid-cooled engines)

Repair and overhaul tools

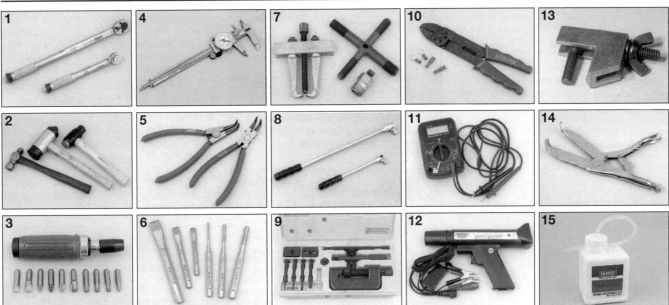

1 Torque wrench
   (small and mid-ranges)
2 Conventional, plastic or
   soft-faced hammers
3 Impact driver set
4 Vernier gauge
5 Circlip pliers (internal and
   external, or combination)
6 Set of cold chisels
   and punches
7 Selection of pullers
8 Breaker bars
9 Chain breaking/
   riveting tool set
10 Wire stripper and
   crimper tool
11 Multimeter (measures
   amps, volts and ohms)
12 Stroboscope (for
   dynamic timing checks)
13 Hose clamp
   (wingnut type shown)
14 Clutch holding tool
15 One-man brake/clutch
   bleeder kit

Specialist tools

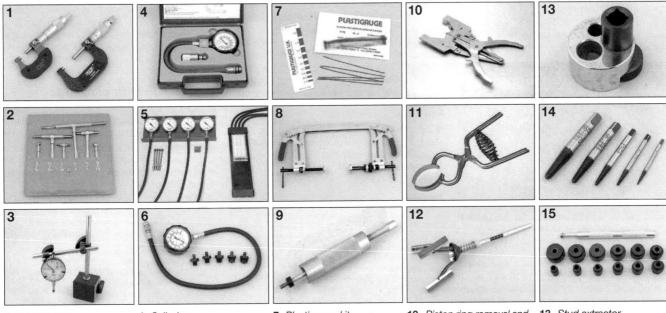

1 Micrometers
   (external type)
2 Telescoping gauges
3 Dial gauge
4 Cylinder
   compression gauge
5 Vacuum gauges (left) or
   manometer (right)
6 Oil pressure gauge
7 Plastigauge kit
8 Valve spring compressor
   (4-stroke engines)
9 Piston pin drawbolt tool
10 Piston ring removal and
   installation tool
11 Piston ring clamp
12 Cylinder bore hone
   (stone type shown)
13 Stud extractor
14 Screw extractor set
15 Bearing driver set

1 Workshop equipment and facilities

The workbench

● Work is made much easier by raising the bike up on a ramp - components are much more accessible if raised to waist level. The hydraulic or pneumatic types seen in the dealer's workshop are a sound investment if you undertake a lot of repairs or overhauls (see illustration 1.1).

1.1 Hydraulic motorcycle ramp

● If raised off ground level, the bike must be supported on the ramp to avoid it falling. Most ramps incorporate a front wheel locating clamp which can be adjusted to suit different diameter wheels. When tightening the clamp, take care not to mark the wheel rim or damage the tyre - use wood blocks on each side to prevent this.
● Secure the bike to the ramp using tie-downs (see illustration 1.2). If the bike has only a sidestand, and hence leans at a dangerous angle when raised, support the bike on an auxiliary stand.

1.2 Tie-downs are used around the passenger footrests to secure the bike

● Auxiliary (paddock) stands are widely available from mail order companies or motorcycle dealers and attach either to the wheel axle or swingarm pivot (see illustration 1.3). If the motorcycle has a centrestand, you can support it under the crankcase to prevent it toppling whilst either wheel is removed (see illustration 1.4).

1.3 This auxiliary stand attaches to the swingarm pivot

1.4 Always use a block of wood between the engine and jack head when supporting the engine in this way

Fumes and fire

● Refer to the Safety first! page at the beginning of the manual for full details. Make sure your workshop is equipped with a fire extinguisher suitable for fuel-related fires (Class B fire - flammable liquids) - it is not sufficient to have a water-filled extinguisher.
● Always ensure adequate ventilation is available. Unless an exhaust gas extraction system is available for use, ensure that the engine is run outside of the workshop.
● If working on the fuel system, make sure the workshop is ventilated to avoid a build-up of fumes. This applies equally to fume build-up when charging a battery. Do not smoke or allow anyone else to smoke in the workshop.

Fluids

● If you need to drain fuel from the tank, store it in an approved container marked as suitable for the storage of petrol (gasoline) (see illustration 1.5). Do not store fuel in glass jars or bottles.

1.5 Use an approved can only for storing petrol (gasoline)

● Use proprietary engine degreasers or solvents which have a high flash-point, such as paraffin (kerosene), for cleaning off oil, grease and dirt - never use petrol (gasoline) for cleaning. Wear rubber gloves when handling solvent and engine degreaser. The fumes from certain solvents can be dangerous - always work in a well-ventilated area.

Dust, eye and hand protection

● Protect your lungs from inhalation of dust particles by wearing a filtering mask over the nose and mouth. Many frictional materials still contain asbestos which is dangerous to your health. Protect your eyes from spouts of liquid and sprung components by wearing a pair of protective goggles (see illustration 1.6).

1.6 A fire extinguisher, goggles, mask and protective gloves should be at hand in the workshop

● Protect your hands from contact with solvents, fuel and oils by wearing rubber gloves. Alternatively apply a barrier cream to your hands before starting work. If handling hot components or fluids, wear suitable gloves to protect your hands from scalding and burns.

What to do with old fluids

● Old cleaning solvent, fuel, coolant and oils should not be poured down domestic drains or onto the ground. Package the fluid up in old oil containers, label it accordingly, and take it to a garage or disposal facility. Contact your local authority for location of such sites or ring the oil care hotline.

OIL CARE
FOLLOW THE CODE
OIL BANK LINE
0800 66 33 66
www.oilbankline.org.uk

Note: It is antisocial and illegal to dump oil down the drain. To find the location of your local oil recycling bank, call this number free.

In the USA, note that any oil supplier must accept used oil for recycling.

2 Fasteners -
screws, bolts and nuts

Fastener types and applications

Bolts and screws

● Fastener head types are either of hexagonal, Torx or splined design, with internal and external versions of each type (see illustrations 2.1 and 2.2); splined head fasteners are not in common use on motorcycles. The conventional slotted or Phillips head design is used for certain screws. Bolt or screw length is always measured from the underside of the head to the end of the item (see illustration 2.11).

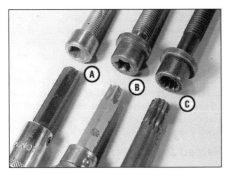

2.1 Internal hexagon/Allen (A), Torx (B) and splined (C) fasteners, with corresponding bits

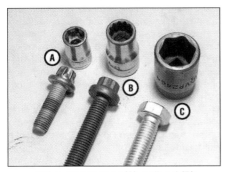

2.2 External Torx (A), splined (B) and hexagon (C) fasteners, with corresponding sockets

● Certain fasteners on the motorcycle have a tensile marking on their heads, the higher the marking the stronger the fastener. High tensile fasteners generally carry a 10 or higher marking. Never replace a high tensile fastener with one of a lower tensile strength.

Washers (see illustration 2.3)

● Plain washers are used between a fastener head and a component to prevent damage to the component or to spread the load when torque is applied. Plain washers can also be used as spacers or shims in certain assemblies. Copper or aluminium plain washers are often used as sealing washers on drain plugs.

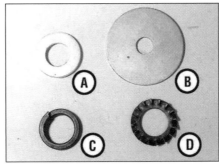

2.3 Plain washer (A), penny washer (B), spring washer (C) and serrated washer (D)

● The split-ring spring washer works by applying axial tension between the fastener head and component. If flattened, it is fatigued and must be renewed. If a plain (flat) washer is used on the fastener, position the spring washer between the fastener and the plain washer.

● Serrated star type washers dig into the fastener and component faces, preventing loosening. They are often used on electrical earth (ground) connections to the frame.

● Cone type washers (sometimes called Belleville) are conical and when tightened apply axial tension between the fastener head and component. They must be installed with the dished side against the component and often carry an OUTSIDE marking on their outer face. If flattened, they are fatigued and must be renewed.

● Tab washers are used to lock plain nuts or bolts on a shaft. A portion of the tab washer is bent up hard against one flat of the nut or bolt to prevent it loosening. Due to the tab washer being deformed in use, a new tab washer should be used every time it is disturbed.

● Wave washers are used to take up endfloat on a shaft. They provide light springing and prevent excessive side-to-side play of a component. Can be found on rocker arm shafts.

Nuts and split pins

● Conventional plain nuts are usually six-sided (see illustration 2.4). They are sized by thread diameter and pitch. High tensile nuts carry a number on one end to denote their tensile strength.

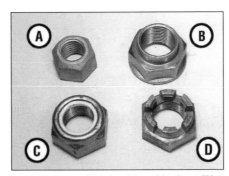

2.4 Plain nut (A), shouldered locknut (B), nylon insert nut (C) and castellated nut (D)

● Self-locking nuts either have a nylon insert, or two spring metal tabs, or a shoulder which is staked into a groove in the shaft - their advantage over conventional plain nuts is a resistance to loosening due to vibration. The nylon insert type can be used a number of times, but must be renewed when the friction of the nylon insert is reduced, ie when the nut spins freely on the shaft. The spring tab type can be reused unless the tabs are damaged. The shouldered type must be renewed every time it is disturbed.

● Split pins (cotter pins) are used to lock a castellated nut to a shaft or to prevent slackening of a plain nut. Common applications are wheel axles and brake torque arms. Because the split pin arms are deformed to lock around the nut a new split pin must always be used on installation - always fit the correct size split pin which will fit snugly in the shaft hole. Make sure the split pin arms are correctly located around the nut (see illustrations 2.5 and 2.6).

2.5 Bend split pin (cotter pin) arms as shown (arrows) to secure a castellated nut

2.6 Bend split pin (cotter pin) arms as shown to secure a plain nut

Caution: If the castellated nut slots do not align with the shaft hole after tightening to the torque setting, tighten the nut until the next slot aligns with the hole - never slacken the nut to align its slot.

● R-pins (shaped like the letter R), or slip pins as they are sometimes called, are sprung and can be reused if they are otherwise in good condition. Always install R-pins with their closed end facing forwards (see illustration 2.7).

2.7 Correct fitting of R-pin. Arrow indicates forward direction

Circlips (see illustration 2.8)

● Circlips (sometimes called snap-rings) are used to retain components on a shaft or in a housing and have corresponding external or internal ears to permit removal. Parallel-sided (machined) circlips can be installed either way round in their groove, whereas stamped circlips (which have a chamfered edge on one face) must be installed with the chamfer facing away from the direction of thrust load **(see illustration 2.9)**.

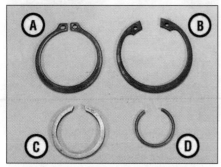

2.8 External stamped circlip (A), internal stamped circlip (B), machined circlip (C) and wire circlip (D)

● Always use circlip pliers to remove and install circlips; expand or compress them just enough to remove them. After installation, rotate the circlip in its groove to ensure it is securely seated. If installing a circlip on a splined shaft, always align its opening with a shaft channel to ensure the circlip ends are well supported and unlikely to catch **(see illustration 2.10)**.

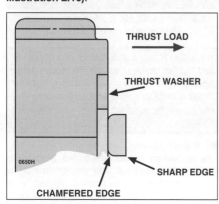

2.9 Correct fitting of a stamped circlip

THRUST LOAD

THRUST WASHER

SHARP EDGE

CHAMFERED EDGE

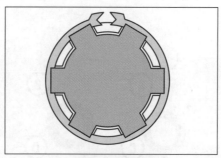

2.10 Align circlip opening with shaft channel

● Circlips can wear due to the thrust of components and become loose in their grooves, with the subsequent danger of becoming dislodged in operation. For this reason, renewal is advised every time a circlip is disturbed.

● Wire circlips are commonly used as piston pin retaining clips. If a removal tang is provided, long-nosed pliers can be used to dislodge them, otherwise careful use of a small flat-bladed screwdriver is necessary. Wire circlips should be renewed every time they are disturbed.

Thread diameter and pitch

● Diameter of a male thread (screw, bolt or stud) is the outside diameter of the threaded portion **(see illustration 2.11)**. Most motorcycle manufacturers use the ISO (International Standards Organisation) metric system expressed in millimetres, eg M6 refers to a 6 mm diameter thread. Sizing is the same for nuts, except that the thread diameter is measured across the valleys of the nut.

● Pitch is the distance between the peaks of the thread **(see illustration 2.11)**. It is expressed in millimetres, thus a common bolt size may be expressed as 6.0 x 1.0 mm (6 mm thread diameter and 1 mm pitch). Generally pitch increases in proportion to thread diameter, although there are always exceptions.

● Thread diameter and pitch are related for conventional fastener applications and the accompanying table can be used as a guide. Additionally, the AF (Across Flats), spanner or socket size dimension of the bolt or nut **(see illustration 2.11)** is linked to thread and pitch specification. Thread pitch can be measured with a thread gauge **(see illustration 2.12)**.

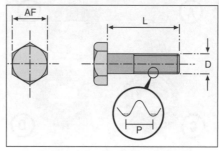

2.11 Fastener length (L), thread diameter (D), thread pitch (P) and head size (AF)

AF L D P

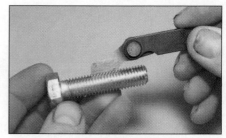

2.12 Using a thread gauge to measure pitch

AF size	Thread diameter x pitch (mm)
8 mm	M5 x 0.8
8 mm	M6 x 1.0
10 mm	M6 x 1.0
12 mm	M8 x 1.25
14 mm	M10 x 1.25
17 mm	M12 x 1.25

● The threads of most fasteners are of the right-hand type, ie they are turned clockwise to tighten and anti-clockwise to loosen. The reverse situation applies to left-hand thread fasteners, which are turned anti-clockwise to tighten and clockwise to loosen. Left-hand threads are used where rotation of a component might loosen a conventional right-hand thread fastener.

Seized fasteners

● Corrosion of external fasteners due to water or reaction between two dissimilar metals can occur over a period of time. It will build up sooner in wet conditions or in countries where salt is used on the roads during the winter. If a fastener is severely corroded it is likely that normal methods of removal will fail and result in its head being ruined. When you attempt removal, the fastener thread should be heard to crack free and unscrew easily - if it doesn't, stop there before damaging something.

● A smart tap on the head of the fastener will often succeed in breaking free corrosion which has occurred in the threads **(see illustration 2.13)**.

● An aerosol penetrating fluid (such as WD-40) applied the night beforehand may work its way down into the thread and ease removal. Depending on the location, you may be able to make up a Plasticine well around the fastener head and fill it with penetrating fluid.

2.13 A sharp tap on the head of a fastener will often break free a corroded thread

● If you are working on an engine internal component, corrosion will most likely not be a problem due to the well lubricated environment. However, components can be very tight and an impact driver is a useful tool in freeing them **(see illustration 2.14)**.

2.14 Using an impact driver to free a fastener

● Where corrosion has occurred between dissimilar metals (eg steel and aluminium alloy), the application of heat to the fastener head will create a disproportionate expansion rate between the two metals and break the seizure caused by the corrosion. Whether heat can be applied depends on the location of the fastener - any surrounding components likely to be damaged must first be removed **(see illustration 2.15)**. Heat can be applied using a paint stripper heat gun or clothes iron, or by immersing the component in boiling water - wear protective gloves to prevent scalding or burns to the hands.

2.15 Using heat to free a seized fastener

● As a last resort, it is possible to use a hammer and cold chisel to work the fastener head unscrewed **(see illustration 2.16)**. This will damage the fastener, but more importantly extreme care must be taken not to damage the surrounding component.

Caution: Remember that the component being secured is generally of more value than the bolt, nut or screw - when the fastener is freed, do not unscrew it with force, instead work the fastener back and forth when resistance is felt to prevent thread damage.

2.16 Using a hammer and chisel to free a seized fastener

Broken fasteners and damaged heads

● If the shank of a broken bolt or screw is accessible you can grip it with self-locking grips. The knurled wheel type stud extractor tool or self-gripping stud puller tool is particularly useful for removing the long studs which screw into the cylinder mouth surface of the crankcase or bolts and screws from which the head has broken off **(see illustration 2.17)**. Studs can also be removed by locking two nuts together on the threaded end of the stud and using a spanner on the lower nut **(see illustration 2.18)**.

2.17 Using a stud extractor tool to remove a broken crankcase stud

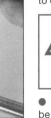

2.18 Two nuts can be locked together to unscrew a stud from a component

● A bolt or screw which has broken off below or level with the casing must be extracted using a screw extractor set. Centre punch the fastener to centralise the drill bit, then drill a hole in the fastener **(see illustration 2.19)**. Select a drill bit which is approximately half to three-quarters the

2.19 When using a screw extractor, first drill a hole in the fastener . . .

diameter of the fastener and drill to a depth which will accommodate the extractor. Use the largest size extractor possible, but avoid leaving too small a wall thickness otherwise the extractor will merely force the fastener walls outwards wedging it in the casing thread.

● If a spiral type extractor is used, thread it anti-clockwise into the fastener. As it is screwed in, it will grip the fastener and unscrew it from the casing **(see illustration 2.20)**.

2.20 . . . then thread the extractor anti-clockwise into the fastener

● If a taper type extractor is used, tap it into the fastener so that it is firmly wedged in place. Unscrew the extractor (anti-clockwise) to draw the fastener out.

> ⚠️ *Warning: Stud extractors are very hard and may break off in the fastener if care is not taken - ask an engineer about spark erosion if this happens.*

● Alternatively, the broken bolt/screw can be drilled out and the hole retapped for an oversize bolt/screw or a diamond-section thread insert. It is essential that the drilling is carried out squarely and to the correct depth, otherwise the casing may be ruined - if in doubt, entrust the work to an engineer.

● Bolts and nuts with rounded corners cause the correct size spanner or socket to slip when force is applied. Of the types of spanner/socket available always use a six-point type rather than an eight or twelve-point type - better grip

2.21 Comparison of surface drive ring spanner (left) with 12-point type (right)

is obtained. Surface drive spanners grip the middle of the hex flats, rather than the corners, and are thus good in cases of damaged heads **(see illustration 2.21)**.

● Slotted-head or Phillips-head screws are often damaged by the use of the wrong size screwdriver. Allen-head and Torx-head screws are much less likely to sustain damage. If enough of the screw head is exposed you can use a hacksaw to cut a slot in its head and then use a conventional flat-bladed screwdriver to remove it. Alternatively use a hammer and cold chisel to tap the head of the fastener around to slacken it. Always replace damaged fasteners with new ones, preferably Torx or Allen-head type.

HAYNES HINT

A dab of valve grinding compound between the screw head and screwdriver tip will often give a good grip.

Thread repair

● Threads (particularly those in aluminium alloy components) can be damaged by overtightening, being assembled with dirt in the threads, or from a component working loose and vibrating. Eventually the thread will fail completely, and it will be impossible to tighten the fastener.

● If a thread is damaged or clogged with old locking compound it can be renovated with a thread repair tool (thread chaser) **(see illustrations 2.22 and 2.23)**; special thread

2.22 A thread repair tool being used to correct an internal thread

2.23 A thread repair tool being used to correct an external thread

chasers are available for spark plug hole threads. The tool will not cut a new thread, but clean and true the original thread. Make sure that you use the correct diameter and pitch tool. Similarly, external threads can be cleaned up with a die or a thread restorer file **(see illustration 2.24)**.

2.24 Using a thread restorer file

● It is possible to drill out the old thread and retap the component to the next thread size. This will work where there is enough surrounding material and a new bolt or screw can be obtained. Sometimes, however, this is not possible - such as where the bolt/screw passes through another component which must also be suitably modified, also in cases where a spark plug or oil drain plug cannot be obtained in a larger diameter thread size.

● The diamond-section thread insert (often known by its popular trade name of Heli-Coil) is a simple and effective method of renewing the thread and retaining the original size. A kit can be purchased which contains the tap, insert and installing tool **(see illustration 2.25)**. Drill out the damaged thread with the size drill specified **(see illustration 2.26)**. Carefully retap the thread **(see illustration 2.27)**. Install the

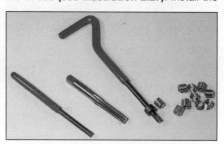

2.25 Obtain a thread insert kit to suit the thread diameter and pitch required

2.26 To install a thread insert, first drill out the original thread . . .

2.27 . . . tap a new thread . . .

2.28 . . . fit insert on the installing tool . . .

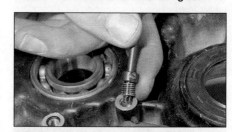

2.29 . . . and thread into the component . . .

2.30 . . . break off the tang when complete

insert on the installing tool and thread it slowly into place using a light downward pressure **(see illustrations 2.28 and 2.29)**. When positioned between a 1/4 and 1/2 turn below the surface withdraw the installing tool and use the break-off tool to press down on the tang, breaking it off **(see illustration 2.30)**.

● There are epoxy thread repair kits on the market which can rebuild stripped internal threads, although this repair should not be used on high load-bearing components.

Thread locking and sealing compounds

● Locking compounds are used in locations where the fastener is prone to loosening due to vibration or on important safety-related items which might cause loss of control of the motorcycle if they fail. It is also used where important fasteners cannot be secured by other means such as lockwashers or split pins.

● Before applying locking compound, make sure that the threads (internal and external) are clean and dry with all old compound removed. Select a compound to suit the component being secured - a non-permanent general locking and sealing type is suitable for most applications, but a high strength type is needed for permanent fixing of studs in castings. Apply a drop or two of the compound to the first few threads of the fastener, then thread it into place and tighten to the specified torque. Do not apply excessive thread locking compound otherwise the thread may be damaged on subsequent removal.

● Certain fasteners are impregnated with a dry film type coating of locking compound on their threads. Always renew this type of fastener if disturbed.

● Anti-seize compounds, such as copper-based greases, can be applied to protect threads from seizure due to extreme heat and corrosion. A common instance is spark plug threads and exhaust system fasteners.

3 Measuring tools and gauges

Feeler gauges

● Feeler gauges (or blades) are used for measuring small gaps and clearances **(see illustration 3.1)**. They can also be used to measure endfloat (sideplay) of a component on a shaft where access is not possible with a dial gauge.

● Feeler gauge sets should be treated with care and not bent or damaged. They are etched with their size on one face. Keep them clean and very lightly oiled to prevent corrosion build-up.

3.1 Feeler gauges are used for measuring small gaps and clearances - thickness is marked on one face of gauge

● When measuring a clearance, select a gauge which is a light sliding fit between the two components. You may need to use two gauges together to measure the clearance accurately.

Micrometers

● A micrometer is a precision tool capable of measuring to 0.01 or 0.001 of a millimetre. It should always be stored in its case and not in the general toolbox. It must be kept clean and never dropped, otherwise its frame or measuring anvils could be distorted resulting in inaccurate readings.

● External micrometers are used for measuring outside diameters of components and have many more applications than internal micrometers. Micrometers are available in different size ranges, eg 0 to 25 mm, 25 to 50 mm, and upwards in 25 mm steps; some large micrometers have interchangeable anvils to allow a range of measurements to be taken. Generally the largest precision measurement you are likely to take on a motorcycle is the piston diameter.

● Internal micrometers (or bore micrometers) are used for measuring inside diameters, such as valve guides and cylinder bores. Telescoping gauges and small hole gauges are used in conjunction with an external micrometer, whereas the more expensive internal micrometers have their own measuring device.

External micrometer

Note: *The conventional analogue type instrument is described. Although much easier to read, digital micrometers are considerably more expensive.*

● Always check the calibration of the micrometer before use. With the anvils closed (0 to 25 mm type) or set over a test gauge (for

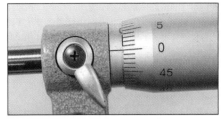

3.2 Check micrometer calibration before use

the larger types) the scale should read zero **(see illustration 3.2)**; make sure that the anvils (and test piece) are clean first. Any discrepancy can be adjusted by referring to the instructions supplied with the tool. Remember that the micrometer is a precision measuring tool - don't force the anvils closed, use the ratchet (4) on the end of the micrometer to close it. In this way, a measured force is always applied.

● To use, first make sure that the item being measured is clean. Place the anvil of the micrometer (1) against the item and use the thimble (2) to bring the spindle (3) lightly into contact with the other side of the item **(see illustration 3.3)**. Don't tighten the thimble down because this will damage the micrometer - instead use the ratchet (4) on the end of the micrometer. The ratchet mechanism applies a measured force preventing damage to the instrument.

● The micrometer is read by referring to the linear scale on the sleeve and the annular scale on the thimble. Read off the sleeve first to obtain the base measurement, then add the fine measurement from the thimble to obtain the overall reading. The linear scale on the sleeve represents the measuring range of the micrometer (eg 0 to 25 mm). The annular scale

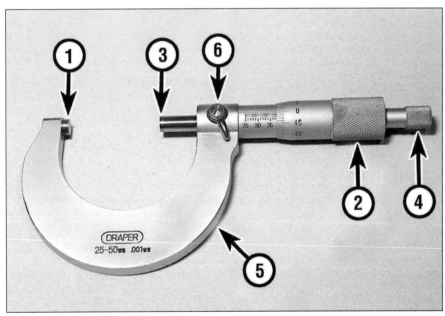

3.3 Micrometer component parts

1 Anvil	3 Spindle	5 Frame
2 Thimble	4 Ratchet	6 Locking lever

on the thimble will be in graduations of 0.01 mm (or as marked on the frame) - one full revolution of the thimble will move 0.5 mm on the linear scale. Take the reading where the datum line on the sleeve intersects the thimble's scale. Always position the eye directly above the scale otherwise an inaccurate reading will result.

In the example shown the item measures 2.95 mm (see illustration 3.4):

Linear scale	2.00 mm
Linear scale	0.50 mm
Annular scale	0.45 mm
Total figure	**2.95 mm**

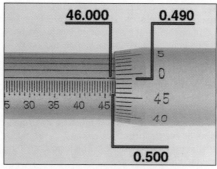

3.5 Micrometer reading of 46.99 mm on linear and annular scales . . .

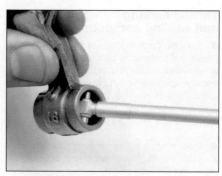

3.7 Expand the telescoping gauge in the bore, lock its position . . .

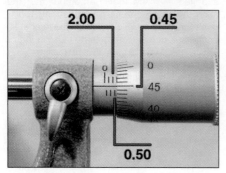

3.4 Micrometer reading of 2.95 mm

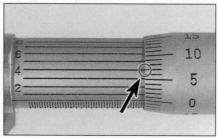

3.6 . . . and 0.004 mm on vernier scale

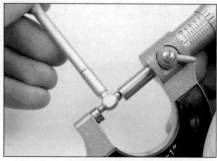

3.8 . . . then measure the gauge with a micrometer

Most micrometers have a locking lever (6) on the frame to hold the setting in place, allowing the item to be removed from the micrometer.
● Some micrometers have a vernier scale on their sleeve, providing an even finer measurement to be taken, in 0.001 increments of a millimetre. Take the sleeve and thimble measurement as described above, then check which graduation on the vernier scale aligns with that of the annular scale on the thimble **Note:** *The eye must be perpendicular to the scale when taking the vernier reading - if necessary rotate the body of the micrometer to ensure this.* Multiply the vernier scale figure by 0.001 and add it to the base and fine measurement figures.

In the example shown the item measures 46.994 mm (see illustrations 3.5 and 3.6):

Linear scale (base)	46.000 mm
Linear scale (base)	00.500 mm
Annular scale (fine)	00.490 mm
Vernier scale	00.004 mm
Total figure	**46.994 mm**

Internal micrometer

● Internal micrometers are available for measuring bore diameters, but are expensive and unlikely to be available for home use. It is suggested that a set of telescoping gauges and small hole gauges, both of which must be used with an external micrometer, will suffice for taking internal measurements on a motorcycle.
● Telescoping gauges can be used to

measure internal diameters of components. Select a gauge with the correct size range, make sure its ends are clean and insert it into the bore. Expand the gauge, then lock its position and withdraw it from the bore **(see illustration 3.7)**. Measure across the gauge ends with a micrometer **(see illustration 3.8)**.
● Very small diameter bores (such as valve guides) are measured with a small hole gauge. Once adjusted to a slip-fit inside the component, its position is locked and the gauge withdrawn for measurement with a micrometer **(see illustrations 3.9 and 3.10)**.

Vernier caliper

Note: *The conventional linear and dial gauge type instruments are described. Digital types are easier to read, but are far more expensive.*
● The vernier caliper does not provide the precision of a micrometer, but is versatile in being able to measure internal and external diameters. Some types also incorporate a depth gauge. It is ideal for measuring clutch plate friction material and spring free lengths.
● To use the conventional linear scale vernier, slacken off the vernier clamp screws (1) and set its jaws over (2), or inside (3), the item to be measured **(see illustration 3.11)**. Slide the jaw into contact, using the thumb-wheel (4) for fine movement of the sliding scale (5) then tighten the clamp screws (1). Read off the main scale (6) where the zero on the sliding scale (5) intersects it, taking the whole number to the left of the zero; this provides the base measurement. View along the sliding scale and select the division which

3.9 Expand the small hole gauge in the bore, lock its position . . .

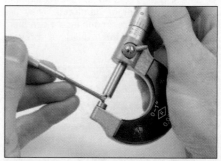

3.10 . . . then measure the gauge with a micrometer

lines up exactly with any of the divisions on the main scale, noting that the divisions usually represents 0.02 of a millimetre. Add this fine measurement to the base measurement to obtain the total reading.

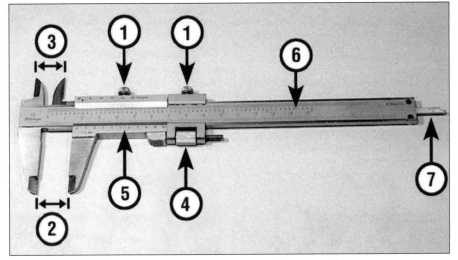

3.11 Vernier component parts (linear gauge)

1	Clamp screws	3	Internal jaws	5	Sliding scale
2	External jaws	4	Thumbwheel	6	Main scale
				7	Depth gauge

In the example shown the item measures 55.92 mm **(see illustration 3.12)**:

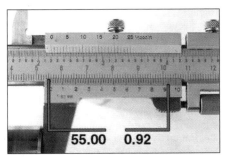

3.12 Vernier gauge reading of 55.92 mm

Base measurement	55.00 mm
Fine measurement	00.92 mm
Total figure	**55.92 mm**

● Some vernier calipers are equipped with a dial gauge for fine measurement. Before use, check that the jaws are clean, then close them fully and check that the dial gauge reads zero. If necessary adjust the gauge ring accordingly. Slacken the vernier clamp screw (1) and set its jaws over (2), or inside (3), the item to be measured **(see illustration 3.13)**. Slide the jaws into contact, using the thumbwheel (4) for fine movement. Read off the main scale (5) where the edge of the sliding scale (6) intersects it, taking the whole number to the left of the zero; this provides the base measurement. Read off the needle position on the dial gauge (7) scale to provide the fine measurement; each division represents 0.05 of a millimetre. Add this fine measurement to the base measurement to obtain the total reading.

In the example shown the item measures 55.95 mm **(see illustration 3.14)**:

Base measurement	55.00 mm
Fine measurement	00.95 mm
Total figure	**55.95 mm**

3.14 Vernier gauge reading of 55.95 mm

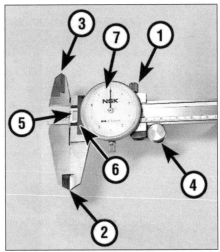

3.13 Vernier component parts (dial gauge)

1	Clamp screw	5	Main scale
2	External jaws	6	Sliding scale
3	Internal jaws	7	Dial gauge
4	Thumbwheel		

Plastigauge

● Plastigauge is a plastic material which can be compressed between two surfaces to measure the oil clearance between them. The width of the compressed Plastigauge is measured against a calibrated scale to determine the clearance.

● Common uses of Plastigauge are for measuring the clearance between crankshaft journal and main bearing inserts, between crankshaft journal and big-end bearing inserts, and between camshaft and bearing surfaces. The following example describes big-end oil clearance measurement.

● Handle the Plastigauge material carefully to prevent distortion. Using a sharp knife, cut a length which corresponds with the width of the bearing being measured and place it carefully across the journal so that it is parallel with the shaft **(see illustration 3.15)**. Carefully install both bearing shells and the connecting rod. Without rotating the rod on the journal tighten its bolts or nuts (as applicable) to the specified torque. The connecting rod and bearings are then disassembled and the crushed Plastigauge examined.

3.15 Plastigauge placed across shaft journal

● Using the scale provided in the Plastigauge kit, measure the width of the material to determine the oil clearance **(see illustration 3.16)**. Always remove all traces of Plastigauge after use using your fingernails.

Caution: Arriving at the correct clearance demands that the assembly is torqued correctly, according to the settings and sequence (where applicable) provided by the motorcycle manufacturer.

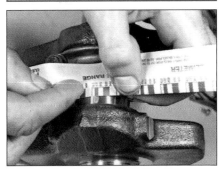

3.16 Measuring the width of the crushed Plastigauge

Dial gauge or DTI (Dial Test Indicator)

● A dial gauge can be used to accurately measure small amounts of movement. Typical uses are measuring shaft runout or shaft endfloat (sideplay) and setting piston position for ignition timing on two-strokes. A dial gauge set usually comes with a range of different probes and adapters and mounting equipment.
● The gauge needle must point to zero when at rest. Rotate the ring around its periphery to zero the gauge.
● Check that the gauge is capable of reading the extent of movement in the work. Most gauges have a small dial set in the face which records whole millimetres of movement as well as the fine scale around the face periphery which is calibrated in 0.01 mm divisions. Read off the small dial first to obtain the base measurement, then add the measurement from the fine scale to obtain the total reading.

In the example shown the gauge reads 1.48 mm **(see illustration 3.17)**:

Base measurement	1.00 mm
Fine measurement	0.48 mm
Total figure	**1.48 mm**

3.17 Dial gauge reading of 1.48 mm

● If measuring shaft runout, the shaft must be supported in vee-blocks and the gauge mounted on a stand perpendicular to the shaft. Rest the tip of the gauge against the centre of the shaft and rotate the shaft slowly whilst watching the gauge reading **(see illustration 3.18)**. Take several measurements along the length of the shaft and record the

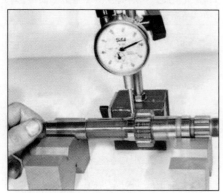

3.18 Using a dial gauge to measure shaft runout

maximum gauge reading as the amount of runout in the shaft. **Note:** *The reading obtained will be total runout at that point - some manufacturers specify that the runout figure is halved to compare with their specified runout limit.*
● Endfloat (sideplay) measurement requires that the gauge is mounted securely to the surrounding component with its probe touching the end of the shaft. Using hand pressure, push and pull on the shaft noting the maximum endfloat recorded on the gauge **(see illustration 3.19)**.

3.19 Using a dial gauge to measure shaft endfloat

● A dial gauge with suitable adapters can be used to determine piston position BTDC on two-stroke engines for the purposes of ignition timing. The gauge, adapter and suitable length probe are installed in the place of the spark plug and the gauge zeroed at TDC. If the piston position is specified as 1.14 mm BTDC, rotate the engine back to 2.00 mm BTDC, then slowly forwards to 1.14 mm BTDC.

Cylinder compression gauges

● A compression gauge is used for measuring cylinder compression. Either the rubber-cone type or the threaded adapter type can be used. The latter is preferred to ensure a perfect seal against the cylinder head. A 0 to 300 psi (0 to 20 Bar) type gauge (for petrol/gasoline engines) will be suitable for motorcycles.
● The spark plug is removed and the gauge either held hard against the cylinder head (cone type) or the gauge adapter screwed into the cylinder head (threaded type) **(see illustration 3.20)**. Cylinder compression is measured with the engine turning over, but not running - carry out the compression test as described in

3.20 Using a rubber-cone type cylinder compression gauge

Fault Finding Equipment. The gauge will hold the reading until manually released.

Oil pressure gauge

● An oil pressure gauge is used for measuring engine oil pressure. Most gauges come with a set of adapters to fit the thread of the take-off point **(see illustration 3.21)**. If the take-off point specified by the motorcycle manufacturer is an external oil pipe union, make sure that the specified replacement union is used to prevent oil starvation.

3.21 Oil pressure gauge and take-off point adapter (arrow)

● Oil pressure is measured with the engine running (at a specific rpm) and often the manufacturer will specify pressure limits for a cold and hot engine.

Straight-edge and surface plate

● If checking the gasket face of a component for warpage, place a steel rule or precision straight-edge across the gasket face and measure any gap between the straight-edge and component with feeler gauges **(see illustration 3.22)**. Check diagonally across the component and between mounting holes **(see illustration 3.23)**.

3.22 Use a straight-edge and feeler gauges to check for warpage

3.23 Check for warpage in these directions

- Checking individual components for warpage, such as clutch plain (metal) plates, requires a perfectly flat plate or piece or plate glass and feeler gauges.

4 Torque and leverage

What is torque?

- Torque describes the twisting force about a shaft. The amount of torque applied is determined by the distance from the centre of the shaft to the end of the lever and the amount of force being applied to the end of the lever; distance multiplied by force equals torque.
- The manufacturer applies a measured torque to a bolt or nut to ensure that it will not slacken in use and to hold two components securely together without movement in the joint. The actual torque setting depends on the thread size, bolt or nut material and the composition of the components being held.
- Too little torque may cause the fastener to loosen due to vibration, whereas too much torque will distort the joint faces of the component or cause the fastener to shear off. Always stick to the specified torque setting.

Using a torque wrench

- Check the calibration of the torque wrench and make sure it has a suitable range for the job. Torque wrenches are available in Nm (Newton-metres), kgf m (kilograms-force metre), lbf ft (pounds-feet), lbf in (inch-pounds). Do not confuse lbf ft with lbf in.
- Adjust the tool to the desired torque on the scale (see illustration 4.1). If your torque wrench is not calibrated in the units specified, carefully convert the figure (see Conversion Factors). A manufacturer sometimes gives a torque setting as a range (8 to 10 Nm) rather than a single figure - in this case set the tool midway between the two settings. The same torque may be expressed as 9 Nm ± 1 Nm. Some torque wrenches have a method of locking the setting so that it isn't inadvertently altered during use.

4.1 Set the torque wrench index mark to the setting required, in this case 12 Nm

- Install the bolts/nuts in their correct location and secure them lightly. Their threads must be clean and free of any old locking compound. Unless specified the threads and flange should be dry - oiled threads are necessary in certain circumstances and the manufacturer will take this into account in the specified torque figure. Similarly, the manufacturer may also specify the application of thread-locking compound.
- Tighten the fasteners in the specified sequence until the torque wrench clicks, indicating that the torque setting has been reached. Apply the torque again to double-check the setting. Where different thread diameter fasteners secure the component, as a rule tighten the larger diameter ones first.
- When the torque wrench has been finished with, release the lock (where applicable) and fully back off its setting to zero - do not leave the torque wrench tensioned. Also, do not use a torque wrench for slackening a fastener.

Angle-tightening

- Manufacturers often specify a figure in degrees for final tightening of a fastener. This usually follows tightening to a specific torque setting.
- A degree disc can be set and attached to the socket (see illustration 4.2) or a protractor can be used to mark the angle of movement on the bolt/nut head and the surrounding casting (see illustration 4.3).

4.2 Angle tightening can be accomplished with a torque-angle gauge . . .

4.3 . . . or by marking the angle on the surrounding component

Loosening sequences

- Where more than one bolt/nut secures a component, loosen each fastener evenly a little at a time. In this way, not all the stress of the joint is held by one fastener and the components are not likely to distort.
- If a tightening sequence is provided, work in the REVERSE of this, but if not, work from the outside in, in a criss-cross sequence (see illustration 4.4).

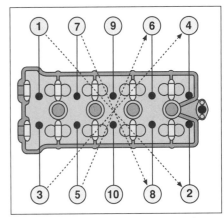

4.4 When slackening, work from the outside inwards

Tightening sequences

- If a component is held by more than one fastener it is important that the retaining bolts/nuts are tightened evenly to prevent uneven stress build-up and distortion of sealing faces. This is especially important on high-compression joints such as the cylinder head.
- A sequence is usually provided by the manufacturer, either in a diagram or actually marked in the casting. If not, always start in the centre and work outwards in a criss-cross pattern (see illustration 4.5). Start off by securing all bolts/nuts finger-tight, then set the torque wrench and tighten each fastener by a small amount in sequence until the final torque is reached. By following this practice,

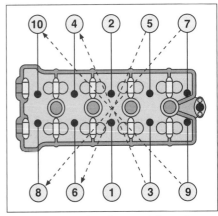

4.5 When tightening, work from the inside outwards

the joint will be held evenly and will not be distorted. Important joints, such as the cylinder head and big-end fasteners often have two- or three-stage torque settings.

Applying leverage

● Use tools at the correct angle. Position a socket wrench or spanner on the bolt/nut so that you pull it towards you when loosening. If this can't be done, push the spanner without curling your fingers around it (see illustration 4.6) - the spanner may slip or the fastener loosen suddenly, resulting in your fingers being crushed against a component.

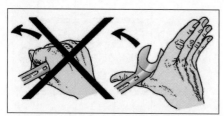

4.6 If you can't pull on the spanner to loosen a fastener, push with your hand open

● Additional leverage is gained by extending the length of the lever. The best way to do this is to use a breaker bar instead of the regular length tool, or to slip a length of tubing over the end of the spanner or socket wrench.
● If additional leverage will not work, the fastener head is either damaged or firmly corroded in place (see Fasteners).

5 Bearings

Bearing removal and installation

Drivers and sockets

● Before removing a bearing, always inspect the casing to see which way it must be driven out - some casings will have retaining plates or a cast step. Also check for any identifying markings on the bearing and if installed to a certain depth, measure this at this stage. Some roller bearings are sealed on one side - take note of the original fitted position.
● Bearings can be driven out of a casing using a bearing driver tool (with the correct size head) or a socket of the correct diameter. Select the driver head or socket so that it contacts the outer race of the bearing, not the balls/rollers or inner race. Always support the casing around the bearing housing with wood blocks, otherwise there is a risk of fracture. The bearing is driven out with a few blows on the driver or socket from a heavy mallet. Unless access is severely restricted (as with wheel bearings), a pin-punch is not recommended unless it is moved around the bearing to keep it square in its housing.

● The same equipment can be used to install bearings. Make sure the bearing housing is supported on wood blocks and line up the bearing in its housing. Fit the bearing as noted on removal - generally they are installed with their marked side facing outwards. Tap the bearing squarely into its housing using a driver or socket which bears only on the bearing's outer race - contact with the bearing balls/rollers or inner race will destroy it (see illustrations 5.1 and 5.2).
● Check that the bearing inner race and balls/rollers rotate freely.

5.1 Using a bearing driver against the bearing's outer race

5.2 Using a large socket against the bearing's outer race

Pullers and slide-hammers

● Where a bearing is pressed on a shaft a puller will be required to extract it (see illustration 5.3). Make sure that the puller clamp or legs fit securely behind the bearing and are unlikely to slip out. If pulling a bearing

5.3 This bearing puller clamps behind the bearing and pressure is applied to the shaft end to draw the bearing off

off a gear shaft for example, you may have to locate the puller behind a gear pinion if there is no access to the race and draw the gear pinion off the shaft as well (see illustration 5.4).

Caution: Ensure that the puller's centre bolt locates securely against the end of the shaft and will not slip when pressure is applied. Also ensure that puller does not damage the shaft end.

5.4 Where no access is available to the rear of the bearing, it is sometimes possible to draw off the adjacent component

● Operate the puller so that its centre bolt exerts pressure on the shaft end and draws the bearing off the shaft.
● When installing the bearing on the shaft, tap only on the bearing's inner race - contact with the balls/rollers or outer race with destroy the bearing. Use a socket or length of tubing as a drift which fits over the shaft end (see illustration 5.5).

5.5 When installing a bearing on a shaft use a piece of tubing which bears only on the bearing's inner race

● Where a bearing locates in a blind hole in a casing, it cannot be driven or pulled out as described above. A slide-hammer with knife-edged bearing puller attachment will be required. The puller attachment passes through the bearing and when tightened expands to fit firmly behind the bearing (see illustration 5.6). By operating the slide-hammer part of the tool the bearing is jarred out of its housing (see illustration 5.7).
● It is possible, if the bearing is of reasonable weight, for it to drop out of its housing if the casing is heated as described opposite. If this

5.6 Expand the bearing puller so that it locks behind the bearing . . .

5.7 . . . attach the slide hammer to the bearing puller

method is attempted, first prepare a work surface which will enable the casing to be tapped face down to help dislodge the bearing - a wood surface is ideal since it will not damage the casing's gasket surface. Wearing protective gloves, tap the heated casing several times against the work surface to dislodge the bearing under its own weight **(see illustration 5.8)**.

5.8 Tapping a casing face down on wood blocks can often dislodge a bearing

● Bearings can be installed in blind holes using the driver or socket method described above.

Drawbolts

● Where a bearing or bush is set in the eye of a component, such as a suspension linkage arm or connecting rod small-end, removal by drift may damage the component. Furthermore, a rubber bushing in a shock absorber eye cannot successfully be driven out of position. If access is available to a engineering press, the task is straightforward. If not, a drawbolt can be fabricated to extract the bearing or bush.

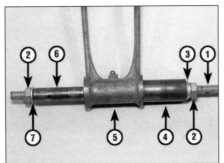

5.9 Drawbolt component parts assembled on a suspension arm

1   Bolt or length of threaded bar
2   Nuts
3   Washer (external diameter greater than tubing internal diameter)
4   Tubing (internal diameter sufficient to accommodate bearing)
5   Suspension arm with bearing
6   Tubing (external diameter slightly smaller than bearing)
7   Washer (external diameter slightly smaller than bearing)

5.10 Drawing the bearing out of the suspension arm

● To extract the bearing/bush you will need a long bolt with nut (or piece of threaded bar with two nuts), a piece of tubing which has an internal diameter larger than the bearing/bush, another piece of tubing which has an external diameter slightly smaller than the bearing/bush, and a selection of washers **(see illustrations 5.9 and 5.10)**. Note that the pieces of tubing must be of the same length, or longer, than the bearing/bush.

● The same kit (without the pieces of tubing) can be used to draw the new bearing/bush back into place **(see illustration 5.11)**.

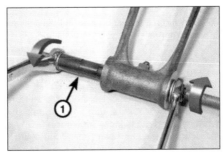

5.11 Installing a new bearing (1) in the suspension arm

Temperature change

● If the bearing's outer race is a tight fit in the casing, the aluminium casing can be heated to release its grip on the bearing. Aluminium will expand at a greater rate than the steel bearing outer race. There are several ways to do this, but avoid any localised extreme heat (such as a blow torch) - aluminium alloy has a low melting point.

● Approved methods of heating a casing are using a domestic oven (heated to 100°C) or immersing the casing in boiling water **(see illustration 5.12)**. Low temperature range localised heat sources such as a paint stripper heat gun or clothes iron can also be used **(see illustration 5.13)**. Alternatively, soak a rag in boiling water, wring it out and wrap it around the bearing housing.

> ⚠ **Warning: All of these methods require care in use to prevent scalding and burns to the hands. Wear protective gloves when handling hot components.**

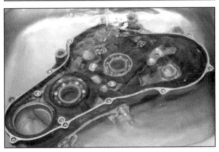

5.12 A casing can be immersed in a sink of boiling water to aid bearing removal

5.13 Using a localised heat source to aid bearing removal

● If heating the whole casing note that plastic components, such as the neutral switch, may suffer - remove them beforehand.

● After heating, remove the bearing as described above. You may find that the expansion is sufficient for the bearing to fall out of the casing under its own weight or with a light tap on the driver or socket.

● If necessary, the casing can be heated to aid bearing installation, and this is sometimes the recommended procedure if the motorcycle manufacturer has designed the housing and bearing fit with this intention.

● Installation of bearings can be eased by placing them in a freezer the night before installation. The steel bearing will contract slightly, allowing easy insertion in its housing. This is often useful when installing steering head outer races in the frame.

Bearing types and markings

● Plain shell bearings, ball bearings, needle roller bearings and tapered roller bearings will all be found on motorcycles **(see illustrations 5.14 and 5.15)**. The ball and roller types are usually caged between an inner and outer race, but uncaged variations may be found.

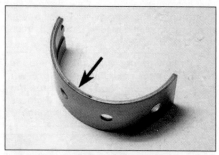

5.14 Shell bearings are either plain or grooved. They are usually identified by colour code (arrow)

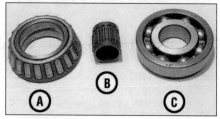

5.15 Tapered roller bearing (A), needle roller bearing (B) and ball journal bearing (C)

● Shell bearings (often called inserts) are usually found at the crankshaft main and connecting rod big-end where they are good at coping with high loads. They are made of a phosphor-bronze material and are impregnated with self-lubricating properties.
● Ball bearings and needle roller bearings consist of a steel inner and outer race with the balls or rollers between the races. They require constant lubrication by oil or grease and are good at coping with axial loads. Taper roller bearings consist of rollers set in a tapered cage set on the inner race; the outer race is separate. They are good at coping with axial loads and prevent movement along the shaft - a typical application is in the steering head.
● Bearing manufacturers produce bearings to ISO size standards and stamp one face of the bearing to indicate its internal and external diameter, load capacity and type **(see illustration 5.16)**.
● Metal bushes are usually of phosphor-bronze material. Rubber bushes are used in suspension mounting eyes. Fibre bushes have also been used in suspension pivots.

5.16 Typical bearing marking

Bearing fault finding

● If a bearing outer race has spun in its housing, the housing material will be damaged. You can use a bearing locking compound to bond the outer race in place if damage is not too severe.
● Shell bearings will fail due to damage of their working surface, as a result of lack of lubrication, corrosion or abrasive particles in the oil **(see illustration 5.17)**. Small particles of dirt in the oil may embed in the bearing material whereas larger particles will score the bearing and shaft journal. If a number of short journeys are made, insufficient heat will be generated to drive off condensation which has built up on the bearings.

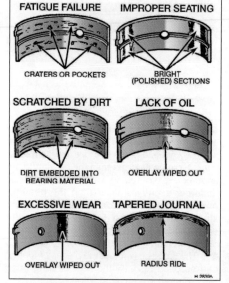

5.17 Typical bearing failures

● Ball and roller bearings will fail due to lack of lubrication or damage to the balls or rollers. Tapered-roller bearings can be damaged by overloading them. Unless the bearing is sealed on both sides, wash it in paraffin (kerosene) to remove all old grease then allow it to dry. Make a visual inspection looking to dented balls or rollers, damaged cages and worn or pitted races **(see illustration 5.18)**.
● A ball bearing can be checked for wear by listening to it when spun. Apply a film of light oil to the bearing and hold it close to the ear - hold the outer race with one hand and spin the inner

5.18 Example of ball journal bearing with damaged balls and cages

5.19 Hold outer race and listen to inner race when spun

race with the other hand **(see illustration 5.19)**. The bearing should be almost silent when spun; if it grates or rattles it is worn.

6   Oil seals

Oil seal removal and installation

● Oil seals should be renewed every time a component is dismantled. This is because the seal lips will become set to the sealing surface and will not necessarily reseal.
● Oil seals can be prised out of position using a large flat-bladed screwdriver **(see illustration 6.1)**. In the case of crankcase seals, check first that the seal is not lipped on the inside, preventing its removal with the crankcases joined.

6.1 Prise out oil seals with a large flat-bladed screwdriver

● New seals are usually installed with their marked face (containing the seal reference code) outwards and the spring side towards the fluid being retained. In certain cases, such as a two-stroke engine crankshaft seal, a double lipped seal may be used due to there being fluid or gas on each side of the joint.

● Use a bearing driver or socket which bears only on the outer hard edge of the seal to install it in the casing - tapping on the inner edge will damage the sealing lip.

Oil seal types and markings

● Oil seals are usually of the single-lipped type. Double-lipped seals are found where a liquid or gas is on both sides of the joint.
● Oil seals can harden and lose their sealing ability if the motorcycle has been in storage for a long period - renewal is the only solution.
● Oil seal manufacturers also conform to the ISO markings for seal size - these are moulded into the outer face of the seal (see illustration 6.2).

6.2 These oil seal markings indicate inside diameter, outside diameter and seal thickness

7 Gaskets and sealants

Types of gasket and sealant

● Gaskets are used to seal the mating surfaces between components and keep lubricants, fluids, vacuum or pressure contained within the assembly. Aluminium gaskets are sometimes found at the cylinder joints, but most gaskets are paper-based. If the mating surfaces of the components being joined are undamaged the gasket can be installed dry, although a dab of sealant or grease will be useful to hold it in place during assembly.
● RTV (Room Temperature Vulcanising) silicone rubber sealants cure when exposed to moisture in the atmosphere. These sealants are good at filling pits or irregular gasket faces, but will tend to be forced out of the joint under very high torque. They can be used to replace a paper gasket, but first make sure that the width of the paper gasket is not essential to the shimming of internal components. RTV sealants should not be used on components containing petrol (gasoline).
● Non-hardening, semi-hardening and hard setting liquid gasket compounds can be used with a gasket or between a metal-to-metal joint. Select the sealant to suit the application: universal non-hardening sealant can be used on virtually all joints; semi-hardening on joint faces which are rough or damaged; hard setting sealant on joints which require a permanent bond and are subjected to high temperature and pressure. **Note:** *Check first if the paper gasket has a bead of sealant*

impregnated in its surface before applying additional sealant.
● When choosing a sealant, make sure it is suitable for the application, particularly if being applied in a high-temperature area or in the vicinity of fuel. Certain manufacturers produce sealants in either clear, silver or black colours to match the finish of the engine. This has a particular application on motorcycles where much of the engine is exposed.
● Do not over-apply sealant. That which is squeezed out on the outside of the joint can be wiped off, whereas an excess of sealant on the inside can break off and clog oilways.

Breaking a sealed joint

● Age, heat, pressure and the use of hard setting sealant can cause two components to stick together so tightly that they are difficult to separate using finger pressure alone. Do not resort to using levers unless there is a pry point provided for this purpose (see illustration 7.1) or else the gasket surfaces will be damaged.
● Use a soft-faced hammer (see illustration 7.2) or a wood block and conventional hammer to strike the component near the mating surface. Avoid hammering against cast extremities since they may break off. If this method fails, try using a wood wedge between the two components.

Caution: If the joint will not separate, double-check that you have removed all the fasteners.

7.1 If a pry point is provided, apply gently pressure with a flat-bladed screwdriver

7.2 Tap around the joint with a soft-faced mallet if necessary - don't strike cooling fins

Removal of old gasket and sealant

● Paper gaskets will most likely come away complete, leaving only a few traces stuck on

Most components have one or two hollow locating dowels between the two gasket faces. If a dowel cannot be removed, do not resort to gripping it with pliers - it will almost certainly be distorted. Install a close-fitting socket or Phillips screwdriver into the dowel and then grip the outer edge of the dowel to free it.

the sealing faces of the components. It is imperative that all traces are removed to ensure correct sealing of the new gasket.
● Very carefully scrape all traces of gasket away making sure that the sealing surfaces are not gouged or scored by the scraper (see illustrations 7.3, 7.4 and 7.5). Stubborn deposits can be removed by spraying with an aerosol gasket remover. Final preparation of

7.3 Paper gaskets can be scraped off with a gasket scraper tool . . .

7.4 . . . a knife blade . . .

7.5 . . . or a household scraper

7.6 Fine abrasive paper is wrapped around a flat file to clean up the gasket face

7.7 A kitchen scourer can be used on stubborn deposits

the gasket surface can be made with very fine abrasive paper or a plastic kitchen scourer **(see illustrations 7.6 and 7.7)**.

● Old sealant can be scraped or peeled off components, depending on the type originally used. Note that gasket removal compounds are available to avoid scraping the components clean; make sure the gasket remover suits the type of sealant used.

8 Chains

Breaking and joining final drive chains

● Drive chains for all but small bikes are continuous and do not have a clip-type connecting link. The chain must be broken using a chain breaker tool and the new chain securely riveted together using a new soft rivet-type link. Never use a clip-type connecting link instead of a rivet-type link, except in an emergency. Various chain breaking and riveting tools are available, either as separate tools or combined as illustrated in the accompanying photographs - read the instructions supplied with the tool carefully.

> ⚠ **Warning: The need to rivet the new link pins correctly cannot be overstressed - loss of control of the motorcycle is very likely to result if the chain breaks in use.**

● Rotate the chain and look for the soft link. The soft link pins look like they have been

8.1 Tighten the chain breaker to push the pin out of the link . . .

8.2 . . . withdraw the pin, remove the tool . . .

8.3 . . . and separate the chain link

deeply centre-punched instead of peened over like all the other pins **(see illustration 8.9)** and its sideplate may be a different colour. Position the soft link midway between the sprockets and assemble the chain breaker tool over one of the soft link pins **(see illustration 8.1)**. Operate the tool to push the pin out through the chain **(see illustration 8.2)**. On an O-ring chain, remove the O-rings **(see illustration 8.3)**. Carry out the same procedure on the other soft link pin.

> **Caution: Certain soft link pins (particularly on the larger chains) may require their ends to be filed or ground off before they can be pressed out using the tool.**

● Check that you have the correct size and strength (standard or heavy duty) new soft link - do not reuse the old link. Look for the size marking on the chain sideplates **(see illustration 8.10)**.

● Position the chain ends so that they are engaged over the rear sprocket. On an O-ring

8.4 Insert the new soft link, with O-rings, through the chain ends . . .

8.5 . . . install the O-rings over the pin ends . . .

8.6 . . . followed by the sideplate

chain, install a new O-ring over each pin of the link and insert the link through the two chain ends **(see illustration 8.4)**. Install a new O-ring over the end of each pin, followed by the sideplate (with the chain manufacturer's marking facing outwards) **(see illustrations 8.5 and 8.6)**. On an unsealed chain, insert the link through the two chain ends, then install the sideplate with the chain manufacturer's marking facing outwards.

● Note that it may not be possible to install the sideplate using finger pressure alone. If using a joining tool, assemble it so that the plates of the tool clamp the link and press the sideplate over the pins **(see illustration 8.7)**. Otherwise, use two small sockets placed over

8.7 Push the sideplate into position using a clamp

8.8 Assemble the chain riveting tool over one pin at a time and tighten it fully

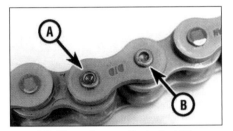

8.9 Pin end correctly riveted (A), pin end unriveted (B)

the rivet ends and two pieces of the wood between a G-clamp. Operate the clamp to press the sideplate over the pins.

● Assemble the joining tool over one pin (following the maker's instructions) and tighten the tool down to spread the pin end securely (see illustrations 8.8 and 8.9). Do the same on the other pin.

 Warning: Check that the pin ends are secure and that there is no danger of the sideplate coming loose. If the pin ends are cracked the soft link must be renewed.

Final drive chain sizing

● Chains are sized using a three digit number, followed by a suffix to denote the chain type (see illustration 8.10). Chain type is either standard or heavy duty (thicker sideplates), and also unsealed or O-ring/X-ring type.

● The first digit of the number relates to the pitch of the chain, ie the distance from the centre of one pin to the centre of the next pin (see illustration 8.11). Pitch is expressed in eighths of an inch, as follows:

8.10 Typical chain size and type marking

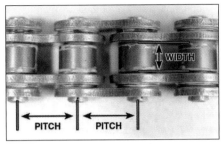

8.11 Chain dimensions

Sizes commencing with a 4 (eg 428) have a pitch of 1/2 inch (12.7 mm)

Sizes commencing with a 5 (eg 520) have a pitch of 5/8 inch (15.9 mm)

Sizes commencing with a 6 (eg 630) have a pitch of 3/4 inch (19.1 mm)

● The second and third digits of the chain size relate to the width of the rollers, again in imperial units, eg the 525 shown has 5/16 inch (7.94 mm) rollers (see illustration 8.11).

9 Hoses

Clamping to prevent flow

● Small-bore flexible hoses can be clamped to prevent fluid flow whilst a component is worked on. Whichever method is used, ensure that the hose material is not permanently distorted or damaged by the clamp.

a) A brake hose clamp available from auto accessory shops (see illustration 9.1).

b) A wingnut type hose clamp (see illustration 9.2).

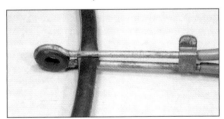

9.1 Hoses can be clamped with an automotive brake hose clamp . . .

9.2 . . . a wingnut type hose clamp . . .

c) Two sockets placed each side of the hose and held with straight-jawed self-locking grips (see illustration 9.3).

d) Thick card each side of the hose held between straight-jawed self-locking grips (see illustration 9.4).

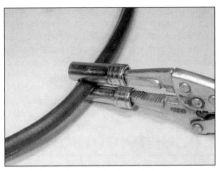

9.3 . . . two sockets and a pair of self-locking grips . . .

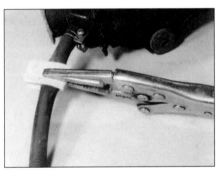

9.4 . . . or thick card and self-locking grips

Freeing and fitting hoses

● Always make sure the hose clamp is moved well clear of the hose end. Grip the hose with your hand and rotate it whilst pulling it off the union. If the hose has hardened due to age and will not move, slit it with a sharp knife and peel its ends off the union (see illustration 9.5).

● Resist the temptation to use grease or soap on the unions to aid installation; although it helps the hose slip over the union it will equally aid the escape of fluid from the joint. It is preferable to soften the hose ends in hot water and wet the inside surface of the hose with water or a fluid which will evaporate.

9.5 Cutting a coolant hose free with a sharp knife

Introduction

In less time than it takes to read this introduction, a thief could steal your motorcycle. Returning only to find your bike has gone is one of the worst feelings in the world. Even if the motorcycle is insured against theft, once you've got over the initial shock, you will have the inconvenience of dealing with the police and your insurance company.

The motorcycle is an easy target for the professional thief and the joyrider alike and the official figures on motorcycle theft make for depressing reading; on average a motorcycle is stolen every 16 minutes in the UK!

Motorcycle thefts fall into two categories, those stolen 'to order' and those taken by opportunists. The thief stealing to order will be on the look out for a specific make and model and will go to extraordinary lengths to obtain that motorcycle. The opportunist thief on the other hand will look for easy targets which can be stolen with the minimum of effort and risk.

Whilst it is never going to be possible to make your machine 100% secure, it is estimated that around half of all stolen motorcycles are taken by opportunist thieves. Remember that the opportunist thief is always on the look out for the easy option: if there are two similar motorcycles parked side-by-side, they will target the one with the lowest level of security. By taking a few precautions, you can reduce the chances of your motorcycle being stolen.

Security equipment

There are many specialised motorcycle security devices available and the following text summarises their applications and their good and bad points.

Once you have decided on the type of security equipment which best suits your needs, we recommended that you read one of the many equipment tests regularly carried out by the motorcycle press. These tests compare the products from all the major manufacturers and give impartial ratings on their effectiveness, value-for-money and ease of use.

No one item of security equipment can provide complete protection. It is highly recommended that two or more of the items described below are combined to increase the security of your motorcycle (a lock and chain plus an alarm system is just about ideal). The more security measures fitted to the bike, the less likely it is to be stolen.

Lock and chain

Pros: *Very flexible to use; can be used to secure the motorcycle to almost any immovable object. On some locks and chains, the lock can be used on its own as a disc lock (see below).*

Cons: *Can be very heavy and awkward to carry on the motorcycle, although some types will be supplied with a carry bag which can be strapped to the pillion seat.*

● Heavy-duty chains and locks are an excellent security measure **(see illustration 1)**. Whenever the motorcycle is parked, use the lock and chain to secure the machine to a solid, immovable object such as a post or railings. This will prevent the machine from being ridden away or being lifted into the back of a van.

● When fitting the chain, always ensure the chain is routed around the motorcycle frame or swingarm **(see illustrations 2 and 3)**. Never merely pass the chain around one of the wheel rims; a thief may unbolt the wheel and lift the rest of the machine into a van, leaving you with just the wheel! Try to avoid having excess chain free, thus making it difficult to use cutting tools, and keep the chain and lock off the ground to prevent thieves attacking it with a cold chisel. Position the lock so that its lock barrel is facing downwards; this will make it harder for the thief to attack the lock mechanism.

Ensure the lock and chain you buy is of good quality and long enough to shackle your bike to a solid object

Pass the chain through the bike's frame, rather than just through a wheel . . .

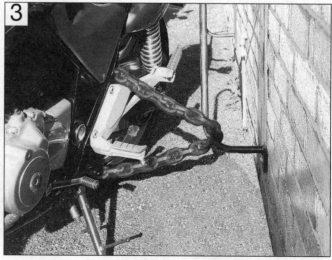

. . . and loop it around a solid object

U-locks

Pros: *Highly effective deterrent which can be used to secure the bike to a post or railings. Most U-locks come with a carrier which allows the lock to be easily carried on the bike.*

Cons: *Not as flexible to use as a lock and chain.*

● These are solid locks which are similar in use to a lock and chain. U-locks are lighter than a lock and chain but not so flexible to use. The length and shape of the lock shackle limit the objects to which the bike can be secured **(see illustration 4)**.

Disc locks

Pros: *Small, light and very easy to carry; most can be stored underneath the seat.*

Cons: *Does not prevent the motorcycle being lifted into a van. Can be very embarrassing if you*

U-locks can be used to secure the bike to a solid object – ensure you purchase one which is long enough

forget to remove the lock before attempting to ride off!

● Disc locks are designed to be attached to the front brake disc. The lock passes through one of the holes in the disc and prevents the wheel rotating by jamming against the fork/brake caliper **(see illustration 5)**. Some are equipped with an alarm siren which sounds if the disc lock is moved; this not only acts as a theft deterrent but also as a handy reminder if you try to move the bike with the lock still fitted.

● Combining the disc lock with a length of cable which can be looped around a post or railings provides an additional measure of security **(see illustration 6)**.

Alarms and immobilisers

Pros: *Once installed it is completely hassle-free to use. If the system is 'Thatcham' or 'Sold Secure-approved', insurance companies may give you a discount.*

Cons: *Can be expensive to buy and complex to install. No system will prevent the motorcycle from being lifted into a van and taken away.*

● Electronic alarms and immobilisers are available to suit a variety of budgets. There are three different types of system available: pure alarms, pure immobilisers, and the more expensive systems which are combined alarm/immobilisers **(see illustration 7)**.

● An alarm system is designed to emit an audible warning if the motorcycle is being tampered with.

● An immobiliser prevents the motorcycle being started and ridden away by disabling its electrical systems.

● When purchasing an alarm/immobiliser system, check the cost of installing the system unless you are able to do it yourself. If the motorcycle is not used regularly, another consideration is the current drain of the system. All alarm/immobiliser systems are powered by the motorcycle's battery; purchasing a system with a very low current drain could prevent the battery losing its charge whilst the motorcycle is not being used.

A typical disc lock attached through one of the holes in the disc

A disc lock combined with a security cable provides additional protection

A typical alarm/immobiliser system

8

Indelible markings can be applied to most areas of the bike – always apply the manufacturer's sticker to warn off thieves

9

Chemically-etched code numbers can be applied to main body panels . . .

10

. . . again, always ensure that the kit manufacturer's sticker is applied in a prominent position

Security marking kits

Pros: *Very cheap and effective deterrent. Many insurance companies will give you a discount on your insurance premium if a recognised security marking kit is used on your motorcycle.*

Cons: *Does not prevent the motorcycle being stolen by joyriders.*

● There are many different types of security marking kits available. The idea is to mark as many parts of the motorcycle as possible with a unique security number **(see illustrations 8, 9 and 10)**. A form will be included with the kit to register your personal details and those of the motorcycle with the kit manufacturer. This register is made available to the police to help them trace the rightful owner of any motorcycle or components which they recover should all other forms of identification have been removed. Always apply the warning stickers provided with the kit to deter thieves.

Ground anchors, wheel clamps and security posts

Pros: *An excellent form of security which will deter all but the most determined of thieves.*

Cons: *Awkward to install and can be expensive.*

● Whilst the motorcycle is at home, it is a good idea to attach it securely to the floor or a solid wall, even if it is kept in a securely locked garage. Various types of ground anchors, security posts and wheel clamps are available for this purpose **(see illustration 11)**. These security devices are either bolted to a solid concrete or brick structure or can be cemented into the ground.

11

Permanent ground anchors provide an excellent level of security when the bike is at home

Security at home

A high percentage of motorcycle thefts are from the owner's home. Here are some things to consider whenever your motorcycle is at home:
✔ Where possible, always keep the motorcycle in a securely locked garage. Never rely solely on the standard lock on the garage door, these are usual hopelessly inadequate. Fit an additional locking mechanism to the door and consider having the garage alarmed. A security light, activated by a movement sensor, is also a good investment.

✔ Always secure the motorcycle to the ground or a wall, even if it is inside a securely locked garage.
✔ Do not regularly leave the motorcycle outside your home, try to keep it out of sight wherever possible. If a garage is not available, fit a motorcycle cover over the bike to disguise its true identity.
✔ It is not uncommon for thieves to follow a motorcyclist home to find out where the bike is kept. They will then return at a later date. Be aware of this whenever you are returning

home on your motorcycle. If you suspect you are being followed, do not return home, instead ride to a garage or shop and stop as a precaution.
✔ When selling a motorcycle, do not provide your home address or the location where the bike is normally kept. Arrange to meet the buyer at a location away from your home. Thieves have been known to pose as potential buyers to find out where motorcycles are kept and then return later to steal them.

Security away from the home

As well as fitting security equipment to your motorcycle here are a few general rules to follow whenever you park your motorcycle.
✔ Park in a busy, public place.
✔ Use car parks which incorporate security features, such as CCTV.

✔ At night, park in a well-lit area, preferably directly underneath a street light.
✔ Engage the steering lock.
✔ Secure the motorcycle to a solid, immovable object such as a post or railings with an additional lock. If this is not possible,

secure the bike to a friend's motorcycle. Some public parking places provide security loops for motorcycles.
✔ Never leave your helmet or luggage attached to the motorcycle. Take them with you at all times.

Lubricants and fluids

A wide range of lubricants, fluids and cleaning agents is available for motor-cycles. This is a guide as to what is available, its applications and properties.

Four-stroke engine oil

● Engine oil is without doubt the most important component of any four-stroke engine. Modern motorcycle engines place a lot of demands on their oil and choosing the right type is essential. Using an unsuitable oil will lead to an increased rate of engine wear and could result in serious engine damage. Before purchasing oil, always check the recommended oil specification given by the manufacturer. The manufacturer will state a recommended 'type or classification' and also a specific 'viscosity' range for engine oil.

● The oil 'type or classification' is identified by its API (American Petroleum Institute) rating. The API rating will be in the form of two letters, e.g. SG. The S identifies the oil as being suitable for use in a petrol (gasoline) engine (S stands for spark ignition) and the second letter, ranging from A to J, identifies the oil's performance rating. The later this letter, the higher the specification of the oil; for example API SG oil exceeds the requirements of API SF oil. **Note:** *On some oils there may also be a second rating consisting of another two letters, the first letter being C, e.g. API SF/CD. This rating indicates the oil is also suitable for use in a diesel engines (the C stands for compression ignition) and is thus of no relevance for motorcycle use.*

● The 'viscosity' of the oil is identified by its SAE (Society of Automotive Engineers) rating. All modern engines require multigrade oils and the SAE rating will consist of two numbers, the first followed by a W, e.g. 10W/40. The first number indicates the viscosity rating of the oil at low temperatures (W stands for winter – tested at –20°C) and the second number represents the viscosity of the oil at high temperatures (tested at 100°C). The lower the number, the thinner the oil. For example an oil with an SAE 10W/40 rating will give better cold starting and running than an SAE 15W/40 oil.

● As well as ensuring the 'type' and 'viscosity' of the oil match the recommendations, another consideration to make when buying engine oil is whether to purchase a standard mineral-based oil, a semi-synthetic oil (also known as a synthetic blend or synthetic-based oil) or a fully-synthetic oil. Although all oils will have a similar rating and viscosity, their cost will vary considerably; mineral-based oils are the cheapest, the fully-synthetic oils the most expensive with the semi-synthetic oils falling somewhere in-between. This decision is very much up to the owner, but it should be noted that modern synthetic oils have far better lubricating and cleaning qualities than traditional mineral-based oils and tend to retain these properties for far longer. Bearing in mind the operating conditions inside a modern, high-revving motorcycle engine it is highly recommended that a fully synthetic oil is used. The extra expense at each service could save you money in the long term by preventing premature engine wear.

● As a final note always ensure that the oil is specifically designed for use in motorcycle engines. Engine oils designed primarily for use in car engines sometimes contain additives or friction modifiers which could cause clutch slip on a motorcycle fitted with a wet-clutch.

Two-stroke engine oil

● Modern two-stroke engines, with their high power outputs, place high demands on their oil. If engine seizure is to be avoided it is essential that a high-quality oil is used. Two-stroke oils differ hugely from four-stroke oils. The oil lubricates only the crankshaft and piston(s) (the transmission has its own lubricating oil) and is used on a total-loss basis where it is burnt completely during the combustion process.

● The Japanese have recently introduced a classification system for two-stroke oils, the JASO rating. This rating is in the form of two letters, either FA, FB or FC – FA is the lowest classification and FC the highest. Ensure the oil being used meets or exceeds the recommended rating specified by the manufacturer.

● As well as ensuring the oil rating matches the recommendation, another consideration to make when buying engine oil is whether to purchase a standard mineral-based oil, a semi-synthetic oil (also known as a synthetic blend or synthetic-based oil) or a fully-synthetic oil. The cost of each type of oil varies considerably; mineral-based oils are the cheapest, the fully-synthetic oils the most expensive with the semi-synthetic oils falling somewhere in-between. This decision is very much up to the owner, but it should be noted that modern synthetic oils have far better lubricating properties and burn cleaner than traditional mineral-based oils. It is therefore recommended that a fully synthetic oil is used. The extra expense could save you money in the long term by preventing premature engine wear, engine performance will be improved, carbon deposits and exhaust smoke will be reduced.

● Always ensure that the oil is specifically designed for use in an injector system. Many high quality two-stroke oils are designed for competition use and need to be pre-mixed with fuel. These oils are of a much higher viscosity and are not designed to flow through the injector pumps used on road-going two-stroke motorcycles.

Transmission (gear) oil

● On a two-stroke engine, the transmission and clutch are lubricated by their own separate oil bath which must be changed in accordance with the Maintenance Schedule.
● Although the engine and transmission units of most four-strokes use a common lubrication supply, there are some exceptions where the engine and gearbox have separate oil reservoirs and a dry clutch is used.
● Motorcycle manufacturers will either recommend a monograde transmission oil or a four-stroke multigrade engine oil to lubricate the transmission.
● Transmission oils, or gear oils as they are often called, are designed specifically for use in transmission systems. The viscosity of these oils is represented by an SAE number, but the scale of measurement applied is different to that used to grade engine oils. As a rough guide a SAE90 gear oil will be of the same viscosity as an SAE50 engine oil.

Shaft drive oil

● On models equipped with shaft final drive, the shaft drive gears are will have their own oil supply. The manufacturer will state a recommended 'type or classification' and also a specific 'viscosity' range in the same manner as for four-stroke engine oil.
● Gear oil classification is given by the number which follows the API GL (GL standing for gear lubricant) rating, the higher the number, the higher the specification of the oil, e.g. API GL5 oil is a higher specification than API GL4 oil. Ensure the oil meets or

exceeds the classification specified and is of the correct viscosity. The viscosity of gear oils is also represented by an SAE number but the scale of measurement used is different to that used to grade engine oils. As a rough guide an SAE90 gear oil will be of the same viscosity as an SAE50 engine oil.
● If the use of an EP (Extreme Pressure) gear oil is specified, ensure the oil purchased is suitable.

Fork oil and suspension fluid

● Conventional telescopic front forks are hydraulic and require fork oil to work. To ensure the forks function correctly, the fork oil must be changed in accordance with the Maintenance Schedule.
● Fork oil is available in a variety of viscosities, identified by their SAE rating; fork oil ratings vary from light (SAE 5) to heavy (SAE 30). When purchasing fork oil, ensure the viscosity rating matches that specified by the manufacturer.
● Some lubricant manufacturers also produce a range of high-quality suspension fluids which are very similar to fork oil but are designed mainly for competition use. These fluids may have a different viscosity rating system which is not to be confused with the SAE rating of normal fork oil. Refer to the manufacturer's instructions if in any doubt.

Brake and clutch fluid

● All disc brake systems and some clutch systems are hydraulically operated. To ensure correct operation, the hydraulic fluid must be changed in accordance with the Maintenance Schedule.
● Brake and clutch fluid is classified by its DOT rating with most motorcycle manufacturers specifying DOT 3 or 4 fluid. Both fluid types are glycol-based and can be mixed together without adverse effect; DOT 4 fluid exceeds the requirements of DOT 3

fluid. Although it is safe to use DOT 4 fluid in a system designed for use with DOT 3 fluid, never use DOT 3 fluid in a system which specifies the use of DOT 4 as this will adversely affect the system's performance. The type required for the system will be marked on the fluid reservoir cap.
● Some manufacturers also produce a DOT 5 hydraulic fluid. DOT 5 hydraulic fluid is silicone-based and is not compatible with the glycol-based DOT 3 and 4 fluids. Never mix DOT 5 fluid with DOT 3 or 4 fluid as this will seriously affect the performance of the hydraulic system.

Coolant/antifreeze

● When purchasing coolant/antifreeze, always ensure it is suitable for use in an aluminium engine and contains corrosion inhibitors to prevent possible blockages of the internal coolant passages of the system. As a general rule, most coolants are designed to be used neat and should not be diluted whereas antifreeze can be mixed with distilled water to

provide a coolant solution of the required strength. Refer to the manufacturer's instructions on the bottle.
● Ensure the coolant is changed in accordance with the Maintenance Schedule.

Chain lube

● Chain lube is an aerosol-type spray lubricant specifically designed for use on motorcycle final drive chains. Chain lube has two functions, to minimise friction between the final drive chain and sprockets and to prevent corrosion of the chain. Regular use of a good-quality chain lube will extend the life of the drive chain and sprockets and thus maximise the power being transmitted from the transmission to the rear wheel.

● When using chain lube, always allow some time for the solvents in the lube to evaporate before riding the motorcycle. This will minimise the amount of lube which will 'fling' off from the chain when the motorcycle is used. If the motorcycle is equipped with an 'O-ring' chain, ensure the chain lube is labelled as being suitable for use on 'O-ring' chains.

Degreasers and solvents

● There are many different types of solvents and degreasers available to remove the grime and grease which accumulate around the motorcycle during normal use. Degreasers and solvents are usually available as an aerosol-type spray or as a liquid which you apply with a brush. Always closely follow the manufacturer's instructions and wear eye protection during use. Be aware that many solvents are flammable and may give off noxious fumes; take adequate precautions when using them (see Safety First!).
● For general cleaning, use one of the many solvents or degreasers available from most motorcycle accessory shops. These solvents are usually applied then left for a certain time before being washed off with water.

Brake cleaner is a solvent specifically designed to remove all traces of oil, grease and dust from braking system components. Brake cleaner is designed to evaporate quickly and leaves behind no residue.

Carburettor cleaner is an aerosol-type solvent specifically designed to clear carburettor blockages and break down the hard deposits and gum often found inside carburettors during overhaul.

Contact cleaner is an aerosol-type solvent designed for cleaning electrical components. The cleaner will remove all traces of oil and dirt from components such as switch contacts or fouled spark plugs and then dry, leaving behind no residue.

Gasket remover is an aerosol-type solvent designed for removing stubborn gaskets from engine components during overhaul. Gasket remover will minimise the amount of scraping required to remove the gasket and therefore reduce the risk of damage to the mating surface.

Spray lubricants
● Aerosol-based spray lubricants are widely available and are excellent for lubricating lever pivots and exposed cables and switches. Try to use a lubricant which is of the dry-film type as the fluid evaporates, leaving behind a dry-film of lubricant. Lubricants which leave behind an oily residue will attract dust and dirt which will increase the rate of wear of the cable/lever.

● Most lubricants also act as a moisture dispersant and a penetrating fluid. This means they can also be used to 'dry out' electrical components such as wiring connectors or switches as well as helping to free seized fasteners.

Greases

● Grease is used to lubricate many of the pivot-points. A good-quality multi-purpose grease is suitable for most applications but some manufacturers will specify the use of specialist greases for use on components such as swingarm and suspension linkage bushes. These specialist greases can be purchased from most motorcycle (or car) accessory shops; commonly specified types include molybdenum disulphide grease, lithium-based grease, graphite-based grease, silicone-based grease and high-temperature copper-based grease.

Gasket sealing compounds
● Gasket sealing compounds can be used in conjunction with gaskets, to improve their sealing capabilities, or on their own to seal metal-to-metal joints. Depending on their type, sealing compounds either set hard or stay relatively soft and pliable.

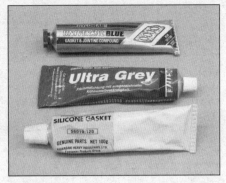

● When purchasing a gasket sealing compound, ensure that it is designed specifically for use on an internal combustion engine. General multi-purpose sealants available from DIY stores may appear visibly similar but they are not designed to withstand the extreme heat or contact with fuel and oil encountered when used on an engine (see 'Tools and Workshop Tips' for further information).

Thread locking compound
● Thread locking compounds are used to secure certain threaded fasteners in position to prevent them from loosening due to vibration. Thread locking compounds can be purchased from most motorcycle (and car) accessory shops. Ensure the threads of the both components are completely clean and dry before sparingly applying the locking compound (see 'Tools and Workshop Tips' for further information).

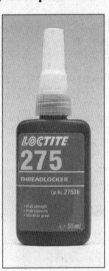

Fuel additives
● Fuel additives which protect and clean the fuel system components are widely available. These additives are designed to remove all traces of deposits that build up on the carburettors/injectors and prevent wear, helping the fuel system to operate more efficiently. If a fuel additive is being used, check that it is suitable for use with your motorcycle, especially if your motorcycle is equipped with a catalytic converter.

● Octane boosters are also available. These additives are designed to improve the performance of highly-tuned engines being run on normal pump-fuel and are of no real use on standard motorcycles.

Conversion Factors

Length (distance)

Inches (in)	x 25.4	= Millimetres (mm)	x 0.0394	= Inches (in)
Feet (ft)	x 0.305	= Metres (m)	x 3.281	= Feet (ft)
Miles	x 1.609	= Kilometres (km)	x 0.621	= Miles

Volume (capacity)

Cubic inches (cu in; in³)	x 16.387	= Cubic centimetres (cc; cm³)	x 0.061	= Cubic inches (cu in; in³)
Imperial pints (Imp pt)	x 0.568	= Litres (l)	x 1.76	= Imperial pints (Imp pt)
Imperial quarts (Imp qt)	x 1.137	= Litres (l)	x 0.88	= Imperial quarts (Imp qt)
Imperial quarts (Imp qt)	x 1.201	= US quarts (US qt)	x 0.833	= Imperial quarts (Imp qt)
US quarts (US qt)	x 0.946	= Litres (l)	x 1.057	= US quarts (US qt)
Imperial gallons (Imp gal)	x 4.546	= Litres (l)	x 0.22	= Imperial gallons (Imp gal)
Imperial gallons (Imp gal)	x 1.201	= US gallons (US gal)	x 0.833	= Imperial gallons (Imp gal)
US gallons (US gal)	x 3.785	= Litres (l)	x 0.264	= US gallons (US gal)

Mass (weight)

Ounces (oz)	x 28.35	= Grams (g)	x 0.035	= Ounces (oz)
Pounds (lb)	x 0.454	= Kilograms (kg)	x 2.205	= Pounds (lb)

Force

Ounces-force (ozf; oz)	x 0.278	= Newtons (N)	x 3.6	= Ounces-force (ozf; oz)
Pounds-force (lbf; lb)	x 4.448	= Newtons (N)	x 0.225	= Pounds-force (lbf; lb)
Newtons (N)	x 0.1	= Kilograms-force (kgf; kg)	x 9.81	= Newtons (N)

Pressure

Pounds-force per square inch (psi; lbf/in²; lb/in²)	x 0.070	= Kilograms-force per square centimetre (kgf/cm²; kg/cm²)	x 14.223	= Pounds-force per square inch (psi; lbf/in²; lb/in²)
Pounds-force per square inch (psi; lbf/in²; lb/in²)	x 0.068	= Atmospheres (atm)	x 14.696	= Pounds-force per square inch (psi; lbf/in²; lb/in²)
Pounds-force per square inch (psi; lbf/in²; lb/in²)	x 0.069	= Bars	x 14.5	= Pounds-force per square inch (psi; lbf/in²; lb/in²)
Pounds-force per square inch (psi; lbf/in²; lb/in²)	x 6.895	= Kilopascals (kPa)	x 0.145	= Pounds-force per square inch (psi; lbf/in²; lb/in²)
Kilopascals (kPa)	x 0.01	= Kilograms-force per square centimetre (kgf/cm²; kg/cm²)	x 98.1	= Kilopascals (kPa)
Millibar (mbar)	x 100	= Pascals (Pa)	x 0.01	= Millibar (mbar)
Millibar (mbar)	x 0.0145	= Pounds-force per square inch (psi; lbf/in²; lb/in²)	x 68.947	= Millibar (mbar)
Millibar (mbar)	x 0.75	= Millimetres of mercury (mmHg)	x 1.333	= Millibar (mbar)
Millibar (mbar)	x 0.401	= Inches of water (inH₂O)	x 2.491	= Millibar (mbar)
Millimetres of mercury (mmHg)	x 0.535	= Inches of water (inH₂O)	x 1.868	= Millimetres of mercury (mmHg)
Inches of water (inH₂O)	x 0.036	= Pounds-force per square inch (psi; lbf/in²; lb/in²)	x 27.68	= Inches of water (inH₂O)

Torque (moment of force)

Pounds-force inches (lbf in; lb in)	x 1.152	= Kilograms-force centimetre (kgf cm; kg cm)	x 0.868	= Pounds-force inches (lbf in; lb in)
Pounds-force inches (lbf in; lb in)	x 0.113	= Newton metres (Nm)	x 8.85	= Pounds-force inches (lbf in; lb in)
Pounds-force inches (lbf in; lb in)	x 0.083	= Pounds-force feet (lbf ft; lb ft)	x 12	= Pounds-force inches (lbf in; lb in)
Pounds-force feet (lbf ft; lb ft)	x 0.138	= Kilograms-force metres (kgf m; kg m)	x 7.233	= Pounds-force feet (lbf ft; lb ft)
Pounds-force feet (lbf ft; lb ft)	x 1.356	= Newton metres (Nm)	x 0.738	= Pounds-force feet (lbf ft; lb ft)
Newton metres (Nm)	x 0.102	= Kilograms-force metres (kgf m; kg m)	x 9.804	= Newton metres (Nm)

Power

Horsepower (hp)	x 745.7	= Watts (W)	x 0.0013	= Horsepower (hp)

Velocity (speed)

Miles per hour (miles/hr; mph)	x 1.609	= Kilometres per hour (km/hr; kph)	x 0.621	= Miles per hour (miles/hr; mph)

Fuel consumption*

Miles per gallon (mpg)	x 0.354	= Kilometres per litre (km/l)	x 2.825	= Miles per gallon (mpg)

Temperature

Degrees Fahrenheit = (°C x 1.8) + 32

Degrees Celsius (Degrees Centigrade; °C) = (°F - 32) x 0.56

It is common practice to convert from miles per gallon (mpg) to litres/100 kilometres (l/100km), where mpg x l/100 km = 282

About the MOT Test

In the UK, all vehicles more than three years old are subject to an annual test to ensure that they meet minimum safety requirements. A current test certificate must be issued before a machine can be used on public roads, and is required before a road fund licence can be issued. Riding without a current test certificate will also invalidate your insurance.

For most owners, the MOT test is an annual cause for anxiety, and this is largely due to owners not being sure what needs to be checked prior to submitting the motorcycle for testing. The simple answer is that a fully roadworthy motorcycle will have no difficulty in passing the test.

This is a guide to getting your motorcycle through the MOT test. Obviously it will not be possible to examine the motorcycle to the same standard as the professional MOT tester, particularly in view of the equipment required for some of the checks. However, working through the following procedures will enable you to identify any problem areas before submitting the motorcycle for the test.

It has only been possible to summarise the test requirements here, based on the regulations in force at the time of printing. Test standards are becoming increasingly stringent, although there are some exemptions for older vehicles. More information about the MOT test can be obtained from the TSO publications, *How Safe is your Motorcycle* and *The MOT Inspection Manual for Motorcycle Testing*.

Many of the checks require that one of the wheels is raised off the ground. If the motorcycle doesn't have a centre stand, note that an auxiliary stand will be required. Additionally, the help of an assistant may prove useful.

Certain exceptions apply to machines under 50 cc, machines without a lighting system, and Classic bikes - if in doubt about any of the requirements listed below seek confirmation from an MOT tester prior to submitting the motorcycle for the test.

Check that the frame number is clearly visible.

> **HAYNES HINT**
> *If a component is in borderline condition, the tester has discretion in deciding whether to pass or fail it. If the motorcycle presented is clean and evidently well cared for, the tester may be more inclined to pass a borderline component than if the motorcycle is scruffy and apparently neglected.*

Electrical System

Lights, turn signals, horn and reflector

✔ With the ignition on, check the operation of the following electrical components. **Note:** *The electrical components on certain small-capacity machines are powered by the generator, requiring that the engine is run for this check.*

a) *Headlight and tail light. Check that both illuminate in the low and high beam switch positions.*

b) *Position lights. Check that the front position (or sidelight) and tail light illuminate in this switch position.*

c) *Turn signals. Check that all flash at the correct rate, and that the warning light(s) function correctly. Check that the turn signal switch works correctly.*

d) *Hazard warning system (where fitted). Check that all four turn signals flash in this switch position.*

e) *Brake stop light. Check that the light comes on when the front and rear brakes are independently applied. Models first used on or after 1st April 1986 must have a brake light switch on each brake.*

f) *Horn. Check that the sound is continuous and of reasonable volume.*

✔ Check that there is a red reflector on the rear of the machine, either mounted separately or as part of the tail light lens.

✔ Check the condition of the headlight, tail light and turn signal lenses.

Headlight beam height

✔ The MOT tester will perform a headlight beam height check using specialised beam setting equipment **(see illustration 1)**. This equipment will not be available to the home mechanic, but if you suspect that the headlight is incorrectly set or may have been maladjusted in the past, you can perform a rough test as follows.

✔ Position the bike in a straight line facing a brick wall. The bike must be off its stand, upright and with a rider seated. Measure the height from the ground to the centre of the headlight and mark a horizontal line on the wall at this height. Position the motorcycle 3.8 metres from the wall and draw a vertical

Headlight beam height checking equipment

line up the wall central to the centreline of the motorcycle. Switch to dipped beam and check that the beam pattern falls slightly lower than the horizontal line and to the left of the vertical line **(see illustration 2)**.

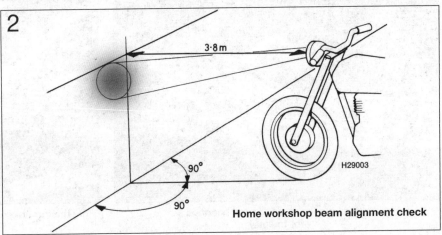

3·8 m

90°

90°

H29003

Home workshop beam alignment check

Exhaust System and Final Drive

Exhaust

✔ Check that the exhaust mountings are secure and that the system does not foul any of the rear suspension components.
✔ Start the motorcycle. When the revs are increased, check that the exhaust is neither holed nor leaking from any of its joints. On a linked system, check that the collector box is not leaking due to corrosion.

✔ Note that the exhaust decibel level ("loudness" of the exhaust) is assessed at the discretion of the tester. If the motorcycle was first used on or after 1st January 1985 the silencer must carry the BSAU 193 stamp, or a marking relating to its make and model, or be of OE (original equipment) manufacture. If the silencer is marked NOT FOR ROAD USE, RACING USE ONLY or similar, it will fail the MOT.

Final drive

✔ On chain or belt drive machines, check that the chain/belt is in good condition and does not have excessive slack. Also check that the sprocket is securely mounted on the rear wheel hub. Check that the chain/belt guard is in place.
✔ On shaft drive bikes, check for oil leaking from the drive unit and fouling the rear tyre.

Steering and Suspension

Steering

✔ With the front wheel raised off the ground, rotate the steering from lock to lock. The handlebar or switches must not contact the fuel tank or be close enough to trap the rider's hand. Problems can be caused by damaged lock stops on the lower yoke and frame, or by the fitting of non-standard handlebars.
✔ When performing the lock to lock check, also ensure that the steering moves freely without drag or notchiness. Steering movement can be impaired by poorly routed cables, or by overtight head bearings or worn bearings. The tester will perform a check of the steering head bearing lower race by mounting the front wheel on a surface plate, then performing a lock to lock check with the weight of the machine on the lower bearing (see illustration 3).
✔ Grasp the fork sliders (lower legs) and attempt to push and pull on the forks (see illustration 4). Any play in the steering head bearings will be felt. Note that in extreme cases, wear of the front fork bushes can be misinterpreted for head bearing play.
✔ Check that the handlebars are securely mounted.
✔ Check that the handlebar grip rubbers are secure. They should by bonded to the bar left end and to the throttle cable pulley on the right end.

Front wheel mounted on a surface plate for steering head bearing lower race check

Front suspension

✔ With the motorcycle off the stand, hold the front brake on and pump the front forks up and down (see illustration 5). Check that they are adequately damped.

Checking the steering head bearings for freeplay

Hold the front brake on and pump the front forks up and down to check operation

Inspect the area around the fork dust seal for oil leakage (arrow)

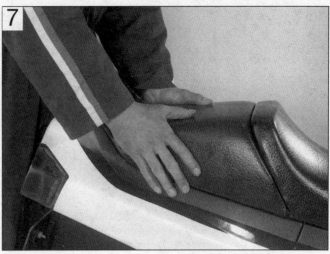

Bounce the rear of the motorcycle to check rear suspension operation

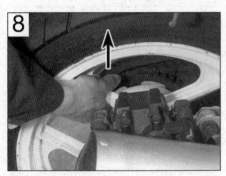

Checking for rear suspension linkage play

✔ Inspect the area above and around the front fork oil seals **(see illustration 6)**. There should be no sign of oil on the fork tube (stanchion) nor leaking down the slider (lower leg). On models so equipped, check that there is no oil leaking from the anti-dive units.

✔ On models with swingarm front suspension, check that there is no freeplay in the linkage when moved from side to side.

Rear suspension

✔ With the motorcycle off the stand and an assistant supporting the motorcycle by its handlebars, bounce the rear suspension **(see illustration 7)**. Check that the suspension components do not foul on any of the cycle parts and check that the shock absorber(s) provide adequate damping.

✔ Visually inspect the shock absorber(s) and check that there is no sign of oil leakage from its damper. This is somewhat restricted on certain single shock models due to the location of the shock absorber.

✔ With the rear wheel raised off the ground, grasp the wheel at the highest point and attempt to pull it up **(see illustration 8)**. Any play in the swingarm pivot or suspension linkage bearings will be felt as movement. **Note:** *Do not confuse play with actual suspension movement.* Failure to lubricate suspension linkage bearings can lead to bearing failure **(see illustration 9)**.

✔ With the rear wheel raised off the ground, grasp the swingarm ends and attempt to move the swingarm from side to side and forwards and backwards - any play indicates wear of the swingarm pivot bearings **(see illustration 10)**.

Worn suspension linkage pivots (arrows) are usually the cause of play in the rear suspension

Grasp the swingarm at the ends to check for play in its pivot bearings

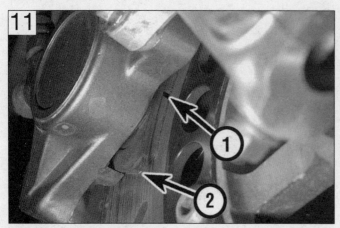

Brake pad wear can usually be viewed without removing the caliper. Most pads have wear indicator grooves (1) and some also have indicator tangs (2)

On drum brakes, check the angle of the operating lever with the brake fully applied. Most drum brakes have a wear indicator pointer and scale.

Brakes, Wheels and Tyres

Brakes

✔ With the wheel raised off the ground, apply the brake then free it off, and check that the wheel is about to revolve freely without brake drag.

✔ On disc brakes, examine the disc itself. Check that it is securely mounted and not cracked.

✔ On disc brakes, view the pad material through the caliper mouth and check that the pads are not worn down beyond the limit **(see illustration 11)**.

✔ On drum brakes, check that when the brake is applied the angle between the operating lever and cable or rod is not too great **(see illustration 12)**. Check also that the operating lever doesn't foul any other components.

✔ On disc brakes, examine the flexible hoses from top to bottom. Have an assistant hold the brake on so that the fluid in the hose is under pressure, and check that there is no sign of fluid leakage, bulges or cracking. If there are any metal brake pipes or unions, check that these are free from corrosion and damage. Where a brake-linked anti-dive system is fitted, check the hoses to the anti-dive in a similar manner.

✔ Check that the rear brake torque arm is secure and that its fasteners are secured by self-locking nuts or castellated nuts with split-pins or R-pins **(see illustration 13)**.

✔ On models with ABS, check that the self-check warning light in the instrument panel works.

✔ The MOT tester will perform a test of the motorcycle's braking efficiency based on a calculation of rider and motorcycle weight. Although this cannot be carried out at home, you can at least ensure that the braking systems are properly maintained. For hydraulic disc brakes, check the fluid level, lever/pedal feel (bleed of air if its spongy) and pad material. For drum brakes, check adjustment, cable or rod operation and shoe lining thickness.

Wheels and tyres

✔ Check the wheel condition. Cast wheels should be free from cracks and if of the built-up design, all fasteners should be secure. Spoked wheels should be checked for broken, corroded, loose or bent spokes.

✔ With the wheel raised off the ground, spin the wheel and visually check that the tyre and wheel run true. Check that the tyre does not foul the suspension or mudguards.

✔ With the wheel raised off the ground, grasp the wheel and attempt to move it about the axle (spindle) **(see illustration 14)**. Any play felt here indicates wheel bearing failure.

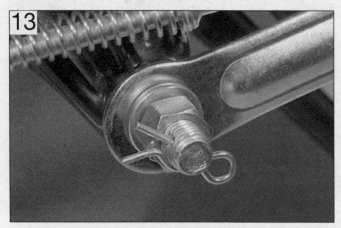

Brake torque arm must be properly secured at both ends

Check for wheel bearing play by trying to move the wheel about the axle (spindle)

Checking the tyre tread depth

Tyre direction of rotation arrow can be found on tyre sidewall

Castellated type wheel axle (spindle) nut must be secured by a split pin or R-pin

Two straightedges are used to check wheel alignment

✔ Check the tyre tread depth, tread condition and sidewall condition **(see illustration 15)**.
✔ Check the tyre type. Front and rear tyre types must be compatible and be suitable for road use. Tyres marked NOT FOR ROAD USE, COMPETITION USE ONLY or similar, will fail the MOT.

✔ If the tyre sidewall carries a direction of rotation arrow, this must be pointing in the direction of normal wheel rotation **(see illustration 16)**.
✔ Check that the wheel axle (spindle) nuts (where applicable) are properly secured. A self-locking nut or castellated nut with a split-pin or R-pin can be used **(see illustration 17)**.
✔ Wheel alignment is checked with the motorcycle off the stand and a rider seated. With the front wheel pointing straight ahead, two perfectly straight lengths of metal or wood and placed against the sidewalls of both tyres **(see illustration 18)**. The gap each side of the front tyre must be equidistant on both sides. Incorrect wheel alignment may be due to a cocked rear wheel (often as the result of poor chain adjustment) or in extreme cases, a bent frame.

General checks and condition

✔ Check the security of all major fasteners, bodypanels, seat, fairings (where fitted) and mudguards.

✔ Check that the rider and pillion footrests, handlebar levers and brake pedal are securely mounted.

✔ Check for corrosion on the frame or any load-bearing components. If severe, this may affect the structure, particularly under stress.

Sidecars

A motorcycle fitted with a sidecar requires additional checks relating to the stability of the machine and security of attachment and swivel joints, plus specific wheel alignment (toe-in) requirements. Additionally, tyre and lighting requirements differ from conventional motorcycle use. Owners are advised to check MOT test requirements with an official test centre.

Preparing for storage

Before you start

If repairs or an overhaul is needed, see that this is carried out now rather than left until you want to ride the bike again.

Give the bike a good wash and scrub all dirt from its underside. Make sure the bike dries completely before preparing for storage.

Engine

● Remove the spark plug(s) and lubricate the cylinder bores with approximately a teaspoon of motor oil using a spout-type oil can (see illustration 1). Reinstall the spark plug(s). Crank the engine over a couple of times to coat the piston rings and bores with oil. If the bike has a kickstart, use this to turn the engine over. If not, flick the kill switch to the OFF position and crank the engine over on the starter (see illustration 2). If the nature on the ignition system prevents the starter operating with the kill switch in the OFF position,

remove the spark plugs and fit them back in their caps; ensure that the plugs are earthed (grounded) against the cylinder head when the starter is operated (see illustration 3).

⚠ *Warning: It is important that the plugs are earthed (grounded) away from the spark plug holes otherwise there is a risk of atomised fuel from the cylinders igniting.*

> **HAYNES HINT** *On a single cylinder four-stroke engine, you can seal the combustion chamber completely by positioning the piston at TDC on the compression stroke.*

● Drain the carburettor(s) otherwise there is a risk of jets becoming blocked by gum deposits from the fuel (see illustration 4).

● If the bike is going into long-term storage, consider adding a fuel stabiliser to the fuel in the tank. If the tank is drained completely, corrosion of its internal surfaces may occur if left unprotected for a long period. The tank can be treated with a rust preventative especially for this purpose. Alternatively, remove the tank and pour half a litre of motor oil into it, install the filler cap and shake the tank to coat its internals with oil before draining off the excess. The same effect can also be achieved by spraying WD40 or a similar water-dispersant around the inside of the tank via its flexible nozzle.

● Make sure the cooling system contains the correct mix of antifreeze. Antifreeze also contains important corrosion inhibitors.

● The air intakes and exhaust can be sealed off by covering or plugging the openings. Ensure that you do not seal in any condensation; run the engine until it is hot,

Squirt a drop of motor oil into each cylinder

Flick the kill switch to OFF . . .

. . . and ensure that the metal bodies of the plugs (arrows) are earthed against the cylinder head

Connect a hose to the carburettor float chamber drain stub (arrow) and unscrew the drain screw

Exhausts can be sealed off with a plastic bag

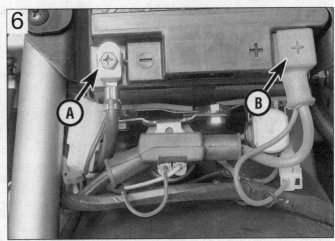

Disconnect the negative lead (A) first, followed by the positive lead (B)

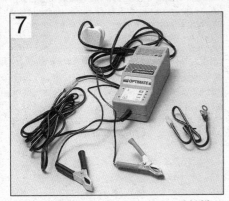

Use a suitable battery charger - this kit also assess battery condition

then switch off and allow to cool. Tape a piece of thick plastic over the silencer end(s) **(see illustration 5)**. Note that some advocate pouring a tablespoon of motor oil into the silencer(s) before sealing them off.

Battery

● Remove it from the bike - in extreme cases of cold the battery may freeze and crack its case **(see illustration 6)**.

● Check the electrolyte level and top up if necessary (conventional refillable batteries). Clean the terminals.
● Store the battery off the motorcycle and away from any sources of fire. Position a wooden block under the battery if it is to sit on the ground.
● Give the battery a trickle charge for a few hours every month **(see illustration 7)**.

Tyres

● Place the bike on its centrestand or an auxiliary stand which will support the motorcycle in an upright position. Position wood blocks under the tyres to keep them off the ground and to provide insulation from damp. If the bike is being put into long-term storage, ideally both tyres should be off the ground; not only will this protect the tyres, but will also ensure that no load is placed on the steering head or wheel bearings.
● Deflate each tyre by 5 to 10 psi, no more or the beads may unseat from the rim, making subsequent inflation difficult on tubeless tyres.

Pivots and controls

● Lubricate all lever, pedal, stand and footrest pivot points. If grease nipples are fitted to the rear suspension components, apply lubricant to the pivots.
● Lubricate all control cables.

Cycle components

● Apply a wax protectant to all painted and plastic components. Wipe off any excess, but don't polish to a shine. Where fitted, clean the screen with soap and water.
● Coat metal parts with Vaseline (petroleum jelly). When applying this to the fork tubes, do not compress the forks otherwise the seals will rot from contact with the Vaseline.
● Apply a vinyl cleaner to the seat.

Storage conditions

● Aim to store the bike in a shed or garage which does not leak and is free from damp.
● Drape an old blanket or bedspread over the bike to protect it from dust and direct contact with sunlight (which will fade paint). This also hides the bike from prying eyes. Beware of tight-fitting plastic covers which may allow condensation to form and settle on the bike.

Getting back on the road

Engine and transmission

● Change the oil and replace the oil filter. If this was done prior to storage, check that the oil hasn't emulsified - a thick whitish substance which occurs through condensation.
● Remove the spark plugs. Using a spout-type oil can, squirt a few drops of oil into the cylinder(s). This will provide initial lubrication as the piston rings and bores comes back into contact. Service the spark plugs, or fit new ones, and install them in the engine.

● Check that the clutch isn't stuck on. The plates can stick together if left standing for some time, preventing clutch operation. Engage a gear and try rocking the bike back and forth with the clutch lever held against the handlebar. If this doesn't work on cable-operated clutches, hold the clutch lever back against the handlebar with a strong elastic band or cable tie for a couple of hours **(see illustration 8)**.
● If the air intakes or silencer end(s) were blocked off, remove the bung or cover used.
● If the fuel tank was coated with a rust

Hold clutch lever back against the handlebar with elastic bands or a cable tie

preventative, oil or a stabiliser added to the fuel, drain and flush the tank and dispose of the fuel sensibly. If no action was taken with the fuel tank prior to storage, it is advised that the old fuel is disposed of since it will go off over a period of time. Refill the fuel tank with fresh fuel.

Frame and running gear

● Oil all pivot points and cables.
● Check the tyre pressures. They will definitely need inflating if pressures were reduced for storage.
● Lubricate the final drive chain (where applicable).
● Remove any protective coating applied to the fork tubes (stanchions) since this may well destroy the fork seals. If the fork tubes weren't protected and have picked up rust spots, remove them with very fine abrasive paper and refinish with metal polish.
● Check that both brakes operate correctly. Apply each brake hard and check that it's not possible to move the motorcycle forwards, then check that the brake frees off again once released. Brake caliper pistons can stick due to corrosion around the piston head, or on the sliding caliper types, due to corrosion of the slider pins. If the brake doesn't free after repeated operation, take the caliper off for examination. Similarly drum brakes can stick due to a seized operating cam, cable or rod linkage.
● If the motorcycle has been in long-term storage, renew the brake fluid and clutch fluid (where applicable).
● Depending on where the bike has been stored, the wiring, cables and hoses may have been nibbled by rodents. Make a visual check and investigate disturbed wiring loom tape.

Battery

● If the battery has been previously removal and given top up charges it can simply be reconnected. Remember to connect the positive cable first and the negative cable last.
● On conventional refillable batteries, if the battery has not received any attention, remove it from the motorcycle and check its electrolyte level. Top up if necessary then charge the battery. If the battery fails to hold a charge and a visual checks show heavy white sulphation of the plates, the battery is probably defective and must be renewed. This is particularly likely if the battery is old. Confirm battery condition with a specific gravity check.
● On sealed (MF) batteries, if the battery has not received any attention, remove it from the motorcycle and charge it according to the information on the battery case - if the battery fails to hold a charge it must be renewed.

Starting procedure

● If a kickstart is fitted, turn the engine over a couple of times with the ignition OFF to distribute oil around the engine. If no kickstart is fitted, flick the engine kill switch OFF and the ignition ON and crank the engine over a couple of times to work oil around the upper cylinder components. If the nature of the ignition system is such that the starter won't work with the kill switch OFF, remove the spark plugs, fit them back into their caps and earth (ground) their bodies on the cylinder head. Reinstall the spark plugs afterwards.
● Switch the kill switch to RUN, operate the choke and start the engine. If the engine won't start don't continue cranking the engine - not only will this flatten the battery, but the starter motor will overheat. Switch the ignition off and try again later. If the engine refuses to start, go through the fault finding procedures in this manual. **Note:** *If the bike has been in storage for a long time, old fuel or a carburettor blockage may be the problem. Gum deposits in carburettors can block jets - if a carburettor cleaner doesn't prove successful the carburettors must be dismantled for cleaning.*

● Once the engine has started, check that the lights, turn signals and horn work properly.

● Treat the bike gently for the first ride and check all fluid levels on completion. Settle the bike back into the maintenance schedule.

This Section provides an easy reference-guide to the more common faults that are likely to afflict your machine. Obviously, the opportunities are almost limitless for faults to occur as a result of obscure failures, and to try and cover all eventualities would require a book. Indeed, a number have been written on the subject.

Successful troubleshooting is not a mysterious 'black art' but the application of a bit of knowledge combined with a systematic and logical approach to the problem. Approach any troubleshooting by first accurately identifying the symptom and then checking through the list of possible causes, starting with the simplest or most obvious and progressing in stages to the most complex.

Take nothing for granted, but above all apply liberal quantities of common sense.

The main symptom of a fault is given in the text as a major heading below which are listed the various systems or areas which may contain the fault. Details of each possible cause for a fault and the remedial action to be taken are given, in brief, in the paragraphs below each heading. Further information should be sought in the relevant Chapter.

1 Engine doesn't start or is difficult to start

- [ ] Starter motor doesn't rotate
- [ ] Starter motor rotates but engine does not turn over
- [ ] Starter works but engine won't turn over (seized
- [ ] No fuel flow
- [ ] Engine flooded
- [ ] No spark or weak spark
- [ ] Compression low
- [ ] Stalls after starting
- [ ] Rough idle

2 Poor running at low speed

- [ ] Spark weak
- [ ] Fuel/air mixture incorrect
- [ ] Compression low
- [ ] Poor acceleration

3 Poor running or no power at high speed

- [ ] Firing incorrect
- [ ] Fuel/air mixture incorrect
- [ ] Compression low
- [ ] Knocking or pinging
- [ ] Miscellaneous causes

4 Overheating

- [ ] Engine overheats
- [ ] Firing incorrect
- [ ] Fuel/air mixture incorrect
- [ ] Compression too high
- m Engine load excessive
- [ ] Lubrication inadequate
- [ ] Miscellaneous causes

5 Clutch problems

- [ ] Clutch slipping
- [ ] Clutch not disengaging completely

6 Gearchange problems

- [ ] Doesn't go into gear, or lever doesn't return
- [ ] Jumps out of gear
- [ ] Overselects

7 Abnormal engine noise

- [ ] Knocking or pinging
- [ ] Piston slap or rattling
- [ ] Valve noise
- [ ] Other noise

8 Abnormal driveline noise

- [ ] Clutch noise
- [ ] Transmission noise
- [ ] Final drive noise

9 Abnormal frame and suspension noise

- [ ] Front end noise
- [ ] Shock absorber noise
- [ ] Brake noise

10 Oil pressure indicator light comes on

- [ ] Engine lubrication system
- [ ] Electrical system

11 Excessive exhaust smoke

- [ ] White smoke
- [ ] Black smoke
- [ ] Brown smoke

12 Poor handling or stability

- [ ] Handlebar hard to turn
- [ ] Handlebar shakes or vibrates excessively
- [ ] Handlebar pulls to one side
- [ ] Poor shock absorbing qualities

13 Braking problems

- [ ] Brakes are spongy, don't hold
- [ ] Brake lever or pedal pulsates
- [ ] Brakes drag

14 Electrical problems

- [ ] Battery dead or weak
- [ ] Battery overcharged

1 Engine doesn't start or is difficult to start

Starter motor doesn't rotate

☐ Engine kill switch OFF.
☐ Fuse blown. Check main fuse and starter circuit fuse (Chapter 8).
☐ Battery voltage low. Check and recharge battery (Chapter 8).
☐ Starter motor defective. Make sure the wiring to the starter is secure. Make sure the starter relay clicks when the start button is pushed. If the relay clicks, then the fault is in the wiring or motor.
☐ Starter relay faulty. Check it according to the procedure in Chapter 8.
☐ Starter switch not contacting. The contacts could be wet, corroded or dirty. Disassemble and clean the switch (Chapter 8).
☐ Wiring open or shorted. Check all wiring connections and harnesses to make sure that they are dry, tight and not corroded. Also check for broken or frayed wires that can cause a short to earth (see wiring diagram, Chapter 8).
☐ Ignition (main) switch defective. Check the switch according to the procedure in Chapter 8. Replace the switch with a new one if it is defective.
☐ Engine kill switch defective. Check for wet, dirty or corroded contacts. Clean or replace the switch as necessary (Chapter 8).

Starter motor rotates but engine does not turn over

☐ Starter motor clutch defective. Inspect and repair or replace (Chapter 2).
☐ Damaged idle or starter gears. Inspect and replace the damaged parts (Chapter 2).

Starter works but engine won't turn over (seized)

☐ Seized engine caused by one or more internally damaged components. Failure due to wear, abuse or lack of lubrication. Damage can include seized valves, camshafts, pistons, crankshaft, connecting rod bearings, or transmission gears or bearings. Refer to Chapter 2 for engine disassembly.

No fuel flow

☐ No fuel in tank.
☐ Fuel pump failure (see Chapter 3A, 3B or Chapter 8 according to model).
☐ Fuel filter blocked (see Chapter 1).
☐ Fuel tank breather hose (early SS/SL models) or breather hole in filler cap (all other models) obstructed.
☐ Fuel line clogged. Refer to Chapter 3A or B for fuel line detachment details.
☐ Float needle valve clogged (carburettor models). For the valve in both carburettors to be clogged, either a very bad batch of fuel with an unusual additive has been used, or some other foreign material has entered the tank. Many times after a machine has been stored for many months without running, the fuel turns to a varnish-like liquid and forms deposits on the inlet needle valves and jets. The carburettors should be removed and overhauled if draining the float chambers doesn't solve the problem.
☐ Faulty injection system relay or injectors (see Chapter 3B)

Engine flooded – carburettor models

☐ Float height too high – refer to the Note in Chapter 3A.
☐ Float needle valve worn or stuck open. A piece of dirt, rust or other debris can cause the valve to seat improperly, causing excess fuel to be admitted to the float chamber. In this case, the float chamber should be cleaned and the needle valve and seat inspected. If the needle and seat are worn, then the leaking will persist and the parts should be replaced with new ones (Chapter 3A).
☐ Starting technique incorrect. Under normal circumstances the machine should start with little or no throttle. When the engine is cold, the choke should be ON and the engine started without opening the throttle. When the engine is at operating temperature, only a very slight amount of throttle should be necessary.

Engine flooded – fuel injection models

☐ Faulty pressure regulator – if it is stuck closed there could be excessive pressure in the fuel rail. Check as described in Chapter 4.
☐ Injector(s) stuck open, allowing a constant flow of fuel into the engine. Check as described in Chapter 4.
☐ Starting technique incorrect. When the engine is cold, use the fast idle lever on the handlebar and no throttle. When the engine is warm use a small amount of throttle.

No spark or weak spark

☐ Ignition switch OFF.
☐ Engine kill switch turned to the OFF position.
☐ Battery voltage low. Check and recharge the battery as necessary (Chapter 8).
☐ Spark plugs dirty, defective or worn out. Locate reason for fouled plugs using spark plug condition chart and follow the plug maintenance procedures (Chapter 1).
☐ Spark plug caps or secondary (HT) wiring faulty. Check condition. Replace either or both components if cracks or deterioration are evident (Chapter 4).
☐ Spark plug caps not making good contact. Make sure that the plug caps fit snugly over the plug ends.
☐ Ignition control unit or ECU (according to model) defective. Check the unit, referring to Chapter 3B or 4 for details.
☐ Pick-up coil or timing sensor (according to model) defective. Check the unit, referring to Chapter 3B or 4 for details.
☐ Ignition HT coils defective. Check the coils, referring to Chapter 4.
☐ Ignition or kill switch shorted. This is usually caused by water, corrosion, damage or excessive wear. The switches can be disassembled and cleaned with electrical contact cleaner. If cleaning does not help, replace the switches (Chapter 8).
☐ Wiring shorted or broken between:
 a) Ignition (main) switch and general relay
 b) General relay and engine kill switch (or blown fuse)
 c) Engine kill switch and HT coils
 d) Ignition HT coils and spark plugs
 e) Ignition control units and pick-up coils
 f) Ignition control units and HT coils
☐ Make sure that all wiring connections are clean, dry and tight. Look for chafed and broken wires (Chapters 4 and 8).

Compression low

☐ Spark plugs loose. Remove the plugs and inspect their threads. Reinstall and tighten to the specified torque (Chapter 1).
☐ Cylinder head not sufficiently tightened down. If the cylinder head is suspected of being loose, then there's a chance that the sealing surfaces are damaged or that a cylinder stud has broken. The head nuts should be tightened to the proper torque in the correct sequence (Chapter 2).
☐ Improper valve clearance. This means that the valve is not closing completely and compression pressure is leaking past the valve. Check and adjust the valve clearances (Chapter 1).
☐ Cylinder and/or piston worn. Excessive wear will cause compression pressure to leak past the rings. This is usually accompanied by worn rings as well. A top-end overhaul is necessary (Chapter 2).
☐ Piston rings worn, weak, broken, or sticking. Broken or sticking piston rings usually indicate a lubrication or carburation problem that causes excess carbon deposits or seizures to form on the pistons and rings. Top-end overhaul is necessary (Chapter 2).

1 Engine doesn't start or is difficult to start (continued)

Compression low (continued)

☐ Piston ring-to-groove clearance excessive. This is caused by excessive wear of the piston ring lands. Piston replacement is necessary (Chapter 2).

☐ Cylinder head warped. This is caused by overheating or improperly tightened head nuts. Machine shop resurfacing or head replacement is necessary (Chapter 2).

☐ Valve not seating properly. This is caused by a bent valve (from over-revving or improper valve adjustment), burned valve or seat (improper carburation) or an accumulation of carbon deposits on the seat (from carburation or lubrication problems). The valves must be cleaned and/or replaced and the seats serviced if possible (Chapter 2).

Stalls after starting

☐ Improper choke action. Check the choke operating cable and choke linkage on the carburettors (Chapter 3A).

☐ Ignition malfunction. See Chapter 4.

☐ Carburettor or fuel injection system malfunction. See Chapter 3A or B.

☐ Fuel contaminated. The fuel can be contaminated with either dirt or water, or can change chemically if the machine is allowed to sit for several months or more. Drain the tank and float chambers (Chapter 3A).

☐ Intake air leak. On carburettor models check for a loose joint at the carburettor inlet ducts, loose or missing vacuum gauge adapter screws or hoses, or loose carburettor tops (Chapter 3A). On all models check the ducts between the carburettors or throttle bodies and the cylinder head.

☐ Engine idle speed incorrect (see Chapter 1).

Rough idle

☐ Ignition malfunction. See Chapter 4.

☐ Idle speed incorrect. See Chapter 1.

☐ Carburettors or throttle bodies not synchronised. Adjust as described in Chapter 1.

☐ Carburettor or fuel injection system malfunction. See Chapter 3A or B.

☐ Fuel contaminated. The fuel can be contaminated with either dirt or water, or can change chemically if the machine is allowed to sit for several months or more. Drain the tank and float chambers (Chapter 3A).

☐ Intake air leak. Check for a loose joint at the carburettor inlet ducts, loose or missing vacuum gauge adapter screws or hoses, or loose carburettor tops (Chapter 3A).

☐ Air filter clogged. Replace the air filter element (Chapter 1).

2 Poor running at low speeds

Spark weak

☐ Battery voltage low. Check and recharge battery (Chapter 8).

☐ Spark plugs fouled, defective or worn out. Refer to Chapter 1 for spark plug maintenance.

☐ Spark plug cap or HT wiring defective. Refer to Chapters 1 and 4 for details on the ignition system.

☐ Spark plug caps not making contact.

☐ Incorrect spark plugs. Wrong type, heat range or cap configuration. Check and install correct plugs listed in Chapter 1.

☐ Ignition control unit defective. See Chapter 4.

☐ Pick-up coil defective. See Chapter 4.

☐ Ignition HT coils defective. See Chapter 4.

Fuel/air mixture incorrect – carburettor models

☐ Pilot screws out of adjustment (Chapter 3A).

☐ Pilot jet or air passage clogged. Remove and overhaul the carburettors (Chapter 3A).

☐ Air bleed holes clogged. Remove carburettor and blow out all passages (Chapter 3A).

☐ Air filter clogged, poorly sealed or missing (Chapter 1).

☐ Air filter housing poorly sealed. Look for cracks, holes or loose clamps and replace or repair defective parts.

☐ Fuel level too high or too low – refer to Note in Chapter 3A concerning float height.

☐ Fuel tank breather hose (SS/SL models) or breather hole in filler cap (Monsters) obstructed.

☐ Carburettor inlet ducts loose or gasket leaking. Check the inlet duct adapters for cracks, breaks, tears or loose clamps. Replace the adapters if split or perished.

Fuel/air mixture incorrect – fuel injection models

☐ Fuel injection system malfunction (see Chapter 4).

☐ Fuel injector clogged (see Chapter 4).

☐ Fuel pump or pressure regulator faulty (see Chapter 4).

☐ Throttle body intake manifolds loose. Check for cracks, breaks, tears or loose clamps. Renew the rubber intake manifold joints if split or perished.

☐ Air filter clogged, poorly sealed or missing (Chapter 1).

☐ Air filter housing poorly sealed. Look for cracks, holes or loose clamps and renew or repair defective parts.

☐ Fuel tank breather hose obstructed.

Compression low

☐ Spark plugs loose. Remove the plugs and inspect their threads. Reinstall and tighten to the specified torque (Chapter 1).

☐ Cylinder head not sufficiently tightened down. If the cylinder head is suspected of being loose, then there's a chance that the sealing surfaces are damaged or that a cylinder stud has broken. The head nuts should be tightened to the proper torque in the correct sequence (Chapter 2).

☐ Improper valve clearance. This means that the valve is not closing completely and compression pressure is leaking past the valve. Check and adjust the valve clearances (Chapter 1).

☐ Cylinder and/or piston worn. Excessive wear will cause compression pressure to leak past the rings. This is usually accompanied by worn rings as well. A top-end overhaul is necessary (Chapter 2).

☐ Piston rings worn, weak, broken, or sticking. Broken or sticking piston rings usually indicate a lubrication or carburation problem that causes excess carbon deposits or seizures to form on the pistons and rings. Top-end overhaul is necessary (Chapter 2).

☐ Piston ring-to-groove clearance excessive. This is caused by excessive wear of the piston ring lands. Piston replacement is necessary (Chapter 2).

☐ Cylinder head warped. This is caused by overheating or improperly tightened head nuts. Machine shop resurfacing or head replacement is necessary (Chapter 2).

☐ Valve not seating properly. This is caused by a bent valve (from over-revving or improper valve adjustment), burned valve or seat (improper carburation) or an accumulation of carbon deposits on the seat (carburation, lubrication problems). The valves must be cleaned and/or replaced and the seats serviced if possible (Chapter 2).

2 Poor running at low speeds

Poor acceleration

☐ Carburettors or throttle bodies leaking or dirty. Overhaul them (Chapter 3A).

☐ Fuel injection system malfunction, faulty fuel pump, or pressure regulator – see Chapter 4.

☐ Timing not advancing. The pick-up coils or the ignition control units (carburettor models), or the timing sensor or ECU (fuel injection models) may be defective. If so, they must be replaced

with new ones, as they can't be repaired.

☐ Carburettors or throttle bodies not synchronised. Adjust them (Chapter 1).

☐ Engine oil viscosity too high. Using a heavier oil than that recommended in Chapter 1 can damage the oil pump or lubrication system and cause drag on the engine.

☐ Brakes dragging. Usually caused by debris which has entered the brake piston seals, or from a warped disc or bent axle. Repair as necessary (Chapter 6).

3 Poor running or no power at high speed

Firing incorrect

☐ Air filter restricted. Clean or replace filter (Chapter 1).

☐ Spark plugs fouled, defective or worn out. See Chapter 1 for spark plug maintenance.

☐ Spark plug caps or HT wiring defective. See Chapters 1 and 4 for details of the ignition system.

☐ Spark plug caps not in good contact. See Chapter 4.

☐ Incorrect spark plugs. Wrong type, heat range or cap configuration. Check and install correct plugs listed in Chapter 1.

☐ Ignition control unit defective. See Chapter 4.

☐ Ignition HT coils defective. See Chapter 4.

Fuel/air mixture incorrect – carburettor models

☐ Main jet clogged. Dirt, water or other contaminants can clog the main jets. Clean the fuel filters, the float chamber area, and the jets and carburettor orifices (Chapter 3A).

☐ Main jet wrong size. The standard jetting is for sea level atmospheric pressure and oxygen content.

☐ Air bleed holes clogged. Remove and overhaul carburettors (Chapter 3A).

☐ Air filter clogged, poorly sealed, or missing (Chapter 1).

☐ Air filter housing poorly sealed. Look for cracks, holes or loose clamps, and replace or repair defective parts (Chapter 3A).

☐ Fuel level too high or too low – refer to the Note concerning float height in Chapter 3A.

☐ Fuel tank breather hose (SS/SL models) or breather hole in filler cap (Monsters) obstructed.

☐ Carburettor inlet ducts loose or gasket leaking. Check the inlet duct adapters for cracks, breaks, tears or loose clamps. Replace the adapters if split or perished.

Fuel/air mixture incorrect – fuel injection models

☐ Fuel injection system malfunction (see Chapter 4).

☐ Fuel injector clogged (see Chapter 4).

☐ Fuel pump or pressure regulator faulty (see Chapter 4).

☐ Throttle body intake manifolds loose. Check for cracks, breaks, tears or loose clamps. Renew the rubber intake manifold joints if split or perished.

☐ Air filter clogged, poorly sealed or missing (Chapter 1).

☐ Air filter housing poorly sealed. Look for cracks, holes or loose clamps and renew or repair defective parts.

☐ Fuel tank breather hose obstructed.

Compression low

☐ Spark plugs loose. Remove the plugs and inspect their threads. Reinstall and tighten to the specified torque (Chapter 1).

☐ Cylinder head not sufficiently tightened down. If the cylinder head is suspected of being loose, then there's a chance that the sealing surfaces are damaged or that a cylinder stud has broken. The head nuts should be tightened to the proper torque in the correct sequence (Chapter 2).

☐ Improper valve clearance. This means that the valve is not closing

completely and compression pressure is leaking past the valve. Check and adjust the valve clearances (Chapter 1).

☐ Cylinder and/or piston worn. Excessive wear will cause compression pressure to leak past the rings. This is usually accompanied by worn rings as well. A top-end overhaul is necessary (Chapter 2).

☐ Piston rings worn, weak, broken, or sticking. Broken or sticking piston rings usually indicate a lubrication or carburation problem that causes excess carbon deposits or seizures to form on the pistons and rings. Top-end overhaul is necessary (Chapter 2).

☐ Piston ring-to-groove clearance excessive. This is caused by excessive wear of the piston ring lands. Piston replacement is necessary (Chapter 2).

☐ Cylinder head warped. This is caused by overheating or improperly tightened head nuts. Machine shop resurfacing or head replacement is necessary (Chapter 2).

☐ Valve not seating properly. This is caused by a bent valve (from over-revving or improper valve adjustment), burned valve or seat (improper carburation) or an accumulation of carbon deposits on the seat (from carburation or lubrication problems). The valves must be cleaned and/or replaced and the seats serviced if possible (Chapter 2).

Knocking or pinking

☐ Carbon build-up in combustion chamber. Use of a fuel additive that will dissolve the adhesive bonding the carbon particles to the crown and chamber is the easiest way to remove the build-up. Otherwise, the cylinder head will have to be removed and decarbonised (Chapter 2).

☐ Incorrect or poor quality fuel. Old or improper grades of fuel can cause detonation. This causes the piston to rattle, thus the knocking or pinging sound. Drain old fuel and always use the recommended fuel grade.

☐ Spark plug heat range incorrect. Uncontrolled detonation indicates the plug heat range is too hot. The plug in effect becomes a glow plug, raising cylinder temperatures. Install the proper heat range plug (Chapter 1).

☐ Improper air/fuel mixture. This will cause the cylinder to run hot, which leads to detonation. Clogged jets or an air leak can cause this imbalance. See Chapter 3A or B.

Miscellaneous causes

☐ Throttle valve doesn't open fully. Adjust the throttle cable freeplay (Chapter 1).

☐ Clutch slipping. May be caused by loose or worn clutch components. Refer to Chapter 2 for clutch overhaul procedures.

☐ Timing not advancing (see Chapter 4).

☐ Engine oil viscosity too high. Using a heavier oil than the one recommended in Chapter 1 can damage the oil pump or lubrication system and cause drag on the engine.

☐ Brakes dragging. Usually caused by debris which has entered the brake piston seals, or from a warped disc or bent axle. Repair as necessary (Chapter 6).

4 Overheating

Firing incorrect

☐ Spark plugs fouled, defective or worn out. See Chapter 1 for spark plug maintenance.
☐ Incorrect spark plugs.
☐ Faulty ignition HT coils (Chapter 4).

Fuel/air mixture incorrect – carburettor models

☐ Main jet clogged. Dirt, water and other contaminants can clog the main jets. Clean the fuel filters, the float chamber area and the jets and carburettor orifices (Chapter 3A).
☐ Main jet wrong size. The standard jetting is for sea level atmospheric pressure and oxygen content.
☐ Air filter clogged, poorly sealed or missing (Chapter 1).
☐ Air filter housing poorly sealed. Look for cracks, holes or loose clamps and replace or repair (Chapter 3A).
☐ Fuel level too low – refer to the Note in Chapter 3A concerning float height.
☐ Fuel tank breather hose (SS/SL models) or breather hole in filler cap (Monsters) obstructed.
☐ Carburettor inlet ducts loose or gasket leaking. Check the inlet duct adapters for cracks, breaks, tears or loose clamps. Replace the adapters if split or perished.

Fuel/air mixture incorrect – fuel injection models

☐ Fuel injection system malfunction (see Chapter 4).
☐ Fuel injector clogged (see Chapter 4).
☐ Fuel pump or pressure regulator faulty (see Chapter 4).
☐ Throttle body intake manifolds loose. Check for cracks, breaks, tears or loose clamps. Renew the rubber intake manifold joints if split or perished.
☐ Air filter clogged, poorly sealed or missing (Chapter 1).
☐ Air filter housing poorly sealed. Look for cracks, holes or loose clamps and renew or repair defective parts.
☐ Fuel tank breather hose obstructed.

Compression too high

☐ Carbon build-up in combustion chamber. Use of a fuel additive that will dissolve the adhesive bonding the carbon particles to the piston crown and chamber is the easiest way to remove the build-up. Otherwise, the cylinder head will have to be removed and decarbonised (Chapter 2).

Engine load excessive

☐ Clutch slipping. Can be caused by damaged, loose or worn clutch components. Refer to Chapter 2 for overhaul procedures.
☐ Engine oil level too high. The addition of too much oil will cause pressurisation of the crankcase and inefficient engine operation. Check oil level (Daily (pre-ride) checks).
☐ Engine oil viscosity too high. Using a heavier oil than the one recommended in Chapter 1 can damage the oil pump or lubrication system as well as cause drag on the engine.
☐ Brakes dragging. Usually caused by debris which has entered the brake piston seals, or from a warped disc or bent axle. Repair as necessary (Chapter 6).

Lubrication inadequate

☐ Engine oil level too low. Friction caused by intermittent lack of lubrication or from oil that is overworked can cause overheating. The oil provides a definite cooling function in the engine. Check the oil level (Chapter 1).
☐ Poor quality engine oil or incorrect viscosity or type. Oil is rated not only according to viscosity but also according to type. Some oils are not rated high enough for use in this engine. Check the Specifications section and change to the correct oil (Chapter 1).
☐ Oil cooler matrix blocked or oil cooler pipes damaged (Chapter 2).

Miscellaneous causes

☐ Modification to exhaust system. Most aftermarket exhaust systems cause the engine to run leaner, which make them run hotter. When installing an accessory exhaust system, always check whether it is necessary to rejet the carburettors.

5 Clutch problems

Clutch slipping

☐ No clutch lever freeplay. Check and adjust (Chapter 1).
☐ Excess fluid in clutch reservoir (Daily (pre-ride) checks).
☐ Friction plates worn or warped. Overhaul the clutch assembly (Chapter 2).
☐ Plain plates warped (Chapter 2).
☐ Clutch springs broken or weak. Old or heat-damaged (from slipping clutch) springs should be replaced with new ones (Chapter 2).
☐ Clutch release mechanism defective. Replace any defective parts (Chapter 2).
☐ Clutch centre or housing worn. This causes improper engagement of the plates. Replace the damaged or worn parts (Chapter 2).

Clutch not disengaging completely (drag)

☐ Insufficient fluid in clutch reservoir (Daily (pre-ride) checks).

☐ Air in hydraulic line. Bleed clutch (Chapter 2).
☐ Clutch plates warped or damaged. This will cause clutch drag, which in turn will cause the machine to creep. Overhaul the clutch assembly (Chapter 2).
☐ Clutch spring tension uneven. Usually caused by a sagged or broken spring. Check and replace the springs as a set (Chapter 2).
☐ Engine oil deteriorated on wet clutches. Old, thin, worn out oil will not provide proper lubrication for the plates, causing the clutch to drag. Replace the oil and filter (Chapter 1).
☐ Engine oil viscosity too high on wet clutches. Using a heavier oil than recommended in Chapter 1 can cause the plates to stick together, putting a drag on the engine. Change to the correct weight oil (Chapter 1).
☐ Clutch release mechanism defective (Chapter 2).
☐ Loose clutch centre nut. Causes drum and centre misalignment putting a drag on the engine. Engagement adjustment continually varies. Overhaul the clutch assembly (Chapter 2).

6 Gearchange problems

Doesn't go into gear or lever doesn't return

- [ ] Clutch not disengaging. See Section 5.
- [ ] Selector fork(s) bent or seized. Often caused by dropping the machine or from lack of lubrication. Overhaul the transmission (Chapter 2).
- [ ] Selector drum endfloat excessive. Check and re-shim if necessary (Chapter 2).
- [ ] Gear(s) stuck on shaft. Most often caused by a lack of lubrication or excessive wear in transmission bearings and bushings. Overhaul the transmission (Chapter 2).
- [ ] Selector drum binding. Caused by lubrication failure or excessive wear (Chapter 2).
- [ ] Gearchange lever return spring weak or broken (Chapter 2).
- [ ] Gearchange lever broken. Splines stripped out of lever or shaft,

caused by allowing the lever to get loose or from dropping the machine. Replace necessary parts (Chapter 2).
- [ ] Gearchange mechanism centring incorrect (Chapter 2).

Jumps out of gear

- [ ] Selector fork(s) worn. Overhaul the transmission (Chapter 2).
- [ ] Gear groove(s) worn. Overhaul the transmission (Chapter 2).
- [ ] Gear dogs or dog slots worn or damaged. The gears should be inspected and replaced. No attempt should be made to service the worn parts.
- [ ] Gearchange mechanism centring incorrect (Chapter 2).

Overselects

- [ ] Selector drum detent assembly malfunctioning (Chapter 2).
- [ ] Gearchange mechanism centring incorrect (Chapter 2).

7 Abnormal engine noise

Knocking or pinking

- [ ] Carbon build-up in combustion chamber. Use of a fuel additive that will dissolve the adhesive bonding the carbon particles to the piston crown and chamber is the easiest way to remove the build-up. Otherwise, the cylinder head will have to be removed and decarbonised (Chapter 2).
- [ ] Incorrect or poor quality fuel. Old or improper fuel can cause detonation. This causes the pistons to rattle, thus the knocking or pinking sound. Drain the old fuel and always use the recommended grade fuel (Chapter 3A).
- [ ] Spark plug heat range incorrect. Uncontrolled detonation indicates that the plug heat range is too hot. The plug in effect becomes a glow plug, raising cylinder temperatures. Install the proper heat range plug (Chapter 1).
- [ ] Improper air/fuel mixture. This will cause the cylinders to run hot and lead to detonation. Clogged jets or an air leak can cause this imbalance. See Chapter 3A or B.

Piston slap or rattling

- [ ] Cylinder-to-piston clearance excessive. Caused by improper assembly. Inspect and overhaul top-end parts (Chapter 2).
- [ ] Connecting rod bent. Caused by over-revving, trying to start a badly flooded engine or from ingesting a foreign object into the combustion chamber. Replace the damaged parts (Chapter 2).
- [ ] Piston pin or piston pin bore worn or seized from wear or lack of lubrication. Replace damaged parts (Chapter 2).
- [ ] Piston ring(s) worn, broken or sticking. Overhaul the top-end (Chapter 2).

- [ ] Piston seizure damage. Usually from lack of lubrication or overheating. Replace the pistons and bore the cylinders, as necessary (Chapter 2).
- [ ] Connecting rod upper or lower end clearance excessive. Caused by excessive wear or lack of lubrication. Replace worn parts.

Valve noise

- [ ] Incorrect valve clearances. Adjust the clearances by referring to Chapter 1.
- [ ] Camshaft or cylinder head worn or damaged. Lack of lubrication at high rpm is usually the cause of damage. Insufficient oil or failure to change the oil at the recommended intervals are the chief causes (Chapter 2).

Other noise

- [ ] Cylinder head-to-barrel joint leaking. Caused by damaged joint surface or broken cylinder stud.
- [ ] Exhaust pipe leaking at cylinder head connection. Caused by improper fit of pipe(s) or loose exhaust flange. All exhaust fasteners should be tightened evenly and carefully. Failure to do this will lead to a leak.
- [ ] Crankshaft runout excessive. Caused by a bent crankshaft (from over-revving) or damage from an upper cylinder component failure. Can also be attributed to dropping the machine on either of the crankshaft ends.
- [ ] Engine mounting bolts loose. Tighten all engine mount bolts (Chapter 2).
- [ ] Crankshaft bearings worn (Chapter 2).

8 Abnormal driveline noise

Clutch noise

- [ ] Clutch housing/friction plate clearance excessive (Chapter 2).
- [ ] Loose or damaged clutch pressure plate and/or bolts (Chapter 2).

Transmission noise

- [ ] Bearings worn. Also includes the possibility that the shafts are worn. Overhaul the transmission (Chapter 2).
- [ ] Gears worn or chipped (Chapter 2).

- [ ] Metal chips jammed in gear teeth. This will cause early bearing failure (Chapter 2).
- [ ] Engine oil level too low (Daily (pre-ride) checks). Causes a howl from transmission.

Final drive noise

- [ ] Incorrectly adjusted or worn drive chain and sprockets (Chapter 1).
- [ ] Worn cush drive in rear wheel hub (Chapter 6).
- [ ] Loose sprocket retaining bolts/nuts (Chapter 6).

9 Abnormal frame and suspension noise

Front end noise

☐ Low fluid level or improper viscosity oil in forks. This can sound like spurting and is usually accompanied by irregular fork action (Chapter 5).

☐ Spring weak or broken. Makes a clicking or scraping sound. Fork oil, when drained, will have a lot of metal particles in it (Chapter 5).

☐ Steering head bearings loose or damaged. Clicks when braking. Check and adjust or replace as necessary (Chapters 1 and 5).

☐ Fork yoke clamps loose. Make sure all clamp pinch bolts are tight (Chapter 5).

☐ Fork tube bent. Good possibility if machine has been dropped. Replace both tubes with a new ones (Chapter 5).

☐ Front wheel axle or axle clamp bolt loose. Tighten them to the specified torque (Chapter 6).

Shock absorber noise

☐ Fluid level incorrect. Indicates a leak caused by defective seal. Shock will be covered with oil. Replace shock or seek advice on repair from a Ducati dealer (Chapter 5).

☐ Defective shock absorber with internal damage. Have the shock overhauled by a Ducati dealer or suspension specialist.

Brake noise

☐ Squeal caused by dust on brake pads. Usually found in combination with glazed pads. Clean using brake cleaning solvent (Chapter 6).

☐ Contamination of brake pads. Oil, brake fluid or dirt causing brake to chatter or squeal. Clean or replace pads (Chapter 6).

☐ Pads glazed. Caused by excessive heat from prolonged use or from contamination. Do not use sandpaper, emery cloth, carborundum cloth or any other abrasive to roughen the pad surfaces as abrasives will stay in the pad material and damage the disc. A very fine flat file can be used, but pad replacement is suggested as a cure (Chapter 6).

☐ Disc warped. Can cause a chattering, clicking or intermittent squeal. Usually accompanied by a pulsating lever and uneven braking. Replace the disc (Chapter 6).

☐ Loose or worn wheel bearings. Check and replace as needed (Chapter 6).

10 Oil pressure indicator light comes on

Engine lubrication system

☐ Engine oil pump defective, blocked oil filter gauze or failed pressure relief valve. Carry out oil pressure check (Chapter 1).

☐ Engine oil level low. Inspect for leak or other problem causing low oil level and add recommended oil (Daily (pre-ride) checks).

☐ Engine oil viscosity too low. Very old, thin oil or an improper weight of oil used in the engine. Change to correct oil (Chapter 1).

☐ Blocked oilways in the crankshaft and cylinders.

Electrical system

☐ Oil pressure switch defective. Check the switch according to the procedure in Chapter 8. Replace it if it is defective.

☐ Oil pressure indicator light circuit defective. Check for pinched, shorted, disconnected or damaged wiring (Chapter 8).

11 Excessive exhaust smoke

White smoke

☐ Piston oil scraper ring worn. The ring may be broken or damaged, causing oil from the crankcase to be pulled past the piston into the combustion chamber. Replace the rings with new ones (Chapter 2).

☐ Cylinders worn, cracked, or scored. Caused by overheating or oil starvation. The cylinders will have to be renewed and new pistons installed – they cannot be rebored.

☐ Valve oil seal damaged or worn. Replace oil seals with new ones (Chapter 2).

☐ Valve guide worn. Perform a complete valve job (Chapter 2).

☐ Engine oil level too high, which causes the oil to be forced past the rings. Drain oil to the proper level (Daily (pre-ride) checks).

☐ Failure of an O-ring at cylinder head-to-barrel joint (Chapter 2).

☐ Abnormal crankcase pressurisation, which forces oil past the rings. Clogged crankcase breather is usually the cause.

Black smoke

☐ Air filter clogged. Clean or replace the element (Chapter 1).

☐ Main jet too large or loose. Compare the jet size to the Specifications (Chapter 3A).

☐ Choke cable or linkage shaft stuck, causing fuel to be pulled through choke circuit (Chapter 3A).

☐ Fuel level too high – refer to the Note concerning float height in Chapter 3A.

☐ Float needle valve held off needle seat. Clean the float chambers and fuel line and replace the needles and seats if necessary (Chapter 3A).

Brown smoke

☐ Main jet too small or clogged. Lean condition caused by wrong size main jet or by a restricted orifice. Clean float chambers and jets and compare jet size to Specifications (Chapter 3A).

☐ Fuel flow insufficient. Float needle valve stuck closed due to chemical reaction with old fuel. Float height incorrect. Restricted fuel line. Clean line and float chamber and adjust floats if necessary (Chapter 3A).

☐ Carburettor or throttle body inlet ducts loose, or inlet duct adapters leaking (Chapter 3A or B).

☐ Air filter poorly sealed or not installed (Chapter 1).

12 Poor handling or stability

Handlebar hard to turn

☐ Steering head bearing adjuster nut too tight. Check adjustment as described in Chapter 1.

☐ Bearings damaged. Roughness can be felt as the bars are turned from side-to-side. Replace bearings and races (Chapter 5).

☐ Races dented or worn. Denting results from wear in only one position (e.g. straightahead), from a collision or hitting a pothole or from dropping the machine. Replace races and bearings (Chapter 5).

☐ Steering stem lubrication inadequate. Causes are grease getting hard from age or being washed out by high pressure car washes. Disassemble steering head and repack bearings (Chapter 5).

☐ Steering stem bent. Caused by a collision, hitting a pothole or by dropping the machine. Replace damaged part. Don't try to straighten the steering stem (Chapter 5).

☐ Front tyre air pressure too low (Daily (pre-ride) checks).

Handlebar shakes or vibrates excessively

☐ Tyres worn or out of balance (Chapter 5).

☐ Swingarm bearings or pivot worn. Replace worn components (Chapter 5).

☐ Wheels warped or damaged. Inspect wheels for runout (Chapter 6).

☐ Wheel bearings worn. Worn front or rear wheel bearings can cause poor tracking. Worn front bearings will cause wobble (Chapter 6).

☐ Handlebar clamp bolts loose (Chapter 5).

☐ Fork yoke clamp bolts loose. Tighten them to the specified torque (Chapter 5).

☐ Engine mounting bolts loose. Will cause excessive vibration with increased engine rpm (Chapter 2).

Handlebar pulls to one side

☐ Frame bent. Definitely suspect this if the machine has been dropped. May or may not be accompanied by cracking near the bend. Replace the frame (Chapter 5).

☐ Wheels out of alignment. Caused by improper location of axle spacers or from bent steering stem or frame (Chapter 6).

☐ Swingarm bent or twisted. Caused by age (metal fatigue) or impact damage. Replace the arm (Chapter 5).

☐ Steering stem bent. Caused by impact damage or by dropping the motorcycle. Replace the steering stem (Chapter 5).

☐ Fork tube bent. Disassemble the forks and replace the damaged parts (Chapter 5).

☐ Fork oil level uneven. Check and add or drain as necessary (Chapter 5).

Poor shock absorbing qualities

☐ Too hard:

a) Fork oil level excessive (Chapter 5).

b) Fork oil viscosity too high. Use a lighter oil (see the Specifications in Chapter 5).

c) Fork tube bent. Causes a harsh, sticking feeling (Chapter 5).

d) Shock shaft or body bent or damaged (Chapter 5).

e) Fork internal damage (Chapter 5).

f) Shock internal damage (Chapter 5).

g) Tyre pressure too high (Daily (pre-ride) checks).

☐ Too soft:

a) Fork or shock oil insufficient and/or leaking (Chapter 5).

b) Fork oil level too low (Chapter 5).

c) Fork oil viscosity too light (Chapter 5).

d) Fork springs weak or broken (Chapter 5).

e) Shock internal damage or leakage (Chapter 5).

13 Braking problems

Brakes are spongy, don't hold

- [ ] Air in brake line. Caused by inattention to master cylinder fluid level or by leakage. Locate problem and bleed brakes (Chapter 6).
- [ ] Pad or disc worn (Chapters 1 and 6).
- [ ] Brake fluid leak from hoses or seals. Renew as necessary (Chapter 6).
- [ ] Contaminated pads. Caused by contamination with oil, grease, brake fluid, etc. Clean or replace pads. Clean disc thoroughly with brake cleaner (Chapter 6).
- [ ] Brake fluid deteriorated. Fluid is old or contaminated. Drain system, replenish with new fluid and bleed the system (Chapter 6).
- [ ] Master cylinder internal parts worn or damaged causing fluid to bypass (Chapter 6).
- [ ] Master cylinder bore scratched by foreign material or broken spring. Repair or replace master cylinder (Chapter 6).
- [ ] Disc warped. Replace disc (Chapter 6).

Brake lever or pedal pulsates

- [ ] Disc warped. Replace disc (Chapter 6).
- [ ] Wheel axle bent. Replace axle (Chapter 6).
- [ ] Brake caliper bolts loose (Chapter 6).
- [ ] Wheel warped or otherwise damaged (Chapter 6).
- [ ] Wheel bearings damaged or worn (Chapter 6).

Brakes drag

- [ ] Incorrect brake lever or pedal freeplay (Chapter 1).
- [ ] Master cylinder piston seized. Caused by wear or damage to piston or cylinder bore (Chapter 6).
- [ ] Lever balky or stuck. Check pivot and lubricate (Chapter 6).
- [ ] Brake caliper pistons seized in their bores. Caused by wear or ingestion of road salt and dirt past deteriorated seal (Chapter 6).
- [ ] Brake pad damaged. Pad material separated from backing plate. Usually caused by faulty manufacturing process or from contact with chemicals. Replace pads (Chapter 6).
- [ ] Pads improperly installed (Chapter 6).

14 Electrical problems

Battery dead or weak

- [ ] Battery faulty. Caused by sulphated plates which are shorted through sedimentation. Also, broken battery terminal making only occasional contact (Chapter 8). Refer to *Fault Finding Equipment* for battery voltage and specific gravity checks.
- [ ] Battery cables making poor contact (Chapter 8).
- [ ] Load excessive. Caused by addition of high wattage lights or other electrical accessories.
- [ ] Ignition (main) switch defective. Switch either earths internally or fails to shut off system. Replace the switch (Chapter 8).
- [ ] Regulator/rectifier defective (Chapter 8).
- [ ] Alternator stator coil open or shorted (Chapter 8).
- [ ] Wiring faulty. Wiring earthed or connections loose in ignition, charging or lighting circuits (Chapter 8).

Battery overcharged

- [ ] Regulator/rectifier defective. Overcharging is noticed when battery gets excessively warm (Chapter 8).
- [ ] Battery defective. Replace battery with a new one (Chapter 8).
- [ ] Battery amperage too low, wrong type or size. Install manufacturer's specified amp-hour battery to handle charging load (Chapter 8).

Checking engine compression

● Low compression will result in exhaust smoke, heavy oil consumption, poor starting and poor performance. A compression test will provide useful information about an engine's condition and if performed regularly, can give warning of trouble before any other symptoms become apparent.

● A compression gauge will be required, along with an adapter to suit the spark plug hole thread size. Note that the screw-in type gauge/adapter set up is preferable to the rubber cone type.

● Before carrying out the test, first check the valve clearances as described in Chapter 1.

1 Run the engine until it reaches normal operating temperature, then stop it and remove the spark plug(s), taking care not to scald your hands on the hot components.

2 Install the gauge adapter and compression gauge in No. 1 cylinder spark plug hole **(see illustration 1)**.

Screw the compression gauge adapter into the spark plug hole, then screw the gauge into the adapter

3 On kickstart-equipped motorcycles, make sure the ignition switch is OFF, then open the throttle fully and kick the engine over a couple of times until the gauge reading stabilises.

4 On motorcycles with electric start only, the procedure will differ depending on the nature of the ignition system. Flick the engine kill switch (engine stop switch) to OFF and turn the ignition switch ON; open the throttle fully and crank the engine over on the starter motor for a couple of revolutions until the gauge reading stabilises. If the starter will not operate with the kill switch OFF, turn the ignition switch OFF and refer to the next paragraph.

5 Install the plugs back in their caps and arrange the plug electrodes so that their metal bodies are earthed (grounded) against the cylinder heads; this is essential to prevent damage to the ignition system **(see illustration 2)**. Position the plugs well away from the plug holes otherwise there is a risk of

All spark plugs must be earthed (grounded) against the cylinder head

atomised fuel escaping from the plug holes and igniting. As a safety precaution, cover the cylinder head covers with rag and disconnect the fuel pump wiring connector (see Chapter 3A or B). Turn the ignition switch and kill switch ON, open the throttle fully and crank the engine over on the starter motor for a couple of revolutions until the gauge reading stabilises.

6 After one or two revolutions the pressure should build up to a maximum figure and then stabilise. Take a note of this reading and on multi-cylinder engines repeat the test on the remaining cylinders.

7 The correct pressures are given in Chapter 1 Specifications. If the results fall within the specified range and on multi-cylinder engines all are relatively equal, the engine is in good condition. If there is a marked difference between the readings, or if the readings are lower than specified, inspection of the top-end components will be required.

8 Low compression pressure may be due to worn cylinder bores, pistons or rings, failure of the cylinder head gasket, worn valve seals, or poor valve seating.

9 To distinguish between cylinder/piston wear and valve leakage, pour a small quantity of oil into the bore to temporarily seal the piston rings, then repeat the compression tests **(see illustration 3)**. If the readings show

Bores can be temporarily sealed with a squirt of motor oil

a noticeable increase in pressure this confirms that the cylinder bore, piston, or rings are worn. If, however, no change is indicated, the cylinder head gasket or valves should be examined.

10 High compression pressure indicates excessive carbon build-up in the combustion chamber and on the piston crown. If this is the case the cylinder head should be removed and the deposits removed. Note that excessive carbon build-up is less likely with the used on modern fuels.

Checking battery open-circuit voltage

 Warning: The gases produced by the battery are explosive - never smoke or create any sparks in the vicinity of the battery. Never allow the electrolyte to contact your skin or clothing - if it does, wash it off and seek immediate medical attention.

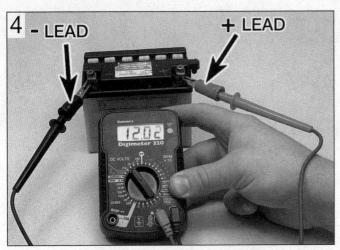

Measuring open-circuit battery voltage

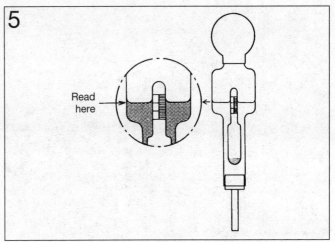

Float-type hydrometer for measuring battery specific gravity

● Before any electrical fault is investigated the battery should be checked.

● You'll need a dc voltmeter or multimeter to check battery voltage. Check that the leads are inserted in the correct terminals on the meter, red lead to positive (+ve), black lead to negative (-ve). Incorrect connections can damage the meter.

● A sound fully-charged 12 volt battery should produce between 12.3 and 12.6 volts across its terminals (12.8 volts for a maintenance-free battery). On machines with a 6 volt battery, voltage should be between 6.1 and 6.3 volts.

1 Set a multimeter to the 0 to 20 volts dc range and connect its probes across the battery terminals. Connect the meter's positive (+ve) probe, usually red, to the battery positive (+ve) terminal, followed by the meter's negative (-ve) probe, usually black, to the battery negative terminal (-ve) **(see illustration 4)**.

2 If battery voltage is low (below 10 volts on a 12 volt battery or below 4 volts on a six volt battery), charge the battery and test the voltage again. If the battery repeatedly goes flat, investigate the motorcycle's charging system.

Checking battery specific gravity (SG)

 Warning: The gases produced by the battery are explosive - never smoke or create any sparks in the vicinity of the battery. Never allow the electrolyte to contact your skin or clothing - if it does, wash it off and seek immediate medical attention.

● The specific gravity check gives an indication of a battery's state of charge.

● A hydrometer is used for measuring specific gravity. Make sure you purchase one

which has a small enough hose to insert in the aperture of a motorcycle battery.

● Specific gravity is simply a measure of the electrolyte's density compared with that of water. Water has an SG of 1.000 and fully-charged battery electrolyte is about 26% heavier, at 1.260.

● Specific gravity checks are not possible on maintenance-free batteries. Testing the open-circuit voltage is the only means of determining their state of charge.

1 To measure SG, remove the battery from the motorcycle and remove the first cell cap. Draw

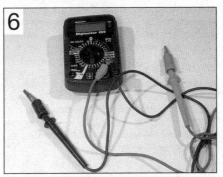

Digital multimeter can be used for all electrical tests

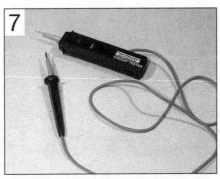

Battery-powered continuity tester

some electrolyte into the hydrometer and note the reading **(see illustration 5)**. Return the electrolyte to the cell and install the cap.

2 The reading should be in the region of 1.260 to 1.280. If SG is below 1.200 the battery needs charging. Note that SG will vary with temperature; it should be measured at 20°C (68°F). Add 0.007 to the reading for every 10°C above 20°C, and subtract 0.007 from the reading for every 10°C below 20°C. Add 0.004 to the reading for every 10°F above 68°F, and subtract 0.004 from the reading for every 10°F below 68°F.

3 When the check is complete, rinse the hydrometer thoroughly with clean water.

Checking for continuity

● The term continuity describes the uninterrupted flow of electricity through an electrical circuit. A continuity check will determine whether an **open-circuit** situation exists.

● Continuity can be checked with an ohmmeter, multimeter, continuity tester or battery and bulb test circuit **(see illustrations 6, 7 and 8)**.

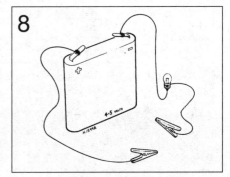

Battery and bulb test circuit

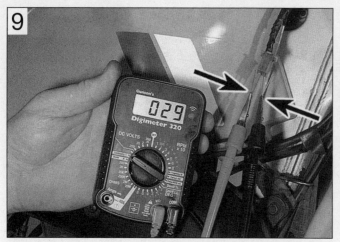

Continuity check of front brake light switch using a meter - note split pins used to access connector terminals

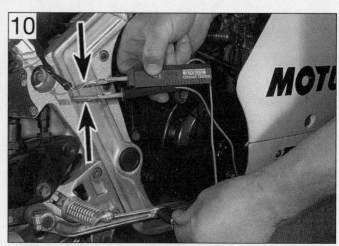

Continuity check of rear brake light switch using a continuity tester

● All of these instruments are self-powered by a battery, therefore the checks are made with the ignition OFF.

● As a safety precaution, always disconnect the battery negative (-ve) lead before making checks, particularly if ignition switch checks are being made.

● If using a meter, select the appropriate ohms scale and check that the meter reads infinity (∞). Touch the meter probes together and check that meter reads zero; where necessary adjust the meter so that it reads zero.

● After using a meter, always switch it OFF to conserve its battery.

Switch checks

1 If a switch is at fault, trace its wiring up to the wiring connectors. Separate the wire connectors and inspect them for security and condition. A build-up of dirt or corrosion here will most likely be the cause of the problem - clean up and apply a water dispersant such as WD40.

2 If using a test meter, set the meter to the ohms x 10 scale and connect its probes across the wires from the switch (see illustration 9). Simple ON/OFF type switches, such as brake light switches, only have two wires whereas combination switches, like the

ignition switch, have many internal links. Study the wiring diagram to ensure that you are connecting across the correct pair of wires. Continuity (low or no measurable resistance - 0 ohms) should be indicated with the switch ON and no continuity (high resistance) with it OFF.

3 Note that the polarity of the test probes doesn't matter for continuity checks, although care should be taken to follow specific test procedures if a diode or solid-state component is being checked.

4 A continuity tester or battery and bulb circuit can be used in the same way. Connect its probes as described above (see illustration 10). The light should come on to indicate continuity in the ON switch position, but should extinguish in the OFF position.

Wiring checks

● Many electrical faults are caused by damaged wiring, often due to incorrect routing or chaffing on frame components.

● Loose, wet or corroded wire connectors can also be the cause of electrical problems, especially in exposed locations.

1 A continuity check can be made on a single length of wire by disconnecting it at each end and connecting a meter or continuity tester

across both ends of the wire (see illustration 11).

2 Continuity (low or no resistance - 0 ohms) should be indicated if the wire is good. If no continuity (high resistance) is shown, suspect a broken wire.

Checking for voltage

● A voltage check can determine whether current is reaching a component.

● Voltage can be checked with a dc voltmeter, multimeter set on the dc volts scale, test light or buzzer (see illustrations 12 and 13). A meter has the advantage of being able to measure actual voltage.

● When using a meter, check that its leads are inserted in the correct terminals on the meter, red to positive (+ve), black to negative (-ve). Incorrect connections can damage the meter.

● A voltmeter (or multimeter set to the dc volts scale) should always be connected in parallel (across the load). Connecting it in series will not harm the meter, but the reading will not be meaningful.

● Voltage checks are made with the ignition ON.

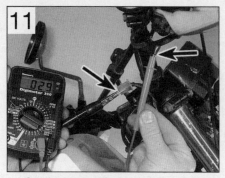

Continuity check of front brake light switch sub-harness

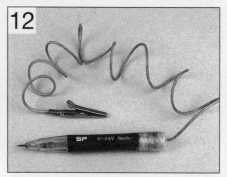

A simple test light can be used for voltage checks

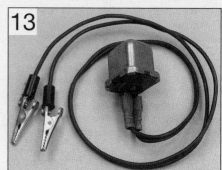

A buzzer is useful for voltage checks

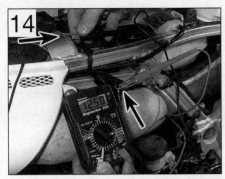

Checking for voltage at the rear brake light power supply wire using a meter . . .

1 First identify the relevant wiring circuit by referring to the wiring diagram at the end of this manual. If other electrical components share the same power supply (ie are fed from the same fuse), take note whether they are working correctly - this is useful information in deciding where to start checking the circuit.

2 If using a meter, check first that the meter leads are plugged into the correct terminals on the meter (see above). Set the meter to the dc volts function, at a range suitable for the battery voltage. Connect the meter red probe (+ve) to the power supply wire and the black probe to a good metal earth (ground) on the motorcycle's frame or directly to the battery negative (-ve) terminal **(see illustration 14)**. Battery voltage should be shown on the meter

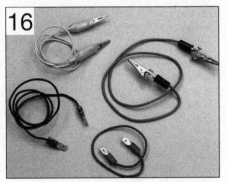

A selection of jumper wires for making earth (ground) checks

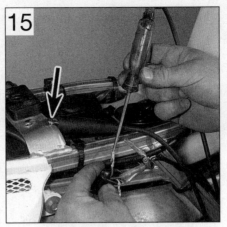

. . . or a test light - note the earth connection to the frame (arrow)

with the ignition switched ON.

3 If using a test light or buzzer, connect its positive (+ve) probe to the power supply terminal and its negative (-ve) probe to a good earth (ground) on the motorcycle's frame or directly to the battery negative (-ve) terminal **(see illustration 15)**. With the ignition ON, the test light should illuminate or the buzzer sound.

4 If no voltage is indicated, work back towards the fuse continuing to check for voltage. When you reach a point where there is voltage, you know the problem lies between that point and your last check point.

Checking the earth (ground)

● Earth connections are made either directly to the engine or frame (such as sensors, neutral switch etc. which only have a positive feed) or by a separate wire into the earth circuit of the wiring harness. Alternatively a short earth wire is sometimes run directly from the component to the motorcycle's frame.

● Corrosion is often the cause of a poor earth connection.

● If total failure is experienced, check the security of the main earth lead from the

negative (-ve) terminal of the battery and also the main earth (ground) point on the wiring harness. If corroded, dismantle the connection and clean all surfaces back to bare metal.

1 To check the earth on a component, use an insulated jumper wire to temporarily bypass its earth connection **(see illustration 16)**. Connect one end of the jumper wire between the earth terminal or metal body of the component and the other end to the motorcycle's frame.

2 If the circuit works with the jumper wire installed, the original earth circuit is faulty. Check the wiring for open-circuits or poor connections. Clean up direct earth connections, removing all traces of corrosion and remake the joint. Apply petroleum jelly to the joint to prevent future corrosion.

Tracing a short-circuit

● A short-circuit occurs where current shorts to earth (ground) bypassing the circuit components. This usually results in a blown fuse.

● A short-circuit is most likely to occur where the insulation has worn through due to wiring chafing on a component, allowing a direct path to earth (ground) on the frame.

1 Remove any bodypanels necessary to access the circuit wiring.

2 Check that all electrical switches in the circuit are OFF, then remove the circuit fuse and connect a test light, buzzer or voltmeter (set to the dc scale) across the fuse terminals. No voltage should be shown.

3 Move the wiring from side to side whilst observing the test light or meter. When the test light comes on, buzzer sounds or meter shows voltage, you have found the cause of the short. It will usually shown up as damaged or burned insulation.

4 Note that the same test can be performed on each component in the circuit, even the switch.

Note: *References throughout this index are in the form* **"Chapter number"** • **"Page number"**. *So, for example, 2•15 refers to page 15 of Chapter 2.*

A

Air filter
clean – 1•16
housing removal and
installation – 3A•12, 3B•5
Alternator
removal and installation – 2•21, 8•23
stater coils – 8•24

B

Battery
electrolyte level check – 1•7
charging – 8•3
removal and refitting – 8•2
specifications – 8•1
Bearings
connecting rod – 2•54 to 2•55
steering head – 1•20, 5•18
swingarm – 5•25
wheel – 1•21, 6•16
Brakes
bleeding system – 6•11
caliper
front – 6•3
rear – 6•7
checks – 1•17
disc
front – 6•4
rear – 6•8
hoses – 1•22
hydraulic fluid change – 1•20
hydraulic fluid level check – 0•14
light switches – 8•11
master cylinder
front – 6•5
rear – 6•9
pad replacement
front – 6•2
rear – 6•6
pad wear check – 1•19
specifications – 6•1
Bulbs
replacement – 8•5
wattages – 8•2

C

Cables
choke – 3A•10
fast idle – 3B•11
speedometer/tachometer – 8•11
throttle – 3A•10, 3B•11
Caliper (brake)
front – 6•3
rear – 6•7

Cam belts
checks – 1•10
replacement – 1•22
removal and installation – 2•8
Cam belt pulleys and drive – 2•9
Camshafts – 2•13
Carburettors
disassembly, cleaning and
inspection – 3A•5
overhaul (general) – 3A•4
reassembly and float height
check – 3A•8
removal and installation – 3A•4
separation and joining – 3A•7
specifications – 3A•1
synchronisation – 1•16
warmer kit – 2•48
Charging system
alternator – 8•23
leakage and output test – 8•23
specifications – 8•1
testing – 8•22
Choke cable
adjustment – 1•14
removal and installation – 3A•10
Clutch
fluid change – 1•20
fluid top-up – 0•13
hydraulic system – 2•44
master cylinder – 2•43
removal, inspection and
installation – 2•28 to 2•42
release cylinder – 2•42
Connecting rods
bearings – 2•53
general information – 2•55
Control cables and pivot points – 1•19
Conversion factors – REF•26
Crankcases
inspection – 2•51
separating and joining – 2•49
Crankshaft – 2•52
Cush drive check – 1•21, 5•27
Cylinder barrels
removal, inspection and
installation – 2•18
Cylinder heads
removal and installation – 2•11
overhaul – 2•13

D

Daily (pre-ride) checks – 0•12
Dimensions – 0•9
Drive chain
check, adjustment and lubrication – 1•6
removal, cleaning and installation – 5•26

E

ECU – 3B•9
Electrical system
alternator – 2•21, 8•23
battery – 8•2, 8•3
brake light – 8•10
charging system – 8•22
fault finding – 8•2
fuel pump – 8•19
fuses – 8•4
general relay – 8•18
headlight – 8•5, 8•6
handlebar switches – 8•16
horn – 8•18
ignition (main) switch – 8•15
instrument cluster – 8•11, 8•12, 8•14
lighting system – 8•5
low fuel level sensor – 8•18
neutral switch – 8•17
oil pressure switch – 8•15
regulator/rectifier – 8•24
sidestand switch – 8•17
specifications – 2•1
starter motor – 8•20
starter relay – 8•19
tail light – 8•7
turn signals – 8•8
wiring diagrams – 8•25 to 8•36
Engine – 2•1 *et seq*
alternator rotor, starter clutch and
starter drive – 2•21
bearings – 2•53, 1•20, 1•21, 6•16
cam belt removal and refitting – 2•8
camshafts – 2•13
compression check – 1•17
connecting rods – 2•55
crankcases – 2•49, 2•51
crankshaft – 2•52
cylinder barrels – 2•18
cylinder heads – 2•11
engine transmission removal and
refitting – 2•5
gearchange mechanism – 2•26
idle speed – 1•15
oil and filter change – 1•8
oil level check – 0•12
oil pressure check – 1•17
oil pump – 2•45
pistons – 2•19
piston rings – 2•21
primary drive gear – 2•46
removal and installation – 2•5
specifications – 2•1
valves – 2•13
valve clearances – 1•9
valves and seats – 2•18

Index REF•49

Note: *References throughout this index are in the form* **"Chapter number"** • **"Page number"**. *So, for example, 2•15 refers to page 15 of Chapter 2.*

Engine number – 0•11
Exhaust system – 3A•13

F

Fast idle cable – 3B•11
Fault finding – REF•35 to REF•43
Fairing – 7•2, 7•3
Filter
air – 1•16
fuel – 1•13
oil – 1•8
Footrests and brackets – 5•3
Fuel injectors – 3B•1
Frame inspection and repair – 5•3
Frame number – 0•11
Front forks
adjustment – 5•23
disassembly, inspection and reassembly – 5•7
oil change – 1•22
removal and installation – 5•6
Front mudguard – 7•5
Front wheel
bearings – 6•15
removal and installation – 6•12
Fuel filter – 1•13
Fuel injection system – 3B•7
air temperature sensor – 3B•8
atmospheric pressure sensor – 3B•9
fuel level sensor – 8•18
specifications – 3B•1
timing sensor – 3B•9
throttle position sensor – 3B•8
Fuel pump
carburettor models – 8•19
injection models – 3B•4
Fuel system
carburettor models – 3A•1 *et seq*
check – 1•22
fuel injection models – 3B•1 *et seq*
Fuel tank
cleaning and repair – 3A•4, 3B•3
removal and installation – 3A•3, 3B•2
Fuses – 8•2, 8•4

G

Gearshafts and selector drum/forks – 2•56, 2•57
Gearchange mechanism (external) – 2•26
General relay – 8•18

H

Handlebars
removal and installation – 5•5
switches – 8•16
Headlight
beam height – 8•7
bulb replacement – 8•5
unit removal and installation – 8•5

Horn – 8•18
Hoses (brake and clutch) – 1•22, 6•11
HT coils – 4•2

I

Idle fuel/air mixture adjustment – 3A•4
Idle speed – 1•15
Ignition control units – 4•5
Ignition main switch – 8•15
Ignition system
check – 4•2
control unit – 4•5
ECU – 3B•9
HT coils – 4•2
pick-up coils – 4•4
Ignition timing – 4•5
Immobiliser system – 4•6
Initial start up after overhaul – 2•62
Instrument cluster
bulb replacement – 8•14
check and replacement – 8•12
removal and installation – 8•11

L

Lighting system – 8•5
Lubricants – 1•3, REF•23

M

Maintenance – 1•1 *et seq*
Main bearings – 2•52
Master cylinder
clutch – 2•43
front brake – 6•5
rear brake – 6•9
MOT test checks – REF•27 to REF•31
Mudguards – 7•5

N

Neutral switch – 8•17
Nuts and bolts tightness check – 1•22

O

Oil (engine) – 1•3
Oil (front forks) – 5•2
Oil cooler – 2•48
Oil pressure check – 1•17
Oil pressure relief valve – 2•48
Oil pressure switch – 8•15
Oil pump – 2•45
Oil strainer – 1•19

P

Pads (brake) – 6•2, 6•6
Passenger grab rail – 7•6
Pick-up coils – 4•4

Pistons
removal, inspection and installation – 2•19
rings – 2•21
Primary drive gear – 2•46
Pump
fuel (carburettor models) – 8•19
fuel (injection models) – 3B•4
oil – 2•45

R

Rear mudguard – 7•5
Rear shock absorber
adjustment – 5•23
removal, inspection and installation – 5•19
Rear suspension linkage (Monster models) – 5•21
Rear wheel
bearings
check – 1•21
renewal – 6•15
coupling/rubber dampers – 5•27
cush drive check – 1•21
removal and installation – 6•14
Rear view mirrors – 7•4
Regulator/rectifier – 8•24
Running in procedure – 2•62

S

Safety precautions – 0•10
Seat – 7•5
Security – REF•20 to REF•22
Selector drum and forks – 2•61
Side panels – 7•4
Sidestand
removal and installation – 5•5
switch – 8•17
Specifications
brakes – 6•1
clutch – 2•2
engine – 2•1
electrical system – 8•1
front forks – 5•1
fuel system
carburettor – 3A•1
injection – 3B•1
general – 0•8
ignition system – 4•1
wheels and tyres – 6•1
Spark plugs – 1•2, 1•12
Speedometer – 8•11, 8•12
Sprockets – 5•26
Starter clutch and drive – 2•21
Starter motor – 8•20
Starter relay – 8•19
Steering stem – 5•17
Steering head bearings
check and adjustment – 1•20
inspection and replacement – 5•18
lubrication – 1•22
Storage – REF•32
Suspension
adjustments – 5•23
check – 1•21
front forks – 5•23
rear linkage – 5•21
rear shock absorber – 5•19

Note: *References throughout this index are in the form* "**Chapter number**" • "**Page number**". *So, for example, 2•15 refers to page 15 of Chapter 2.*

Swingarm
  inspection and bearing
    replacement – 1•22, 5•25
  removal and installation – 5•24
Switches
  handlebar – 8•16
  ignition – 8•15
  neutral – 8•17
  oil pressure – 8•15
  sidestand – 8•17

T

Tachometer – 8•11
Tail light – 8•7
Throttle body assembly – 3B•10
Throttle cable
  freeplay – 1•14
  removal and installation – 3A•10, 3B•11
Tools – REF•2 to REF•19
Torque settings – 1•3, 2•4, 3A•2, 3B•1, 4•1,
  5•3, 6•1, 8•2

Transmission
  removal and installation – 2•5
  gearshafts and selector
    drum/forks – 2•55
Turn signals
  assemblies – 8•9
  bulb replacement – 8•8
  circuit check and relay – 8•10
Tyres
  general information and fitting – 6•17
  pressures and tread depth – 0•16
  sizes – 6•1

V

Valves
  clearances check – 1•9
  overhaul – 2•13
  servicing – 2•18
Vacuum fuel pump (Monster
  models) – 3A•11

W

Weights – 0•9
Wheel
  alignment check – 6•11
  bearings – 1•21, 6•15
  cush drive check (rear) – 1•21
  inspection and repair – 6•11
  removal and installation – 6•14
Windshield – 7•3
Wiring diagrams – 8•25 to 8•36

Preserving Our Motoring Heritage

> <
> *The Model J Duesenberg Derham Tourster. Only eight of these magnificent cars were ever built – this is the only example to be found outside the United States of America*

Almost every car you've ever loved, loathed or desired is gathered under one roof at the Haynes Motor Museum. Over 300 immaculately presented cars and motorbikes represent every aspect of our motoring heritage, from elegant reminders of bygone days, such as the superb Model J Duesenberg to curiosities like the bug-eyed BMW Isetta. There are also many old friends and flames. Perhaps you remember the 1959 Ford Popular that you did your courting in? The magnificent 'Red Collection' is a spectacle of classic sports cars including AC, Alfa Romeo, Austin Healey, Ferrari, Lamborghini, Maserati, MG, Riley, Porsche and Triumph.

A Perfect Day Out

Each and every vehicle at the Haynes Motor Museum has played its part in the history and culture of Motoring. Today, they make a wonderful spectacle and a great day out for all the family. Bring the kids, bring Mum and Dad, but above all bring your camera to capture those golden memories for ever. You will also find an impressive array of motoring memorabilia, a comfortable 70 seat video cinema and one of the most extensive transport book shops in Britain. The Pit Stop Cafe serves everything from a cup of tea to wholesome, home-made meals or, if you prefer, you can enjoy the large picnic area nestled in the beautiful rural surroundings of Somerset.

> *John Haynes O.B.E., Founder and Chairman of the museum at the wheel of a Haynes Light 12.*

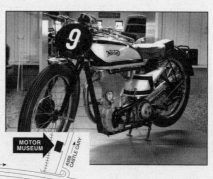

> <
> *The 1936 490cc sohc-engined International Norton – well known for its racing success*

The Museum is situated on the A359 Yeovil to Frome road at Sparkford, just off the A303 in Somerset. It is about 40 miles south of Bristol, and 25 minutes drive from the M5 intersection at Taunton.
Open 9.30am - 5.30pm (10.00am - 4.00pm Winter) 7 days a week, *except Christmas Day, Boxing Day and New Years Day*
Special rates available for schools, coach parties and outings Charitable Trust No. 292048